D1542992

To
Tom Stater
with best wishes !

M. T. Carleton

5/17/91

The Louisiana Governors

Consulting Editors

Mark T. Carleton
Jack D. L. Holmes
Joe Gray Taylor
Joseph G. Tregle, Jr.

The Louisiana
GOVERNORS

FROM IBERVILLE TO EDWARDS

Edited by Joseph G. Dawson III

LOUISIANA STATE UNIVERSITY PRESS

Baton Rouge and London

Copyright © 1990 by Louisiana State University Press
All rights reserved
Manufactured in the United States of America
First printing
99 98 97 96 95 94 93 92 91 90   5 4 3 2 1
Designer: Patricia Douglas Crowder
Typeface: Linotron 202 Aldus
Typesetter: G & S Typesetters, Inc.
Printer and binder: Thomson-Shore, Inc.

LIBRARY OF CONGRESS CATALOGING-IN-PUBLICATION DATA
The Louisiana governors : From Iberville to Edwards / edited by Joseph G. Dawson III.
    p.   cm.
    Includes bibliographical references.
    ISBN 0-8071-1527-4 (alk. paper)
    1. Louisiana—Governors—Biography.   2. Louisiana—Politics and government.
I. Dawson, Joseph G., 1945–
F368.L68   1990
976.3'0092'2—dc20
[B]   89-27333
                                                                       CIP

The paper in this book meets the guidelines for permanence and durability of the Committee on
Production Guidelines for Book Longevity of the Council on Library Resources. ∞

TO

Joseph Green Dawson, Jr., and Susan Hubbell Dawson

AND

Everette Leon Stokes and Maribess Temple Stokes

AND

Jack D. L. Holmes

Contents

Acknowledgments

This book is a collective effort, and it is appropriate to acknowledge the work of the many who helped bring it to completion.

First I would like to thank the Consulting Editors, Jack Holmes, Joe Tregle, and Joe Gray Taylor, who each read sections of the manuscript—covering the colonial period, 1803–1860, and 1860–1900, respectively. I owe thanks as well to Tom Carleton, who read the section on the twentieth century. The suggestions and other assistance of these scholars were invaluable.

Next I must thank the writers of the essays. Our goal was to bring together essays that give an objective introduction to and an interpretive analysis of Louisiana's governors. In addition, my hearty thanks must go to Margaret Dalrymple, editor in chief at Louisiana State University Press, for her patience, encouragement, and advice on a project that took much longer than either of us expected. Thanks are due, too, to Brady Banta and Mike Mulhern for their assistance.

On behalf of the contributors, I would like to acknowledge the many archivists and librarians who aided our efforts, particularly Stone Miller and the staff of the Department of Archives and Manuscripts and the Troy H. Middleton Library, of Louisiana State University, Baton Rouge; Mrs. Harriet Callahan, of Louisiana State Library, Baton Rouge; and the staff members of many other institutions: the John B. Cade Library, of Southern University, Baton Rouge; the Department of Archives at Sandel Library, of Northeast Louisiana University, Monroe; the Dupre Library, of the University of Southwestern Louisiana, Lafayette; the Lether E. Frazar Memorial Library, of McNeese State University, Lake Charles, La.; the Linus A. Sims Memorial Library, of Southeastern Louisiana University, Hammond; the Allen J. Ellender Memorial Library, of Nicholls State University, Thibodaux, La.; the Earl K. Long

Library, of the University of New Orleans; the New Orleans Public Library; the Fondren Library, of Rice University, Houston; the M. D. Anderson Memorial Library, of the University of Houston; the Library of Texas A & M University at Galveston; and the Sterling Evans Library, of Texas A & M University, College Station.

Introduction

For three centuries the governor has been the pivotal figure in Louisiana politics. Maligned or revered, soft-spoken or brash, sophisticated or uncultured, Louisiana's governors have used politics for personal and partisan advantage. The same is true of many governors in other states in America, but throughout Louisiana's history, its governors have wielded extraordinary legal power and have often exercised influence above what their official authority appeared to permit.

Of course, Louisiana's governors have worked under restraints and limits, including, at various times, a council or cabildo, assembly or legislature, or intendants or judges, not to mention supporters and opponents, constitutions and laws, and bureaucrats and journalists. Rivals and detractors have sometimes portrayed French and Spanish colonial governors as military despots or underhanded dictators. But that the governors were military officers did not require them to be despotic. As Stephen S. Webb has pointed out, the English as well as the French and Spanish relied for their colonial governors on men who made their mark in the army. Colonization and military reach went hand in hand. Overseas outposts needed an alert defense, and therefore, naturally, European monarchs selected military officers as governors-general.[1] In British North America, however, the governors encountered restraints that were absent in French and Spanish colonies, including English common law, jury trials, functioning legislatures, and the payment of salaries by the legislature rather than the crown. No matter the nationality, colonial governors made as much as they could of their appointive office and took advantage of the distance separating their colony from Europe: a regal commission meant that governors-general spoke and acted on behalf of the monarch. Though military officers, judges, coun-

1. Stephen S. Webb, *The Governors-General: The English Army and the Definition of the Empire, 1569–1681* (Chapel Hill, N.C., 1979), *passim*.

cilmen, or intendants might circumvent their governor, they were often frustrated by their inability to overcome the governor's authority.

The composite profile of the governor of the French colonial period in Louisiana (including explorer Pierre Lemoyne, Sieur d'Iberville) would be of a white male military officer (six came from the army and five from the navy) from either France (seven) or Canada (four), who was about forty-one years old when arriving in Louisiana to assume his responsibilities. Of the many French colonial governors, one was exceptional: Jean-Baptiste Lemoyne, Sieur de Bienville, Iberville's brother. His patience, stamina, and hard work, and his beguiling adroitness in political maneuvering and bargaining mark him as the model of the successful governor in Louisiana history. Both popular and controversial, Bienville was a leader, whether in or out of office.[2] Living in a colony that, besides having military vulnerabilities, was often on the edge of economic collapse, Bienville sometimes skirted the law if doing so suited his purpose. Often his purpose and the good of the colony coincided. As Bienville and other governors knew, the requirements of administering a distant imperial possession were often in conflict with the rules of the imperial game. For instance, according to mercantilist laws, Louisiana was supposed to trade only with the mother country or its other colonies, and smuggling was to be punished. But if Bienville had completely forbidden smuggling, he would have risked seeing Louisiana fail for want of needed supplies. By allowing the commerical laws to be broken, he helped the colony survive and himself to prosper. His choice to permit the illegal shipments of goods may now seem to have been obvious, even logical, given the alternative of colonial collapse. But once broken, laws became easier to disregard.

The breaking and ignoring of laws and regulations matured into a tradition during Louisiana's Spanish period. The Spanish governors dealt with many of the same kinds of problems that Bienville and the French had faced. The composite profile of the Spanish colonial governor of Louisiana would be of a white male army officer (only Antonio de Ulloa was in the navy) who was about forty-eight years old when he took on his gubernatorial duties. Six of the governors were from Spain; four were from other colonies or countries. The Spanish sent men who possessed scientific expertise (such as Ulloa), daring and charisma (such

2. Charles E. O'Neill, "Jean-Baptiste Le Moyne de Bienville," *Dictionary of Canadian Biography* (11 vols.; Toronto, 1974), III, 370–84; Joe Gray Taylor, *Louisiana: A Bicentennial History* (New York, 1976), 13.

as Bernardo de Gálvez), ironclad determination (such as Alexander O'Reilly), or diplomatic skill (such as Manuel Gayoso de Lemos). Still, none of them dominated the Spanish period as Bienville had the French years. But the argument can be made that the example of French and Spanish colonial administration contributed to Louisiana's predisposition toward strong governors and its tolerance of corruption in state government.

In the transition from European to American control, Louisiana had one guide, William C. C. Claiborne. A young lawyer from Virginia, Claiborne dominated Louisiana's years as a territory and its first four years as a state. In his late twenties when President Thomas Jefferson appointed him territorial governor in 1803, Claiborne exercised virtually dictatorial power during the first eight months of his administration, in a way that many Louisianians must have found familiar. On the other hand, the govenor set about establishing the fundamentals of Anglo-American law and preparing residents of the territory for statehood, which they achieved in 1812.[3] According to data supplied by Roy R. Glashan, only two of the other sixteen territorial governors who served during the years 1803–1812 were in their twenties, and the average age when assigned was forty-one.[4] Nine were attorneys, four soldiers, one a farmer, one a planter, and one a businessman.

As territorial governor, Claiborne disputed with the Spanish over the boundaries between Louisiana and Spain's colonies, took advantage of circumstances to acquire additional lands during the West Florida Rebellion of 1810, and saw to the writing of the state's first constitution. The Constitution of 1812, under which Claiborne was elected the state's first governor, borrowed heavily from the Kentucky state constitution. It was aristocratic in tone and elitist in practice. According to it, gubernatorial candidates were limited to men at least thirty-five years of age who were residents of Louisiana for six years and owners of land valued at five thousand dollars or more (an indication of wealth in the early nineteenth century). Of course, governors had to be United States citizens, a requirement in all subsequent Louisiana state constitutions as well. Voters were limited to white males aged twenty-one or over who

3. Joseph T. Hatfield, *William Claiborne: Jeffersonian Centurion in the American Southwest* (Lafayette, La., 1976), 96–276. See also George Dargo, *Jefferson's Louisiana: Politics and the Clash of Legal Traditions* (Cambridge, Mass., 1975), 23–50 and *passim*.

4. Roy G. Glashan (comp.), *American Governors and Gubernatorial Elections, 1775–1978* (Westport, Conn. 1979), *passim*. Glashan's book is arranged alphabetically by state, then chronologically by gubernatorial term.

were residents of a Louisiana county (a voting district that could comprise two parishes) for one year and who had paid state taxes. Even by 1840, only half of Louisiana's white adult men paid state tax. Gubernatorial candidates could announce for office individually, or small informal groups of the state's political, social, and economic elite could meet to promote a particular man. Upon the decline of the Federalist party, after 1816, the Democratic-Republicans, who were Jefferson's party, divided into factions. According to the provisions of the Constitution of 1812, the state assembly—the legislature—would select as governor one or other of the two top vote getters in the general election. The Constitution of 1812 did not provide for a lieutenant governor: if the governor died or was removed from office, the president of the state senate succeeded him. The governor was ineligible to succeed himself but could serve again after another four years. He had vast appointive powers, continuing the colonial tradition of a strong and influential executive. Under the Constitution of 1812, he appointed all major state officeholders (secretary of state, attorney general, state treasurer, state judges), as well as other officers such as local sheriffs.[5] The constitutional provisions made the Louisiana governor one of the most powerful state executives in the United States and, because of the qualifications for holding the office, sure to be a slaveowner or directly associated—as an attorney or businessman—with the slaveowning aristocracy. The composite profile of the governor during the years 1816–1860 is of a white male planter or lawyer, or both, about age forty-seven when taking office, with some political experience in state politics, such as holding a seat in one or both houses of the legislature. Ten of the fifteen governors from 1816 through 1860 had been state legislators or senators.[6] The Whig party was a force in Louisiana during its period of national influence (about 1832–1853), with two members of that party being governor (1835–1843), but the Democrats—the party of Andrew Jackson—controlled the governorship in the state between 1843 and 1860.

Louisiana's governors from 1816 to 1860 were generally similar to other Deep South governors during those years, according to the data compiled by Glashan.[7] Florida, for instance, also elected two Whigs; the

5. Benjamin W. Dart (ed.), *Constitutions of the State of Louisiana* (Indianapolis, 1932), 499–507, esp. 501–503; Perry H. Howard, *Political Tendencies in Louisiana,* rev. and exp. ed. (Baton Rouge, 1971), 20–21.

6. Glashan (comp.), *American Governors, passim.*

7. *Ibid.*

typical Florida govenor was a white male lawyer or planter who took office at about age forty-eight. In other nearby states, Arkansas and Alabama, the governor's average age on beginning his term was forty-one and forty-two, respectively, but neither state elected a Whig to the office. In Mississippi and Georgia, the governor's average age on beginning his term was forty-three and forty-five, respectively, and each state elected only one Whig.

When Louisiana drafted and ratified a new constitution in 1845, the general profile of men holding the governor's office remained consistent with what it had been under the Constitution of 1812. The Constitution of 1845 required candidates for governor to be white males, at least thirty-five years of age and residents of the state for *fifteen* years. In an important change, the property requirement was dropped completely for both gubernatorial candidacy and voting. Voters had to be white males aged at least twenty-one and residents of the state for two years. The Constitution of 1845 established the office of lieutenant governor and put him first in the line of succession. It also reduced the governor's broad appointive powers (for example, sheriffs were to be elected by parish voters) and required that governors be elected by popular vote rather than the state assembly. But legislative apportionment was by total population, including slaves, who could not vote or hold office.[8] Thus the slaveowning plantation operators—whether Whigs or Democrats—continued to dominate the politics of the state. They nominated such men as Alexandre Mouton, Isaac Johnson, and Joseph M. Walker, each of whom loyally represented the state's planter-business oligarchy.

The Whigs dominated the constitutional convention of 1852 (eighty-five Whigs to forty-five Democrats), which drafted a state charter whose primary significance lay in reducing again the number of offices appointed by the governor. Legislative apportionment continued to be based on total population, however, which meant that slaveowners kept their disproportionate influence in the state. Gubernatorial candidates had to be white males at least twenty-eight years old and residents of the state for four years. Under the Constitution of 1852, voters had to be at least twenty-one and residents of the state for one year.[9]

Louisiana's slaveowning planters controlled the process that resulted

8. Dart (ed.), *Constitutions of Louisiana*, 508–22, esp. 511–13; Howard, *Political Tendencies*, 48–49.

9. Dart (ed.), *Constitutions of Louisiana*, 523–36, esp. 526–528; Howard, *Political Tendencies*, 69–71.

in the state's secession from the Union in 1861 and, soon thereafter, its move to join the Confederate States of America. In 1862, Union forces occupied a significant portion of Louisiana, including New Orleans, at that time the South's largest city. The defeat of the Confederacy resulted in two new constitutions for the state. The short-lived Constitution of 1864 was significant for abolishing the institution of slavery.[10] The Constitution of 1868 authorized black men to vote, required only one year's residence for voting, based legislative apportionment on total population, called for integrated public schools, and overall, was the most democratic constitution for Louisiana since statehood. Qualifications for the governorship under the Constitution of 1868 were unusually brief: candidates had to be male citizens who had resided in the state for two years. If the governor was impeached, he was to be suspended from office pending the outcome of a trial in the state senate; meanwhile the lieutenant governor was to serve as acting governor.[11]

The leading Republican in Louisiana during Reconstruction was Governor Henry Clay Warmoth, one of the most detested and, undoubtedly, one of the most controversial men elected to the state's highest office. Warmoth remains enigmatic to historians. His inaugural address on July 13, 1868, was idealistic and high-minded; his administration was shot through with corruption. He entered office a man of only moderate means; he left it wealthy. As governor, Warmoth developed a highly sophisticated repertoire of political tools: he acquired the authority to fill vacancies in many state and local offices; he employed the New Orleans Metropolitan Police to carry out his orders across the state; he manipulated vote counts through the State Returning Board, a special agency established by law to certify the state's election returns; and he held signed but undated resignations from leading state officeholders in order to secure their continuing cooperation. Edwin A. Davis calls Warmoth a dictator for conducting his office in this manner. The turmoil of the era grew when Warmoth was impeached.[12] Lieutenant

---

10. Dart (ed.), *Constitutions of Louisiana*, 537–52, esp. 537.
11. *Ibid.*, 553–69, esp. 558–60; Taylor, *Louisiana: A Bicentennial History*, 106.
12. Sidney J. Romero (ed.), *"My Fellow Citizens . . .": The Inaugural Addresses of Louisiana's Governors* (Lafayette, La., 1980), 144–46. The most complete account of Warmoth's political career is F. Wayne Binning's "Henry Clay Warmoth and Louisiana Reconstruction" (Ph.D. dissertation, University of North Carolina, 1969). See also Joe Gray Taylor, *Louisiana Reconstructed, 1863–1877* (Baton Rouge, 1974), 175, 179, 181–82, 208, 216; Richard N. Current, *Three Carpetbag Governors* (Baton Rouge, 1967), 36–66; and Edwin A. Davis, *Louisiana: A Narrative History* (3rd ed.; Baton Rouge, 1971), 270.

Governor P. B. S. Pinchback became acting governor, the only black to serve as governor in United States history prior to 1990.

Overlooking the political shenanigans of Democratic boss John Slidell in the antebellum years, former Confederates claimed that Warmoth and other Republican carpetbaggers had corrupted them and their state. Warmoth responded with what may be one of the most quoted statements about Louisiana: "Why, damn it, everybody is demoralized down here. Corruption is the fashion."[13] Indeed, Richard N. Current concludes that "if Warmoth was corrupt, it would be nearer the truth to say that Louisiana corrupted *him* than to say that *he* corrupted Louisiana."[14] T. Harry Williams, in his biography of Huey P. Long, compares the Kingfish and the young carpetbagger, concluding that Long may have followed some of Warmoth's political tactics. According to Williams, Warmoth recognized that "the politics of his adopted state was peculiar, differing subtly from the art as practiced in any other state." Williams continues, "Louisiana politics was speculative, devious, personal, exuberant, and highly professional. The objective was to win, and in no other state were the devices employed to win—stratagems, deals, oratory—so studied and so admired by the populace. It had been like this in the antebellum era, it was like this in Warmoth's time, and it would be like this in the future."[15] In fact, in the future it would become worse.

Some Louisianians mistakenly believed that Warmoth and the Republicans represented the nadir of graft and dishonesty; certainly that was what the Democrats claimed in the following years. But only a little later, native Louisiana Democrats dealt the state perhaps the worst, most corrupt years in its history. To further their own designs, the Democrats called a constitutional convention, the result of which was the Constitution of 1879. This granted a twenty-five-year charter to the corrupt Louisiana Lottery Company, a nefarious business that co-opted governors, state officials, judges, and members of the legislature. Since the Democratic governor Francis R. T. Nicholls opposed the Lottery, the Constitution of 1879 rescheduled the next election, cutting Nicholls' term by one year; at the same time, it increased the official powers of appointment of the governor almost to the levels of the

13. Roger W. Shugg, *Origins of Class Struggle in Louisiana: A Social History of White Farmers and Laborers During Slavery and After, 1840–1875* (Baton Rouge, 1939), 227.
14. Current, *Three Carpetbag Governors,* 63.
15. T. Harry Williams, *Huey Long: A Biography* (New York, 1969), 183–84.

Constitution of 1812. Warmoth had maneuvered to gain power over appointments while he was in office; under the Constitution of 1879, the Democrats would enjoy all of Warmoth's powers and others as well. Furthermore, despite a flurry of interest in the Populist party in the 1890s, the state remained essentially a one-party state from the 1870s to the 1970s. A provision in the Constitution of 1879 allowed Louisiana governors to succeed themselves for the first time in the state's history; candidates had to be male citizens thirty or older residing in the state for at least ten years. Voters had to be men at least twenty years old who had resided in the state for one year.[16]

Under the so-called Bourbon Democrats, led by Samuel D. McEnery, the governor from 1881 to 1888, flagrant graft and embezzlement became a demented art form in the hands of the conniving state treasurer, Edward A. Burke, who absconded to Honduras with $1 million in 1888. Meanwhile, the Bourbons condoned the sordid convict lease system operated by Samuel L. James. Under Murphy J. Foster, a Bourbon first elected governor in 1892 and reelected in 1896, vote fraud reached new heights in the Louisiana elections of 1896. In that election, an unusual fusion of the Republican and Populist parties challenged the Democrats. Several parishes recorded no votes at all for Foster's Republican-Populist opponent, John N. Pharr, who campaigned on the novel platform of honestly tabulating all the votes—of blacks and whites, rich and poor. Warmoth and his cronies had adjusted voting returns from certain parishes, but the wholesale vote tampering of the Bourbons surpassed the Republicans' in bravado and venality. Foster, in his second inaugural, on May 18, 1896, unblushingly conceded that the massive vote fraud "may have been the result of undue or overzealous partisanship." Foster wielded such great power that he, too, earned the epithet of dictator.[17]

The Louisiana Constitution of 1898 capped the Bourbon period. This antipopulist, antiblack charter established a literacy test for voters, which was waived in the case of ownership of property valued at three hundred dollars or more. Voters, in addition to being men at least twenty-one years old and state residents for two years, had to show

16. Dart (ed.), *Constitutions of Louisiana*, 570–604, esp. 577–79; Howard, *Political Tendencies*, 149; William I. Hair, *Bourbonism and Agrarian Protest: Louisiana Politics, 1877–1900* (Baton Rouge, 1969), 108–109, 141, 258–67.

17. Romero (ed.), "My Fellow Citizens . . . ," 224; Bennett H. Wall (ed.), *Louisiana: A History* (Arlington Heights, Ill., 1984), 267.

their poll-tax receipts for the previous two years when they cast their ballots. The Constitution of 1898 retained the requirement that gubernatorial candidates be at least thirty years old and residents of the state for ten years. The new charter forbade governors to succeed themselves and authorized the legislature to establish a primary system in which each party would hold elections to select the party's nominees for state offices, including that of governor; the nominees would then run in the general election.[18] The legislature soon established a primary system that practically made winning the Democratic primary tantamount to election. Other former Confederate states had their own Bourbon Democrats who operated convict lease systems, manipulated the vote count, dabbled in fiscal corruption, rewrote state constitutions, and established the primary system to favor their state's Democratic party. But Louisiana's Bourbons were unsurpassed masters of all these political and economic tactics.

The corrupt Bourbons and their successors had politics their way from the 1870s to the early years of the twentieth century. "Progressive" reforms of the early 1900s seemed tepid in the South and hardly penetrated Louisiana. But an exceptional governor, John M. Parker (1920–1924), managed to introduce some of progressivism's benefits, high-mindedly aiming for honesty and efficiency in a state government that had known little of either.[19]

Louisiana governors from 1900 to 1928 present the composite profile of a white male attorney with some political experience, about age fifty when taking office, and a member of the Democratic party. Parker, however, was the exception to this profile: he was fifty-seven when he became governor and was a former planter and reform crusader with little political experience. Across the Deep South the profile is close to the Louisiana composite: all the governors were Democrats, most were lawyers with officeholding experience, and the average age on assuming office ran from forty-one in Arkansas to forty-three in Florida, forty-four in Texas, forty-five in Mississippi, and fifty-three in Alabama and Georgia.[20]

18. Dart (ed.), Constitutions of Louisiana, 605–61, esp. 612–15; Howard, Political Tendencies, 188–93; Taylor, Louisiana: A Bicentennial History, 143–44; Hair, Bourbonism and Agrarian Protest, 276–77; Wall (ed.), Louisiana: A History, 235.

19. For Parker's political career, see Matthew J. Schott, "John M. Parker and the Varieties of American Progressivism" (Ph.D. dissertation, Vanderbilt University, 1969).

20. Glashan (comp.), American Governors, passim.

In Louisiana, Parker worked closely with the legislature to promulgate a state severence tax on oil and other natural resources, provide additional funding for Louisiana State University, and broaden the powers of the Railroad Commission (redesignated the Public Service Commission). Some of his goals he accomplished through the new state constitution in 1921, which continued to concede to the governor extensive appointive powers. Gubernatorial candidates had to be at least thirty years old and state residents for at least ten years. Voters had to be at least twenty-one years old and state residents for at least two years. They also had to pass a literacy test. By the terms of the Constitution of 1921, women as well as men could vote.[21] On the other hand, Parker had opposed ratification of the Women's Suffrage Amendment (1920) to the United States Constitution and later shrank from supporting higher state taxes for business and industry. A harbinger of things to come, Parker could not bring about change as quickly as some Louisianans wanted. Making things worse for Parker's objectives, the two governors who followed him appeared generally satisfied with conservative approaches to state government and did not build on Parker's accomplishments in order to gain further reforms.

Louisiana's progressives made such little headway that many voters in the state were willing to take a chance on a political maverick named Huey P. Long. Historians and political scientists still debate the meaning of his governorship, but scholars have agreed that Long's policies had a far-reaching influence on the state. Long invigorated people's hopes and expectations during the campaign, and in his inaugural address pledged to "eliminate all means and avenues of waste, extravagance and plunder."[22] He failed to live up to his promises, but his dynamic leadership and controversial programs propelled Louisiana from the nineteenth century to the twentieth.

Williams prefers the term *mass leader* to characterize Long, but most writers and scholars who have studied Long's governorship judge him a dictator. Allan P. Sindler uses the phrase *ruthless bossdom* to describe Long's "highly personal dictatorship." V. O. Key says that Long created a "virtual dictatorship in Louisiana." Arthur M. Schlesinger, Jr., connects Long with the state's Latin heritage, writing that "Huey Long resembled, not a Hitler or a Mussolini, but a Latin American dictator, a

21. Dart (ed.), *Constitutions of Louisiana*, 88, 92, 231–32; Howard, *Political Tendencies*, 216–17.
22. Romero (ed.), "*My Fellow Citizens . . .* ," 295.

Vargas or a Peron." And according to Joe Gray Taylor, Long "made himself as near absolute dictator of Louisiana as was possible under a federal system of government." Michael Kurtz agrees that *dictator* is the best word for characterizing Long. But Coleman Ransone believes that Long was not a dictator and argues that Long built a "powerful political machine" and then concentrated executive power as it had never been concentrated before.[23] If powerful governors preceded Long, none before him in the twentieth century amassed authority as he did; the other Louisiana governors who served between 1900 and 1928 appear lackluster when contrasted to the flamboyant Kingfish.

Huey Long was aged thirty-four when he was sworn in as governor. Most American governors in the years 1928–1935 were in their fifties or sixties, although eleven state executives—two from Texas—were in their thirties when they took office during those years.[24] Several governors provided distinctive administrations between 1928 and 1935, including Richard Russell (aged thirty-three when elected) in Georgia, Philip La Follette (also aged thirty-three when first elected) in Wisconsin, Franklin D. Roosevelt in New York, Alfred Landon in Kansas, and Theodore Bilbo in Mississippi. Governor Harry F. Byrd, Sr., and the Byrd machine of Virginia rivaled Huey Long in exercising power within an individual state, but Long had greater influence on national politics.

Of the several governors since Huey Long—including Huey's brother Earl K. Long, who was twice elected governor himself—none seems to have held the office with the same combination of personal flair and political daring as Edwin Edwards. Although Huey Long and Edwards came from different backgrounds—Long's heritage was north Louisiana hill-country Protestant whereas Edwards' mother was a south Louisiana Roman Catholic—Edwards' flamboyance harkened back to Huey's white suits, freewheeling exchanges with journalists, and jaunty campaign swings across the state. Edwards had political substance—and greatly benefited from the boom in international oil and gas prices—to go along with the Las Vegas gambling sorties. The political analyst Larry

23. Williams, *Huey Long,* 414–15; Allan P. Sindler, *Huey Long's Louisiana: State Politics, 1920–1952* (Baltimore, 1956), 99, 110; V. O. Key, *Southern Politics in State and Nation* (New York, 1949), 156; Arthur M. Schlesinger, Jr., *The Politics of Upheaval* (Boston, 1960), 68; Taylor, *Louisiana: A Bicentennial History,* 155; Michael L. Kurtz, in Wall (ed.), *Louisiana: A History,* 267; Coleman B. Ransone, Jr., *The Office of Governor in the United States* (University, Ala., 1956), 373. See also Edward Renwick, "The Governor," in James Bolner (ed.), *Louisiana Politics: Festival in a Labyrinth* (Baton Rouge, 1982), 85.

24. Glashan (comp.), *American Governors, passim.*

Sabato recognizes two "outstanding" governors in Louisiana during the years 1950–1975: Earl Long and Edwards. By the time of his unprecedented third election to the governorship in 1983, political friends and opponents could agree with Kurtz's assessment that in spite of the legal imbroglios of "Brilab" and "Koreagate," Edwards had become the "most powerful political leader in Louisiana since Huey Long."[25]

Edwards fits the general profile of Louisiana governors from 1940 to the 1980s. All but Jimmie Davis were lawyers. All acquired political experience before running for governor, but they gained their experience in a variety of offices—on the Public Service Commission, in the legislature, holding a judgeship, or serving in Congress. Governors in Louisiana since 1940 have been white, male, and with one significant exception, members of the Democratic party. Most were in their forties when inaugurated, with an average age of forty-six upon taking office. Most other Deep South governors since 1904 have been male lawyers with political experience who took office in their forties. Two southern states, however, have had women governors: Miriam A. Ferguson in Texas, 1925–1927, and Lurleen Wallace in Alabama, 1967–1968. Only three other states—Wyoming, Washington, and Connecticut—have had women governors; Louisiana has yet to elect its first female chief executive.[26]

Edwards, like Huey Long, was the product of an essentially one-party state, notwithstanding the arguments over Long-inspired bifactionalism.[27] Louisiana, like the other ten states of the Old Confederacy, has been overwhelmingly Democratic since Reconstruction, electing only one Republican governor since 1877. (Three former Confederate states have elected at least one Republican governor, but Virginia has had three, Tennessee four, and in Texas, Republican William Clements was elected twice.) Although the Republicans showed some signs of revival in the 1950s, it was during the 1970s and 1980s that the Republican party really began to make a comeback in Dixie, electing an occasional governor, including David Treen in Louisiana in 1979, and some United States senators and congressmen. Moreover, Republican presidential candidates have done well in the South since 1952. The votes of Loui-

25. Larry Sabato, *Goodbye to Good-Time Charlie: The American Governor Transformed, 1950–1975* (Lexington, Mass., 1978), 52; Kurtz, in Wall (ed.), *Louisiana: A History*, 372.

26. Glashan (comp.), *American Governors, passim.*

27. On the Louisiana Democratic party's factionalism and its similarity to a two-party structure, see, for example, Key, *Southern Politics*, 168–80; Sindler, *Huey Long's Louisiana*, 75, 115, 248–249; and Howard, *Political Tendencies*, 251–52, 258–59, 376–79.

sianians resulted in the awarding of the state's electoral votes to Republicans in six of the ten presidential contests between 1952 and 1988. The rebirth of the Republican party in the South has reduced the importance of the antiquated state primary system and increased the significance of the general election.[28] To counteract the move toward a modern, two-party system, Louisiana and several other southern states have scheduled gubernatorial elections in off-presidential years. Thus they avoid the possibility that a groundswell of support for the Republican presidential candidate will influence the state election.[29]

Edwards was undoubtedly able to build his political power in virtue of being reelected in 1975, but Louisiana, throughout most of its history since statehood, has prohibited successive terms by its governors. From 1812 to 1879, governors could not stand for reelection until after they had sat out one term, and during those years only one governor, André Bienvenu Roman, served two terms. Between 1879 and 1898, governors were allowed to succeed themselves. Murphy J. Foster was elected in 1892 and again in 1896. The Constitution of 1898 restored the requirement that governors wait four years before seeking another term. In 1966, through an amendment to the Constitution of 1921, John J. McKeithen became eligible to run for a second term in 1967, which he won. Provisions in the Constitution fo 1974 allow for a governor to hold office for two terms, sit out a term, and then run again. Edwards followed that path to his third election in 1983.[30] By permitting the governor to succeed himself, Louisiana aligned itself with the trend in many state constitutions across the nation.[31]

The Constitution of 1974 helped bring a modern appearance to the state's politics.[32] Gubernatorial candidates could now be as young as twenty-five and needed only a residence of five years in Louisiana. The minimum voting age had been lowered in 1971 to eighteen by federal mandate, but the Constitution of 1974 virtually did away with the residence requirements by allowing instant voter registration.

28. For excellent coverage of the topic, see Alexander P. Lamis, *The Two-Party South* (New York, 1984).

29. Coleman B. Ransome, Jr., *The Office of Governor in the South* (University, Ala., 1951), 51–52, 65; Key, *Southern Politics*, 619–20, 625–42; Howard, *Political Tendencies*, 211–397.

30. Renwick, "The Governor," 76.

31. Ransone, *Governor in the South*, 59; Thad L. Beyle, "Governors," in Virginia Gray, Herbert Jacob, and Kenneth N. Vines (eds.), *Politics in the American States: A Comparative Analysis* (4th ed.; Boston, 1983), 196, 214.

32. Wall (ed.), *Louisiana: A History*, 358–59; Mark T. Carleton, "The Louisiana Constitution of 1974," in Bolner (ed.), *Louisiana Politics*, 15–41.

The governor's patronage power remains substantial under the Constitution of 1974, but other aspects of the modern governorship distinguish it from the office in bygone times. The powers and responsibilities of a modern governor are clearly spelled out in a public document, in contrast to the individual commissions or assignments of colonial governors.[33] And governors since the 1930s have had to deal with the modern media, not only newspapers and magazines but also radio and, especially, since the 1960s, television. Several notable governors from other eras might have been failures in the electronic age. Even Earl Long seemed anachronistic at the time of his death in 1960, though he had just won an election to the United States Congress.[34] Some of Edwards' popularity in the 1970s was due to his talent for using television to his own advantage, especially in news conferences and through coverage of his out-of-state trips. In Louisiana, as in other states, the size of the governor's staff has also grown remarkably in the past fifty years. Governors retain a variety of paid advisers and experts to help them with budgets, pollution and the environment, education, health care, welfare, law enforcement and prisons, media and public relations, and the like. Furthermore, in the 1960s, governors took on the responsibility of administering federal revenue-sharing programs.[35]

There is also the matter of campaign financing. Gubernatorial candidates have always needed money to conduct their campaigns, but the costs of running for office, especially in Louisiana, have reached outrageous levels. In fact, Louisiana politicians hold the dubious distinction of conducting the most expensive campaigns for state office in the United States. According to Thad Beyle, during the late 1970s and early 1980s Louisiana politicians greatly exceeded the reported national average for gubernatorial campaign costs of $3.5 million for two candidates. In 1979, the Republican candidate, Treen, and several Democratic contenders spent a combined total of more than $20 million trying to win the governor's chair. Four years later, Treen and Edwards together

33. Joseph E. Kallenbach, *The American Chief Executive: The Presidency and the Governorship* (New York, 1966), Chap. 1.

34. For an insightful account of Earl Long, see A. J. Liebling, *The Earl of Louisiana* (New York, 1961; rpr. Baton Rouge, 1970). See also Beyle, "Governors," 210; and Renwick, "The Governor," 85.

35. Beyle, "Governors," 205; Sabato, *Goodbye to Good-Time Charlie* (2nd ed.; Washington, D.C., 1983), 82–86, 164–69; J. Oliver Williams, "Changing Perspectives on the American Governor," in Thad Beyle and J. Oliver Williams (eds.), *The American Governor in Behavioral Perspective* (New York, 1972), 2. See also Coleman B. Ransone, Jr., *The American Governorship* (Westport, Conn., 1982), *passim*.

spent nearly another $20 million for an elective office that had a budgeted annual salary of only $73,000 in 1984. Spending so much money, solicited from wealthy contributors and special interests, makes a mockery of representative democracy.[36]

As readers of the following essays will discover, Louisiana's democracy in the nineteenth and twentieth centuries has sometimes been less than honest and equitable. Unfortunately for Louisiana's voters, the state's leaders have not always allowed eligible citizens to register to vote, or permitted those registered to exercise the franchise, or even conceded that those voting would determine the outcome of the elections. Modern-day stories of vote fraud—recalling Slidell's manipulation of the votes of immigrants and the heavy turnouts from cemeteries in Foster's day—remind us that representative democracy needs both honest officials and fair elections to function properly.

JOSEPH G. DAWSON III

BIBLIOGRAPHY

Alexander, Herbert E. "Financing Gubernatorial Election Campaigns." *State Government*, LIII (1980), 140–43.

Bass, Jack, and Walter DeVries. *The Transformation of Southern Politics: Social Change and Political Consequence Since 1945*. New York, 1976.

Beyle, Thad L. "Governors." In *Politics in the American States: A Comparative Analysis*, edited by Virginia Gray, Herbert Jacob, and Kenneth N. Vines. 4th ed. Boston, 1983.

Binning, F. Wayne, "Henry Clay Warmoth and Louisiana Reconstruction." Ph.D. dissertation, University of North Carolina, 1969.

Brinkley, Alan. *Voices of Protest: Huey Long, Father Coughlin, and the Great Depression*. New York, 1982.

Current, Richard N. *Three Carpetbag Governors*. Baton Rouge, 1967.

Dargo, George. *Jefferson's Louisiana: Politics and the Clash of Legal Traditions*. Cambridge, Mass., 1975.

Dart, Benjamin W., ed. *Constitutions of the State of Louisiana*. Indianapolis, 1932.

Davis, Edwin A. *Louisiana: A Narrative History*. 3rd ed. Baton Rouge, 1971.

Glashan, Roy R., comp. *American Governors and Gubernatorial Elections, 1775–1978*. Westport, Conn., 1979.

Hair, William I. *Bourbonism and Agrarian Protest: Louisiana Politics, 1877–1900*. Baton Rouge, 1969.

Hatfield, Joseph T. *William Claiborne: Jeffersonian Centurion in the American Southwest*. Lafayette, La., 1976.

Howard, Perry H. *Political Tendencies in Louisiana*. Rev. and exp. ed. Baton Rouge, 1971.

36. Beyle, "Governors," 187–90; Kurtz, in Wall (ed.), *Louisiana: A History*, 372; Renwick, "The Governor," 75. See also Ransone, *Governor in the United States*, 105–106; Sabato, *Goodbye to Good-Time Charlie* (2nd ed.), 147–53; Herbert E. Alexander, "Financing Gubernatorial Election Campaigns," *State Government*, LIII (1980), 140–43.

Kallenbach, Joseph E. *The American Chief Executive: The Presidency and the Governorship.* New York, 1966.

Key, V. O. *Southern Politics in State and Nation.* New York, 1949.

Lamis, Alexander P. *The Two-Party South.* New York, 1984.

Leibling, A. J. *The Earl of Louisiana.* New York, 1961; rpr. with a foreword by T. Harry Williams, Baton Rouge, 1970.

Murray, Richard, and Arnold Vedlitz. "Racial Voting Patterns in the South: An Analysis of Major Elections from 1960–1977 in Five Cities." *Annals of the American Academy of Political and Social Science,* September, 1978, pp. 29–39.

Ransone, Coleman B., Jr. *The American Governorship.* Westport, Conn., 1982.

———. *The Office of Governor in the South.* University, Ala., 1951.

———. *The Office of Governor in the United States.* University, Ala., 1956.

———. "Political Leadership in the Governor's Office." In *The American South in the 1960's,* edited by Avery Leiserson, 197–220. New York, 1964.

Renwick, Edward. "The Governor." In *Louisiana Politics: Festival in a Labyrinth,* edited by James Bolner, 75–88. Baton Rouge, 1982.

Romero, Sidney J., ed. *"My Fellow Citizens . . .": The Inaugural Addresses of Louisiana's Governors.* Lafayette, La., 1980.

Sabato, Larry, *Goodbye to Good-Time Charlie: The American Governor Transformed, 1950–1975.* Lexington, Mass., 1978; 2nd ed., Washington, D.C., 1983.

Sears, Louis M. *John Slidell.* Durham, N.C., 1925.

Schlesinger, Arthur M., Jr. *The Politics of Upheaval.* Boston, 1960.

Schott, Matthew J. "John M. Parker and the Varieties of American Progressivism." Ph.D. dissertation, Vanderbilt University, 1969.

Sindler, Allan P. *Huey Long's Louisiana: State Politics, 1920–1952.* Baltimore, 1956.

Taylor, Joe Gray. *Louisiana: A Bicentennial History.* New York, 1976.

———. *Louisiana Reconstructed, 1863–1877.* Baton Rouge, 1974.

Wall, Bennett H., ed. *Louisiana: A History.* Arlington Heights, Ill., 1984. Contributions by Charles E. O'Neill, Joe Gray Taylor, William I. Hair, Mark T. Carleton, and Michael L. Kurtz.

Webb, Stephen S. *The Governors-General: The English Army and the Definition of the Empire, 1569–1681.* Chapel Hill, N.C., 1979.

Williams, J. Oliver. "Changing Perspectives on the American Governor." In *The American Governor in Behavioral Perspective,* edited by Thad Beyle and J. Oliver Williams. New York, 1972.

Williams, T. Harry. *Huey Long: A Biography.* New York, 1969.

———. *Romance and Realism in Southern Politics.* Athens, Ga., 1961.

The Louisiana Governors

Governors of the French Colonial Period

Pierre Lemoyne, Sieur d'Iberville et d'Ardillières
Colonial Explorer, 1699–1702

IBERVILLE, Pierre Lemoyne, Sieur d' (b. Montreal, Canada, July 16 [?], 1661; d. Havana, Cuba, July 9, 1706), French army officer and colonial explorer and administrator. Iberville, descendant of a remarkable Norman family whose exploits helped create permanent French Canadian settlements from the pristine wilderness, was baptized at Ville-Marie parish on July 20, 1661. Before his early death, probably from yellow fever, he demonstrated martial skills against the Indians and the English alike, and between 1686 and 1697 he won virtually every battle against the enemies of France

PIERRE LEMOYNE, SIEUR D'IBERVILLE ET D'ARDILLIÈRES. *Photograph courtesy of State Library of Louisiana, from Alcée Fortier's* A History of Louisiana *(4 vols.; New York, 1904), I, 50.*

in Canada. For several decades the success of Iberville forestalled the monopoly of the English on the Canadian fur trade. After the Treaty of Ryswick, in 1697 (ending the War of the League of Augsburg, 1688–1697), France expanded from the St. Lawrence River south along the vital communication arteries binding the Ohio, Mississippi, and Tombigbee rivers with the Gulf of Mexico. In the establishment of French Louisiana, Iberville played a major role and, in keeping with French maritime policy, blocked both the English and the Spanish expansion into North America's heartland.

In his first of three voyages from the French part of the island of Santo Domingo (modern Haiti), and with the *Badine* and *Marin* as his ships, Iberville sailed for the Gulf by way of the Florida Channel on December 31, 1698. By May 31, 1699, he was heading back to France. Although the Spaniards beat the French in the race to fortify Pensacola Bay, Iberville established the first French settlements around Biloxi Bay. From 1699 to 1763, French Louisiana would extend from Mobile Bay along the Gulf Coast at least to the "Isle of New Orleans" east of the Mississippi, and possibly as far as the Red River settlement of Natchitoches, which had been created as a trading post in Spanish Texas. Iberville played a major role in the early exploration of this vast hinterland.

The second of his voyages to the Gulf left Cap Haitien, on the northern shore of Santo Domingo, on December 22, 1699. With the ships *Renommée* and *Gironde*, Iberville sailed to the Mississippi, where he encountered an English corvette under Captain Lewis Bond. When Iberville explained that France had already claimed the area, the English ship departed, leaving to the site the name English Turn, which survives to this day. On this expedition, Iberville sent his younger brother Jean Baptiste Lemoyne, Sieur de Bienville, to meet with the Taensas, Yatachés, and other Indians in the lower Mississippi Delta between March 22 and May 18, 1700. The fragmentary documentation of that journey affords the earliest ethnography of the lower Mississippi Valley.

Iberville's third voyage to the Gulf, aboard the *Renommée*, took place, according to his diary, between December 15, 1701, and April 27, 1702. He had ordered the construction of Fort Saint-Louis, at Mobile, which served as the cradle of French Louisiana until the capital was removed to New Orleans in 1718.

Although Iberville invariably won in conflicts with the English, he was less successful against the Spanish. An international struggle for control over the Gulf of Mexico began with his arrival in 1699 and plunged France into incessant conflicts, especially before 1763. But Iberville left Louisiana in 1702, never to see his colony again. In France, he drafted numerous reports that indicated his sustained affection for the region, some of the accounts, however, exaggerating resistance by both the English and the native population.

Though it is true that Iberville entrusted most of the administration of Louisiana to his younger brother Bienville, the elder Lemoyne must be included in any list of early Louisiana governors. He was a conqueror first of all, yet without his influence the roots of French colonization and settlement in Louisiana might not have taken hold.

❧

Legends, mythology, and uncertainties surround the life of Iberville, from the correct date of his birth to the name of the church where he was interred. One fact emerges unchallenged, however: in the age of international rivalry over North American power, Iberville played a pivotal role in staking France's claims to Louisiana.

For the territory, he coordinated initial Indian policy and created the economic base on which later French governors and intendants could build and expand. Iberville's understanding of the needs and cultural differences of the French and the Indians, his facility in speaking to the natives in their own tongues, his success in Canada—these talents established patterns of control over the Indians that were the key to continued French success vis-à-vis the English. The French followed his example of bestowing presents upon friendly tribes and countering with the musket those who opposed French policies. Not until the policy drafted by Thomas Jefferson ended the practice of giving annual presents in favor of "civilizing" the American Indians did the wise policy of Iberville cease. The English in West Florida, too, and after them, the Spanish, adhered to the French approach that had succeeded so well. Iberville introduced sugarcane into Louisiana on his second voyage, and the crop ultimately became one of the state's most important.

He was called the Canadian Cid or the Great Conqueror in an effusive display of hyperbole that sometimes distorts his historical role. In order to place Iberville in his proper place, a new generation of historians must carry out a new, critical examination of *all* documents, including his own flawed memoir.

JACK D. L. HOLMES

BIBLIOGRAPHY

Crouse, Nellis M. *LeMoyne d'Iberville: Soldier of New France.* Ithaca, N.Y., 1954.
Davis, Andrew M. "Canada and Louisiana." In *Narrative and Critical History of America,* edited by Justin Winsor. Vol. V of 8 vols., 1–78. Boston, 1887.
Frégault, Guy. *Iberville le conquérant.* Montreal, 1944.
———. *Pierre LeMoyne d'Iberville.* Montreal and Paris, 1968.
McWilliams, Richebourg Gaillard. "Iberville and the Southern Indians." *Alabama Review,* XX (1967), 243–62.
———. "Iberville at the Birdfoot Subdelta: Final Discovery of the Mississippi River." In *Frenchmen and French Ways in the Mississippi Valley,* edited by John Francis McDermott, 127–40. Urbana, Ill., 1969.

————, trans. and ed. *Iberville's Gulf Journals.* University, Ala., 1981.
Pothier, Bernard. "LeMoyne d'Iberville." *Dictionary of Canadian Biography.* Vol. II of 11 vols., 390–401. Toronto, 1969.

Sieur de Sauvole

Colonial Governor, 1699–1700

SIEUR DE SAUVOLE (b. France [?], *ca.* 1660; d. Fort Maurepas, Louisiana Colony [Biloxi, Mississippi], August 22, 1700), French naval officer and colonial administrator. Very little is known about Sauvole, *enseigne de vasseau, lieutenant de compagnie de Bellecourt,* before his connection with the nascent Louisiana colony. Any claim to a family relationship with the Lemoyne brothers (Iberville and Bienville) or to the sobriquet "de La Villantry" has been disproved; Marcel Giraud has suggested that Sauvole's family came from the province of Guyenne, but no evidence of his birthplace or the date of his birth has been unearthed. His identification as the first governor of Louisiana is more a *de facto* than a *de jure* one, too, since he was placed in charge of what must be considered a beachhead while the commander of the expedition, Iberville, returned to France to fetch the settlers and material for the colony's true foundation.

The chronology of Sauvole's brief moment of historical visibility begins with his arrival on the Gulf Coast with Iberville's first expedition, in 1699. From the beginning the entries in Iberville's logs make it obvious that he was an important member of the expedition. The frequency with which Iberville called upon him to make important channel soundings suggests that Sauvole may have had training as an engineer; certainly the commander viewed him as a reliable officer. The fact that Iberville chose Sauvole to take command of the little garrison left behind at Old Biloxi when he departed for France on May 2, with Bienville serving as his second-in-command, implies, too, that he was somewhat older and more responsible than the explorer's younger brother.

While Iberville was present, the expeditions that Sauvole undertook required diplomatic contacts with Indians, and he showed some adeptness in dealing with the country's natives. The journal that Sauvole kept from May 3, 1699, to April 1, 1700, shows that he handled this aspect of the commandant's job quite well on his own. During Iberville's absence, Bienville, who is better known for his skill in Indian diplomacy, was often away from the Old Biloxi base on explorations of the Mississippi. With apparent aplomb, Sauvole entertained several delegations of Bayougoula, Pascagoula, Biloxi, and Choctaw Indians, establishing the good relations that would be vital to the colony's survival.

At the same time, he went assiduously about the task of building the security of his post, sending men into the hinterlands to explore Mobile Bay, the Pascagoula River, and Lakes Maurepas and Pontchartrain. Closer to the post, he led a reconnaissance to find a secure water source and oversaw the planting of several crops, which failed in the unusually dry summer weather. To increase his manpower, Sauvole wrote to Canada to invite experienced voyageurs to join him at the new post. Sauvole was in charge of a crucial message center, collecting intelligence reports on the surrounding countryside and its inhabitants and initiating expeditions to collect such intelligence from greater distances when it did not come to him without his efforts, as when the Canadian missionaries, having heard of the French presence on the coast, came down from the Tunicas and the Taensa to report alarming activities of the English among the Chickasaw Indians. Perhaps the most important event during this period was the turning-back of an English ship, away from the waters of the Mississippi, by Bienville, but Bienville was under Sauvole's orders at the time.

Iberville returned with the second expedition on January 9, 1700. Sauvole, as his first duty, went aboard Iberville's ship to report the events of the preceding months, with particular emphasis on repelling the English and on the visit of the two missionaries with news of English activity inland. During Iberville's second sojourn, Sauvole was set to work on new projects important to the colony's future. On his report that one proposed site for the main French center was unsuitable for settlement, he was authorized to begin serious work on the fortifications that would become Fort Maurepas. He was granted men and material for the task and doubtless prepared the fort to accommodate the eight cannon that had been brought from France. During this time, while Iberville was absent on further Mississippi explorations, Sauvole seems to have been left in command of the expedition's ships anchored at Ship Island. To satisfy the interest that France had shown in the reputed presence of pearls, he also oversaw pearl fishing, but this effort failed because of swollen currents in what later would be known as the Pearl River.

Although Iberville was supposed to have brought adequate provisions from France, the garrison ran short of food soon after Iberville departed. To seek relief, Sauvole twice sent the small ship *Enflammé* to Santo Domingo and sent some of his men to aid the Tohomé and Mobilian Indians in defending themselves against other Indians, since the men would be fed by their hosts and would be able to trade for additional foodstuffs while among them.

During this second period of command, Sauvole had to deal with several other problems, among them the unruliness of the Canadians when confined to the garrison, a serious outbreak of tertian fever, and the awkwardness of having to send visiting missionaries away after a brief stay because they were a drain on food supplies. Throughout that hot summer, Sauvole continued with the important tasks of dispatching exploration parties, receiving Indian embassies, and collecting information. In his journal he expressed a wistful envy of men like Le Sueur and Bienville, whose discoveries brought exciting reports. His wish to take part in the excitement of the exploratory journeys was not to be fulfilled, however; he contracted the fever that was ravaging the fort and died of it. Bienville, as second-in-command, succeeded him.

☙

Sauvole never bore the title of governor of the Louisiana colony, nor did he command much more than Fort Maurepas, at Old Biloxi. Yet he did on a small scale what later on in the history of the colony several men did who bore the title. The problems he had to deal with—crop failures and food shortages, ignorance of the interior, the maintenance of successful relations with Indians, manpower shortages, indiscipline among the men he did have, and most devastating of all, uncontrollable disease—were dealt with no more successfully by his successors, if the relative scale of his and their problems is considered.

His successful dealings with the Indians of the Gulf Coast should not be overshadowed by Bienville's later reputation as Indian diplomat *extraordinaire*. It must be remembered that Bienville did not have serious dealings with the coastal Indians until after Sauvole's death, and since the center of the colony was for the first eighteen years of its existence the coast—first at Old Biloxi, then at Mobile and New Biloxi—the importance of Sauvole's own diplomatic maneuvers cannot be exaggerated. If Sauvole had training as an engineer, it is even more evident why he would have been considered by the court the most appropriate commander for the small garrison, since the ability to construct a reliable fortification and to direct marine and land surveys was especially important in the early stages of the colony.

Sauvole's journals may appear somewhat querulous regarding the conduct of missionaries and voyageurs, but probably to his superiors his concern with these matters seemed justified by prudence. We see the other Sauvole, the one who would rather be involved in the adventure of exploration, only briefly; to the good of the colony, Sauvole's mature common sense prevailed, and he disciplined himself to the discretion that makes him seem less colorful than many of his contemporaries. That he would have been capably employed in explorations is evident from the few expeditions he led before taking command of the fort, but his apparent conscientiousness toward any responsibility he was assigned bespeaks the disciplined naval officer more than the unimaginative bureaucrat.

PATRICIA KAY GALLOWAY

BIBLIOGRAPHY

French, Benjamin F., trans. and ed. *Historical Collections of Louisiana*, Part III. New York, 1851.

Giraud, Marcel. *The Reign of Louis XIV, 1698–1715*. Translated by Joseph C. Lambert. Baton Rouge, 1974. Vol. I of Giraud, *A History of French Louisiana*. 4 vols.

Higginbotham, Jay. "Who Was Sauvole?" *Louisiana Studies*, VIII (1968), 144–48.

———, trans. and ed. *The Journal of Sauvole*. Mobile, Ala., 1969.

McWilliams, Richebourg Gaillard, trans. and ed. *Iberville's Gulf Journals*. University, Ala., 1981.

Rowland, Dunbar, and Albert G. Sanders, trans. and eds. *Mississippi Provincial Archives: French Dominion*. Vol. II of 5 vols. Jackson, Miss., 1929.

Jean Baptiste Lemoyne, Sieur de Bienville

Colonial Governor, 1701–1713, 1716–1717, 1718–1725, 1733–1743

BIENVILLE, Jean Baptiste Lemoyne, Sieur de (b. Montreal, Canada, February, 1680; d. Paris, France, March 7, 1767), French military officer and colonial governor. Bienville was the father of Louisiana—that vast territory stretching from Canada to the Gulf of Mexico and wedged between Spanish Florida and Spanish Texas. He may, with some justification, be considered the founder of Alabama and Mississippi, which formed the first French settlements at the beginning of the eighteenth century. The son of Charles Lemoyne and Catherine Thierry Primot, he was baptized in the Montreal parish of Ville-Marie on February 23, 1680.

During Bienville's lifetime, the critical struggle between France and England for supremacy in North America reached its greatest intensity, and he was an important leader in French expansion toward the Gulf of Mexico in the aftermath of Sieur de La Salle's claim to the Louisiana region for King Louis XIV in 1682. Bienville carried scars of an engage-

JEAN BAPTISTE LEMOYNE, SIEUR DE BIEN-VILLE. *Photograph courtesy of State Library of Louisiana, from Fortier's* History of Louisiana, *I, 128.*

ment in 1697 with the English in America, when he was a callow youth in the *garde-marin*. He recuperated in France and, with his elder brothers, sailed from Brest on October 24, 1698, aboard the squadron, comprising the *Badine* and the *Marin*, that the French sent to carry out their plan of establishing French colonies on the Gulf of Mexico. Throughout the spring of 1699, the Lemoynes explored the area, and on March 2 sailed into the Mississippi, which Sieur de La Salle had rediscovered and explored years earlier. At English Turn, the French compelled the English captain Lewis Bond to withdraw from an attempt to settle the area, and Bienville explored the lower Red and Ouachita rivers. He also commanded Fort de La Boulaye, located about thirty miles south of New Orleans. On August 22, 1701, upon the death of Sieur de Sauvole, Bienville's first term as governor of Louisiana began.

Bienville encountered logistical problems when the English cut his supply lines during the War of the Spanish Succession (or Queen Anne's War, 1702–1713) but succeeded in creating the capital of Louisiana at 27-Mile Bluff, on the Mobile River, with a naval port on Dauphin Island, just below Mobile Bay. He led efforts to cooperate with his Spanish neighbors at Pensacola, Havana, and Veracruz and supplied the French colonists with needed provisions during the so-called starving time. By alliances with the Choctaws and other powerful Indian tribes, the French under Bienville opposed English attempts to push the

Charleston fur trade to the Gulf. French success was doomed, however, because of a defect in the form of colonial government, which permitted vicious quarrels between Bienville, the commissary (*commissaire or-donnateur*) Nicholas de La Salle, and Father Henri Roulleaux de La Vente. It was, unfortunately, one of the many internecine struggles Bienville experienced in his political career.

The remarkable Lemoyne influence over Louisiana suffered with Iberville's death in 1706, and Bienville's ever-present enemies at the French court conspired to replace him with Nicholas Daneau, Sieur de Muy, in 1707. Muy died on the way to his post at Mobile, but the com-missioner, Jean Baptiste Martin d'Artaguette Diron, conducted his own investigation of Bienville's handling of government affairs. To his sur-prise, he learned that Bienville was an effective leader, popular with the colonists and most of the Indians.

Still, Bienville could do only so much with the colonists the French government sent to Louisiana. Louisiana needed working hands—farmers, laborers, and soldiers. Bureaucrats and sons of the gentry—drones—came instead. Facing economic failure in the province, Louis XIV turned to Antoine Crozat and, on September 14, 1712, the creation of a private, fifteen-year proprietary colony under Crozat's direction. The signing of the Treaty of Utrecht in the following year diminished Franco-Spanish rivalry for a time, and the new proprietary governor, Antoine de Lamothe, Sieur de Cadillac, arrived in June, 1713, to suc-ceed Bienville.

Cadillac complained about his command and the environment from the moment he landed. Four years later, after a surge of turbulent poli-tics and economic failures, France looked again to Bienville: he was named military commander of the Mississippi, from the mouth of the Ohio River to the Gulf. His major task was to undo the alienation of the Indian nations that had once been a basic support of French colonial efforts. But Bienville's and Cadillac's conflicting personalities defeated any hope of cooperative success. Each official undercut the authority and efforts of the other. Bienville's reaction to the murder of several Canadians by the Natchez Indians in 1716 was to build Fort Rosalie at Natchez and to make a show of force that temporarily impressed the Indians.

Upon returning to Mobile, Bienville learned that he had been named acting governor pending the arrival of Jean-Michiel, Seigneur de Lép-inay et de La Longueville. But when the new governor arrived in

March, 1717, tension arose between the two colonial administrators that was as debilitating to effective rule as that between Bienville and Cadillac had been. In the end, John Law's Company of the West (later called the Company of the Indies) reorganized the colonial government, and Bienville had to be content to serve as commandant general of the colony, with the right to wear the Cross of St. Louis.

It was during his third tenure as governor (1718–1725) that Bienville recorded some of his most notable achievements. On a site at an ancient Indian trade center, where there was a portage from the Mississippi to Lake Pontchartrain, Bienville in 1718 established the town of New Orleans. During the Franco-Spanish War (1719–1722), he defended Mobile and Dauphin Island against enemy attacks and succeeded twice in capturing Spanish Pensacola. French conquests pushed the colonial boundary to St. Joseph's Bay, although the Perdido River was accepted at the close of the war. French Canadian attempts to expand to Natchitoches in 1714, however, were met in 1718 by Spain's establishment of Los Adaes (modern Robeline, Louisiana) as the capital of Spanish Texas.

Law's dream of funding colonization through paper currency and a thriving bond market was too advanced for its time. The runaway speculation of the Mississippi Bubble created a negative public image for the Louisiana colony, and Bienville suffered as a result. His supporters lost a crucial political struggle in 1726, and on August 9 of that year Etienne de Perier succeeded him. Bienville and his younger brother, Chateaugay, returned to France in 1727. But, myopic colonial policies once more endangered Louisiana. On November 28, 1729, the antagonized Natchez Indians massacred virtually the entire French command and civilian population. In 1731, Louisiana became a royal colony once more, and the crown recalled Bienville to duty. For his fourth and final period as governor (1733–1743), he received an unwieldy set of instructions that the French government had drafted on February 2, 1732.

Bienville's final administration helped heal the breaches in the Franco-Indian alliances. By a successful use of the roller-type cotton gin, he helped introduce a valuable agricultural staple. To avoid the high cost of tallow wax, he urged settlers to process the native bayberry laurel into wax. He named a military commission to improve fortifications and defenses. He provided succor to the victims of the hurricane of 1740 and joined with sailor Jean Louis in promoting the establishment of a charity hospital—the forerunner of St. Charles Charity Hospital. Bienville supported the work of the St. Louis parish church, the predecessor of the present-day New Orleans cathedral, and he backed the priests who tried to soften the negative effects of the harsh Code Noir of 1724 governing slaves. In that, he often worked in opposition to the selfish wishes of the colony's plantation owners. With Edme Gatien Salmon, he proposed in 1742 the teaching of geography, geometry, and the humanities at a college to be created under the direction of the Jesuit fathers.

Bienville's military failure against the Chickasaw Indians, including the defeat on May 25, 1736, at the village of Ackia, led him to extend the French forts to the Chickasaw Bluffs (modern Memphis, Tennessee), where in 1738 he established Fort Assumption. The Indian campaigns caused Bienville anguish and physical pain, and he asked to be relieved of command. Sciatica and the Chickasaws had done him in.

On August 17, 1743, he returned to Paris and life in retirement on a modest government pension.

❧

Bienville seems to reverse the fate that Mark Antony spoke of in his funeral oration for Julius Caesar: "The evil that men do lives after them, / The good is oft interred with their bones." Historians over the centuries have interred the evil with Bienville's bones and made of him almost a saint. As Jo Ann Carrigan writes in her commentary on Alcée Fortier's *History of Louisiana,* "It is high time that someone attempted a reevaluation of Jean Baptiste Lemoyne, Sieur de Bienville, his character, his motivation, and the nature and worth of his influence on the history of French colonial Louisiana." Carrigan notes that Bienville "was almost constantly embroiled in bitter disputes with the commissary or members of the council; when he was reduced to second in command, he always fought the governor, sometimes forming an alliance with the commissary." Although Bienville is given credit for bringing the Ursuline nuns to Louisiana to run the schools, careful scholarship discloses that the nuns' duty was primarily to manage the hospital, only "secondarily to direct the school."[1]

As Carrigan points out, controversy continues to surround a number

1. Jo Ann Carrigan, "Commentary," in Alcée Fortier, *Early Explorers and the Domination of the French, 1512–1768,* ed. Jo Ann Carrigan (Baton Rouge, 1966), 291, Vol. I of Fortier, *A History of Louisiana,* 2 vols. in 2nd ed.

of aspects of Bienville's career in Louisiana. General histories of the colony and state have not placed enough emphasis on Bienville's questionable decisions or on his encouragement of factionalism at the expense of the colony's well-being. Twice recalled to France (in 1708 and 1724), Bienville faced charges of corruption and malfeasance in office—charges that were directed against other governors as well during the colonial era. Bienville's appointment of family members—a younger brother, a cousin, and a nephew—stamp him with the disrepute of nepotism, although his own time found no fault with such family favors. In answering the charges against him, Bienville often emerged victorious, and that may explain Fortier's traditional view of the father of Louisiana as innocent of misconduct. On the other hand, some sources suggest that Bienville practiced political intrigue to keep himself at the center of Louisiana's stage, or at least ever in the wings, eager to reappear in order to right the wrongs as he saw them. He was the quintessential politician, anxious to serve the people and ever mindful of feathering his own nest. The Lake Pontchartrain site for New Orleans may have been an unhealthy one, but it is obvious that the choice of location made Bienville wealthy. Bienville traded with France's enemies, the English and the Spanish, notwithstanding official directives, and he thereby helped establish through quasi-legal channels the means to supply Louisiana colonists, and to add to his personal wealth. It is moot, perhaps, whether his fostering of political corruption in early Louisiana affairs has had a part in institutionalizing the shady in the Bayou State's history.

Still, the balance sheet for Bienville is in his favor. He contributed much to the creation of France's largest colony in the Americas, and if he did so under the calumny of his detractors, he earns comparison with another founding father, George Washington. Though of different ethnic and national backgrounds, Bienville and Washington had much in common: both faced cabals against them; both were military leaders who rose above temporary defeat to prevail; and both suffered the physical torments that the flesh is heir to. In the final analysis, too, both succeeded in surmounting bureaucratic impediments to extend the power of their governments to the western frontiers. And both were victims of the fake-lore and mythology of well-meaning writers. It is time for historians to examine anew Bienville's role in France's colonial history.

JACK D. L. HOLMES

BIBLIOGRAPHY

Cruzat, Heloise H. "New Orleans Under Bienville." *Louisiana Historical Quarterly*, I (1918), 55–86.

Fortier, Alcée. *Early Explorers and the Domination of the French, 1512–1768.* 2nd ed. Edited with commentary by Jo Ann Carrigan. Baton Rouge, 1966. Vol. I of Fortier, *A History of Louisiana.* 2 vols. in 2nd ed.

Giraud, Marcel. *Histoire de la Louisiane française.* 4 vols. Paris, 1953–74.

Higginbotham, Jay. *Old Mobile: Fort Louis de la Louisiane, 1702–1711.* Mobile, Ala., 1977.

King, Grace Elizabeth. *Jean-Baptiste Le Moyne Sieur de Bienville.* New York, 1893.

O'Neill, Charles E. "Jean-Baptiste Le Moyne de Bienville." *Dictionary of Canadian Biography.* Vol. III of 11 vols., 379–84. Toronto, 1974.

Rowland, Dunbar, and Albert G. Sanders, trans. and eds. *Mississippi Provincial Archives, French Dominion.* 3 vols. Jackson, Miss., 1927–32.

Antoine de Lamothe, Sieur de Cadillac

Colonial Governor, 1713–1716

CADILLAC, Antoine de Lamothe, Sieur de (b. Lauments, France, March 5, 1658; d. Castelsarrasin, France, October 16, 1730), colonial military officer and colonial governor. The man born Antoine Laumet in a small village of Gascony died Antoine de Lamothe, Sieur de Cadillac, having been in the meantime seigneur in Acadia, commandant at Michilimackinac, proprietor of Detroit, and governor of Louisiana. He carefully engineered his own social ascension, with the help of shady dealings, falsified credentials, and bald-faced lies.

The son of Jean Laumet, a minor provincial judge, Cadillac first appeared on the North American continent around 1683 when he settled at Port Royal, in Acadia (Nova Scotia). He sailed for a while under the privateer François Guion, whose niece Marie-Thérèse he married in 1687. On the marriage certificate, he dubbed himself "Antoine de Lamothe, Sieur de Cadillac," and claimed to be the son of "Jean de la Mothe, Seigneur de dict lieu de Cadillac, de Launay et Semontel."[1] Cadillac's social advancement had begun. He settled with his wife on his small Acadian seigneurie until 1691, when his quarrels with the governor, Louis-Alexandre des Friches de Meneval, and the destruction of his house during a British raid against Port Royal drove him and his family to Quebec.

1. Nouvelles acquisitions, Fonds français, 9229, folio 2, in Bibliothèque Nationale, Paris.

In New France (Canada), he impressed Governor Louis de Buade, Comte de Frontenac, who gave him a half-pay commission in the Troupes of the Marine. A true son of Gascony, Cadillac was never at a loss for words, especially in praise of himself and in defense of his projects, and Frontenac named him commandant at Michilimackinac, the most important military and commercial post in western Canada. In 1698, the French crown decided to close the western beaver trade, the French market being flooded with more pelts than it could use. Cadillac embarked for France, where he presented an ambitious new project to the Ministry of the Marine: the founding of a post at Detroit. He succeeded in convincing the minister, Jérome de Phelypeaux, Comte de Pontchartrain, that a settlement at Detroit would slow down the beaver trade, hamper English expansion, and serve as a focal point for the Western Indian tribes. In 1701, Cadillac arrived in Detroit with about one hundred men.

Dissension quickly arose between Cadillac and Philippe de Rigaud, Marquis de Vaudreuil, who had become governor of New France in 1703. Finally, Pontchartrain sent an investigator to report on Detroit and Cadillac. The report filed by François Clairambault d'Aigremont indicted Cadillac's conduct and impugned his character to such a degree that the Gascon should have been finished in the royal service. Instead, Pontchartrain, whether because he was reluctant to admit he had long supported an incompetent rascal or because the golden-tongued Cadillac cast doubts on the validity of the report, named Cadillac governor of Louisiana on May 5, 1710.

Louisiana, at the time, was a poor, struggling outpost that the crown considered an expensive burden. Pontchartrain was eager to lay down the burden and was eyeing Antoine Crozat, the wealthy financier, as the man who could relieve France by becoming proprietor of the province. Cadillac, named governor of a province he had never visited, was chosen to persuade Crozat. He used his not inconsiderable rhetorical powers on the reluctant financier, addressing to him a memoir on the area's potential mineral wealth (June 29, 1712). Persuaded, Crozat took on the colony, agreeing to send two ships a year, each with ten young settlers, in exchange for a monopoly on the Louisiana trade. Pontchartrain confirmed Cadillac in his functions as governor and selected a commissioner of the marine, Jean-Baptiste Du Bois Du Clos, as *ordonnateur*.

On February 6, 1713, Cadillac, his wife and daughters, Du Bois Du

Clos, and twelve marriageable girls sailed on the *Baron de la Fauche*. The crossing was not without incident. The two men entrusted with the future of the colony laid down the basis of steady enmity. Du Clos took notes so that he might tattle effectively to the minister. On June 5, the *Baron de la Fauche* arrived at Dauphin Island, and Cadillac took his first look at his domain. He was not impressed.

In fact, there is a strong suggestion that the governor had been deluded by his own grandiose descriptions and that his bitter attacks on Louisiana, which he called "not worth a straw,"[2] owed in part to his disappointment when he had to face reality. He found on Dauphin Island (off the coast of modern Alabama) a nasty little garden with twelve fig trees, three pear trees, three apple trees, one plum tree, and thirty feet of vineyards with rotten grape clusters: "This," he exclaimed, "is the terrestrial paradise" he had been led to expect.[3] Moreover, a prim and proper family man, Cadillac was scandalized by the moral tone prevailing in Louisiana. "There is a woman on Dauphin Island," he wrote his minister, "who yields herself to all comers."[4]

Poverty and immorality, however, were secondary problems compared with the factional divisions that soon arose between Cadillac and his *ordonnateur*, Du Bois Du Clos, who allied himself with Jean-Baptiste Lemoyne de Bienville and the Jesuits, whom the governor heartily detested. Louisiana, like French provinces and other colonies, was plagued by a dual form of government with the *ordonnateur* and governor sharing powers and responsibilities. The *ordonnateur* administered the colony's finances and supervised commerce while the governor controlled the military; they shared responsibility for police and land grants. In fact, the neat division did not work, and quarrels over prerogatives were as frequent during Cadillac's tenure as during Bienville's administration. The situation was aggravated by Bienville's presence. Embittered at the appointment of Cadillac to a post he thought rightfully his, Bienville did nothing to facilitate the task of the new governor. Cadillac had been ordered to conduct an investigation into Bienville's actions. This investigation yielded no results: the charges against Bienville were too old, the testimony too contradictory. The irascible Canadian, however, held a grudge against Cadillac. Du Clos, out of per-

2. Cadillac to Comte de Pontchartrain, October 26, 1713, in Correspondance générale, Louisiane, C 13a, Vol. 3, folio 47, Archives des Colonies, Paris.

3. *Ibid.*, folio 9.

4. Cadillac to Council, January 2, 1716, in Correspondance générale, Louisiane, C 13a, Vol. 4, folios 530–31, Archives des Colonies.

sonal animoisty toward the governor, had refused to participate in the investigation. Du Clos and Bienville thus found themselves allies against Cadillac.

Cadillac did make some effort to develop what he considered the only hope for Louisiana, namely, mines and trade with Mexico. He went to the Illinois country and located mines, but nothing was done to exploit them except for lead. He tried to trade with the Spanish colonies but met with official opposition in both Pensacola and Veracruz. The colonists, on the other hand, circumvented Crozat's monopoly whenever possible and traded personally with the Spaniards despite strict interdictions. Du Clos, who was supposed to regulate the colony's commerce, closed his eyes to the settlers' actions and participated wholeheartedly in the illegal trade. When Cadillac attempted to curb these activities, he was branded a company man.

Crozat became increasingly disillusioned with both the colony and his governor. In January, 1717, he petititoned for an end to his monopoly; on August 23, 1717, the council freed him of his responsibilities. In the same month, John Law's Company of the West was chartered. Law, a Scotsman given to outlandish financial schemes, decided to try his hand at managing Louisiana. With this, Cadillac's Louisiana involvement ended definitively.

Replaced as governor, Cadillac sailed for France, where John Law had unleashed a remarkable propaganda blitz about Louisiana. For once, the Gascon was on the side of the truth as he tried to present a more realistic view of the colony. This unwonted venture into honesty served him badly. On September 27, 1717, he was sent to the Bastille. Freed after four months' imprisonment, and granted the Cross of St. Louis and salary arrears as consolation, Cadillac ceased to have any influence in colonial affairs and retired to Gascony. In 1723, he bought the governorship at Castelsarrasin, and it was there that he died seven years later.

☙

Cadillac's contributions to Louisiana were slight. He left the administrative system unchanged, compounded the dissension among officials, failed to develop either trade or industry, and certainly did not reform the moral laxity he deplored. On the one hand, his pessimistic accounts of Louisiana's poverty and sterility were forgotten after his brief tenure. On the other hand, his trip to the Illinois country and his favorable report on mine prospects helped to keep alive the dreams of mineral wealth and to lure unsuspecting immigrants to the Gulf shore during Law's control of the colony. Cadillac may have the distinction of being Louisiana's most colorful governor of the colonial period, and may rank with Huey P. Long, Earl K. Long, and Edwin Edwards in personal flair.

MATHÉ ALLAIN

BIBLIOGRAPHY

Delanglez, Jean, S.J., "Antoine Laumet, Alias Cadillac." *Mid America*, XXVII (1945), 108–32, 188–216, 232–56.

———. "Cadillac at Detroit." *Mid America*, XXX (1948), 152–76.

———. "Cadillac, Proprietor of Detroit," *Mid America*, XXXII (1950), 155–88, 226–58.

———. "Cadillac's Early Years in America." *Mid America*, XXVI (1944), 3–39.

———. "Cadillac's Last Years." *Mid America*, XXXIII (1951), 3–42.

———. "The Genesis and Building of Detroit." *Mid America*, xxx (1948), 75–104.

Giraud, Marcel. *Années de transition, 1715–1717*. Paris, 1958. Vol. II. of Giraud, *Histoire de la Louisiane française*. 4 vols.

O'Neill, Charles Edwards. *Church and State in French Colonial Louisiana: Policy and Politics to 1732*. New Haven, 1966.

Wall, Bennett H., ed. *Louisiana: A History*. Arlington Heights, Ill., 1984.

Zoltvany, Yves F. "Antoine Laumet, Sieur de Cadillac." *Dictionary of Canadian Biography*. Vol. II of 8 vols., 351–56. Toronto, 1969.

———. "New France and the West, 1701–1713." *Canadian Historical Review*, XLVI (1965), 302–22.

Jean-Michiele Lépinay

Colonial Governor, 1717–1718

LÉPINAY, JEAN-MICHIELE, SEIGNEUR DE LÉPINAY ET DE LA LONGUEVILLE (also rendered L'Epinay, Lespinay, La Espinay; b. Fougères, France, *ca.* 1665; d. Fort-Royal, Martinique, French West Indies, January 3, 1721), French naval officer and colonial governor. Fougères, where Lépinay was born, is a small manufacturing town in Brittany, northeast of Rennes. Of Lépinay's early life little is known. He entered royal service in 1683 as a midshipman in the French navy and was assigned to duty at Rochefort, the new military port and arsenal established by Jean-Baptiste Colbert. He accompanied French forces to Canada in 1687, serving first as ensign and later as lieutenant. His actions recommended him to the Comte de Frontenac, governor of New France (Canada), who rewarded him with the honorary position of port captain of Quebec. After eight years of service in Canada, on April 20, 1695, Lépinay re-

ceived permission to return to France, where he was again posted to
Rochefort. On November 1, 1705, he was promoted to lieutenant com-
mander. In this capacity he came to the attention of the Comte de
Toulouse, head of the Conseil de la Marine. Agreeing with Antoine
Crozat, Toulouse recommended Lépinay for the position of governor of
Louisiana in 1716, and this nomination was confirmed by the Conseil
on March 16, 1716.

Lépinay's delay in taking up his new position was the result of the
lengthy preparations needed for a major expedition to Louisiana. Before
setting out, Lépinay petitioned for the Cross of St. Louis, which he received on October 21, 1716. Finally, on December 21, 1716, the expedition departed from Rochefort. It included two hundred soldiers, eighty-
one settlers, the new governor, Marc-Antoine Hubert as *commissaire
ordonnateur*, and Sr. de Artus as engineer in chief and director of fortifications in Louisiana. Both Lépinay and Artus brought their personal
servants; some of the officers brought their parents, brothers, sisters,
and wives. Their numbers were so great that the original two royal vessels commissioned for the expedition proved inadequate and a third ship
was readied at the last moment. Including over one hundred sailors, the
expedition came to more than four hundred persons. After a very
stormy crossing, the ships reached Mobile Bay on March 9, 1717. Lépinay took up residence on Dauphin Island.

Lépinay's first impressions of the frontier colony were distinctly unfavorable. On May 30, 1717, he wrote the Conseil de la Marine that
supplies were short, settlers were fleeing the colony for Mobile, Old
Biloxi, and new settlements, soldiers were refusing to accept maize flour
in place of wheat, and only twenty thousand livres remained in the
treasury to rebuild fortifications on Dauphin Island and at Mobile. He
added that inflation was rampant, credit nonexistent, and foodstuffs in
short supply. To alleviate a shortage of supplies, Lépinay allowed two
distressed English vessels to sell their cargoes in Louisiana and sent a
ship to Havana to purchase cattle. The governor encouraged prospect-
ing and exploration of the interior, established a new post among the
Alibamones, and recommended changes in the French colonial uniform
(hatchets were substituted for rapiers and swordbelts entirely eliminated), but he was unsuccessful in fulfilling his orders on several other
counts.

By October, relations between the governor and the *ordonnateur*,

Hubert, were openly hostile. Hubert wrote the Conseil de la Marine to complain that Lépinay was arrogant and despotic, treated the Superior Council with disdain, and had usurped police and judicial powers. Hubert added that Lépinay was so inept in dealing with the Indians that he was driving them to the English. The chiefs of twenty-four Indian tribes had visited with the new governor during the summer of 1717, and they had been well received and rewarded with suitable gifts. But Lépinay was less generous with those who could not make the trip to Mobile. Both the *ordonnateur* and the former governor, Bienville, claimed that Lépinay had been extremely stingy with gifts, leading to considerable dissatisfaction among certain tribes. In subsequent letters, Hubert questioned Lépinay's honesty and made allusions to his scandalous life in the colony.

While discord reigned in Louisiana, affairs in France took a dramatic turn that shortened the tenure of the new governor. In August, 1717, Antoine Crozat, anxious to become disengaged fom his monopoly of trading privileges in Louisiana, surrendered these rights to a trading company newly created by John Law, the Company of the West. On September 12, 1717, the company received proprietorship over Louisiana for twenty-five years, with permission to nominate all administrative officials. Almost immediately the Company of the West exercised this right, ordering the recall of Lépinay and replacing him with Bienville.

Lépinay received news of his recall on February 9, 1718, and promptly turned over the government to Bienville. He was also informed of his nomination as governor of Grenada, an appointment dated November 1, 1717. Accompanied by Artus, who had also been recalled, and a large number of servants, he departed from Louisiana for France in the summer of 1718. Once he was back in France, his conduct as governor was the subject of a lengthy investigation, since it was rumored that he had brought back a sizable fortune. All of his possessions were sequestered at Rochefort, and he was forced to remain in France during the whole of 1719. Perhaps he was the victim of slander or simply of libelous letters from Louisiana by Hubert and Bienville; in the end, no charges could be proved against him.

On May 18, 1720, he set sail for Grenada to assume the position he had been appointed to more than two years before. After a speedy crossing, he landed on June 28, 1720. Scarcely six months later, he was dead, the rigors of colonial service having taken their toll. He died on January 3, 1721, while visiting the governor-general of the French West Indies, at Fort-Royal, Martinique.

∝

Lépinay's instructions from the Conseil de la Marine called for him to adjudicate pending conflicts; gather information about the conduct of his predecessor, Antoine de Lamothe, Sieur de Cadillac; appease dissension; work in harmony with the new *ordonnateur*; and involve Louisiana more fully in the life of the French Empire. With regard to foreign policy, he was to keep friendly relations with neighboring Spanish settlements, provide for reciprocal restitution of deserters and exchange of prisoners, and maintain a stable peace through the generous provision of gifts to the Indian tribes. Domestically, he was to enforce the restriction against mixed marriages in the colony, thus promoting the morals of the colony in order that the officers, soldiers, and settlers might serve as good examples to the Indians. He was also to encourage the cultivation of tobacco, mulberry trees, and indigo, and to increase the pelt trade. Lépinay hardly had time to carry out these tall orders.

Because of previous jurisidictional disputes between governor and *ordonnateur*, Lépinay's powers as governor were expanded, he was given the right to make "extraordinary expenditures," and he took on added responsibilities for the hospital, the king's storehouses, provisions for the troops, and other areas traditionally the prerogative of the *ordonnateur*. The additional powers, as well as the fact that he drew a higher salary (two thousand livres a year for two years) than Hubert (fifteen hundred livres), placed Lépinay in a much more advantageous position than the one his predecessor, Cadillac, held. In addition, the new governor was granted a 2-percent commission on all exports and the right to bring with him six tons of salable merchandise and a large quantity of flour and brandy for his personal use.

If the additional powers and privileges were designed to end the constant wrangling between colonial officials, they had just the opposite effect. Rather than being content, Lépinay sought to enlarge his privileges, exceeded his instructions, and usurped police and justice powers assigned to the *ordonnateur*. His actions had the effect of continuing the long-standing conflict between governor and *ordonnateur*. Hubert became so disgruntled that he proposed dividing the colony into two sectors, with Bienville holding responsibilities in the western part. For

Lépinay, his recall and promotion to the governorship of Grenada could not have been altogether unpleasant, since it freed him from a desperately poor, neglected frontier colony riddled with opposing factions.

BRIAN E. COUTTS

BIBLIOGRAPHY

Giraud, Marcel. *Années de Transition, 1715–1717.* Paris, 1958. Vol. II of Giraud, *Histoire de la Louisiane française.* 4 vols.
————. *L'Epoque de John Law, 1717–1720.* Paris, 1966. Vol. III of Giraud, *Histoire.*
Lauvrière, Emile. *Histoire de la Louisiane française, 1673–1939.* Paris, 1940; Baton Rouge, 1940.
Rowland, Dunbar, and Albert G. Sanders, trans. and eds. *Mississippi Provincial Archives: French Dominion.* Vols. II and III of 5 vols. Jackson, Miss., 1929–32.
Taillemite, Etienne. "Jean-Michel de Lespinay." *Dictionary of Canadian Biography.* Vol. II of 11 vols., 425–26. Toronto, 1969.

Pierre Sidrac Dugué de Boisbriand

Acting Colonial Governor, 1725–1726

DUGUÉ DE BOISBRIAND, Pierre (also rendered Boisbriant; b. Montreal, Canada, February 21, 1675; d. France, June 7, 1736), French naval and army officer, commandant of the Mobile and Illinois districts, and acting colonial governor. Dugué was one of nine children of Michel-Sidrac and Marie Moyen. His father, one of the first seigneurs in the region of Montreal, served as the commander of the military garrison there and was rewarded with the seigneury of Senneville, on Montreal Island. He later sold this property and in 1683 obtained the seigneury of Mille-Iles. Despite extensive landholdings, his primary interest was in the fur trade.

Inheriting the love of the frontier from his father, Dugué followed an older brother into military service. With the patronage of the Comte de Frontenac, a family friend, he entered military service as a half-pay ensign in 1691. Three years later, he was promoted to ensign and in 1696 served with his cousin, Pierre Lemoyne d'Iberville, in an attack on English-held Newfoundland. In 1697, he accompanied Iberville on a successful conquest of Fort Bourbon, on Hudson Bay.

The peace brought by the Treaty of Ryswick in 1697 also brought unemployment for Dugué. Along with sixty Canadian compatriots, he sailed to France and resided at La Rochelle on half pay awaiting reassignment.

Iberville recruited most of the Canadians, including Dugué and Louis Juchereau de Saint-Denis, for his second expedition to Louisiana. They departed in the fall of 1699 on board two ships and arrived off the Mississippi coast in January, 1700. Dugué, along with the future governor Jean Baptiste Lemoyne de Bienville, led numerous reconnaissance missions for Iberville. When the main French settlement was moved to Mobile, Dugué aided in the construction of Fort Louis de Louisiane. In the town laid out behind the fort, he received several lots immediately in front of the parade ground.

Promoted to major, Dugué remained in Mobile for the next dozen years, using it as a base for numerous expeditions into the interior. Apart from a brief affair with Marie Françoise de Boisrenaud, who had led twenty-three women to Mobile in 1704, he remained a bachelor. (Several sources mention that he suffered from a deformed back, perhaps the result of a childhood spinal injury.) Although seriously considered for the post of commandant of the newly established Natchez district in 1714, Dugué was passed over in favor of Captain Chavagne de Richebourg. Two years later, in 1716, he was, however, named garrison adjutant, and in 1717, he became commandant of the Mobile and Dauphin Island district.

After sixteen years of continuous service in Louisiana, Dugué returned to France in 1717 on the grounds of having to settle the estate of Charles Le Vasseur de Ruessavel, for which he was acting as executor. Meeting regularly with colonial officials in Paris, he lobbied in favor of Bienville's promotion to commandant general of the colony. He also informed officials of the sad condition of the colonial troops, explaining that they were forced to live marginally because of their poor pay and the high costs on the frontier. Dugué met with leading scientists, officers from the naval council, and concessionaires and members of various colonization societies, furnishing them with a great deal of practical knowledge about the colony.

His lobbying may have had some effect. Bienville was appointed commandant general in March, 1718, shortly before Dugué returned to Louisiana with a new commission as lieutenant. On April 17, less than a month after arriving, he was rewarded by being named commandant of the Illinois district.

At the urging of John Law's Company of the West, Dugué led a group of a hundred men, including sixty-eight soldiers and several French mining experts, to the Illinois district. He aimed to discover rich silver mines and reinforce the defense of the region. Leaving New Orleans in December, 1718, he encountered high water on the Mississippi, which delayed the arrival at Kaskaskia until May, 1719. Some twenty kilometers from there, on the east bank of the Mississippi, Dugué supervised the construction of Fort Chartres, named in honor of the Duke of Chartres. When completed in 1720, the fort consisted of a wooden stockade, a commandant's house, a barracks, a storehouse, and a blacksmith's shop. To fulfill his second objective, that of discovering rich silver mines, he led several explorations. On one of these, a small lead mine was discovered that also yielded a small quantity of silver. Samples of the ore were shipped to Bienville in New Orleans for forwarding to company officials in France.

As commandant of the Illinois district, Dugué enjoyed a good deal of success. Despite jurisdictional disputes with the governor of Canada and religious disputes with the Jesuits, he did much to solidify French control in the region. Fluent in the Illinois language, he successfully pacified several of the many tribes of the area.

Remaining at Fort Chartres until late 1724, Dugué obeyed orders to return to New Orleans to replace Bienville, who had been recalled to France. Arriving in New Orleans in January, 1725, Dugué served as acting commandant general until the arrival of Etienne de Périer in March, 1727, at which time he resumed his postion as king's lieutenant.

Dugué left New Orleans for the last time in November, 1728, reaching France in the spring of 1729. There, caught in the middle of anti-Bienville sentiment, he suffered censure and dismissal from royal service. But on the basis of his thirty-six years of service to the crown, the king awarded him a modest pension of eight hundred livres in 1730. Three years later, he learned that Bienville had returned to America as governor of Louisiana.

⬥

Dugué de Boisbriand served as acting commandant general or governor—the term *governor* was not used until 1732—of Louisiana from February, 1725, when Bienville departed, until March 15, 1727, when Périer arrived. He was ill suited for the task. His intimate connections with his cousin Bienville and the pro-Bienville faction in the colony brought him into repeated conflicts with Jacques de La Chaise, chief financial officer representing the Company of the West.

As commandant general, Dugué occupied a house owned by the crown and staffed by three European servants and one black and four Indian domestic slaves. His salary remained at five thousand livres per annum, the amount he had received as king's lieutenant. The Superior Council, of which he was president, did repay him for the personal funds he had advanced for Indian gifts and for the three thousand some livres he had paid to his interpreter during a five-year residence in Illinois. He repeatedly complained that five thousand livres was insufficient to maintain the dignity of his office. He devoted much of his time to lobbying for increased benefits for the troops. One critic, writing to the company officials from Louisiana, reported that Dugué had allowed them virtually to clean out the company stores.

By late 1725, La Chaise was remonstrating to company officials that Dugué was derelict in performing his duties, that he encouraged assemblies of dissident officers, and that he had slandered other members of the Superior Council. Another critic grumbled that, although no criticism could be made about Dugué's personal conduct, the man was a weak leader, one who lacked the qualities necessary to bring the warring factions of society under control.

The appointment of Périer as commandant general in August, 1726, and the recall of several of Bienville's supporters further weakened Dugué's position in New Orleans. As one contemporary put it, Dugué was a good Canadian, accustomed to the life of the Indians and so slack that he would never exercise his authority unless forced to. Although the criticism may be a little overdrawn, Dugué certainly lacked the strong, objective qualities of leadership necessary to restore harmony in the colony.

Stripped of his honors and rank when he returned to France in 1729, Dugué had the satisfaction of knowing that Bienville assumed the governorship three years later. Dugué's death in 1736 brought to a close the life of one of Louisiana's little-known founding fathers.

BRIAN E. COUTTS

BIBLIOGRAPHY

Giraud, Marcel. *Histoire de la Louisiane française.* 4 vols. Paris, 1953–74.
Reid, W. Stanford. "Pierre Dugué de Boisbriand." *Dictionary of Canadian Biography.* Vol. II of 11 vols., 203–204. Toronto, 1969.

Rowland, Dunbar, and Albert G. Sanders, trans. and eds. *Mississippi Provincial Archives: French Dominion*. Vols. I–III of 5 vols. Jackson, Miss., 1927–32.

Etienne de Périer

Colonial Governor, 1727–1733

PÉRIER, Etienne de (b. Le Havre, France, *ca.* 1690; d. Brest, France, *ca.* 1755), French naval officer, captain in the merchant fleet of the Company of the Indies, and colonial governor. Located 134 miles west-northwest of Paris, the seaport of Le Havre, in Normandy, was a major center for the French navy. Little is known about Périer's early life there. Along with his younger brother Antoine Alexis, he was attracted to a naval career at an early age. A few sources suggest that he fought valiantly as a naval officer in the latter stages of the War of the Spanish Succession (1701–1713).

At the end of the war, Périer entered the services of the Company of the West and later served its successor, the Company of the Indies, in a variety of capacities. Several sources indicate his strong loyalty and dedicated efforts in behalf of company interests. His efforts prompted the directors of the company to choose Périer as commandant general—in effect, the governor—of Louisiana, then a colony under company control. On August 9, 1726, the king ratified the company's nomination.

Prior to his departure for Louisiana, Périer received lengthy instructions from company officials. The orders, dated September 30, 1726, directed him to confer in New Orleans with the company's commissary, Jacques de La Chaise, to arrange for the prompt departure of his predecessor, Dugué de Boisbriand, a supporter of the former commandant general Bienville, and to reorganize thoroughly the company's operations in the colony.

Périer, accompanied by his wife, Catherine Le Chibelier, and his stepson de Chambellan, departed Lorient on board a company ship on December 1, 1726. Fellow passengers included the Jesuit superior of Louisiana, Father Beaubois, as well as Jesuit and Capuchin missionaries. After a brief stop for provisions in Cap Français (in modern Haiti), the Périers and Beaubois reached New Orleans at daybreak on March 15,

1727. Later that day, Périer presented his credentials to the Superior Council, reviewed the troops, and met with colonists. Soon he was installed as commandant general.

That Périer took seriously the company's instructions to see to the improvement of the colony is attested by his personal involvement in almost every aspect of Louisiana's administration. During his first year in Louisiana, he ascended the Mississippi as far as the Arkansas River, visiting and conciliating various Indian tribes. In succeeding years, he inspected settlements at Bay St. Louis, Biloxi, Pascagoula, and Mobile. Governing the colony, Périer encountered a host of discordant personalities. Although he maintained cordial and correct relations with La Chaise, who remained commissary, and members of the Superior Council, Périer complained to the company's directors that neither was very trustworthy. Trying to maintain strict neutrality between the Jesuits and the Capuchins proved to be difficult for the commandant general. Despite Périer's dedicated efforts to improve the colony's economy, the disastrous Natchez massacre on November 28, 1729, focused attention on his ineffectiveness in dealing with the Indians. That eventually led to his recall, in March, 1733, and his replacement by the former commandant general Bienville.

Périer and his family returned to France in the spring of 1733. Retiring from royal service, rewarded with the Cross of St. Louis and a modest pension, he established his family in the busy seaport of Brest, in Brittany. He and his wife had two children, with the second, a son, named after the parents' Louisiana plantation, Monplaisir.

᳁

Company officials, in their instructions to Périer in the fall of 1726, stressed the importance of developing tobacco cultivation and the significance of the company's settlement at Natchez.

En route to Louisiana, Périer recruited three Englishmen in Cap Français, supposed experts from the Carolinas, to instruct local planters to grow tobacco in the best English manner. Two years later, in 1728, company officials in Paris engaged a Swiss Protestant named Lunel, who had observed tobacco cultivation in Virginia, to go to Louisiana to teach the settlers to cultivate and prepare tobacco in the Virginia style. Nevertheless, planter resistance, a shortage of slaves, inconsistent quality, and the vagaries of the Louisiana climate conspired to prevent the rapid development of tobacco culture. Although some good tobacco was arriving in France from Louisiana by 1729, it cost more than double what came from Virginia and was inferior in quality to it.

A lack of manufactured goods and a shortage of specie plagued Périer's administration. Six months after arriving, Périer wrote the directors of the company that there was not a single sou in the treasury and that he was more than two months behind in paying salaries to soldiers and workmen. The colony suffered from persistent shortages of rope, sailcloth, windowpane glass, coal, blankets, and medicines.

To alleviate shortages and improve conditions in the colony, Périer made a number of attempts to promote economic development. He asked company officials to send fruit trees to develop a citrus industry. He suggested that if each planter was required to plant one tree for every three slaves he owned, citrus products would soon become an important commercial export. Furthermore, in 1729, he concluded that the land was suitable for silk production. To begin the project, he asked company officials to send two women silkmakers from France along with a spinning wheel and a pound of silkworm eggs. In return, he promised the company all the silk produced during the first two years at no cost. Despite the initial enthusiasm of a number of settlers, neither citrus products nor the silk industry became commercially profitable.

To reduce food shortages in the colony and to improve the livestock, Périer attempted to secure cattle from Spanish Florida in 1728, sending his stepson de Chambellan to St. Marks to complete negotiations. Before arrangements were completed, however, war broke out between Spain and England, and British troops laid siege to the Florida ports. Other attempts to obtain cattle from Campeche in New Spain (Mexico) were equally fruitless.

Périer's greatest successes came in the area of public and charitable works. He supervised construction of a levee above and below New Orleans to reduce the danger from flooding. Using an appropriation of five thousand livres, he undertook the deepening of the mouth of the main channel of the Mississippi from twelve feet to seventeen feet. During his administration, work on a prison and a conservatory were completed, and construction was begun on the Ursuline convent. Colonial workers dug a ditch around the central city to drain off water and completed the canal linking the city to Lake Pontchartrain. Périer also took a sincere interest in the morality of the local inhabitants. He received approval for his plan to provide rations for orphan boys and an allowance for the Ursulines to care for orphan girls. He attempted to restrict the traditional vices and asked the company to send women to become wives of the settlers.

The disastrous Indian attack on the Natchez settlement nullified all the careful efforts of Périer's tenure. On November 28, 1729, a large group of Natchez Indians raiders killed 145 men, 35 women, and 56 children, and captured numerous others, including a large number of slaves. Because the man chiefly responsible for provoking the Natchez, a Captain Chepart, had been appointed by Périer, the tragedy reflected negatively on the commandant general. To reduce fears of a general Indian uprising in the colony, 350 men under the command of Périer's younger brother Antoine Périer de Salvert arrived in New Orleans from France on September 16, 1730. They formed the largest part of an expeditionary force that left New Orleans on December 9, 1730, in search of the Natchez raiders. On January 21, 1731, French forces led by the Périers struck a Natchez stronghold between the Black and Red rivers (in modern Concordia Parish), taking 450 prisoners who were later sold into slavery in St. Domingue (Haiti). More than 200 other Indians managed to escape, and they continued to harass the French until they were finally subdued later in the year.

The Natchez massacre accelerated the desire of the Company of the Indies to divest itself of what was a highly unprofitable venture. When offered an opportunity to buy their way out of their obligations in Louisiana, the company's directors eagerly accepted. On July 1, 1731, Louisiana once again became a crown colony of France, and Périer was promoted in title to governor. The promotion was short-lived, however, since officials at the Ministry of the Marine were eager to rid the colony of all who had been company officials. On March 2, 1733, Périer was informed of his recall. The next day, Bienville arrived as his replacement.

BRIAN E. COUTTS

BIBLIOGRAPHY

Heinrich, Pierre. *La Louisiane sous la compagnie des Indes, 1717–1731*. Paris, 1908.
O'Neill, Charles Edwards. *Church and State in French Colonial Louisiana: Policy and Politics to 1732*. New Haven, 1966.
Price, Jacob M. *France and the Chesapeake: A History of the French Tobacco Monopoly*. 2 vols. Ann Arbor, Mich., 1973.
Rowland, Dunbar, and Albert G. Sanders, trans. and eds. *Mississippi Provincial Archives: French Dominion*. Vols. I–III of 5 vols. Jackson, Miss., 1927–32.
Wall, Bennett H., ed. *Louisiana: A History*. Arlington Heights, Ill., 1984.

Woods, Patricia D. *French-Indian Relations on the Southern Frontier, 1699–1762.* Ann Arbor, Mich., 1980.

Pierre François de Rigaud, Marquis de Vaudreuil

Colonial Governor, 1743–1753

VAUDREUIL, Pierre François de Rigaud, Marquis de (b. Quebec, Canada, November 22, 1698; d. Paris, France, August 4, 1788), French army officer and colonial governor. Vaudreuil was the fourth son of Phillippe de Rigaud, Marquis de Vaudreuil, and Louise Elizabeth de Jaybert. Both parents possessed considerable influence in the royal court at Versailles; the elder Vaudreuil and each of his sons achieved distinguished careers. Reared in Montreal, young Vaudreuil moved with the family to Quebec when his father became governor of New France (Canada).

PIERRE FRANÇOIS DE RIGAUD, MARQUIS DE VAUDREUIL. *Photograph courtesy of State Library of Louisiana, from Fortier's* History of Louisiana, *I, 136.*

In 1699, Jérome de Pontchartrain became secretary of state in the French government, a position he held until 1715, from which, as friend of the elder Vaudreuil, he exerted considerable influence upon the careers of the family.

In 1713, the younger Vaudreuil was sent to France to deliver colonial correspondence to Pontchartrain and to win his favor. By 1715, Vaudreuil had returned to New France, where he observed his father's art of governing; the young man's goal was someday to become governor of Canada. In 1720, promoted to lieutenant in the army, he took the first of many steps toward that end. In 1723, Maurepas, the son of Pontchartrain, became minister of marine. The good contacts between Maurepas and Vaudreuil's mother assured Vaudreuil of steady promotions. Maurepas would also later provide protection when Vaudreuil served as governor of Louisiana.

From 1733 to 1742, Vaudreuil was governor of the Trois-Rivières region of New France. His sensitivity and firmness caused him to be both admired and feared by the people he governed, and his reputation eventually reached Paris. In the summer of 1741, while sojourning in France, Vaudreuil learned that he would be named governor of Louisiana. The nomination was made on July 1, 1742, and Vaudreuil arrived in New Orleans on May 10, 1743.

Vaudreuil injected life and direction into Louisiana, a colony that had been in decline. Engaged in last-ditch attempts to revitalize the colony, France supported his efforts to increase Louisiana's population, improve harvests, and strengthen the military force. The census of 1744 showed somewhat more than 5,000 persons (approximately 3,000 of whom were white) and 800 soldiers. By 1746, the number of settlers had increased to 8,830 (4,000 whites), and by 1750, the garrison had grown to nearly 2,000 soldiers.

The years 1740–1748 were difficult for Louisiana, because the War of Austrian Succession reduced trade between the colony and France substantially. Vaudreuil combated the near–economic strangulation of his colony by encouraging unauthorized trade with the Spanish colonies. Technically illegal, the trade enabled Louisiana to survive.

As a result of Vaudreuil's actions, the decade of his administration was remembered as rich and brilliant. Agriculture prospered and produced surpluses for export. Manufacturers satisfied home needs and provided some material for trade. Vaudreuil mounted military campaigns between 1747 and 1752 to defeat the Chickasaws and pacify the Choctaws; he secured relative safety for the colony during a period in which Indian unrest ravaged much of the Mississippi Valley.

Vaudreuil's service pleased Maurepas, and others took note of his accomplishments; as early as 1750 some leaders in New France sought his appointment as governor. In 1752, Vaudreuil learned that he would hold the office for which he had worked so long: he would be appointed governor-general of New France. The king signed Vaudreuil's commission as governor of New France on January 1, 1755.

But Vaudreuil seemed to have lost the powers and abilities that had brought him to his long-sought goal. He allowed François Bigot, intendant of New France, to make a pawn of him in financial manipulations that defrauded the French treasury. He relied heavily on and appointed to responsible positions Canadian associates and relatives who proved to be incompetent. He floundered in matters of broad military strategy, and this deficiency placed him at odds with the Marquis de Montcalm, the most effective military leader in New France. Vaudreuil, who originally won respect from the Indians for his stern but fair treatment, became indulgent of atrocities and military indiscipline. And despite his reputation for decisiveness in Louisiana, he often vacillated in New France and failed to handle decisively the crises he faced. Vaudreuil's deficiences contributed greatly to the loss of Canada to the British in the Seven Years' War (1756–1763).

Vaudreuil returned to France after the surrender of Canada in late 1760. He was tried in court, with François Bigot, on charges of maladministration arising out of Bigot's longtime fiscal manipulations. Although Vaudreuil was acquitted, his reputation suffered, and he retired from government service.

ↄₐ

Vaudreuil enjoyed several advantages in his successful career in Louisiana, advantages that would have served him well anywhere. Member of an old and noble family, he was the titled son of an illustrious man who gave him excellent contacts at Versailles. Furthermore, he had both military and political experience and was respected by the Indians. An American both by birth and in outlook, Vaudreuil was sensitive to colonial trends and understood the meaning behind events. His ability to anticipate what would happen enabled him to operate well within the system of governance France used in its American colonies.

The French colonial system rested on the eighteenth-century mercantilist premise that a colony existed solely for the benefit of the mother country. Louisiana was seen as a foothold at the mouth of the Mississippi to keep foreign powers out of the Mississippi Valley and to make commercial gains at the expense of Spain. New France was expected to anchor the northern Mississippi Valley, to control commerce and the Indian populations, and to bar the British from the Great Lakes region and the Ohio River valley.

Vaudreuil's success in Louisiana and his failure in New France were determined largely by the degree of support he received from France in the two cases. Though France never provided consistent or abundant support for its colonies, Vaudreuil was able in Louisiana to obtain aid from Versailles to increase both the number of settlers and the size of the budget. During his time in Canada, however, France was unable to provide such aid, because of the war with Britain.

The French system arranged the two leading offices of a colony so that they supported—and checked—each other. The governor (the military and administrative official) and the *commissaire ordonnateur* (a fiscal and administrative offical) were often at odds, and their efforts were frequently mutually negating. A strong man with ability, family connections, and good contacts in Versailles could, however, prosper as governor. Vaudreuil had the necessary qualifications and in Louisiana was successful in part because he stood head and shoulders above the crowd of petty noblemen and plantation owners. In New France, he was merely one important man among many. Moreover, Vaudreuil's influence at Versailles, which he had previously used so effectively, lost most of its value when the conflict with the British closed off support from France.

Both the French colonial system and Vaudreuil left strong and lasting imprints upon Louisiana and its politics. The French system was established to produce strong leaders capable of meeting and overcoming opposition. The juxtaposition of governor and *commissaire ordonnateur* ensured, through systemic competition, that capable individuals would be pushed to their limits of development. As a successful product of that system, Vaudreuil, "le grand marquis," was remembered fondly, and several generations of Louisianians praised his administration. Like their ancestors, modern Louisianians often demand that a governor have the stength and ability to overcome the objections of his *commissaire ordonnateur*—the elected legislature. Therefore the governor of Louisiana is perhaps the most legitimately powerful of state chief executives. In Louisiana, the guidelines established by the French colonial system and the example set by Vaudreuil have made the exercise of gubernatorial power a way and a fact of life.

DONALD J. LEMIEUX

BIBLIOGRAPHY

Eccles, W. J. *France in America.* New York, 1972.
Fregault, Guy. *Le Grand Marquis: Pierre de Rigaud de Vaudreuil, et da Louisiane.* Montreal, 1952.
Gayarré, Charles. *History of Louisiana.* 5th ed. 4 vols. New Orleans, 1965.
Giraud, Marcel. "France and Louisiana in the Eighteenth Century." *Mississippi Valley Historical Review,* XXXVI (1950), 657–74.
Lanctot, Gustave. *A History of Canada.* Translated by Margaret M. Cameron. 3 vols. Cambridge, Mass., 1965.
Lemieux, Donald J. "The Office of 'Commissaire Ordonnateur' in French Louisiana, 1731–1763: A Study in French Colonial Administration." Ph.D. dissertation, Louisiana State University, 1972.
Surrey, N. M. M. *The Commerce of Louisiana During the French Regime, 1699–1763.* New York, 1916.
Wall, Bennett H., ed. *Louisiana: A History.* Arlington Heights, Ill., 1984.

Louis Billouart, Chevalier de Kerlerec

Colonial Governor, 1753–1763

KERLEREC, Louis Billouart, Chevalier de (b. Quimper, France, June 26, 1708; d. Brittany, France, September 8, 1770), French army officer and colonial governor. The son of Guillaume Billouart de Kerlerec and Louise de Lansullyen, Louis Billouart was a veteran of twenty-five years of active military service, in which he had frequently been commended for bravery and had risen to the rank of captain, when as a reward for faithful and distinguished service to the French crown, he was appointed to the governorship of Louisiana in February, 1752. He reached New Orleans on February 6, 1753, and was officially installed in office on February 12, 1753.

LOUIS BILLOUART, CHEVALIER DE KERLEREC. *Photograph courtesy of State Library of Louisiana, from Fortier's* History of Louisiana, *I, 154.*

Kerlerec was noted, in both his official and his personal capacities, as a man of severe discipline and honesty. The new governor needed such traits of character in Louisiana. Whereas European events had caused France to give special attention to the needs of the colony during the administration of his predecessor, the Marquis de Vaudreuil, the Continental situation brought almost total neglect during Kerlerec's time in office. The governor endured two years in which he received no communications from his superiors in France and another four years during which the mother country was unable to send supplies to its colony.

In part, negligence reflected the normal policies of mercantilist France for a colony that had proved commercially disappointing. To a greater extent, however, the situation was exacerbated by the Great War for Empire (1756–1763). That conflict (also known as the French and Indian War and the Seven Years' War) erupted in the Ohio River valley in May, 1754, and escalated from mere skirmishes to pitched battles along the colonial frontier into Canada.

The war had a detrimental impact on Louisiana. Speculation in treasury bills of exchange and profiteering on goods created spiraling inflation, sapping the treasury and emptying both private and government warehouses. Colonial society became increasingly nonproductive and parasitic. As Kerlerec's successor, Jean-Jacques-Blaise d'Abbadie, observed in 1764, three-fourths of the inhabitants were in a state of insolvency. The intentness of some colonists on trafficking in bills of exchange and merchandise from the king's warehouses meant that too few people were cultivating the land and pursuing other productive occupations.

That Kerlerec was able to function in this stultifying situation is a credit to the man. Knowing full well Louisiana's military value for controlling the Mississippi Valley, he requested additional troops and supplies, and money for fortifications. France gave no sign of hearing his appeals. Nevertheless, he managed to strengthen the Ship Island defenses and refurbish the Mississippi River posts. Out of necessity, he also reinstituted contraband trade with the Spanish in Mexican, Caribbean, and Gulf Coast colonies in order to obtain munitions and vital supplies. The number of soldiers under his command increased somewhat in 1758, when, after the fall of Fort Duquesne, at the forks of the Ohio, the complement from that fort reached New Orleans by way of the Ohio and Mississippi rivers.

Meanwhile, the local Indian tribes had become restive. Their loyalty had earlier been won by generous shipments of trade goods, which gained Kerlerec the title of father of the Choctaws. The lack of supplies during the years when France neglected the colony, however, caused the tribes to doubt the governor's abilities. Only the arrival of goods in 1758 enabled Kerlerec to retain the allegiance of the Choctaw and Alibamon nations, who furnished hundreds of warriors toward colonial defense. At this time, the governor proposed an attempt to unite all the Mississippi Valley tribes for diversionary strikes against the western frontiers of the British coastal colonies. His plan, which might have relieved beleaguered Canada, went unsupported by France.

The fall of Canada to the English caused many Nova Scotians to follow earlier Acadians to Louisiana, and the British acquisition of the Floridas from Spain prompted several Indian tribes to relocate to French territory. Kerlerec arranged for a suitable settlement of these peoples.

Kerlerec was also hampered throughout much of his term by systematic opposition from the colony's financial officers. In particular, the *commissaire ordonnateur,* Vincent-Gaspard-Pierre de Rochemore, a man with a reputation as a cheat and a spendthrift, mounted a campaign to discredit Kerlerec in Versailles, possibly in the hope of diverting attention from his own activities. Kerlerec's charges eventually obtained Rochemore's recall, but the campaign was continued by Rochemore's successor. Relieved by d'Abbadie on June 29, 1763, Kerlerec returned to France to face charges of maladministration. He was sent to the Bastille.

After Kerlerec was freed through solicitations by his friends, he lived in Brittany until his death. Although he was never fully exonerated, the parliament of Brittany revoked most of the debts attached to his estate. Furthermore, in 1774, his son received letters of commendation highly praising the career accomplishments of the elder Kerlerec.

The governors and *commissaires ordonnateurs* of the French colony of Louisiana invariably faced a difficult task. By eighteenth-century French mercantilist standards, which held that a colony had value only so far as the mother country benefited from it, Louisiana was a liability rather than an asset. The colony seldom produced raw materials in the volume required to make trade commercially attractive and to become a stable market for goods produced in France and its other colonies. Something always seemed to be lacking. When ships were available, Louisiana rarely had products to trade, and when production was high, there were wars or commerical restrictions imposed by France which severely hampered exchange. Contraband trade with the neighboring Spanish colonies produced the few prosperous periods for Louisiana during this period.

Drained by wars and other conflicts, France no longer possessed the material and moral resources that had permitted the successful colonization of New France (Canada) and the French Caribbean islands. The French expected the colony in Louisiana to serve two purposes: as a military bastion against another nation's gaining a foothold in the Mississippi Valley, and as a vehicle for obtaining a share of Spanish commerce. When Louisiana failed to make inroads upon Spanish trade, France either could not or would not make the financial investment necessary to put the colony on a sound fiscal base but left it a weak and dependent possession. France could ill afford to retain the colony, but for strategic reasons, the French equally could not afford to relinquish it. The shortage of specie was a perennial problem in Louisiana. Silver earned in the sporadic Spanish trade, as well as the gold frugally allotted by France, flowed from the colony in payment for supplies. The resulting reliance within the colony upon unsecured paper money and bills of exchange created circumstances in which speculation and inflation were rampant.

To maintain order in Louisiana, French policy provided for a colonial government headed by two substantially equal administrators. The governor was supreme in military matters, the *commissaire ordonnateur* ascendant in matters of royal finance and commerce. General administration was a shared concern. This administrative structure, intended as a means of establishing checks and balances—and serving that purpose reasonably well—encouraged the development of an adversary relationship between the two officials. Even under the best of conditions, with full and amicable cooperation between the two, resources were so sparce that success was possible only if France provided generous assistance. But the attitudes of the officials toward each other ranged more characteristically from passive obstruction to debilitating intransigence.

The Kerlerec-Rochemore administration was typical in that regard. Rochemore, through speculation and peculation, drove the colony to the brink of economic ruin. Meanwhile, perhaps as a cover for his activities, he systematically opposed Kerlerec's every action. Kerlerec was compelled to respond in kind if he expected to maintain any semblance of colonial stability and morale. The battle was decided, as always, by the administrative superiors in Versailles to whom both officials reported. The confrontation of the two men was ultimately eased with the recall of Rochemore, but the conflict was not over. A colonial administrator could advance in the French system if he had both political ability and influence at Versailles. Rochemore had the latter if not the former, and his successor as *ordonnateur*, with the connivance of Rochemore's supporters in Versailles, continued the harassment that in the end led to Kerlerec's downfall.

Kerlerec was perhaps a better than average governor, but he was typical of the system that shaped and then discarded him. His achievements, especially considering the circumstances, were impressive, but he was by no means innovative. He was essentially a competent, workmanlike governor who was content to follow standard procedures in order to function within and maintain an established system.

DONALD J. LEMIEUX

BIBLIOGRAPHY

Gayarré, Charles. *History of Louisiana.* 5th ed. 4 vols. New Orleans, 1965.
Giraud, Marcel. "France and Louisiana in the Eighteenth Century." *Mississippi Valley Historical Review,* XXXVI (1950), 657–74.
———. *Histoire de la Louisiane française.* 4 vols. Paris, 1953–74.
LaFargue, André. "The French Governors of Louisiana." *Mississippi Valley Historical Review,* XIV (1927), 156–67.
Lauvrière, Emile. *Histoire de la Louisiane française, 1673–1939.* Paris, 1940; Baton Rouge, 1940.
Lemieux, Donald J. "The Office of 'Commissaire Ordonnateur' in French Louisiana, 1731–1763: A Study in French Colonial Administration." Ph.D. dissertation, Louisiana State University, 1972.
Lyon, E. Wilson. *Louisiana in French Diplomacy, 1759–1804.* Rev. ed. Norman, Okla., 1974.
Smith, Ronald D. "French Interests in Louisiana: From Choiseul to Napoleon." Ph.D. dissertation, University of Southern California, 1964.
Surrey, N. M. M. *The Commerce of Louisiana During the French Regime, 1699–1763.* New York, 1916.
———. "The Development of Industries in Louisiana During the French Regime, 1673–1763." *Mississippi Valley Historical Review,* IX (1922), 227–35.
Wall, Bennett H., ed. *Louisiana: A History.* Arlington Heights, Ill., 1984.

Jean-Jacques-Blaise d'Abbadie

Colonial Governor, 1763–1765

D'ABBADIE, Jean-Jacques-Blaise (b. Chateau d'Audoux, France, 1726; d. New Orleans, Louisiana, February 4, 1765), French naval officer and colonial governor. D'Abbadie's early life, at Chateau d'Audoux, near Navarrenx, Basse-Pyrénées, is largely obscure, but the Midi nobleman's personal correspondence indicates that he attended College d'Harcourt, graduating in 1742. Upon leaving the Jesuit institution of higher learning, d'Abbadie entered the Ministry of the Marine's Rochefort office as a clerk, thereby following the example of his father, a former chief clerk of the bureau's naval department.

After one year of service at Rochefort, d'Abbadie was promoted to the rank of royal scribe in the comptroller's office, and in 1744, he was assigned to the Rochefort mast yard. In 1751, after shipboard duty in the Americas, he was appointed chief clerk of the artillery department, and four years later he was transferred to the Ministry of the Marine's colonial department. After the outbreak of the Seven Years' War, in

1756, d'Abbadie was again assigned to active duty in the French navy. In 1757, holding the rank of commissary, he served aboard a "small naval division"[1] that unsuccessfully attempted to deliver provisions to Louisbourg, the French fortress on Cape Breton Island, off Canada. He subsequently returned to the Ministry of the Marine's Rochefort office, where he remained until his appointment as Louisiana's *commissaire ordonnateur,* or administrative chief, around December 14, 1761.

Invested on January 18, 1762, with royal authority to establish and maintain good relations between Louisiana's feuding religious orders, the Jesuits and Capuchins, and to administer the colony's financial, police, and judicial affairs, d'Abbadie traveled to Bordeaux, where Daubenton, the intendant, was organizing a four-vessel supply expedition to Louisiana. The convoy was intercepted, however, in early April, 1762, by a sixty-ship British fleet in the Bay of Biscay, only one hour after its departure from Bordeaux. Three of the ships escaped and made safe passage to Louisiana. But the British captured the fourth ship and detained d'Abbadie and other officers at Barbados. D'Abbadie returned to France after his release, and by October, 1762, he was reassigned to Louisiana. His departure from France and the issuance of his new commission as director general (governor and administrative chief) of Louisiana was postponed until the signing of the Treaty of Paris, on February 10, 1763.

D'Abbadie's commission as director general of Louisiana reflected recent French political and diplomatic developments. First, through the Treaty of Paris, France ceded trans-Appalachian Louisiana to England. Second, through the Treaty of Fontainebleau, in October, 1762, the portion of Louisiana lying west of the Mississippi and the Isle of Orleans had been ceded to Spain. Finally, the influential relatives of the former Louisiana *commissaire ordonnateur* Vincent de Rochemore, who had been summoned to France in 1761 to face charges of corruption and insubordination brought against him by Governor Louis Billouart de Kerlerec, secured Kerlerec's recall. With Louisiana's government thus in a shambles, d'Abbadie, through his commission as director general, was invested with the powers of governor and chief administrator. Such centralization of authority would not only terminate the dangerous governmental infighting that had plagued the colony since

1. Carl A. Brasseaux (trans. and ed.), *A Comparative View of French Louisiana, 1699 and 1762: The Journals of Pierre Le Moyne d'Iberville and Jean-Jacques-Blaise d'Abbadie* (Lafayette, La., 1979), 85.

its inception but would also facilitate the transfer of the colony to England and Spain.

The strain of the rapidly deteriorating intercolonial and Franco-Indian relations, as well as the demands of governing a colony without the necessary resources, quickly took their toll upon d'Abbadie's health. In the late fall of 1764, he was confined to bed by a nervous disorder; serveral months later he died of a stroke.

ↄ∾

The instructions to d'Abbadie clearly showed the importance placed by the French government on the speedy and orderly transfer of Louisiana to England and Spain. As the first step of the French withdrawal from the Mississippi Valley, the director general would transfer all but two hundred colonial regulars to St. Domingue (Haiti). French colonists in Louisiana would be permitted to live under English or Spanish domination, but settlers wishing to relocate would be transferred, at royal expense, to the French colony of their choice, where they would be given concessions equivalent to their Louisiana land grants. Moreover, d'Abbadie was ordered to devote the "greatest attention to the maintenance of good relations with the [Indian] tribes and the avoidance of problems which a change of domination could occasion." In order to expedite the "change of domination," the director general was to remit to the incoming English and Spanish commissaries, upon completion of a detailed inventory, the magazines, barracks, hospitals, artillery, and "all royal property" in their respective portions of Louisiana.[2]

Upon arrival with his wife and children at New Orleans in late June, 1763, d'Abbadie quickly prepared to discharge his government responsibilities. Most of the colonial regulars were transferred to the colonial capital, where, in early October, 1763, they were placed aboard chartered merchantmen bound for St. Domingue. The departure of the greater part of the colonial garrison coincided with the arrival of English representatives at Mobile. In order to facilitate their occupation of trans-Appalachian Louisiana, d'Abbadie personally supervised the dismantling of the French bureaucracy and the remaining military outposts in present-day Alabama and Mississippi. In addition, the director general addressed representatives of the area's most powerful Francophile tribes and succeeded in establishing a fragile working relationship between them and their new English overlords.

2. Royal memoir to serve as d'Abbadie's instructions, February 10, 1763, in Correspondance Générale, Louisiane, C 13a, Vol. 43, folio 221vo, Archives des Colonies, Paris.

French efforts to establish harmonious Anglo-Indian relations in the upper trans-Appalachian area, however, were far less successful. Franco-Indian diplomacy in this region was doomed to failure by the outbreak of Pontiac's uprising. Indeed, the Ohio Valley tribes, agitated by the great Ottawa chief, exerted great pressure on the French Louisiana government to continue and even expand arms shipments. In order to prevent the Indian uprising from engulfing the entire region, however, d'Abbadie suspended the shipment of all munitions and foodstuffs to the embattled tribes.

The Indian unrest, coupled with the English occupation of trans-Appalachian Louisiana, precipitated a massive exodus of the French from the present states of Illinois and Alabama. Under d'Abbadie's direction, these refugees were settled in Missouri, along the Mississippi above New Orleans, and in southwestern Louisiana on land grants issued by the French colonial government. With the relocation of the displaced French settlers in 1764, d'Abbadie had discharged his duties as director general. During the following months, he presided over a caretaker government plagued by supply shortages and financial instability—the difficulties of a colony that was completely neglected by France. He desperately awaited the arrival of the Spanish occupational force, and he expected to return to France.

Though his Louisiana career was short-lived, d'Abbadie left a permanent mark on the history of the Mississippi Valley. His adept supervision of the transfer of eastern colonial Louisiana to England precluded any popular uprising against the new administration, unlike the less tranquil governmental transition in western Louisiana. Moreover, the director general's Indian diplomacy doomed Pontiac's rebellion to failure and ultimately permitted English occupation and settlement of northeastern colonial Louisiana. The rich cultural mix of southwestern Louisiana and St. Genevieve, Missouri, are living testimony to the effectiveness of d'Abbadie's settlement policies for trans-Appalachian refugees.

CARL A. BRASSEAUX

BIBLIOGRAPHY

"Abbadie (d')." *Dictionnaire de biographie française.* Vol. I of 16 vols., 32–33. Paris, 1933.
Brasseaux, Carl A., trans. and ed. *A Comparative View of French Louisiana, 1699 and 1762: The Journals of Pierre Le Moyne d'Iberville and Jean-Jacques-Blaise d'Abbadie.* Lafayette, La., 1979.

Charles Philippe Aubry
Colonial Governor, 1765–1766

Aubry, Charles Philippe (b. France, 17??; d. near Bordeaux, France, February 17, 1770), French army officer and colonial governor. Aubry's early life is obscure. It is certain, however, that he was a native of France and that he entered the Lyonnais Infantry Regiment as a second lieutenant on November 6, 1742. He was transferred to a company of grenadiers on April 1, 1743, and was later promoted to lieutenant. As a grenadier officer, Aubry served the French crown with distinction during the War of the Austrian Succession (1742–1748). After his discharge in 1748, he apparently encountered difficulty in securing employment in postwar France. In 1750, he was commissioned captain of the colonial troops and assigned to Louisiana.

The years immediately following his arrival in Louisiana were filled with routine administrative duties, primarily in the Illinois district. At the outset of the Seven Years' War, in 1754, however, Aubry, one of the most experienced and capable officers in the Louisiana garrison, was quickly pressed into duty. In 1755, he commanded an expedition, laden with war munitions, to Fort Duquesne (later the site of Pittsburgh). This foray was followed by other expeditions into the interior. During September, 1758, Aubry joined in the defense of Fort Duquesne, leading a detachment in the virtual annihilation of Colonel James Grant's invading British Army. The following October, in the face of another British attack, he participated in a successful delaying action designed to permit the evacuation of Fort Duquesne. Subsequently, Aubry returned to Illinois. In July, 1759, in a skirmish with superior enemy forces, his Indian allies deserted him. The French captain was captured, tortured by Indians allied with the English, and then sent to New York for permanent detention.

Aubry's detention there, however, was brief. In 1760, after the capitulation of the final pockets of French resistance in Canada, the French prisoners of war in North America were transported to France. While in the mother country, Aubry petitioned the French government for both the Cross of St. Louis, France's most prestigious colonial decoration, and a dangerous new assignment; both prayers were answered.

In March, 1763, Aubry was placed in command of Louisiana's garrison. Since Louisiana had been ceded to England and Spain through the recently concluded treaties of Paris and Fontainebleau, however, the colonial garrison was to consist of only four companies of troops. Despite the reduction of his command, the former prisoner of war was obviously eager to resume his duties in the field. Therefore, upon his return to the colony in June, 1763, he immediately assumed an active role in the colony's military affairs.

In October, 1763, for example, Aubry accompanied Governor Jean-Jacques-Blaise d'Abbadie to Mobile, where the French officials attempted to persuade the assembled representatives of the major southeastern tribes to accept their new English overlords. Upon returning to New Orleans in January, 1764, Aubry assessed the deficiencies of the colonial garrison, reported his findings to France, and prepared to return to the mother country after the anticipated arrival of Spanish occupational forces. But the Spaniards failed to appear as soon as expected, thus delaying Aubry's departure. When Governor d'Abbadie died suddenly on February 4, 1765, Aubry, the colony's ranking military officer, was compelled to take charge of the government.

Aubry's administration was brief but turbulent. He encouraged Acadian immigration from Canada, changing south Louisiana's cultural complexion. His efforts to solve other thorny administrative problems, however, were less successful. He had particular difficulty in dealing with the new Spanish governor, Antonio de Ulloa, who was a brilliant scientist but who had deficiencies as a governor. Aubry attempted to shield his Spanish counterpart from growing internal dissent while permitting him to manipulate the government without formally assuming the responsibility of governing. The result was a leadership vacuum that spawned political and economic chaos, and ultimately rebellion.

In response to the Rebellion of 1768, the Spanish sent General Alexander O'Reilly to Louisiana to pacify the colony. Aubry cooperated with O'Reilly for a time and then departed to France. Aubry's ship was wrecked off the French coast, and he died without regaining French soil.

⮬

Aubry could hardly have become acting governor at a worse time. Because of France's growing neglect of Louisiana, he lacked the authority, finances, and troops to administer the colony adequately. His routine problems were further complicated by the arrival of 383 destitute Acadian refugees. Moved by compassion for the displaced Francophones—

for he had encountered several Acadians during his yearlong detention in New York—the new colonial executive mobilized the colony's meager resources to settle them in south Louisiana.

Aubry's problems in governing the virtually bankrupt colony were compounded by the arrival, in early March, 1766, of a Spanish representative equally unprepared to rule Louisiana. Lacking adequate military and financial resources to secure and maintain control of the colony, the Spanish governor Ulloa refused to take up the reins of government. Aubry, on the other hand, demonstrated equal insubordination, refusing to transfer authority immediately, as explicitly required by ministerial decree, and by permitting the colony's caretaker French government to serve as an administrative facade for the phantom Spanish regime.

In this manner, Aubry permitted Ulloa to promulgate restrictive Spanish commerical decrees, while shielding the Spaniard from the colonists' harsh response. Though initially successful, Aubry's efforts to protect the increasingly unpopular Spanish colonial powers progressively lost their effectiveness, and in addition, Ulloa's persistent refusal to take possession of the colony in a public ceremony created a leadership vacuum. The inevitable result was rebellion.

Hundreds of armed Louisianians gathered at New Orleans on the morning of October 29, 1768, to demand the expulsion of Ulloa. Aubry, opposing the rebels with only 110 wavering militiamen, vainly attempted to quell the uprising, and in the end Louisiana's first Spanish governor was compelled to flee to Havana.

Because of his unshakable support of the Spanish regime, Aubry was discredited in Louisiana. He, therefore, maintained a very low profile during the aftermath of the rebellion. With the arrival of a large Spanish army commanded by O'Reilly and sent to restore Spanish rule in Louisiana forcibly, Aubry's political position was rehabilitated. Aubry gratefully collaborated with O'Reilly in bringing to justice the rebel leaders.

His cooperation did not go unrewarded. Indeed, he received at least ten thousand livres in Spanish silver for his assistance in prosecuting the rebels of 1768—the so-called Louisiana martyrs. Like Judas, however, Aubry suffered an untimely death before he could spend his ill-gotten gain. He perished aboard the *Père de Famille*, a merchantman, as it foundered within sight of the French coast.

CARL A. BRASSEAUX

BIBLIOGRAPHY

Brasseaux, Carl A. "L'Officier de Plume: Denis-Nicolas Foucault, Commissaire-ordonnateur of French Louisiana, 1762–1769." M.A. thesis, University of Southwestern Louisiana, 1975.

Chandler, R. E. "Aubry: Villain or Hero?" *Louisiana History*, XXVI (1985), 241–70.

Moore, Preston. *Revolt in Louisiana: The Spanish Occupation, 1766–1769.* Baton Rouge, 1976.

Wall, Bennett H., ed. *Louisiana: A History.* Arlington Heights, Ill., 1984.

Governors of the Spanish Colonial Period

Antonio de Ulloa

Colonial Governor, 1766–1768

ULLOA, Antonio de (b. Seville, Spain, January 12, 1716; d. Cádiz, Spain, July 5, 1795), Spanish naval officer, scientist, and colonial governor. Of the lesser aristocracy, Don Antonio de Ulloa y de la Torre-Guiral was educated at the Colegio de Santo Tomás, in Seville, where he received a basic knowledge of the classics and mathematics, which stood him well later. Because of the boy's fragile constitution, his father secured a place for his son, then thirteen years of age, as cabin boy on a ship cruising to the Indies. At the end of the voyage, the youngster entered the newly founded naval academy at Cádiz, where he excelled in his studies.

ANTONIO DE ULLOA. *Photograph courtesy of Spanish Naval Museum, Madrid.*

An aptitude for mathematics led to Ulloa's designation by King Philip V as one of two Spanish representatives to an important scientific mission organized by the French Academy of Science to measure one degree of latitude at the equator in Ecuador, the results of which would prove or disprove Sir Isaac Newton's concept of the shape of the earth. The fruit of almost eleven years of travel and scientific observation in the Indies was the publication by Ulloa, in collaboration with his companion Jorge Juan, in 1748, of the *Relación histórica del viaje a la América Meridional* (A voyage to South America). The work won immediate international acclaim for both men. Election to England's prestigious Royal Society and other renowned organizations attested to their high standing in European intellectual circles. Because of their concern over the future of America, Ulloa and Juan prepared for the Marqués de Ensenada, minister of the navy and the Indies, a confidential report on political, economic, and social condtions in the colonies. Modern historians regard this report as an exceedingly valuable source of information on the eighteenth-century Spanish Empire. Consulted by government officials, it remained in manuscript form until a copy was clandestinely obtained by an Englishman, who published it in 1826 under the title *Noticias Secretas de América* (Secret information on Spanish America).

Subsequent government service employed Ulloa's skills in the Iberian Peninsula and abroad. He was an engineer in the construction of the Canal of Castile, which was designed to improve internal transportation and communication. He headed a mission to European countries to observe and report on naval bases and on mining technologies. Because of his knowledge of mining, the crown dispatched him in 1758 to Peru as governor of Huancavelica to increase the output of mercury, a material essential in the production of silver. The reforms that he recommended in Peru could not be applied, owing primarily to the venality of the miners' guild and the secret opposition of colonial officials.

Ulloa's next assignment was the governorship of Louisiana. The colony was acquired by Spain from France in 1762 in the Treaty of Fontainebleau, drawn up near the end of the Seven Years' War. Ulloa resided in Louisiana from March 5, 1766, to November 1, 1768, when he was expelled in an uprising of the resident French colonists.

This setback did not affect Ulloa's status in the navy. He was promoted to the rank of rear admiral and eventually to that of admiral of the fleet. During the war between Spain and England (1779–1783), he commanded a squadron operating against English raiders in the Azores.

Although he was a naval officer of some repute, his literary and scientific contributions were of greater significance. A founder of the natural history museum in Madrid, he was responsible for much of the royal collection, as well as for conducting experiments in electricity and magnetism. He was the first European scientist to identify platinum as a separate metal.

His chief work in later years was the *Noticias Americanas* (Spanish-American notes), a comparative study of data drawn from observations in Ecuador, Peru, Panama, and Louisiana, and treating geographical, sociological, and ethnological features of these regions. His last publication bears the title *Conversaciones de Ulloa con sus trest hijos* (Conversations of Ulloa with his three sons), a storehouse of information on ships, naval customs, and meteorology. Some of his literary productions remain in manuscript, the most outstanding being a survey of the navies of Europe (1750), the introduction of which contains a plea for disarmament unique in his age.

How does one assess Ulloa's role as the first Spanish governor? Victim of an unforeseen revolt on the part of the leading French merchants and landowners, he had only two and a half years to bring about the recovery of a region that had been neglected by the French court during the Seven Years' War. Ulloa had not been successful in Peru, but the crown believed that he possessed the qualifications requisite for assimilating the colony to the empire. Having firsthand experience in the Americas and knowing that the English had attacked Spanish Florida and Havana in the recent war, Ulloa perceived the threat of English aggrandizement. His response to the English threat—the construction of forts on the frontier—was imaginative though impractical and costly.

Rehabilitation of Louisiana's economy would have tested the sagacity and patience of the best of administrators. There is no question of Ulloa's genuine sincerity in the establishment of a sound currency and the promotion of commerce and agriculture. Like his French predecessors, he realized the necessity of subsidies, for the colony could not be self-supporting. When the flow of pesos from Mexico was interrupted for any period of time, the consequences were serious. Hence, Ulloa's appeals for funds from the ministry in Madrid and from the viceroy of New Spain were constant and, toward the end of his governorship, when the worst shortage occurred, desperate. The implementation of commercial policies was premised on the acceptance of restrictive mercantilism, which was difficult to maintain, even for the older Spanish colonies. Orders for the elimination of contraband, the lifeblood of Louisiana, came from high-level ministry officials; and Ulloa, as an obedient subordinate, made efforts to enforce them despite the risk of alienating traders and landowners. Expenditures for the restoration of government facilities and churches, neglected during the Seven Years'

War, taxed the colony's resources. In the face of these difficulties, winning the loyalty and confidence of the French population proved impossible.

The solution of these vexatious problems required acumen and diplomacy on the part of the governor and unconditional support by the ministry. Perseverance, imagination, obedience, integrity, and racial tolerance were Ulloa's virtues. It has been customary to dwell on his weaknesses: brusqueness towards his subordinates, a martinetlike enforcement of regulations, and a distaste for conviviality—all of which might be summed up as a lack of the "common touch," not rare among men of high intelligence. The modern specialist finds it hard to grasp the encyclopedic range of interests of Ulloa, a paramount exemplar of the Spanish enlightenment. Hours unspent in the performance of official duties he filled with the examination of the flora and fauna of the subtropical climate, of meteorological phenomena, and of the mores of the natives, material he recorded subsequently in his work on the American scene and in correspondence with European scientists. Unquestionably, he was the most illustrious Spaniard to visit or hold office in the colony of Louisiana.

Conditions outside Ulloa's control were primarily responsible for his downfall as governor of Louisiana. The lack of funds, a weak military posture, the indifference of the ministry, and the xenophobic attitude of the French colonials largely explain his removal. Ulloa's experience as the first Spanish governor impressed upon the crown the need for adopting policies more beneficial to the colonists and for selecting as governors men knowledgeable in administration and well endowed in the qualities of leadership.

J. PRESTON MOORE

BIBLIOGRAPHY

Gayarré, Charles. *History of Louisiana*, 5th ed. 4 vols. New Orleans, 1965.
Moore, J. Preston. "Anglo-Spanish Rivalry on the Louisiana Frontier, 1763–1768." In *The Spanish in the Mississippi Valley, 1762–1804*, edited by John F. McDermott, 72–86. Urbana, Ill., 1974.
———. "Antonio de Ulloa: Profile of the First Spanish Governor of Louisiana." *Louisiana History*, VIII (1967), 189–218.
———. *Revolt in Louisiana: The Spanish Occupation, 1766–1770*. Baton Rouge, 1976.
Wall, Bennett H., ed. *Louisiana: A History*. Arlington Heights, Ill., 1984.
Whitaker, Arthur P. "Antonio de Ulloa." *Hispanic American Historical Review*, XV (1935), 155–94.

Alexander O'Reilly

Colonial Governor, 1769–1770

O'REILLY Y MCDOWELL, Alexander (also rendered Alejandro; b. Beltrasna, County Meath, near Dublin, Ireland, October 24, 1723; d. Bonete, Murcia, Spain, March 23, 1794), Spanish army officer and colonial governor. The son of Thomas O'Reilly and Rosa McDowell, Alexander O'Reilly y McDowell was an indifferent student who enlisted in the Hibernian Infantry Regiment as a cadet at the age of ten. He served in several European wars and in 1766 earned the gratitude of Carlos III by crushing mobs who assaulted the royal palace in the Esquilache riots. He won rewards for

ALEXANDER O'REILLY. *Photograph courtesy of Jack D. L. Holmes, from oil painting in Ayuntamiento, Cádiz.*

his courageous actions during Spanish campaigns, particularly in Portugal at the time of the Seven Years' War (1756–1763). O'Reilly served as a military consultant on Prussian organization for the postwar structuring of the Spanish army, and he went on to devise important changes for the militia and regular army in Puerto Rico and Cuba. After promotion to lieutenant general, he sailed from Spain to Havana and then to Louisiana, to crush the revolt there in 1768 against Spanish rule and Governor Antonio de Ulloa. The far-reaching religious, political, economic, and social reforms O'Reilly introduced in incorporating Louisiana into Spain's American empire served for almost four decades, and his measures were approved by the Council of the Indies and Carlos III.

O'Reilly's troops arrived at New Orleans, 2,100-strong, on July 24, 1769. He arrested the organizers of the 1768 revolt and conducted an intensive investigation of events. Except for the leaders, five of whom were shot and six imprisoned, most of the Louisiana rebels won an amnesty by signing oaths of allegiance to the Spanish sovereign.

Ulloa had instructions not to change the form of Louisiana government and not to try to integrate the French colony into the Spanish-American system, but the revolt ended that policy. O'Reilly had orders to adapt the Spanish laws, particularly the *Recopilación de las leyes de los reinos de Indias*, to the new Spanish colony. The so-called Code O'Reilly was the result, and it covered a host of political, economic, and military matters. It was O'Reilly who created the unique Louisiana political division of parishes by establishing a religious structure for the settlers under the *patronato real*, the system by which the Spanish government appointed priests, covered their wages, and provided a subvention for church expenses. The people of Louisiana had no tithes to pay. O'Reilly promoted Spanish as the language of Louisiana by setting up Spanish public schools and fixing the requirements for teachers. Louisiana never accepted the language, but the vernacular Creole combined African, Spanish, French, and English into the unique Louisiana patois.

O'Reilly rented out houses flanking the Plaza de Armas (modern Jackson Square), in New Orleans, to bring in revenue for the city. He set anchorage duties and customs on imports. He enacted regulations for the conduct of billiard parlors, taverns, inns, and lemonade stands. He modified the French slave code of 1724 with a new Code Noir but insisted that Indian slaves be freed. In medicine, the O'Reilly regulations of 1770 are considered the most advanced rules on pharmacy and for physicians and surgeons in North America. To ensure the defenses, O'Reilly cut back on some fortifications but reorganized both the regular force (Regimiento Fixo de Infantería de Luisiana) and the various militia units throughout the province. He encouraged Negro and mulatto militia units and formed a cadre of experienced officers that resulted in the praetorian tradition of later years.

To replace the Superior Council of the French, O'Reilly created the Cabildo, with a set number of officers who bought their offices and who were elected each year to fill various committee assignments touching not only on municipal government but also on affairs of the entire province. Although not as democratic as the New England town meeting, the Cabildo in New Orleans gave to the city's leaders a degree of self-government unusual in Spain's American colonies. As in so many of the Spanish institutions established in Louisiana, expediency dictated a new look in colonial attitudes. Marriage between Spanish governors and the Creoles, the indigenous population of European descent, was discouraged throughout the rest of Spanish America, but in Louisiana it was not only tolerated but encouraged. O'Reilly's successor, Luis de Unzaga, who came with him in 1769, selected as his wife a daughter of the wealthy merchant Gilbert Antoine de St. Maxent. The match was such a success that Unzaga's successor, Bernardo de Gálvez, chose another of the comely St. Maxent girls for his wife. Thus some of the Creole French who lived in Louisiana not only accepted Spanish rule but enjoyed it in a fully participating way.

O'Reilly named Pedro Piernas lieutenant governor for Upper Louisiana (present-day Missouri, with the capital at St. Louis), and Athanase de Mézières for Natchitoches, on the Texas frontier. O'Reilly drafted complete instructions for them and named captains for each of the settlements in Louisiana. He also established the system of grants by which potential settlers received free parcels of land measured in arpents. Public improvements such as fences and levees were the responsibility of landowners, and failure to maintain a property resulted in its return to the crown. O'Reilly continued to take an interest in Louisiana even after he returned to Spain. Documents show that he made recommendations for budgets and more efficient government. Unfortunately, he commanded the disastrous campaign against the Algiers pirates in February, 1775, which left a blot on his otherwise distinguished military dossier. When his ally, the Marqués de Grimaldi, fell from power in Madrid, the resulting cabals forced O'Reilly into retirement as captain general at Cádiz. Only in 1793, when his adopted land needed his military acumen once more, to lead the army of Rosellon, did he come out of retirement. He died on the field, on the way to join his command.

❧

Recent scholarship has tempered the harsh criticism of O'Reilly in Louisiana. Gone are the days of Alcée Fortier and Henry Dart, true Hispanophobes who could not see the woods for the trees. Bloody O'Reilly is the substance of mythology, serving emotional fervor more than reflecting a historical basis. One can discount the execution of a few French malcontents and the romanticized folklore that grew up around the rebels who tried to overthrow Spanish rule. Then one can credit O'Reilly's blanket amnesty for Louisiana and the creation of a vast body of laws, many of which still guide the courts in determining the rights of litigants. O'Reilly emerges in a more reasonable way; indeed, he may be considered one of Louisiana's greatest colonial governors.

Nothing seemed to escape his administrative eye: social, economic, political, military, religious—even the pool halls! Except for the assumption of the power to grant lands by the intendant Juan Ventura Morales in 1799, the power of the colonial government remained as it had been under O'Reilly in 1770. O'Reilly seems to epitomize the Spanish philosophy of the enlightened Bourbon monarchs Carlos III and Carlos IV that governors who carried out their duties with mildness, firmness, and mercy would earn the most respect from the people they governed. The Conde de Floridablanca expressed it best in 1787: governors should have "uprightness, ethical integrity, moderation, and zeal."[1] O'Reilly was one governor who met the count's requirements.

JACK D. L. HOLMES

BIBLIOGRAPHY

Beerman, Eric. "Un bosquejo biográfico y genealógico del General Alejandro O'Reilly." *Hidalguía* (Madrid), March–April, 1981, pp. 225–40.

Bjork, David K. "The Establishment of Spanish Rule in the Province of Louisiana, 1762–1770." Ph.D. dissertation, University of California, 1923.

Fortier, Alcée. *A History of Louisiana.* 4 vols. New York, 1904.

Holmes, Jack D. L. "O'Reilly's 1769 Commission: A Personal View." *Louisiana History,* XXIV (1983), 307–13.

———. "Some Irish Officers in Spanish Louisiana." *Irish Sword* (Dublin), VI (1964), 234–40.

Montero de Pedro, José (Marqués de Casa Mena). *Españoles en Nueva Orleáns y Luisiana.* Madrid, 1979.

Moore, J. Preston. *Revolt in Louisiana: The Spanish Occupation, 1766–1770.* Baton Rouge, 1976.

Rodríguez Casado, Vicente. *Primeros años de dominación española en la Luisiana.* Madrid, 1942.

Texada, David Ker. *Alejandro O'Reilly and the New Orleans Rebels.* Lafayette, La., 1970.

Torres Ramírez, Bibiano. *Alejandro O'Reilly en las Indias.* Seville, 1969.

Luis de Unzaga y Amezaga

Colonial Governor, 1770–1777

UNZAGA Y AMEZAGA, Luis de (b. Málaga, Spain, 1717; d. Málaga, July 21, 1793), Spanish army officer and colonial governor. Unzaga entered

---

1. Floridablanca's "Instrucción reservada" to the Junta de Estado, July 8, 1787, paragraph clx, in José Monino, Conde de Floridablanca, *Obras originales del Conde de Floridablanca, y escritos referentes a su persona,* ed. Antonio Ferrer del Río, Biblioteca de Autores Espanoles, LIX (Madrid, 1952), 237.

the Spanish army at the age of sixteen, in the Fixed Regiment of Lusitania, where he mustered with the Dragoons, rising to the rank of captain after meritorious service in the Italian campaigns of the 1730s. He received his first important command in 1740 as a battalion commander in the Fixed Regiment of Havana. By the early 1760s, he had risen to commandant of the garrison at Santiago, Cuba. In this capacity, he led a valiant but unsuccessful attempt to reinforce Havana during the British attack of 1762.

Unzaga's skills at administration later caught the attention of General Alexander O'Reilly, who in 1769 organized an expedition to reassert Spanish control over Louisiana. Unzaga received appointment as O'Reilly's second-in-command, and the governorship of Louisiana once Spanish rule had been successfully reestablished. Unzaga arrived in New Orleans with O'Reilly in August, 1769. He technically held the title of governor from the moment of his arrival, although General O'Reilly clearly commanded while in the colony.

There has thus been historical confusion about exactly when Unzaga began his term of office. His official appointment papers carry the date of April 21, 1769. O'Reilly proclaimed Unzaga governor to the people of New Orleans on December 1, 1769. To compound the problem, O'Reilly failed to execute the necessary papers relinquishing command to Unzaga until October 29, 1770, with the Council of the Indies granting formal approval on January 28, 1771. As a practical solution, most historians date the start of Unzaga's term of office from March, 1770, when General O'Reilly left Louisiana.

Unzaga's tenure as governor lasted six and a half years. Unzaga worked to reconcile the French Creoles to Spanish domination. His marriage to Marie Elizabeth St. Maxent, eldest daughter of the New Orleans planter Gilbert Antoine St. Maxent, assisted him in this effort. As an active military officer, he naturally placed emphasis on Louisiana's military defenses.

On January 1, 1777, Unzaga relinquished the post of governor and received appointment as captain general of Caracas, where he remained until 1782. In that year, he became captain general of Cuba, where he implemented Spanish military policy regarding the war with Great Britain, reorganized the tobacco monopoly, and attempted to check the growing influence of American merchants at Havana. He accordingly ordered the controversial arrest and imprisonment at Havana of a number of American traders, including Oliver Pollock, the former congressional agent at New Orleans, then residing in Cuba.

In 1785, Unzaga received assignment as lieutenant general of the regiment of Galicia, in Spain. In his advanced age, the cold climate of northern Spain proved too much for his constitution, and he successfully sought reassignment to his native Málaga, on the Mediterranean. There Unzaga remained until his death.

෴

The governorship of Unzaga marked the peaceful transition to Spanish rule in Louisiana. He exhibited many characteristics of a pacifier, having skill as an organizer, a calm temperament, a deliberativeness in decision making, an evenhandedness, and a methodical nature that sometimes frustrated subordinates who sought quick and expedient action. Unzaga maintained the almost bland style of leadership that Louisiana badly needed in the early 1770s. To his credit, he presided over a significant period of political healing.

Unzaga dealt with a series of problems for which he provided moderate solutions. He strengthened the Spanish judicial system, in addition to winning the support of the French Creole community. He undertook the founding of a Spanish-style academy, which became a reality but never grew to the size Unzaga envisioned. On religious matters, he successfully defused a potentially explosive ecclesiastical dispute between French and Spanish friars that permitted the bishop of Cuba to assert jurisdiction over Louisiana.

Unzaga addressed the commerical problems of the colony by taking an almost laissez-faire approach in spite of Spanish trade policies to the contrary. Louisiana had traditionally relied upon trade connections outside the Spanish commercial system. To an extent, the colony also depended upon illicit trade with the British. The governor's complicity in permitting contraband trade allowed the functioning of a commerce that, although illegal under Spanish law, eased Louisiana's economic problems. He thus fostered a limited, local prosperity where none would have otherwise been possible. In this, he walked a delicate line between unofficially sanctioning contraband activity and upholding royal trade regulations. For example, in 1772, he attempted, without much vigor, to expel British traders from the province in response to pressures from Spain. Both king and Creoles seemed satisfied with his handling of the episode.

As a career military officer, Unzaga concerned himself with improving the military defenses of Louisiana. He attempted to improve the frontier posts, especially the one at Natchitoches, in which he took a personal interest. Spanish parsimony thwarted many of his efforts, and Unzaga remained in almost perpetual frustration over the lack of resources. He did manage to increase the level of preparedness of the Louisiana regiment, although it remained understaffed and undersupplied throughout his administration. Unzaga attempted as best he could to meet the ever-present threat of conflict with the British in neighboring West Florida. In the event of a strong attack, however, the Spanish court preferred that Unzaga retreat to Mexico rather than maintain an expensive military establishment in Louisiana. Unzaga enjoyed greater success in his dealings with the Indians. In 1770 and 1771, he negotiated a series of treaties with many of the tribes along the lower Mississippi, thereby giving some strength to his military position. He also began sending secret agents to spy on the British in the Floridas and along the Atlantic coast, establishing the basis of what eventually became an important Spanish espionage network during the American Revolution.

The American Revolution presented Unzaga with his final and most perplexing crisis. Unlike the Spanish policy for his immediate successor, Bernardo de Gálvez, regulations from Spain during his time demanded the strictest neutrality between the "British and American English." This greatly circumscribed his activities, and both parties in the conflict came to suspect his favoritism toward the other side. The governor did show limited consideration and support for the Americans. He permitted a merchant, Oliver Pollock, to operate in New Orleans on behalf of the rebellious colonies. Unzaga cordially received the mission headed by the American lieutenant George Gibson and sold the rebel officer gunpowder from the royal warehouse.

In 1777, Unzaga left almost as many problems as he found when he assumed the governorship in 1770. A troubled and weak economy, a widespread contraband trade in violation of Spanish law, strained relations with the English, and a poorly equipped military force became a legacy for Gálvez. Almost all Unzaga's problems stemmed, however, from a consistent withholding of full support by Spain, especially in financial matters. Spain's attitude also undermined the effectiveness of Unzaga's successors in office. At bottom, the Spanish court viewed the province as little more than an inconsequential backwater far from the center of the empire.

LIGHT TOWNSEND CUMMINS

BIBLIOGRAPHY

Caughey, John W. *Bernardo de Gálvez in Louisiana, 1776–1783.* Berkeley, Calif., 1934; rpr. with intro. by Jack D. L. Holmes, Gretna, La., 1972.

Cummins, Light T. "Spanish Agents in North America During the Revolution, 1775–1779." Ph.D. dissertation, Tulane University, 1977.

Din, Gilbert C., trans. and ed. *Louisiana in 1776: A Memoria of Francisco Bouligny.* New Orleans, 1977.

Gayarré, Charles. *History of Louisiana.* 5th ed. 4 vols. New Orleans, 1965.

Kinnaird, Lawrence, trans. and ed. *Spain in the Mississippi Valley, 1765–1794.* Part I of Kinnaird (trans. and ed.), *The Revolutionary Period, 1765–1781.* 3 parts. In *Annual Report of the American Historical Association for the Year 1945.* Vol. II of 4 vols. Washington, D.C., 1947.

Wall, Bennett H., ed. *Louisiana: A History.* Arlington Heights, Ill., 1984.

Bernardo de Gálvez

Colonial Governor, 1777–1785

GÁLVEZ, Bernardo de (b. Macharaviaya, Spain, July 23, 1746; d. near Mexico City, Mexico, November 30, 1786), Spanish army officer and colonial governor. Gálvez ranks among the most capable military governors-general in the annals of Spanish Louisiana. The son of Matías de Gálvez García Madrid y Cabrera and of Josefa Gallardo Madrid, and the nephew of King Carlos III's vigorous colonial minister, José de Gálvez, Marqués de Sonora, the nineteen-year-old Bernardo accompanied his uncle to New Spain (Mexico) in 1765 after achieving distinction as a lieutenant during the Portuguese campaign in 1762. Captain Bernardo was wounded in warfare against the Apaches, but he also arranged important alliances

BERNARDO DE GÁLVEZ. *Photograph courtesy of Jack D. L. Holmes, from Jacobo de la Pezuela's* Crónica de las Antillas *(Madrid, 1871).*

among the peaceful Indians, a tactic that served him well later in his official positions. Returning to the Old World, Gálvez was wounded again on July 8, 1775, in the disastrous Algerian campaign. The campaign's failure led to the downfall of its commander, Alexander O'Reilly, who had been colonial governor of Louisiana in 1769.

Appointed to command the Louisiana infantry battalion in 1776, Gálvez came to New Orleans with the added commission of governor ad interim dating from July 10, 1776. He was sworn in as the successor of Luis de Unzaga y Amezaga on January 1, 1777. On November 2, 1777, he became Unzaga's brother-in-law through marriage to the twenty-one-year-old Felicité St. Maxent, the widow of Jean Baptiste Destrehan and a prominent New Orleans beauty from distinguished French Creole families. The marriage proved decisive for Gálvez' attempt to win the loyalty of the Louisiana settlers, which would have additional military importance with the Spanish declaration of war against Great Britain in 1779.

Prior to hostilities, the Spaniards had been supplying American revolutionary insurgents with money, supplies, and ammunition, largely through the intermediary Oliver Pollock. Gálvez cooperated closely with Pollock in their "common cause" against the British, and Spanish money, supplies, and soldiers diverted British attention along the Gulf and throughout the Mississippi Valley, enabling the Americans to fight a smaller British force in the Southern campaigns during 1780 and 1781.

Gálvez, in New Orleans, received news of the declaration of war before the British governor Peter Chester or the military commander in Pensacola, General John Campbell. Gálvez knew that New Orleans was all but defenseless against a British attack, so he resolved to strike first and have the element of surprise on his side against the British posts along the Mississippi. Before he left New Orleans in 1779, he issued detailed instructions to the senior Spanish military officer left behind, the sergeant major (brevet lieutenant colonel) of the Louisiana infantry regiment, Pedro Joseph Piernas. Gálvez included contingency plans in the nineteen paragraphs of instructions, which Piernas apparently exceeded in cooperation with the Cabildo during the three years he was left in interim command of the Louisiana government. In 1782, an enraged Gálvez removed Piernas and replaced him with Esteban Rodríguez Miró. Yet it was Piernas who, on September 8, 1779, officially announced to the colony that war existed between Spain and England. Miró later wrote that Piernas had served in interim command of Louisiana during the Gálvez expeditions to the complete satisfaction of his superiors and was "praised by the late Conde de Gálvez."[1] On various occasions during the years Piernas had been assigned to Louisiana, he had served as interim commander.

Despite a disastrous hurricane on August 18, 1779, Gálvez managed to assemble white militiamen from among the Acadian and French Creole settlers, as well as recruit some black volunteers. Enlisting friendly Choctaws to join the expedition—even when that meant they had to fight pro-British Choctaws—and reinforced besides by a handful of regular veterans from Spanish line units and the untried Louisiana infantry regiment, he captured Fort Bute, at Manchac, and Fort New Richmond, at Baton Rouge, in September, 1779. The capitulation signed by Lieutenant Colonel Alexander Dickson included the peaceable surrender of Fort Panmure, at Natchez, with its large Anglo-American population.

With additional Spanish regular soldiers sent from Cuba, Gálvez' forces lay siege to Fort Charlotte, the British bastion on the western shore of Mobile Bay, which an experienced British garrison under the command of Elias Durnford ably defended. But a spirited exchange of cannon fire resulted in critical damage to the fort, and on March 14, 1780, Durnford surrendered, just before reinforcements that General Campbell was sending from Pensacola were able to arrive. Gálvez next aimed to take Pensacola, but he was short of supplies and requested reinforcements. In October, one of the worst hurricanes in Gulf history destroyed and scattered the attack fleet he had assembled.

Undaunted, and armed with appointment as commander in chief, Gálvez convoked a meeting of Cuban generals and admirals to discuss the strategy for capturing Pensacola and defeating the British. Eventually, four expeditions were launched, and the most important—the one directed against Pensacola—Gálvez commanded himself. In a daring maneuver calculated to demonstrate his bravery to cautious Cuban naval leaders, he sailed his small brig, the *Gálveztown*, past the British harbor defenses. The action boosted his troops' morale and probably meant the difference between success and failure in the battle for Pensacola. The fighting was fierce, with heavy casualties on both sides;

---

1. Testimonial from Esteban Miró, New Orleans, January 29, 1791, in Papeles procedentes de la isla de Cuba, legajo 122-b, Archivo General de Indias, Seville.

Gálvez himself suffered two wounds during the campaign. Some of the British surrendered on May 8, 1781, and the rest followed two days later. Gálvez triumphantly sent the captured English banners home to Spain.

Rewarding the officer's heroic acts, King Carlos III promoted Gálvez to lieutenant general and named him governor and captain general of the provinces of West Florida and Louisiana. To Gálvez and his descendants, the crown granted the title of count, with a special coat of arms showing a brig and the motto "Yo Solo" ("I Alone").

Gálvez returned briefly to Spain to discuss Louisiana affairs in 1783–1784. He sailed back to Veracruz when his father, then viceroy of New Spain, died in office. The son succeeded him in 1785, but in the following year, after suffering from a mysterious ailment, Gálvez was laid to rest in the San Fernando Church, where his father's remains were interred.

❧

Gálvez' conquests were important. The governor had captured by force of arms the British province of West Florida; subsequent peace treaties granted East Florida to Spain as well. In 1800, Spain retroceded Louisiana to France. The French soon sold Louisiana to the United States in violation of the treaty, and those portions of West Florida *east* of Bayou Manchac were no longer considered by the international community to be part of French Louisiana but were thought of, rather, as British West Florida conquered by Spain. Thus, the United States pretension to an eastern boundary at the Perdido River for Louisiana was totally without merit.

Less attention is usually given to Gálvez' nonmilitary exploits in Louisiana and, later, in Mexico. Yet he was as capable in his administrative career as he was in the arts of war. He encouraged trade with the French and persuaded the crown to reduce duties on Louisiana exports to Spain and to eliminate duties on Spanish imports to New Orleans. He set a tariff schedule for tobacco and established regulations governing its cultivation and export. He devised sound rules for the slave trade and set prices on food and other basic necessities. A census taken at his direction indicated that Louisiana had 17,926 people in 1777.

Because of the possibility of war between England and Spain over the Falkland Islands (las Malvinas) in the late 1770s, Gálvez spent considerable time organizing and reorganizing military units, including a militia company of free mulattoes and another group, the Distinguished Company of Carbineer Militia of New Orleans, members of the city's elite Creole families.

To solve the problem of runaway slaves, he enforced the regulation that decreed the reimbursement of owners for runaways executed by the government or shot in flight. He worked closely with his lieutenant governor, Francisco Bouligny, in founding settlements of the Malagueños at New Iberia. He opposed Bouligny's application for a franchise (*asiento*) to supply Louisiana with slaves, because that would have eliminated competititon and raised prices. Gálvez refused to accept Bouligny's rights as lieutenant governor, and the dispute continued for several years.

Franco-Spanish rivalry abated under Gálvez' governorship. Moreover, he laid the foundation for important alliances with the Indian nations and was able to win the support of the formerly pro-British Choctaws. He extended the boundaries of Louisiana into West Florida as far as Fort San Marcos de Apalache; no other governor increased the size of Spanish Louisiana's jurisdiction the way he did.

Upon the beginning of his expeditions, he left Pedro Piernas, lieutenant colonel of the Louisiana infantry regiment, in charge of the governor's office ad interim, and after 1782, Colonel Esteban Miró held the post. Gálvez never returned to Louisiana, but his imprint on its government and military organization was a memorial to his wise programs. So impressive was he that he was exempt from the *residencia*, the official judicial inquiry into the conduct of a governor's term of office. Because of his accomplishments and the pride he instilled of being a Louisiana Creole, Spanish or French, he is generally considered one of the best Spanish governors of the province.

JACK D. L. HOLMES

BIBLIOGRAPHY

Boeta, José Rodulfo. *Bernardo de Gálvez*. Madrid, 1976.
Caughey, John Walton. *Bernardo de Gálvez in Louisiana, 1776–1783*. Berkeley, 1934; rpr. with intro. by Jack D. L. Holmes, Gretna, La., 1972.
Holmes, Jack D. L. "Bernardo de Gálvez: Spain's 'Man of the Hour' During the American Revolution." In *Cardinales de dos independencias (Noreste de México—Sureste de los Estados Unidos)*, edited by Beatriz Ruiz Gaytán *et al.*, 161–74. Mexico City, 1978.
———. *Gálvez*. Birmingham, Ala., 1980.
Whitaker, Arthur P., "Bernardo de Gálvez." *Dictionary of American Biography*. Vol. VII of 20 vols., 119–20. New York, 1931.

Woodward, Ralph Lee, Jr., trans. and ed. *Tribute to Don Bernardo de Gálvez: Royal Patents and an Epic Ballad Honoring the Spanish Governor of Louisiana.* New Orleans, 1979.

Esteban Rodríguez Miró

Colonial Governor, 1782–1791

MIRÓ, Esteban Rodríguez (b. Reus, Catalonia, Spain, 1744; d. Spanish Pyrenees, June, 1795), Spanish army officer and colonial governor. Miró entered the army as a cadet in the Zamora Regiment in 1760 and participated in the Spanish campaign against Portugal in 1762. During the next eight years he served in the Corona Regiment in Mexico as an aide (*ayudante*), returning to Spain as a lieutenant. Miró was part of General Alexander O'Reilly's disastrous expedition against Algiers in 1775, and he completed a course of study at the Escuela Militar de Avila in 1777–1778.

ESTEBAN RODRÍGUEZ MIRÓ. *Photograph courtesy of State Library of Louisiana, from Fortier's* History of Louisiana, *II, 110.*

When he arrived in Louisiana in 1778, Miró became the highest ranking officer (brevet lieutenant colonel) in the Louisiana Fixed Regiment after Governor Bernardo de Gálvez. In the war against Britain, Miró accompanied Gálvez on the Mississippi campaign in 1779, traveled to Havana to obtain troops for the conquests of Mobile and Pensacola, and served as Gálvez' aide-de-camp at Pensacola in 1781. For the faithful completion of his duties, he was promoted to permanent lieutenant colonel, in 1780, and to colonel, in 1781.

Because Gálvez was called to Guarico, Haiti, to plan a campaign against Jamaica, he appointed Miró acting governor of Louisiana and West Florida on January 20, 1782. Miró received the position of proprietary governor by a commission dated August 19, 1785, and served until December 30, 1791, when the Baron de Carondelet replaced him. Miró also acquired the post of intendant in 1788 upon Martín Navarro's retirement. He petitioned successfully for the rank of brigadier general in 1789. In 1779, Miró married Marie Céleste Elénore de Macarty, of a prominent New Orleans family; their only child was a daughter who died while young.

After ten years as governor of Louisiana—the longest term of any Spanish governor—and three as intendant, Miró returned to Spain. Instead of receiving an active military assignment, he remained at the Spanish court between 1792 and 1793, occasionally reporting on Louisiana affairs. He was promoted to field marshal in 1793 and returned to active duty in the war against the revolutionary French republic, during which he saw action on the Franco-Spanish frontier in the Pyrenees. Miró died at the front from natural causes in June, 1795.

༜

Miró became governor of Louisiana and West Florida in the final year of the American Revolution. Between 1782 and 1783, he had to contend with "river pirates" led by James Colbert, a self-styled British officer, who seized American and Spanish boats on the Mississippi and attacked the Spanish Arkansas post in April, 1783. Miró personally led reinforcements to Natchez in the summer of 1782 and sent men and material on to Arkansas Post. After the war, invasion fears did not subside, and rumors flooded the Mississippi Valley each summer. Several of the invasion scares stemmed from Spain's closing of the Mississippi to United States citizens in 1784 because no boundary agreement existed between the two nations. The controversy arose as a result of Britain's having made separate and different treaties with the United States and Spain over former British lands on the Mississippi's east bank. The United States claimed that side of the Mississippi down to the thirty-first parallel, including the Natchez district of West Florida, which Spain had conquered during the war and then occupied. Spain also claimed lands far above Natchez.

In order to retain the regions Spain won in the war, Miró negotiated treaties with the southern Indians, who also objected to American encroachment on their territories. In 1784, Miró held congresses in Pensacola and Mobile with various tribes that pledged to support Spain. He acquired the assistance of the English firm of Panton, Leslie, and Company, to supply the southern Indians with merchandise from Pensacola. Miró also successfully warded off the Georgia commissioners who in 1785 asserted that the Natchez district was their state's Bourbon County. Although he asked for large numbers of soldiers and artillery pieces from Cuba and Mexico, he learned that he had to protect Louisiana with the undermanned Louisiana Fixed Regiment. Moreover, Louisiana was starved for funds in the 1780s, and the governor had to economize wherever possible. The support of the Indians was dubious at best, and when Miró stopped supplying them with arms in the late 1780s, they turned away from Spain briefly.

Because of American discontent in the West and George Rogers Clark's seizure in 1786 of Spanish goods on the Mississippi in retaliation for the river's closure, Miró and Navarro were drawn to General James Wilkinson's scheme to separate the American West from the United States and form an alliance with Spain. They passed the proposal on to the Spanish court in September, 1787, wholeheartedly endorsing Wilkinson's second proposal—which in reality was Miró's—for Anglo-Americans to settle in the Natchez district as a countercolonizing presence balancing the rapid and alarming growth in population of the American West. Miró hoped to convert and assimilate the Protestant immigrants through the use of English-speaking Irish missionaries.

Miró's administration was generally mild, and he encouraged commerce and agriculture. He often stated his wish that the fur traders would settle down and become productive farmers. He helped the Natchez planters by having the crown purchase their tobacco harvests for several years and thus stimulated economic activity in that area before the advent of cotton. When a great fire struck New Orleans in 1788 and burned some 805 buildings, Miró reacted energetically to relieve the population's suffering. A major part of the city was rebuilt, including the government buildings around the Plaza de Armas (Jackson Square). Miró also assisted Canadian and Acadian immigrants who entered Louisiana during his administration, and he settled them in uninhabited areas in lower Louisiana. Because the crown declined to continue backing expensive projects to bring immigrants from Europe, he sought to attract settlers from the United States and to convert them into loyal, Catholic, and productive subjects.

In the late 1780s and after the outbreak of the French Revolution, Louisiana again appeared to be vulnerable. Miró led the effort to shore up the colony's fortifications, which had badly deteriorated after the war. By 1787, a battalion had been authorized for Pensacola, the Third Battalion of the Louisiana regiment. Nogales (modern Vicksburg) also replaced Natchez as the principal Spanish defensive fortification above New Orleans on the Mississippi. Work on Nogales had only begun when Miró's tenure as governor ended.

A number of charges were made against Miró during his *residencia*, the official investigation into wrongdoing that might have occurred during his term in office. The charges appear to have been instigated by a New Orleans cabal led by José Orue, with whom Miró had had unpleasant working relations. He successfully defended himself against them, but the investigation was not completed before his death in 1795. Owing to wartime delays, a judge arrived in New Orleans only in 1802 to liquidate the final accusations, which turned out to have been petty and ill founded.

As governor, Miró was active, imaginative, and generally popular. Louisiana's population and commerce increased during his administration. But he was hampered by a perpetual shortage of funds, and that hurt his ability to do more for the provinces in his care.

GILBERT C. DIN

BIBLIOGRAPHY

Burson, Caroline Maude. *The Stewardship of Don Esteban Miró, 1782–1792.* New Orleans, 1940.

Din, Gilbert C. "The Immigration Policy of Governor Esteban Miró in Spanish Louisiana." *Southwestern Historical Quarterly,* LXXIII (1969), 155–75.

———. "Proposals and Plans for Colonization in Spanish Louisiana, 1781–1790." *Louisiana History,* XI (1970), 197–213.

———. "War Clouds on the Mississippi: Spain's 1785 Crisis in West Florida." *Florida Historical Quarterly,* LX (1981), 51–76.

Wall, Bennett H., ed. *Louisiana: A History.* Arlington Heights, Ill., 1984.

Whitaker, Arthur P. *The Spanish-American Frontier, 1783–1795.* Boston, 1927.

François-Louis Hector, Baron de Carondelet et Noyelles

Colonial Governor, 1791–1797

CARONDELET, Francois-Louis Hector, Baron de (b. Cambray, France, July 29, 1747; d. Quito, Ecuador, August 10, 1807), Spanish army officer and colonial governor. Scion of a distinguished Burgundian family, Carondelet was the son of Jean-Louis de Carondelet et Noyelles, the thirteenth Baron de Carondelet. Little is known about his childhood except that he entered the service of the Hapsburgs at an early age.

In 1762, he was named captain (apparently an honorary title) in the
Walloon Royal Guards. He subsequently joined the Spanish army
and, while serving under Alexander
O'Reilly, was severely wounded in
the ill-fated Spanish invasion of Algiers (1775). Once recovered from
his injuries, he was assigned to the
New World, where, in 1781, he
participated in the Spanish siege of
Pensacola as commander of the 4th
Division of Walloon Guards. In
recognition of his meritorious services, he was commissioned lieutenant colonel in 1781. On June 11,
1789, he was named governor and
intendant of San Salvador, then a province of Guatemala. Carondelet's
administrative career in Central America was short-lived; he succeeded
Esteban Rodríguez Miró as governor and intendant of Louisiana and
West Florida on December 30, 1791.

FRANÇOIS-LOUIS HECTOR, BARON DE CAR-
ONDELET ET NOYELLES. *Photograph courtesy of State Library of Louisiana, from Fortier's* History of Louisiana, *II, 152.*

Carondelet was governor of Louisiana for nearly six years, and his
unpopular policies not only cost him the intendancy in 1793 but also
fed the controversy and turmoil that plagued his administration. His
incumbency is best remembered for his use of Indian diplomacy as a
means of keeping the United States out of the Gulf South and his
efforts to combat republican agitation in Louisiana. The abortive Pointe
Coupee slave insurrection (1795) resulted from his confusing slave policy. The New Orleans fire of 1794, the construction of the Carondelet
Canal (1794–1796), and the establishment of the diocese of New Orleans (1795) were other important events during his governorship.

On August 5, 1797, he relinquished his position to accept the presidency of the Royal Audiencia of Quito. He assumed this office on February 20, 1799, and served Spain in it until his death. He was interred
in St. Peter Cathedral, Quito.

&

Once hailed as a model administrator, Carondelet has fallen in the es-
timation of recent historians and has become one of the more controversial figures in Spanish Louisiana historiography. James Thomas

McGowan in his work on colonial slavery has identified Carondelet's indecisiveness as the source of late Spanish Louisiana's vacillating and ineffective slave policies. Indeed, in McGowan's lengthy examination of slavery in the 1790s, Carondelet emerges as a rank opportunist who expediently sided with the region's powerful, albeit Hispanophobic, planter aristocracy when, inadvertently, his humanitarian reforms threatened to spark a general servile insurrection.

Most recent works on the Spanish borderlands offer more positive views of the governor. In them, Carondelet comes across as an energetic, capable leader, whose actions were impaired by a marked lack of pragmatism. In *Spanish War Vessels on the Missisippi*, Abraham P. Nasatir, for example, notes that the governor was "a choleric and quick-nerved warrior, a strategist of wide views and agile combinations, but often deficient in precise knowledge of the instruments and conditions of the game he was taking over and somewhat deficient, it may be, in practical realities. But he had in recompense a prophetic vision of the magnitude of the issues at stake."[1]

It was precisely Carondelet's "vision of the magnitude of the issues" that shaped the meandering course of his administration. Though at odds over his ethics, if not his overall effectiveness, Carondelet's defenders and detractors concur regarding the governor's propensity to view threats to Louisiana's internal and external security on a grand scale. Panicked by rumors of sedition within the colony and of impending attack by land-hungry American and French revolutionaries, Carondelet developed a siege mentality and labored to strengthen the colony's defenses.

Fearing American encroachments into the Spanish Gulf South, the governor in 1792–1793 forged alliances with the region's most powerful tribes. In addition, he expanded Spain's military presence in the portion of the Mississippi Valley lying north of the thirty-first parallel, the ownership of which was disputed by the United States. He ordered construction of a fleet of armed galleys to meet waterborne invaders and supported the ultimately unsuccessful schemes of the Marquis de Maison Rouge, the Baron de Bastrop, and Delassus as a means of increasing the population and thus bolstering the local militia, the backbone of Louisiana's defense system. In 1793, Carondelet organized the mercantile Company of the Missouri, ostensibly to find a route to the

1. Abraham P. Nasatir, *Spanish War Vessels on the Mississippi, 1792–1796* (New Haven, 1968), 29.

Pacific but actually to combat the increasing influence of English traders and smugglers in the upper Great Plains.

While preparing for an invasion that never materialized, Carondelet took measures to defend his militarily weak regime against sedition. Reports of the successes of the French Revolution reached Louisiana in early 1793, evoking displays of revolutionary and French sympathies. Moreover, fifty New Orleans merchants sent representatives to France to express their support for the revolutionary government. Fearing that this act presaged an uprising in the colony, Carondelet quickly took steps to consolidate what he perceived to be a tenuous position. He summoned troops from Havana and, after promulgating the declaration of Franco-Hispanic hostilities in June 1793, extracted oaths of allegiance from all residents who had immigrated since 1790.

These measures, along with the reports of Spain's military victories in Europe and the liberal commercial policies initiated by Spanish authorities at the outset of the war, temporarily suppressed prorevolutionary agitation. Working surreptitiously, however, the colony's revolutionaries sought assistance from Edmund Genêt, French minister to the United States. Copies of Genêt's inflammatory address were soon circulating throughout Louisiana, and by the fall of 1793, the French population of New Orleans was animated with revolutionary fervor. Again anticipating an upheaval, Carondelet summoned from Natchez to the colonial capital three hundred of English ancestry and Tory inclination. With the assistance of these loyalists, the governor managed, through arrests, intimidation, and banishments, to end once again the public demonstration of loyalty to France. In addition, he reorganized the New Orleans militia, the keystone of the colonial defense, and placed in leadership positions persons of proven devotion to Spain. Thereafter the threat of rebellion in New Orleans dissipated.

Though Carondelet's measures were effective in Louisiana's one urban center, revolutionary agitation continued in the rural settlements, especially in Natchitoches. By January, 1796, anarchy reigned at Natchitoches, and Carondelet dispatched a militia detachment to restore order, but he could not deal so easily with the activities of the revolutionary underground working quietly among the servile population.

From the very outset of his administration, Carondelet feared that the Saint Domingue (Haitian) slave insurrection would spread to the Mississippi Valley. He also believed that the colony's black population had to be tied to the Spanish administration as a hedge against the doubtful loyalty of the planter class. Convinced that the cruelty of French slaveholders had been the principal cause of the Haitian revolution, he determined that his Spanish government would regulate slave affairs in such a way as to curb abuses, thereby minimizing the threat of servile insurrection. Carondelet quickly established himself with free blacks and urged them to tell enslaved friends and relatives that he would hear and act upon their complaints at his office.

Carondelet's humanitarian slave policy had far-reaching effects in the colony. First, the governor earned the undying animosity of Louisiana's powerful, predominantly French planter class. Second, emboldened by the governor's promised protection, slaves throughout Louisiana began to challenge their masters' authority, organizing work slowdowns and strikes to protest plantation conditions. Realizing that his measures were counterproductive, Carondelet quickly retreated and promulgated a code that barred slaves from direct access to his office, invested local commandants with both enforcement and surveillance responsibilities, and reduced to a token level fines on planters who abused their slaves.

Carondelet also vacillated over the question of Indian slavery, which had been raised by the colony's free black population. Indian slavery had been banned by O'Reilly in 1769, but the institution had persisted into the 1790s. In response to the governor's paternalistic overtures of 1792, the colony's free blacks filed numerous suits during the next year for the manumission of enslaved blacks of Indian descent. Unable to avoid prosecuting the cases if he wanted to maintain his image as the benefactor of the black population, yet fearful of a white backlash against problack decisions, Carondelet heard the cases but waited more than two years before issuing a decision. During that time, free blacks faithfully reported the anti-Spanish sympathies of planters and their violations of Carondelet's humanitarian code. The planters retaliated with a vicious campaign of intimidation against free blacks, threatening to enslave them once the colony fell into French hands.

The governor's failure to protect his informants, his procrastination in issuing decisions in the controversial Indian slavery cases, and his shifting slave policies undermined Carondelet's credibility among Louisiana's nonwhites. Consequently, when rumors reached the colony's slaves that the Spanish king had ordered their emancipation, they took matters into their own hands. Assisted by French republican sympathizers in the colonial garrison and disenchanted free blacks, the slaves prepared to break their shackles. In the ensuing weeks, numerous conspiracies were conceived, the most notable of which resulted in the abortive slave insurrection at Pointe Coupee in 1795.

At the news of that uprising, Carondelet demonstrated a marked inability to act forcefully to allay the fears of the panic-stricken Creole planters. As a result, the Creoles, represented by Attorney General Michel Fortier, attempted to impose changes by which the supervision of slaves would be vested in the native white population.

Carondelet responded by issuing a comprehensive police code in June, 1795. The new code established a draconian slave regime under which all blacks were subject to the complete authority of any and all whites, regardless of whether the whites owned them.

The governor's paternalistic slave policy was just one of his programs that recoiled on him. Carondelet's massive defense expenditures in the early 1790s depleted the colonial treasury and thus, when fire destroyed New Orleans in 1794, the Louisiana government was incapable of assisting the victims. His efforts to bring the southeastern Indians into the Spanish sphere of influence and to build fortifications in disputed territory undermined Spain's official policy of achieving a negotiated settlement with the United States.

Carondelet's achievements—such as the establishment, with his support, of theaters and newspapers in the colonial capital (1792–1795), the construction of a canal linking New Orleans with Bayou St. John (1794–1796), and the installation of oil-burning streetlights in New Orleans to reduce street crimes (1796)—were clearly overshadowed by his failures, which perhaps stemmed less from circumstances than from personal shortcomings. Though a man of remarkable energy, he often lacked the persistence to see projects, such as the implementation of his paternalistic slave policies, to fruition. Quick tempered, impulsive, and extremely gullible, the governor was prone to rash decisions based on inadequate or faulty information. Executive policies were thus unsteady, and in many instances only the timely intercession of Lieutenant Governor Manuel Gayoso de Lemos prevented serious international repercussions when Carondelet acted precipitately. In the absence of capable direction, Carondelet's administration bequeathed a legacy of administrative ineffectiveness, political oppression, and social repression.

CARL A. BRASSEAUX

BIBLIOGRAPHY

Beerman, Eric. "XV Baron de Carondelet: Gobernador de la Luisiana y la Florida, 1791–1797." *Hidalguía* (Madrid), March–April, 1978, pp. 3–15.

Bork, Albert W., and Georg Maier, comps. *Historical Dictionary of Ecuador.* Metuchen, N.J., 1973.

Fiehrer, Thomas M. "The Baron de Carondelet as Agent of Bourbon Reform: A Study of Spanish Colonial Administration in the Years of the French Revolution." Ph.D. dissertation, Tulane University, 1977.

Gayarré, Charles E. *History of Louisiana.* 5th ed. 4 vols. New Orleans, 1965.

Liljegren, Ernest R. "Jacobinism in Spanish Louisiana." *Louisiana Historical Quarterly,* XXII (1939), 47–97.

McGowan, James Thomas. "Creation of a Slave Society: Louisiana Plantations in the Eighteenth Century." Ph.D. dissertation, University of Rochester, 1976.

Nasatir, Abraham P. *Spanish War Vessels on the Mississippi, 1792–1796.* New Haven, 1968.

Nasatir, Abraham P., and Ernest R. Liljegren. "Materials Relating to the History of the Mississippi Valley, from the Minutes of the Spanish Supreme Council of State, 1787–1797." *Louisiana Historical Quarterly,* XXI (1938), 5–75.

O'Callaghan, Mary A. "An Indian Removal Policy in Spanish Louisiana." In *Greater America: Essays in Honor of Herbert Eugene Bolton,* edited by Adele Ogden and Engel Sluitar. Berkeley, Calif., 1945.

Wall, Bennett H., ed. *Louisiana: A History.* Arlington Heights, Ill., 1984.

Whitaker, Arthur P. "Carondelet, Francisco Luis Hector." *Dictionary of American Biography.* Vol. II of 20 vols., 507–508. New York, 1929.

Manuel Gayoso de Lemos

Colonial Governor, 1797–1799

GAYOSO DE LEMOS, Manuel (b. Oporto, Portugal, May 30, 1747; d. New Orleans, Louisiana, July 18, 1799), Spanish army officer, diplomat, and colonial governor. Born in Portugal, where his father was serving as Spanish consul general, Gayoso consistently maintained that he was a native of Pontevedra, in Galicia, where the family estate was located. The boy's mother was Doña Theresa Angelica de Amorín y Magallanes, a native of Portugal. The youth was educated at Westminister, in England, from which he returned to Spain to join the Lisbon Infantry Regiment as a cadet in 1771. His flair for diplomacy, his broad understanding of politics, economics, languages, and the law, and his family connections won him rapid advancement in the service of King Carlos III. During the Spanish siege of Gibraltar (1779–1783), the combined

Franco-Spanish forces assembled at
Cádiz, where Alexander O'Reilly
was captain general and Gayoso
was aide-de-camp to the formidable
Irishman.

When the Spanish government
reorganized the Natchez district,
which it had won from the British
in 1779, the need was for a diplomatic English-speaking governor
skilled in dealing with a polyglot
population that was accustomed to
non-Spanish political traditions.
Spain hoped to make of this district
a buffer zone separating Spanish
Louisiana and West Florida from
the restless American frontiersmen.

MANUEL GAYOSO DE LEMOS. *Photograph
courtesy of Jack D. L. Holmes, from portrait
ca. 1798.*

Alliances with the surrounding Indian tribes—Choctaws, Cherokees,
Chickasaws, and Creeks—complemented the Spanish design. Gayoso
had the responsibility for carrying out and advancing the grand plan.

Gayoso reached Natchez in 1789 and served as governor of the
Natchez district until 1797. During his tenure there, he dealt with numerous problems, including discontented farmers, the maintenance of
communications with New Orleans, and the establishment of new military posts and defenses. One of his primary duties was to keep on good
terms with the Indians of the region, and his skill at diplomacy was put
to use.

In 1797, when Gayoso became governor-general of Louisiana, at
New Orleans, his concern with the redrawing of the boundary between
United States and Spanish territory had to continue. In New Orleans,
Gayoso reorganized colonial defenses, reevaluated several municipal
ordinances, and prepared to make his permanent home in the Crescent
City. His administration as Louisiana's governor-general, filled with
promise after his experiences in Natchez, was cut short, however, by an
outbreak of yellow fever, from which Gayoso died.

❧

Gayoso arrived in Natchez in 1789, a time of economic difficulties for
the planters, who had mortgaged heavily and owed much to their credi-

tors. The crown declined to renew its commitment to purchase all the tobacco produced. To prevent economic panic, Gayoso arranged for a moratorium on debts for a five-year period. Under his administration, indigo and, later, cotton became staple exports of Natchez. At the same time, he laid out a plan for developing the city along the bluff above the Mississippi landing, and he improved mail communication with New Orleans and several military posts. Two posts in which he took a personal interest were Los Nogales, established at the confluence of the Yazoo and Mississippi rivers during the governorship of Esteban Rodríguez Miró and completed in 1791, and Barrancas de Margot, at the Chickasaw Bluffs, where Gayoso erected Fort San Fernando de las Barrancas in 1795. From these frontier posts grew, respectively, the cities of Vicksburg and Memphis.

Gayoso granted the Indians permission to trade with licensed traders, particularly the Scot-dominated firm of Panton, Leslie, and Forbes. Because of Panton's contacts in Jamaica, Nassau, and London, trade goods from England circulated in Louisiana and West Florida. Gayoso kept close watch over Indian commerce and encouraged prominent chiefs among the Choctaws and Chickasaws to send their sons to him for education. He signed important treaties such as the Treaty of Natchez (1792), by which Spain acquired the small plot of land on which Fort Nogales was erected; the Treaty of Nogales (1793), which bound all the southern tribes into a strong defensive alliance with Spain; and the Chickasaw Bluffs cession (1795), by which the Chickasaws ceded the land for Fort San Fernando de las Barrancas.

In his government at Natchez, Gayoso had the able support of fellow *gallego* José (or Joseph) Vidal, his secretary. He was capably assisted, too, by the post adjutant, Stephen Minor, a Pennsylvania native who became a Spanish subject and was the last Spanish governor of the Natchez district before American occupation in 1798. Because the settlers of Natchez had a strong tradition of conservative respect for the rights embodied in English law, Gayoso's task was simpler than that of his American successors, who encountered high-spirited frontiersmen anxious to avoid government control. Gayoso could act the enlightened or paternal Spanish governor ever anxious to show courtesy and suave diplomacy.

Under the terms of the Treaty of San Lorenzo (1795), Spain relinquished exclusive control over the Mississippi River, recognized the thirty-first parallel as the northern limit of Spanish East and West Florida, and agreed to provide a place of deposit at New Orleans for American boats carrying the produce of the Ohio and Mississippi valleys to world markets. The United States Senate named the brilliant astronomer and mathematician Andrew Ellicott the boundary commissioner, and he presented his credentials to Gayoso in the spring of 1797. The discovery of an English plan to invade Spanish Louisiana (Blount's Conspiracy) and the resistance of several Spanish district governors to the evacuation of posts north of the thirty-first parallel strained relations between Ellicott and Gayoso. The two men fixed the initial point for the agreed boundary on the basis of astronomical observations by Ellicott and the Spanish commissioner William Dunbar, a Scot who had changed allegiance from Great Britain to Spain and who would later become an American citizen. After Gayoso and Ellicott's agreement, Minor replaced Dunbar and continued the work as far as the St. Mary's River in East Florida.

Gayoso took his oath as governor-general in New Orleans in August, 1797, but he maintained a close watch on the boundary commission. He carried out the remaining provisions of the Treaty of San Lorenzo by evacuating Natchez and Fort Nogales in March, 1798, and Fort San Esteban, in Alabama, in 1799. With a view to reorganizing Louisiana's defenses, he established a defensive line across Baton Rouge, repaired the galleys in the river-defense squadron, increased its personnel and firepower, and established frontier settlements at the Feliciana parishes and in Concordia parish opposite Natchez.

Under Gayoso's supervision, municipal changes were made in New Orleans. These included increasing the number of night watchmen (*serrenos*), placing pumps and buckets conveniently in order to fight fires, organizing a volunteer force of fire fighters, regulating cart traffic, putting matters of weights and measures under government control, and renewing the slave trade that had been halted by the fear of slave revolts. A host of regulations aimed for "good government," and some of them covered taverns, inns, and billiard parlors.

Gayoso renovated a home near the government house and brought his new wife and infant son, Fernando, from Natchez to the Crescent City. Gayoso married three times. His first wife and a native of Lisbon, Theresa Margarita Hopman y Pereira, died shortly after the Gayosos arrived in Natchez in 1789, as did an infant daughter. A son remained in Portugal with maternal relatives. Gayoso's second wife, Elizabeth Watts, the daughter of a prominent British settler, moved from Baton Rouge to Natchez after the American Revolution. When Elizabeth died, Gayoso remarried once more, this time to Elizabeth's sister, Margaret Watts.

As Louisiana's governor-general, Gayoso had a series of political disputes with the proud and jealous intendant, Juan Buenaventura Morales. He was beginning to have to face as well American expansion into the Old Southwest, migration he had blocked during his decade of service in Natchez. But just as he was turning attention to these matters, he suffered an attack of yellow fever, from which he died. He was interred in the St. Louis Cathedral, in New Orleans. During the critical decade preceding his death, Gayoso had managed to spread benevolent Spanish rule into northern Missouri and to retard for a few years what became the Manifest Destiny of westward expansion by the United States. His honesty and sense of fair play endeared him to those who valued those qualities in their governor.

JACK D. L. HOLMES

BIBLIOGRAPHY

Holmes, Jack D. L. *Gayoso: The Life of a Spanish Governor in the Mississippi Valley, 1789–1799.* Baton Rouge, 1965.
Leonard, Irving A. "A Frontier Library, 1799." *Hispanic American Historical Review,* XXIII (1943), 21–51.
Whitaker, Arthur P. "Gayoso de Lemos, Manuel." *Dictionary of American Biography.* Vol. VII of 20 vols., 201–202. New York, 1931.

Francisco Bouligny
Marqués de Casa-Calvo
Manuel Juan de Salcedo
Pierre Clément, Baron de Laussat

Colonial Governors, 1799–1803

From the death of Manuel Gayoso de Lemos, on July 18, 1799, to December 20, 1803, when American authorities took charge of Louisiana, four men served as governors of the province. Of these men—Francisco Bouligny, the Marqués de Casa-Calvo, Manuel Juan de Salcedo, and Pierre Clément, Baron de Laussat—Salcedo alone enjoyed a regular appointment as governor. The others served on an ad interim basis. Spain's last years in Louisiana were dismal. Its power in the colony declined, since it intended to divest itself of the troublesome possession. Spanish military strength there steadily deteriorated, shipments of the subsidy arrived late and were often incomplete, and the continuing European wars frequently resulted in blockades at the mouth of the Mississippi and threats of invasion from Canada. The short tenures of the governors—and in the case of Salcedo, the unfitness of the man—contributed to the general worsening of conditions. Petty disputes, corruption, and an overall inefficiency in administration characterized affairs in Louisiana during those years.

The first of the four governors, Bouligny, was born to a merchant family in Alicante, Spain, on September 4, 1736. He entered the army as a cadet in 1758. Five years later, as a lieutenant, he arrived in Cuba, where he remained until 1769. That year, he joined General Alexander O'Reilly's expedition from Havana to Louisiana to recover the colony after the French Creole rebellion. Bouligny volunteered to remain as a captain in the newly created Louisiana Fixed Battalion. Except for two years (1775–1777) when he was on leave in Spain, Bouligny spent the rest of his life in Louisiana. In Spain in 1776, he presented a *memoria* on conditions in the colony, with recommendations to build up its agriculture, industry, and commerce. He became for a brief time the lieutenant governor for Indians, commerce, and settlements. In the war against Britain (1779-1783), he participated in the Mississippi River campaign and at the sieges of Mobile and Pensacola. In 1782, he served temporarily as acting governor, as he would do again for short periods. In 1791, upon the death of Colonel Pedro Joseph Piernas, commandant of the Louisiana Fixed Regiment, Bouligny assumed command and held the post until his own demise on November 25, 1800. He was promoted to colonel in 1791 and to brigadier general in 1800.

Bouligny's brief periods as governor did not permit him to initiate policy or to influence the office appreciably. Nevertheless, he appears to have exercised authority energetically, especially in military matters. In 1784, he ordered expeditions that defeated and captured runaway slaves. On the death of Governor Manuel Gayoso de Lemos, in July, 1799, he became acting military governor. But almost immediately he fell sick. By August, when he had recovered, some Americans had began to penetrate the *barrera*, encroaching on Spanish territory. Although Bouligny wanted the appointment as proprietary governor, his replacement, Casa-Calvo, took charge on September 18, 1799.

Casa-Calvo (Sebastián Nicolas de Bari Calvo de la Puerta y O'Farrill) was born in Havana on August 11, 1751. He began his military career on April 1, 1763, as a cadet in the Company of Nobles. In 1769, he accompanied O'Reilly's expedition to Louisiana, and he fought with Bernardo de Gálvez against the British at Mobile in 1780 and at Pensacola in 1781. In 1794, he served in Santo Domingo during Spain's brief war against republican France. Casa-Calvo became a captain of cavalry in 1769, a lieutenant colonel in 1786, and a colonel in 1802. He achieved knighthood in the Order of Santiago and received his title of nobility in 1786. At the time of Gayoso's death, Casa-Calvo held the position of judge advocate in Havana. Captain General Someruelos, of Cuba, sent him to Louisiana as ad interim governor, where he served from September 18, 1799, to July 14, 1801. Because of Spain's cession of Louisiana to France, Casa-Calvo returned to Louisiana on April 10, 1803, so as to assist Governor Salcedo in turning the colony over to Napoleon's agents. He remained nearly three years as commissioner of limits, to work out a boundary between Spanish Texas and American Louisiana. Finally, in early 1806, the first American governor, William C. C. Claiborne, expelled him. Casa-Calvo retreated to Spain and, at the time of the French invasion of that nation in 1808, sided with the Bonapartists. He became a lieutenant general in the service of King Joseph I, Napoleon's brother, and upon the French defeat in 1813, was forced to leave Spain. He died on May 20, 1820, in exile in Paris.

Casa-Calvo's tenure as ad interim governor was prolonged as a result of the time it took his successor, Salcedo, to arrive. Although Casa-Calvo was not of great ability, he had a mind of his own and enjoyed the esteem of Louisiana's Creoles. He tried to keep the attention of his subordinates on government business. He did not get along with Dr. Nicholás María Vidal, who had ad interim civil authority and who undermined Casa-Calvo's power. The marqués later recommended that the military and civil jurisdictions of the office of governor not be left divided. He also quarreled with the Cabildo and contributed to the decline of its power and influence. More than anything else, Casa-Calvo simply attempted to keep affairs functioning smoothly. He was hampered in his duties by the war against Britain that often closed the mouth of the Mississippi with blockades and impeded commerce. Delays in the arrival of the subsidy from Veracruz kept him short of money, and military defenses continued to deteriorate. The possibility of invasion from Canada loomed in the spring of both 1800 and 1801. The real threat to Spanish power, however, came from William Augustus Bowles, who captured Fort San Marcos de Apalache in 1800. Although the fort was quickly recovered, Bowles remained a danger to Spanish authority until 1802. During Casa-Calvo's term as governor and the term of his successor, Americans entered Spanish territory at will to settle, trade, and carry out their designs. Despite his efforts to restrain American penetration, he could not stem the tide of intruders. The helplessness of the Spaniards in Louisiana increased under the next governor.

Salcedo, who was born in Bilbao, Spain, in 1743, had forty-two years of national service and was fifty-eight years of age when he became governor of Louisiana. On November 18, 1799, when the crown appointed him governor, he was a colonel and the king's lieutenant at Santa Cruz, on the island of Tenerife, in the Canaries. Accompanied by his wife, Francisca Quiruga y Manso, and two sons, he began in August, 1800, a journey that turned into an odyssey. He was delayed in Puerto Rico and, later, in Cuba; his wife died; he almost lost his own life; and one son remained behind temporarily. He assumed office on July 14, 1801, and stayed until France took charge. During that time, he often relied on his son Manuel María de Salcedo, who was later governor of Texas. Salcedo showed little liking for Louisiana and repeatedly petitioned the crown to permit him to retire to the more benign environs of the Canaries with the rank of brigadier. The government at last acceded to his request, granting him an annual pension of three thousand pesos and permitting his sons to accompany him.

Contemporaries of Salcedo who visited New Orleans, the captain general of Cuba, and later historians share in the concensus that Salcedo was unfit for office. He evidently sought to profit from his post and frequently abused his authority. He acted in concert with his older son, Manuel María, and with the judge advocate, Vidal, both of whom were charged with corruption. Like a number of governors before him, Salcedo quarreled with the Cabildo. He boycotted its meetings, humiliated its members, and further contributed to the institution's decline. He refused to permit inoculation (variolation) in the smallpox epidemic of 1802, here too blocking the Cabildo. He allowed an antagonism to develop between himself and the commandant of the Louisiana regiment, Lieutenant Colonel Carlos Howard. His relations were no better with the intendant, Juan Ventura Morales, with Joseph Martínez de la Pedrera, a lawyer, or with his French successor, Laussat. Although Salcedo pushed Spanish exploration up the Missouri River and tried to control the Indians on the waterway, he canceled Auguste Chouteau's trade monopoly over the Osage Indians, which had been useful in dominating that worrisome tribe. The Spanish government lacked confidence in Salcedo and did not

PIERRE CLÉMENT, BARON DE LAUSSAT. *Photograph courtesy of State Library of Louisiana, from Fortier's* History of Louisiana, *II, 224.*

inform him of the secret orders to the intendant, Morales, to suspend the right of deposit of the Americans. Nor did the captain general of Cuba believe Salcedo fit to surrender the colony to the French in 1803. He sent Casa-Calvo back to assist Salcedo, and the marqués seems to have done most of the work.

Laussat was born in Pau, France, on November 23, 1756. Trained for government service, he held a number of posts at the local level prior to the French Revolution. He survived and adapted to several changes in government. When France regained Louisiana, Laussat obtained appointment as prefect. He was named to his position, which was the highest civilian post in the new French government for Louisiana, on August 20, 1802. He and his party arrived in New Orleans in March, 1803, but Napoleon sold the province to the United States during the very next month, and Laussat became the commissioner charged with receiving Louisiana from Spain and delivering it to the Americans. Upon leaving New Orleans, Laussat served as prefect in Martinique (1804–1809) and in Antwerp and Jemmapes (1810–1814). In 1815, during Napoleon's brief return to power, he was a member of the Chamber of Deputies. In the Bourbon restoration, he was appointed governor of French Guiana, and he received a baronage upon his return to France. In poor health, he retired to his chateau at Bernadets, where he died in 1835.

As governor of Louisiana for twenty days—November 30 to December 20, 1803—Laussat had little impact on his office. He spent much of his time attending to ceremonial matters, and he appointed French and Creoles to temporary offices and prepared to surrender the colony. Haughty when he arrived in Louisiana, Laussat alienated many of the Spaniards, but he learned a measure of humility when he received word that his supreme act in the colony was to be arranging for its transfer.

GILBERT C. DIN

BIBLIOGRAPHY

DeConde, Alexander. *This Affair of Louisiana.* New York, 1976.

Din, Gilbert C., trans. and ed. *Louisiana in 1776: A Memoria of Francisco Bouligny.* New Orleans, 1977.

Din, Gilbert C. and Abraham P. Nasatir. *The Imperial Osages.* Norman, Okla., 1983.

Laussat, Pierre Clément de. *Memoirs of My Life.* Translated and introduced by Agnes-Josephine Pastwa. Edited by Robert D. Bush. Baton Rouge, 1978.

Lyon, E. Wilson. *Louisiana in French Diplomacy, 1759–1804.* Rev. ed. Norman, Okla., 1974.

Morazán, Ronald R. "Letters, Petitions, and Decrees of the Cabildo of New Orleans, 1800–1803." Ph.D. dissertation, Louisiana State University, 1972.

Whitaker, Arthur P. *The Mississippi Question, 1795–1803: A Study in Trade, Politics, and Diplomacy.* New York, 1934.

Territorial and State Governors of the Nineteenth Century

William C. C. Claiborne

Territorial Governor, 1803–1812; Governor, 1812–1816

CLAIBORNE, William Charles Cole (b. Sussex County, near Richmond, Virginia, 1775; d. New Orleans, Louisiana, November 23, 1817), Tennessee congressman, territorial governor of Mississippi, governor of the territory of Orleans (Louisiana), governor, and United States senator-elect. Claiborne was the son of William Claiborne, a colonel of militia during the American Revolution, and Mary Leigh. Apparently, Colonel Claiborne suffered bankruptcy soon after the Revolution, but his son received a sound education at the Richmond Academy and attended William and

WILLIAM C. C. CLAIBORNE. *Photograph courtesy of State Library of Louisiana, from Fortier's* History of Louisiana, *III, 20.*

Mary College for a time. At age fifteen, he went to New York, then the national capital, and was employed by the clerk of the Congress. While working in this position, first at New York and later at Philadelphia, he met John Sevier and Thomas Jefferson, both of whom would have a great effect on his career.

At Sevier's urging, he returned to Virginia and read law in a judge's office for three months; this enabled him to pass the state bar examination. Virginia was full of lawyers, however, and Claiborne emigrated to what is now Sullivan County, Tennesse. Despite his youth, he conducted a highly successful frontier law practice, but in 1796, his service in the convention that drew up Tennessee's first state constitution led him into public life. Sevier was elected the first governor of the new state, and he appointed Claiborne, then twenty-one years old, as a justice on the Tennessee Supreme Court. A year later, Andrew Jackson resigned from the Congress, and Claiborne was elected to the vacant seat in the United States House of Representatives. In 1798, he was reelected to a full term.

As a Tennessee congressman, Claiborne helped hold his state's vote for Jefferson when the choice between Jefferson and Aaron Burr was thrown into the House of Representatives in 1801. When the governorship of the territory of Mississippi became vacant, Jefferson appointed Claiborne to that office and also named him commissioner of Indian affairs for the territory. Before leaving Nashville for Natchez, Claiborne married Eliza Lewis, a young woman of good family and considerable wealth. In 1803, when news of the Louisiana Purchase reached Jefferson, he appointed Claiborne and General James Wilkinson as United States commissioners to take possession of the new territory. This they did on December 20, 1803.

For the first few months of American possession of the Louisiana lands, Claiborne was for all practical purposes dictator, but an unorganized territorial government was established in 1804, with Claiborne as governor of the territory of Orleans, which comprised modern Louisiana without the Florida Parishes. In 1805, the territory was organized with an elected lower house of the legislature. Five years later, after the West Florida Rebellion, the part of Florida west of the Perdido River was added to Claiborne's domain. Jefferson at one time considered replacing him, but when the Marquis de Lafayette rejected the position, Claiborne remained in office.

In 1805, Major General Wilkinson, the senior officer in the United States Army, became governor of the Louisiana district, the Purchase north of the thirty-third parallel; he was also a Spanish secret agent, and he was deeply involved in Aaron Burr's conspiratorial plans. When in December, 1806, Wilkinson betrayed Burr and declared martial law in New Orleans, Claiborne gave him his full support. This was one of the more unglorious deeds of the governor's career, though it must be said that Wilkinson's duplicity was not known at the time.

Meanwhile, Claiborne, well aware of rebellion in Haiti—the slave uprising from 1794 to 1803 led by Toussaint L'Ouverture—had feared a slave revolt from the time he arrived in Louisiana, and establishing a militia was one of his highest priorities. Indeed, he found the French and Spanish slave regulations lax in comparison with those in the United States. The slave revolt that he had long feared came in 1811, when approximately five hundred, and perhaps many more, slaves in St. John the Baptist Parish rose in rebellion. Fortunately, most of the rebels were armed with agricultural tools rather than firearms, and the largest slave revolt in United States history was crushed quickly. Most of the slaves fled, but some sixty-six were killed, and sixteen captured leaders were promptly executed. Their heads were placed on poles along the Mississippi as an example to others. Louisiana had no other major revolt so long as slavery lasted.

Claiborne and President Jefferson had agreed from the beginning that the people of Louisiana needed experience in representative government before statehood could be considered. The early attitude of Louisianians was demonstrated by the fact that many men resented voting and jury duty as impositions. That a decennial census would be taken by the federal government in 1810 afforded a good excuse for delay, since the census would establish the population. This did not sit at all well with some people, Creoles and Americans, who wanted immediate statehood and who resented the separation of the territory of Orleans from the rest of the Louisiana Purchase. Daniel Clark was one of the governor's political opponents, and their bitterly expressed disagreements led in 1807 to a duel in which Claiborne was seriously wounded in the thigh.

After 1810, there was no reason to delay statehood; a constitution, modeled on the charter then in effect in Kentucky, was drawn up by a convention and approved by Congress. On April 30, 1812, Louisiana, including part of West Florida, became the eighteenth state of the United States. The state's constitution called for a two-step gubernatorial election—first an election by qualified voters, and then a choice by the legislature of one of the two candidates who had the highest number of votes in the popular contest. Claiborne, probably much to his surprise, ran well ahead of his nearest rival, Jacques Villeré, in the popular vote, and the legislature, despite a Creole majority, voted overwhelmingly to keep him in office. Claiborne read his inaugural address on July 31, 1812.

Louisiana had achieved statehood just in time for participation in the War of 1812, which had begun on June 18, and Claiborne called again and again for strengthening the militia. The militia in the countryside responded to his pleas, but in New Orleans the response was far less enthusiastic. Apparently more than a few of the Creole leaders believed that the United States would not or could not defend New Orleans against the British. Doubts as to American determination ended when Andrew Jackson arrived on the scene, but then the city leaders feared that the general might burn New Orleans rather than give it up. In the end, urged on by Claiborne and inspired by Jackson, the New Orleans militia fought as well as any other troops in the Battle of New Orleans.

Under Louisiana's Constitution of 1812, Claiborne was not eligible for a second successive term as governor. He was, however, elected by the legislature to the United States Senate. He did not return, however, to Washington, D.C., that raw capital city he had left to go to Mississippi fifteen years earlier, for he came down with a fatal liver ailment, only forty-two years of age.

Little is known of Claiborne's personal life; almost all his correspondence deals with official matters. His first wife died in 1804, and he married for a second time in 1806, taking Clarissa Duralde, of Louisiana, as his bride. She and a daughter she bore him died a few years later. His third and final wife was Suzette Bosque, whom he married in 1812. She bore him a daughter and a son and survived him. Claiborne apparently participated fully in the social activities of New Orleans, but few details are available concerning his social and family life.

Claiborne faced a task never faced before by an American official. Previous American territories had been inhabited by people who spoke the English language, who were Protestant, and who had experience in representative government. The people of Louisiana were predominantly French in culture; they were Catholic; and nothing in their history had given them experience in representative government. The French prefect, Pierre Clément de Laussat, remained in New Orleans for some time, and a former Spanish governor, the Marqués de Casa-Calvo, remained in the territory, even pretentiously visiting various places in the interior, until Claiborne ordered him to leave. Furthermore, the people of Louisiana had no love for the people of the United States. The Americans they had known had been pioneers from Kentucky and Tennessee, "Kaintucks" to the people of New Orleans, whose most notable characteristics had been their drinking, wenching, and brawling.

The people of Louisiana also quickly became disgusted with the judicial system that the Americans brought with them. In Spanish and French Louisiana, there had been no trial by jury, no right on the part of a defendant to confront the witnesses against him, and therefore no need for lawyers. What must have seemed a plague of lawyers descended on the territory after 1803, and since they knew no French, court proceedings already strange to the Louisianians were further confused by being carried on through interpreters. Congress did not make Claiborne's task any easier when, in 1808, it outlawed the foreign slave trade in Louisiana at a time when sugar and cotton culture was expanding rapidly.

Yet Claiborne accomplished his task. He sometimes seemed indecisive, and he sometimes demonstrated the all too human disposition to believe that anyone who disagreed with him had to have some malevolent purpose and be opposed to his government or to the United States, but Louisiana was gradually Americanized. A flood of refugees from the revolution in St. Domingue (modern Haiti) continued to arrive at New Orleans, bringing with them, in many cases, slaves who had absorbed revolutionary ideas. From France, too, came refugees from one change or another in the French government, until the "foreign French" came to be significant constituency in Louisiana politics. Claiborne realized that one of the greatest needs of the people of Louisiana was education, and under his leadership a preparatory school, the University of Orleans, was established, but very little was accomplished by this institution.

In many ways, by the time he had been elected governor in 1812, Claiborne had already made his most important contribution—that of supervising the gradual changes toward Americanization that had occurred while Louisiana was a territory. During his elected term, the War of 1812 consumed much of the talk and time of Louisianians. Claiborne cooperated closely with General Jackson and helped bring the state militia to duty. The governor had an important role in recruiting Jean Lafitte's Baratarians to serve with Jackson's forces (which included United States Army regulars, Louisiana militia, Tennessee volunteers, Kentucky militia, and Mississippi dragoons) fighting against the invading British army of veterans of the Napoleonic wars in Europe.

For a nonimperial nation, the United States has produced some outstanding proconsuls: Leonard Wood, in Cuba, William Howard Taft, in the Philippines, and Douglas McArthur, in Japan, come to mind. But of all these, Claiborne must rank as the most successful. He took over an indifferent, if not hostile, province, and in less than a decade brought it into the Union as one of eighteen equal states. He did not accomplish this through any brilliant stratagem or bold policy. Rather he met each crisis as it came, and simply did the best he could. In retrospect, his best seems to have been very good indeed. It is difficult to see how any other man could have accomplished so much so permanently in so short a time. He richly deserved the thanks of his countrymen, including the Louisianians he had led into his country.

JOE GRAY TAYLOR

BIBLIOGRAPHY

Abernethy, Thomas P. *The Burr Conspiracy.* New York, 1954.
Carter, Clarence E., ed. *The Territory of Mississippi, 1797–1817.* Washington, D.C., 1937. Vols. V and VI of Carter (ed.), *The Territorial Papers of the United States.* 25 vols.
———, ed. *The Territory of Orleans, 1803–1812.* Washington, 1940. Vol. IX of Carter (ed.), *The Territorial Papers.*
Dargo, George. *Jefferson's Louisiana: Politics and the Clash of Legal Traditions.* Cambridge, Mass., 1974.
DeConde, Alexander. *This Affair of Louisiana.* New York, 1976.
DeGrummond, Jane L. *The Baratarians and the Battle of New Orleans.* Baton Rouge, 1961.
Hatfield, Joseph T. *William Claiborne: Jeffersonian Centurion in the American Southwest.* Lafayette, La., 1976.
Reilly, Robin. *The British at the Gates: The New Orleans Campaign in the War of 1812.* New York, 1974.
Rowland, Dunbar, ed. *Official Letter Books of W. C. C. Claiborne, 1801–1816.* 6 vols. Jackson, Miss., 1917.
Winters, John D. "William C. C. Claiborne: Profile of a Democrat." *Louisiana History,* X (1969), 189–209.

Jacques Philippe Villeré

Governor, 1816–1820

VILLERÉ, Jacques Philippe (b. "German Coast," probably St. John the Baptist Parish, Louisiana colony, 1761; d. Conseil Plantation, St. Ber-

nard Parish, March 7, 1830), governor. Villeré's parents, Joseph Roy
Villeré and Marguerita de La Chaise,
ranked among the first families of
Louisiana. Yet, status in this for-
lorn outpost of the French Empire
merely meant that the Villerés had
a better chance of surviving the
austere frontier conditions than
most other colonials.

Such advantage, small as it was,
did not last long for the Villerés.
Among Villeré's earliest memories
were the excited discussions of his
father and his numerous cousins
concerning Louisiana's transfer to
Spain. With a child's enthusiasm,

Jacques Philippe Villeré. *Photograph
courtesy of State Library of Louisiana, from
Fortier's* History of Louisiana, *III, 206.*

he undoubtedly thought that the resistance to Spanish rule that his father, his cousin Nicholas de Lafrenière, and others planned would be a
great adventure. When, however, his father spoke of fleeing the colony
to avoid punishment, fear and uncertainty quenched his enthusiasm.
News of his father's arrest and death staggered the eight-year-old Villeré, and bitter hatred of the Spanish became the all-consuming passion
of the young man and his entire family. Indeed, when Villeré was thirteen years old, his mother arranged to have him spirited away from
Louisiana rather than see him join the militia and take an oath of allegiance to Spain.

In 1774, he went to the Caribbean and arrived in St. Domingue
(modern Haiti), where with the aid of his cousin, Captain de Villars, he
joined the French army. Villeré received the only formal education he
was ever to have in 1775–1776, when he was sent to France, where
he enrolled in a military academy. Second Lieutenant Villeré returned
to his duties in St. Domingue in 1776, and two years later, while on
leave, he came to Louisiana to visit his family. Spanish authorities were
understandably suspicious of this young man who had fled the colony
and now served France and whose father had behaved so reprehensibly.
Thus, when Villeré attempted to return to St. Domingue, Spanish officials refused to grant him permission to leave the Spanish colony. For

several years his status was uncertain, but circumstances soon made it imperative that he come to terms with Spanish rule.

Villeré's mother died in 1782, and in the same year he met and began to court Jeanne Henriette de Fazende. Spurred on by the necessity of gaining his inheritance and securing his marriage, Villeré finally took the oath of allegiance to Spain in 1784. In the same year, he married, and his wife brought considerable wealth and prestige to her husband, whose status in the community grew apace.

During the twenty days of French rule in 1803, Villeré sought and secured a place on the municipal council of New Orleans. Like most other colonials, he found the transfer to America disturbing. But his anxiety was soothed when he received appointment as justice of the peace for St. Bernard Parish. He served the new American administration as a major general in the territorial militia, as a member of the police jury for the county of Orleans, and as a delegate to the Louisiana constitutional convention of 1811–1812.

Throughout the territorial period, Louisiana politics had included factional bickering between Americans, foreign French, and Creoles. The large Gallic population chafed under American control and looked forward to ousting William C. C. Claiborne in the state's first gubernatorial race, in 1812, the year Louisiana achieved statehood. Villeré's years of service, his ownership of broad acres and many slaves, and his popularity with the Gallic population made him a strong candidate. But division in the Gallic forces between Villeré and Jean d'Estrehan made Claiborne's victory in 1812 easier than it might otherwise have been.

Villeré had little time to lament his defeat. The outbreak of war in 1812 between the United States and Great Britain found him busily preparing Louisiana's defenses. As commander of the First Division of the Louisiana Militia, he was assigned to the area near Lake Borgne and along the narrow area of Bayou Dupre. While he was thus engaged, Villeré's plantation, Conseil, was overrun by British forces. Property destruction, the discomfort of his family, and the loss of fifty-two slaves to the British must have tempered his elation with the great American victory by Andrew Jackson at Chalmette on January 8, 1815.

Peace returned Villeré to the thick of political life, and in 1816 he made his second bid for the governorship. Once again the election revolved about personality and nationality—American against Creole. In a very close contest, Villeré emerged victorious over Joshua Lewis on July 1, 1816, and took office on December 17.

Circumstances were kind to Louisiana's first native-born governor. The population increased, and unheard-of prosperity came to the state during his tenure of office. Cotton, sugar, and numerous other crops, as well as trade goods and settlers, floated downriver from the entire Mississippi-Ohio Valley complex to turn New Orleans into a major commercial center. Befitting a new state, the Louisiana legislature passed many new laws, but Villeré took little direct role in legislative affairs. He did seek, however, to act as a mediator between recent settlers—the Anglo-Americans—and Louisiana's Creoles. He spent much of his term trying to accommodate the two factions, and the efforts of Villeré's administration held the promise of accord in the future.

Unfortunately, this promise was not to be realized once Villeré left office. In the 1820s, factional strife erupted again, and the issue of ethnicity provided a focal point for the 1824 gubernatorial election. Villeré's Creole faction called him from retirement in spite of his advanced years and presented him as a candidate. Bernard Marigny, a prominent leader of the Gallic forces, refused to support Villeré and sought the governorship himself. The Creoles were thrown into disarray as a consequence of this divison. Indeed, Marigny spent his time denouncing Villeré's submission to the Americans and insisting that a continuation of Villeré's kindness and condescension would lead to "slavery." Factionalism ensured the election of the American candidate, Henry S. Johnson.

The last years of Villeré's life were devoted to his estate, his wife, their eight children, and their numerous grandchildren. Jeanne Villeré died in 1826. Some months later Villeré was again called from retirement and selected as presidential elector for John Quincy Adams. Louisianians expressed intense interest in the presidential election of 1828, and the fledgling beginnings of political organizations took shape in the state.

By 1828, Villeré was seriously ill. For the most part he was confined to Conseil for the next two years, and he died there.

⚘

Louisiana's first native-born governor has been neglected by historians, perhaps because he was not very articulate and his tenure as governor was unspectacular. He did not possess that colorful political flair which endears politicians to Louisianians. Villeré witnessed the transfers of Louisiana between Spain, France, and the United States, and understood from personal experience the necessity of accommodating the inevitable. Thus, from the beginning of American administration, Villeré offered his service and allegiance to the new government. From 1803 until his election as governor in 1816, he saw the great tide of American immigration into Louisiana, and he realized that factionalism based upon ethnic origin meant political doom for the Creole population.

During Villeré's administration, the legislature passed many bills, including a judicial law that reconstructed the whole framework of local justice. But in the main, Villeré was a follower rather than a leader. Unlike the governors in other states, the governor of Louisiana could control enormous power. Yet Villeré did not exercise that power to secure political victories. His experience was rooted in the French-Spanish tradition—a tradition devoid of political democracy and political parties. Villeré was not a politician, nor did he believe that he should be. Unlike several other Louisiana governors, he viewed the role of the chief executive as a ceremonial one, and his major concern was to conciliate and mediate, not to initiate or lead.

The role of mediator ideally suited Villeré's temperament. Possessed of common sense and good will, the governor enjoyed enormous popularity with both recently arrived Americans and established Creoles. Through his efforts, the bitter hostility of ethnic factionalism temporarily subsided. To the patronage posts in his giving, Villeré appointed 155 Americans, 50 foreign French, and 34 Creoles. Villeré focused his attention upon healing the breach between the Americans and Gallic populations, but in the final analysis, the unassuming and often inarticulate governor brought only a brief respite to the racial and personal antagonisms that so often characterized Louisiana politics.

CAROLYN E. DeLATTE

BIBLIOGRAPHY

Arthur, Stanley, and George C. H. de Kernion. *Old Families of Louisiana*. Baton Rouge, 1971.

Chambers, Henry E., *A History of Louisiana Wilderness—Colony—Province—Territory—State—People*. 3 vols. New York, 1925.

Hatfield, Joseph T. *William Claiborne: Jeffersonian Centurion in the American Southwest*. Lafayette, La., 1976.

Tregle, Joseph G., Jr. "Louisiana in the Age of Jackson." Ph.D. dissertation, University of Pennsylvania, 1954.

Villeré, Sidney Louis. *Jacques Philippe Villeré: First Native-Born Governor of Louisiana, 1816–1820*. New Orleans, 1981.

Thomas Bolling Robertson

Governor, 1820–1824

ROBERTSON, Thomas Bolling (b. Prince George County, Virginia, 1773; d. White Sulphur Springs, Virginia, October 5, 1828), secretary of the territory of Orleans, congressman, governor, and federal judge. It was the questionable distinction of Robertson to be governor of Louisiana during what were probably the most fiercely divisive years of ethnic conflict in the state's history. Born of impressive family connections, he was the son of William Robertson, a Petersburg merchant who served as a member and secretary of the Council of Virginia for many years, and Elizabeth

THOMAS BOLLING ROBERTSON. *Photograph courtesy of Special Collections, Hill Memorial Library, Louisiana State University, from O. B. Steele Photograph Collection.*

Bolling, who claimed direct descent from Pocahontas. Robertson took frequent and expansive delight in this ancestry, as he did in the accomplishments of his brothers. John became attorney general and chancellor of Virginia, and Wyndham became governor of their native state in 1836. In the mid-1820s, Robertson married Lelia Skipwith, of Baton Rouge, the daughter of Fulwar Skipwith, a former American consul in Paris more notable as the governor of the short-lived West Florida Republic. Robertson and his wife had no children.

After graduation from William and Mary College in 1797, Robertson practiced law in Virginia until his appointment by President Thomas Jefferson on August 12, 1807, as secretary of the territory of Orleans. While in that position, he also served as one of three federal land commissioners for eastern Orleans and, briefly, as attorney general of the territory (March 8–September 3, 1808). His tenure was marked by continuous confrontation with the territorial governor, William C. C. Claiborne, who counted Robertson among a coterie of enemies plotting his political destruction. Much like Claiborne in his first years in Orleans, Robertson found his new locale barbarous and unenlightened. "For all purposes of Government," he wrote James Madison in 1809, "there is here a more obvious unfitness, a more deplorable destitution of talents than in any other part of our Country."[1]

By 1812, the attractive opportunities of statehood were too seductive to resist, whatever Robertson's private misgivings as to the viability of the republican process among his new neighbors. Obviously unaware of his jaundiced view of them, Louisiana voters sent Robertson to Washington in 1812 as the first, and for a time the only, Louisiana member of the House of Representatives. His main service there was in vigorously defending the sugar tariff that protected Louisiana's still infant industry.

The enticement of more challenging and remunerative engagement back home in Louisiana persuaded Robertson to decline reelection to Congress in 1818, largely to prepare for the 1820 campaign for the governor's chair. The incumbent, Jacques Philippe Villeré, had committed his administration to peace between the Gallic and American political factions in the state, hoping to establish a rotation of the governorship from one to the other. It was this situation which Robertson chose to exploit. His principal rivals were a fellow American, Abner L. Duncan, and a "foreign Frenchman," Pierre Derbigny. Duncan's failing health reduced his political attractiveness; Derbigny was heavily burdened by popular antagonism to the immigrant French even among the Gallic Creoles, and particularly by the wide acceptance of the Villeré position that this was now the American turn. Robertson won a plurality of the popular votes cast, then swept to unanimous selection by the legislature, which under the Constitution of 1812 chose the governor from the two candidates with the largest vote in the public poll. All these subleties of the Louisiana political scene seem completely to have escaped Robertson's notice. Accepting his new position as if it were the natural consequence of his own virtue, an ascendancy for which he owed no thanks and in which he was obliged to render little accounting, he proceeded in the next four years to give substance to the judgment of an old foe, Alexander Porter, that "he does not believe that other men are made *with* him, but *for* him."[2]

1. Thomas B. Robertson to James Madison, May 24, [1809], in Clarence Carter (ed.), *The Territory of Orleans, 1803–1812* (Washington, D.C., 1940), 841, Vol. IX of Carter (ed.), *The Territorial Papers of the United States*, 25 vols.

2. Alexander Porter to Josiah Stoddard Johnston, April 4, 1826, in Josiah Stoddard Johnston Papers, Historical Society of Pennsylvania, Philadelphia.

There was no immediate break between Robertson and the Gallic community. But it was soon clear that he was intent on aggrandizing Anglo-American political strength at the expense of the French. This perceived betrayal of the amicable evenhandedness preached and practiced by Villeré convinced many of the Gallic leaders that honorable compromise with the Americans was impossible, Bernard Marigny warning, "Virginia will exhaust itself before a Louisianian is made governor in his country."[3]

The steadily roiling conflict boiled over in January, 1823, when the governor's hand was seen in an attempt to push through the legislature a measure moving the state capital to Baton Rouge, a long-held dream of the Anglo-American-dominated Florida region in which Robertson had his closest connections. The Gallic forces led by Louis Moreau Lislet responded with an attempt to expel Florida members from the Louisiana Senate, arguing that Congress' addition of their district to the old territory of Orleans was unconstitutional. Armed conflict was avoided only by joint withdrawal from political positions which had blown up a tempest frightening to both factions.

But the Florida bill had unchained passions which were not to be brought under control during the remainder of Robertson's term. His veto of a usury bill (1823) in the name of free enterprise and the inviolability of contracts brought down on his head perhaps the most concentrated criticism of his governorship, exposing him to violent attack as the defender of "shavers" and usurers, most of whom, the Gallic press insisted, were to be found among his aristocratic Anglo-American favorites.

For their part, the Anglo-American forces attempted to justify their moves against Gallic dominance by maintaining that Louisiana was in the clutch of a foreign faction intent on delivering the state to the royalist mercies of Louis XVIII and the Concert of Europe. The Americans refused to obey orders of unnaturalized officers in the state militia, precipitating a quarrel among the military companies in New Orleans in 1823–1825, which produced violent riots in the city and came perilously close to open civil war. Robertson essentially turned his back on the turmoil, which continued to disrupt the community until put to rest in 1825 by the political skill of Henry S. Johnson.

3. *Mémoire de Bernard Marigny, habitant de la Louisiane, addressé à ses concitoyens* (Paris, 1822), 36.

Despite Robertson's own general ineptness, his administration stimulated the state's infant internal-improvements program, opening the Pearl and Red rivers to navigation and building Louisiana's portion of the national road from Madisonville to Nashville. Economic constriction was loosened with the creation of the Bank of Louisiana in 1824, and the College of Orleans and the state's Charity Hospital enjoyed increased funding of five thousand dollars annually from the licensing of six gambling houses in New Orleans. Largely in response to Robertson's insistence, moreover, plans were begun for a new state penitentiary and the federal government pledged greater attention to the defense of the highly vulnerable borders of the state.

But none of this brought popularity to the beleaguered governor, whose increasingly violent temper and haughty disdain for his associates finally eroded his acceptability even in his home district of the Florida Parishes. Beset by monetary problems as well, he resigned the governorship in November, 1824, to assume the federal district judgeship vacated by the death of John Dick.

Robertson's judicial career was distinctly unimpressive, for he was notoriously ill read in the law—a deficiency he brushed aside with the assurance that he possessed a more important judicial qualification, political genius. What remained of his reputation was shattered when, in 1826, during the impeachment trial of a Florida Parishes judge for not forwarding election returns to the governor, Robertson reported to the legislature that "thanks to God and His prophets," he had finally found the missing returns in the bed of his greyhound bitch.[4]

He fought vigorously against being passed over for appointment to a federal circuit judgeship in 1826, a humiliation prevented by Congressional refusal to create the new position. Failing health and a realistic appraisal of his political fortunes led him to reject offers of support for the governorship in 1828.

In national politics, Robertson was a consistent champion of John Quincy Adams and Henry Clay. He was particularly sympathetic to Clay's concerns in promoting Latin American independence and highly critical of the Adams-Onis Treaty, which he considered to have surrendered legitimate United States claims to Texas.

Robertson made his home at Montesano Bluffs, five miles above

---

4. Alexander Porter to Josiah Stoddard Johnston, April 14, 1826, in Johnston Papers.

Baton Rouge, but he died at White Sulphur Springs, Virginia, where he is buried.

⤞

The "time of troubles" during the Robertson years tends to overshadow the more admirable features of Robertson's administration. If he were judged simply by the content of his messages to the legislature, he might well be seen today as a visionary liberal reformer, for he continually called for abolition of imprisonment for debt, an improved penal system, advancement of public education, greater accessibility of judicial services, restriction of the governor's vast appointive powers, expansion of state welfare agencies such as asylums and hospitals, and speedier transfer of land ownership from federal to state and private hands. But these rhetorical commitments foundered on Robertson's vitiating weakness—unreasonable championing of the Anglo-American faction in state affairs, closed-mindedness as to the ethnic and cultural traditions of the area in which he had chosen to relocate, and determination to advance his second-rate talents through a network of political favoritism linked to Virginia connections. Vain, supercilious, and essentially stupid, he looked upon his place in Louisiana as akin to that of a Roman proconsul ruling over barbarians of the empire. By inflaming ethnic passion in the state, he doomed his administration to ineffectiveness and nearly brought Louisianians to violence.

Perhaps the most significant aspect of Robertson's term, however, lies in its demonstration of how deeply the mass of native Louisianians were committed to their union with the United States. Despite hoary legends of New Orleanians weeping as the American flag was raised over the city in 1803, there is no evidence of any tendency in the annexed population, then or later, to question the wisdom and desirability of partnership in the Republic. In all the extensive testimony of the Aaron Burr trial, for example, there is not one whisper of complicity on the part of a native Louisianian. Even in the most bitter ethnic quarrels engendered by Robertson's policies, with fiery Gallic reproaches against *les Américains*, one finds no attack upon the inviolability of the Purchase treaty.

Robertson was in many respects the personification of the Anglo-American presence in Louisiana in the early years of its statehood. Migrating there in territorial days, he brought with him the whole package of cultural and political conceits which were to prove so hateful and provocative to Creole and French antagonists like Marigny and Moreau Lislet. His governorship was consequently a major stimulus to the emergence of Creole champions like André Bienvenu Roman and Alexandre Mouton and largely fixed the dimensions of Louisiana politics until these yielded to the growing dominance of national political parties in the mid-1840s.

JOSEPH G. TREGLE, JR.

BIBLIOGRAPHY

Patton, James S. *The Family of William and Elizabeth Bolling Robertson.* Gay Mount, Va., 1975.

Robertson, Wyndam. *Pocahontas and Her Descendants.* Richmond, 1887.

There is no biography of Robertson nor any specific study of his political career. The Virginia Historical Society holds a fragmentary early diary detailing his journey to Louisiana, and he figures prominently in the Josiah Stoddard Johnston Papers, at the Historical Society of Pennsylvania, in Philadelphia.

Henry S. Thibodaux

Governor, 1824

THIBODAUX, Henry Schuyler (b. Albany, New York, 1769; d. Bayou Terrebone, Louisiana, October 24, 1827), state legislator and governor. The many paradoxes of antebellum Louisiana society are epitomized in the fact that the governor whose surname is most redolent of traditional Gallic, Cajun essence was in actuality an immigrant from New York. Born to Alexis Thibodaux, a French Canadian, and Anne Blanchard, Thibodaux lost his parents early in life but found warm refuge in the family of General Philip Schuyler, scion of one of the great landed aristocratic clans of New York, revolutionary protagonist, and father-in-law of Alexander Hamilton. This formidable association showered substantial opportunities on Thibodaux, including formal education in Scotland, but the young man was not temperamentally attracted to a life of patronage or family advancement, preferring instead to launch an independent career in Louisiana shortly after 1790. His marriage to Felicité Bonvillain, of Acadia, Louisiana (in modern St. James Parish) was blessed with three children. A second marriage, to Bridgette Belanger, on May 20, 1800, produced five children, one of whom, Bannon Goforth, became a Whig congressman from Louisiana in the 1840s.

Shortly after his first marriage, Thibodaux moved from Acadia to the Bayou Lafourche district. Louisiana was then a Spanish colony. The Lafourche district remained the fundamental base of his growing influence in what became the parishes of Terrebonne, Assumption, and Lafourche after the Purchase of 1803.

Despite the aristocratic and affluent character of his New York upbringing, Thibodaux was quintessentially the humble, unpretentious, unsophisticated southwest Louisianian of the early 1800s. Completely sloughing off his American background to take on the role of *père* to the sprawling Gallic community in Lafourche, he entered political service as a member of the legislature of the territory of Orleans in 1805, moved on to become justice of the peace for Lafourche County after 1808, and helped draft the first Louisiana state constitution in 1811–1812. By that time, he had become the undisputed arbiter of political power along Bayou Lafourche, which he represented in the state senate from 1812 until November, 1824, when as president of that body, he succeeded to the governorship upon the resignation of Thomas Bolling Robertson. At that time, Henry Johnson had already been elected to a gubernatorial term beginning in December, 1824. Thibodaux' one-month tenure gave him little chance to establish any kind of executive record, but it steered him inexorably to candidacy for a full term in the succeeding election, in 1828. His chances for success were mixed, at best. Though he enjoyed almost total support from the Lafourche district, and a generous following among Anglo-Americans elsewhere who would have balked at backing a truly French candidate, Thibodaux was burdened by the very characteristics which made him so attractive to the plain folk who accepted him as their natural spokesman. His simple contentment with life as a humble shoemaker verged on the bizarre in a community dominated by men on the make in a world of planters, bankers, lawyers, and merchant princes, while his blithe ignorance of belles lettres, classical languages, and the arts seemed beneath what many deemed the necessary dignity of the governorship.

All these considerations proved academic in the end, for he died in the midst of the campaign, at Bayou Terrebonne on October 24, 1827, of what his associates identified as an abscessed liver. He is buried in St. Bridget's Church, Schriever, Louisiana.

❧

Although there is little in his career that was of major importance, Thibodaux stands as a prime exemplar of the paternalistic politics which played so large a part in the early history of Louisiana and helped to impart so much of what is still distinctive to the state's public personality.

JOSEPH G. TREGLE, JR.

BIBLIOGRAPHY

There are no Thibodaux manuscripts extant, but Thibodaux is frequently referred to in the Josiah Stoddard Johnston Papers, at the Historical Society of Pennsylvania, in Philadelphia, and in the William S. Hamilton Papers, at the Troy H. Middleton Library, of Louisiana State University, in Baton Rouge. See also Marguerite Watkins, "History of Terrebonne Parish to 1861" (M.A. thesis, Louisiana State University, 1939). Thibodaux' succession, dated January 5, 1828, is filed in the office of the clerk of court, Lafourche Parish, Louisiana.

Henry S. Johnson

Governor, 1824–1828

JOHNSON, Henry S. (b. Virginia, September 14, 1783; d. Pointe Coupee Parish, Louisiana, September 4, 1864), state judge, United States senator, governor, and congressman. For many antebellum Louisianians, officeholding was a predominant preoccupation. For Johnson, officeholding was an absolute obsession: from 1809 until 1850, he was either in public service or an office seeker—in the eyes of his contemporaries the very model of the professional politician.

Born in Virginia on September 14, 1783, Johnson came to Louisiana in 1809 as clerk of the second

HENRY S. JOHNSON. *Photograph courtesy of State Library of Louisiana, from Fortier's History of Louisiana, III, 206.*

superior court of the territory of Orleans. By 1811, he was a judge in St. Mary Parish and a delegate from Attakapas to the first Louisiana constitutional convention. Losing his bid to become the state's original federal representative, in 1812, to Thomas Bolling Robertson, Johnson busied himself in a prosperous legal practice in Donaldsonville until chosen in 1818 to fill the United States Senate seat vacated by the death of William C. C. Claiborne.

With typical assiduity, Johnson had already mastered the French language, ingratiated himself with the Creole and "foreign French" populations, and identified with the issues most important to his constituency. Nothing loomed larger in their concern than the validation of the murky land claims they held from the Spanish and French, and the opening of the federal domain to private settlement. These were the areas in which Johnson worked most diligently and effectively while in Washington. His unflagging attention to duty easily won him reelection in 1823, though there were reports that he further eased his continuation by promising ambitious colleagues that he would not seek the governorship in 1824.

If he made the pledge, he soon broke it. The furious ethnic quarrel in the state occasioned by Governor Robertson's anti-Gallic policies removed all hopes for a frictionless rotation of the governor's office between the French and American factions. Old Jacques Philippe Villeré was being pushed forward again, as a kind of reproach to the Anglo-Americans for having rejected his earlier pleas of harmony. Just returned from France, Bernard Marigny heaped curses upon all Creole moderates such as Villeré, whose softness toward the Anglo-Americans he saw as suicidal; at the same time, he excoriated the "foreign French" for their scornful exploitation of the native Gallic community. Only he, Marigny swore, was capable of crushing *all* outlanders and restoring Louisiana to its true and proper masters, the Gallic Creoles. In the Florida Parishes, Thomas Butler and Philemon Thomas appeared to challenge Johnson's claims to the Anglo-American vote, but Butler was tainted by suspicions of connections with the infamous Aaron Burr, and Thomas by advanced age and a reputation as a perennial and ineffective candidate.

United in their fury against Anglo-American domination, Creoles and "foreign French" alike rebuked Johnson for abandoning his old Gallic attachments. But the anger centered on him was as nothing compared with the violence of the Villeré and Marigny camps in attacking each other for the right to represent the Gallic cause. The irreparable breach in French ranks gave Johnson an easy plurality in the popular vote in 1824, a victory confirmed by his formal election by the legislature, despite the efforts of some irreconcilables to save Gallic honor by having the legislative vote thrown to the second-place Villeré because of American betrayal of the rotation principle.

However much his ascendancy might be attributed to the stupidity of his opponents, Johnson soon demonstrated his vaunted political skills, and his administration stands as one of the most productive of the antebellum period. Exploiting the mythic popularity of the Marquis de Lafayette in both ethnic populations, he used the hero's visit to Louisiana in 1825 to damp the almost hysterical factional wars which had blighted the Robertson years. The old controversy over the location of the state capital was brought to a compromise by providing for a shift of the seat of government to Donaldsonville in 1829, thus guaranteeing its removal from the supposed iniquitous influence of New Orleans while retaining it within traditionally Gallic precincts. Economic well-being was greatly stimulated by creation of the Louisiana State Bank in 1824 and the Consolidated Association of Planters of Louisiana in 1827, the latter an ingenious and novel property bank designed to assist planters by lending on mortgage security, though it quite quickly moved into more traditional commercial discounting. These agencies of expanded capital aided Johnson's campaign for extensive internal improvements— mainly roads and canals—backed by an Internal Improvement Board, created in 1825. Acreage under agrarian cultivation multiplied rapidly, especially in those areas suited to cane, with the result that by 1828 sugar had become the crop of greatest monetary value in Louisiana.

Dissatisfaction with the system of letting the state legislature choose presidential electors, which had proved embarrassing in the election of 1824, led to adoption of the popular ballot for the state's five members of the electoral college in time for the next canvass, in 1828. The state, not unfittingly, played host to a tumultuous campaign visit by Andrew Jackson in January of the election year.

By 1825, the never-prosperous College of Orleans was still reeling from the fatal leadership of the regicide Joseph Lakanal, so much the victim of old ethnic hatreds that the legislature adopted Johnson's proposal terminating state support, which was shifted to the College of Louisiana, in Jackson. The Gallic community had its victory in the final adoption of the great 1825 Louisiana Civil Code drafted by Edward Livingston, Louis Moreau Lislet, and Pierre Derbigny.

It was strong commitment to balance and moderation which most characterized Johnson's administration. That did little, however, to endear the governor to his contemporaries, projecting him as cold and cal-culating rather than warm and sympathetic. "He acts," one of his asso-ciates remarked, "on the principle of Sir Peter Pearle in the play, who says, this is 'at best a very wicked world, and the fewer people we praise in it the better.'"[1]

Johnson's genius for political intrigue had full play in the various campaigns of 1828, during which he successfully guided Edward D. White to a congressional victory over Livingston and masterminded enough of a shuffling of election judges in the gubernatorial and state legislative contests in New Orleans to clinch a landslide victory for those favorable to his presidential candidate, John Quincy Adams. Among the winners he helped in 1828 was his successor, Derbigny. Johnson was not so fortunate in promoting his own preferment. Facing loss of office in 1829, he moved to contest for the United States Senate seat held by the French Creole Dominique Bouligny, thus once again infuriating the Gallic forces by what they saw as his insatiable thirst for position. The rivals agreed to unite behind whichever of them won the higher vote on the legislative first ballot, which proved to be Bouligny. When Johnson coolly refused to honor his pledge and remained in the race, irate supporters of Bouligny joined rival Jacksonians to make Livingston the new United States senator, in what Henry Adams Bul-lard called the "most singular election ever known in the state."[2]

In 1834, however, Johnson succeeded his old protégé White in the House of Representatives when White assumed the governorship. Johnson's hopes for the Whig gubernatorial nomination in 1838 evapo-rated before the strength of the native son André Bienvenu Roman, and White resumed his old seat in Congress. But in 1842, Johnson was back in the field as the Whig candidate for governor against the Jacksonian Creole Alexandre Mouton. Rising Jacksonian numbers in the great ur-ban center of New Orleans and in the opening hill parishes of northern Louisiana crippled his chances, as did what he himself called the "deter-mining issue" of the Creole question. Mouton's victory by 9,669 to 8,104 votes sent Johnson into brief eclipse, but Alexander Porter's death in 1844 opened the way to a new stint in the United States Senate, where he served until 1849, in a term marked by his vigorous support of Texas annexation. The capture of his Senate seat by a Jacksonian was

1. Alexander Porter to Josiah Stoddard Johnston, January 12, 1827, in Josiah Stoddard Johnston Papers, Historical Society of Pennsylvania, Philadelphia.
2. Henry Adams Bullard to Josiah Stoddard Johnston, January 13, 1829, in Johnston Papers.

followed in 1850 by the even more humiliating loss to a fellow Whig, Bullard, in a race for the House of Representatives.

Retiring to Point Coupee Parish, Johnson continued the practice of law until his death. Long before, in 1829, he had married Elizabeth Key, of Maryland. They had no children. He is buried on his plantation at the juncture of Bayous Grosse Tete and Maringouin.

&

The successive administrations of Robertson and Johnson provide particularly revealing insight into the singular problems which pervaded the early political life of Louisiana in the years following the Purchase. The overriding needs of the community—land-title security, expansion of internal improvements, broadening of credit accessibility, nourishment of the two great staples of cotton and sugar—were highlighted in their terms, and it was the special strength of Johnson to articulate these needs so well and respond to them so effectively. Constitution making, defense of the state's peculiar protectionist tariff posture in an otherwise free-trade South, championship of the vigorous American territorial impulse—all reflected Johnson's skillful exploitation of the interests of his adopted community.

But like Robertson before him, Johnson was widely perceived in Louisiana as a symbol of supposed Creole incapacity to govern and Anglo-American determination to monopolize the political life of the state. The simple fact was that the Gallic Creoles had not been able in the first decades after the Purchase to bring forward native-born leaders with sufficient political skills to challenge the more experienced and sophisticated Anglo-Americans. It could hardly have been otherwise, given the pervasive isolation and illiteracy which were the heritage of colonial submission to France and Spain. If there were no Gallic natives expert in political leadership, neither were there any in medicine, the law, journalism, or the other learned professions. Talent abounded among the "foreign French" from the Continent and St. Domingue (modern Haiti), but they were relatively few and always suspect as interlopers with alien loyalties. These fundamental weaknesses were compounded by factionalism in the Gallic ranks, so that Anglo-Americans like Robertson and Johnson rose to power almost as a matter of default.

Robertson's insensitivity and Johnson's unappeased hunger for office were seen by the Gallic community as typical American vices. In fact, they were conceits matched by equally exclusionary views among those who resented them, but even so, they were to carry a heavy price. In

1828, Gallic frustration and anger reached heights against Anglo-American arrogance sufficient to overcome Creole antiforeigner sentiment and take Derbigny, one of the "foreign French," to the governorship.

Unlike Robertson before him, Johnson brought talent and effectiveness to his leadership of the state, and his meticulous attention to the humdrum workings of the political process was of immeasurable value to Louisiana. Ambitious, manipulative, office-hungry he most certainly was, but he delivered conscientious and productive service to his adopted community—and in no capacity more notably than as governor. His inability ever to rewin that position speaks volumes about the ethnic dimension of Louisiana politics in the 1830s and 1840s.

JOSEPH G. TREGLE, JR.

BIBLIOGRAPHY

Tregle, Joseph G., Jr. "Louisiana in the Age of Jackson." Ph.D. dissertation, University of Pennsylvania, 1954.

There are no Henry Johnson papers extant, but individual letters by and about him may be found in the Josiah Stoddard Johnston Papers, at the Historical Society of Pennsylvania, in Philadelphia; in the Henry Clay Papers, at the Library of Congress; and in the William Johnson Papers, at the Mississippi Department of Archives and History, in Jackson, Miss.

Pierre Auguste Bourguignon Derbigny
Arnaud Julie Beauvais
Jacques Dupré

Governors, 1828–1831

Pierre Auguste Bourguignon Derbigny was born into a noble family at Laon, near Lille, in France, on June 30, 1769, the eldest child of Augustin d'Herbigny and Louise Angelique Blondela. He left France in 1791 with the family of Pierre Charles deHault de Lassus de Luzières and traveled to St. Domingue (modern Haiti) and then Pittsburgh. There and at other posts in the Illinois country, he served as an English-language interpreter for the Spanish authorities for several years. He married Félicité Odile deHault de Lassus at Pittsburgh on June 29, 1791. They had five daughters and two sons. One son, Charles Zenon Derbigny, was an active Whig in the 1840s and a leader of the American (Know-Nothing) party during the 1850s in Louisiana. They arrived in New Orleans in 1797.

Holding a variety of appointive posts during the territorial period, Derbigny became a part of Louisiana's political establishment. He was secretary to the municipality of New Orleans in 1803, interpreter for the territory beginning in 1803, and clerk of the court of common pleas and secretary of the legislative council of the territory by 1804. By 1807, he was an attorney employed by the city of New Orleans in a lawsuit brought against the city by Edward Livingston for possession of the waterfront area known as the Batture. In 1804 and 1805, as a leader of the protest against the act

PIERRE AUGUSTE BOURGUIGNON DER-
BIGNY. *Photograph courtesy of State Li-
brary of Louisiana, from Fortier's* History of
Louisiana, *III, 206.*

of Congress of 1804, he was one of three selected to carry a memorial to Congress urging full self-government for Louisiana and the reopening of the slave trade. Partially as a result of the memorialists' lobbying, Congress in 1805 provided for an elected lower house in the territorial legislature. Upon returning to Louisiana, Derbigny was among those who opposed the adoption of British common law in Louisiana. He also led the movement that established the College of Orleans, the first institution of higher learning in what became the state.

After Louisiana achieved statehood in 1812, Derbigny served briefly as secretary of the senate and then, in 1814, was appointed a justice of the supreme court of Louisiana. During the War of 1812, he served in Captain Chauveneau's Company of Cavalry in the Louisiana Militia at the Battle of New Orleans (January 8, 1815). In 1819, Derbigny, Livingston, and Louis Moreau Listlet began work on what was to become the 1825 Civil Code of Louisiana. In 1820, Derbigny belonged to a group that was issued the first license to operate a steam ferry at New Orleans. By 1820, he was generally perceived as a moderate working to ease tensions between the French and Anglo-American groups in New Orleans, and he resigned from the supreme court to make a bid for the governorship, which was unsuccessful. He served as secretary of state from 1820 to 1828, when he again ran for governor, this time as a supporter of John Quincy Adams and Henry Clay, both of whom were

National Republicans in the emerging party divisions. In 1828, he won his first elective post: the governorship of the state of Louisiana. The election, held on July 7, 1828, pitted Derbigny against three contenders. The Louisiana State Assembly confirmed Derbigny's election.

In his inaugural address, on December 15, 1828, he lamented the discord and disorder evident in the recent presidential election and encouraged economy in government. Furthermore, he recommended the appointment of an unpaid inspector of schools to report annually to the legislature, and he expressed support for state assistance for internal improvements. He also asked that the legislature adopt safety regulations for steamboats operating in the state. The legislature moved in the area of internal improvements, incorporating the New Orleans Gas Light company and two companies to improve the navigation of the bayous, and taking over operation of the Orleans Navigation Company. The state assembly also passed a major bill setting criteria for the construction and repair of levees and levee roads and authorizing a program of regular levee inspections. And responding to fears that rebellious slaves from other states were being sold in Louisiana, the legislature established regulations for the introduction of slaves into the state.

After only ten months as governor, Derbigny was thrown from his carriage while riding in Gretna. He died a few days later, on October 6, 1829. He is buried at St. Louis Roman Catholic Church Cemetery, in New Orleans.

Arnaud Julie Beauvais was born in Point Coupee Parish on September 6, 1783, the youngest son of eight children of Pierre Charles St. James Beauvais and Marie Françoise Richer. In 1806, at the age of twenty-two, he bought the family plantation, consisting of eleven arpents of frontage on the Mississippi and twenty-one slaves, from his mother. He married Louise Delphine Labatut, of New Orleans, on January 24, 1811. They had no children.

In 1810, William C. C. Claiborne named Beauvais justice of the peace for Point Coupee Parish. In 1814, Beauvais was elected to the Louisiana House of Representatives; voters returned him to the house in 1816 and 1820. He served on the election committee, the committee on propositions and grievances, and a select committee on the militia before being elected speaker of the house in 1820. In 1822, he was elected to the Louisiana Senate, holding his seat continuously throughout the 1820s. On January 1, 1827, fellow senators elected him president of the senate, and he continued in that capacity until the death of Pierre Derbigny, on October 6, 1829. Under the Constitution of 1812, the president of the senate assumed the duties of governor whenever the governor was unable to perform them. Beauvais served as acting governor from October 6, 1829, until January 14, 1830, during the period that the legislature was out of session and the seat of government was being moved from New Orleans to Donaldsonville. When the legislature convened in early January, he reported that administrative duties had kept him very busy and that the process of moving to Donaldsonville prevented him from being able to report on the finances of the state. But he recommended legislation restricting the importation of adult slaves, he renewed the efforts to get the federal government to move rapidly in the sale of public lands, and he urged that Louisiana's representatives in Congress oppose any reduction in the sugar tariff. Focusing instead on the question of the succession, the state senate maintained that each newly elected President of the senate should assume the duties of the still-vacant office of governor. The house resisted until a compromise was reached that provided that though each newly elected president of the senate would assume the duties of governor, an election would be held in July to elect a new governor for a four-year term. When that resolution passed, the senate elected Jacques Dupré as its president, and he assumed the duties of governor on January 14, 1830, while continuing to serve as president of the senate.

Beauvais had considerable support for becoming president pro tempore of the senate, but lost on the fourth ballot. He remained very active during the session, serving on the committee on the audit and introducing legislation on public education, roads and levees, and the licensing of gambling establishments. He ran for governor in the July election but finished third. Both Beauvais and André Bienvenu Roman, who won the election, were supporters of Henry Clay in national politics. Beauvais returned to the senate in late January, 1833, and served until the following year, filling out the unexpired term of a senator who had resigned. He was adversely affected by the depression of 1837; owing to insolvency, all his property—consisting of landholdings in Point Coupee and West Feliciana parishes and thirty-nine slaves—was sold at public auction in 1839. Beauvais and his wife moved to Orleans Parish in 1840. He died on November 18, 1843, at the age of sixty.

Jacques Dupré was born in New Orleans on February 12, 1773, the eldest son of Laurent Dupré dit Terrebone and Marie Josephe Fontenot, residents of St. Landry Parish. Dupré's father died when he was ten, and his mother later married "Grand Louis" Fontenot, owner of more than twenty thousand head of cattle and a plantation on the road about halfway between Opelousas and Washington. In 1791, Dupré and his two brothers each received from the king of Spain land grants of forty arpents of frontage on the Bayou Boeuf. Dupré married Theotiste Roy, of Point Coupee, at Opelousas on May 19, 1792, and they had seven children. By 1810, Dupré had acquired twelve slaves. Buying land in the Plaisance area, northwest of Opelousas, the family raised large herds of cattle. By the 1830s, Dupré was recognized as one of Louisiana's major cattlemen.

Dupré served as major in the 16th Regiment of the Louisiana Militia at the Battle of New Orleans; his two eldest sons served with him. In 1816, he was elected, at the age of forty-three, to the Louisiana House of Representatives; he was reelected in 1822 and 1824. In 1828, district voters sent him to the Louisiana Senate, where he served for the rest of his life. On January 14, 1830, he was elected president of the senate and immediately assumed the duties of governor. Dupré, of course, had had no opportunity to prepare recommendations for the legislature, but even so the assembly was active during the session of 1830. It continued the tradition of the previous decade of involvement in the economic development of the state, incorporating a railroad company, a canal company, two companies for improving the navigation of various bayous, the Merchants' Insurance Company of New Orleans, and a company to refine sugar by a new process. It passed a resolution objecting to the extreme southern position with regard to the Tariff of 1828 and stating that the tariff was neither unconstitutional nor harmful to the southern states. It also passed a series of acts responding to the fears generated by the new hostility of the abolitionists and by slave insurrection—or threats of it—in other states. The legislation included a prohibition on further immigration of free persons of color into the state, with the expulsion of those who had entered the state since 1825; tightening of the restrictions on slaves and free persons of color; and penalties for writing, speaking, or distributing anything likely to cause slave unrest. In Dupré's final message to the legislature, he reported the treasury to be in good condition, expressed concern about the likelihood of a reduction in the sugar tariff, urged more attention to public education, and recommended the establishment of a state penitentiary.

After Roman became governor in January, 1831, Dupré resigned as president of the senate. During his next sixteen years in the senate, he served on many committees, including the committee on claims, the committee on internal improvements, and the committee on commerce, agriculture, and manufactures. He served as an anti-Jacksonian, or Whig, elector in the presidential contests of 1832, 1836, 1840, and 1844. He continued to prosper, possessing 205 slaves in 1840. He died on September 14, 1846, and is buried in St. Landry Roman Catholic Cemetery, in Opelousas.

Despite the death of Governor Derbigny and a dispute regarding the succession, the state of Louisiana was able to function effectively during these two years. The legislature later amended the constitution to provide for the office of lieutenant governor. The next governors, like those before, continued to focus on promoting the economic growth of the state, on trying to provide for public education without a great expenditure of money, and on responding to events initiated outside the state. The dispute over who should act as governor, despite the fact that Derbigny, Beauvais, and Dupré were all nascent Whigs, is evidence of the rudimentary state of political party development in Louisiana around 1830.

JUDITH F. GENTRY

BIBLIOGRAPHY

Acts of the Ninth Legislature of the State of Louisiana. New Orleans and Donaldson-
    ville, La., 1829–30.
D'Herbigny, Michel. Pierre Bourguignon-d'Herbigny, 1769–1829, Governor of Loui-
    siana, and His Descendants in U.S.A. Lille, 1979.
Fortier, Alcée. A History of Louisiana. 4 vols. New York, 1904.
Journal of the Louisiana House of Representatives. New Orleans and Donaldsonville,
    La., 1812–31.
Journal of the Louisiana Senate. New Orleans and Donaldsonville, La., 1812–47.
Tregle, Joseph G., Jr. "The Governors of Louisiana." Louisiana History, XXII (1981),
    298, 368, 418.

André Bienvenu Roman

Governor, 1831–1835, 1839–1843

ROMAN, André Bienvenu (b. Opelousas district, Louisiana, March 5, 1795; d. New Orleans, Louisiana, January 26, 1866), state representative, speaker of the Louisiana House of Representatives, and governor. Roman was the son of Jacques Etienne Roman and Marie Louise

Patin. After a childhood spent on the family plantation in what is now St. James Parish, he attended St. Mary's College, in Maryland, from which he graduated in 1815. The following year he married Aimée Françoise Parent, by whom he fathered eight children and with whom he settled on his own sugar plantation in St. James.

Elected in 1818 to the Louisiana House of Representatives, he served as speaker of that body from 1822 to 1826. A two-year term as parish judge in St. James was followed in 1828 by a return to his old post as house speaker, a move that placed

ANDRÉ BIENVENU ROMAN. *Photograph courtesy of State Library of Louisiana, from Fortier's History of Louisiana, III, 206.*

him in a particularly advantageous position in the constitutional crisis that erupted in 1829. Governor Pierre Derbigny's death that year so confused the succession that the legislature called for a special, highly questionable, gubernatorial election in 1830.

It came at a time of confused disarray in the ranks of the Gallic Creoles. The vicious split of their forces in 1824 between followers of the flamboyantly anti-Anglo-American Bernard Marigny and the moderate, conciliatory Jacques Philippe Villeré still rankled, and there was little hope of rallying a united front behind either man. Neither Arnaud Julie Beauvais nor Jacques Dupré, Derbigny's successors, commanded any broad-based support, while Martin Duralde, son-in-law of Henry Clay (United States senator from Kentucky) and the most popular and politically powerful Creole in the state, was strangely self-effacing. Roman had no hesitancy in moving into the breach. Unlike Marigny, Villeré, and Duralde, he attracted few by force of his personality or character, for he was notoriously cold of temperament and of a demeanor described by an associate as "rigidly formal and conventional."[1] But this lack of personal magnetism was offset by qualities recognizably lacking in his Creole competitors: sound educational preparation and a disciplined grounding in the essentials of responsible

1. Cyprien Dufour, "Local Sketches," *Louisiana Historical Quarterly*, XIV (1931), 399.

statecraft. True to his reputation as a man of fixity of purpose which "often rose to obstinacy,"[2] Roman rejected all appeals to submit to Duralde's leadership, and equally true to form, Duralde refused to divide Creole strength by vying with the younger newcomer. Only the unyielding Beauvais continued to compete for the Gallic vote.

In the opposing Anglo-American camp, things were equally unsettled. Those favorable to Henry Clay's expected bid for the presidency in 1832 were loath to allow the governor's race to split his support along ethnic lines, while the champions of Andrew Jackson were in confusion stemming from the almost pathological determination of one of their number, Martin Gordon, collector of customs at New Orleans, to exercise absolute control of his party throughout the state. Leading Jacksonians in the Florida Parishes refused to knuckle under, and when Gordon's handpicked candidate for governor, Walter H. Overton, declined to run in the face of the strong intention of the Floridian William S. Hamilton to make the race, the New Orleans Custom House Coterie simply lost interest in the contest. In the critical month of January, 1830, Henry Clay took up residence in New Orleans, from which he coordinated the Roman campaign. The result was a resounding victory for the young contender, who won 3,638 votes to Hamilton's 2,701, Beauvais' 1,478, and the 463 of David Randall, another Anglo-American Jacksonian.

Taking office on January 31, 1831, Roman was governor during years marked by vigorous economic growth, yellow-fever epidemics, and rumblings of portentous political discord. The number of banks in the state jumped from five to eleven, with a book-capital expansion from nine to forty million dollars. One of the banks, the Canal Bank, Louisiana's first improvement company, built the New Basin Canal from Lake Pontchartrain into the heart of the American section of New Orleans. The Pontchartrain Railroad, the first line west of the Alleghenies, opened its run, using horse-drawn carriages, from the Mississippi to Milneburg, on the lakefront in 1831. A locomotive went into service in September, 1832. An innovative penitentiary system was established in Baton Rouge; the state capital was returned to New Orleans in 1830, after a single session in Donaldsonville; and state support was broadened for elementary and secondary schools. In 1831, a College of Jefferson was opened in St. James Parish and a College of Frank-

2. *Ibid.*

lin in St. Landry Parish, and although they were private institutions, they owed much to the personal patronage of Roman. The Louisiana Agricultural Society, pushed by Governor Henry S. Johnson back in 1826, was finally organized in 1833, with Roman as its first president, and it was largely through his efforts that the state acquired its first copy of the elephant folios of Audubon's *Birds of America.*

Not everything was so productive and rewarding. In the successive seasons of 1832 and 1833, the state was ravaged by a joint visitation of yellow fever and cholera, the deadliest epidemic of its entire history. Those same terrible months brought to a climax South Carolina's nullification controversy, a quarrel that saw most Louisianians following Roman in uncharacteristic fervid support of President Andrew Jackson's stout nationalistic stand in support of federal authority against a recalcitrant South Carolina.

Despite the obvious political success of Roman's administration, his attempt to step into a United States Senate seat at the end of his term was blocked by the rising young Creole champion, Alexandre Mouton, who possessed in bountiful supply the qualities of galvanic personality so lacking in his opponent. In 1838, however, Roman was the overwhelming Whig choice to succeed his own successor in the governor's chair. Mouton was still in Washington, and more significant, Democratic strength had been shaken in the state by the Panic of 1837. Roman's task was made somewhat easier by the vulnerability of his Jacksonian opponent, New Orleans Mayor Denis Prieur, who was notoriously indolent and self-indulgent and who was living openly with a quadroon mistress. But Prieur was favored by nature with very handsom features and a seductiveness of manner, and Roman was hard put to defeat him, 7,590 to 6,782. He took office for the second time on February 4, 1839.

The game was hardly worth the candle, for the effects of the Panic of 1837 were so devastating as to make Roman's second term the most economically distressed of the entire antebellum period. Some relief was found in record crop production and trade through New Orleans in 1839–1840, but in 1841–1842, severe contractions and liquidations in the banking community produced unprecedented economic hardship. Legislative attempts to expand capital by chartering new development banks met with repeated vetoes by Roman, until in 1842 a whole new direction was given to Louisiana banking by passage of the famous Bank Act of 1842, which replaced the earlier easy credit system with a sounder, more restrictive policy. In a not unrelated move, the state had in 1840 abolished imprisonment for debt.

In his later years, Roman served as a delegate to the state constitutional conventions of 1845 and 1852, as the European agent arranging extension of bond redemption by the Citizens Bank and the Consolidated Association of Planters, and as a delegate to the Louisiana secession convention of 1861. Fiercely opposed to disunion, he voted against secession, but he could not abandon his state in its final decision to separate from the Union. In 1861, the Confederate government appointed him, along with John Forsyth and Martin J. Crawford, to seek a peaceful compromise with the United States, but the mission was aborted by Secretary of State William Seward's refusal to grant them an audience.

In 1866, his fortunes ruined by the Civil War, Roman gratefully accepted appointment by Governor James Madison Wells as recorder of deeds and mortgages in New Orleans. But before he could take office, he died while walking on Dumaine Street in that city. He is buried on the family estate in St. James Parish.

❧

The first three decades of the nineteenth century were years of remarkable ambivalence for the Gallic Creoles of Louisiana. Generally convinced of the economic and political advantages of their new membership in the American Union, they were humiliated and distressed by the cultural and political primitiveness of their society, which exposed them to the insulting and condescending tutelage and leadership of "foreign French" immigrants and Anglo-American newcomers. Gubernatorial elections of 1820 and 1824 threatened to fasten upon them a local Virginia dynasty, and the 1828 ascendancy of the Frenchman Derbigny did little to assuage their injured pride. It was in this context that Roman appeared upon the scene as the long-sought Creole David. Antebellum Louisiana's only two-term governor, he experienced the heady satisfaction of one administration blessed by lively growth and the gloomy despair of a second term blighted by the worst economic depression of the pre–Civil War years.

Roman's significance in the history of the state lies most likely in neither the prosperity nor the economic contraction during his time in office. Rather, the Creole population, after years of self-doubt and debilitating failure in political mastery, found in him one of their own capable of vying with the most formidable Anglo-American or "foreign French" challenger. It is no accident that after his election in 1830 there was never again to be a foreign-born *éminence grise* such as Etienne Mazureau behind the governor's chair, nor the threat of a Virginia dynasty like that of Thomas Bolling Robertson or Henry S. Johnson. In large measure, Roman gave Louisiana back to Louisianians.

JOSEPH G. TREGLE, JR.

BIBLIOGRAPHY

"A. B. Roman of Louisiana." *De Bow's Review*, XI (1851), 436–43.
Burge, Dennis F. "Louisiana Under Governor André Bienvenu Roman, 1831–1835, 1839–1843." M.A. thesis, Louisiana State University, 1937.
Dufour, Cyprien. "Local Sketches." *Louisiana Historical Quarterly*, XIV (1931), 399.
Green, George D. *Finance and Economic Development in the Old South: Louisiana Banking, 1804–1861*. Stanford, Calif., 1972.
Meynier, Arthur. *Louisiana Biographies*. New Orleans, 1882.

Edward Douglass White

Governor, 1835–1839

WHITE, Edward Douglass (also rendered Edward Douglas, but documents in the archives of the Louisiana Supreme Court establish the other spelling; b. Maury County, Tennessee, March 3, 1795; d. New Orleans, Louisiana, April 18, 1847), congressman and governor. White was the son of James White and Mary Wilcox, who brought him to St. Martin Parish in 1799, where the elder White was to become a district judge after the Louisiana Purchase. A graduate of the University of Nashville in 1815, he studied law under Alexander Porter, a well-known Louisiana attorney and political figure, and eventually went into practice at Donaldsonville. After a brief term, from 1825 to 1828, as judge of the New Orleans city court, he turned to sugar planting along Bayou Lafourche, from which he was almost immediately diverted by a successful campaign to claim Edward

EDWARD DOUGLASS WRIGHT. *Photograph courtesy of State Library of Louisiana, from Fortier's* History of Louisiana, *III, 224.*

Livingston's seat in the national House of Representatives. Supporters of Livingston had ridiculed the challenge of this "callow" and "presumptuous" young man, but White profited from Livingston's notorious neglect of constituents and from the skillful grooming he himself received from his old tutor, Porter, then a justice of the Louisiana Supreme Court, and Henry S. Johnson, the incumbent governor.

He was aided immeasurably as well by what was always to prove one of his great political assets: a warmth and generosity of spirit that won the hearts of almost all who knew him. Even his political foes attested to his winning ways. Duff Green, a staunch Democratic newspaper editor, once remarked that no other public figure in Washington "had more endeared himself to his numerous friends, than this excellent and amiable man."[1] But White's amiability was wedded to a brusque and blunt manner of address that gave him a reputation for being "highly eccentric" in personality.[2] On one occasion, at least, his eccentricity exploded into violence. In the 1828 campaign, he attempted to kill with his dirk an old political foe taunting him with pro-Livingston oratory.

White's congressional tenure was marked by his steady support of policies propounded by Henry Clay, a United States senator from Kentucky. White supported Clay's policies even to the extent of backing the Compromise Tariff, which reduced protection of the Louisiana sugar industry. A close escape from death in the 1833 explosion of the Red River steamboat *Lioness* only briefly interrupted his campaign for the governorship in 1834.

Jacksonian opposition to White was once again directed by the New Orleans collector of customs, Martin Gordon, whose ineffective role in the 1830 contest won by André Bienvenu Roman had convinced him that victory could be assured only by a union of his Custom House Coterie with other Democratic forces in the Florida parishes. Moving quickly to end the threat of a run by Denis Prieur, mayor of New Orleans and part of the John Slidell faction expelled by Gordon from the Democratic fold, the collector threw his support to John B. Dawson, of West Feliciana. Dawson was a foppish poseur given to effusive and florid expression. Empty of thought and political philosophy, and dominated by what he himself called his capacity for "malignant hatred,"[3]

1. Washington (D.C.) *United States Telegraph*, June 12, 1833.
2. Alexander Porter to J. Burton Harrison, March 6, 1835, in J. Burton Harrison Papers, Manuscript Division, Library of Congress, Washington, D.C.
3. John B. Dawson to William S. Hamilton, June 29, 1824, in William S. Hamilton Papers, Troy H. Middleton Library, Louisiana State University, Baton Rouge.

he depended for support upon his uncritical dedication to the Jackson cause and his ability to cadge ideas and speeches from his brother-in-law, Isaac Johnson, and old cronies such as William S. Hamilton.

For his part, White commanded the loyalty of the Clay factions, both Anglo-American and Gallic, as well as that of many Jacksonian Latin Creoles willing to forget national party ties in order to assure a governorship friendly to their ethnic concerns.

Despite the national debate concerning nullification, tariff policy, and the Bank of the United States, the campaign was almost devoid of any substantive political discourse; it centered instead on personal vilification and the supposed "aristocratic" or "democratic" leanings of the two candidates. That was the kind of battle most congenial to Gordon's press hacks, and it was made easy by the gaffes of White's supporters, like Etienne Mazureau, who scornfully remarked that votes for Dawson could be bought by the gift of drams of whiskey. A preference for whiskey immediately became the symbol of Dawson's democratic egalitarianism, in contrast to the aristocratic fondness for claret and champagne which the Dawson forces imputed to White and his friends despite common knowledge that White's life-style was as plain as a toothpick compared with that of the resplendent Dawson. Much was made, as well, of the alleged domination of White by Porter, whom Gordon attacked as an "Irish foreigner" of uncertain citizenship and questionable dedication to American democratic institutions. It was only relatively late in the campaign that the economic stringency of 1834 became an issue. Although the Jacksonians argued fervidly that the hardship was traceable to curtailments by the Bank of the United States, some Democrats moved to White's side in the belief that the mischief stemmed from Jackson's vindictive removal of federal deposits from the bank.

In the end, White's broad appeal to Louisianians who supported Clay's national Whig ideals and to many of the state's Gallic voters proved too strong for the Dawson effort. White got the vote of New Orleans and every parish south of the Red River except Plaquemines. The Democrats swept the Florida Parishes and all of north Louisiana save Avoyelles and Concordia, for a total of 4,149 votes against White's 6,065.

White was to find this moment of victory more pleasurable than anything in his governorship, which began on February 2, 1835. His four years in office were crowded with bitter quarrels over his patronage, with charges that he was anti-American in his appointment policies, with growing popular paranoia centered on abolitionists and slave insurrections, and with the dreadful effects of the Panic of 1837. It was his misfortune, he would claim later, to have won the governorship in a striking victory, so that vast numbers of persons thought they could demand appointment to state office confident that they had been the architect of his success. The hordes of patronage seekers doomed to inevitable disappointment turned against him loudly, in constant criticism of his actions. Also troublesome was the involvement of Louisiana in the Texas independence movement and the Seminole War in Florida, which put White in the vexing posture of having to suppress the illegal enlistment of Louisianians in their western neighbor's fight against Mexico while he labored to fill the state's quota of troops to serve in campaigns against the Indians.

Even more clamorous than his unsatisfied friends were the Democrats under the always-resourceful Gordon, who set up the cry that White, as a tool of the hated Irishman Porter, was delivering the state to the domination of foreigners. It was this hysteria which produced the Native American movement in Louisiana under the direction of the Democrat William Christy, with its heritage of years of divisiveness and violence.

All White's burdens were particularly disheartening in light of the unparalleled financial boom in the first two years of his administration, which saw the chartering of six new banks capitalized at sixteen million dollars and dedicated to the construction of two new railroads, the St. Charles and St. Louis Hotels in New Orleans, and the city's gas street lighting. But it was precisely the freezing of the banks' assets in such improvement projects that made these institutions vulnerable in the Panic of 1837 and led to the failure of all of them by 1847. On the positive side, White in 1837 signed the charter creating the Medical College of Louisiana, forerunner of Tulane University.

At the end of his governorship, White returned to Congress for two additional terms, 1839–1843, during which he worked diligently for advancement of the United States mint in New Orleans and for increased commerce between Mexico and the United States. Upon retirement from political life, he settled on his plantation near Thibodaux, on Bayou Lafourche. On September 22, 1834, he had married Catherine Sidney Lee Ringgold (known as Sidney), daughter of Tench Ringgold, marshal of the federal district under Presidents James Madison and James Monroe. Their children were Susan, James, Eliza, Edward Douglass, Jr., and Mary Sidney. James became a prominent physician, Edward Douglass a member of the United States Supreme Court in 1894 and chief justice of the United States in 1910.

❧

White, except for Robert Wickliffe the last nonnative governor of antebellum Louisiana, was in fact the one of his breed most acceptable to the Latin Creole community of the state. Indeed, as was true of the New York–born Henry S. Thibodaux, White's extended and intimate identification with the Acadian community along Bayou Lafourche made him as much a member of the Gallic political faction as of the Anglo-American, to which he belonged by birth.

It was the irony of White's governorship that he, a longtime favorite of the Gallic Creole class, presided over a term that saw the birth in Louisiana of the viciously bigoted Native American movement. Taken up at first ostensibly to protect the rights of all native-born Louisianians, Latin Creoles as well as others, it soon revealed itself to be a depository of hatred and antagonism to anything not traditionally Anglo-American Protestant in nature. It engendered passions that helped divide New Orleans into three distinct municipalities in 1836 and poisoned all the ethnic relationships that White had once been in a position to improve. Neither his vaunted personal charm nor his unparalleled appeal to the Gallic segment of the community could minimize the cleavages in the state. Not until the very end of the antebellum period did Louisianians again entrust the governorship to a nonnative, whatever his personal appeal.

But White's four-year tenure was portentous in other ways as well. The presidential election of 1836, midway in his term, focused on slavery in a way unknown in previous canvasses. The public hysteria generated by fears of slave insurrection and the supposed plottings of subversive abolitionists led eventually to more and more restrictive state strictures in racial matters, which were particularly damaging to the famously robust and creative free black population of the community. More even than the grievous effects of the Panic of 1837, this pollution of the public atmosphere caused White pain and regret as he surveyed the ruin of his administration.

JOSEPH G. TREGLE, JR.,

BIBLIOGRAPHY

Green, George D. *Finance and Economic Development in the Old South: Louisiana Banking, 1804–1861.* Stanford, Calif., 1972.

Ramke, Diedrich. "Edward Douglas White, Sr., Governor of Louisiana, 1835–1839." *Louisiana Historical Quarterly*, XIX (1936), 273–327.

Sparks, W. H. *The Memories of Fifty Years*. Philadelphia, 1870.

Tregle, Joseph G., Jr. "Louisiana in the Age of Jackson." Ph.D. dissertation, University of Pennsylvania, 1954.

Alexandre Mouton

Governor, 1843–1846

MOUTON, Alexandre (b. Attakapas district [Lafayette Parish], Louisiana, November 18, 1804; d. Vermilionville [Lafayette], Louisiana, February 12, 1885), state legislator, speaker of the Louisiana House of Representatives, United States senator, governor, and chairman of the Louisiana Secession Convention. The sixth child of Jean Mouton and Marie Martha Bordat, Mouton was born on his family's plantation on Bayou Carencro. Both his parents were of Acadian origin, and his father was considered the founder of Vermilionville (modern Lafayette). In 1820, Mouton was graduated

ALEXANDRE MOUTON. *Photograph courtesy of Lafayette Museum, Lafayette, La., from Currier and Ives print of painting by Charles Fenderich.*

from Georgetown College, in Washington, D.C.; he then read law in the offices of Charles Antoine and Edward Simon, of St. Martinville, and was admitted to the bar in 1825. After practicing law for a few years, Mouton turned his attention to the cultivation of cotton and sugar cane on Ile Copal Plantation, which his father had given him as a wedding present. In 1826, Mouton married Celia Rousseau, granddaughter of Jacques Dupré, a wealthy cattle rancher in the Opelousas region and a prominent local politician; they had five children before Celia died. In 1842, he married Emma Kitchell Gardner; they had six children.

Although the prairie and bayou sugarcane region was later a stronghold of the Whig party, Mouton became a supporter of the Jacksonian

Democrats and rose to prominence within his party. He served as a Democratic presidential elector in 1828, 1832, and 1836, and represented Louisiana at the Democratic national conventions in 1856 and 1860. He served in the lower house of the Louisiana legislature from 1826 to 1832—the last two years as speaker of the house—and again from 1836 to 1837. As a legislator, he supported internal improvements and the chartering of banks, and encouraged the rapid sale of federal lands in Louisiana. In 1832, he cast the tie-breaking vote in favor of chartering the Union Bank of Louisiana, which was designed to make credit available to rural areas through eight branches; the state guaranteed the bonds of the bank in order to facilitate their sale in Europe. In 1834, Mouton became president of the bank's Vermilionville branch.

Mouton was elected by the state legislature to the United States Senate in 1837 and served until 1842. As a strong Jacksonian senator from Louisiana, he gave attention to better mail service, the settlement of land claims, the more rapid sale of federal lands in Louisiana, the distribution to the state of a portion of the proceeds from the sale of federal lands, and the support of internal improvement projects in Louisiana by the federal government. He opposed rechartering the Bank of the United States, and he was against the protective tariff.

In 1842, at the request of Democratic party leaders in Louisiana, Mouton resigned from the Senate in order to run for the governorship of the state. The Democrats were criticizing the Whigs for the economic difficulties the state was experiencing. Hardships associated with the depression that had begun in 1837 intensified in 1842. The legislature passed the Bank Act of 1842, intended to maintain the fiscal integrity of the state's economy. Subsequently, however, nine of Louisiana's fourteen banks went into liquidation, resulting in a serious shortage of money and credit. The state owed $1.2 million in short-term debt to the banks and had additional millions of dollars of long-term debt and other obligations.

Mouton won the election with 60 percent of the popular vote and on January 30, 1843, took the oath as the first Democratic governor of Louisiana. In office, Mouton developed controversial economic policies for Louisiana—including balancing the budget in a time of economic depression. Whereas Governor André Bienvenu Roman had pursued a policy of frugality and urged tax increases, Mouton further reduced state expenditures and liquidated state assets in order to balance the budget and meet bond obligations without raising taxes. He sold all the bank stock held by the state and applied the proceeds of the sales to the short-term debts of the state to the banks. He also sold steamboats, equipment, and slaves owned by the state, which had been employed since 1834 under a program inaugurated by Roman to remove the Red River Raft and make other internal improvements. In contrast to his actions as a legislator, Mouton as governor opposed virtually all expenditures for internal improvements. He initiated a program of leasing out the state penitentiary with its labor and textile machinery, in order to relieve the state of the cost of operating the system. He supported limitations on state borrowing and advocated using all state income to pay the debt, except for proceeds of the sale of public lands dedicated to education.

In the 1842 gubernatorial campaign and during Mouton's governorship, the Democrats supported the calling of a constitutional convention. Along with many Democrats, Mouton favored the removal of property qualifications for suffrage and officeholding, and the election of all local officials and most judges. The two required referenda were conducted while Mouton was governor, delegates to the convention were elected, and a new constitution was written and ratified by the voters in 1845. A majority of the delegates were Democrats, but a radical-conservative split among Democrats allowed a Whig–conservative Democratic alliance to wield influence. Consequently, Mouton was unable to exert the influence in the convention that he might have, and several of the provisions of the Constitution of 1845 bore the mark of many compromises.

After his governorship, Mouton retired to the life of a sugar planter and railroad promoter. In 1851, he became vice-president of the newly formed New Orleans, Algiers, Attakapas, and Opelousas Railroad.

As a member of the Louisiana delegation to the national Democratic convention in 1860, Mouton presented the resolution that demanded the right for slaveowners to take slaves into any territory of the United States; when the motion was rejected, he joined in the walkout by Deep South Democrats. A supporter of immediate secession, he was elected to the Louisiana Secession Convention, for which the delegates chose him chairman. Mouton stood for election to the senate of the Confederate States of America but was defeated. During the Civil War, he was once arrested by, and once had to flee from, Union troops, who used Ile Copal Plantation as a headquarters and burned the sugar mill and other work buildings. As a result of the Union victory, Mouton's 120 slaves were freed. The destruction and economic hardship of the war years contributed to Mouton's declining wealth, although he continued to own the 1,900 acres that Ile Copal comprised.

◈

Mouton's decision to balance the state budget during a time of depression had important political and economic consequences intensifying the hard times and making recovery difficult. The decrease in bank-note circulation necessitated by his policies caused a severe contraction of money and credit. Mouton, however, was acting in accordance with the best financial and economic understanding of the day. Balancing the budget was not a party issue; both Whigs and most Democrats were committed to that goal. Mouton left the governorship with a $225,000 surplus for his last year of office (compared with a $200,000 deficit for the year before he took office) and a significantly reduced state debt. But his stringent fiscal retrenchment was only partially responsible for the improved financial condition of the state government. The most important cause was the general economic recovery, a development Mouton's programs had retarded rather than advanced.

Perhaps the most important accomplishment of Mouton's term was the writing of the Constitution of 1845. This new constitution reflected a strong North-South split in the state, and indicated some anticity bias, against New Orleans. Although the property requirements for suffrage and officeholding were eliminated, provisions designed to maintain political control by wealthy planters were introduced. For the first time, the state Senate was to be apportioned on the basis of total population—including voteless slaves—and New Orleans was to be limited to no more than one-eighth of the membership. The design was to give the slaveholding parishes, with their greater total population, more votes in the state senate than the northern, hill-country parishes and the city of New Orleans. A two-year residence requirement for voting, instead of the previous one-year requirement, would delay the enfranchisement of recently arrived men from other states and newly arrived, generally poor, immigrants from abroad. The proponents of democratic reform was successful, however, in providing for the direct election of the governor by the voters and the election of most local officials. The reapportionment in the Constitution of 1845 reduced the power of the French-speaking Roman Catholics of South Louisiana, who were an overwhelming majority of the state's population when the Constitution of 1812 had been written. The new charter also provided for regular reapportionment in the future.

Furthermore, the Constitution of 1845 included restrictions on state aid to economic enterprise, as well as limitations on borrowing. It prohibited the legislature from granting any monopoly for more than twenty years, from incorporating or renewing the charters of any banks, and from guaranteeing the bonds of any person, corporation, or body politic. The legislature was prohibited from incurring debts totaling more than $100,000 without providing for the taxes necessary to extinguish the debt. It was required to establish a free public-education system, but the limitations on going into debt and the restrictions against guaranteeing the bonds of any body politic made it difficult to comply with that mandate.

Both Whigs and Democrats were dissatisfied with the Constitution of 1845. Both parties mildly supported the ratification of the new constitution, but both also proved willing to call a new constitutional convention only seven years later. Thus Mouton's support for the Constitution of 1845 had created only a short-lived state charter.

JUDITH F. GENTRY

BIBLIOGRAPHY

Ferguson, Ted. "The Louisiana Constitution of 1845." M.A. thesis, Louisiana State University, 1948.

Gayarré, Charles. *The American Domination*. 5th ed. New Orleans, 1965. Vol. IV of Gayarré, *History of Louisiana*. 4 vols.

Green, George D. *Finance and Economic Development in the Old South: Louisiana Banking, 1804–1861*. Stanford, Calif., 1972.

Perrin, William Henry, ed. *Southwest Louisiana: Biographical and Historical*. New Orleans, 1891.

Schumacher, Elizabeth M. "The Political Career of Alexandre Mouton." M.A. thesis, Louisiana State University, 1935.

Isaac Johnson

Governor, 1846–1850

JOHNSON, Isaac (b. West Feliciana Parish, Louisiana, November 1, 1803; d. New Orleans, Louisiana, March 15, 1853), state legislator, state judge, governor, and state attorney general. Johnson, fourth of the numerous progeny of John Hunter Johnson and Thenia Munson, was born at his father's plantation, Troy. The influential Johnson clan had been established by his grandfather, who had come to the area from England in the 1770s. Johnson's father played a leading role in the West

Florida Rebellion, prospered as a successful lawyer and planter, and served the parish as sheriff and judge.

Surrounded by many brothers, sisters, and cousins, young Johnson spent his childhood at Troy plantation. The Feliciana of his youth was a frontier where riding, hunting, and shooting absorbed the attention of all males, whether young or old, and owners of large estates were plagued by a shortage of labor, a lack of ready cash, and an abundance of debts. Private tutors attended to his early education, and later he probably read law under

ISAAC JOHNSON. *Photograph courtesy of State Library of Louisiana, from Fortier's* History of Louisiana, *III, 224; and Chambers'* History of Louisiana, *I, 608.*

the supervision of his father and his uncle, Joseph E. Johnson. In 1828, Johnson began to practice law, and in the same year, he married Charlotte McDermott. Shortly afterward, he joined his uncle and his brother William in a partnership. The Johnson firm prospered, and Johnson's legal reputation spread throughout the Felicianas.

Johnson soon became involved in local politics in the Democratic party, and in 1833, he won a seat in the Louisiana State Assembly. At the end of his term, he returned to his law practice until he was appointed judge of the third district court in 1839, a post he held with one brief interruption until he received the Democratic nomination for governor in 1845. The Whig party selected William De Buys to oppose Johnson. In a campaign marked by an unresponsive electorate and the absence of the usual personal invective, the "boy of Feliciana," as the phrase the opposition coined to emphasize Johnson's youth and inexperience described him, defeated De Buys on January 19, 1846, by a margin of 2,491 votes.

Johnson's administration was filled with political turmoil. Implementing the new state constitution that had been ratified in 1845 was a large undertaking and caused acrimonious debates over matters large and small. The inaugural ceremony, held February 12, 1846, itself occasioned the first difficulty to confront the new governor. Some maintained that Johnson had taken an improper oath and therefore was not legally governor of the state. Hardly had the courts attended to that matter—in Johnson's favor—than the ancient feud between city and country erupted over the removal of the capital from New Orleans. In a similar way, debates over the Public School Law and over providing appropriations to implement that legislation caused internal political divisions. Johnson was consistently concerned about the state of education in Louisiana.

At the same time, political attention focused upon the war between the United States and Mexico (1846–1848), after which the controversy over the expansion of slavery in the new territories became heated. Johnson, like most Louisianians, responded enthusiastically to the war with Mexico. Indeed, he advocated annexing all of Mexico. His ardor cooled considerably when he was bombarded with complaints from Louisiana's soldiers, who maintained that they had not been paid and that they had no funds to return home. Johnson engaged in a sharp exchange with the United States Army's paymaster general, and he criticized the federal government for not sharing the expenses for equipping the state's militia. Throughout the troubled years of his administration, the governor upheld a strict interpretation of the constitution and states' rights, and he vehemently denounced the Wilmot Proviso, a resolution introduced in Congress by the Pennsylvania congressman David Wilmot to prohibit slavery in the territories obtained from Mexico.

More important, Johnson faced a difficult political situation in Louisiana. By 1846, the fortunes of the Democratic party were on the rise. After years of frustration, party leaders such as John Slidell had succeeded in molding a disciplined organization. Yet their efforts seemed worthless when "Taylor Democrats" (supporters of General Zachary Taylor) carried the state for the Whigs in the 1848 presidential election and factional disputes within the party threatened to deprive it of gains so recently made. Johnson's leadership proved a disappointment to Democratic party leaders. An affable man who enjoyed being popular, he could not accept the tenets of strict party discipline. He appointed Whigs to office, much to the chagrin of Democratic leaders and much to the delight of the opposition. By 1848, Johnson was out of favor with the party chieftains who had secured his election.

In addition to the difficulties of his office, Johnson had to contend with a personal tragedy during his administration. In 1847, Charlotte Johnson died, leaving the governor with three children to raise. Johnson married again, but his second marriage appears to have been based upon convenience rather than geniune affection.

In 1849, Johnson and the principal state officials moved to the new capital in Baton Rouge, and when the legislature met there in 1850, the governor delivered his final message. He requested funds for the repair and construction of levees damaged in the severe flood of 1849, and he took great pleasure in reporting an increased enrollment in the state's public schools. He retired from office on January 28, 1850.

Johnson's retirement from public life was short. On February 15, 1850, Governor Joseph M. Walker, his successor, appointed him attorney general of Louisiana. He served as the state's top legal officer for two years, and he represented the state well in a number of important cases. In 1852, he again returned to his estate in West Feliciana, where it appeared he would retire for good. In 1853, however, Johnson announced his candidacy for associate justice on the state supreme court and again embarked upon the campaign trail. Johnson was not to see the results of this election, because before it took place, he suffered a heart attack and died in his room at the Verandah Hotel, in New Orleans. Burial ceremonies at Troy, in West Feliciana, were hardly completed when tragedy again struck the Johnson family. For later in the same year his two sons were stricken with yellow fever and died.

ॐ

Johnson was only forty-three years old when he became Louisiana's chief executive. Although an impressive physical figure with an open, easygoing manner, Johnson had little political experience and few of the qualities essential in a decisive politician or strong executive leader. During his brief tenure in the state legislature, he did not participate in any of the heated debates. Nor did he seek reelection when his term ended in 1835. As governor, he rapidly succeeded in alienating leaders of his own Democratic party by giving patronage appointments to rival Whigs. Political confrontations and the give-and-take of debate held little fascination for him. He was more comfortable preparing a legal brief or defining or ruling on a point of law. A Louisiana facsimile of President and Chief Justice William Howard Taft, Johnson had talents and interests that were legal rather than political.

Unquestionably, Johnson was a fine lawyer. It was from the bench of the third judicial district court that Johnson's reputation and popularity originated, prompting Democrats to select him as the party's gubernatorial nominee in 1845. Indeed, Johnson died amid a campaign to secure a seat on the state supreme court—a post he would almost surely have won had he lived.

Although Johnson was more judge than politician, Louisiana made progress during his administration. Health conditions improved, school attendance and the population increased, and prosperity grew apace. And Johnson's contemporaries, whether friend or foe, appraised him as a man of unquestionable honesty and integrity.

CAROLYN E. DeLATTE

BIBLIOGRAPHY

Adams, William H. *The Whig Party of Louisiana.* Lafayette, La., 1973.

Arthur, Stanley, and George C. H. de Kernion. *Old Families of Louisiana.* Baton Rouge, 1971.

Aucoin, Sidney J. "The Political Career of Isaac Johnson, Governor of Louisiana, 1846–1850." *Louisiana Historical Quarterly,* XXVIII (1945), 941–89.

Chambers, Henry. *A History of Louisiana Wilderness—Colony—Province—Territory—State—People.* Vol. I of 3 vols. New York, 1925.

Joseph M. Walker

Governor, 1850–1853

WALKER, Joseph Marshall (b. New Orleans, Louisiana, July ?, 1786; d. Rapides Parish, Louisiana, January 26, 1856), state legislator, state senator, state treasurer, and governor. Walker was born to Peter Walker and Constantia Revoli. As a man in his twenties, he went to Mexico, joined the Spanish military service, was commissioned lieutenant of dragoons, and became master of the military school at Chihuahua. When he resigned his commission, he remained in Mexico as a horse trader and cattle dealer.

During the War of 1812, when the British threatened Louisiana,

JOSEPH M. WALKER. *Photograph courtesy of State Library of Louisiana, from Fortier's* History of Louisiana, *III, 224.*

Walker returned to his native state. He enlisted in the state militia, served with volunteer forces under Andrew Jackson at Chalmette (the Battle of New Orleans), and later became brigadier general of the 1st Brigade of the state militia. After the War of 1812, he moved to Rapides Parish, where he became a cotton planter. He and his wife, Catherine Carter, of Adams County, Mississippi, settled in Rapides and reared three daughters and seven sons.

In 1820, Walker began his political career by being elected to the lower house of the state legislature. The voters reelected him in 1822. While in the lower house, and because of his service and interest in the state militia, he served as chairman of the committee on the state militia. Walker subsequently served in the Louisiana Senate. His only electoral defeat occurred in 1834, when a Whig, Alexander Porter, defeated him for a United States Senate seat. As a Democrat, Walker won a seat as delegate to the Louisiana constitutional convention of 1845, and his colleagues elected him president of the convention.

In the following year, the Louisiana voters elected Walker state treasurer, and in 1849, the Democratic party nominated him as its candidate for governor.

Walker was not, however, the unanimous choice of the Democrats, and he encountered some opposition to his nomination. There was a segment of the Democratic party that believed Walker to have some attachments to the Whigs. These Democrats feared that as governor, Walker would appoint Whigs to office. The Democrats and Walker expected a difficult campaign in which nativism and the national issue of slavery in the territories would predominate.

Ironically, during the 1849 campaign, the Whigs, who had been associated with antiforeign sentiment, charged Walker with nativism. Hoping to capture the office of governor, as they had so recently captured the presidency, they alleged that Walker had called Porter a "damned Irishman" after Porter defeated Walker for the Senate seat in 1834. The Whigs accused the Democratic candidate of opposition to electing or appointing naturalized citizens to high posts. They dragged out Walker's legislative voting record to support their allegations. They asserted that Walker had voted against an appropriation for the Catholic Male Orphan Asylum, in New Orleans, which aided immigrant children. Overcoming these allegations, Walker narrowly defeated his Whig opponent, Alexander De Clouet, with a majority of slightly more than one thousand votes out of more than thirty-four thousand cast. The Whigs must have had difficulty accepting the loss, convinced as they were that the Democrats had manipulated the foreign-born voters.

On January 28, 1850, Walker became the first Louisiana governor inaugurated at the new statehouse in Baton Rouge. After his inauguration, Governor Walker set the goals for his administration. Following the lead of his predecessor, Isaac Johnson, Walker wanted to improve the public schools of the state. He also advocated internal improvements and the election of judges by the voters. To achieve the latter, he called for a consitutional amendment. Education continued to progress under Walker, but what success there was should be credited to a vigorous state superintendent rather than to the governor or to the legislature. Despite Walker's interest in internal improvements, they received little funding during his tenure, and it was not until the creation of the Swamp Land Fund in the administration of Governor Paul Octave Hébert that they again received practical attention in the state.

The paramount domestic issue to arise during Walker's administration concerned the calling of a constitutional convention. The commercial interests of Louisiana chafed under the Constitution of 1845, which they considered restrictive. The main objections focused on the limited right of the legislature to borrow money, the prohibition against public loans for internal improvements (which helps explain why so little progress was made in that area), the forbidding of the general assembly (the legislature) to charter banks, and the limitation of all corporations to a twenty-five-year tenure. The restrictions were supported by the Democrats in general, and by Governor Walker in particular. The voters of the state, however, sought constitutional changes to extend the democratic reforms begun in 1845. Walker and the majority of the Democrats, although in favor of democratic political reforms, wanted to use the slower process of constitutional amendments. Although Walker opposed the calling of a constitutional convention, as in his admonition to the general assembly in his message of January, 1852, where he said that "forms of government should not be changed for light, trivial causes,"[1] a determined and well-organized Whiggery had already won the state election of 1851 on a platform endorsing constitutional change, and it elected a majority of the convention delegates in 1852.

The adoption of the Constitution of 1852 forced Governor Walker to

1. Charles Gayarré, *The American Domination* (5th ed.; New Orleans, 1965), 674, Vol. IV of Gayarré, *History of Louisiana*, 4 vols.

leave office a year earlier than he would have done under the 1845 charter. He retired to cotton planting at his plantation in Rapides Parish, refusing to be nominated to other offices, including the United States Senate. Walker apparently preferred the company of his large family.

❧

Walker secured some of the political changes he desired: the practice of choosing judges by election and the reduction of the age requirement for the governor and lieutenant governor. But he was particularly disappointed by the removal of the prohibitions on state borrowing and on the chartering of banking institutions by the state. The electorate, apparently less reluctant than Walker—particularly in its desire to speed political reform—ratified the Constitution of 1852 by a sizable majority.

Governor Walker's apprehension of chartered banks, state debt, and corporations dated back at least to the constitutional convention of 1845, over which he had presided. In his last message to the general assembly, on January 17, 1853, he urged the legislature to use its newly acquired right to contract debts "with extreme caution," and he questioned the "expediency of flooding the country with bank issues."[2] But Walker's failure—as well as the failure of the Democrats in general—to exert more leadership during the debate over whether to call a constitutional convention was, in part at least, responsible for the changes Walker opposed. Moreover, while the governor may have been satisfied with the reforms in the judicial and executive branches, the Constitution of 1852 required the lower house of the legislature to be apportioned by total population. This feature, already applied to the senate in 1852, transferred control of the legislature "from the people to property."[3]

With national controversies such as the expansion of slavery in the western territories prominent in Walker's 1849 campaign, it is not surprising that he offered a defense of the South's peculiar institution while he was governor. Walker regarded himself as a Southern Rights Democrat, one who advocated equality for the South within the Union, or else secession. His determination is evident in one of his many addresses on the subject of southern rights, when he declared that if the

2. *Ibid.*, 675.

3. Roger W. Shugg, *Origins of Class Struggle in Louisiana: A Social History of White Farmers and Laborers During Slavery and After, 1840–1875* (Baton Rouge, 1939), 139.

South could not receive its rights, "we are prepared to make common cause with our neighbors of the slaveholding states, and pronounce the Union at an end."[4] Walker's pronouncement anticipated Louisiana's secession nine years after he retired from politics.

MARIUS M. CARRIERE, JR.

BIBLIOGRAPHY

Carriere, Marius M., Jr. "The Know Nothing Movement in Louisiana." Ph.D. dissertation, Louisiana State University, 1977.

Fortier, Alcée. A History of Louisiana. Vol. III of 4 vols. New York, 1904.

Gayarré, Charles. The American Domination. 5th ed. New Orleans, 1965. Vol. 4 of Gayarré, History of Louisiana. 4 vols.

Greer, James K. "Louisiana Politics, 1845–1861." Louisiana Historical Quarterly, XII (1929), 570–610.

Shugg, Roger W. Origins of Class Struggle in Louisiana: A Social History of White Farmers and Laborers During Slavery and After, 1840–1875. Baton Rouge, 1939.

Paul Octave Hébert

Governor, 1853–1856

HÉBERT, Paul Octave (b. Iberville Parish, Louisiana, December 12, 1818; d. New Orleans, Louisiana, August 29, 1880), state engineer, army officer, governor, and Confederate general. Hébert was graduated first in his class in 1836 from Jefferson College, Louisiana, and at the head of his class from the United States Military Academy, at West Point, in 1840. He was posted as acting assistant professor of engineering at West Point in 1841, and then was appointed assistant engineer at the port of New Orleans. On August 2, 1842, he married Cora Wills Vaughn, the daughter of a sugar planter. Hébert resigned from the army in 1845.

PAUL OCTAVE HÉBERT. Photograph courtesy of State Library of Louisiana, from Fortier's History of Louisiana, IV, 62.

4. Gayarré, The American Domination, 674.

On February 28, 1845, Governor Alexandre Mouton appointed Hébert to the office of civil engineer for the state of Louisiana. Governor Isaac Johnson reappointed him on March 23, 1846. Hébert resigned this position in April, 1847, to fight in the Mexican War. He served as lieutenant colonel of the United States 14th Infantry Regiment and fought at the battles of Contreras, Churubusco, Molino del Rey, Chapultepec, and Mexico City. He received an honorable discharge at New Orleans on July 25, 1848.

After briefly trying his hand at sugar planting, Hébert began his political career as a Democrat, in 1849. His bid for a state senate seat from the Whig party stronghold of Iberville Parish failed by nine votes. After this defeat, he returned to sugar planting. Subsequently, a division among Iberville Whigs permitted him to win a delegate's seat to the constitutional convention of 1852.

John Slidell, the top leader in the Louisiana Democratic party, focused his interest on national office, opening the way for Democrats to turn to Hébert in 1852 and nominate him their gubernatorial candidate. Campaigning for the governorship, Hébert opposed what he called the "anti-republican features of the new constitution."[1] All Democrats opposed this "Whig document,"[2] but Hébert's campaign was not limited to the negative. He called for internal improvements, reform of the state militia, a banking system created by general laws, and immediate redemption in specie of all paper money. During the 1852 campaign, as during Hébert's gubernatorial term, there was a resurgent nativism. He tried to stress internal improvements and education, and defeated the Whig candidate, Louis Bordelon, by two thousand votes.

Hébert took the oath of office on January 1, 1853, and within four years guided the legislature toward making improvements in water commerce and railroad construction. It was through his efforts that the legislature approved an enlargement of the formerly neglected school for the deaf, mute, and blind. The issue of nativism and the rapid rise of the Know-Nothing party distracted the governor from his reform goals and caused him concern. Twice, party regulars mentioned him as a possible candidate for the United States Senate, but Slidell's influence was greater. In January, 1856, Hébert retired to Iberville Parish and the life of a gentleman planter.

1. Albert L. Duport, "The Career of Paul O. Hébert, 1853–1856," *Louisiana Historical Quarterly*, XXXI (1948), 501–502.
2. *Ibid.*, 499.

With the election of Abraham Lincoln in the fall national election, the Democratic governor Thomas O. Moore in December, 1860, appointed Hébert to a military board that was to reorganize the state's militia and defenses. Hébert received a commission as a colonel of the 1st Louisiana Artillery, and in April, 1861, he became a brigadier general in the state forces. He obtained a commission as brigadier general in the provisional army of the Confederacy in August, 1861, and later received the same rank in the Confederate army. The Confederacy placed him in command of troops in Louisiana. Later assignments included temporary command of the Trans-Mississippi Department, in August, 1861, and of the Department of Texas, in 1862. He assumed the command of the subdistrict of north Louisiana and aided in the defense of Vicksburg. The only battle of any consequence in which Hébert participated was the Battle of Milliken's Bend, Louisiana, in June, 1863. He was back in Texas in August, 1864, and remained there until the fall of the Confederacy. He returned to Louisiana in 1865 and received a pardon from President Andrew Johnson that same year.

Although Hébert returned to sugar planting after the war, he became active in politics during Reconstruction. A supporter of the Liberal Republican movement, he attended the Liberal Republican state convention in New Orleans. He endorsed the Liberal Republican presidential candidacy of Horace Greeley in 1872 and opposed the Louisiana Custom House Republican faction. He also supported the Republican governor of Louisiana, Henry Clay Warmoth. After Greeley's defeat in 1872, Hébert changed his support to Ulysses S. Grant and called for a third term for the incumbent president. His new allegiance to Grant secured him an appointment by Governor William Pitt Kellogg to the Board of State Engineers in 1873. The next year, President Grant made him a member of the Commission of Engineers. This commission paid particular attention to Mississippi River projects, one of Hébert's special interests. Hébert shifted political allegiances again in 1876, supporting the Democratic candidates in the state election.

જી

Hébert's engineering background could help explain his particular emphasis on encouraging internal improvements in Louisiana. It was during his administration that four major railroad corporations received their charters, including the New Orleans, Jackson, and Great Northern Railroad Company. His goal was to see that "every part of the State

will be connected [by rail] with the Great Emporium [New Orleans]."[3]
He was not, however, notably successful with land reclamation projects
and even encountered stiff opposition from his own Democratic party.

In contrast to many antebellum southern governors, Hébert took a
serious interest in public education. In his 1855 annual message, he
characterized the educational system of the state as "lame and ineffi-
cient."[4] He called for a total reform of the system, and on March 15,
1855, the legislature responded by providing a free education for all
white children between six and sixteen, with the funding coming from
an annual levy of one mill on all taxable property. Hébert was also interested in higher education. The Constitution of 1845 had provided for
a seminary of learning, but it was not until March 31, 1853, in Hébert's
term, that the legislature undertook its establishment at Alexandria.
The Charity Hospital and education of the deaf, mute, and blind also
received strong support from Hébert. Deeply in debt when he took
office, the Charity Hospital benefited from his attention, and during
1855 and 1856, the institution generated a surplus. The governor's attention to the school for the deaf, mute, and blind considerably improved instruction and care for the children enrolled there.

During Hébert's campaign for governor, Whig newspapers attempted to discredit him with both the Anglo-American and Creole
communities, and he continued to be saddled with the problems of
nativism and Know-Nothingism while in office. The Whig, and later
the Know-Nothing, newspapers claimed that Governor Hébert had become disenchanted with his Democratic party and was ready to effect an
alliance with the Know-Nothings. The Democratic press vehemently
denied the charges. But the embarrassment of the Democrats must
have been intense, considering Hébert's independence when it came to
the exercise of appointment power. On several occasions as governor,
he named Whigs to minor offices. With the advent of the Know-
Nothings, he made several appointments of members of that party to
lucrative posts. Whether he really favored practical rotation in office or
was a disappointed aspirant to the United States Senate who was taking
out his frustrations on his own party, as some claimed, is difficult to
determine. He removed several loyal Democrats after the state legislature selected Slidell as senator in 1855, but he never officially deserted

3. *Ibid.,* 511.
4. *Ibid.,* 515.

the Democrats while he was governor. He did, however, become increasingly aware of growing opposition within his party to some of his projects.

MARIUS M. CARRIERE, JR.

BIBLIOGRAPHY

Carriere, Marius M., Jr. "The Know Nothing Movement in Louisiana." Ph.D. dissertation, Louisiana State University, 1977.
Dupont, Albert L. "The Career of Paul O. Hébert, 1853–1856." *Louisiana Historical Quarterly*, XXXI (1948), 491–552.
McLure, Mary Lilla. *Louisiana Leaders, 1830–1860.* Shreveport, La., 1935.
Soulé, Leon C. *The Know Nothing Party in New Orleans: A Reappraisal.* Baton Rouge, 1961.

Robert C. Wickliffe

Governor, 1856–1860

WICKLIFFE, Robert Charles (b. Bardstown, Kentucky, January 6, 1819; d. Bardstown, April 18, 1895), state senator and governor. Wickliffe was graduated from Centre College of Kentucky. When his father became postmaster general under President John Tyler, Wickliffe moved to Washington, D.C., where he studied law under Hugh Legare, the attorney general of the United States. Wickliffe was admitted to the Kentucky bar. In February, 1843, he married Anna Dawson, daughter of the Louisiana congressman John B. Dawson and niece of governor Isaac Johnson.

ROBERT C. WICKLIFFE. *Photograph courtesy of State Library of Louisiana, from Fortier's History of Louisiana, III, 224.*

Subsequently, Wickliffe came to Louisiana to recover from pneumonia. He lived at his wife's home, Wyoming, in St. Francisville. In 1846, he began a law practice there. During the Mexican War (1846–1848), he won a brevet colonelcy for gallantry while serving with the army of General Winfield Scott in the campaign against Mexico City.

Wickliffe began his political career in 1851, winning a seat in the Louisiana Senate as a Democrat. In 1853, he was reelected. Working with a Democratic majority in the legislature, Wickliffe became chairman of the committee on public education, and his colleagues unanimously elected him president pro tempore of the senate. In the fall of 1854, when the lieutenant governor died, Wickliffe became president of the senate.

Wickliffe had hesitated to let his name be brought forward for the governorship in 1855. But Know-Nothing reverses in Virginia and the rebuff of the Louisiana Know-Nothing delegation at the party's national convention convinced Wickliffe that the party could be beaten. Therefore, he sought and obtained the Democratic gubernatorial nomination and defeated Charles Derbigny, the Know-Nothing candidate, by more than three thousand votes. He carried thirty-one of forty-eight parishes.

In his inaugural address, on January 29, 1856, Wickliffe set the tone for his four years in office. Deprecating congressional interference with domestic institutions—with slavery in particular—Wickliffe advocated a united Democratic South to protect the rights of the states. The governor believed that the Union should be abandoned when northerners outnumbered southerners in the United States Senate. Throughout his administration, he remained preoccupied with southern rights. To secure these rights, he championed a vigorous expansionistic policy for the United States. In his annual message of 1857 to the Louisiana General Assembly, he called for America to annex territories in the Caribbean. Obviously, the governor wanted slavery to spread to "regions so palpably pointed to, by the finger of destiny"—including Cuba, Mexico, and Central America.[1]

Wickliffe was fortunate to have a Democratic legislature during his term as governor, and he devoted some effort to the subjects of banking and railroads. Blaming the loosely managed Board of Currency for the Panic of 1857 in Louisiana, Governor Wickliffe urged the legislature to provide a secretary for that board. The general assembly complied, and Louisiana's banks had to make weekly statements to the secretary of the Board of Currency. While Wickliffe had been a state senator, he had favored state subscription to railroad companies, and he encouraged continued railroad building during his governorship.

1. *Louisiana House Journal*, 1858, p. 7.

Something of a reformer in education while a senator, Wickliffe as governor demonstrated little leadership in that area. He readily admitted a preference for higher education and, while serving as governor, offered not a single suggestion about increasing the attention paid general public education or the funding it received. The proportion of educable children in school was smaller at the end of his term than it had been ten years earlier. A tightfisted legislature reduced Wickliffe's recommended budget of twenty-five thousand dollars for higher education to twenty thousand dollars.

Eventually, Wickliffe's dealings with the Know-Nothing party, his rivalry with the New Orleans city leadership, and his fight against John Slidell, kingpin of the Louisiana Democratic party, were the most salient features of his term as governor. After Wickliffe left office, he returned to his law practice, but he remained active in Democratic politics. In the national election of 1860, he broke with Slidell and sided with Pierre Soulé in support of the presidential candidacy of Stephen A. Douglas, a United States senator from Illinois. Wickliffe was a delegate for Douglas at the national Democratic convention in Baltimore, where Douglas was nominated. Wickliffe was not active in the secession crisis, and during the Civil War he attempted to act as an intermediary between the Confederacy and the Union.

He returned to politics in the postwar period and presided over the Democratic party's convention in New Orleans in 1865. Although the voters in the Third Congressional District elected Wickliffe, Congress denied him a seat in the House of Representatives because of arguments and disagreements in Washington over Reconstruction. He then went into temporary political retirement.

But in time Wickliffe resumed political activity. Twice, in 1876 and 1884, he served as a delegate to the Democratic national convention, supporting respectively Samuel J. Tilden (who lost the election) and Grover Cleveland (who won the presidency). On the state level, in 1892, Wickliffe was the nominee of the Louisiana Lottery faction of the Democratic party for lieutenant governor, but he lost out to the anti-Lottery Democrats led by Murphy J. Foster.

Wickliffe spent most of his last years in Kentucky, and he died in the same town in which he was born.

~

The rapid growth of the Know-Nothing party—also known as the American party—in the United States and Louisiana coincided with

Wickliffe's early administration, and the governor played an important role in opposing the Know-Nothings in the state. He devoted much attention to curtailing election violence in New Orleans, which he and the Democrats associated with the success of the Know-Nothing movement. The Democrats were concerned with the amount of control New Orleans had in the Louisiana General Assembly, as well as the city's influence in general elections. As governor, Wickliffe urged the legislature to impose restrictions upon New Orleans "to prevent her corporate power from becoming abused to promote party purposes."[2] The Democrats in control of the legislature were receptive, and the governor secured a registry law and new city charter for New Orleans in 1856. Wickliffe hoped that the government of New Orleans, which the Know-Nothings dominated, would no longer taint the "purity of the ballot box."[3] The Know-Nothing activities continued in New Orleans, however, and Wickliffe called for, and the legislature passed, a stronger registry law in 1857. But in his message to the legislature in January, 1858, the governor acknowledged that the new and stronger election law for New Orleans had not proved especially successful. Faced with continued election violence in New Orleans, Wickliffe finally sent militia to that city, in 1858. Wickliffe had succeeded in securing legislative controls for New Orleans, but he left office with the Know-Nothings firmly in control of the city's government.

Perhaps Wickliffe's greatest challenge as governor, and his most significant role in state politics, was his contest with Slidell over leadership of the Louisiana Democratic party. During the state elections of 1857, Wickliffe opposed Slidell's choice of candidate in the third Congressional District and backed another candidate. The governor's candidate lost. Wickliffe defied Slidell again by joining Soulé in support of Douglas in the 1860 presidential election. Slidell backed the former Democratic vice-president, John C. Breckinridge, of Kentucky, for president in that campaign. Breckinridge went on to carry Louisiana's electoral votes, although Abraham Lincoln won the national election. Slidell became minister to France for the Confederacy after Louisiana seceded from the Union. Wickliffe's attempt to challenge Slidell for control—or partial control—of the state party leadership had failed.

MARIUS M. CARRIERE, JR.

2. Sidney J. Romero (ed.), *"My Fellow Citizens . . .": The Inaugural Addresses of Louisiana's Governors* (Lafayette, La., 1980), 111.
3. *Ibid.*, 110.

BIBLIOGRAPHY

Carriere, Marius M., Jr. "The Know Nothing Movement in Louisiana." Ph.D. dissertation, Louisiana State University, 1977.

Landry, Thomas R. "The Political Career of Robert Charles Wickliffe, Governor of Louisiana, 1856–1860." *Louisiana Historical Quarterly*, XXV (1942), 670–727.

McLure, Mary Lilla. *Louisiana Leaders, 1830–1860*. Shreveport, La., 1935.

Soulé, Leon C. *The Know Nothing Party in New Orleans: A Reappraisal*. Baton Rouge, 1961.

Thomas O. Moore

Confederate Governor, 1860–1864

MOORE, Thomas Overton (b. Sampson County, North Carolina, April 10, 1804; d. near Alexandria, Louisiana, June 25, 1876), state representative, state senator, and governor. Moore attended schools in Sampson County, North Carolina, and apparently aided his father in running their plantation. At the age of twenty-five, he moved to Rapides Parish, Louisiana, to live with an uncle, Walter H. Overton. The next year, 1830, Moore married Bethiah Jane Leonard, and their union produced five children. He managed Overton's sugar plantation for several years and eventually

THOMAS O. MOORE. *Photograph courtesy of State Library of Louisiana, from Chambers' History of Louisiana, I, 611.*

purchased property of his own. In time, Moore's landholdings increased until he became one of the leading planters in the state. Early, he developed an interest in local politics and served several terms on the parish police jury. In 1848, the people of Rapides Parish elected him to the state house of representatives. He ran successfully for a seat in the state senate in 1856. During his time in the state legislature, he served as a supporter of Governor Joseph M. Walker, another planter from Rapides Parish. Upon Walker's death, Moore became head of the Democratic party in central Louisiana.

John Slidell, head of the regular faction of the state Democratic party, chose Moore as his faction's gubernatorial candidate in 1859. The opposition faction, led by Pierre Soulé, nominated Thomas Jefferson Wells, a native of Rapides Parish. Moore defeated Wells by a vote of 24,434 to 15,587 and took the oath as governor on January 23, 1860.

The growing sectional crisis dominated Moore's early months in office. When the national Democratic party's convention split into northern and southern wings at Charleston, South Carolina, he threw his support to the ticket headed by states' rights advocate John C. Breckinridge, of Kentucky. Moore's considerable influence aided Breckinridge in carrying Louisiana in the 1860 presidential election. The election of the Republican candidate, Abraham Lincoln, however, caused Moore to recommend that the legislature call a convention to decide what course the state would follow. Prior to the convening of the convention, Moore ordered the state militia to seize all federal military installations in Louisiana. When the convention met in January, 1861, its members voted to approve an ordinance of secession. Moore soon appointed Braxton Bragg as a brigadier general to head a state army authorized by the legislature. Moore recognized the need for cooperation among the southern states in secession, and he strongly supported the formation of the Confederate States of America, which the Louisiana legislature voted to join in March, 1861.

Moore encouraged the organization of local defense companies throughout the state and established supply depots and food-processing plants at several locations. The Confederate president, Jefferson Davis, asked Louisiana to supply three thousand men for the Confederate army, and with the outbreak of war after the bombardment of Fort Sumter, in Charleston, South Carolina (April 12–13, 1861), Moore asked for an additional five thousand men to respond to the president's call.

New Orleans was the South's largest financial center, and its banks held a large reserve of gold and silver. Moore asked the banks in the Crescent City to halt payments in specie and ordered them to begin using Confederate treasury notes. He urged Confederate authorities to establish a strong defense system for New Orleans, which he realized would be a major target for attack by United States military forces.

As Moore feared, the Federals, under Flag Officer David G. Farragut, mounted an attack against New Orleans, which fell in April, 1862. Baton Rouge also came under Federal assault. Therefore, in May, 1862,

Moore moved the state capital to Opelousas; later he moved it to Shreveport. After a short stay at Camp Moore, near Tangipahoa, the governor went to Opelousas to direct the state's war effort. From there, he issued an appeal for continued resistance, even though no organized military force remained in the part of the state west of the Mississippi. He called out the state militia to do active duty until regular Confederate units could reach south Louisiana, and he began organizing companies of partisan rangers. Moore issued orders forbidding trade with the enemy and mandating the burning of cotton that might fall into hostile hands. The Confederate War Department ordered Major General Richard Taylor to assume command of all military forces in western Louisiana in July, 1862. Moore cooperated with Taylor in every way he could. He persuaded the legislature to appropriate money for the construction of defensive fortifications and to provide slave labor to aid in the construction. The legislature created a state guard to be filled by men exempt from conscription. This guard would serve as reinforcements to Taylor's regular Confederate army when needed. Moore also obtained legislation to provide support for families whose men were in the army or had died or been disabled in service.

In January, 1864, Moore relinquished the governor's chair to Henry Watkins Allen and retired to his plantation south of Alexandria. A Federal raid up the Red River in the spring of that year forced Moore and his family to become refugees. Union soldiers burned Moore's plantation home and many of its buildings in May, 1864. At the end of the war, Moore again had to flee, because the Union government of the state had ordered his arrest. Moore, Allen, and a number of other former Confederate officials went to Mexico. Moore did not remain there long but made his way to Havana. Eventually, President Andrew Johnson granted him a full pardon, allowing him to return to his home. During the remaining years of his life, he attempted to rebuild his fortunes as a planter but kept clear of any involvement in politics.

∂

Some historians have viewed Moore as a puppet or tool of Slidell in the secession crisis. Moore's political philosophy made him acceptable to the Slidell faction, but his record of support for the idea of secession probably contradicts the idea that he was merely a pawn. Moore recognized very early that for secession to be valid, the Southern states would have to cooperate in forming a new national government. He worked with the Confederate States authorities in forwarding men and supplies to threatened areas, sometimes to the detriment of the defenses of his own state.

Moore's constant warnings about the vulnerability of New Orleans and the lower Mississippi to Federal attack went unheeded by the Confederate high command. He recognized the geographical, political, and economic importance of the Crescent City to the new nation and did not make his requests for aid out of narrow, local interest. Federal occupation of New Orleans and Baton Rouge and enemy incursions into the rich parishes along the Mississippi made Moore's job as governor extremely difficult.

In contrast to Governors Zebulon Vance, of North Carolina, and Joe Brown, of Georgia, Moore firmly supported President Jefferson Davis and the Confederate government. He did not hesitate to apply to President Davis for authority to declare martial law in his own Rapides and several other parishes to quell Union sympathies. Moore supported enforcement of the Confederate Conscription Act and aided in establishing camps of instruction in north and south Louisiana. He recognized the effects of Union control of the Mississippi and became one of the first officials to request a unified military command over the states west of the river. Contemporary accounts attest to Moore's genuine concern for the well-being not only of the soldiers in the field but the families they left at home.

Beset by numerous difficulties and obstacles, Moore performed his job as well as could be expected under trying circumstances.

ARTHUR W. BERGERON, JR.

BIBLIOGRAPHY

Bearss, Edwin C. "The Seizure of the Forts and Public Property in Louisiana." *Louisiana History*, II (1961), 401–409.

Bragg, Jefferson Davis. *Louisiana in the Confederacy*. Baton Rouge, 1941.

Dufour, Charles L. *The Night the War Was Lost*. Garden City, N.Y., 1960.

Greer, J. K. "Louisiana Politics, 1845–1861." *Louisiana Historical Quarterly*, XII (1929), 381–402, 555–610, XIII (1930), 67–116, 257–303, 444–83, 617–54.

McLure, Mary Lilla. "The Elections of 1860 in Louisiana." *Louisiana Historical Quarterly*, IX (1926), 601–702.

Odom, Van D. "The Political Career of Thomas Overton Moore, Secession Governor of Louisiana." *Louisiana Historical Quarterly*, XXVI (1943), 975–1054.

Shugg, Roger W. *Origins of Class Struggle in Louisiana: A Social History of White Farmers and Laborers During Slavery and After, 1840–1875*. Baton Rouge, 1939.

Whittington, G. P. "Thomas O. Moore, Governor of Louisiana, 1860–1864." *Louisiana Historical Quarterly*, XII (1930), 5–31.

Winters, John D. *The Civil War in Louisiana*. Baton Rouge, 1963.

Yearns, W. Buck, ed. *The Confederate Governors*. Athens, Ga., 1985.

Henry Watkins Allen

Confederate Governor, 1864–1865

ALLEN, Henry Watkins (b. Farmville, Virginia, April 29, 1820; d. Mexico City, Mexico, April 22, 1866), Mississippi state representative, Louisiana state representative, Confederate general, and Confederate governor. The son of a well-to-do physician and planter, Allen attended a local county school. In 1833, three years after his mother's death, his father moved the family to Ray County, Missouri. Allen attended Marion College, in Philadelphia, Missouri, but did not graduate. He moved to Grand Gulf, Mississippi, in 1837, and worked as a tutor on a nearby

HENRY WATKINS ALLEN. *Photograph courtesy of State Library of Louisiana.*

plantation for two years. Allen studied law and gained admittance to the Mississippi bar in 1841. He volunteered for a company formed to serve in the Texas militia in early 1842 and became its captain. His unit saw some skirmishing along the Mexican border during the summer of that year. After his company disbanded, Allen resumed his law practice at Grand Gulf. He married Salome Ann Crane on July 2, 1844, who died in January, 1851. They had no children. He served one term (1845–1847) in the Mississippi House of Representatives.

Allen moved to West Baton Rouge Parish, Louisiana, in 1852 and acquired a large sugar plantation. He succeeded in forming a company that built a railroad from the town of West Baton Rouge (modern Port Allen) to Rosedale, on Bayou Grosse Tete. After an unsuccessful attempt to gain election to the Louisiana Senate in 1855, he won a seat in the Louisiana House of Representatives in 1857 as a member of the Know-Nothing (American) party. Switching to the Democratic party late in 1859, he became an administration floor leader. He helped to reorganize the Louisiana Historical Society and became its president in February, 1861.

Allen volunteered as a private in the Delta Rifles Company in December, 1860, and participated in the seizure of the federal arsenal in Baton Rouge on January 13, 1861. After aiding in the formation of several military companies, Allen received an appointment as lieutenant colonel of the 4th Louisiana Infantry Regiment on May 1, 1861. His regiment occupied Ship Island, Mississippi, and Berwick Bay before going to Tennessee in February, 1862. On March 21, 1862, Allen received promotion to colonel of the 4th Louisiana. At the Battle of Shiloh, in Tennessee (April 6–7, 1862), Allen suffered a bullet wound through the cheek. He later commanded a brigade in the Battle of Baton Rouge (August 5, 1862). At Baton Rouge, while leading an attack on a Union artillery battery, Allen fell severely wounded and crippled in both legs. He resigned as colonel of the 4th Louisiana in January, 1863, and served briefly on a military court at Jackson, Mississippi. Governor Thomas O. Moore appointed him major general of the Louisiana militia, but Allen never exercised that command. The Confederate congress promoted Allen to brigadier general on August 19, 1863, and the War Department ordered him to Shreveport to organize paroled prisoners of war.

On November 2, 1863, voters of Confederate Louisiana elected Allen governor. After his inauguration on January 25, 1864, he worked hard to aid both the civilian population of the state and the Confederate war effort. He persuaded the legislature to appropriate money to purchase cotton cards (wire-toothed brushes used to prepare lint cotton for spinning) and medicines for distribution either at cost or free of charge. Eventually, Allen established a state factory to manufacture cotton cards and two facilities for the manufacture of cotton cloth. He tried to control paper money and establish a uniform currency in the state. Allen set up state-operated stores all over the western part of Louisiana. At those facilities citizens might purchase food, clothing, kitchen utensils, shoes, and household goods at low prices if they could afford to do so; if they could not, they received the articles free of charge. Allen supervised a large-scale program to collect cotton for trade and to circumvent the Union blockade by transporting the product through

Texas and Mexico. He established a state laboratory at Mount Lebanon University (a women's academy), in Minden, to make and distribute medicine, and he started a medical dispensary in Shreveport. Allen authorized a geologic survey of the state to locate needed raw materials, and he set up a state mining and manufacturing bureau. In a bold move, he supported the idea of arming slaves to fight for the Confederacy.

In early 1864, Allen raised two battalions of state guards to assist regular Confederate military units, particularly in the apprehension of jayhawkers, draft dodgers, and deserters. These two battalions became the 8th Louisiana Cavalry Regiment late in that year. Upon hearing of General Robert E. Lee's surrender in Virginia, Allen at first advocated continued resistance in the Trans-Mississippi Department but soon urged the surrender of Confederate armies there. He issued a farewell message on June 2, 1865, and went into exile.

Allen crossed into Mexico with other Confederate military and governmental leaders and reached Mexico City in July, 1865. There he published a newspaper in English called the *Mexican Times*. Against his wishes, Allen's supporters in Louisiana placed his name on the gubernatorial ballot in November, 1865. Thousands of men voted for Allen, and he carried five parishes. After his death, Allen's friends buried his body in the American Cemetery in Mexico City. Friends in Louisiana reinterred his remains in New Orleans in January, 1867, and finally, on the grounds of the state capitol in Baton Rouge in 1885.

☙

Though of short duration, the administration of Henry Watkins Allen showed many positive accomplishments. The historian Douglas Southall Freeman has dubbed Allen "the single great administrator produced by the Confederacy."[1]

Allen's programs brought much-needed relief to the destitute citizens of the state and succeeded in raising hundreds of thousands of dollars for the state treasury. His agents supplied soldiers and civilians alike with food, clothing, and medicines. He strongly supported public schools, kept them operating, and sponsored the publication of books for children. Allen's financial reforms made state-issued money more valuable than Confederate notes by the end of the war. Though he had some disagreements with Confederate authorities over the irregular

---

1. Douglas Southall Freeman, "Henry Watkins Allen," *Dictionary of American Biography*, (20 vols.; New York, 1928–44), I, 193.

impressment of animals and provisions, he worked well with General Edmund Kirby Smith and adhered to the Confederate cause until he saw that there remained no hope of success.

Vincent Cassidy and Amos Simpson, Allen's most recent biographers, have aptly summed up his term as governor: "Allen had established order, had restored confidence, had demonstrated the concern of the state for the welfare of its people."[2]

ARTHUR W. BERGERON, JR.

BIBLIOGRAPHY

Bragg, Jefferson Davis. *Louisiana in the Confederacy*. Baton Rouge, 1941.

Cassidy, Vincent H., and Amos E. Simpson. *Henry Watkins Allen of Louisiana*. Baton Rouge, 1964.

Chandler, Luther E. "The Career of Henry Watkins Allen." Ph.D. dissertation, Louisiana State University, 1940.

Dorsey, Sarah A. *Recollections of Henry Watkins Allen, Brigadier-General, Confederate States Army, Ex-Governor of Louisiana*. New York, 1866.

East, Charles E. "The Journalistic Career of Henry Watkins Allen." M.A. thesis, Louisiana State University, 1962.

Freeman, Douglas Southall. "Henry Watkins Allen." *Dictionary of American Biography*. Vol. I of 20 vols., 191–93. New York, 1928.

Simpson, Amos E., and Vincent H. Cassidy. "The Wartime Administration of Governor Henry W. Allen." *Louisiana History*, V (1964), 257–69.

Winters, John D. *The Civil War in Louisiana*. Baton Rouge, 1963.

Yearns, W. Buck, ed. *The Confederate Governors*. Athens, Ga., 1985.

George F. Shepley

Military Governor, 1862–1864

SHEPLEY, George Foster (b. Saco, Maine, January 1, 1819; d. Portland, Maine, July 20, 1878), judge, army officer, and military governor. Shepley was the son of Ether Shepley and Ann Foster. His father was a prominent Democrat in Maine politics and served as a United States senator and as chief justice of the state's supreme court. Shepley was graduated from Dartmouth College in 1837. After reading law for a time at Harvard and with his father, he was admitted to the bar and began his practice at Bangor, Maine, in 1839. In 1844, he married Lucy Ann Hayes, and in that year, he moved to Portland, Maine, where he

---

2. Vincent H. Cassidy and Amos E. Simpson, *Henry Watkins Allen of Louisiana* (Baton Rouge, 1964), 113.

acquired a large law practice and, in 1848–1849, served as the United States district attorney for Maine. Shepley lost that position when Zachary Taylor, a Whig, became president. But in 1853, he was reappointed by the Democratic president, Franklin Pierce, and he continued to serve through the administration of James Buchanan, also a Democrat.

Shepley was a delegate to the Democratic national convention at Charleston, South Carolina, in 1860, and to the adjourned convention at Baltimore, where he supported the candidacy of Senator Stephen A.

GEORGE F. SHEPLEY. *Photograph from* Photographic History of the Civil War, *ed. F. T. Miller (10 vols.; New York, 1912), X, 211.*

Douglas, of Illinois. At Baltimore, Shepley formed a close relationship with another candidate, Benjamin Franklin Butler. With the outbreak of war in 1861, he obtained a commission as colonel of the 12th Maine Volunteer Infantry, and because of his friendship with Butler, his regiment was incorporated into the Federal expedition against New Orleans. By the time the city was captured, he was acting brigadier general in command of the 3rd Brigade.

After the fall of New Orleans on May 1, 1862, Shepley was appointed commandant of the city, and he was given the duties of acting mayor once General Butler had removed the mayor and city council. He served in that capacity until June 2, 1862, when he was appointed military governor of Louisiana. In the following month, he was promoted to brigadier general. Butler remained as commander of the Department of the Gulf, with headquarters in New Orleans. The appointment of Shepley as military governor placed a buffer between the tactless Butler and foreign diplomats, who had complained of his heavy-handed dealings with the consulates in the Crescent City.

Shepley's chief function as military governor was to preside over the embryo civil government in the part of Louisiana occupied by Federal troops, which included New Orleans and the several surrounding parishes. When Major General Nathaniel Prentiss Banks replaced Butler as commander of the Gulf department in December, 1862, the first positive steps were taken to move the occupied parishes of Louisiana toward full civil government. In the following year, contending factions in Louisiana debated the crucial questions of the status of slavery and free blacks, under the watchful eyes of the Lincoln administration and the close supervision of General Banks. During this time, Governor Shepley served as little more than a functionary who received the petitions of citizens' groups and acted as spokesman for the authorities in Washington. Subsequently, an election of state officers was held in fourteen parishes in southeastern Louisiana. On February 22, 1864, Michael Hahn was elected the first civil governor of the state under federal authority since secession.

After Hahn was inaugurated on March 4, Shepley was transferred to the Virginia theater. He was given command of the eastern district of Virginia in May, 1864, within the department commanded by his old friend Butler. When Butler was removed by General Ulysses S. Grant the following November, Shepley was investigated for mishandling the administration of his district. The investigation seems to have been perfunctory and merely a means of demoting a close associate of Butler's. Afterward, Shepley served on the staff of Major General Godfrey Weitzel, commander of the XXV Army Corps. When Richmond fell on April 3, 1865, Shepley became military governor of the former Confederate capital, and he occupied that office until the end of June.

Shepley resigned from the army in late June and returned to Maine, where he resumed the practice of law at Portland. He declined a seat on the United States Supreme Court, but from 1869 until death he was United States judge for the First Judicial District of Maine. His first wife having died in 1859, he married Helen Merrill in 1872. In 1878, Dartmouth College conferred on him an honorary doctorate of laws. He died in Portland, reportedly of Asiatic cholera and is buried there in Evergreen Cemetery.

❧

The ultimate problem in evaluating Shepley's career is that he was never his own man. He always acted on the order or carried out the policy of someone else. One authority holds Shepley as culpable for the corruption charged to Butler as Butler himself, simply because he was Butler's right-hand man. While serving as military governor, Shepley presided over the events of early Reconstruction in Louisiana in name only. For nearly two years, during a time of turmoil and uncertainty, when momentous decisions were being made, he never participated in those decisions and had only a perfunctory role in carrying them out. Shepley's career would seem to present the happy, and perhaps rare, circumstance of the man of limited ability who is accorded limited authority.

F. WAYNE BINNING

BIBLIOGRAPHY

Caskey, Willie M. *Secession and Restoration of Louisiana.* Baton Rouge, 1938.
Dawson, Joseph G. III. *Army Generals and Reconstruction: Louisiana, 1862–1877.* Baton Rouge, 1982.
McCrary, Peyton. *Abraham Lincoln and Reconstruction: The Louisiana Experiment.* Princeton, 1978.
Ripley, C. Peter. *Slaves and Freedmen in Civil War Louisiana.* Baton Rouge, 1976.
Taylor, Joe Gray. *Louisiana Reconstructed, 1863–1877.* Baton Rouge, 1974.
Trefousse, Hans L. *Ben Butler: The South Called Him Beast!* New York, 1957.
West, Richard S. *Lincoln's Scapegoat General: A Life of Benjamin F. Butler, 1818–1893.* Boston, 1965.

Michael Hahn

Governor, 1864–1865

HAHN, Georg Michael Decker (b. Klingemunster, Bavaria [Germany], November 24, 1830; d. Washington, D.C., March 15, 1886), congressman, governor, state representative, speaker of the state house of representatives, and federal judge. Hahn was short and dark complexioned, with a broad, square face and dark, curly hair. One leg was shorter than the other, and he walked with a crutch. The facts concerning his birth and early childhood are obscure. He was born Georg Michael Decker, the child of Mrs. Hahn (née Decker), who had been widowed for almost two years

MICHAEL HAHN. *Photograph courtesy of State Library of Louisiana.*

when she gave birth to her son. The mother and her five children emigrated to America; they stayed briefly in New York, then moved to

Texas, and had settled in New Orleans in the city's German community by 1840. One year later, Hahn's mother died during a yellow-fever epidemic.

Orphaned and thrown upon his own resources, young Hahn completed his elementary education in the New Orleans public schools. At the age of nineteen, he began reading law under the direction of Christian Roselius, a prominent Whig politician and an able attorney. Hahn also studied law at the University of Louisiana (modern Tulane University). After his graduation from the law department, on April 7, 1851, Hahn entered into the civic and political life of New Orleans. Elected at the age of twenty-two to the city school board, he served for several years as either a school director or president of the school system.

The young, ambitious attorney joined the Democratic party and allied himself with the faction headed by Pierre Soulé. Locally, the Soulé Democrats stood opposed to John ("King John") Slidell. In national politics, they supported Stephen A. Douglas, a senator from Illinois. During the 1860 presidential election, Hahn served on the state committee that ran Douglas' campaign in Louisiana.

In the secession crisis, Hahn emerged as an outspoken Unionist. At a mass meeting held in Lafayette Square on May 8, 1860, he delivered an ardent antisecessionist speech and put forth a list of pro-Union resolutions. During the brief period of Confederate rule in New Orleans, he cleverly avoided taking the oath of allegiance to the rebel government, although he did become a notary public under the regime. When the United States Army liberated the city, Hahn immediately associated himself with the Federal occupation, helping to organize Union associations and working closely with the military commanders.

As a result of President Abraham Lincoln's design for restoring civil government, elections were ordered for the First and Second Congressional Districts, the districts then controlled by the Union army. Lincoln hoped that the elections would encourage Unionism and thereby weaken the Confederate cause. Facing three opponents, Hahn entered the race for the Second District seat with the strong backing of the city's German immigrants. The complete returns were never published, but Hahn won easily. Two months later, the United States House of Representatives voted by a wide margin to seat Hahn and Benjamin Franklin Flanders, the winner in the First District. Their tenure, however, was short: they were seated on February 3, 1863, but the Thirty-seventh Congress adjourned on March 4, 1863. While in Washington, Hahn voted with the Republican administration and developed a close relationship with Abraham Lincoln that continued when Hahn returned home. The president, who took a keen interest in Louisiana politics, relied upon Hahn for political intelligence and patronage recommendations. Hahn himself became a federal prize commissioner in New Orleans.

From June to November, 1863, little progress was made toward the restoration of civil government in the Pelican State despite Lincoln's requests for action. Lincoln demanded that the issue be pressed, and directed that Major General Nathaniel Prentiss Banks assume control of Reconstruction in the state. To speed up the process, Banks decided to hold state elections on February 22, 1864, and then call a constitutional convention. Thus the election was to be held on the basis of the old proslavery Constitution of 1852. Flanders and Thomas Jefferson Durant, two prominent radical Union men, opposed the plan. Hahn, however, was more than willing to cooperate with Banks. At this point, Hahn purchased a proslavery newspaper, the New Orleans *True Delta*, and converted it to moderate Unionism. Hahn rode to victory on a military bandwagon. He won 6,183 votes, or 54 percent of the 11,411 votes cast. The conservative candidate, J. Q. A. Fellows, came in second, with 2,996 votes, or 26 percent of the total. Flanders, the radical candidate, ran third with 2,232, or 20 percent. Encouraged by the victory, Lincoln added to Hahn's authority the duties and powers of military governor.

As governor, Hahn played a leading role in the state constitutional convention of 1864 and worked closely with the new state legislature. But despite his new authority and President Lincoln's good will, Hahn ran into opposition from Major General Stephen A. Hurlbut, the recently appointed commander of the Department of the Gulf, an officer concerned chiefly with civil affairs in the occupied region. General Hurlbut insisted that until Congress approved Lincoln's plan of Reconstruction, the army was supreme in Louisiana. Although Hahn appealed to the president, the new governor was nearly impotent politically in the face of General Hurlbut's refusal to recognize his authority in any important matter, like government appointments. Angered and frustrated, Hahn reluctantly accepted nomination by the state legislature to the United States Senate. Elected senator in January, 1865, he resigned the governorship on March 3. After Lincoln's assassination the next month, the Congress was unwilling to seat senators and representatives fom the South, and Hahn's claims to the office were never pressed.

Hahn then allied himself with the Louisiana Radicals and became a leader in calling for a convention to revise the Constitution of 1864 to include a provision for black suffrage. The state's former Confederates adamantly opposed black rights, and black suffrage in particular. The conservative leaders of New Orleans and the state did nothing to prevent violence from being used to disrupt the Radicals' convention. Hahn was nearly murdered by white thugs during the New Orleans police riot of July 30, 1866. But he proved indefatigable. In 1867, he became editor and manager of the New Orleans *Republican*, where he continued his career in journalism until 1871.

In 1872, Hahn went to live on his sugar plantation in St. Charles Parish. There he founded the village of Hahnville and set up a local newspaper, the *St. Charles Herald*. He became a public-school director and in 1872 served as president of the Louisiana state education convention. He was elected to three terms in the state legislature in 1872, 1874, and 1876. During his tenure, he served as chairman of the judiciary committee and, for a time, as speaker of the house. He was appointed state registrar of voters on August 15, 1876, and was superintendent of the United States mint at New Orleans from June, 1878, to January, 1879, and federal district judge for St. John, St. Charles, and Jefferson parishes from 1879 to 1885. During the 1880 elections, he founded and edited yet another newspaper, the New Orleans *Ledger*, to promote Republican candidates.

Although he first refused the nomination, Hahn became the Republican candidate for Congress in the Second District in the election of 1884. The district was heavily Democratic, but Hahn won with a majority of 1,300 votes. He did not live to complete his term. A bachelor, he died at the age of fifty-five, alone in his room at the Willard Hotel, in Washington, D.C., of a ruptured blood vessel near the heart. He was later buried in Metairie, Louisiana.

Unlike many Louisiana politicians, Hahn died broke.

❧

Hahn's inauguration ceremony in 1864 was a lavish spectacle. The event began with eight thousand school children signing "Hail Columbia." After the inaugural address, an orchestra of five hundred musicians played the "Anvil Chorus," accompanied by forty blacksmiths keeping time on their anvils and fifty pieces of artillery booming in cadence. The featured speaker was General Banks. The presence of the Union officer and the salute of the Yankee guns were clear indications of the basis of Hahn's political power during his brief, unhappy tenure. Once that support was withdrawn and power was unequally divided between military officers and civilians, the governor's position became untenable.

After the "redemption" of Louisiana by the conservative Democrats, Hahn remained active in state politics—evidence that he had made peace with his political enemies. The Democrats approved of his essential conservatism and considered him the least objectionable of the leading Republicans. Indeed, Hahn was one of the few politicians, Republican or Democrat, to emerge from Reconstruction and the Gilded Age with his reputation intact.

Yet he deserves more credit than that. With Lincoln's aid and encouragement, he had been in the forefront of the movement to advance the cause of black rights in Louisiana. During his administration, Louisiana abolished slavery and adopted a constitutional provision that allowed for the future enfranchisement of black men. During this time, the state laid the foundations of a black school system and began the process of Reconstruction. That these achievements were limited and later frustrated does not negate the importance of Hahn's contribution. What he attempted was remarkable considering the intransigence of white Louisianians, the Unionist factionalism, and the lack of popular support for racial reform in the state except among blacks and a handful of carpetbaggers and scalawags. What Hahn attempted took a good measure of idealism and a great deal of courage.

FRANK J. WETTA

BIBLIOGRAPHY

Cox, Lawanda. *Lincoln and Black Freedom: A Study in Presidential Leadership.* Columbia, S.C., 1981.

Dawson, Joseph G. III. *Army Generals and Reconstruction: Louisiana, 1862–1877.* Baton Rouge, 1982.

Simpson, Amos E., and Vaughan B. Baker. "Michael Hahn, Steady Patriot." *Louisiana History,* XIII (1972), 229–52.

McCrary, Peyton. *Abraham Lincoln and Reconstruction: The Louisiana Experiment.* Princeton, 1978.

Vandal, Gilles. *The New Orleans Riot of 1866: Anatomy of a Tragedy.* Lafayette, La., 1983.

Wetta, Frank J. "The Louisiana Scalawags." Ph.D. dissertation, Louisiana State University, 1977.

James Madison Wells

Governor, 1865–1867

WELLS, James Madison (b. near Alexandria, Louisiana, January 8, 1808; d. Lecompte, Louisiana, February 18, 1899), lieutenant governor, governor, and chairman of the State Returning Board. Samuel Levi Wells, Wells's father, sired a family of fourteen children and acquired large landholdings in central Louisiana. Left an orphan at the age of eight, Wells came under the care of paternal aunts. He was sent north for most of his schooling, matriculating at St. Joseph's College, a Jesuit institution, in Bardstown, Kentucky, and at Alden Partridge's Academy, in Middletown, Con-

JAMES MADISON WELLS. *Photograph courtesy of State Library of Louisiana.*

necticut. Wells completed his education at the Cincinnati Law School. In Cincinnati, he also read law in the offices of the attorney Charles Hammond. Evidently, being educated in the North and exposed to Hammond's nationalist convictions had a great influence on Wells.

Returning to his native state in 1830, he operated three plantations in central Louisiana. In 1833, he married fifteen-year-old Mary Ann Scott; the couple had fourteen children. During the 1850s, Wells increased his property in dairy cattle. By 1860, he had purchased nearly one hundred slaves. A Whig in politics, he served as sheriff of Rapides Parish on the appointment of Governor André Bienvenu Roman.

After the breakup of the national Whig party, Wells was a political orphan. During the exciting presidential election of 1860, he cast his ballot for the Democrat Stephen A. Douglas. In 1861, Wells's outspoken devotion to the Union and his opposition to secession brought criticism from some of his neighbors, including his brother, Montfort Wells.

Wells remained loyal to the Union during the Civil War. Confederate officials arrested him for his Union sympathies, and he fled to the woods to escape arrest on two other occasions. In 1864, he helped form the Unconditional Union Club of Western Louisiana. By that time, the Federal army controlled all or part of seventeen parishes in south Louisiana.

In 1864, Wells, because of his well-known Unionism, was nominated for the office of lieutenant governor by both factions of the Free State (Unionist) party—the radicals, led by Benjamin Franklin Flanders, and the moderates, by Michael Hahn. Wells kept silent during the campaign, not revealing his conservative opposition to black rights. The election was held under President Abraham Lincoln's Reconstruction plan and supervised by the United States Army. Wells was elected easily, and Hahn won the governor's race. They were inaugurated on March 4, 1864.

As lieutenant governor, Wells attended the constitutional convention of 1864 and supported the conservative position of compensated emancipation. The new constitution abolished slavery—without compensation to owners—and provided increased funding for public education but did not authorize black suffrage. In an unusual move, the president of the convention adjourned the body subject to future recall. On January 9, 1865, the new state legislature elected Governor Hahn to the United States Senate. Hahn's resignation took effect on March 3, and Wells was inaugurated as governor on March 4.

Wells's governorship was stormy and marked by widespread political animosity. Under the unique conditions of the postbellum period, the United States Army's orders could overrule those of civil officials. Wells took steps to implement President Andrew Johnson's lenient plan of Reconstruction. In the process, however, Wells ran afoul of both the military authorities and former Confederates. On June 3, 1867, after Congress had passed the Military Reconstruction Acts of 1867, giving the army unusual powers within southern military districts, General Philip H. Sheridan removed Wells from office for acting as an "impediment to Reconstruction." Wells went home to Rapides Parish.

Returning to politics in 1872, Wells supported the reelection of Republican President Ulysses S. Grant. The following year, the Louisiana Republicans made Wells chairman of the State Returning Board, an influential agency that could determine the legality of election ballots and discard fraudulent votes. As chairman of the returning board, Wells helped to give a slight edge to the Republicans in 1874. In reward, he was appointed surveyor of customs for the port of New Orleans. In the crucial election of 1876, the State Returning Board decided that the Democrats had used fraud and intimidation, and it canceled enough Democratic ballots to give Louisiana's electoral count to Rutherford B. Hayes, the Republican presidential candidate. Hayes went on to win the presidency and permitted Francis R. T. Nicholls, a Democrat, to become governor of Louisiana as a part of the Compromise of 1877. Wells was surveyor of customs until 1880, when he retired.

꼐

Taking office under difficult circumstances, Wells had a question to answer. What was his constituency—moderate Unionists, Republicans, and blacks (who could not yet vote), or conservative Unionists, former Confederates, and Confederate sympathizers? There were more men in the second group, and Wells sided with the conservatives, most of whom were Democrats. For an inexperienced leader, Wells dared to take politicial risks: opposing General Banks, the Union officer who had patched together Louisiana's Free State party; supporting former secessionist Hugh Kennedy for the mayorship of New Orleans; and appointing numerous former Confederates to state and local offices. In a meeting with President Johnson, Wells seemed to find a comrade; the two southern Unionists and former slaveowners wanted a mild Reconstruction, and both had doubts about the trustworthiness of Yankee "radicals."

Running as a Democrat on November 6, 1865, Wells was elected governor in a special election over the former Confederate governor Henry Watkins Allen, an exile in Mexico, by a count of 22,312 to 5,497. Allen's surprising strength (he was a write-in candidate) may have pushed Wells more toward the conservatives. In a special message to the new legislature, which was heavily peppered with Democrats, Wells recommended dismantling public education. He urged that only taxes from blacks should be used to fund freedmen's schools. Wells also asked the legislature to appropriate money for levee repairs, a new state capital, and a new state penitentiary. The legislature ignored his suggestions, spending its time electing United States senators (whom Congress rejected) and passing a series of laws known as black codes, which restricted the rights of freedmen.

The next session intensified the rivalry between the governor and the legislature. Wells vetoed bills to permit new elections in New Orleans and other locales; the legislature passed the bills over his veto. The next mayor of New Orleans had been mayor during the Civil War, and the sheriff a former Confederate officer. They gained office by defeating candidates favored by Wells. The governor and the onetime Confederates had broken ranks.

To the surprise of many, Wells supported the reconvocation of the constitutional convention of 1864—which appeared bent on giving blacks the right to vote—despite the dubious legality of recalling it. Like a chameleon, Wells had gone from conservative to radical almost overnight. During July, 1866, emotions for and against the convention ran high. Finally, on July 30, a race riot occurred at the site of the convention. Wells and other state and city officials had taken few precautions to prevent violence, and General Sheridan, a Radical Republican and the senior army officer in the state, held Wells responsible.

During the remainder of 1866, Wells appointed some Unionists to office, urged the legislature to ratify the proposed Fourteenth Amendment to the United States Constitution (it was rejected), and sought funding for black schools. Despite Wells's apparent change of political heart, Sheridan did not trust him. Using an argument over the proper membership on the state's levee board as a ploy, Sheridan removed the vacillating governor from office, remarking that Wells's "conduct has been as sinuous as the mark left in the dust by the movement of a snake."[1] Sheridan chose Flanders as the new governor.

Wells, in his checkered career, made no major contribution to the development of the Louisiana executive branch beyond continuing the time-honored tradition of battling with the legislature. In fact, his political vacillation probably hurt the state when it most needed moderate, consistent, and farsighted leadership. No one doubted Wells's loyalty to the Union, but he gambled that Reconstruction would be simple and that returning Confederates would run state government. He was wrong on both counts. Wells, who was not an experienced politician, misjudged the political winds, especially those blowing from the North after Lincoln's assassination. He failed to cooperate satisfactorily with the army generals sent to supervise the postwar government, at the same time that he was insufficiently conservative to placate former Confederates. Ironically, Wells returned to politics as a Republican, be-

1. Philip H. Sheridan to Edwin M. Stanton, June 3, 1867, in *House Executive Documents,* 40th Cong., 1st Sess., No. 20, p. 65. See also Joseph G. Dawson III, *Army Generals and Reconstruction: Louisiana, 1862–1877* (Baton Rouge, 1982), 53–54.

coming a scalawag in the 1870s. It is no wonder that he was known as Mad Wells.

JOSEPH G. DAWSON III

BIBLIOGRAPHY

Dawson, Joseph G. III. *Army Generals and Reconstruction: Louisiana, 1862–1877.* Baton Rouge, 1982.

Lowrey, Walter M. "The Political Career of James Madison Wells." *Louisiana Historical Quarterly,* XXXI (1948), 995–1123.

McCrary, Peyton. *Abraham Lincoln and Reconstruction: The Louisiana Experiment.* Princeton, 1978.

Taylor, Joe Gray. *Louisiana Reconstructed, 1863–1877.* Baton Rouge, 1974.

Vandal, Gilles. *The New Orleans Riot of 1866: Anatomy of a Tragedy.* Lafayette, La., 1983.

Wetta, Frank J. "The Louisiana Scalawags." Ph.D. dissertation, Louisiana State University, 1977.

Benjamin Franklin Flanders

Military Governor, 1867–1868

FLANDERS, Benjamin Franklin (b. Bristol, New Hampshire, January 26, 1816; d. near Youngstown, Louisiana, March 13, 1896), congressman, treasury agent, governor, and mayor of New Orleans. Fourth son of Jospeh Flanders and Relief Brown, Flanders attended New Hampton Academy, New Hampshire, and graduated from Dartmouth College in 1842. He moved to New Orleans one year later, and read law under Charles M. Emerson, a fellow Dartmouth graduate. Deciding not to pursue a legal career, Flanders became a principal and teacher in the New

BENJAMIN FRANKLIN FLANDERS. *Photograph courtesy of State Library of Louisiana, from Edwin L. Jewel's* Crescent City Illustrated, *143.*

Orleans schools during 1844–1845. In 1847, he returned to Bristol, New Hampshire, to marry Susan H. Sawyer. Their union produced six children. From 1848 until 1852, Flanders served as an alderman representing the third municipal district of New Orleans. In 1852, he became the secretary and treasurer of the Opelousas and Great Western Railroad. He remained in that position until January, 1862.

When the Civil War broke out, Flanders opposed the secessionists and demonstrated his Unionist sympathies by displaying the American flag. Angered by his act of bravado, a vigilante committee drove him from New Orleans. Fleeing northward, he left his wife and children behind, barely escaping with his life. He made his way to Cairo, Illinois, and Columbus, Ohio, and wound up in New York City. But he returned to Louisiana soon after Federal troops liberated the Crescent City in April, 1862.

Major General Benjamin Franklin Butler appointed Flanders city treasurer, and he served in that capacity from July 20 until December 10, 1862. He resigned the position when he was elected to Congress under unusual circumstances. As part of President Abraham Lincoln's "plan" of Reconstruction, special elections were held in the two congressional districts then under Union control. Butler initiated the first phase in the reestablishment of civil government in Louisiana when he ordered that an election be held on December 12, 1862, for congressmen to represent the First and Second Congressional Districts. Unionists endorsed Flanders for the First District seat. He won easily over an independent candidate, John Bouligny. The United States House of Representatives voted by a narrow margin to seat Flanders and Michael Hahn, the winner in the Second District. Their tenures were brief (February 3–March 3, 1863) and ended when the Thirty-seventh Congress adjourned.

On July 13, 1863, Flanders was made a captain of Company C of the 5th Regiment of Louisiana Volunteers, a Union regiment. He left the service with an honorable discharge on August 12, 1863. By that time, President Lincoln valued Flanders' suggestions regarding patronage and his observations on political developments in Louisiana. In 1863, Salmon P. Chase, the secretary of the treasury, appointed Flanders the supervising special agent of the Treasury Department of the southern region (Louisiana, Texas, Mississippi, Alabama, and western Florida). He held that position, which was a patronage plum, until 1866, earning almost three thousand dollars in commissions from the sale of confiscated cotton. Meanwhile, he remained active in Louisiana politics. He campaigned for the governorship in 1864. In a special election managed by the army, Flanders, considered a radical Unionist, ran a weak third against the former congressman Michael Hahn, a moderate Unionist, and J. Q. A. Fellows, a conservative Unionist. He won only 20 percent of the vote. Nevertheless, he retained his support in Washington. After the election, he became the first supervising special agent of the Freedmen's Bureau in the Department of the Gulf.

Flanders was a leader in the movement that led to the creation of the Republican party in Louisiana. In reaction to President Andrew Johnson's Reconstruction policies and the conservatism of Governor James Madison Wells, a fellow Unionist then in temporary alliance with the former rebels, Flanders and the scalawag leaders formed the Friends of Universal Suffrage. The object was to promote black suffrage and to secure the repeal of the Louisiana black codes. The formation of the Friends marked the transformation of a rather loosely organized pressure group into a tightly structured political-action committee. The next step was the creation of a formal party apparatus. Flanders stood out among the 111 scalawag, carpetbagger, and black delegates who in September, 1865, held meetings that gave birth to the Republican party in Louisiana. Reading the first public statement of the new party, Flanders said that the people of Louisiana had to accept certain revolutionary developments: slavery was dead, "swept away by the tempest of war," and "the people of African descent [were] now free and as free as all other men."[1] Accordingly, white men would be required to do more than uphold the narrow legal aspects of emancipation. All were "now bound in conscience and honor to treat each man as he himself would be treated."[2]

On June 9, 1867, Major General Philip H. Sheridan, commander of the Fifth Military District under the congressional Military Reconstruction Acts of 1867, used his authority to remove Governor Wells from office and appointed Flanders military governor of Louisiana. As governor, Flanders served under Sheridan (June 9–September 5, 1867), Brevet Major General Charles Griffin (September 5–15, 1867), and Brevet Major General Joseph A. Mower (September 15–November 29, 1867). On January 1, 1868, after Major General Winfield Scott Hancock, a conservative Democrat, took command of the district, Flanders resigned in protest over Hancock's removal of Radicals from state offices.

1. *Proceedings of the Convention of the Republican Party of Louisiana, Held at Economy Hall, New Orleans, September 25, 1865* (N.p., n.d.), 18–19.
2. *Ibid.*, 19–20.

In May, 1870, the young carpetbag governor Henry Clay Warmoth appointed Flanders mayor of New Orleans. In November of that year, he was elected to a two-year term as mayor. Three years later, President Ulysses S. Grant made Flanders assistant treasurer of the United States at New Orleans. Flanders remained in that federal job until 1882. In 1888, he was the unsuccessful Republican candidate for state treasurer. Despite his failure to return to elective office, the post-Reconstruction years seem to have been economically good ones for Flanders. He died on his plantation, Ben Alva, in Lafayette Parish.

⤙

Although a Northerner by birth, Flanders lived in Louisiana eighteen years prior to the Civil War; he was a Louisianian by adoption. Well educated and financially successful, he did not see in the disruptive years of war and Reconstruction a chance to rise above a hardscrabble existence at the expense of the old ruling class. Nor was Flanders a political adolescent; he demonstrated a talent for politics and had experience in city government during the antebellum years. He was motivated by a strong sense of nationalism; his Republicanism can be seen as an extension of his wartime Unionism. Thus in economic, social, educational, and political background, Flanders was similar to some of the more important southern white Republican leaders—the so-called scalawags—in Louisiana and the South.

During the hectic years of military occupation and political upheaval, Flanders allied with the Radical wing of the Unionist movement. He championed the emancipation of the slaves, the confiscation of rebel property, the recruitment of black soldiers, and the granting of black suffrage. But George Denison, a fellow Radical, noted, "Politically Mr. F. is an Abolitionist, but not of the bloodthirsty kind." Denison implied that Flanders came to support Negro voting rights only reluctantly.[3]

White collaborationists, like Flanders, and their carpetbag and black allies formed the bone and sinew of the Republican party. Nevertheless, Flanders and his associates were not always united on either political strategy or objectives. He and other Unionist Republicans were deeply involved in the self-destructive factional wars over control of the party and spoils of office that sapped the strength and weakened the cohesion of the Republican movement in Louisiana.

3. George S. Denison to Salmon P. Chase, November 28, 1862, in *Diary and Correspondence of Salmon P. Chase, Annual Report of the American Historical Association* (2 vols.; Washington, D.C., 1903), II, 335.

In sum, Flanders will be remembered not for his seven months as governor of Louisiana but for his role in the creation of the state Republican party. The litany of his service to the Republican party and his officeholding indicate that he was a shrewd Gilded Age politician—a faithful soldier in Lincoln's Republican army. Thus, Flanders is best described as a middle-level politician and party functionary.

FRANK J. WETTA

BIBLIOGRAPHY

Caskey, Willie M. *Secession and Restoration of Louisiana.* Baton Rouge, 1938.

Cox, LaWanda. *Lincoln and Black Freedom: A Study in Presidential Leadership.* Columbia, S.C., 1981.

Dawson, Joseph G. III. *Army Generals and Reconstruction: Louisiana, 1862–1877.* Baton Rouge, 1982.

McCrary, Peyton. *Abraham Lincoln and Reconstruction: The Louisiana Experiment.* Princeton, 1978.

Taylor, Joe Gray. *Louisiana Reconstructed, 1863–1877.* Baton Rouge, 1974.

Wetta, Frank J. "The Louisiana Scalawags." Ph.D. dissertation, Louisiana State University, 1977.

Joshua Baker

Military Governor, 1868

BAKER, Joshua (b. Mason County, Kentucky, March 23, 1799; d. Lynne, Connecticut, April 15, 1885), army officer, engineer, and governor. In 1803, Baker's parents moved from Kentucky to Mississippi, and in 1811, they settled at Oak Lawn Plantation in St. Mary Parish, Louisiana. Baker received his elementary education at Lexington Academy, in Kentucky. Upon the recommendation of Henry Clay, of Kentucky, then speaker of the United States House of Representatives, Baker entered the United States Military Academy, at West Point, on October 25, 1817. An able student, he

JOSHUA BAKER. *Photograph courtesy of Special Collections, Hill Memorial Library, Louisiana State University, from oil painting attributed to Adolph D. Rinck, used by permission of Mrs. C. A. Lanaux Rareshide.*

completed all the required courses within two years and graduated tenth in a class of twenty-nine cadets. On July 1, 1819, he was commissioned a second lieutenant of artillery. In October, he returned to West Point to become an assistant professor of "natural and experimental philosophy." He remained in that position until October 31, 1820, when his resignation from the army took effect.

After leaving the army, Baker studied law in Kentucky and was admitted to the bar. Moving to Opelousas, in the Attakapas region of Louisiana, he opened a law office with John Bronson and practiced law from 1822 to 1829 and from 1832 to 1838 but did not confine his activities to legal work. He served as engineer of the Plaquemines Company (1827–1829), judge of St. Mary Parish and judge of probate *ex officio* for the parish (1829–1839), assistant engineer of the state of Louisiana (1833–1838), director of public works of the state of Louisiana (1840–1845), colonel in the Louisiana Militia (1826–1829), militia captain of cavalry (1846–1851), and member of the board of visitors to the United States Military Academy (1853–1861). In addition, he owned three sugar plantations, one on Bayou Black, in Terrebonne Parish, one on the Grand River in St. Martin Parish, and the third, Fairfax Plantation, in St. Mary Parish. Besides having planting interests, he also invested in steamboat properties.

In politics, Baker allied himself with the conservative Democrats. Although a Southerner by adoption, he opposed secession and later collaborated with the Federal army of occupation. On January 8, 1868, General Winfield Scott Hancock, a fellow conservative Democrat, appointed him military governor of Louisiana after Benjamin Franklin Flanders had resigned the office on January 1, 1868. Baker gained his appointment through his support for the lenient program of Reconstruction advocated by President Andrew Johnson.

Baker married twice. His first wife was Fanny Assherton, whom he married at Opelousas, Louisiana, on November 25, 1825. The union produced three children. After the death of Fanny, on August 17, 1831, he married Catherine Patton, of Fairfax, Virginia. Two children were born of the second marriage. Baker died while visiting at a daughter's home in Connecticut in 1885.

☙

When General Hancock assumed command of the Fifth Military District, encompassing Louisiana and Texas, under the provisions of the congressional Military Reconstruction Acts of 1867, he planned to oust

Radical Republicans from state and local offices and thereby ensure a conservative restoration of civil government. Thus he began to reverse the policies of General Philip H. Sheridan, the former commander, who had sought to build a new state government on a sound Republican foundation. In clear violation of the intent of the congressional Republicans who had seized control of the Reconstruction process from President Johnson, Hancock cautiously began to remove certain Radicals from office and appoint men in sympathy with his conservative political objectives. When Flanders resigned in protest over these removals, the general appointed Baker military governor of the state. This was a shrewd maneuver, since Baker was a well-known Unionist but also a solid conservative.

Soon after Baker assumed office, in fact, there was an attempt to unseat him. Baker had taken a loyalty oath on January 8, 1868, swearing that he had never voluntarily given aid and comfort to the Confederates during the war. Later it was alleged that he had indeed aided the rebels by placing barricades along Bayou Teche in an attempt to prevent a Union force from advancing up the waterway. A federal marshal arrested Baker on March 10, 1868, and brought him before R. H. Shannon, a United States commissioner. Charged with perjury and released on a three-thousand-dollar bond, Baker agreed to appear on March 19 for an examination. One witness, however, testified that the charges were trumped up, since it was widely known that Baker had always been a loyal Union man. Another witness stated that Baker had never willingly aided the rebel cause. The charges were dropped. Perhaps the whole affair was a Republican plot to embarrass General Hancock.

Baker exerted little influence on the operation of the state government during his short time in office. United States senators and congressmen from Louisiana were not yet permitted to take seats in the nation's capital, and all acts of the state government, including orders from the executive, were provisional. General Hancock could override Governor Baker at any time, according to the Military Reconstruction Acts. When Hancock removed nine New Orleans city councilmen from office, Ulysses S. Grant, the general-in-chief of the United States Army, countermanded the order. Frustrated and angry, Hancock asked to be reassigned to another post. His replacement arranged for new elections in April, 1868, and a young carpetbagger, Henry Clay Warmoth, became governor on June 27 of that year.

Although Baker had impressive qualifications for holding high office, little can be said of his tenure; he was nothing more than a political pawn in the contest for control of the state. Only a footnote in the history of Louisiana, Baker provided an illustration of the confusion and chaos brought on by the revolutionary conditions of the war years and the failure of the government in Washington to devise a consistent and coherent policy of Reconstruction.

FRANK J. WETTA

BIBLIOGRAPHY

Baker, Joshua. File. United States Military Academy Archives, West Point, New York.
Dawson, Joseph G. III. *Army Generals and Reconstruction: Louisiana, 1862–1877.* Baton Rouge, 1982.
Reeves, Mirian G. *The Governors of Louisiana.* Gretna, La., 1972.
Seymour, W. H. Papers. Department of Archives and Manuscripts, Troy H. Middleton Library, Louisiana State University, Baton Rouge.
Wetta, Frank J. "The Louisiana Scalawags." Ph.D. dissertation, Louisiana State University, 1977.

Henry Clay Warmoth

Governor, 1868–1872

WARMOTH, Henry Clay (b. McLeansboro, Illinois, May 9, 1842; d. New Orleans, Louisiana, September 30, 1931), army officer, governor, and collector of customs. Warmoth's schooling was irregular but thorough, and after reading law books owned by his father, a justice of the peace, he migrated to Lebanon, Missouri. There, a month before his nineteenth birthday, he began the practice of law. The ability to charm and influence people which characterized Warmoth later must have developed early, because after the firing on Fort Sumter and the beginning of the Civil War, he quickly became a colonel of Missouri militia and then lieutenant colonel

HENRY CLAY WARMOTH. *Photograph courtesy of Library of Congress.*

of the 32nd Missouri Infantry Regiment. When General John A. Mc-
Clernand organized troops for the Vicksburg campaign, Warmoth became a member of his staff while retaining his place in the infantry
regiment.

General Ulysses S. Grant, at the conclusion of the Vicksburg campaign, relieved McClernand of his command, seeing to it that Warmoth,
who had been severely wounded in the fighting, received a dishonorable
discharge for "circulating false reports." Warmoth thereupon went
to Washington, had an audience with President Abraham Lincoln,
and recovered his commission. He participated in the Battle of Look-
out Mountain and then was transferred to Louisiana, where General
Nathaniel Prentiss Banks made him judge of the provost court of occupied New Orleans. In November, 1864, his decimated regiment was
consolidated with others, and his military service came to an end.

Warmoth then began the private practice of law in New Orleans, and
he obviously prospered. He became more and more interested in politics as the war ended, and he was one of the earliest members of the
Republican party in Louisiana. He quickly became the leader of a small
group of carpetbaggers who took over control of the new organization,
displacing native Radical Republicans, who included a number of well-
educated free men of color. Meanwhile, he ostensibly accepted the
"state suicide" theory of Reconstruction set forth by Radicals in Washington. When Governor James Madison Wells called an election for
state officials and members of Congress in November, 1865, Warmoth
ran for the position of "territorial" representative from Louisiana in an
extralegal election in which he encouraged blacks to vote. Thus, Warmoth early advocated black suffrage, something that was essential if
Republicans were to have any chance of winning elections in Louisiana.
The effort to achieve black suffrage led to the New Orleans riot of July
30, 1866, in which scores of blacks and a number of white Republicans
were killed or wounded. Warmoth was a witness to this riot and wrote
a vivid account of what he saw.

The Military Reconstruction Acts that Congress passed in 1867
called for black suffrage and made Republican control of Louisiana a real
possibility. Warmoth was not a member of the Louisiana constitutional
convention of 1867–1868, but he had enough influence to make certain
that the minimum age for the governor was low enough for him to
qualify at age twenty-six. He won the Republican nomination for the

governorship over Major Francis E. Dumas, a free man of color, and with a former slave, Oscar J. Dunn, as his running mate, he easily won election.

By the end of his four-year term as governor, people all over the United States accused Warmoth of being a prince of corruptionists. They accused him, among other things, of taking bribes on a number of occasions. There is room for doubt that he ever accepted bribes, but if he did, bribery was not then illegal in Louisiana. He definitely profited hugely from part ownership of the newspaper with the contract for state printing. He also bought and sold state bonds and state treasury notes, engaging in a speculation at which he could hardly lose, because he was able to bring about changes in the price of these securities. He left office a wealthy man. The state debt rose while he was governor, as did taxes, but this would almost certainly have been true in any administration that sought to promote public education and internal improvements, including road and levee repairs and the construction of public buildings, in the ravaged Louisiana that emerged from the Civil War.

Despite his advocacy of black suffrage, Warmoth shared the racial prejudices of most white Louisianians. He very effectively prevented the implementation of the civil-rights provisions of the Constitution of 1868, but he got no credit for this from his Democratic political opponents.

Even though the Republican vote in April, 1868, had been more than ample to ratify the new constitution and to elect not only Warmoth but also other Republican state officials and a strong Republican majority in the legislature, the Democrat Horatio Seymour carried Louisiana seven months later, in the presidential election, over General Grant, the Republican candidate. The reversal of Republican fortunes was brought about by the Knights of the White Camellia and other terrorist organizations modeled after the Ku Klux Klan. To keep these forces from prevailing in other elections, Warmoth pushed through the legislature a new election law that created the State Returning Board, to which all election returns were to be reported and which was to have the power to throw out the vote from any precinct or parish if it was distorted by fraud or intimidation. The returning board was created to prevent Democrats from stealing elections. In practice, it enabled Republicans to steal elections from the Democrats, though it could be argued that the

Republicans were merely stealing the elections back. Louisiana did not have a single honest state election between April, 1868, and 1900.

Warmoth amassed more power than any other governor of Louisiana had exercised, but it was not enough to keep him in office. His racial prejudices contributed to his downfall, as did the enmity of President Grant. The Republican party in Louisiana developed two factions, one headed by Warmoth and composed largely of state employees, the other led by federal employees and usually called the Custom House Ring. President Grant supported the latter, especially after Warmoth prevented the election of James F. Casey, Mrs. Grant's brother-in-law, to the United States Senate. Other supporters of the Custom House Ring included black leaders like Dunn and, eventually, P. B. S. Pinchback. With that faction on one side and the Democrats (or Conservatives as many of them preferred to be called) on the other, Warmoth struggled for his political life during the last two years of his administration.

In 1872, when the Republican party split nationally, Warmoth supported the Liberal Republican candidate for president, Horace Greeley, against the regular Republican candidate, Grant. In Louisiana, Warmoth supported John D. McEnery, a Democrat, against William Pitt Kellogg, the regular Republican and Custom House candidate. No one will ever know who won this election, or who would have won if fraud and intimidation had been eliminated. As it was, no fewer than three returning boards were in action before the maneuvering was over. President Grant chose to recognize the results reported by a board that had no returns to work with but that concluded anyway that Kellogg had won the election. After the election, Warmoth was impeached though never brought to trial. He was thus suspended from office for the last thirty-five days of his term.

Warmoth's career as an officeholder ended before his thirty-first birthday, but he lived sixty more years. At age thirty-five, he married an heiress from New Jersey; they lived comfortably on his 2,700-acre sugar plantation in Plaquemines Parish. He remained active in Republican politics and was a hopeless candidate for governor in 1888. In 1890, ironically, President Benjamin Harrison named him collector of customs in New Orleans, and he served until removed by President Grover Cleveland. In his later years, he lived in the St. Charles Hotel, in New Orleans. Still handsome and erect, he became one of the sights of the city. He published his memoirs at eighty-seven and died in his nine-tieth year.

❧

Warmoth was one of the only two Republicans elected governor of Louisiana before 1979. In office, he gathered power into his own hands to such an extent that two noted historians, T. Harry Williams and Richard N. Current, have concluded that he was a model for Huey P. Long. If they are right, his influence on Long was the most significant result of his career. The internal improvements he sponsored were al-most entirely failures, the illegally segregated public schools established during his administration did not evolve into anything close to univer-sal public education until the twentieth century, and the Republican party in Louisiana remained in disarray for a century after Recon-struction.

Nonetheless, Warmoth continues to fascinate students of Louisiana history. Perhaps that is because this young lawyer, Union soldier, car-petbagger, and Radical Republican almost perfectly represented the type of politician many Louisianians admire. He was tall and handsome and exuded a charm that reaches across the decades to those who peruse his papers or his memoirs. When attacked by political enemies, he pre-ferred to counterattack rather than to defend himself, and he liked best of all to turn aside criticism with a quip or a good story. He did not deny being corrupt in the common sense of the word. Once, indeed, he confirmed it. He knew well that Louisianians, however much they de-plored shady political profit taking, admired the politician who took his cut with skill, aplomb, a smile, and a wink. Nor must we forget that Warmoth outlived all his enemies and, in his 1930 memoirs, could leave his own unchallenged version of his dealings with them.

JOE GRAY TAYLOR

BIBLIOGRAPHY

Binning, F. Wayne. "Henry Clay Warmoth and Louisiana Reconstruction." Ph.D. dissertation, University of North Carolina, 1969.
Current, Richard N. *Three Carpetbag Governors*. Baton Rouge, 1967.
Dawson, Joseph G. III. *Army Generals and Reconstruction: Louisiana, 1862–1877*. Baton Rouge, 1982.
Dufour, Charles L. "The Age of Warmoth." *Louisiana History*, VI (1965), 335–64.
Lonn, Ella. *Reconstruction in Louisiana After 1868*. New York, 1918.
Pitre, Althea D. "The Collapse of the Warmoth Regime, 1870–1872." *Louisiana History*, VI (1965), 161–87.
Taylor, Joe Gray. *Louisiana Reconstructed, 1863–1877*. Baton Rouge, 1975.

Warmoth, Henry Clay. *War, Politics, and Reconstruction: Stormy Days in Louisiana.* New York, 1930.

P. B. S. Pinchback

Governor, 1872–1873

PINCHBACK, Pinckney Benton Stewart (b. near Macon, Georgia, May 10, 1837; d. Washington, D.C., December 21, 1921), army officer, lieutenant governor, and governor. Pinchback spent his childhood years in comfort on a plantation in Holmes County, Mississippi.[1] His father, William Pinchback, a white planter, and his mother, Eliza Stewart, a recently manumitted mulatto, had been traveling to Mississippi from Virginia when Pinckney was born. In 1846, Pinchback and his older brother, Napoleon, were sent to Cincinnati to attend the Gilmore

P. B. S. PINCHBACK. *Photograph courtesy of Library of Congress.*

School. The brothers attended classes for under two years, leaving Cincinnati when they learned that their father was ill. They returned home shortly before he died. When Napoleon became mentally ill, twelve-year-old Pinckney had to take responsibility for supporting the family, which had moved to Ohio to avoid the risk of being sold into slavery.

Pinchback took a job as a cabin boy on canal boats plying the Miami, Toledo, and Fort Wayne canals. Later, from 1854 to 1862, the young man worked aboard steamboats on the Missouri, Red, and Mississippi rivers. His diligence paid off: he earned the position of steward, the best riverboat job a black could get during the years of slavery.

Some months after the outbreak of the Civil War, Pinchback decided

---

1. The author wishes to thank the Southern Fellowships Fund and the Rockefeller Archive Center for aiding his research on a larger project of which this essay is a part.

to enlist in the cause of the Union. He made his way to New Orleans and joined the 1st Louisiana Volunteer Infantry—a white regiment—and served with it from August 18, 1862, to October 5, 1862. Meanwhile, Major General Benjamin Franklin Butler, commander of the Department of the Gulf, had announced that he advocated the formation of regiments of free men of color. Pinchback obtained permission to recruit a company of black volunteers. The company—Company A, 2nd Regiment, Louisiana Native Guards—was raised, and Pinchback was designated its captain, holding the rank from October 6, 1862, to September, 17, 1863. Racial hostility from white army officers caused him to resign with an honorable discharge. Still willing to fight for the Union, Pinchback applied for and received a commission from Major General Nathaniel Prentiss Banks to raise a cavalry company. Using his own money, Pinchback raised the company but was denied the opportunity to serve with it because he was black.

After the war ended, Pinchback lived in Alabama for almost two years. He spoke out in support of education for blacks and praised their many examples of valor during the war. Advocating civil and political rights for his race, the former army officer pressed reluctant veterans to demand the franchise.

With the advent of congressional Reconstruction, Pinchback naturally entered the political arena himself. He moved to New Orleans in early 1867 and organized the Fourth Ward Republican Club. Using the club as a base, he served in the Republican state convention in June, 1867, and accepted the honor of being one of the ten vice-presidents of the assemblage. In September, he was elected a delegate to the Louisiana constitutional convention and drafted Article 13, the constitution's important civil-rights article. In the subsequent election, the Constitution of 1868 was ratified and Pinchback was chosen state senator from the Second Senatorial District (New Orleans). He served from August, 1868, to December 7, 1871, when he was elected lieutenant governor by a special vote of the state senate after the death of Lieutenant Governor Oscar J. Dunn, another black politician. When the Louisiana House of Representatives impeached Governor Henry Clay Warmoth for supposed "high crimes and misdemeanors," Pinchback became acting governor. Although Warmoth never acknowledged Pinchback's right to the office, ten acts of the legislature became law during his tenure as governor. His brief time as Louisiana's chief executive, from December 9, 1872, to January 13, 1873, ended with Pinchback's yielding the office to a fellow Republican, William Pitt Kellogg. Pinchback had been governor for thirty-five days.

He continued to be an important politician. The legislature elected him to the United States Senate, but that body refused him his seat. Nevertheless, while his status was being debated, the Senate voted him pay totaling $16,666, the sum he would have received if he had served. Pinchback held a variety of other offices, on the State Board of Education (1877), as internal-revenue agent (1879–1882), as surveyor of customs for the port of New Orleans (1882), and on the board of trustees of Southern University (1883 and 1885). As a delegate from Madison Parish to the constitutional convention of 1879, he had urged that a college for blacks be built in Louisiana. Southern University, the institution established largely as a result of Pinchback's efforts, became one of the world's largest predominantly black institutions of higher learning.

Pinchback invested in several businesses during and after Reconstruction. His ventures included operating a cotton factorage, jointly owning a newspaper—the New Orleans *Louisianian*—and serving as president of the Mississippi River Packet Company. White-owned transportation companies practiced Jim Crowism, and Pinchback's company was designed to accommodate black passengers.

Around 1883, Pinchback left New Orleans with his family and went to Washington, D.C. In 1895, the Pinchbacks moved to New York, where he was employed as a United States marshal. In 1909, he set up a law practice in the nation's capital. Pinchback died in Washington but was buried in Metairie Ridge Cemetery, in New Orleans.

⁙

Pinchback was the only black to become governor of a southern state during Reconstruction. Although blacks served conspicuously in many political offices in the South—as legislators, sheriffs, city councilmen, militiamen, superintendents of education, and lieutenant governors— none was elected governor. Thus, Pinchback's position, however he obtained it, makes him unique. His time in office was short and relatively inconsequential in itself.

Louisiana's backstabbing political rivals—factions and splinter groups of Republicans and Democrats—were uncooperative and bitterly antagonistic. In a clever political maneuver, Pinchback claimed the governorship when the state house of representatives impeached Governor Warmoth. The ousted carpetbagger had already changed sides, abandoning the regular Republicans to support the Democrats. It was no wonder that Warmoth challenged Pinchback's right to the office: the state senate never convicted him on the charges listed by the house. In the midst of this turmoil, Pinchback, supported by federal soldiers under the command of Brevet Major General William H. Emory, stabilized the chaotic political climate, consolidated some of the Republican factions, and helped to arrange for the orderly transfer of power to Governor Kellogg.

CHARLES VINCENT

BIBLIOGRAPHY

Grosz, Agnes Smith. "The Political Career of Pinckney Benton Stewart Pinchback." *Louisiana Historical Quarterly*, XXVII (1944), 526–632.

Haskins, James. *Pinckney Benton Stewart Pinchback*. New York, 1973.

Taylor, Joe Gray. *Louisiana Reconstructed, 1863–1877*. Baton Rouge, 1974.

Vincent, Charles. *Black Legislators in Louisiana During Reconstruction*. Baton Rouge, 1976.

Weisberger, Bernard A. "The Carpetbagger [Pinchback]: A Tale of Reconstruction." *American Heritage*, XXV (1973), 70–77.

William Pitt Kellogg

Governor, 1873–1876

KELLOGG, William Pitt (b. Orwell, Vermont, December 8, 1831; d. Washington, D.C., August 30, 1918), territorial judge, collector of customs, governor, United States senator, and congressman. Kellogg attended Norwich Military Institute, in Northfield, Vermont, before his family migrated to Peoria County, Illinois, about 1848. There he taught school for several years while reading law. Admitted to the bar in 1853, he opened a practice in Canton, Illinois. In 1856, he attended the convention at Bloomington that established the state's Republican party. Four years later,

WILLIAM PITT KELLOGG. *Photograph courtesy of Library of Congress.*

he attended the convention in Chicago that nominated Abraham Lincoln, and in the same year, as an Illinois presidential elector, he voted for his party's nominee. Lincoln, less than a month into his presidency, appointed Kellogg chief justice of the Nebraska Territory. At the outbreak of the Civil War, Kellogg returned to Illinois, where he recruited and became a colonel of the 7th Illinois Volunteer Cavalry. He later commanded a cavalry brigade, but ill health forced him to leave the army. He resumed his judicial responsibilities in Nebraska until, as Lincoln's last appointment, on April 13, 1865, he was named collector of customs at New Orleans. In June, 1865, he married Mary E. Wills, of Canton, and thereafter moved to New Orleans as chief of the Custom House. He occupied that post until July, 1868, when the Louisiana legislature elected him to the United States Senate. On November 1, 1872, he resigned from the Senate to accept the Republican nomination for the governorship of Louisiana. His Democratic opponent was John D. McEnery, a native son.

At the end of a bitter campaign, each man claimed victory. Kellogg obtained an injunction against the State Returning Board, controlled by Governor Henry Clay Warmoth, a McEnery supporter, to prevent promulgation of returns favorable to the Democrats. A rival board was organized reporting in favor of Kellogg. McEnery still claimed the governorship; two inaugurations were celebrated and two legislatures convened. Congress investigated and then temporized. Finally, President Ulysses S. Grant issued an executive order on May 22, 1873, recognizing Kellogg as the legitimate governor of the state.

Governor Kellogg's problems were just beginning. Many Louisianians refused to accept his right to govern. Some citizens—mostly former Confederates—refused to pay their taxes. Lawlessness was rampant in some of the hinterland parishes. Kellogg was the object of an assassination attempt. On the afternoon of September 14, 1874, an armed force of Democrats, most of them former Confederate soldiers, marched on the statehouse in New Orleans and overthrew the state government. Kellogg fled to the protection of the Custom House on Canal Street, from which he appealed to President Grant for military intervention to restore the Republican state administration. United States troops returned Kellogg to office. In February, 1876, the Democratic state house of representatives voted charges of impeachment, but the Republican senate refused to convict.

National weariness with civil disorder and reported outrages from

Louisiana provided the background for the election of 1876. To succeed Kellogg, the Republicans chose the United States marshal and president of the Republican state central committee, Stephen B. Packard; the Democrats chose a former Confederate brigadier and a native Louisianian, Francis R. T. Nicholls. In the disputed election of 1876, Louisiana's electoral vote was counted for Rutherford B. Hayes, the Republican, but in the ensuing political settlement—part of the Compromise of 1877—the Hayes administration abandoned Packard and recognized the election of the Democratic "redeemer," Nicholls. At the same time, the Democrats in the Louisiana legislature elected Kellogg to serve a full term in the United States Senate, where he sat without particular distinction until 1883. He followed his senatorial career with election to one term in the House of Representatives (1883–1885) from the sugar district of Bayou Teche. In 1885, his political career as an officeholder ended, although he continued to attend Republican national conventions as a delegate until 1896. He moved to Washington, D.C., where he had substantial real-estate investments. At his death, in 1918, he left an estate valued in excess of $300,000.

Kellogg suffered through a four-year term that presented repeated challenges to his governorship—perhaps challenges greater than those faced by any other Louisiana chief executive. Electoral disputes, legal controversies, an assassination attempt, civil insurrection, and finally, impeachment forced him to devote most of his time and energy to maintaining himself in office. Throughout his governorship, Louisiana's Republican ranks remained divided—between Warmoth and Custom House factions, whites and blacks, reformers and profligates, outsiders and natives. Adding to his difficulties were the turmoils and the economic dislocation of the Panic of 1873.

Above all, Kellogg remained a dedicated party man. He arrived in New Orleans in 1865 to head the largest civilian organ of the federal government in the state, and he promptly set about using his position as collector of customs to build the Republican party. Kellogg naturally supported President Grant and survived as governor because of the support President Grant provided. Federal troops defended Kellogg's trembling Republican regime against threats of violence from rampaging Democrats.

Many Louisianians never viewed Kellogg as a resident. Although he purchased a fashionable house on St. Charles Avenue, in New Orleans, city directories of the period suggest he never lived there. His speeches and his extant correspondence reflect no particular feeling for the Bayou State. During each of his four years as governor, Kellogg made lengthy trips north. Republican newspapers reported these trips as involving state business, but his absences frequently corresponded to the late summer and early fall, when fevers plagued the Crescent City.

The years as collector of customs provided Kellogg with a unique vantage point from which to survey the Louisiana economy. He understood that the New Orleans port needed rail connections with Texas to the west and Shreveport to the north. He saw that without such improvements in transportation, it would be impossible for Louisiana to realize its economic potential. As governor, he endeavored to bring order to the fiscal chaos he inherited from the Warmoth administration. His economic program included funding the state debt while repudiating an illegal portion of that debt, reducing taxes, and operating state government more honestly and efficiently. His funding plan succeeded, but many of his initiatives failed in the legislature because he never wielded enough influence to compel their passage into law. Nor was he able to fulfill the hopes of some that he might lure northern investment capital into the state.

In his inaugural address, Kellogg identified the major problems confronting Louisiana, and in statesmanlike language, he professed both good intentions and sound ideas. He remained faithful to his Radical Republicanism during his Louisiana years, in a partisanship that, however, understandably obscured his positive initiatives in the eyes of equally partisan Democrats. Kellogg's commitment to blacks—evidenced by his including a large number of blacks in state government and by his support of programs to advance the welfare of the freedmen—produced hostility in the Democratic press and strengthened the determination of native whites to recover control of the state's government. The national depression of the 1870s hurt Louisiana's economy during Kellogg's term. Furthermore, flourishing commerce required public order and political stability on the local level; so long as former Confederates were determined to use violence to oust him, Kellogg could provide neither. In a violent period, speedy justice was imperative; yet because of the Democrats' use of violence, state courts functioned in some areas only when the presence of federal soldiers protected them. As the problems mounted, the Democrats hypocritically condemned Kellogg for his inability to govern.

Some of Kellogg's successors copied his policies of reducing expenditures, lowering taxes, and attempting to improve transportation facilities. But for better than a century after Kellogg's term, Democratic politicians decried the evils of "black-Republican" rule. The Democrats attached this stigma so effectively that it took more than a hundred years for Louisianians to elect another Republican governor. If Kellogg made a lasting impression on the state's government, it was because his opponents made of him the prototypical Louisiana carpetbagger.

C. HOWARD NICHOLS

BIBLIOGRAPHY

Dawson, Joseph G. III. *Army Generals and Reconstruction: Louisiana, 1862–1877*. Baton Rouge, 1982.

Gillette, William. *Retreat from Reconstruction, 1869–1879*. Baton Rouge, 1980.

Gonzales, John E. "William Pitt Kellogg, Reconstruction Governor of Louisiana, 1873–1877." *Louisiana Historical Quarterly*, XXIX (1946), 394–495.

Hair, William I. *Bourbonism and Agrarian Protest: Louisiana Politics, 1877–1900*. Baton Rouge, 1969.

Lonn, Ella. *Reconstruction in Louisiana After 1868*. New York, 1918.

McGinty, Garnie W. *Louisiana Redeemed: The Overthrow of Carpetbag Rule, 1876–1880*. New Orleans, 1941.

Rable, George C. *But There Was No Peace: The Role of Violence in the Politics of Reconstruction*. Athens, Ga., 1984.

Taylor, Joe Gray. *Louisiana Reconstructed, 1863–1877*. Baton Rouge, 1974.

Francis R. T. Nicholls

Governor, 1877–1880, 1888–1892

NICHOLLS, Francis Redding Tillou (b. Donaldsonville, Louisiana, August 20, 1834; d. Thibodaux, Louisiana, January 4, 1912), Confederate general, governor, and chief justice and associate justice of the Louisiana Supreme Court. Born to the large family—five sons and one daughter—of Judge Thomas Clark Nicholls and Louise Hannah Drake, Francis attended the Jefferson Academy, in New Orleans. In 1851, he was appointed to the United States Military Academy, at West Point; he graduated twelfth out of thirty-four in the class of 1855. Commissioned a brevet second lieutenant in the 2nd Artillery Regiment, Nicholls served briefly in Florida and California, and resigned his commission in 1856, apparently for reasons of health. He studied law at the University of Louisiana (modern Tulane University) but left before he earned a degree. He passed the bar examination and became a successful attorney in Napoleonville. He married Caroline Guion on April 20, 1860, and by her fathered one son and five daughters.

At the start of the Civil War, Nicholls helped to raise an infantry company for Confederate service and was elected its captain. Later, he was made lieutenant colonel of the 8th Louisiana Infantry Regiment. Nicholls went east with his regiment and fought at First Manassas. Subsequently, in Virginia, Nicholls was twice wounded, losing his left arm after the Battle of

FRANCIS R. T. NICHOLS. *Photograph courtesy of State Library of Louisiana.*

Winchester (May 25, 1862) and his left foot at the Battle of Chancellorsville (May 4, 1863), where he commanded the 2nd Louisiana Brigade with the rank of brigadier general. Crippled, he carried out administrative duties until the war ended, when he reestablished his law practice in Napoleonville.

Throughout Reconstruction, Nicholls disdained politics, but in 1876, he decided to run for governor and in a controversial election emerged the winner. Two groups, one comprising Democrats and the other mostly Republicans, each claimed to be the state legislature. They met separately in New Orleans. Stooping to take money from the nefarious Louisiana Lottery Company, Nicholls paid the salary of some Republicans who joined his Democratic assembly, giving it a quorum and making it the official legislature.

Inaugurated on January 8, 1877, Nicholls was a patrician Democrat—a fiscally conservative elitist who favored many aspects of the *ancien régime* of antebellum days but claimed to act in the best interest of all. Actually, he had fallen into a den of thieves. The state treasurer, Edward A. Burke, was one of the biggest crooks in Louisiana history. Samuel L. James operated the state's brutal convict lease system for tremendous personal profit. The original lease had been granted by the Republicans during Reconstruction, but James shifted political gears to mesh smoothly with the Democratic machine. Lieutenant Governor

Louis A. Wiltz became a willing tool of the Louisiana Lottery Company, which also had been chartered under the Republicans, and he permitted its corrupt influence to spread throughout the state.

By necessity, Nicholls had enlisted Republicans to consolidate the legislature, but when he appointed other Republicans—including a few blacks—to state offices, Wiltz and others criticized him for mishandling party patronage. In reply, the governor castigated his fellow Democrats for using violence and fraud to carry black precincts in the state election of 1878. When Nicholls recommended amending the state's Constitution of 1868, which had been written by the Republicans, rather than drafting a new charter, an open split occurred among the Democrats.

Wiltz presided over the constitutional convention of 1879. The new charter reapportioned the legislature and reduced its authority vis-à-vis the governor, knocked down taxes to a very low rate, and moved the capital from New Orleans back to Baton Rouge. Moreover, the convention called for a special election for state officials at the same time that voters approved or rejected the new constitution. Nicholls would not be renominated; the twist of holding a special election cut a year from his term. Not surprisingly, Wiltz was the Democratic nominee, and he swept into office in the election of December, 1879. Nicholls resumed his law practice.

Wiltz and his lieutenant governor, Samuel D. McEnery, who succeeded to the governorship on Wiltz's death in 1881, operated a venal administration tied to the Louisiana Lottery. By 1887, some Democrats supported an Anti-Lottery League and looked again to Nicholls for the appearance of honesty. He agreed to run and on April 17, 1888, defeated Republican carpetbagger Henry Clay Warmoth.

Nicholls' second term, which opened on May 21, 1888, was mainly a crusade against the Louisiana Lottery Company. The Lottery's charter was to run out at the end of 1893, and Nicholls struck a blow for honesty when the Lottery-owned legislators passed a joint resolution rechartering the syndicate. Hoping for Nicholls' approval, the Lottery offered a gift of more than one million dollars to the state treasury. Then the Lottery proposed to pay an *annual* fee of one million dollars to the state. Despite the offered generosity, Nicholls vetoed the resolution. But the state supreme court, in an unusual move, reversed Nicholls' action by voting to support recharter. Still, the Lottery had struggled in vain. For the United States Congress passed legislation forbidding lotteries from using the federal mails to sell their tickets across the nation, and deprived of a necessary source of revenue, the Louisiana Lottery Company moved in 1894 to Honduras, where it eked out a small income for a few more years.

Nicholls continued his public service after leaving the governorship for the second time. His successor, Murphy J. Foster, appointed him the chief justice of the Louisiana Supreme Court, a position he held from 1892 to 1904. He remained on the high court from 1904 to his retirement, in 1911, as an associate justice.

∝

Twice, Nicholls was called upon to rescue Louisiana from the grip of corruption, and each time he was less than completely successful.

In 1876, the state Democratic party was in the hands of archconservatives, including John D. McEnery, who claimed in 1872 to be elected governor, David B. Penn, who led an armed revolt against Governor William P. Kellogg, and Mayor Wiltz, of New Orleans. Wiltz led on the first three ballots at the Democratic convention, but the delegates ended by nominating "all that was left" of the war-ravaged Nicholls for governor, and Wiltz for lieutenant governor.

The campaign of 1876 was bitter and violent, as was common enough in Louisiana politics. The Democrats denounced Stephen B. Packard, the Republican candidate. Originally from Maine, Packard served as a captain in the Union army and opened a law office in New Orleans after the Civil War. He was appointed United States marshal for Louisiana and became a force in state politics. The Democrats charged that Republican carpetbaggers had stolen state funds, manipulated election returns, and misspent state monies. These accusations were true. On the other hand, the Republicans had also rebuilt roads and levees, reestablished and expanded public education for blacks and whites, and promoted civil and political rights for the freedmen. Nicholls and the Democrats claimed that they would continue public education, allow blacks to keep the rights gained under the Fourteenth and Fifteenth Amendments to the United States Constitution, and stop the hemorrhage of public funds into private pockets. The Democratic appeal to black voters seemed necessary, for in 1876, Louisiana had 115,168 black men registered, contrasted with 92,354 white men. But the Bourbons were determined to gain control of the state government by any means—whether lies, threats, intimidation, murder, or fraud. Nicholls may have believed that he could temper the zeal of unscrupulous fellow "redeemers"—men out to redeem the state from so-called Republican misrule. Nicholls' glorious war record and personal honesty helped lead the Democrats to a victory reinforced by "bulldozers" who had practiced terrorism against Republicans in several parishes before the election.

Both sides manipulated the vote count. The Democrats stopped *any* Republican votes from being counted in the Feliciana parishes, where blacks were in the majority, and in a time-honored ploy, the Bourbons laced the New Orleans voting rolls with names of the dead. Nicholls came out leading by eight thousand votes. The Republicans called together the State Returning Board, which had legal power to evaluate the returns and discard fraudulent ballots. Chaired by the former governor James Madison Wells, the returning board nullified enough of Nicholls' votes to give Packard the governorship and to deprive Samuel J. Tilden, the Democratic nominee for president, of Louisiana's electoral votes, which went instead to the Republican, Rutherford B. Hayes. John McEnery, however, declared Nicholls the winner.

Complicating matters on the national scene, two other southern states, South Carolina and Florida, also reported dual sets of returns to Congress, which established a unique electoral commission to decide the validity of the returns. The commission found in favor of Hayes in every case, but Democrats in Congress blocked an official vote count. While Congress debated, politicians from both parties—including Edward A. Burke and other Louisianians—and railroad promoters met semisecretly in Washington and negotiated the Compromise of 1877, which included the promise from Hayes's friend that Nicholls would be Louisiana's governor.

In 1876–1877, Nicholls found that he was unable to control his fellow redeemers. As Republican Henry Clay Warmoth observed, the regular Democrats were "running over [Nicholls] while . . . using him."[1] Nicholls gave scant attention to public education, and under his successors, education, even for whites, would get short shrift. Virtually none of the promises made by the Democrats were fulfilled. The main result of Nicholls' first term was to remove from power a Republican administration of questionable honesty and replace it with a Democratic administration of questionable honesty.

The Wiltz and Samuel McEnery administrations, which separated

1. William I. Hair, *Bourbonism and Agrarian Protest: Louisiana Politics, 1877–1900* (Baton Rouge, 1969), 21.

Nicholls' two terms in office, were destitute of accomplishment; even some Bourbons were embarrassed by James's operation of the brutal convict lease system, by revelations of venality, including a state land fraud scheme involving the governor's brother, John McEnery, and by the rottenness of the Lottery.

Before his second administration, Nicholls had to make a deal with Samuel McEnery. In order to avoid McEnery's threat in 1888 to hold a "fair count" (an honest election in which the Republicans might have a chance of winning), Nicholls agreed to appoint McEnery to the state supreme court. Ensuring his own election, Nicholls sanctioned the use of vote fraud against blacks and some protesting white farmers and laborers in 1888—the kind of Democratic manipulation that later grew to massive proportions in 1896, when Bourbons nullified the votes of thousands of white Populists. But at least Nicholls removed one blight from the body politic by cutting Burke from the ticket in 1888. Forced from office, Burke absconded to Honduras with his embezzlements. An audit of the state records revealed that he had stolen more than $1,200,000 from the state treasury during his ten years in office; how much more he took through bribes from the Lottery will never be known.

Nicholls' record is not without its blemishes. In 1876, he struck a bargain with rascals in order to return the state to the hands of the Democratic party. Like most Bourbons, he considered disfranchisement a logical solution to the problem of what to do with illiterate voters, both black and white. He acquiesced in a gradual reduction of state funding for public schools, which resulted in nearly three generations of blacks being educationally handicapped.

In his own defense, Nicholls could point to his consistent opposition to the Lottery. He opposed the Lottery during 1877–1879, when a weaker man could have given in to the syndicate's blandishments. In an oft-quoted statement, Nicholls said his veto of the Lottery's recharter in 1890 came from his determination that "under no circumstances will I permit one of my hands to aid in degrading what the other was lost in seeking to uphold . . . the honor of my native state."[2]

JOSEPH G. DAWSON III

2. Joy J. Jackson, *New Orleans in the Gilded Age: Politics and Urban Progress, 1880–1896* (Baton Rouge, 1969), 127.

BIBLIOGRAPHY

Alwes, Berthold C. "The History of the Louisiana State Lottery Company." *Louisiana Historical Quarterly*, XXVII (1944), 964–1118.

Carleton, Mark T. *Politics and Punishment: The History of the Louisiana State Penal System*. Baton Rouge, 1971.

Dawson, Joseph G. III. *Army Generals and Reconstruction: Louisiana, 1862–1877*. Baton Rouge, 1982.

Hair, William I. *Bourbonism and Agrarian Protest: Louisiana Politics, 1877–1900*. Baton Rouge, 1969.

Lathrop, Barnes F., ed. "An Autobiography of Francis T. Nicholls, 1834–1881." *Louisiana Historical Quarterly*, XVII (1934), 246–67.

McDaniel, Hilda. "Francis T. Nicholls and the End of Reconstruction." *Louisiana Historical Quarterly*, XXXII (1949), 357–509.

McGinty, Garnie W. *Louisiana Redeemed: The Overthrow of Carpetbag Rule, 1876–1880*. New Orleans, 1941.

Nichols, C. Howard. "Francis Tillou Nicholls, Bourbon Democrat." M.A. thesis, Louisiana State University, 1959.

Taylor, Joe Gray. *Louisiana Reconstructed, 1863–1877*. Baton Rouge, 1974.

Wall, Bennett H., ed. *Louisiana: A History*. Arlington Heights, Ill., 1984.

Louis A. Wiltz

Governor, 1880–1881

WILTZ, Louis Alfred (b. New Orleans, Louisiana, October 22, 1843; d. New Orleans, October 16, 1881), Confederate army officer, mayor of New Orleans, speaker of the state house of representatives, lieutenant governor, and governor. The son of J. B. Theophile Wiltz and Louise Irene Villaneuva left public school at the age of fifteen and went to work in a mercantile establishment as a clerk. When Louisiana seceded in 1861, Wiltz enlisted in a New Orleans Confederate artillery unit stationed at Fort Jackson, below New Orleans. Wiltz was elected captain and was captured when the

LOUIS A. WILTZ. *Photograph courtesy of State Library of Louisiana, from Fortier's History of Louisiana, IV, 120.*

fort surrendered to Union forces in April, 1862. After being exchanged, he returned to military service as a provost marshal. In 1862, he married Michaela Bienvenu, of St. Martinville, Louisiana. They were the parents of seven children. Wiltz's first postwar employment was as an accountant in a commission house; later he was engaged in the banking business.

His political career as a member of the Democratic party coincided with the stormy Reconstruction and Bourbon periods of Louisiana history. He was a member of the Democratic state central committee and the Orleans Parish central committee. At various times he was also a member of the state house of representatives, a member of the New Orleans city council, mayor of New Orleans, and speaker of the state house of representatives. He became lieutenant governor on the ticket headed by Francis R. T. Nicholls in the famous disputed election of 1876 and served as president of the state constitutional convention of 1879. On December 8, 1879, he was elected the first governor under the new constitution, and he was inaugurated on January 14, 1880. Twenty-two months later, he died in office, a victim of tuberculosis.

Wiltz exerted his main influence on Louisiana politics before he became governor. He was a leader of the New Orleans Ring–Louisiana Lottery wing of the Conservative-Democratic party and as such played a role in the significant political events of the turbulent post–Civil War era.

As mayor of New Orleans, he did not participate in the Battle of Liberty Place. In the fighting on September 14, 1874, the White League, mostly former Confederates, attempted to overthrow the carpetbag regime of the Republican governor William Pitt Kellogg. After their apparent victory, however, Wiltz congratulated the citizens of New Orleans on the "restoration of the duly elected and rightful state authorities,"[1] referring to Democrats John D. McEnery and David B. Penn, who claimed to be governor and lieutenant governor respectively. The "victory" proved short-lived when President Ulysses S. Grant authorized the use of federal troops to quell the insurrection.

In January, 1875, Wiltz became speaker of the state house of representatives through a Democratic coup. He tried through the appoint-

1. Stuart O. Landry, *The Battle of Liberty Place: The Overthrow of Carpetbag Rule in New Orleans, September 14, 1874* (New Orleans, 1955), 140.

ment process to set up a Democratic majority in the house to offset the Radical Republican majority in the senate. The intervention of United States Army troops, which caused Wiltz's coup to fail, was one of the most controversial events of Louisiana's Reconstruction and received national attention. Subsequently, in February, 1876, the house of representatives voted to impeach Governor Kellogg. Wiltz was named one of the trial managers. But the Republican senate acquitted the governor without a trial.

Wiltz was a major contender for nomination as governor in the Conservative-Democratic convention of July, 1876, but he lost out to Nicholls. Although he was no friend of the nominee, Wiltz was nominated as lieutenant governor to balance the ticket between Nicholls' Conservative-patrician faction and the Bourbon-Ring-Lottery faction of the Democratic party.

Nicholls and Wiltz were recognized as the legal executive officers of Louisiana in the Compromise of 1877. This extraordinary political arrangement settled the crisis arising out of the disputed election of 1876, giving the office of president to Republican Rutherford B. Hayes. President Hayes ordered the removal of some federal troops from New Orleans, indicating that the soldiers would not be used to prop up the government of the Republican gubernatorial claimant, Stephen B. Packard.

Within a few months of taking office, the Bourbon-Ring-Lottery Democrats demanded that a new constitution reflecting their political philosophy be written to replace the Constitution of 1868, which had been put together by the Republicans. Wiltz was a leader in this movement. The delegates elected him president of the constitutional convention of 1879. Over the strong opposition of the Nicholls Conservative-patrician faction, the new charter included a special clause favoring the continued operation of the Louisiana Lottery Company, the state's politically powerful gambling enterprise. Furthermore, in order to advance their basic scheme, Wiltz and his political ally, the state treasurer Edward A. Burke, obtained from the convention an extraordinary resolution: a year would be cut from Nicholls' term and a state election would be held early.

In the special election of 1879, Wiltz headed the Democratic ticket and was elected governor, easily defeating Taylor Beattie, a weak Republican candidate. In the same election, the voters ratified the Constitution of 1879. As William I. Hair concludes, "Thus simultaneously vanished from state government both Radical law and patrician conservatism."[2]

In his inaugural address, Wiltz suggested enactment of laws "relating to the lien of mechanics and other laborers so that capital and labor would each receive adequate and equal protection under law,"[3] the establishment of both a board of health to combat epidemics and a bureau of agriculture and immigration, a more humane method of capital punishment than hanging, and the promotion of public education. It is not known how hard he pressed for the passage of his proposals, some of which seem unusually liberal for the times.

He died after serving less than two uneventful years in office. But Wiltz was important because he typified the conservative Bourbon political philosophy of the New Orleans Ring–Louisiana Lottery faction of the Democratic party of Louisiana.

PHILIP D. UZEE

BIBLIOGRAPHY

Dawson, Joseph G. III. *Army Generals and Reconstruction: Louisiana, 1862–1877.* Baton Rouge, 1982.

Hair, William I. *Bourbonism and Agrarian Protest: Louisiana Politics, 1877–1900.* Baton Rouge, 1969.

Landry, Stuart O. *The Battle of Liberty Place: The Overthrow of Carpetbag Rule in New Orleans, September 14, 1874.* New Orleans, 1955.

Lonn, Ella. *Reconstruction in Louisiana After 1868.* New York, 1918.

Taylor, Joe Gray. *Louisiana Reconstructed, 1863–1877.* Baton Rouge, 1974.

Samuel D. McEnery

Governor, 1881–1888

McENERY, Samuel Douglas (b. Monroe, Louisiana, May 28, 1837; d. New Orleans, Louisiana, June 28, 1910), lieutenant governor, governor, associate justice of the Louisiana Supreme Court, and United States senator. McEnery attended Spring Hill College, in Mobile, Alabama, the United States Naval Academy (from which he resigned

---

2. William I. Hair, *Bourbonism and Agrarian Protest: Louisiana Politics, 1877–1900* (Baton Rouge, 1969), 99.

3. Alcée Fortier, *Louisiana: Comprising Sketches of Parishes, Towns, Events, Institutions, and Persons, Arranged in Cyclopedic Form* (3 vols.; n.p., 1914), II, 654.

shortly before graduation), and the University of Virginia. Upon the death of his father, in 1857, McEnery decided to switch his studies from Virginia to the State and National Law School, in Poughkeepsie, New York. He received his law degree from that institution and was admitted to the New York bar in 1859. But on the urging of a former naval-academy classmate from Missouri, McEnery decided to practice in Maryville, Missouri.

SAMUEL D. MCENERY. *Photograph courtesy of State Library of Louisiana, from Fortier's History of Louisiana, IV, 146.*

The coming of the Civil War forced him to reconsider his loyalties. By 1860, he had come back to Louisiana, and he was one of the founders of a volunteer company, the Pelican Grays, which became part of the 2nd Louisiana Regiment. In 1862, he was commissioned a lieutenant in the provisional army of the Confederacy. At the end of the war, he was in command of the Confederate training camp at Trenton, Louisiana. In 1865, McEnery taught school in Monroe while he prepared for the Louisiana bar examination. He was certified to practice law in Louisiana in 1866 and began legal practice in his hometown.

Taking an active part in politics during the turbulent Reconstruction period was natural to McEnery. His father, Henry O'Neil McEnery, was an Irish immigrant who became a prominent north Louisiana planter and was twice registrar of the land office at Monroe. One of his brothers was a physician, and two were lawyers. His brother John D. McEnery, who also served as registrar of the land office, was the Democratic candidate for governor in 1872, but his claim to have won the election was denied by the federal authorities.

In 1879, Samuel McEnery was elected lieutenant governor on the Democratic ticket headed by Louis A. Wiltz. When Governor Wiltz died in October, 1881, McEnery succeeded him. He was elected to a term of his own in 1884 and served as governor until May, 1888, when Francis R. T. Nicholls replaced him as the Democratic nominee and was thus the assured winner against Republican oposition.

After McEnery left office in 1888, Nicholls appointed him to the post of associate justice of the state supreme court for a twelve-year term. He was again a candidate for governor on the pro-Lottery ticket in 1892 but lost to Murphy J. Foster, the anti-Lottery candidate. But just as Nicholls had done before him, Foster chose McEnery for an important political position. To keep a coalition of Republicans and Populists from securing a United States Senate seat for their candidate, Foster persuaded the Democrats in the state senate to elect McEnery. He served from March, 1897, until his death in 1910. In the Senate, McEnery broke sharply with Democratic policy, voting for the high, Republican-sponsored Dingley Tariff. During his last years, McEnery was handicapped by severe deafness, but his careful reading of the *Congressional Record* and his remarkably retentive memory aided him in keeping up with Senate business. McEnery was married to Elizabeth Phillips, of Monroe, and had three children—two sons and a daugher.

꙳

The historical evidence reveals two sides to this Gilded Age governor. As an individual, McEnery was a jovial, likable man who was loyal to his friends and honest in his personal dealings. He remained a man of modest means until his death, although Edward A. Burke, a conspicuous figure in his administration who was associated with the Louisiana Lottery Company, amassed a fortune through illegal manipulation of public funds. Burke fled into exile in Honduras at the end of McEnery's term.

As governor, McEnery sincerely tried to provide flood protection through the building of levees and even acquired the nickname of the levee governor. He also wanted to attract new business, industry, and immigrants to Louisiana. The Cotton Centennial Exposition, held in New Orleans in 1884–1885, was an ambitious but frustrating attempt in that direction. But good intentions and personal affability could not make up for McEnery's inherently weak position as governor. When he succeeded Wiltz, it was the state treasurer, Burke, who was the state official with greatest power in state government, through his control of the disbursement of funds. There were almost no legislative or executive checks on Burke's authority. Other powerful influences upon state officials were John Morris and Charles T. Howard, of the Louisiana Lottery Company, and Samuel L. James, the major lessee of convict labor at the state penitentiary and also the man who held a monopoly of levee construction contracts, which he sublet to smaller companies.

Burke operated the state treasurer's office cavalierly, with several important consequences. Certain bondholders might be paid off in full while state employees received, instead of regular salaries, warrants that they had to sell to brokers at a discount. Public institutions, such as the insane asylum, were allowed to deteriorate, and public education—especially for blacks—was woefully neglected. Louisiana went from fifth place in 1880 in illiteracy nationwide to first place in 1890. McEnery's Democratic stalwarts glibly dismissed any criticism of corruption or neglect of the state's public responsibilities, on the grounds that the Civil War and the Republicans' crooked carpetbag regimes were to blame for starting a downward trend in law, order, and fiscal responsibility.

By 1888, nevertheless, McEnery was being called McLottery by critics. A coalition of reform Democrats organized to block his renomination at the party's convention early in 1888, and they succeeded in putting together enough support for Governor Nicholls to ease out McEnery. But in the general election in which Nicholls ran against the Republican Henry Clay Warmoth and defeated him, McEnery threatened to assure a "fair count," which in Louisiana political parlance meant allowing blacks in delta parishes to vote Republican without interference from whites. This did not happen, because the Nicholls faction came to an amicable understanding with the McEnery forces. After Nicholls took office, he appointed McEnery an associate justice to the state supreme court, a move that the historian William I. Hair, in his book *Bourbonism and Agrarian Protest,* interprets as showing that a deal was struck.

Although McEnery was governor for seven years and a United States senator for fourteen, he remains a shadowy, undefined figure in Louisiana history. He destroyed all of his correspondence and other papers, relying instead upon his remarkable total recall for personal references. After his death, only what he had done, or rather failed to do, was left to document his record.

JOY J. JACKSON

BIBLIOGRAPHY

Carleton, Mark T. *Politics and Punishment: The History of the Louisiana State Penal System.* Baton Rouge, 1971.

Hair, William I. *Bourbonism and Agrarian Protest: Louisiana Politics, 1877–1900.* Baton Rouge, 1969.

Jackson, Joy J. *New Orleans in the Gilded Age: Politics and Urban Progress, 1880–1896.* Baton Rouge, 1969.

Kennedy, Lawrence F., comp. *Biographical Directory of the American Congress, 1774–1971.* Washington, D.C., 1971.

Wall, Bennett H., ed. *Louisiana: A History.* Arlington Heights, Ill., 1984.

Murphy J. Foster

Governor, 1892–1900

FOSTER, Murphy James (b. near Franklin, Louisiana, January 12, 1849; d. Dixie Plantation, near Franklin, Louisiana, June 21, 1921), state senator, governor, United States senator, and collector of customs. Foster spent two years after the Civil War in preparatory school at White's Creek, near Nashville, one year at Washington College, in Virginia, and two years at Cumberland University, in Lebanon, Tennessee, where in 1870 he received a B.A. degree. Returning to Louisiana, he earned a law degree from the University of Louisiana (Tulane University) and was admitted to the bar in 1871. That same year he formed a law partnership with his cousin Donelson Caffery, in Franklin, Louisiana.

MURPHY J. FOSTER. *Photograph courtesy of State Library of Louisiana, from Fortier's* History of Louisiana, *IV, 146.*

As a Democrat and supporter of John D. McEnery, Foster ran for the legislature in 1872 but was denied his seat as a result of disputes with Republicans over the result of the election. He subsequently joined the White League, comprising former Confederate soldiers and other Democrats, and worked in St. Mary Parish toward the overthrow of the Republican carpetbag regime of Governor William Pitt Kellogg. In 1879, he won a race to the state senate and was reelected twice, serving until 1892. Foster was president pro tempore of the senate from 1888 to 1890. He stoutly opposed the constitutional amendment to recharter the Louisiana Lottery Company.

In the 1892 canvass, Foster was elected governor on the anti-Lottery Democratic ticket by a vote of 79,270. His main opponent, Samuel D. McEnery, was a former governor who ran on the pro-Lottery Democratic ticket; he received 47,046 votes. Others in the race included the Republicans A. H. Leonard and John E. Breaux, as well as Robert L.

Tannehill, the Populist candidate. The voters overwhelmingly defeated the amendment to recharter the Lottery.

As governor, Foster faced two emergencies. First, in 1892 he had to send state militia into New Orleans to keep the peace during a general strike of forty-two unions which threatened to shut down much of the city's economic activity. After three days, the strikers and their employers reached an agreement on wages and hours. Second, during the spring of 1893, Foster had to deal with severe flooding that drove five thousand persons from their homes and required the setting-up of temporary refugee camps.

Foster made several important appointments during his first term. The former governor Francis R. T. Nicholls was appointed chief justice of the state supreme court. Caffery and Newton Crain Blanchard were both appointed to the United States Senate. Acts passed by the legislature which the governor endorsed established a college at Ruston (later to become Louisiana Tech University), outlawed lotteries in the state, instituted the direct election of police juries, set the time and manner of elections, and put before the voters a suffrage amendment that, if it had been approved in the 1896 election, would have eliminated most blacks and many poor whites from the registration rolls. The legislature also passed a segregation bill affecting railroads in the state. That legal draft set the pattern for legislation concerning separate racial facilities in the state for the next fifty years. The governor signed this bill into law without hesitation.

In the controversial election of 1896, Foster won reelection as the Democratic candidate, with 116,216 votes. His challenger was John N. Pharr, a Populist-Republican fusion candidate who polled 87,698 votes. There was persuasive evidence that the Democrats used fraud in the north Louisiana cotton parishes to carry Foster's reelection. Since the suffrage amendment had been defeated in the 1896 state election by whites who feared it might affect them as well as blacks, Foster called a constitutional convention that rewrote Louisiana law to limit the franchise to those men who were literate, who owned property worth three hundred dollars, or who, through a grandfather clause, could vote because they, their father, or their grandfather had been registered in 1867. That clause—declared unconstitutional in 1915—protected illiterate whites while excluding most blacks.

The Constitution of 1898 also barred Foster from a third consecutive term. He left office on May 21, 1900, and the next day was elected by the state legislature to succeed Caffery in the United States Senate in March, 1901. Foster was reelected in 1906. As a senator, he never became prominent nationally, but he worked diligently to protect the interests of Louisiana sugar planters, to promote levee construction in the lower Mississippi Valley, and to regulate interstate railroad commerce. He was defeated for reelection in 1912 by Congressman Joseph E. Ransdell, of Lake Providence.

After the election in 1912 of the Democratic presidential candidate, Woodrow Wilson, the Louisiana congressional delegation recommended that Foster be appointed collector of customs in New Orleans, and President Wilson acted upon the recommendation in 1914. Foster remained as collector of customs until his death in 1921. He married twice. He wed Daisy Hine in 1877, who died a few months after the wedding. In 1881, he married Rosa Rosetta Ker. They had ten children.

ॐ

Foster's career had two major themes: as a state senator, to fight and destroy the Louisiana Lottery Company, and as governor, to hold the Democratic party together as the dominant political force in Louisiana. In combating the Lottery, he used his flawless reputation (which was altogether free of Lottery taint), his great parliamentary skill, his quiet but magnetic style of oratory, and his organizational ability to pull together planters from southwestern Louisiana and agrarians from north Louisiana. Although he held an essentially Hamiltonian philosophy of government, in which he saw an educated, propertied elite acting as political stewards to govern for the general welfare, he shared with many agrarian Populists an outrage at the corrupt power of the Louisiana Lottery and a religious fervor to destroy it. He also shared their concern for regulating the practices of corporate railroad companies that hurt planter and dirt farmer alike. But the great victory they won in 1892 with Foster's elevation to the governorship marked the beginning of the end of the coalition of Fosterites and agrarians. The rise of the Populists as a viable political party, Foster's own efforts to woo the McEnery Democrats into reconciliation, and defections from the Democratic to the Republican party by south Louisiana planters all drastically affected Louisiana politics and the role Foster played in it between 1896, the year of his reelection, and 1900, when he left office.

During 1896, new factions formed and old adversaries became allies. The Democratic Wilson-Gorman Tariff, passed by Congress in 1894, had removed the bounty on sugar and sent Louisiana sugar planters into the Republican ranks. Another turnabout came when the state legislature voted to fill a United States Senate seat. The threat of a Populist-Republican candidate's getting the post forced Foster to recommend his old adversary, Samuel McEnery, for the job. A cordial political relationship based on mutual interests developed between them. Furthermore, Foster turned in his search for new political allies to the Democratic regular machine in New Orleans, a faction that had opposed him over the Lottery question in 1892.

A man at all times soft-spoken and well groomed (he would not appear at the dining table without a coat and tie), Foster strove to present the image of a stern but paternalistic leader. He saw himself as an enlightened Bourbon, but as the Republicans and Populists made political inroads upon the ranks of the Democrats, he found himself having to assume the role of a political boss and take drastic measures to fight them. Foster sincerely believed that only the educated, white, Democratic property owner could properly vote or rule the state. The use of black votes in the sugar parishes by lily-white Republicans and the rising tide of agrarian poor white Populists in north Louisiana he viewed as threats to the Democratic party, and he moved without hesitation to curb or cut from the state's voting lists the groups he feared. The grandfather clause that protected illiterate white voters he accepted as a compromise.

Foster's tenure as governor was beneficial to the state in its attempts to bring fiscal accountability to state finances and to remove political corruption by outlawing lotteries. But the greatest impact Foster had was negative as far as black citizens were concerned. His term as governor marked the expansion of segregation legislation in the state and the denial of the franchise to most blacks. The image of the Bourbon gentleman turned governor, which he personified, persisted as the model for politicians aspiring to the highest office in the state until the 1920s. Only the rowdy, flamboyant figure of the Kingfish—Huey P. Long—finally supplanted it.

JOY J. JACKSON

BIBLIOGRAPHY

Carleton, Mark T. *Politics and Punishment: The History of the Louisiana State Penal System.* Baton Rouge, 1971.

Hair, William I. *Bourbonism and Agrarian Protest: Louisiana Politics, 1877–1900.* Baton Rouge, 1969.

Jackson, Joy J. *New Orleans in the Gilded Age: Politics and Urban Progress, 1880–1896.* Baton Rouge, 1969.

Romero, Sidney J. "The Political Career of Murphy J. Foster, Governor of Louisiana, 1892–1900." *Louisiana Historical Quarterly*, XXVIII (1945), 1129–1243.

Shugg, Roger W. "The New Orleans General Strike of 1892." *Louisiana Historical Quarterly*, XXI (1938), 547–60.

Uzee, Philip D. "The Republican Party in the Louisiana Election of 1896." *Louisiana History*, II (1961), 332–44.

Wall, Bennett H., ed. *Louisiana: A History*. Arlington Heights, Ill., 1984.

State Governors of the Twentieth Century

William Wright Heard

Governor, 1900–1904

HEARD, William Wright (b. Union
Parish, Louisiana, April 28, 1853;
d. New Orleans, Louisiana, May
31, 1926), state senator and governor. Heard, born in a north-central
parish bordering Arkansas, was the
youngest son of Stephen S. Heard,
a Georgia native, and Mary Wright.

While Heard's older brothers
served in the Confederate army,
William—not yet eight years of
age when Fort Sumter was fired
upon—remained at home and attended local schools, including an
academy in Farmerville, the parish
seat. As Radical Reconstruction in
Louisiana experienced its final dis-

WILLIAM WRIGHT HEARD. *Photograph
courtesy of Special Collections, Hill Memorial Library, Louisiana State University,
from O. B. Steele Photograph Collection.*

integration, Heard entered Democratic politics. In 1876, at age twenty-
three, he was elected Union Parish clerk of court, and he continued either as clerk or as deputy clerk until 1892. During those years, Heard
served as well in the lower house of the state legislature, from 1884
until 1888, and in the state senate, from 1888 to 1892. In his eight years
in the legislature, he consistently opposed the two most powerful and
controversial special interests in post-Reconstruction Louisiana: the en-
trenched, dominating, and widely loathed Louisiana Lottery Company,

and the state's brutal and cynically profit-oriented convict lease system, headed by the former Confederate major Samuel L. James.

As an anti-Lottery and antilease Democrat, Heard became closely associated with his senate colleague, Murphy J. Foster, of St. Mary Parish. Foster emerged as the anti-Lottery Democratic candidate for governor in 1892, on the basis of his leadership of Democratic forces opposed to the Lottery and the lease system in the legislature. Heard, by then a follower and protégé of Foster's, was Foster's choice for the office of state auditor of public accounts on the anti-Lottery Democratic ticket. After an inconclusive primary battle with the pro-Lottery Democratic gubernatorial contender, the former governor Samuel D. McEnery (1881–88), Foster went on to victory in the general election, defeating a divided opposition consisting of two Republicans, a Populist, and for the second time, McEnery. Despite a controversial and repressive first administration, Foster and his associates—including Heard—were reelected in 1896 in what may have been the most hotly contested and fraudulent election Louisiana had yet endured. Although much evidence suggests that Foster's Populist-Republican fusion opponents had the support of a statewide voter majority, the Fusionists were "counted out" in the Democratic-controlled cotton parishes of north Louisiana. Democratic attempts to "stabilize" Louisiana elections came to ultimate fruition in the Constitution of 1898, which prevented or discouraged subsequent registration of most black Republicans and many white Populists by requiring ownership of property or proof of literacy as qualifications for voting.

Thus, by the time Foster's governorship drew to a close, an aggressive and determined Bourbon Democracy—of which Heard was a second-echelon leader—reigned secure in Louisiana, all major sources of discord, division, and partisan opposition having been eliminated or restrained. The infamous Lottery had moved to Honduras in 1894, as the result of both federal action and the expiration of the company's original Louisiana charter. Convict lessee James died that same year and, although his firm remained in business until 1901, the Constitution of 1898 prohibited convict leasing to private firms or individuals after expiration of the James contract. Organized political opposition to the Democratic oligarchy was rendered impotent for years to come by both the disfranchisement provisions of 1898 and the heavy-handed and intimidating conduct of the Fosterites.

As a reward for yeoman service to the triumphant Foster faction of the Democratic party, the reliable and low-keyed Heard received the party's gubernatorial nomination in 1900. He won easily, with 60,206 votes cast in his favor (78 percent of the total) to only 16,664 ballots for a greatly reduced, fragmented, and almost muted opposition. The Heard legislature shortly afterward elevated Foster to the United States Senate, where the most powerful and decisive of Louisiana's Gilded Age politicians remained until 1913.

As a result of the massive reduction in the number of voting Louisianians, both white and black, that occurred between 1898 and 1900, political opposition to Heard's Bourbon Democrats virtually disappeared for several years. Consequently, Heard enjoyed a relatively tranquil administration from 1900 to 1904, having to deal with no major political confrontations or crises. In the relatively calm immediate aftermath of the tumultuous 1890s, Louisiana Democrats apparently felt no need for continued aggressive, decisive leadership. An administrator-custodian in the governor's office was the order of the day, and Heard, with his clerical and accounting background and bland, stable disposition, filled the role admirably.

A lifelong active Baptist, Heard moved to New Orleans with his wife and five of his seven children when his many years of public service ended. There he engaged in accounting and banking until he died at the age of seventy-three. Newspaper editorials and obituaries were brief, recalling only Heard's "charming personality," "abhorrence of enmities," and "innate kindliness."[1] On the threshold of the Huey P. Long era, Louisianians remembered Heard the person with becoming respect but had relegated his efficient but quite modest gubernatorial administration to limbo.

⁓

An orderly and humane transition within the penal system from lessee control to state control headed the list of Heard's significant gubernatorial accomplishments. Subsequently, in fact, so interested and involved was Heard in the details of this process that he himself became enough of an expert in prison management to be named president of the State Penitentiary Board of Control in 1910, serving until 1914.

Other matters—education, legal suits, and agriculture—occupied Heard's attention. In 1902, Heard signed a law creating the first State Board of Education, to include the governor, superintendent of public

1. New Orleans *Times-Picayune*, June 2, 1926.

instruction, and attorney general (all *ex officio*), in addition to seven citizens appointed by the governor, one from each of the state's congressional districts. Parish school boards were also created in 1902. In that same year, Heard initiated a suit against the state of Mississippi in a coastal boundary dispute that in 1906 was resolved in Louisiana's favor by the United States Supreme Court. By 1903, the boll weevil had invaded Louisiana, and at Heard's urgent request a special legislative session created the State Crop Pest Commission to deal with the cotton-consuming insect. The commission, however, was unsuccessful in its efforts. Although Heard was not the initiator, the extraction of oil in Louisiana commenced during his administration.

By 1914, Heard had spent virtually his entire adult life on the public payroll, mostly in second-level administrative positions where little leadership was called for. For that reason, he may possess the distinction of having been the first modern career bureaucrat to occupy Louisiana's political summit. (Oramel H. Simpson, governor from 1926 to 1928, was the second of the type: from 1900 until his election as lieutenant governor in 1924, Simpson served successively as assistant secretary and secretary of the state senate.) There is no biography of Heard. His administration, overshadowed by those of more significant governors who preceded and followed him, has been largely ignored by recent scholarship.

MARK T. CARLETON

BIBLIOGRAPHY

Carleton, Mark T. *Politics and Punishment: The History of the Louisiana State Penal System.* Baton Rouge, 1971.
Fortier, Alcée. *Louisiana: Comprising Sketches of Parishes, Towns, Events, Institutions, and Persons, Arranged in Cyclopedic Form.* Vol. 1 of 3 vols. N.p., 1914.
Howard, Perry H. *Political Tendencies in Louisiana.* Rev. and exp. ed. Baton Rouge, 1971.
New Orleans *Times-Picayune*, June 2, 1926.
Wall, Bennett H., ed. *Louisiana: A History.* Arlington Heights, Ill., 1984.

Newton Crain Blanchard

Governor, 1904–1908

BLANCHARD, Newton Crain (b. near Boyce, Louisiana, January 29, 1849; d. Shreveport, Louisiana, June 22, 1922), congressman, United

States senator, justice of the Louisiana Supreme Court, and governor. Blanchard was born at Rosedale, his father's cotton plantation, in Rapides Parish, central Louisiana. He and his brothers, Frank and Henry, were the sons of Carey Hansford Blanchard, a native Virginian, and Frances Amelia Crain.

Blanchard received as sound an education as a young planter aristocrat could obtain in Louisiana at the time. Private schooling preceded attendance at the Louisiana State Seminary of Learning (forerunner of Louisiana State University) and legal studies at the University of

NEWTON CRAIN BLANCHARD. *Photograph courtesy of Special Collections, Hill Memorial Library, Louisiana State University, from New Orleans* Times-Picayune *photograph in vertical file, Louisiana and Lower Mississippi Valley Collection.*

Louisiana (later Tulane University), which bestowed the LL.B. degree on Blanchard in 1870. The following year Blanchard moved to Shreveport, where he commenced a busy, successful, and lucrative legal practice, specializing in corporation law in the service of railroads. (As governor, Blanchard later supported tax exemptions for railroads constructing additional lines in Louisiana.)

Blanchard was twice married. On December 16, 1873, he wed Emily Barrett, who bore him two children, Ashton and Ethel. The first Mrs. Blanchard died on July 27, 1907, while her husband was governor. On his sixtieth birthday, January 29, 1909, he married Charlotte Tracy, who became the mother of Newton Crain, Jr.

Considering the unpopularity of Radical Reconstruction (1867–1877) among most native white Louisianians—especially among the planter gentry that had produced Blanchard—it was not unnatural that the vigorous young attorney should enter politics as a devoted Bourbon Democrat. His election in 1876 as chairman of the Democratic committee of Caddo Parish launched him on a lifelong career of political activity and government service on both state and national levels.

Blanchard's youthful partisan zeal, however, soon got him into difficulty: federal officials indicted him for intimidating black Republican voters in an 1878 election. Although detained for some time in New Orleans, Blanchard was not convicted of the charge. Caddo voters chose

Blanchard as their delegate to the 1879 Louisiana constitutional convention, where his hard work and sharp intellect distinguished him. In
1880, the Democratic governor Louis A. Wiltz appointed Blanchard to
his staff with the rank of major. After Wiltz died the following year, his
successor, Samuel D. McEnery, renewed Blanchard's appointment.

By 1880, the thirty-one-year-old Blanchard had already reached the
upper level of power and influence in Bourbon Democratic Louisiana.
He remained there for the rest of his life. Elected in 1880 to the lower
house of the United States Congress from Louisiana's Fourth District,
Blanchard retained his seat from 1881 to 1894. Rising to the chair-
manship of the House Committee on Rivers and Harbors, Blanchard
did much to expand federal responsibility for levee construction and
flood control throughout the lower Mississippi Valley. When President
Grover Cleveland elevated Senator Edward D. White to the United
States Supreme Court in 1894, Governor Murphy J. Foster appointed
Blanchard to serve the balance of White's Senate term, to 1897. When
that term expired, Blanchard secured an appointment as associate justice on the supreme court of Louisiana, serving creditably from 1897
until 1903, when he resigned to campaign for the governorship.

Blanchard's opponent in the 1904 Democratic primary was Leon Jastremski, a feisty ultra-Bourbon of Franco-Polish descent. Jastremski's
colorful career included service as a Confederate officer, the editorship
of a prominent newspaper in Baton Rouge (where he was simultaneously the mayor), an appointment as United States consul in Lima,
Peru, and a succession of minor state appointments by Governors
McEnery, Foster, and William Wright Heard. Possibly feeling insecure
in the shadow of Blanchard's more substantial record and experience,
Jastremski charged his opponent with cowardice for having evaded
Confederate military service—a ridiculous accusation in light of the
fact that Blanchard had been only twelve years of age when the Civil
War began and was barely sixteen at its conclusion.

After disposing of his volatile fellow Democrat in the party primary,
Blanchard next defeated a Republican challenger, another former Confederate and a former mayor of New Orleans, in a heavily one-sided
and largely pro forma general election. W. J. Behan, a onetime Democrat who had changed parties in 1894, was Blanchard's hapless Republican victim, receiving only 5,877 votes to Blanchard's 48,345 ballots
statewide. Voter participation in Louisiana had steadily decreased in the

aftermath of the Constitution of 1898, which contained literacy and property-ownership requirements for suffrage designed to prevent or discourage black Republicans and rebellious white Populists from voting. In 1896, the total statewide vote had been 206,354; in 1900, 76,780. Four years later, when Blanchard won the governorship, only 54,222 Louisianians cast ballots, of which almost 90 percent were Democratic.

Although political realities in Louisiana by 1904 would probably have enabled any Democratic nominee to defeat Behan—who, to do him justice, would have been a formidable contender in a less repressive political environment—Blanchard came to Baton Rouge as the most experienced and perhaps best qualified gubernatorial winner in the state's history: no other governor before or since has served sixteen years in both houses of Congress and six years on the state supreme court prior to becoming Louisiana's chief executive. Described, moreover, by his political biographer as an impressive man with a "striking and somewhat pompous appearance,"[1] Blanchard contrasted vividly with his less imposing and more parochial predecessor, Heard. A law partner remembered Blanchard in later years as the "only man I knew who could strut while sitting down."[2] And if Heard had been a manager governor, Blanchard proved to be an innovator governor, especially in the areas of public education, reduction of the governor's appointive powers, and the reform of taxation, elections, and institutions.

At the conclusion of his gubernatorial term, Blanchard returned to his Shreveport law practice. But he remained an active Democrat and public servant. In 1912, he attended the last of four Democratic national conventions as a Louisiana delegate. Elected by Caddo voters to the Louisiana constitutional convention of 1913, Blanchard was the unanimous choice of his fellow delegates for the office of convention president. If he had accepted election to the constitutional convention of 1921, he might have set a record as the only person in Louisiana history to have been a delegate to three such gatherings. But ill health forced him to decline an honor urged upon him by his respectful Caddo neighbors. Blanchard died in Shreveport at the age of seventy-three, one of

1. Hazel Shively, "The Political Career of Newton Crain Blanchard" (M.A. thesis, Louisiana State University, 1945), 4.
2. Thomas A. Harrell, interview with author, November 14, 1987.

the last survivors of those who had "redeemed" Louisiana from "carpetbag misrule."

❧

Governor Blanchard was appalled by the deplorable condition of public education in Louisiana, the result of almost three decades of official neglect and even, at times, hostility by the state's conservative Democrats. When voters defeated a proposed constitutional amendment authorizing the sale of one million dollars' worth of state bonds for construction of new school facilities, he supported a law permitting parish school boards to issue bonds of their own. By the third year of Blanchard's term, 1907, 231 additional public-school buildings had been constructed. Between 1904 and 1908, the number of accredited Louisiana high schools more than doubled, from twenty-six to fifty-three. Blanchard also endorsed legislation providing for state teacher certification and for public-school libraries. State appropriations for public education also more than doubled during Blanchard's administration, from $1,551,000 in 1904 to $3,481,000 in 1908. Working closely with Blanchard in trying to lift Louisiana's schools out of the doldrums was James B. Aswell, the state's first effective superintendent of education.

The extensive appointive powers of Louisiana governors had become an issue by 1904, and Blanchard supported making a number of offices elective—those of the justices of the state supreme court, the register of state lands, the commissioner of agriculture and immigration, the members of parish school boards, and the parish assessors. Not until the administration of Edwin Edwards (1972–1980) would the number of offices filled by gubernatorial appointment again be markedly reduced.

When Blanchard became governor, numerous holdings of private property were not listed on state or parish tax rolls. Blanchard believed that all property should be listed and fairly assessed, so that there could be a reduction of tax rates. Accordingly, he urged the creation of a State Board of Equalization to accomplish comprehensive and equitable assessments and, in 1906, also backed legislation lowering the state property-tax millage from six to five, and the parish millage from ten to eight. Property-tax inequities remained endemic in Louisiana, however, until 1973, when state courts and another constitutional convention brought a degree of order out of confusion and favoritism.

The Democratic primary in which Blanchard defeated Jastremski had been a voluntary process. In 1906, Blanchard signed a law making state primaries mandatory, thereby ending the nomination of party contenders by conventions and caucuses. Insofar as voters rather than party functionaries were to exercise the nomination prerogative, the 1906 law was democratic. But because the Louisiana Democratic party had become, in effect, a white man's party, and because Louisiana's Republicans had been reduced to ineffectiveness by disfranchisement of their black constituents, the 1906 law essentially gave legal control of Louisiana's entire political process to white Democrats, who retained that control without serious opposition until the 1970s.

Blanchard insisted in 1904 that the legislature provide an appropriation to build the state reform school that had been authorized by statute in 1900, since youthful "convicts" ten years of age still languished in the state penitentiary. The legislature complied, but construction did not begin until 1908, and the institution, at Monroe, was not ready for occupancy until 1910. Also in 1904, the legislature, at Blanchard's urging, finally created a visitorial State Board of Charities and Corrections, itself authorized by prior law, but inadequate appropriations reduced the board to uselessness for a long period after 1910. Another institutional reform was the creation, in 1904, of a State Board of Forestry.

Although producing few if any concrete results at the time, Governor Blanchard vocally supported the parish construction of better roads, a state pure-food law, and the diversification of agriculture to lessen the dependence upon cotton. He was an outspoken critic of lynching and mob violence.

The last of the immediate post-Reconstruction Bourbons to govern Louisiana, Blanchard was limited in his perceptions and values by the partisan and segregationist conservatism of his generation. Unlike many of his contemporaries, however, he did not remain a paranoid reactionary; he grew, to some extent, with the changing needs and demands of the time. In historical significance, he stands with John M. Parker (1920–1924) as one of the more constructive governors of the Progressive period. It may be that a man of Blanchard's intelligence, initiative, and forcefulness was somewhat deprived by being born too soon for his natural talents to be developed more freely and employed to greater public usefulness.

MARK T. CARLETON

BIBLIOGRAPHY

Carleton, Mark T. *Politics and Punishment: The History of the Louisiana State Penal System.* Baton Rouge, 1971.

Howard, Perry H. *Political Tendencies in Louisiana*. Rev. and exp. ed. Baton Rouge, 1971.

Shively, Hazel. "The Political Career of Newton Crain Blanchard." M. A. thesis, Louisiana State University, 1945.

Sompayrac, Paul A. "Newton Crain Blanchard, Governor of Louisiana, 1904–1908." *Louisiana Historical Quarterly*, VI (1923), 56–59.

Wall, Bennett H., ed. *Louisiana: A History*. Arlington Heights, Ill., 1984.

J. Y. Sanders

Governor, 1908–1912

SANDERS, Jared Young (b. near Morgan City, Louisiana, January 29, 1869; d. Baton Rouge, Louisiana, March 23, 1944), speaker of the state house of representatives, lieutenant governor, governor, and congressman. Sanders, usually called J. Y., was born on a sugar plantation in St. Mary Parish. His father, a sugar planter, died when he was ony twelve years old, and shortly thereafter his family moved to Franklin, where he spent the rest of his youth. After a series of jobs, he became the editor of the *St. Mary Banner*, a weekly newspaper in Franklin, in 1890. He briefly at-

J. Y. SANDERS. *Photograph courtesy of Special Collections, Hill Memorial Library, Louisiana State University, from J. Y. Sanders Papers.*

tended St. Charles Jesuit College, in Grand Coteau, and in 1893 received his law degree from the Tulane University Law School. Sanders then began the practice of law, eventually setting up offices in Franklin and New Orleans.

While still operating his newspaper, he became interested in state politics. In April, 1892, at the age of twenty-three, he was elected as a Democrat from St. Mary Parish to the state house of representatives. Elected on the anti-Lottery ticket supporting Murphy J. Foster's candidacy for governor, Sanders entered politics as the youngest member of the Louisiana legislature at the time. He served in the house for ten years, from 1892 to 1896 and from 1898 to 1904. In 1898, as a member of the Louisiana constitutional convention, he played a major role in drafting the suffrage provisions of the new state constitution, particularly the so-called grandfather clause, ostensibly designed to permit some illiterate whites to continue voting. Other restrictions in the new constitution, such as literacy tests and property-owning requirements, effectively disfranchised many potential black voters.

In 1900, Sanders was unanimously elected speaker of the house, the first time a unanimous vote for the speakership had occurred in Louisiana political history. Sanders held the position until 1904, when he was elected lieutenant governor on the Democratic ticket led by Newton Crain Blanchard. After a number of disagreements with Governor Blanchard, Sanders emerged in 1907 as the leading contender for the office of governor. He defeated his major Democratic opponent, the former congressman Theodore Wilkinson, of Plaquemines Parish, by a margin of fourteen thousand votes, 60,000 to 46,000, and easily overwhelmed his Republican rival, Henry N. Pharr, in the April, 1908, general election. Sanders' election as governor was the first one held under the state's new mandatory primary law, a measure he had worked hard to pass as lieutenant governor.

Sanders' term as governor, from 1908 to 1912, was marked by the passage of progressive reform legislation in areas such as conservation, child labor, gambling, and prohibition. In July, 1910, near the middle of his term as governor, he was chosen by the state legislature to fill the unexpired term of Senator Samuel D. McEnery, who had died at the end of June. Sanders, whose major ambition had always been to serve in the Senate, reluctantly decided, however, to complete his term as governor, mainly to continue working for selection of New Orleans as the site of the Panama Canal Exposition. In spite of Sanders' efforts, San Francisco was chosen as the exposition site.

After leaving office in 1912, Sanders still participated in Democratic party politics. In 1911–1912, he ran a hard-fought but unsuccessful campaign for the United States Senate. Later he ran for the Senate two more times, in 1920 and 1926, narrowly losing each time. Thwarted in his ambition to serve in the upper chamber, Sanders moved to Bogalusa and in 1916 was elected to the United States House of Representatives from the Sixth Congressional District. He served two terms in Congress, from 1917 to 1921, his last years in elective office.

Sanders maintained an active interest in state politics for the rest of his life. He resumed his successful law practice, and in 1921, as a member of the state constitutional convention, helped formulate the first comprehensive plan for a state highway system. One year later, Sanders became the first attorney for the newly created Louisiana Highway Department, helping put together the plan for the state's first gravel roads. Sanders championed Riley J. Wilson, of Catahoula Parish, against Huey Long in the 1927 race for governor. In November, 1927, one of the most colorful incidents of that campaign occurred—a physical confrontation between Sanders and Long at the Roosevelt Hotel, in New Orleans. Both men remained bitter political enemies for the rest of their careers. Sanders died in Baton Rouge at the age of seventy-five and was buried in his hometown, Franklin.

எ

Sanders' significance as governor lies in his pioneering efforts toward passage of a number of pieces of mildly progressive reform legislation, reflecting some aspects of the so-called progressive movement in vogue nationally. Two of his major contributions came in the areas of conservation and good roads. Sanders was a strong supporter of conservation legislation, and in 1908, with his full backing, the legislature passed a measure creating a State Conservation Commission. That was followed in 1910 with the first legislation calling for the payment of a severance tax by those using the state's raw materials. Although quite small, the first severance tax set a principle that became a part of the state constitution despite the opposition of industrial interests. Sanders also was the first governor to recognize the value of highway construction and pushed for legislation that would bring Louisiana good roads. In 1910, for example, the state legislature passed a constitutional amendment calling for using tax money realized from property subject to state assessment to create a separate fund for the construction and repair of bridges and highways in the state. In addition, it has been estimated that thousands of miles of parish roads were built with the backing of the Sanders administration.

Sanders' governorship was significant also for its passage of moral and social legislation, again reflecting the country's progressive mood. Sanders favored the regulation of gambling and liquor. The legislature, with his support, in 1908 passed the Locke Law, which made it a misdemeanor to operate a betting book or gambling device at a racetrack. Sanders, who later endorsed the national Prohibition Amendment (the

Eighteenth Amendment to the United States Constitution), worked for the approval in 1908 of the Shattuck-Gay Law, which set up the first requirements for the state licensing of saloons. In the area of social legislation, Sanders sought the passage of child labor laws. In 1908, largely through his efforts, the legislature passed a law tightening the minimum age and the hour requirements for employing children in industry.

Sanders' contributions to the development of the Louisiana executive branch rest on his firm leadership in guiding needed legislation through to passage. Whenever administration measures were blocked, Sanders quickly and quietly made certain changes that resolved objections but at the same time preserved the essence of his proposals. Through compromise, Sanders was able to get most of his program through the legislature without serious damage. He was a strong executive who knew how to take charge and a skilled politician who knew how to gain passage of his legislative program. The position of chief executive in Louisiana was certainly strengthened during his term.

LOUIS VYHNANEK

BIBLIOGRAPHY

Kemp, John R., ed. *Martin Behrman of New Orleans: Memoir of a City Boss.* Baton Rouge, 1977.

Reynolds, George M. *Machine Politics in New Orleans, 1897–1926.* New York, 1936.

"Sanders, Jared Young." *National Cyclopaedia of American Biography*, Vol. XLI of 63 vols., 379. New York, 1956.

Sanders, Mary Elizabeth. "Jared Young Sanders in the State Campaign of 1907–1908." *Louisiana Historical Quarterly*, XXXVIII (1955), 65–83.

———. "The Political Career of Jared Young Sanders, 1892–1912." M.A. thesis, Louisiana State University, 1955.

Wall, Bennett H., ed. *Louisiana: A History.* Arlington Heights, Ill., 1984.

Williams, T. Harry. *Huey Long: A Biography*, New York, 1969.

Luther E. Hall

Governor, 1912–1916

HALL, Luther Egbert (b. Bastrop, Louisiana, August 30, 1869; d. New Orleans, Louisiana, November 6, 1921), state senator, state judge, governor, and assistant state attorney general. Hall was born in Morehouse Parish, the only child of a planter whose family roots were in seventeenth-century Virginia. After being educated in the public schools, he attended Tulane University and Washington and Lee College, in Virginia, receiving his A.B. degree from the latter in 1889. In 1892, he obtained a law degree from Tulane. After practicing at the bar in Morehouse and Ouachita parishes for six years, he served out an unexpired term in the Louisiana Senate from 1898 to 1900, then was elected district judge, and from 1907 to 1911 served as a judge on the circuit court of appeals. In 1911, he was nominated by the Democratic party as a candidate for associate justice of the Louisiana Supreme Court.

LUTHER E. HALL. *Photograph courtesy of Special Collections, Hill Memorial Library, Louisiana State University.*

At precisely this juncture, the powerful Democratic party factions, including the New Orleans Choctaw machine under the leadership of Mayor Martin Behrman, split with their upstate allies, the city organization favoring Congressman Louis T. Michel for the governorship against a strong bid by the popular congressman James B. Aswell. The split encouraged a forceful New Orleans antimachine movement, the Good Government League, led by John M. Parker, to persuade Hall to enter the race. Hall's decision to run resulted from a hard sell by the reform faction. Victorious, Hall was inaugurated on May 20, 1912, and Parker's circle of reformers were his most prominent supporters.

Hall's governorship was characterized by weak leadership, albeit the enactment of some reforms identified with progressivism, including passage of a workmen's compensation law, the first enacted in the South, and provision for a commission form of government for New Orleans. His principal initiatives as governor, to introduce constitutional and tax reforms, were unsuccessful.

Later, Hall became embittered by two political setbacks: his failure to gain the endorsement of Democratic leaders in either the Choctaw machine or the reform factions for the United States Senate in 1918, and his inability to secure a position on the Louisiana Supreme Court in 1921. In his legal maneuvering to regain nomination to the court, once won in 1911, he suffered a fatal heart attack. His survivors included his wife, the former Clara Wendell, of Brownsville, Texas, one daughter, and one son.

~

The political career of Hall, from his involvement with the Good Government League, until his death, is a study in the frustration of an apparently honest, well meaning, and conscientious man. Prior to making his run for the Senate, Hall even served for several months in 1918 as Governor Ruffin G. Pleasant's assistant attorney general, but his goal to become a justice of the state supreme court twice eluded him as a result of the conflict between Parker's progressives and Behrman's Choctaw machine. In a sense, Hall's governorship may also be viewed as a lesson in the frustration of progressivism during the years 1911–1920.

Virtually handpicked in 1911 to run on a platform of the New Orleans reformers which emphasized electoral reforms, including the creation of a commission form of government for the city, Hall lacked sufficient legislative support to accomplish an agenda fulfilling his progressive campaign promises without cooperation with Mayor Behrman's allies in Baton Rouge. As various progressive proposals, such as nonpartisan election procedures, the short ballot, and recall, were watered down in the state assembly, Parker condemned Hall. Meanwhile, for reasons having as much to do with his admiration of former President Theodore Roosevelt as his perceived personal betrayal by Hall, Parker joined the Progressive party in 1912, which weakened his influence among Democrats in the reform faction and further undercut Hall. The commission form of government was enacted into law, yet Behrman's regular Democrats won an overwhelming victory in the city election.

Hall's efforts to refund the state debt and raise revenue for increased state services ended in a fiasco. First, he had hoped to accomplish the refunding through a constitutional convention, limited to refunding a legally controversial state bonded debt predating his administration. A convention was held in 1913, but the Supreme Court ruled sections of its new constitution invalid, leaving lawyers muddled about the legality of various contradictory sections of the Constitutions of 1898 and 1913. The only solution was to hold a new convention, which Hall proposed for 1915.

The attempt to convene a new convention foundered amid fractious bickering involving the New Orleans progressives, Mayor Behrman, and other powerful political and economic interest groups. Hall equivocated on the controversial issue of regulation of the American Sugar Refining Company, a progressive goal. Conservative elements feared that the convention would bring about an equalization of assessments, as proposed by a blue-ribbon commission appointed by Hall. Then arose the question of whether the convention's constitution would have to be submitted to the voters. Pleasant, Hall's attorney general and gubernatorial successor, opposed the convention, as did Parker, the latter charging that Behrman would dominate it. In 1915, the voters rejected the convention call.

Mayor Behrman, in his memoirs, wrote in a kindly way about Hall, whose convention call the mayor supported. But Behrman is properly suspect because he probably wanted to dominate the convention and influence it to adopt a conservative posture on the issues of taxation, electoral reform, and the regulation of trusts. Hall, in moving closer to the mayor's political views during the period of his governorship, bears out Behrman's own appraisal of the man: he was not a strong governor, he was given to a too judicious temperament, and he was inconsistent and weak in dealing with friends and foes alike. The enemies from both reform and machine factions could agree on the last assessment. What other reforms were enacted during the Hall administration, such as laws governing factory inspection and workmen's compensation, with some increase in support for public education, heralded the presence of progressivism in Louisiana, but on close examination such accomplishments did not move very far.

Without powerful support from the machine and antimachine factions, Hall failed in his effort to be elected a United States senator. Behrman was perhaps correct in his belief that Hall died of a broken heart when the glimmering of his prospects for nomination to the Supreme Court faded in 1921.

MATTHEW J. SCHOTT

BIBLIOGRAPHY
Burke, William J. "Luther E. Hall." *The Louisiana Historical Quarterly*, VI (1923), 46–55.
Kemp, John R., ed. *Martin Behrman of New Orleans: Memoir of a City Boss*. Baton Rouge, 1977.
Reynolds, George M. *Machine Politics in New Orleans, 1897–1926*. New York, 1936.
Schott, Matthew J. "John M. Parker and the Varieties of American Progressivism." Ph.D. dissertation, Vanderbilt University, 1969.
Wall, Bennett H., ed. *Louisiana: A History*. Arlington Heights, Ill., 1984.

Ruffin G. Pleasant

Governor, 1916–1920

PLEASANT, Ruffin Golson (b. Shiloh, Louisiana, June 2, 1871; d. Shreveport, Louisiana, September 12, 1937), state attorney general and governor. Pleasant was born in Union Parish, the son of Benjamin Franklin Pleasant and Martha Washington Duty. He attended Ruston College and Mount Lebanon College, in Minden, Louisiana, between 1885 and 1889, but received an A.B. degree in 1894 from Louisiana State University, where he became captain of the first L.S.U. football team. He then went north to study law at Harvard College and at Yale College. In the

RUFFIN G. PLEASANT. *Photograph courtesy of Special Collections, Hill Memorial Library, Louisiana State University.*

mid-1890s, Pleasant was an instructor in the L.S.U. Department of Philosophy and Civics. He held the rank of lieutenant colonel in the 1st Louisiana Volunteer Infantry Regiment during the Spanish-American War but evidently saw no overseas service.

Thereafter, Pleasant settled in Shreveport, where he served as city attorney. He married Ann Ector, of Shreveport, in 1906. He sought election as state attorney general in 1908 but was defeated. His state political fortunes until 1916 were variously and inconsistently linked to both the reform and planter-machine groups of the Democratic party.

The office of state attorney general, which Pleasant held from 1912 to 1916, became a springboard for his nomination for governor. That nomination came in 1916 with the support of the New Orleans Choctaw Ring, led by Mayor Martin Behrman. The circumstances behind Pleasant's victory in 1916 involved a serious split in the ranks of Louisiana's reform Democrats. One group challenging his nomination identified with a growing prohibition and antivice movement antagonistic to the city machine; another, disillusioned with the administration of Governor Luther E. Hall, ran John M. Parker as a Progressive party candidate. The 1916 contest between Pleasant and Parker marked the only significant challenge to Democratic party domination between 1896 and 1964. Pleasant outpolled Parker, 80,807 to 48,068. His victory was due to strong support from the Choctaw machine–dominated wards of New Orleans and from north Louisiana. He further benefited from the venomous racist argument that a Progressive party victory would threaten white supremacy. The Progressive party's principal support came from the southern parishes, where there was strong opposition to Democratic President Woodrow Wilson's efforts to eliminate the protective tariff on sugar, one of Louisiana's most important crops.

Governor Pleasant was inaugurated on May 15, 1916. His administration can be characterized as uneventful. Aside from some halfhearted economic initiatives, the most distinctive feature of the term was his support for American participation in the Great War (World War I) after Congress declared war against Germany, on April 6, 1917.

When Pleasant's term as governor was over, he remained active in politics. He was elected to the Louisiana constitutional convention of 1921, where he was a leading opponent of John Parker's proposal to tax natural resources—such as oil, gas, and sulfur—that were "severed" from the ground. Subsequently, however, he became a bitter foe of Huey P. Long, with whom he engaged in a debate over whether convicts at the Angola State Prison should be required to wear distinctive striped uniforms, which had been virtually phased out during Pleasant's gubernatorial term.

෴

According to the New Orleans machine boss Mayor Behrman, Governor Pleasant was a closer thing to what reformers called a "tool of the bosses than any other governor" during the period 1900–1924.[1] Probably Pleasant entered office not as Behrman's first choice but, as the mayor said, the "creature"[2] of Robert Ewing, the powerful and conservative New Orleans ward boss and publisher of the New Orleans *Daily States* and the Shreveport *Times*. But several factors undercut Pleasant's governorship. New Orleans ward leaders became increasingly quarrelsome and divided. There was a growing preoccupation across the state with prohibition and alleged toleration of vice in New Orleans,

1. John R. Kemp (ed.), *Martin Behrman of New Orleans: Memoir of a City Boss* (Baton Rouge, 1977), 290–91.
2. *Ibid.*, 291.

which particularly agitated the predominantly Protestant sections of Louisiana. Those factors, combined with the appeal of Parker as an opponent of all "professional politicians" (such as Pleasant and the New Orleans machine), worked against an effective Pleasant administration.

Pleasant did briefly take steps in 1916 to refund the state debt, and he created a new state tax commission, but proposals for the equitable assessment of property failed. None of the problems left over from the Hall administration—principally the need for tax and constitutional reform—were resolved. Pleasant preoccupied himself with preparedness for war and, later, during World War I, with patriotic mobilization. He typically receives credit for his war-related activities. Given Louisiana's poor economic position relative to many other states, the state ranked high in voluntary manpower and financial contributions. Probably, however, Parker, the machine's old foe, was more responsible for stimulating patriotic efforts. Parker, rather than Pleasant, received the highest national award given for civilian service during World War I.

But in 1920, Pleasant himself, ever the opportunist, supported Parker's gubernatorial nomination. The New Orleans machine was then in disarray, and Huey Long was undercutting the north Louisiana rural base of the conservatives' support while at the same time backing Parker. Consequently, Parker's victory in 1920 may be interpreted in effect as repudiation of Pleasant and of his generally ineffectual or necessarily passive leadership.

Although Huey Long is remembered as the leading opponent of Parker's severance tax proposals at the constitutional convention of 1921, Pleasant, allied with Long, also opposed the taxes. That this was the most significant role Pleasant played as a politician is confirmation of his lack of accomplishment as governor. Then, in about-faces so characteristic of Louisiana politics, Pleasant was a prominent booster of Huey Long in 1928 and a strong anti-Longite thereafter.

MATTHEW J. SCHOTT

BIBLIOGRAPHY

Howard, Perry H. *Political Tendencies in Louisiana.* Rev. and exp. ed. Baton Rouge, 1971.

Kemp, John R., ed. *Martin Behrman of New Orleans: Memoir of a City Boss.* Baton Rouge, 1977.

Pleasant, John R., Jr. "Ruffin G. Pleasant and Huey P. Long in the Prisoner-Stripe Controversy." *Louisiana History,* XV (1974), 357–66.

Schott, Matthew J. "John M. Parker and the Varieties of American Progressivism." Ph.D. dissertation, Vanderbilt University, 1969.

Sindler, Allan P. *Huey Long's Louisiana: State Politics, 1920–1952.* Baltimore, 1955.

Wall, Bennett H., ed. *Louisiana: A History.* Arlington Heights, Ill., 1984.

Williams, T. Harry. *Huey Long: A Biography.* New York, 1969.

John M. Parker

Governor, 1920–1924

PARKER, John Milliken (b. Bethel Church, near Port Gibson, Mississippi, March 16, 1863; d. Pass Christian, Mississippi, May 20, 1939), governor. Parker was the oldest child of John Milliken Parker, Sr., and Roberta Buckner. His maternal grandfather served as chancellor of the Mississippi Supreme Court; his paternal grandfather was a substantial landholder and slaveowner in Mississippi. In 1872, John Parker, Sr., moved his family from Port Gibson to New Orleans, where he prospered as a commission merchant, wholesale grocer, and cotton broker. The se-

JOHN M. PARKER. *Photograph courtesy of State Library of Louisiana, from LSU Gumbo, 1921.*

nior Parker participated in local politics as a member of the anti-Republican White League in the 1870s and of antimachine reform movements in the 1880s.

Young Parker attended school irregularly, at Chamberlain Hunt Academy, at Port Gibson; Belle View Academy, in Virginia; and Eastman's Business School, in Poughkeepsie, New York. Before joining his father's firm in the 1880s, he worked briefly on the family plantation at Bethel Church. His plantation interests led him to become a prominent figure in movements advocating federal programs of flood control in the Mississippi Valley. Until 1912, by when he had sold most of his inherited delta properties, Parker had been regarded as one of the leading cotton planters in Mississippi. He combined traits of daring and shrewdness in eventually taking over and expanding his father's business. Recognized as a leader among the New Orleans commercial establishment, Parker was elected in the 1890s as the youngest president of both the Cotton Exchange and the New Orleans Board of Trade. When elected governor in 1920, he was probably one of Louisiana's wealthiest citizens.

A nominal Presbyterian who as an adult rarely attended church, Parker in 1888 married a socially prominent New Orleans Catholic, Cecille Airey. He disliked the social demands of his wife and the obligations of his status in the city, and he submitted only once, and with distaste, to ruling as king of Comus, New Orleans' most prestigious Mardi Gras krewe. He regarded the formal debut as snobbish and the carnival as a frivolous waste. He looked upon "life in the great out-of-doors" as his religion and was usually eager to get away for his favorite pastimes of fishing and hunting. His love of the hunt was politically significant, cementing a friendship with Theodore Roosevelt, whom Parker met in 1898 and entertained on numerous hunting and fishing trips between 1902 and 1915.

Consistent with the stance of his father and business peers, Parker opposed the New Orleans machine, the Choctaws, which consisted of professional politicians dominated by the ward bosses of the Democratic party. From 1888 until his election as governor, Parker was typically active in mayoralty and gubernatorial campaigns, advocating a commission form of government, the expansion of civil service, the business management of municipal regulatory agencies, and various electoral reforms, including the secret ballot and recall. Parker's political positions reflected the desire of the commercial class for honest and efficient government, as well as his own social disdain for professional politicians as a group. The politicians tended to support unionism among white dockworkers, and the commercial interests to oppose it. As an antimachine reformer, Parker was an organizer of the anti-Lottery Young Men's Democratic Association in 1888, the Citizens' League in 1896, and the Good Government League in 1912. It was Parker who persuaded Luther E. Hall to run for governor in 1912. Parker was disappointed with Hall's performance and in 1912 stunned Louisiana Democrats by answering Roosevelt's call to join his Progressive party. In running for governor as a Progressive in 1916 and as a Democrat in 1920, Parker portrayed the power of the city machine as the leading issue in state politics.

Although Parker's role as an antimachine reformer derived from economically and socially conservative values, he was associated before 1920 with a broad range of progressive movements in the state and nation. As a spokesman for regional agricultural and commercial interests, he attacked northern speculators and monopolies (including Standard Oil) and championed conservation and an increase in state support for public education and roads. He advocated women's suffrage and enactment of child labor laws. Parker's identification with progressivism was greatly affected by his admiration for Theodore Roosevelt who, Parker said, inspired a sense of public duty. Thus between 1912 and 1916, Parker stood alongside T. R. on the "New Nationalism" platform of the Progressive party, which called for a strong expansion of the powers of the federal government to achieve economic and social reform. The platform was considered very liberal, but it appealed to Parker on conservative grounds, for it urged federalization of Mississippi Valley flood control and it endorsed tariff protection, which Parker hoped would apply to agricultural commodities. Parker influenced Roosevelt to allow the southern party to organize on a lily-white basis. Progressive party membership thus provided an alternative to nonpartisan opposition to Democratic rule, which Parker, who after 1892 consistently voted Republican in national elections, had long advocated.

As the Progressive gubernatorial candidate in 1916, Parker polled 38 percent of the vote, running primarily as a foe of the machine, but he received his largest support from sugar planters attracted to his party's tariff stand. The state Democrats waged a vicious racist campaign, maintaining that the Progressive challenge constituted a threat to white supremacy. Two months after Parker's defeat, the Progressives nominated him for vice-president. Roosevelt refused the Progressive presidential nomination and announced his support for Charles Evans Hughes, the Republican nominee against President Woodrow Wilson. Angered by Roosevelt's desertion, Parker campaigned for Wilson, praising the reform record of the incumbent Democratic administration.

In the 1920 gubernatorial campaign, Parker promised increased appropriations for schools, higher education, roads, and eleemosynary institutions. Furthermore, he advocated a new state constitution, cheap natural gas for New Orleans, an end to machine rule, and stronger state regulation of oil pipelines—a move directed against Standard Oil.

Typical of southern progressive governors of the 1920s, Parker combined appeals for improvements and an expansion of state services with a businesslike, efficient, and honest administration. During his term, he aimed toward many political reforms but fell short of most of his goals. He battled against the New Orleans mayor, Martin Behrman, the symbol of the machine politics that Parker so detested. The adoption of the Constitution of 1921 was seen as an important progressive step by contemporaries. Parker initiated new severance taxes on natural resources, such as oil, gas, and sulfur. One of the signal accomplishments of his administration was relocating the campus of Louisiana State University to large grounds south of Baton Rouge. But the political and social threat posed by the Ku Klux Klan drew an increasing amount of Parker's time and energy away from other matters.

In the 1924 gubernatorial contest, Parker supported Lieutenant Governor Hewitt Bouanchaud, a Catholic, against both Huey P. Long and Henry L. Fuqua, the favorite of the New Orleans ward bosses. Long finished a strong third, and Fuqua overwhelmed Bouanchaud in the runoff. The result was interpreted by most Louisianians as a thorough repudiation of the Parker administration.

Embittered by events, Parker intended to retire from politics and devote himself fully to a model farm he owned at St. Francisville. In 1927, he returned to prominence as the director of flood relief after the disastrous Mississippi River floods. He also served as a leader of the anti-Long Constitutional League in 1930. He died in Mississippi, but his cremated remains were entombed at Metairie Cemetery, in New Orleans.

Viewed against its promise, the Parker administration was not entirely successful. For example, Parker failed to challenge the New Orleans utility interests and sponsor legislation to bring cheap gas to the Crescent City. He failed to grasp the legal loopholes in legislation designed to regulate the Louisiana carbon-black industry. His fiscal conservativism led him to oppose bonding a state road-building program, instituting a progressive state income tax, and increasing the millage for school improvements. Although he had enjoyed respect as a fair arbitrator of labor-management disputes, he tended as governor to favor the open shop and strongly opposed the right of public employees to strike. He disappointed advocates of women's suffrage, opposing ratification of the Nineteenth Amendment to the United States Constitution on the grounds that it might establish precedents for black enfranchisement.

Remarkably, in view of his background, Parker not only failed to shake the power of the New Orleans ward bosses and to obtain the passage of significant political reform or the expansion of civil service but he was even subject to the criticism that he lacked the resolve to achieve those ends. He did help to organize a successful movement to oust Behrman, the machine mayor since 1904. The effort was compromised, however, by Parker's cooperation with ward bosses who had broken with Behrman. The reform mayor proved incompetent, and Behrman returned to office in 1925.

The Parker administration was successful in supporting a new state constitution, in increasing the power of the Railroad Commission (renamed the Public Service Commission), in authorizing highway improvements, and imposing a severance tax on natural resources. Students of Louisiana government have been highly critical of the often-amended Constitution of 1921, which became cumbersome and made a mockery of the governor's plea for a short, simple charter. Yet this constitution was quite progressive in authorizing the expansion of the tax base and in expanding and rationalizing the role of state government in the areas of education, highways, conservation, and business regulation—all objectives that Parker supported. A new public utilities commission was created with increased power to regulate pipelines. The idea of raising revenue by imposing a severance tax on oil, gas, sulfur, and lumber appealed to Parker as a conservation measure, with the additional revenue to be earmarked for higher education and eleemosynary institutions, such as hospitals for the insane. The governor was strongly committed to a program to relocate and substantially expand Louisiana State University. Parker deserves considerable credit for laying the foundation for L.S.U.'s growth into an important southern university.

Huey Long and others maintained that Parker should have pushed for a higher severance tax rate (3 as opposed to 2 percent), with more revenue allocated to the parishes. Long also attacked Parker's pipeline legislation as too weak. In particular, he criticized Parker's reliance on corporation attorneys, including Standard Oil's, to assist in drafting the tax and regulatory legislation, and he took exception to the governor's "gentlemen's agreements," in which the companies promised not to litigate against Louisiana in return for concessions from Parker. But Parker apparently had good reason to fear legal delays, and he did finally agree to sign legislation raising the severance rate.

Parker's leadership was also assailed by the strongly anti-Catholic Ku Klux Klan, which from 1921 to 1924 gained a considerable following, especially in north Louisiana, and enlarged its political influence. The governor forcefully condemned the secrecy, religious bigotry, and violent actions of the Klan, and supported legislation to ban the wearing of masks. In August, 1922, two men from Mer Rouge disappeared after they were abducted by Klansmen from nearby Bastrop, in Morehouse Parish. In attempting to determine the fate of the two men, Parker encountered obstruction on the part of local officials sympathetic to the Klan. Mutilated corpses, apparently those of the missing men, were later discovered, but the state was unable to prove the guilt of individual Klansmen. Parker demonstrated decency and courage in his fight against the Klan. He won respect throughout the United States as an opponent of bigotry, and he contributed to the hooded order's declining influence in Louisiana by 1924. Yet the issue diverted him from other problems, and even his friends believed that he was unreasonably gripped by the menace of the Klan.

Parker's administration reflected a progressive thrust in state government and the populistic aspirations of Louisianians. But his leadership suffered from his dislike for "playing politics," as well as from his discomfort with professional spoilsmen and lawyers and with legalistic argument. As a popular leader, Parker was inhibited by a rather strict adherence to the elitist, paternalistic, and capitalistic values least appreciated by his most formidable critics, Huey Long and the New Orleans machine politicians.

MATTHEW J. SCHOTT

BIBLIOGRAPHY

Collin, Richard H. "Theodore Roosevelt's Visit to New Orleans and the Progressive Campaign of 1914." *Louisiana History*, XII (1971), 5–20.

Howard, Perry H. *Political Tendencies in Louisiana.* Rev. and exp. ed. Baton Rouge, 1971.

Kemp, John R., ed. *Martin Behrman of New Orleans: Memoirs of a City Boss.* Baton Rouge, 1977.

Phillips, Spencer. "Administration of Governor Parker." Unpublished M.A. thesis, Louisiana State University, 1933.

Reynolds, George M. *Machine Politics in New Orleans, 1897–1926.* New York, 1936.

Schott, Matthew J. "John M. Parker and the Varieties of American Progressivism." Ph.D. dissertation, Vanderbilt University, 1969.

———. "Progressives Against Democracy: Electoral Reform in Louisiana, 1894–1921." *Louisiana History*, XX (1979), 247–60.

Sindler, Allan P. *Huey Long's Louisiana: State Politics, 1920–1952.* Baltimore, 1956.

Wall, Bennett H., ed. *Louisiana: A History.* Arlington Heights, Ill., 1984.

Williams, T. Harry. *Huey Long: A Biography.* New York, 1969.

Henry L. Fuqua

Governor, 1924–1926

FUQUA, Henry Luse (b. Baton Rouge, Louisiana, November 8, 1865; d. Baton Rouge, October 11, 1926), general manager of the Louisiana State Prison at Angola and governor.[1] Fuqua's father, James Overton Fuqua, was a veteran of the Mexican War and the Civil War and a prominent lawyer during Reconstruction. For a time, young Fuqua attended Magruder's Collegiate Institute, in Baton Rouge. After his father's death, he enrolled as a special student at Louisiana State University from 1875 to 1882, with the help of his father's friend David F. Boyd, the university's president,

HENRY L. FUQUA. *Photograph courtesy of State Library of Louisiana.*

but he did not earn a degree. His first employment was as an assistant to the civil engineer building the Yazoo and Mississippi Valley Railroad, then under construction from New Orleans to Memphis. Once the section of the railroad from Lutcher, Louisiana, to Vicksburg, Mississippi, was completed, Fuqua worked for a contracting firm involved in bridge construction for the Yazoo and Mississippi Valley.

In 1883, he returned to Baton Rouge and clerked for a local hardware company. After nine years as a clerk and traveling salesmen in hardware, he decided in 1892 to organize his own firm, the Fuqua Hardware Company, which developed into one of the largest retail businesses of the kind in the region. Fuqua built a career as a successful businessman with, in addition to his hardware firm, rice, cotton, and sugarcane interests. On June 25, 1890, Fuqua married his childhood sweetheart, Marie L. Matta, and the union produced three children.

In 1916, primarily because of his business ability, Fuqua was chosen

---

1. According to Fuqua's son, the correct spelling of the middle name is *Luse,* not *Luce* as is commonly seen. Henry L. Fuqua, Jr., to Joseph G. Dawson III, April 8, 1984.

by Governor Ruffin G. Pleasant to become the general manager of the state prison at Angola. From 1916 to 1924, Fuqua brought his management skills to bear on the large rice, cotton, and sugarcane operations at the prison, which were worked with the aid of convict labor. Fuqua was so successful in applying business skills to the prison operations that the penitentiary's vast agricultural resources began to turn a profit. He also improved the lives of the inmates and won their trust. But his negative contribution to Louisiana penology was his use of convict guards, or trusties. Though cheaper than hired personnel, convict guards were also more brutal, and in time the convict guard system had to be discontinued. But Fuqua's overall success as general manager is reflected in the fact that he was reappointed by Governor John M. Parker and continued in his position until he resigned in 1924 to run for the governorship.

Fuqua had shown no interest in state politics until that year, when at the urging of friends, he became a candidate for the Democratic gubernatorial nomination. In the primary, Fuqua, a Protestant from south Louisiana, had the backing of the former governors J. Y. Sanders and Ruffin G. Pleasant, along with the powerful political support of the Old Regular machine in New Orleans, headed by Martin Behrman. The Ku Klux Klan proved to be the major issue in the campaign. In January, 1924, Fuqua finished in the first primary second to Hewitt Bouanchaud, of Pointe Coupee Parish, the candidate supported by Governor Parker. Fuqua lost to Bouanchaud in that primary by a little under three thousand votes, 84,162 to 81,382, with Huey P. Long, in his first campaign for governor, running a close third. In the second primary, held in February, Fuqua gained most of Long's country-parish vote and easily defeated Bouanchaud, 125,880 to 92,006. In April, he overwhelmed his Republican opponent in the general election and was elected governor.

Fuqua served only briefly as governor, from May 19, 1924, until October 11, 1926. He is best remembered for the vigorous anti–Ku Klux Klan legislation passed during his term, and he worked hard to suppress Klan activities in Louisiana. He did not, however, live to complete his term. When he died at the age of sixty, criminals incarcerated at Angola reportedly grieved for the paternalistic Marse Henry.[2] Fuqua was succeeded by Lieutenant Governor Oramel H. Simpson.

☙

2. Mark T. Carleton, interview with Joseph G. Dawson III, April 10, 1984.

Although Fuqua served too briefly to have a major impact on Louisiana political history, he took a vigorous stand against the Ku Klux Klan. Early in his term, he brought before the state legislature, and ardently worked for the passage of, several pieces of anti-Klan legislation. The most important of the measures, passed in 1924, made it a misdemeanor to wear a mask in a public place and a felony for a masked person to commit an assault. Both measures had an impact upon the Ku Klux Klan's activities in Louisiana.

Another significant piece of legislation enacted during the Fuqua administration authorized the State Highway Commission to contract with private firms to build a toll bridge east of New Orleans across Lake Pontchartrain. The awarding of the franchise to build this bridge to the Watson-Williams syndicate, who were represented by Sanders, created a great deal of controversy for the Fuqua administration and gave Huey Long an explosive issue for his second campaign for governor, in 1928.

Lacking as he did experience and training in politics, Fuqua, as governor, was not as vigorous a party leader in his dealings with the state legislature as a Sanders, or as flamboyant and dynamic a speaker as a Huey Long. His views reflected the probusiness attitude of state government during the mid-1920s, and his style was to exercise quiet leadership behind the scenes. Fuqua, however, was capable of forceful leadership when necessary, as when he moved quickly to implement anti-Klan legislation during his first few months in office.

Like many a Louisiana governor, Fuqua was devoted to Louisiana State University. University records indicate that he may have been one of the youngest students ever to enroll; he attended classes sporadically from the age of ten until he was seventeen. During his governorship, Fuqua regularly attended L.S.U. football games and even called the team into his office in 1925 to give them a pep talk before the game with archrival Tulane. Fuqua's attention to the university went beyond sports; in 1926, he ushered a special appropriations bill through both houses of the legislature for new construction on the campus.

Fuqua was the last governor elected with the backing of Behrman's New Orleans political machine, which had been a major force in state politics for the first two decades of the twentieth century. Fuqua's death in 1926 and the election of Huey Long as governor in 1928 marked the beginning of a new era in Louisiana politics.

LOUIS VYHNANEK

BIBLIOGRAPHY

Carleton, Mark. T. *Politics and Punishment: The History of the Louisiana State Penal System.* Baton Rouge, 1971.
"Fuqua, Henry Luce." *National Cyclopaedia of American Biography,* Vol. XXII of 63 vols., 180–81. New York, 1956.
Howard, Perry H. *Political Tendencies in Louisiana.* Rev. and exp. ed. Baton Rouge, 1971.
Sindler, Allan P. *Huey Long's Louisiana: State Politics, 1920–1952.* Baltimore, 1956.
Wall, Bennett H., ed. *Louisiana: A History.* Arlington Heights, Ill., 1984.
Williams, T. Harry. *Huey Long: A Biography.* New York, 1969.

Oramel H. Simpson

Governor, 1926–1928

SIMPSON, Oramel Hinckley (b. Washington, Louisiana, March 20, 1870; d. New Orleans, Louisiana, November 17, 1932), lieutenant governor and governor. Simpson was born in St. Landry Parish on March 20, 1870, to Samuel F. Simpson and Mary Esther Beer. He received his A.B. degree from Centenary College, at Jackson, in 1890, and his LL.B. degree in 1893 from Tulane University. Simpson married Louise Pichet, of New Orleans, in 1899. They had no children.

After his graduation from Tulane, Simpson established a law office in New Orleans. He entered

ORAMEL H. SIMPSON. *Photograph courtesy of State Library of Louisiana, from New Orleans* Times-Picayune, *May 17, 1959.*

public service in 1899, when he was appointed warrant clerk at the United States mint. In 1900, he became assistant secretary of the state senate, a post he held until he became secretary in 1908. He remained as secretary until his election as lieutenant governor in 1924. In addition, he served as secretary of the constitutional convention of 1921.

Simpson entered the 1924 race as a candidate for lieutenant governor with support from only a personal organization of state legislators.

After the opponent he was facing in the second Democratic primary, Dr. Paul Cyr, allied himself with the gubernatorial candidate Hewitt Bouanchaud, Simpson formed a ticket with Henry Fuqua, the candidate endorsed by the Old Regulars, the New Orleans Democratic machine. The Fuqua-Simpson ticket handily defeated Bouanchaud and Cyr in the second primary.

Simpson became governor of Louisiana when the Louisiana Supreme Court chief justice, Charles P. O'Neill, administered the oath of office to him in New Orleans at nine-thirty on the evening of Monday, October 11, 1926, after Governor Henry L. Fuqua's death at the executive mansion in Baton Rouge earlier the same evening. Simpson thus became the first Louisiana lieutenant governor to succeed to the governor's office through the death of a governor since Samuel D. McEnery replaced Louis A. Wiltz in 1881.

Simpson dealt with a number of challenges during his term. He became embroiled in a long-standing controversy over bridge construction in the New Orleans area. The terrible Mississippi River floods of 1927 threatened the very life of the city of New Orleans. But when Simpson sought election as governor in his own right in the campaign of 1928, he ran third in a field of three.

Simpson's defeat in the 1928 campaign by no means ended his public career. The new governor, Huey P. Long, appointed him the special representative of the Louisiana Tax Commission in New Orleans. Simpson returned to his old post as secretary of the senate during its 1932 session, and in September, 1932, Governor Oscar K. Allen appointed him attorney for the inheritance tax collector in Orleans Parish, replacing Earl K. Long.

Simpson died of a heart seizure. His funeral was held at the Carrollton Avenue Methodist Church, and he was buried at Greenwood Cemetery.

☙

Although part of the Fuqua ticket in 1924, Simpson had few ties with the Old Regulars. In 1925, he supported the insurgent New Orleans mayoral candidate Paul H. Maloney in his race against Martin Behrman. In 1926, he supported United States Senator Edwin S. Broussard in his reelection race against the Old Regular candidate, J. Y. Sanders, an attorney for the corporation that owned the Pontchartrain toll bridge.

Simpson's steadfast opposition to the Pontchartrain toll bridge aptly represents his relationship with the Old Regulars and their allies. In 1918, the state's electorate had approved a constitutional amendment authorizing construction of a toll-free bridge across Lake Pontchartrain from New Orleans to the Mississippi Gulf Coast, but no construction funds had been provided. Succeeding Louisiana governors also failed to provide funds, but in February, 1925, the highway department awarded a franchise to the Watson-Williams group, a syndicate of private investors allied with the Behrman machine, to build a toll bridge from eastern New Orleans northeasterly toward Slidell. Soon after entering office, however, Governor Simpson announced that the state would construct a rival free bridge along the Chef Menteur–Rigolets route. Later, after he lost his bid for a full term in 1928, Simpson fulfilled a request from Huey Long, the governor-elect, and instituted free ferry service on a route parallel to the toll bridge, thus reducing its revenue.

If political considerations often dominated the Pontchartrain bridge controversy, the great Mississippi River flood of 1927 tested the governor's administrative talents. During the spring of 1927, a record flood swept down the Mississippi Valley and threatened to top the levees protecting New Orleans. On April 26, with several days of hurried conferences behind him, Simpson ordered the Mississippi River levee cut at Caernarvon, on the east bank of the river between Poydras and Braithwaite, south of New Orleans, in order to relieve pressure on the city's sodden levees. Later he called a special legislative session to compensate property owners in Plaquemines and St. Bernard parishes for damages resulting from the Caernarvon crevasse. He furthermore approved the Tri-State Flood Control League, through which Louisiana, Arkansas, and Mississippi lobbied for adequate flood-control measures in Congress.

Simpson's greatest political challenge occurred during the 1928 gubernatorial campaign, in which he faced Huey Long and Congressman Riley J. Wilson. The Old Regulars believed that Simpson was too unpopular and too weak to win, and they detested Long. In persuading Wilson to run, they hoped to capitalize, in the wake of the 1927 flood, on the expertise he gained in fourteen years of service on the flood-control committee in the United States House of Representatives. The move backfired, however, when Long caustically commented that after Wilson's years of attending to flood-control measures, Louisiana had suffered its worst flood on record. The main issues of the campaign were Huey Long and his proposals to improve the conditions of the common people of Louisiana: toll-free bridges, state-owned, "free" school textbooks, increased road construction, improved state social services, and opposition to machine and corporate rule. Wilson, a self-made man and ardent spokesman for conservative beliefs, called for restriction of government, economical government, and low taxes. Simpson recognized the need for an increasingly activist state government, but his statements indicate that his reform streak ran shallow: he favored free textbooks only if the money needed to buy them could be raised without increasing taxes. To combat the rising tide of Longism, Wilson and Simpson tried to persuade Louisiana voters that their opponent represented an attempt by communism to take over the state. But neither Wilson nor Simpson found the political strength to overcome Long's appeal. Simpson finished third in the first Democratic primary with 80,325 votes, compared with Wilson's 81,747 and Long's 126,842. Wilson and the regulars backing him chose not to continue the struggle into the second primary.

T. Harry Williams in his biography of Huey Long correctly maintains that Simpson's political career exhibited a basic conservatism. During his years as secretary of the senate, Simpson acquired a reputation for political accommodation that he brought with him to the governor's office. He was not, however, a man without principle. He fought the Pontchartrain toll bridge in part because of political considerations and in part because of principle, but no matter which consideration dominated his mind, his establishment of the free state bridge alienated one of the strongest power blocs in the state. Moreover, Simpson sought to dismiss Dr. Valentine K. Irion as conservation commissioner when he discovered a $24,500 overdraft in Irion's department. His failure to remove Irion cannot be blamed on apathy or accommodation, for even the master politician Huey Long needed intricate legislative and legal maneuvering in order to topple Irion, as he finally did in 1929.

In retrospect, Simpson functioned as a transitional figure between the old days of Old Regular dominance and the new era of Huey Long. He appeared aware that the regulars and their allies had misused Louisiana's resources and people, but he lacked the personal attributes to implement the political reform that might have arisen from that vague conviction. It did not help Simpson that he had a poor public presence and was a poor speechmaker. As Williams said of him after 1928, he was, even in his days as governor, "at the edges of power, a rather pathetic figure whose abilities were not great enough to accomplish his ambition."[1]

JERRY PURVIS SANSON

BIBLIOGRAPHY

Baton Rouge *Morning Advocate*, May 16, 1932, April 14, 1957.
New Orleans *Times-Picayune*, October 12–November 22, 1926, November 18–20, 1932, April 8, 1971.
Sindler, Allan P. *Huey Long's Louisiana: State Politics, 1920–1952.* Baltimore, 1956.
Wall, Bennett H., ed. *Louisiana: A History.* Arlington Heights, Ill., 1984.
Williams, T. Harry. *Huey Long: A Biography.* New York, 1969.

Huey P. Long

Governor, 1928–1932

LONG, Huey Pierce, Jr. (b. near Winnfield, Louisiana, August 30, 1893; d. Baton Rouge, Louisiana, September 10, 1935), chairman of the Public Service Commission, governor, and United States senator. Huey Long attended the public schools in Winnfield, Louisiana, and enrolled for a time at the University of Oklahoma, at Norman. On April 12, 1913, he married Rose McConnell, and they lived in Memphis, Tennessee, for six months before moving to Winnfield. In 1914, the year of the outbreak of World War I in Europe, Long decided to end his four-year career as a sales-

HUEY P. LONG. *Photograph courtesy of State Library of Louisiana.*

man. He enrolled as a special student for law studies at Tulane University in 1914. Auditing additional courses and reading the law, he worked with a tutor in order to prepare for the bar exam.

Long was admitted to the bar on May 15, 1915, at the age of twenty-

---

1. T. Harry Williams, *Huey Long* (New York, 1969), 278–79.

one, and opened his practice of law in Winnfield. He began to specialize in workmen's compensation cases and in land titles and timber rights. He was elected to the Railroad Commission (later renamed the Public Service Commission) in 1918, in which year he moved his legal practice to Shreveport. Serving on the Railroad Commission until 1928, Long was its chairman from 1921 to 1928. As a Democrat, he unsuccessfully sought the governorship in 1924. He was elected governor of Louisiana in 1928 and used every power the office offered during his term, from May 21, 1928, until January 25, 1932. Stepping into national politics, he won election to the United States Senate in 1930, while still governor of the state. He assumed his duties in the Senate on January 25, 1932, and held the seat until his death. He served as Democratic national committeeman from 1928 to 1935 and as chairman of the Democratic state central committee in 1934 and 1935. Long was shot at the state capitol in Baton Rouge on September 8, 1935, and died on September 10, 1935.

℺

No other governor of Louisiana, and perhaps few Americans, have been so controversial as Huey Long. His programs as governor of Louisiana and his influence as a United States senator enabled him to make modern political and economic history at both the state and the national levels. He strongly influenced contemporary attitudes regarding wealth and poverty and was noticeably moderate on the race issue. No single governor has shaped modern Louisiana political and social development so much as Long has.

In the 1928 Democratic state primary, Long received forty thousand more votes than his closest contender, Riley J. Wilson, with an even larger lead over the third-place contender, Oramel H. Simpson. None of the three candidates received a majority. Wilson decided not to enter into a runoff election; Simpson announced his support for Long. There were no Republican candidates for the governorship, and Long became governor. Long thus entered the governor's office in 1928 without a majority of the popular vote and without the support of a legislative majority.

During his governorship, he increased the spending on public education heavily and strove to improve adult literacy; Louisiana then had the highest rate of illiteracy in the nation. Long's insistence that the state provide free textbooks for school children was both innovative and bold but produced a strong reaction from conservative elements in the state. Long forestalled legal, political, and religious objections to the state funding of texts for parochial schools by having the legislation specify that the spending was for school-age children rather than school systems or institutions. Following the precedent set by Governor John M. Parker, Long increased the funding and enlarged the faculty of Louisiana State University, and he established a medical school. A massive road-building, paving, and graveling program brought Louisiana's road system into the twentieth century. Long launched a highway-building program that added 2,500 miles of paved roads, 1,308 miles of asphalt roads, and 9,000 miles of gravel roads. Under his administration and that of Oscar K. Allen, construction was begun on two bridges across the Mississippi within Louisiana. Long's biggest bridge-building efforts, however, lay in the area of social and economic reform.

Political and economic power were naturally intertwined in Louisiana. Popular government had been more facade than reality. The planter-business interests effectively controlled the state. Moreover, most Louisianians acquiesced in this "gentlemen's rule," either out of frustration or as a result of intimidation. One did not easily vote against the interests of the landlord, the local merchant, and the banker. Black citizens had little more than token respresentation since the approval of provisions limiting suffrage in the Constitution of 1898. Under that constitution, only men who could read or write or who owned at least three hundred dollars' worth of property could vote in elections. These provisions disfranchised practically all blacks and a substantial portion of white citizens. Many white men were reenfranchised by the grandfather clause that allowed a man to vote if his father or grandfather voted before 1868, irrespective of the literacy and property tests. But whites and blacks alike were further discouraged from voting by the requirement of a poll tax as qualification for the suffrage. The state's Constitution of 1921 had not changed the reality of limited suffrage in Louisiana.

Although the power of the so-called Bourbons had clearly been eroded by events of the Populist and Progressive eras, and particularly by Governor John M. Parker's assault on New Orleans' "Ring rule" in 1920, political and economic power in 1924 remained in the hands of the few rather than the many. Long challenged that historic arrogating of power and sought to, and did, create a new popular majority in Louisiana politics comprising primarily small farmers, laborers, the rising urban business interests, a few of the "old guard," and a very small and muted black representation.

Long used several means in leading an assault on machine politics in New Orleans. He waged political warfare on Mayor T. Semms Walmsley, the New Orleans Public Service Company, and the Choctaw Club, the urban bosses who effectively controlled the New Orleans city and parish government. Long had promised during his campaign to bring natural gas to New Orleans consumers, who were paying high prices for the more expensive and less suitable manufactured gas. As governor, he fulfilled his promise.

Long's experiences on the Public Service Commission foreshadowed many of his attitudes and policies as governor. As a new member of the commission, he had secured a P.S.C. endorsement that pipelines were public carriers and subject to the commission's regulation. The legislature and Governor Parker supported the ruling, but Standard Oil succeeded in getting the supporting legislation weakened and attempted to oust Long from his seat on the commission. Long's battles with Standard Oil brought his first statewide recognition as a friend of the common man. That was followed by his dramatic reversal of telephone rate increases, which resulted in large refunds to all telephone customers. In 1922, Long had succeeded in encouraging the legislature to enact a 3 percent severance tax on petroleum. Thus, Long's attacks on the New Orleans Public Service Company, the virtual forcing of a natural-gas agreement on the company (which critics argued surreptitiously benefited the company), the construction of toll-free bridges across the Mississippi and the Chef Menteur–Rigolets route across Lake Pontchartrain, and his anti-big-business attitude endeared him to many Louisianians within and without the city of New Orleans and helped him create a new structure of political power in the state. Long also sponsored the repeal of a recently enacted tax on cigarettes and tobacco products and the imposition of a severance tax on the basis of the quantities of the natural resources extracted rather than their market value. Protests from Standard Oil, Ohio Oil, and other business groups simply convinced the greater number of Louisianians that what Huey Long was doing needed doing and that he was a true champion of the people.

Even more convincing proof of Long's commitment to the common people was the way he persuaded the legislature in 1934 to pass a constitutional amendment removing the poll tax. Although it is estimated that the removal of the tax qualified only an additional 10 percent of the citizenry to vote, a very few of whom were black, symbolically the action appeared pure democracy. More important to the interests of the poorer elements in Louisiana was the approval of a homestead bill, which effectively removed the property tax on the homes of vast numbers of Louisianians, a tax that indeed fell disproportionately on poor and middle-class residents. Long's policies supporting free textbooks, charity hospitals, free night schools for adults, and corporation franchise taxes suggested a Robin Hood morality.

Overlooked was Long's basic political pragmatism: he compromised and negotiated whenever it was in his or his constituents' interests to do so. For example, in the legislative session of 1931, he agreed with his old enemies, the New Orleans Choctaw legislators, to dedicate 45 percent of a new one-cent gasoline tax to pay the debt of the Port of New Orleans and to let $700,000 each year go for street repair in New Orleans and $7 million for bridge construction. In return he got their decisive support of a $75-million highway bond issue, a bill hiking the state gasoline tax to five cents per gallon, approval of bonds for a new state capitol, and the removal of impeachment charges against him.

Earlier, in 1929, the New Orleans Choctaw Club and the Standard Oil Company, among others, had reacted to Long's plan to enact a five-cent-per-barrel tax on refined crude by organizing a legislative bloc that rejected the proposed tax and entered impeachment charges against him. The nineteen impeachment articles charged Long with giving bribes, misusing state funds and property, unconstitutionally disposing of civil authority, carrying concealed weapons, violently abusing officials of the state, committing gross misconduct and blackmail, usurping the authority of the legislature, and acting as an accomplice in a murder. Eight charges reached the state senate. Long reacted with public protests that he was being "crucified" by Standard Oil and that the legislators who voted the impeachment articles were themselves bribed by the company. On the second day of the trial, the names of fifteen senators on a round-robin document presented to the chamber testified that they would vote "for acquittal regardless of any evidence which tended to prove the guilt of Huey Long." Each signer rose and identified himself. A two-thirds vote for impeachment was impossible. The issue was dead. But the impeachment motion was not withdrawn until 1931, after Long had won support with public largess for the city of New Orleans.

One result of the impeachment proceedings in 1929 and the rejection of the governor's multimillion-dollar road-bond issue was Long's determination to take the issues to the people. He did this, curiously, by running for the United States Senate in 1930 while retaining the office of governor. His campaign newspaper, the *Louisiana Progress*, which was published in Mississippi in order to avoid libel laws and suits, announced his senatorial bid in July, 1930. Long defeated the incumbent, Joseph E. Ransdell, with 57 percent of the vote, and he carried fifty-three of the sixty-four parishes in the state. Citing the hostility of his lieutenant governor, Dr. Paul Cyr (who unsuccessfully attempted to have Long removed from the Governor's office on the grounds that it was unconstitutional to hold two offices at once), and his unfinished business in the state, Long did not take his seat in the Senate until 1932.

He left for Washington, D.C., only after securing the victory of an entire slate of pro-Long candidates for state office, headed by Oscar K. Allen. Long immediately became a major political factor in the national elections of 1932 and in the administration of President Franklin D. Roosevelt. Long campaigned for Roosevelt and, after his inauguration, urged Roosevelt to wage war against the "money power" and against poverty. Senator Long became the proponent of the "Share Our Wealth" plan, which would have liquidated personal fortunes in excess of three million dollars and used the money to create a giant public trust to give every family $5000 with which to buy a house, a car, and a radio; to provide a $30 pension for persons over 65; to guarantee a $2,500 minimum salary to workers; to grant cash bonuses to veterans; and to establish a government-paid college education program for qualified youths. In the title words of the song, Long proposed to make "Every Man a King." But many believed that he was most interested in making himself president of the United States, and Long and Roosevelt soon became political adversaries.

Long rapidly expanded his influence through the spread of "Share Our Wealth" clubs, believed by some to be the nucleus of a broad-based political machine. He campaigned actively for anti-Roosevelt candidates for the Senate and House of Representatives, while Roosevelt supporters went into Louisiana to campaign against pro-Long candidates for state offices. The United States Senate conducted an investigation of the 1932 election, which had sent Long's handpicked candidate, John H. Overton, to the Senate. The Internal Revenue Service investigated the personal tax returns of Long and his chief lieutenants. Federal relief funds for Louisiana projects were curtailed. In Louisiana, the Choctaw group ended their uneasy alliance with Long, and anti-Long forces succeeded in winning the New Orleans city government elections. Bitter battles ensued between pro-Long and anti-Long forces throughout the state and in the legislature. Generally, in the confrontations, Long prevailed and his power and persuasion grew. He constantly enhanced the power of the governor's office at the expense of legislative, parish, commission, and municipal authority. His popular appeal also increased. T. Harry Williams identifies Huey Long as a successful "mass leader"— neither a dictator nor a demagogue, as his critics and political enemies contended.

By 1935, according to one authority, Long was making serious inroads in the Democratic following of Roosevelt on a national level. Long accused Roosevelt of "selling out" to big business, of failing to pursue the interests of the "little people," and of being unable to cure the Great Depression. Criticism from Long and others such as Father Charles Coughlin and Dr. Francis Townsend helped precipitate a new reform effort by the New Deal, which produced the steeply graduated income tax and the Social Security Act, of 1935. Although there was considerable debate over whether Long had, in fact, become a serious contender for the presidency in 1936 and a threat to Roosevelt's reelection, the test was never to be. On September 8, 1935, in the state capitol in Baton Rouge, Long was shot by Dr. Carl A. Weiss, Jr., the son-in-law of one of Long's political opponents. Long died two days later.

Huey Long remains a controversial figure in history as in life. He was viewed, on the one hand, as one of America's classic demagogues or dictators and, on the other, as a great democrat and mass leader. Creator of a powerful political machine, often charged with being corrupt, he was one of Louisiana's most despised and disdained figures. Conversely, he both promised and accomplished much, becoming one of Louisiana's most beloved and admired governors. Despite the controversies and the heavy-handed regime he imposed on the state, few can deny that more Louisianians were able to lead better lives because of him.

Henry C. Dethloff

BIBLIOGRAPHY

Brinkley, Alan. *Voices of Protest: Huey Long, Father Coughlin, and the Great Depression.* New York, 1982.

Dethloff, Henry C. "Huey Pierce Long: Interpretations." *Louisiana Studies*, III (1964), 219–32.

————. "The Longs: Revolution or Populist Retrenchment?" *Louisiana History*, XIX (1978), 401–12.

————. *Huey P. Long: Southern Demagogue or American Democrat?* Lexington, Mass., 1967; rpr. Lafayette, La., 1978.

Jeansonne, Glen. "Challenge to the New Deal: Huey P. Long and the Redistribution of National Wealth." *Louisiana History*, XXI (1980), 331–39.

Kane, Harnett T. *Louisiana Hayride: The American Rehearsal for Dictatorship, 1928–1940.* New York, 1941.

Long, Huey P. *Every Man a King.* New Orleans, 1933.

McCoy, Donald R. *Angry Voices: Left-of-Center Politics in the New Deal Era.* Lawrence, Kans., 1958.

Martin, Thomas O. *Dynasty: The Longs of Louisiana.* New York, 1960.

Schlesinger, Arthur M., Jr. *The Politics of Upheaval.* Boston, 1960.

Sindler, Allan P. *Huey Long's Louisiana: State Politics, 1920–1952.* Baltimore, 1956.

Wall, Bennett H., ed. *Louisiana: A History.* Arlington Heights, Ill., 1984.

Williams, T. Harry. "The Gentleman from Louisiana: Demagogue or Democrat?" *Journal of Southern History*, XXVI (1960), 1–21.

————. *Huey Long: A Biography.* New York, 1969.

Zinman, David. *The Day Huey Long Was Shot: September 8, 1935.* New York, 1963.

Alvin Olin King

Governor, 1932

KING, Alvin Olin (b. Leoti, Kansas, June 21, 1890; d. Lake Charles, Louisiana, January 21, 1958), state senator, lieutenant governor, and governor. Born to George Merritt King and Bessie B. Sterling, King was the son of a Kansas farmer and the grandson of a New England Methodist minister. When he was four months old, his family joined other midwesterners in the move to the new rice fields near Lake Charles. There his father began as a farmer but became a leading figure in lumber, rice milling, and the wholesale grocery business. King was educated in public schools and

ALVIN OLIN KING. *Photograph courtesy of State Library of Louisiana, from* Louisiana Conservation Review, May, 1932.

graduated from Lake Charles High School in 1908. He attended Parson (Kansas) Business College, worked one year as a bookkeeper, entered Tulane University School of Law, and received an LL.B. degree in 1915. In 1916, King married Willie Lee Voris. They had two children, Alvin O., Jr., and Voris.

After graduating from Tulane, King returned to Lake Charles to practice law. He entered public service in 1920 as city attorney of Lake Charles. In 1924, he was elected to the Louisiana Senate to represent a five-parish district (Calcasieu, Cameron, Beauregard, Allen, and Jefferson Davis); he was reelected in 1928. In 1930, during the administration of Governor Huey P. Long, he was elected president pro tempore of the senate, an office next in succession to that of the lieutenant governor, second in succession to that of the governor. Within the next two years, in an unprecedented set of circumstances, King succeeded to both executive offices.

King's dramatic accession came as a result of Huey Long's break with his elected lieutenant governor, Dr. Paul Cyr, a dentist from Jeanerette. Cyr himself precipitated the move when he declared that the election of Long to the United States Senate in 1930 (midway through his term as governor) and the transmittal of his credentials to the clerk of the Senate constituted membership in that body. Since Long could not legally hold both positions, Cyr argued that a vacancy in the office of governor existed—even though Long had not gone to Washington to take the oath of office. In the fall of 1931, Cyr declared himself governor, solemnly took oath to that office, and filed an ouster suit against Long in state district court. Long promptly retaliated. He proclaimed that Cyr held no office: Cyr had vacated the office of lieutenant governor by prematurely and illegally assuming the governorship. State courts ultimately accepted Long's argument that only the United States Senate can determine its membership and only the state legislature can remove a governor. Long also cited precedents of governors of other states who, on election to the Senate, completed their terms as governor prior to joining the nation's upper house.

In line with his own pronouncements on Cyr's untimely move, Governor Long called for the legal successor to the lieutenant governor to assume that post. Senator King, in Lake Charles at the time, had taken no role in the proceedings, but as president pro tempore he was summoned to Baton Rouge to take the oath of office. After examining all laws concerning vacancy and succession, conferring with Long, and trying, unsucessfully, to reach Cyr by telephone, King on October 14, 1931, at the age of forty-one, was sworn in as lieutenant governor of the state of Louisiana. With no legal challenge from Cyr, who insisted that he was governor, King immediately assumed all duties of the office formerly held by Cyr.

The second succession came early the next year. After the landslide victory of Long's state ticket in January, 1932, Long took his seat in the United States Senate, leaving King to complete his term as governor. Cyr then came forth with another suit, this time claiming that he, as lieutenant governor, was the rightful heir when Long took the Senate oath. He opened a "seat of government"[1] in a Baton Rouge hotel, accused King of serving at the head of an "insurrection,"[2] and demanded that he vacate the governor's office. King "respectfully declined,"[3] and no favorable court action followed. Cyr's failure to challenge King's succession as lieutenant governor had weakened his claim.

King maintained *de facto* possession of the executive office from January 25 until May 16, 1932, when he presided at the inauguration of Oscar K. Allen. On his accession to the governor's office, he expected merely to tend to paperwork, sign commissions, approve warrants, and transact state business of a routine nature for the three and one-half months until Allen's inauguration. By the end of the first week, however, King was touring flooded areas in north Louisiana by motorboat and facing a major crisis in state finances. Because of the ebbing national bond market, Louisiana was unable to sell highway bonds at an acceptable interest rate. After a conference with the state highway commissioner, Governor King ordered a curtailment of Long's renowned road program and a 50-percent cut in the highway department's payroll and staff. King studied financial problems confronting other state agencies, investigated the efficiency of operations, and continued to stress the need for economic and revenue conservation. In a report to the incoming legislature, he called for a lowering of the tax rate, particularly the levy on improved property, and an overall retrenchment in state expenditures.

On leaving office, he resumed the practice of law in Lake Charles,

1. Baton Rouge *Morning Advocate*, January 28, 1932.
2. Baton Rouge *State-Times*, February 1, 1932; New Orleans *Item*, February 1, 1932.
3. E. A. Conway Scrapbook Collection of Long Materials (Louisiana State Library, Baton Rouge), Vol. V.

later becoming the senior partner in the firm of King, Anderson, and Swift. He also served as chairman of the board of the Powell Lumber Company, the Farmers Land and Canal Company, the Farmers Rice Milling Company, Kelly-Weber and Company, and the Bennett Oil Company. Active in civic and professional organizations, King was president of the Lake Charles Association of Commerce in 1948, national councillor of the United States Chamber of Commerce from 1947 to 1954, and president of the Louisiana State Bar Association from 1952 to 1953.

≈

"The more I try to get out of politics, the more I get into it,"[4] said King as he prepared to be sworn in as governor in 1932. He had already decided not to run for reelection to the state senate and disavowed any plans to run for any other position.

Actually, King was a conservative, an uncommon breed among state officials during the Long years. Politically, he referred to himself as an independent in relation to the bitter pro- and anti-Long factionalism of the time. As a state senator, he had worked with the administration, particularly on measures important to his district. He supported much of Long's legislation, but not all. In 1929, he did not join pro-Long senators in signing the famous Round Robin, which ended impeachment maneuvers against the governor. At home most of his personal and professional associates were anti-Long. In fact, when he left office and returned to Lake Charles, his new law partner was the future governor Sam Jones, already one of the leading opponents of Long in southwest Louisiana.

How had King, with so many anti-Long relationships, come to hold the post in the state senate that was next in the line of executive succession? When King ran for president pro tempore in 1930, Long put up no candidate to oppose him; he asked his followers to support King. Could Long have foreseen the wisdom of having such a person at hand should Cyr try to assume the governorship? Surely it all worked to Long's benefit. King had no difficulty in achieving recognition as governor. The traditionally anti-Long Baton Rouge business community and city administration had a testimonial dinner in his honor; local Boy Scouts recognized him with the presentation of an honorary merit

---

4. Baton Rouge *State-Times*, January 25, 1932.

badge. In court some of the most prominent lawyers in the state came to King's aid in countering Cyr's legal pleas. No volunteers flocked to support the former lieutenant governor's call to evict King.

In all, King's demeanor had a calming effect on Louisiana, and members of both political factions readily accepted him as chief executive. In 1932, observers hoped that this boded well for the Pelican State: perhaps political peace had returned to Louisiana, perhaps the truce would last. The hopes proved wistful.

BETTY M. FIELD

BIBLIOGRAPHY

E. A. Conway Scrapbook Collection of Long Materials. Louisiana State Library, Baton Rouge.
Lake Charles *American Press*, April 23–May 23, 1932.
New Orleans *Times-Picayune*, January 25–May 17, 1932, February 23, 1958.
Sindler, Allan P. *Huey Long's Louisiana: State Politics, 1920–1952*. Baltimore, 1956.
Who's Who In America. Vol. XXX of 36 vols. Chicago, 1958.
Williams, T. Harry. *Huey Long: A Biography*. New York, 1969.

Oscar K. Allen

Governor, 1932–1936

ALLEN, Oscar Kelly (b. near Winnfield, Louisiana, August 8, 1882; d. Baton Rouge, Louisiana, January 28, 1936), state senator, chairman of the Louisiana Highway Commission, and governor. Allen was born on the family farm to Asa L. Allen and Sophronia Perkins. He attended public school in Winnfield, took courses in business and teaching at Springfield (Missouri) Normal and Business College, and Trinity University, then of Waxahatchie, Texas. Allen married Florence Love, of Paris, Texas, in 1912. They had three children: Joyce Love, Oscar Kelly, Jr., and Asa Benton.

OSCAR K. ALLEN. *Photograph courtesy of State Library of Louisiana.*

After attending college, Allen taught in area schools and operated a sawmill in Winn Parish. Subsequently, he operated general mercantile establishments and real-estate businesses, and still later he invested in wildcat oil ventures in the newly discovered fields of north Louisiana. He entered politics in 1916, when he was elected assessor of Winn Parish; in 1924, he became secretary to the Winn Parish police jury.

During those years, Allen became acquainted with Huey P. Long, a young lawyer from Winnfield who shared his political interests. When Allen ran for assessor, Long backed a losing candidate in the first primary but gave his support to Allen in the runoff. In 1918, Allen lent Long five hundred dollars to complete his first political campaign and win north Louisiana's seat on the Railroad Commission (later renamed the Public Service Commission). They became business associates and shared in the ups and downs of early oil operations in Louisiana. In 1924, Allen served as district manager in Long's first gubernatorial campaign and later worked for his reelection to the Public Service Commission. In 1928, he supported Long in his successful bid for the office of governor; in that year, Allen himself won election to the state senate. For one term, he served as floor leader for Long and helped in the adoption of the free-schoolbook bill and the revision of the state severance tax on natural resources. The governor appointed Allen chairman of the Louisiana Highway Commission, where he administered Long's important highway and bridge construction program. In 1932, Long chose Allen to head a "Complete the Work" ticket and succeed him as governor. As Long prepared to take his seat in the United States Senate, voters swept Allen, popularly known as O. K., into office.

It was a victory for Long, and Allen's years as governor were in effect a continuation of the Long administration. Much attention went to carrying out Long's program of tax reform, which included the homestead exemption, the state's first income tax, and the repeal of the poll tax. After Long's death, in September, 1935, Allen sought to complete Long's term in the United States Senate. He easily won the Democratic primary, but seven days later, in the executive mansion in Baton Rouge, he died suddenly of a cerebral hemorrhage.

☙

Long completely dominated Allen's administration, and critics called the new executive a puppet, a weakling, a rubber-stamp governor. Allen rebutted this, but he proudly called his administration the Long-Allen administration, describing himself as Long's chief lieutenant. He readily admitted to frequently consulting with Long; associates later described the long-distance telephone call from Washington each night to get a report on the day's happenings and to give instructions for the following day. When the legislature met, Senator Long came to Baton Rouge to direct the adoption of his program. The governor's office became his office; the governor's chair, his chair. Mocking stories circulated about the role Allen played in state government. A favorite was the tale that while Governor Allen was signing documents approved by Long, a leaf blew in and fell on his desk. Taking no chances, Allen signed the leaf.

Accusations of a Long dictatorship peaked during the Allen administration. Numerous special sessions of the legislature met to take punitive action against the senator's foes, and cities ruled by the opposition faced loss of municipal privileges. Attempts were made to strip New Orleans' mayor of authority. State committees were given the power to oversee the selection of local teachers and city and parish employees. On several occasions, Allen called out the National Guard and instituted what he dubbed "partial martial law."[1] Critics complained, but in fact no military rule resulted.

During these years, public attention was focused on the sensational aspects of the Long-Allen administration. But changes of a more permanent nature also took place. The full impact of the Great Depression hit Louisiana in Allen's first years in office, and the executive's response had a lasting effect on the state. For help in maintaining basic services, local governments turned more and more to the state. Long's governorship had increased state financing of parish schools, but during his term of office local sources of revenue still provided most of the money for school operations. By the time Allen's term ended, the state furnished 60 percent of those funds. The state also appropriated money for the building and maintenance of parish roads and thus relieved police juries of much of that expense. All of these moves further centralized government in Louisiana. Anti-Long forces often charged Long and Allen with consolidating state power for political reasons, and their complaints largely concerned legislation that threatened home rule. Laws authorizing the centralizing of control were later repealed, as future administrations restored municipal rights, but changes wrought by the administration's response to city and parish financial needs were not

1. New Orleans *Times-Picayune*, August 1, 1933.

undone. The state's influence and its responsibility for public services on the local level continued.

There were also important developments at the state level. As tax receipts continued to ebb, the depression threatened the state's financial base. Stringent economies befell most state departments. No money was available to heed the growing call of the unemployed and the poor. The Long-Allen years are often viewed as years when state aid to the needy began. A closer look reveals that this was not at the initiative of the state government. The Long-Allen administration acknowledged the need for government action, but parish requests for state assistance in the relief of the poor could not be met. Where could the state get funds to cope with the problems? The answer was obvious. A coordinated statewide program of aid to the poor and unemployed did come to Louisiana, but it came from Washington with federal funding. Soon after the inauguration of President Franklin D. Roosevelt in 1933, New Deal agencies began operating in Louisiana. On the national scene, Senator Long belittled the effectiveness of much of that program and criticized Roosevelt's failure to end the depression. But Governor Allen made every effort to cooperate with New Deal representatives and gain federal funds for a Louisiana relief program. State departments also applied to another federal agency for loans and grants to undertake public works badly needed by the state—a new Charity Hospital, a Mississippi River bridge at Baton Rouge, more flood control along major rivers, repairs to highways, completion of the farm-to-market road system, and new facilities for Louisiana State University. Allen personally offered advice, assistance, and encouragement to local governments in submitting applications for federal money to build schools, courthouses, jails, roads, sidewalks, housing projects, sewerage systems, and waterworks.

Allen had a role in Louisiana's growing reliance on the national government. Yet he never saw the full benefits of the New Deal in Louisiana. In 1935, the Long-Roosevelt clash came to a head, and the public works program became an early victim of a federal policy geared to hurt Long. Long, in turn, had numerous state laws passed challenging federal authority in Louisiana. Allen, too, voiced hostility toward federal policy. But this would not last. With Long's death in September, 1935, Allen promised to "carry the torch" for his leader, and he continued the public criticism of Roosevelt. But he also helped set the Long organization on a new course with the president. Once again, as in his years with Long, Allen was not the guiding force. But his acquiescence eased the way for New Orleans interests with strong personal motives for mending relations with Washington to take control of the Long organization. At the same time, several in the Long camp had been targets of a federal tax probe in Louisiana, and Allen was also under investigation for unreported income. Within the next year, a new state administration, selected with Allen's support, would make peace with Washington.

Allen tried to smooth over differences within the pro-Long faction. Allen's presence on the ticket allayed some resentment among the rural "Share Our Wealth" proponents who felt left out of the Longite proceedings, but the Long organization had designated someone else to win the full-term Senate seat. And Richard Webster Leche won the governorship and leadership of the state party. New leaders in the organization's inner council set their own course. The torch that Allen had vowed to carry fell elsewhere.

BETTY M. FIELD

BIBLIOGRAPHY

Field, Betty M. "Louisiana and the Great Depression." In *Louisiana Gothic: Recollections of the 1930s,* edited by Glenn R. Conrad and Vaughan B. Baker. Lafayette, La., 1984.

————. "The Politics of the New Deal in Louisiana, 1933–1939." Ph.D. dissertation, Tulane University, 1973.

Kane, Harnett T. *Louisiana Hayride: The American Rehearsal for Dictatorship, 1928–1940.* New York, 1941.

Sindler, Allan P. *Huey Long's Louisiana: State Politics, 1920–1952.* Baltimore, 1956.

Wall, Bennett H., ed. *Louisiana: A History.* Arlington Heights, Ill., 1984.

Williams, T. Harry. *Huey Long: A Biography.* New York, 1969.

James A. Noe

Governor, 1936

NOE, James Albert (b. near West Point, Kentucky, December 21, 1890; d. Houston, Texas, October 18, 1976), state senator and governor. Noe was born on a small farm to John M. Noe and Belle McRae. He attended school in the West Point area and helped on the family farm. On America's entry into World War I, he enlisted in the 369th Infantry Regiment as a private, served two years, much of it in France, obtained a commission, and was discharged in 1919 as a lieutenant. In 1922, he married Anna Gray Sweeney, in Farmerville, Louisiana. They had three children, Gay, James A., Jr., and Linda McRae.

Moving to Louisiana in the early 1920s, Noe found success as an independent wildcat driller in the new oil and gas fields of north Louisiana and south Arkansas. He made his home and established his business headquarters in Monroe. In 1934, through the Win or Lose Corporation, he pioneered in the mineral development of state-owned waterways and river bottoms. Noe later became a leader in the communications field, owning WNOE radio station, in New Orleans, and KNOE radio and television stations, in Monroe.

James A. Noe. *Photograph courtesy of State Library of Louisiana.*

Noe entered politics in 1932, when Huey P. Long, soon to take his seat as a United States senator, asked him to oppose the incumbent state senator from the Ouachita-Jackson district. Noe won the election, served as a Long legislative leader during the administration of Governor Oscar K. Allen, and was chosen president pro tempore of the senate by acclamation in 1935. This, with the office of lieutenant governor then vacant, placed him next in succession for the governorship. Noe planned to run for governor in the approaching election, with the support of the Long organization, but after Long was assassinated in September, 1935, the organization's leaders selected Richard Webster Leche for the office. Noe settled for being reelected to the state senate in January, 1936. One week after the primary, however, the sudden death of Allen, the outgoing governor, thrust the president pro tempore into the office of chief executive.

Noe served as governor from January 28 to May 12, 1936. In those months, he helped secure the release of a six-million-dollar federal allotment for highway projects and authorized preliminary work toward the establishment of a state public welfare department in accordance with the national Social Security program. Other actions contributed to his identification with the late Senator Long. In tribute to Long, Noe appointed Rose McConnell Long to complete her husband's term in the

United States Senate and declared Long's birthday a public-school and legal holiday.

With the inauguration of Leche as governor, Noe returned to the Louisiana Senate for his second four-year term. In 1940, he unsuccessfully sought the Democratic nomination for governor. In 1959, he once again ran for governor but failed to make the second primary.

Noe continued to maintain his home and business offices in Monroe, where he was known for his philanthropy. He died in Methodist Hospital, Houston, Texas, of complications from a heart condition.

☙

Noe's importance for Louisiana history lay not in his short, interim term as governor but in his overall business and political life. In his brief tenure as chief executive, he had little opportunity to make significant changes in program or policy, and his growing variance with the incoming administration further hampered his effectiveness. He and the Long organization's choice for lieutenant governor, Earl K. Long, split bitterly over candidates in the runoff for a legislative seat, and discord remained on the question of leadership in the Long faction. As governor, Noe tried to initiate work on building projects approved in the preceding administration, but incoming officials blocked the release of construction funds until after their own inauguration. Noe did manage to issue finishing contracts for a Ouachita River bridge at Monroe and presided at its dedication. Governor Leche, however, had all reference to Noe removed from the bridge's official plaque.

When Leche assumed office as goveror, Noe took his seat in the state senate and became the voice of opposition to the new administration, charging his successor with departing from the principles of Huey Long. Gathering affidavits that charged blatant irregularities in the use of state funds, Noe set the stage for the breaking of the Louisiana Scandals of 1939–1940. His try to win the governorship in 1940 failed, but his subsequent endorsement of Sam Jones helped defeat Earl Long in the second primary. Yet Noe never identified himself as anti-Long. He later reconciled with Earl Long and in 1959 formed a ticket with him— Noe for governor, Long for lieutenant governor. "The Noe team is the go team," read the campaign slogan. But this last try for office came on the plea of a tired, beleaguered Earl Long. The Noe-Long platform echoed traditional campaign cries: homestead exemptions, three-dollar license plates, better roads and bridges, old-age pensions, free schoolbooks, and hot school lunches. But those appeals no longer sufficed. Time and circumstances had taken their toll, and even the Long family was divided in its support.

Noe had been drawn into politics by Huey Long in 1932. Despite the change in conditions, he could not refuse another call, in 1959. But victory eluded him, and the last campaign ended for a man whose political life had spanned and influenced the vibrant years of bifactionalism in state politics.

BETTY M. FIELD

BIBLIOGRAPHY

Field, Betty M. "The Politics of the New Deal in Louisiana, 1933–1939." Ph.D. dissertation, Tulane University, 1973.

Hebert, F. Edward, with John McMillan. *Last of the Titans: The Life and Times of F. Edward Hebert of Louisiana.* Lafayette, La., 1976.

Jeansonne, Glen. *Race, Religion, and Politics: The Louisiana Gubernatorial Elections of 1959–1960.* Lafayette, La., 1977.

Kane, Harnett T. *Louisiana Hayride: The American Rehearsal for Dictatorship, 1928–1940.* New York, 1941.

Sanson, Jerry Purvis. "The Louisiana Homefront During World War II, 1939–1945." Ph.D. dissertation, Louisiana State University, 1984.

Sindler, Allan P. *Huey Long's Louisiana: State Politics, 1920–1952.* Baltimore, 1956.

Wall, Bennett H., ed. *Louisiana: A History.* Arlington Heights, Ill., 1984.

Williams, T. Harry. *Huey Long: A Biography.* New York, 1969.

Richard Webster Leche

Governor, 1936–1939

LECHE, Richard Webster (b. New Orleans, Louisiana, May 15, 1898; d. New Orleans, February 22, 1965), state judge and governor. Leche, the only Louisiana governor ever to be imprisoned, was the son of the salesman Eustace Leche and the schoolteacher Stella Eloise Richard. Because his father was Catholic and his mother Protestant, Leche—who became an Episcopalian—could present an appealingly mixed religious background to the similarly divided Catholic and Protestant electorate of Louisiana when he ran for governor in 1936.

In 1916, after graduating from Warren Easton High School, Leche enrolled at Tulane University, but he enlisted in the United States Army the following year, when the nation became involved in World War I.

Commissioned a second lieutenant of infantry, Leche never saw combat or even served overseas. In the two years following his discharge, in 1919, he sold automobile parts in Chicago. While there, Leche worked for the Democratic ticket in the 1920 presidential election. That was his first experience in politics. Returning to Louisiana in 1921, he graduated from Loyola University Law School, commenced a New Orleans legal practice in 1923, and began to take part in local political campaigns. In 1928, he ran unsuccessfully for the state senate as a follower of Governor Oramel H.

RICHARD WEBSTER LECHE. *Photograph courtesy of Special Collections, Hill Memorial Library, Louisiana State University, from LSU Gumbo, 1937.*

Simpson, who was defeated in the same election by Huey P. Long. In the meantime, Leche had married Elton Reynolds on October 12, 1927. They had two sons, Richard Webster, Jr., and Charles Eustace.

By 1930, Leche was a disciple of Long, and Leche served as New Orleans manager in Long's victorious campaign that year for the United States Senate. After additional services to the Long organization, the rapidly rising Leche became private secretary to Governor Oscar K. Allen in 1932, not—as many believed—on Allen's initiative but because Long desired a trusted aide near the compliant governor to keep him under control. Two years later, in 1934, Leche received an appointment as a judge on the state court of appeal in New Orleans, a position in which he rendered competent service until becoming governor.

After Senator Long's murder in September, 1935, there followed a brief scramble among Long's underlings to determine his successor. From these Byzantine proceedings, the handsome, impressive (six-foot, 215-pound) Judge Leche emerged as the front man, if not the sole substantial leader of the Long faction in Louisiana. The New Orleans furniture dealer and future mayor Robert Maestri was the strongest of several powerful figures in the background.

Although largely unknown statewide until he became the Long organization's nominee for governor, Leche received 362,502 votes in the

Democratic primary on January 21, 1936, to only 176,150 ballots for Cleveland Dear, the anti-Long candidate. The winner by a landslide, with 67.1 percent of all the ballots cast, Leche, who was unopposed in the general election, seemed destined for a serene and constructive administration. But that was not to be.

As described by the writer of one of his obituaries, Leche in 1935 "represented what the Long machine wanted. He was youthful, alert, and not too aggressive. He had no wealth, and he moved slowly and spoke with great deliberation." Tragically, for himself, for the Long organization, and for Louisiana, the Leche who had no wealth apparently became determined to acquire what he lacked, and with few scruples about the means. Soon after he became governor, the "jovial" Leche was heard to remark, "When I took the oath of office I didn't take any vow of poverty."[1]

On June 26, 1939, Leche resigned the governorship—yielding it to Lieutenant Governor Earl K. Long, Huey's younger brother. Leche said that he relinquished the office "because of my health and on the advice of my physicians."[2] One year later, in 1940, Leche was convicted, however, of using the mails to defraud, in a scheme involving the sale of trucks to the State Highway Department. As the top convicted participant in the Louisiana Scandals of 1939–1940—which resulted in the imprisonment, fining, and suicide of other leading Long loyalists as well—Leche made national headlines by being sentenced to ten years' incarceration in the federal penitentiary at Atlanta. (The relative harshness of the sentence arose from the government's failure to convict Leche on several other charges, including an accusation that the governor had profited from the illegal sale of "hot" oil.)

Paroled in 1945, Leche received a pardon from President Harry S. Truman on January 16, 1953. Prior to securing his pardon, Leche ran a tourist attraction named Bayou Gardens, in Lacombe, Louisiana, just across Lake Pontchartrain from New Orleans in St. Tammany Parish. From 1953 until his death, twelve years later, Leche again practiced law in New Orleans and appeared from time to time as a lobbyist at the state legislature in Baton Rouge. Among his distinguished honorary pallbearers were Governor John J. McKeithen and the former governors Jimmie Davis and Robert F. Kennon; the United States senators

1. New York *Times*, February 23, 1965, p. 33.
2. *Ibid.*

Allen J. Ellender and Russell B. Long; and the congressmen Hale Boggs, F. Edward Hebert, and James Morrison.

❧

Mindful that he was at least the nominal heir to Huey Long, Governor Leche did not turn his back on the thousands of humble Louisianians who had sustained the Kingfish and his retinue in power. It appeared that those who had elected Leche to the governorship assumed he would continue Long's programs. The Leche administration built roads, bridges, and schools, added to the state's medical facilities, and gave Louisiana school children free pencils, tablets, and erasers—to accompany the free textbooks Long had begun to provide in 1928.

At the same time, Leche (more urban and business oriented than Long) moved in three other directions that would have shocked and dismayed his rural, neopopulist mentor. In 1936, the Leche administration originated a ten-year property-tax-exemption program for new business and industry and created the State Department of Commerce and Industry to administer the exemptions. (This strikingly un-Longite program still exists as one of Louisiana's principal industrial inducements.) In 1938, Leche advocated enactment of a 1 percent general sales tax, a source of revenue Long had always opposed because of its regressive effect on low and modest wage earners. Leche also obtained other legislation favorable to business and industry and moved successfully to end the feud dating from at least 1934, between Louisiana's pro-Long camp and the New Deal administration of President Franklin D. Roosevelt. In return for terminating Long's radical "Share Our Wealth" program, which offended Roosevelt, and for supporting New Deal legislation more enthusiastically in Congress, Leche and his associates had federal patronage restored to them and tax-evasion charges pending against prominent members of the Long organization dropped. The resumption of cooperation between Baton Rouge and Washington out of mutual interest was popularly known as the second Louisiana Purchase. A number of observers concluded, however, that the restoration to Roosevelt's good graces was interpreted by some leaders of the Long machine as a mandate to steal freely on the local level.

In any case, once Leche and others had obviously begun to sink, the president not only made no move to support them but unleashed federal investigators and prosecutors, with apparent instructions to obtain as many indictments and convictions as possible. Perhaps for this reason, an embittered Leche professed his innocence to the end, charging that others had made him a scapegoat.

Regardless of the circumstances that initiated or concluded the Louisiana Scandals, their consequences for the Long movement were severe if not fatal: banishment from control of Louisiana's state government for eight years, together with the permanent stigma of being incurably corrupt, venal, and untrustworthy. As for Leche, a comprehensive and judicious assessment of his life and administration awaits the full biographical investigation he has yet to receive.

Mark T. Carleton

BIBLIOGRAPHY

Baton Rouge *State-Times*, February 23, 1965.
Kane, Harnett T. *Louisiana Hayride: The American Rehearsal for Dictatorship, 1928–1940.* New York, 1941.
Leslie, J. Paul. "Louisiana Hayride Revisited." *Louisiana Studies*, XI (1972), 282–94.
New York *Times*, February 23, 1965.
Sanson, Jerry Purvis. "The Louisiana Homefront During World War II, 1939–1945." Ph.D. dissertation, Louisiana State University, 1984.
Sindler, Allan P. *Huey Long's Louisiana: State Politics, 1920–1952.* Baltimore, 1956.
Wall, Bennett H., ed. *Louisiana: A History.* Arlington Heights, Ill., 1984.

Earl K. Long

Governor, 1939–1940, 1948–1952, 1956–1960

Long, Earl Kemp (b. near Winnfield, Louisiana, August 26, 1895; d. Alexandria, Louisiana, September 5, 1960), lieutenant governor and governor. Earl Long, the eighth child of Huey Pierce Long, Sr., and Caledonia Tison, was born in Winn Parish, where the Longs owned almost three hundred acres bordering Winnfield. The income from crops and livestock and the occasional sale of a residential lot enabled the family to live comfortably. More than his three brothers, Earl Long helped his father on the farm. He especially enjoyed caring for the livestock. Often he rode through the nearby woods on horseback rounding up cattle and hogs. This was a special period of his life, and years later the memories would bring him back to Winnfield. Formal schooling never appealed to Long, but he managed "to get by" with the help of his sisters. The only subjects he enjoyed were history and civics. Lack of interest caused him to leave school in 1912 and become a traveling sales-

man. He never received a college degree, but he entered Loyola University, at New Orleans, and learned
enough law to pass the state bar examination in 1926.

From 1912 through 1927, he sold
patent medicines, baking powder,
and shoe polish, earning as much as
ten thousand dollars yearly in the
1920s. The experience provided him
with valuable training for politics.
He traveled throughout the state,
making contacts with local commercial leaders and observing firsthand
the needs of the people. He developed a unique and finely tuned
capacity for dealing directly with

EARL K. LONG. *Photograph courtesy of J.
Paul Leslie, Jr., Nicholls State University.*

individuals. According to his brother Huey, "You give Earl a few dollars and turn him loose on the road, and he will make more contacts and
better contacts than any ten men with a barrel of money."[1]

For most of their lives, Earl and Huey were extremely close. As
youths, they enjoyed baseball and fishing, and even shared a paper
route; occasionally they traveled together as salesmen. Ultimately
Huey's political career drew Earl into politics. Huey entered the political arena in 1918 as a candidate for the Railroad Commission; in 1924
and 1928, he was a gubernatorial candidate. In all these campaigns,
Earl's services proved invaluable. He hung posters and met with local
leaders to obtain their support and raise funds. After the 1928 gubernatorial victory, Huey rewarded his younger brother by appointing
him inheritance-tax attorney for Orleans Parish.

During Huey's governorship, Earl concentrated his efforts on lobbying for the passage of legislation to give Louisiana concrete and asphalt
roads, bridges, and free textbooks for parochial- and public-school children. These programs galvanized the electorate and produced a political
revolution called Longism. Nonetheless, opposition developed. In the
spring of 1929, anti-Long elements mounted a campaign to impeach
Huey. But the proceedings were abruptly halted when Earl and Huey

1. Harley B. Bozeman, interview with author, April 30, 1970, Winnfield, Louisiana.

secured the pledges of fifteen state senators to vote against impeachment charges. Earl had been untiring in Huey's behalf. He was convinced of his own political ability and asked his brother for an endorsement in the 1931 lieutenant governor's race. Huey refused, claiming that the wrong Long would be in control of the state. Instead, he endorsed John B. Fournet and forced Earl to run, unsuccessfully, as an independent. In defeat, Earl turned on his brother and joined the anti-Long forces. For nearly two years he fought administration candidates and legislation. On one occasion he even testified against his brother before a congressional hearing.

The years of political exile were hard for Earl. He tried working as an attorney for the Home Owner's Loan Corporation, in New Orleans. But in 1934, Huey sought Earl out to compromise their differences and promised him greater responsibilities in the Long organization. Huey had suffered several political reversals, and according to one aide, "Huey could get along without Earl when riding high, but he would look Earl up when he got his back to the wall."[2] The assassination of Huey in 1935 brought Earl to the forefront as a leader within the Long faction; from this position he became a successful candidate for lieutenant governor in 1936.

Long's term as lieutenant governor was shaped by his determination to capture the 1940 gubernatorial nomination. He avoided controversy, supported administrative legislation, and campaigned extensively for friends. He became more at ease in public appearances and began to develop a combative delivery, especially when attacking the failures of those opposed to Longism. But in June, 1939, Governor Richard Webster Leche unexpectedly resigned, and Long assumed the governorship. Disclosures of corruption within the Long organization became frequent front-page headlines, and nearly four hundred indictments were issued. Throughout the infamous Louisiana Scandals, Long tried to unravel wrongdoing and direct a gubernatorial campaign. It proved too much. He lost the election by nearly ten thousand votes to an anti-Long candidate, Sam Jones.

Undiscouraged, Long persisted, maintaining a drive for political office that lasted the rest of his life. In 1944, however, an inability to secure funds and support caused him to lose the race for lieutenant governor. Storming back, and with the Louisiana Scandals several years in the

2. Clara Long Knott (Long's sister), interview with author, August 16, 1971, Many, Louisiana.

past, Long ran for governor in 1948 and defeated Jones in the runoff election.

As governor, Earl Long reaffirmed the electorate's identification with Longism. He secured passage of legislation that provided Louisianians with free ambulance service and free hospital beds at private institutions. The state educational system received funding for free lunches and vocational schools; the salaries of black and white school teachers were equalized. Moreover, the State Highway Department began a new program for improving roads and bridges. Still, Long's legislative victories clouded his political judgment. He sought to punish foes of the administration. On the state level, he abolished the state civil service except for those agencies working with federal funds. In New Orleans, he had the legislature restrict Mayor DeLesseps S. Morrison's authority on the commission-council and his control over the police department. City revenues were cut back. Voter disapproval of this spiteful legislation became apparent when Long sought to fill Senator John H. Overton's unexpired term. Overton's death prompted Earl to endorse Huey's son Russell, who won an extremely close election.

In the aftermath Long made peace with his foes. New Orleans had its revenues restored and received a home-rule charter; the administration supported a state civil service system. The electoral reaction was mixed. Russell Long won easy reelection to the Senate in 1952, but voters rejected the man Earl Long had handpicked as his own successor, Carlos Spaht, and elected Robert F. Kennon.

In 1956, Louisianians again elected Long governor, making him the state's first modern three-time chief executive. He started his new term by seeking extensions to the social-welfare benefits of the Long program. The civil-rights revolution, however, had produced a bitter racial atmosphere. Segregationists under the leadership of Judge Leander Perez and the state senator Willie Rainach diverted the legislature's attention by seeking further restrictions on blacks. Earl, like Huey, had never used racism to further his political career. He fought the segregationists, especially their attempt to purge nearly 150,000 blacks from voter registration rolls.

These political battles produced severe physical and mental strains on Long, triggering irrational behavior. He began drinking heavily in public and dating Bourbon Street strippers. Family members tried to have him hospitalized in Galveston, Texas, and would have kept him in Galveston as long as necessary, but he would not stay. Later, the family tried to have him institutionalized for more lengthy observation and treatment. But Long rejected the attempts at imposing medical care and unsuccessfully attempted to secure the office of lieutenant governor in the 1959 primaries. Yet he defied political observers, months later, by defeating Harold B. McSween, the incumbent congressman, in the Eighth Congressional District primary elections. A week later, in Alexandria, he died.

Earl Long's presence in state politics stabilized Longism. He provided the masses with a spokesman who could continue to articulate their needs. Like Huey, Earl vigorously identified with social-welfare legislation—laws that, with the agencies they established, improved the daily lives of thousands of Louisianians. On many occasions, he maintained that "the fortunate should assist the unfortunate, the strong should assist the weak, the rich help the poor."[3] During his three terms as governor, the state improved its highways and bridges, expanded charitable medical facilities, and sought to advance its educational system, especially by providing free school lunches and equalizing the pay of black and white teachers. With a good deal of truth, Long could look back at his record and proclaim, "I've done more for the people of this state than any other governor. The only other governor who came close was my brother, Huey, and he was just starting out."[4]

In spite of his enviable record of legislative and social accomplishments, Long became the object of criticism of academics and popular writers. More often than not, they described him as the epitome of a spoils politician intent on maintaining the incompatibility between his administration and civics-book government and on outspending all previous state administrations; rarely did the critics use such standard political terms as *reactionary, conservative, moderate, liberal,* or *radical* when describing his leadership. Instead, they focused on his fights with Morrison, on intrafactional feuds, or on the tragic events associated with his nervous breakdown. He failed, in other words, to measure up to the popular idea of the American reformer.

Reform politics conjures in the mind stereotypes or pictures of advocates of social improvements and restrictive public-utility legislation, who become the standard for measuring political conduct—past, pres-

---

3. Baton Rouge *Morning Advocate,* May 12, 1948.
4. Stan Opotowsky, *The Longs of Louisiana* (New York, 1960), 140.

ent, and future. Long's rough-and-tumble politics proved distasteful to many observers. "I'm the man who invented rock'em sock'em politics," he often argued. A politician had to be rough in Louisiana, he added; otherwise the length of his political service would be "about as long as a snowball in heaven [sic]."[5]

Rather than cultivate a preconceived image, Long worked hard to present himself to Louisiana's rural majority as a farmer, like them, but one who had turned to politics. When asked to describe himself, he once said, "I'm just a country boy, born and raised in the country, and I like the country."[6] His son-of-the-country identity led him to retreat in moments of anxiety or crisis to a rundown farm in Winn Parish; on this farm, which he called his pea patch, he raised watermelons, peas, poultry, and livestock.

Unsurprisingly, political commentators found Long's raging temper and his habits of uninhibited nose blowing, public cursing, spitting, and rump scratching at odds with their standards of twentieth-century political conduct. Partly for this reason, they dismissed him as but a striking example of gothic politics in the Deep South. It did not especially impress commentators that between 1936 and 1956, Long never received under 40 percent of the popular vote in his five statewide races and that many Louisianians perceived that their standard of living improved while he was governor. Sadly, Long's personal and gubernatorial papers were destroyed after his death.

J. PAUL LESLIE, JR.

BIBLIOGRAPHY

Haas, Edward F. *DeLesseps S. Morrison and the Image of Reform: New Orleans Politics, 1946–1961.* Baton Rouge, 1974.

Jeansonne, Glen. *Race, Religion, and Politics: The Louisiana Gubernatorial Elections of 1959–1960.* Lafayette, La., 1977.

Kane, Harnett T. *Louisiana Hayride: The American Rehearsal for Dictatorship, 1928–1940.* New York, 1941.

Kurtz, Michael L. "Earl Long's Political Relations with the City of New Orleans: 1948–1960." *Louisiana History,* X (1969), 241–254.

Leslie, J. Paul, Jr. "Earl K. Long: The Formative Years, 1895–1940." Ph.D. dissertation, University of Missouri, 1974.

Liebling, A. J. *The Earl of Louisiana.* New York, 1961; rpr. Baton Rouge, 1970.

McCaughan, Richard B. *Socks on a Rooster: Louisiana's Earl K. Long.* Baton Rouge, 1967.

Peoples, Morgan D. "Earl Kemp Long: The Man from Pea Patch Farm." *Louisiana History,* XVII (1976), 365–92.

5. Alexandria (La.) *Daily Town Talk,* July 24, 1960.
6. Winnfield (La.) *News-American,* September 9, 1938.

Sanson, Jerry Purvis. "The Louisiana Homefront During World War II, 1939–1945."
    Ph.D. dissertation, Louisiana State University, 1984.
Sindler, Allan P. *Huey Long's Louisiana: State Politics, 1920–1956.* Baltimore, 1956.
Wall, Bennett H., ed. *Louisiana: A History.* Arlington Heights, Ill., 1984.
Williams, T. Harry. *Huey Long: A Biography.* New York, 1969.

Sam Jones

Governor, 1940–1944

JONES, Sam Houston (b. near Merryville, Louisiana, July 15, 1897; d.
Lake Charles, Louisiana, February
8, 1978), governor. Born in a two-
room log cabin in the piny woods
near Merryville, Jones grew up in
nearby DeRidder. His father, a
teacher, storekeeper, and clerk of
court, emphasized education, and
young Jones soon became a voracious reader and talented speaker.
In 1915, he was graduated from
high school as valedictorian and
class president and won a partial
scholarship to Louisiana State University by placing first in a state or-
atorical contest. Supplementing his

SAM JONES. *Photograph courtesy of The
William W. Jones Memorial Collection,
Manuscripts Section, Howard-Tilton Memo-
rial Library, Tulane University.*

scholarship by waiting upon table, he attended L.S.U. for two years before enlisting in the army when the United States entered World War
I. Discharged after attaining the rank of sergeant but unable to afford to
finish college, he returned to DeRidder. There he worked as deputy
clerk of court under his father and studied law under the tutelage of a
local attorney. He was admitted to the bar in 1922.

A year earlier, he had gained his first political experience by serving
as the youngest delegate to Louisiana's constitutional convention of
1921. In 1923, partly because he opposed the Ku Klux Klan, Jones was
appointed city judge of DeRidder by the reform governor John M.
Parker. Rather than seek reelection, he moved to Lake Charles, where
he was assistant district attorney for nine years. In 1934, he married his

high-school sweetheart and joined a distinguished Lake Charles law firm, which provided his family a comfortable income.

After World War I, Jones became active in the American Legion and was elected state commander in 1920. In that capacity he frequently addressed statewide audiences. His direct and appealing style made him a public figure, and in 1939, a citizen's committee headed by Preston Foster, son of a former governor, persuaded Jones to run for governor. The state was then in the midst of the Louisiana Scandals, a period of exposés and the imprisonment of officials who had plundered the state since the death of Huey P. Long, in 1935. Jones's political inexperience was an asset to an electorate weary of habitually venal officeholders.

Five serious candidates entered the race: Jones; the incumbent governor, Earl K. Long, brother of the martyred Kingfish; James A. ("Jimmie") Noe, a disaffected Longite; James H. ("Jimmie") Morrison, of Hammond; and Vincent Moseley, a Harvard graduate and military aviator. Long led in the first primary, with Jones second, Noe third, Morrison fourth, and Moseley a distant fifth. Noe endorsed Jones; Morrison remained neutral.

The major issue of the runoff was honesty in government. Jones pledged to remove the public school system from politics, open state records to outside inspection, and repeal repressive legislation pertaining to voting, the practice of law, and law enforcement. He committed himself to delivering more state services at lower cost by eliminating corruption and inefficiency. Governor Long belittled Jones as a big shot, high-hat, and a corporate attorney from the "metropolis" of Lake Charles and summoned the legislature into special session to enact popular measures, including tax reductions. Jones employed the radio effectively, while Long induced the former "Share Our Wealth" zealot Gerald L. K. Smith to campaign for him. Receiving a heavy vote in rural parishes to offset Long's lead in New Orleans, Jones won by just over nineteen thousand votes.[1]

The Jones administration faced formidable obstacles: the hostility of the Long faction, inexperienced appointees, restrictions due to World War II, and reliance upon an unstable coalition, including both job-hungry friends and civil service crusaders. Nonetheless, Jones fulfilled most of his pledges, carefully administered the state government, and

1. Allan P. Sindler, *Huey Long's Louisiana: State Politics, 1920–1952* (Baltimore, 1956), 146, 148. See also Glen Jeansonne, "Sam Houston Jones and the Revolution of 1940, *Red River Valley Historical Review*, IV (Summer, 1979), 82.

built a reputation for scrupulous honesty. Unrelenting in his drive to clean up the state, he made enemies by his rigid rejection of pragmatic politics. Jones stripped the office of governor of much of the power it derived from the repressive laws of the Long machine and thereby reduced his own influence.

Moreover, Jones failed to build an organization to continue his policies and was unable to find a committed reformer to follow him. Limited by the constitution to one term, he endorsed Jimmie Davis in 1944. The country singer was elected but soon made peace with Jones' opponents and presided over a complaisant administration of "peace and harmony."

The 1948 gubernatorial election featured a rematch between Jones and Earl Long, along with the perennial candidate Morrison and the Minden circuit judge Robert F. Kennon. The Kingfish's younger brother branded Jones an ineffectual conservative. At a time when the state no longer faced a moral and economic crisis, Long outpromised Jones. He promised better roads, greater old-age pensions, larger homestead exemptions, and a bonus for veterans—all without mentioning increased taxes. Jones responded with speeches that made use of charts crammed with economic statistics documenting the accomplishments of his administration. But the folksy Long was a more effective stump speaker and Jones's reforms were unpopular among laid-off state workers and legislators denied pork-barrel projects. Jones ran second to Long in the primary but lost by a large margin in the runoff.

Jones never sought office again but remained active in politics. He backed the Dixiecrat presidential candidacy of J. Strom Thurmond in 1948 and directed Richard M. Nixon's campaign in Louisiana in 1968. The former governor served on numerous government commissions and advisory committees, including President Dwight D. Eisenhower's commission on intergovernmental relations, Governor Earl Long's committee on penal reform, Governor John J. McKeithen's commission to study the powers of the governor, and McKeithen's biracial committee to foster racial peace. He also helped found the Public Affairs Research Council.

⌇

Following close on the heels of the Louisiana Scandals, the Jones administration counted many successes. The governor doubled old-age pensions and increased aid to the blind and to indigent mothers. He tripled the number of students receiving free hot lunches, expanded the free-textbook program, increased funds for every state-supported college, augmented teachers' salaries, and worked to equalize pay for black teachers. He built hospitals, airports, and roads, ended payroll padding, and enacted a fiscal code that provided for competitive bidding and purchasing. Automobile license fees were slashed from an average of fifteen dollars to a flat three dollars. Jones introduced civil service and abolished annual voter registration. Moreover, he was the first Louisiana governor to undertake the reorganization and consolidation of the state's top-heavy and swollen executive branch of government. His efforts had impermanent results, however, and by 1972 almost three hundred different executive agencies, departments, boards, and commissions had reappeared. In 1974, under the direction of Governor Edwin Edwards, and as mandated by the new state constitution of that year, a reorganization of the executive branch of Louisiana's state government into no more than twenty departments took place. But even with the expenses of an active program, Jones, who had inherited a $10-million deficit from the previous administration, left a $15-million surplus.

Jones's administration was not, however, an unqualified success. He abolished the sales tax, as promised, but reinstated it when constitutional amendments providing for alternative forms of revenue were defeated at the polls. His State Crime Commission, created to unearth corruption, was judicially abolished within a year. Jones dispatched the State Guard to Plaquemines Parish when the local boss, Leander Perez, refused to accept a Jones appointee for the unexpired term of the deceased sheriff. Perez assembled a motley army of parish workers and veterans, which melted away before the state forces. Perez remained in power, however, and ultimately his candidate for sheriff triumphed.

Jones acted throughout his term without employing dictatorial methods and without a trace of corruption. But he lacked charisma, and perhaps because of his mixed record, he never became as popular as Huey or Earl Long, the brothers he fought. Most important, Jones restored respect for the state's government both in Louisiana and in the nation.

GLEN JEANSONNE

BIBLIOGRAPHY

Acadiana Profile, II (October–November, 1971). A special issue devoted to Sam Jones.

Carleton, Mark T. *Politics and Punishment: The History of the Louisiana State Penal System*. Baton Rouge, 1971.

Howard, Perry H. *Political Tendencies in Louisiana.* Rev. and exp. ed. Baton Rouge, 1971.

Jeansonne, Glen. "Sam Houston Jones and the Revolution of 1940." *Red River Valley Historical Review,* IV (1979), 73–87.

Sanson, Jerry Purvis. "The Louisiana Gubernatorial Election of 1940." M.A. thesis, Louisiana State University, 1975.

———. "The Louisiana Homefront During World War II, 1939–1945." Ph.D. dissertation, Louisiana State University, 1984.

Sindler, Allan P. *Huey Long's Louisiana: State Politics, 1920–1952.* Baltimore, 1956.

Wall, Bennett H., ed. *Louisiana: A History.* Arlington Heights, Ill., 1984.

Jimmie Davis

Governor, 1944–1948, 1960–1964

DAVIS, James Houston ("Jimmie") (b. near Beech Springs, Louisiana, September 11, 1901), member of the Public Service Commission and governor. Davis, one of eleven children of Jones Davis and Sara Works, was born in a poor sharecropper's cabin in Jackson Parish, northern Louisiana. When his chores permitted, Davis attended grade school at nearby Quitman, then went on to an improvised high school in Beech Springs, where he was graduated in 1920. That same year, he entered Louisiana College, a Baptist-affiliated institution at Pineville, adjacent to Alexandria. He put himself through the college with the usual menial jobs but also augmented his income by strumming his guitar and singing on the street corners of Alexandria.

JIMMIE DAVIS. *Photograph courtesy of Baton Rouge* State Times *and* Morning Advocate.

After earning his A.B. degree in 1924, he returned to Beech Springs in triumph, taking a job as teacher and basketball coach at the town high school. By 1926, he had saved enough to go to Louisiana State University, at Baton Rouge, where he again became a street troubador, while earning his master's degree in education.

Armed with his graduate degree, Davis took a position at Dodd College, a girls' school in Shreveport, teaching history and social studies. It was during this time that he began to write songs and to sing on Friday nights at KWKH radio under the name of Jimmie Davis. Decca Records heard of him, auditioned him, and signed him to what would be a lifetime contract. His initial record, "Nobody's Darling but Mine," was a song of his own that established him in the country-music field. He soon followed that number with other songs, many of which would also become standards. With his initial success, he formed a traveling band that played throughout northern Louisiana and Texas, but he also worked as a clerk of the criminal court, acting as spokesman for Judge Davis B. Samuel. It was Samuel who suggested to him the possibility of a political career as a way of stabilizing what was still a small income from his music.

In 1936, Davis married Alvern Adams, a young teacher from Shreveport, who was more interested in his political prospects than in his music. Shortly afterward, Davis ran for his first elective office, that of commissioner of public safety in Shreveport. He won as an independent Democrat, which he remained throughout his political career. It was in this canvass that Davis fully recognized the value of entertainment in politics, and his campaigns thereafter stressed his music over his political programs.

His musical popularity led to an occasional part in B-grade movies, usually as the leading man's sidekick. By 1942, Alvern was urging Davis to take advantage of his triple reputation—as a singer, actor, and politician—by running for the politically potent office of member of the Public Service Commission from the third district. Davis agreed, and with Alvern managing his campaign, he sang his way to major political status. As his theme song, he used "You Are My Sunshine," a song he had popularized and that was to become inextricably associated with him.

In 1944, Davis, with the apparent but discreet encouragement of the popular outgoing reform governor, Sam Jones, announced for and was elected governor of Louisiana over the Lewis Morgan–Earl K. Long ticket. A continuation of good government, wartime prosperity, and a mild commitment to the Jones reform program characterized his four-year administration. Governor Davis saw no reason to abandon his music or film activities. In his first administration, he and Alvern adopted a baby boy whom they named James William Davis. A popular if largely absentee governor in his first term, Davis was blessed with unprecedented revenues from a prosperous war economy. He left office with a solid record of accomplishment and a surplus in the state treasury.

In 1960, Davis was elected governor again, but in a campaign marred by racist controversy. His second administration, though not without its successes, was buffeted by charges of racial obstructionism, cronyism, and fiscal irresponsibility. It was also during his second administration that Alvern developed the cancer that caused her death in 1968.

Out of office, Davis emphasized his music once again, writing a total of more than three hundred songs, many of which achieved gold-record status. Davis earned induction into the Country Music Hall of Fame in 1972. An evolving difference, however, in his postgubernatorial career was his increased emphasis on gospel music to the exclusion of most other forms. In 1969, Davis married Anna Gordon, a member of the famous Carter family and of the Chuck Wagon Gang, a gospel-singing group well known to country-music listeners. During the 1970s, he performed throughout the United States, mostly on gospel-singing dates but also for civic functions and as favors to old friends.

In 1971, Davis surprised most political observers by announcing early for the 1972 gubernatorial campaign. His poor showing and failure to make the runoff put a cap on his political career.

❧

General evaluations of Governor Davis vary widely, ranging from "the best damn governor we ever had" to "an embarrassment to the state." The truth, as always, lies somewhere between the extremes.

His two administrations themselves differed in time and circumstances, the first commencing in the bloom of wartime prosperity and ending in peacetime jubilation and hope. His second administration coincided with the onset of a stern economic reality and the national confrontation of the civil-rights movement, and it was marked by racial strife, questionable fiscal policies, and a vacuum of leadership. The controversies obscured some improvements in the state and lent credence to the persistent and pervasive belief that Davis had been guided by others in his first administration.

Another difficulty in evaluating Davis comes from the intertwining of his solid and well-earned reputation as an artist with his seemingly part-time commitment to politics. There is no questioning his musical and showmanship capabilities as a country-gospel singer. Except for a few early risqué aberrations, the songs that Davis wrote and sang were the traditional country, or "white man's blues," songs of love, heartbreak, hope, and faith, possessing simple melodic lines and sung with convincing sincerity. Loving his music, his legions of fans had no difficulty in converting their love into political ballots.

Davis' first administration did nothing to dispel public faith in the man, and when Davis left office in 1948, he was at the height of his popularity. He was prevented from succeeding himself only by the one-term restriction of the constitution. Gracing his first administration were a $38-million surplus in the state treasury, a successful transition of the state from a wartime economy to peacetime prosperity, a strengthening of the civil service program, a start of over $100 million of public improvements, and the establishment of a state retirement system—all with no increase in taxes.

In marked contrast to the peace and harmony of his first administration, his second was secured through some hard bargaining with, and commitments to, anti-integration forces; it was therefore predestined to controversy. Davis seemed to be embarrassed by, and reluctant to accept, his role of anti-integration leader, but he fulfilled most of his commitments.

Like many other Louisiana governors, Davis sought both public approval and immortality through major construction projects, a tactic answering to the 1960s cliché of the "edifice complex." Most of the projects were heavily criticized at the time they were built, especially the Sunshine Bridge over the Mississippi at Donaldsonville (called, among other things, the bridge to nowhere and the bridge connecting a cane field on one side of the river with a cane field on the other side of the river), the stately governor's mansion (located near the capitol building in Baton Rouge), and the Toledo Bend Reservoir, but the projects have been vindicated since then through their use by the public and the knowledge of how inflation would have increased their cost only a few years later.

In seeking to escape the glare of unfavorable publicity—especially in his first term—Davis often left his subordinates with too much authority, disappeared from public view, left the state, and withdrew into the comfort of his entertainment career. Never one to seek office on issues, or to reply to charges, or to respond with counteraccusations, Davis campaigned on his personality, standing on the sturdy legs of music and honor, promising peace and harmony. The turmoil of the second administration damaged the reputation he earned in his first term, and he could not regain the spark for a third trip to the governor's mansion.

The troubles of his second administration left a lasting imprint on Davis. Always a proud man and jealously protective of what he perceived as an honorable reputation, he became suspicous of the media and less accessible to what might develop into an investigative interview. Political observers believe that his surprising entry into the 1972 gubernatorial campaign was less a desire to be governor again than a wish to reestablish a reputation he considered to be unjustly tarnished. His poor showing in that last attempt did little to assuage the hurt he felt.

FLOYD M. CLAY

BIBLIOGRAPHY

Carleton, Mark T. *Politics and Punishment: The History of the Louisiana State Penal System*. Baton Rouge, 1971.
Haas, Edward F. *DeLesseps S. Morrison and the Image of Reform: New Orleans Politics, 1946–1961*. Baton Rouge, 1974.
Howard, Perry H. *Political Tendencies in Louisiana*. Rev. and exp. ed. Baton Rouge, 1971.
Jeansonne, Glen. *Race, Religion, and Politics: The Louisiana Gubernatorial Elections of 1959–1960*. Lafayette, La., 1977.
Sanson, Jerry Purvis. "The Louisiana Homefront During World War II, 1939–1945." Ph.D. dissertation, Louisiana State University, 1984.
Sindler, Allan P. *Huey Long's Louisiana State Politics, 1920–1952*. Baltimore, 1956.
Wall, Bennett H., ed. *Louisiana: A History*. Arlington Heights, Ill., 1984.
Weill, Gus. *You Are My Sunshine: The Jimmie Davis Story*. Waco, Tex., 1977.

Robert F. Kennon

Governor, 1952–1956

KENNON, Robert Floyd (b. near Minden, Louisiana, August 21, 1902; d. Baton Rouge, Louisiana, January 11, 1988), mayor of Minden, district attorney, state judge, army officer, associate justice of the Louisiana Supreme Court, and governor. After attending local grammar and high schools, Kennon entered Louisiana State University and received an A.B. degree in 1923, and an LL.B. in 1925. After earning his law degree, the twenty-three-year-old ran for mayor in Minden and won the race, becoming one of the youngest mayors in the United States. At the end of his two-year term, he practiced law for a couple of years but again entered the political arena in 1930. In that year, he was elected district attorney of the Bossier-Webster district and served in that capacity for ten years. He was elected judge of the Court of Appeals of the Second Circuit of Louisiana in 1940. During World War II, Kennon served with distinction, and he was discharged as a lieutenant colonel in 1945. After his discharge, Governor Jimmie Davis appointed him as an associate justice of the Louisiana Supreme Court, where he served for two years.

In 1948, Kennon ran for governor of Louisiana as an anti-Long reform candidate. Although he lost the race, he did so well that he considered trying again for statewide office. His chance came in August, 1948, when he attempted to gain a seat in the United States Senate but lost a very close race to Russell Long. In 1952, Kennon again ran for governor as anti-Long reform candidate. He came in second in the first primary, then easily defeated his Longite opponent, Judge Carlos Spaht, in the second primary, in February, 1952. In the April general election, Kennon overwhelmed his Republican opponent. He was inaugurated governor on May 13, 1952, and served until May 8, 1956.

ROBERT F. KENNON. *Photograph courtesy of State Library of Louisiana.*

Except for an unsuccessful try for the governorship in 1963, Kennon has remained out of the political field, devoting most of his time to his private law practice. Married in 1931, Kennon and his wife, Eugentia, had three sons and made their home in Baton Rouge.

As governor, Kennon attempted to institute what he called a civics-book approach to state government. For many years, political scientists had noted the numerous deficiencies in the state government. The most glaring of these was the lack of a state civil service system. Established under Governor Sam Jones in 1942, state civil service survived only six years, until its abolition under Governor Earl K. Long in 1948. Kennon restored the state merit system and provided it with many safeguards to protect the jobs of public employees. The Kennon administration also ensured that a two-thirds vote of the state legislature would be necessary to make substantial changes in the system. Unquestionably Kennon's greatest achievement as governor, the state civil service system he initiated has become one of the strongest in the nation.

Kennon also won voter approval for several amendments to the state constitution which greatly reduced the powers of the governor. He supported a bill to make the welfare rolls public, a measure that went a long way toward reducing political interference in the welfare system. He strongly endorsed the home-rule charter for the city of New Orleans, a document that prevented the city's harassment by future gubernatorial administrations. The governor supported a right-to-work bill that outlawed the union shop, thus enabling people to retain jobs without being forced to join labor unions or to pay the equivalent of union dues. Under Kennon, Louisiana became the first state in the nation to have voting machines statewide.

The most controversial of Kennon's reforms was the fight he and his administration mounted against organized crime and vice. Kennon's superintendent of state police, Francis Grevemberg, personally led raids on the wide-open gambling casinos that flourished in south Louisiana. A United States Senate subcommittee, under Senator Estes Kefauver, a Democrat from Tennessee, had uncovered evidence of widespread vice in the state. The state police raided numerous establishments and confiscated thousands of slot machines, pinball machines, and roulette wheels.

On another tack, Kennon sought improvements at Angola, the infamous state prison. He demanded that an experienced, competent penologist be hired to run the facility. Reed Cozart, an administrator with the federal prison system, went to Angola on the temporary assignment of recommending ways to improve conditions at the prison. Under Kennon's prodding, and to the amazement of many, the state legislature appropriated money to put through Cozart's recommendations—including an increase in the prison's budget, higher pay for guards, the recruitment of a professional staff, the implementation of modern procedures, and the construction of new buildings.

During four years as governor, Kennon demonstrated his commitment to the cause of reform. His administration proved freer of graft, corruption, and spoils politics than most others in Louisiana history. Unlike the Long brothers, Kennon did not abuse the office of governor. On the contrary, he actually reduced some of its powers. Unlike most anti-Long politicians, he did not engage in large-scale favoritism, and he frequently disagreed with anti-Long leaders such as Jimmie Davis, Sam Jones, and DeLesseps S. Morrison over matters of patronage and money. Although a Democrat, Kennon gave his party only fleeting support. His disputes with President Harry S. Truman over such issues as tidelands oil were so serious that he endorsed the Republican, Dwight D. Eisenhower, in the 1952 and 1956 presidential elections. A maverick to the end of his administration, Kennon retired in 1956 spurned by professional politicians and rejected by the voters but with an impressive record of political reform and fiscal responsibility.

On the other side of the ledger, most of Kennon's reforms had a certain superficiality. For example, to implement the state civil service system was a step in the right direction, but Kennon excluded from it thousands of state employees who were to be categorized as "unclassified." His endorsement of home rule for New Orleans served only to perpetuate the stranglehold on the city's politics exercised by his political ally, Morrison. Grevemberg's raids on casinos and houses of prostitution hardly eliminated vice in Louisiana. The evidence suggests that the much-heralded crackdown merely drove vice underground and may in the final analysis have increased the influence of organized crime.

Kennon's most glaring shortcoming showed itself after 1954, when the United States Supreme Court announced its famous *Brown* v. *Board of Education of Topeka* school desegregation decision. Instead of leading boldly during those years of crisis, Kennon joined other southern politicians in proclaiming the virtues of racial segregation and in calling for "states' rights," a catchphrase that actually meant upholding segregation. He thereby helped pave the way for the racial violence that followed.

Like the other figures in Louisiana's political history, Kennon had a mixed record. His commitment to reform provided welcome relief from the unbridled political partisanship of the Longs, but his failure to win popular support for truly radical reform of the state political system meant in many respects a continuation of politics as usual in Louisiana.

MICHAEL L. KURTZ

BIBLIOGRAPHY

Carleton, Mark T. *Politics and Punishment: The History of the Louisiana State Penal System*. Baton Rouge, 1971.
Davis, Edwin A. *Louisiana: A Narrative History*. Baton Rouge, 1971.

Howard, Perry H. *Political Tendencies in Louisiana.* Rev. and exp. ed. Baton Rouge, 1971.

Public Affairs Research Council of Louisiana (PAR). *PAR Analysis.* Baton Rouge, 1954–56.

Sindler, Allan P. *Huey Long's Louisiana: State Politics, 1920–1952.* Baltimore, 1956.

Wall, Bennett H., ed. *Louisiana: A History.* Arlington Heights, Ill., 1984.

John J. McKeithen

Governor, 1964–1972

McKEITHEN, John Julian (b. Grayson, Louisiana, May 28, 1918), state representative, member of the Public Service Commission, and governor. The son of a contractor and farmer, McKeithen attended public schools in Caldwell Parish. After brief studies at High Point College, a Methodist-supported institution in North Carolina, he returned to his native state and received the B.S. and LL.B. degrees from Louisiana State University in 1942. Shortly after graduation, he enlisted in the United States Army, and he served honorably during World War II, until his discharge as

JOHN J. McKEITHEN. *Photograph courtesy of State Library of Louisiana.*

a first lieutenant in 1945. McKeithen married Marjorie Howell Funderburk on June 14, 1942, and they have six children.

In 1945, McKeithen opened a law practice in Columbia, Louisiana. Three years later, he was elected to the Louisiana House of Representatives, where he served until 1952. During his service in the house, he acted as a floor leader for Governor Earl K. Long. In 1952, he was an unsuccessful candidate for the Democratic nomination for lieutenant governor on the ticket of Judge Carlos Spaht. McKeithen was elected to the Public Service Commission from Huey P. Long's old north Louisiana district in 1954 and was reelected in 1960. While on the commission, he followed Long's example by attacking a large corporation—in his case, Southern Bell Telephone Company. During his term, he successfully fought to keep the five-cent rate for local pay calls.

McKeithen defeated the former New Orleans mayor DeLesseps S. Morrison for the Democratic nomination for governor in 1964. He then turned back a strong challenge by the Republican candidate, Charlton Lyons, in the general election. McKeithen's inauguration occurred on May 13, 1964.

During the 1963–1964 gubernatorial race, McKeithen had run as a reformer, promising to "clean up the mess in Baton Rouge." His first term did have a strong reform flavor to it. He got a state code of ethics established and a board to enforce it. He compiled a central list of state employees, as well as an inventory of state property. He appointed a commission headed by the former governor Sam Jones to examine the appointive powers of the governor. In 1964, the governor of Louisiana appointed more people to office than any other governor in the United States except New York's. The Jones commission consolidated some offices and made others elective. More jobs were put under state civil service. McKeithen worked hard to get new industry for the state and was truly a supersalesman for Louisiana. Tax concessions were expanded to induce new industry to come to the Pelican State. In 1966–1967, McKeithen conducted a "right to profit" campaign.

McKeithen confronted a racial crisis in Bogalusa in 1965. A showdown between the Ku Klux Klan and the Congress of Racial Equality, backed by the militant Deacons for Defense, seemed certain. Local citizens asked McKeithen to intervene, and he called for a cooling-off period. To preserve law and order, he set up the biracial Louisiana Commission on Human Relations, Rights, and Responsibilities. His moderate position helped to quiet the situation. He realized that if tension and violence were allowed to build and spread, they would hurt the state's image and might discourage new businesses from locating in the state. Racial violence threatened to erupt again in the summer of 1967. McKeithen announced that he would not tolerate any disturbances and threatened to have authorities shoot people caught rioting, looting, and fire-bombing.

McKeithen persuaded the legislature to pass two constitutional amendments of significance in 1965, and the people of Louisiana approved them both in the following year. One called for the state to construct a domed stadium, the Superdome, in New Orleans. In exchange for this, McKeithen got support in the Crescent City for the second amendment, which allowed governors, including him, to serve consecutive terms.

Toward the close of McKeithen's first four years, there were charges of widespread labor-union racketeering in the Baton Rouge area. National publications, such as *Fortune*, publicized what it called the "big shakedown in Baton Rouge." McKeithen appointed members to the Labor-Management Board of Inquiry to investigate the charges. The whole affair hurt his efforts to attract new industry, and it became the chief issue of the gubernatorial primary in late 1967.

Congressman John R. Rarick, from the Sixth District, an archconservative and McKeithen's chief opponent in the Democratic primary, accused the governor of allowing racketeers and organized crime to influence state government. Nevertheless, McKeithen won a crushing victory over Rarick, carrying every parish in the state. With no Republican opposition, McKeithen easily gained a second term and became the first Louisiana governor in the twentieth century to succeed himself.

The McKeithen administration received additional criticism in the national press in 1969 and 1970. Several prominent magazines, most notably *Life*, reported Mafia influence in state government. McKeithen appointed a Mafia probe commission to study the alleged link. By 1972, thirty-nine state, parish, and local officials were under indictment for various crimes.

McKeithen's accomplishments during his second term included reform of the Department of Corrections and improvements in the state prison at Angola. To aid the development of the state's colleges and universities, he set up the Coordinating Council for Higher Education. State employees received a uniform insurance program. Highway construction expanded greatly, as did other capital improvements. Despite legislative opposition, the governor finally succeeded in obtaining tax increases to pay for the expanded programs.

After McKeithen left office in 1972, he ran as an independent candidate for the United States Senate but was defeated by J. Bennett Johnston. McKeithen returned to the practice of law and farming in Columbia.

&

McKeithen's election marked an end, for better or for worse depending upon one's perspective, to the bifactional politics that characterized Louisiana elections from the time of Huey Long. The division between supporters and opponents of the policies and programs of Longism had given the state's voters a clear-cut choice while it existed. McKeithen, in his 1963–1964 campaign, reached across bifactional lines with various public images and attracted voters from both camps.

McKeithen succeeded in enacting a number of reforms while he was governor, particularly during his first term but also into his second. In addition, he attracted a large number of industries to Louisiana. Those industries did bring jobs and money into the state, but they employed relatively few semiskilled and unskilled laborers, who made up the bulk of the state's work force. The people who held most of the skilled jobs came from out of state. For the times, McKeithen adopted a moderate stand on racial problems, and though some racial confrontations occurred, the state did not have the major racial violence that affected other parts of the South.

Although charges of racketeering and organized crime clouded McKeithen's two terms, he was never personally accused of any wrongdoing. He was a popular governor, as evidenced by the passage of the gubernatorial succession amendment and his crushing defeat of Rarick in 1968.

ARTHUR W. BERGERON, JR.

BIBLIOGRAPHY

Bass, Jack, and Walter DeVries. *The Transformation of Southern Politics: Social Change and Political Consequence Since 1945.* New York, 1976.

Carleton, Mark T. *Politics and Punishment: The History of the Louisiana State Penal System.* Baton Rouge, 1971.

Havard, William C. *The Changing of Politics of the South.* Baton Rouge, 1972.

Howard, Perry H. *Political Tendencies in Louisiana.* Rev. and exp. ed. Baton Rouge, 1971.

Life, September 8, 29, 1967.

Reichley, James A. "The Big Shakedown in Baton Rouge." *Fortune,* LXXX (August, 1969), 97–99, 134–37.

Tapp, Charles W. "The Gubernatorial Election of 1964: An Affirmation of Political Trends." *Louisiana Academy of Sciences,* XXVII (1964), 74–87.

Wall, Bennett H., ed. *Louisiana: A History.* Arlington Heights, Ill., 1984.

Edwin Edwards

Governor, 1972–1980, 1984–1988

EDWARDS, Edwin Washington (b. Marksville, Louisiana, August 7, 1927), city councilman, state senator, congressman, and governor.

Edwards' life became for a time a twentieth-century political success story.[1] This son of a sharecropper, after elementary and secondary education in public schools, attended Louisiana State University, where he received his law degree at age twenty-one. According to one of his close associates, Edwards was so poor that he had to hitchhike to New Orleans to take the bar examination.

In 1949, after admission to the bar, Edwards established his law practice in Crowley. He married the former Elaine Schwartzenburg, by whom he has four children, and

EDWIN EDWARDS. *Photograph courtesy of State Library of Louisiana.*

quickly became active in local political affairs. He was elected to the Crowley city council in 1954. He held that position until 1964, when he was elected to the Louisiana Senate. Then, in 1965, he won an election to fill an unexpired term in the United States House of Representatives. He was reelected in 1966, 1968, and 1970.

In 1971, Edwards entered the race for governor in a field of seventeen candidates in the Democratic primary. He led in the first primary with 23.8 percent of the vote, largely as a consequence of very strong support in his native south Louisiana. He defeated J. Bennett Johnston in the runoff by less than eight thousand votes and then defeated the Republican, David C. Treen, in the general election, in February 1972, with over 57 percent of the vote. Once in office, Edwards pushed through the legislature a bill that put Democrats and Republicans on the same ballot, in an open primary. In 1975, he benefited from the new procedure, defeating five opponents with 63 percent of the vote.

In 1979, Edwards was blocked by the state constitution from seeking a third consecutive term, but he made it clear that he would go for another term in 1983. In fact, he opened a campaign office in Baton Rouge

1. The author is indebted to several journalists who have written for the New Orleans *Times-Picayune/States Item,* for their factual and interpretive accounts of Edwards' performance in office and on the campaign trail. The writers include James Gillis, Charles Hargroder, Alan Katz, Iris Kelso, Newton Renfro, and Jack Wardlaw.

upon leaving the governorship and immediately launched his run for a third term. He made himself available as a speaker to virtually every organization in the state and started raising money for the sizable war chest required in Louisiana's gubernatorial campaigns. The 1983 governor's race was a historic first in Louisiana. It pitted an incumbent governor, David Treen, against a former governor, Edwards. It contrasted personalities and styles: Treen, the low-keyed governmental technician, versus the flamboyant Edwards. It was a bitter race in which Treen sought to depict Edwards as corrupt and dishonest. Edwards largely ignored the charges, focusing his campaign on Treen's inaccessibility and alleged ineptitude. Edwards reported expenditures of approximately twelve million dollars and Treen approximately six million—figures that likely translate into the highest spending per voter for any governor's race ever conducted in the United States. When the results were in, Edwards buried Treen with 62 percent of the vote, and a majority in sixty-two of sixty-four parishes.

Within a few months of his third inauguration, Edwards faced a stiff political challenge. In late February, 1985, he was named, along with his brother Marion and other business associates, in a fifty-one-count federal indictment, which listed charges of mail fraud, obstruction of justice, and public bribery. The indictment focused on Edwards' alleged involvement in a complicated scheme that granted preferential state certifications to companies involved in business dealings with Louisiana's state hospitals. The allegation was that Edwards had illegally received $1.95 million, which, if he had been found guilty, could have been reclaimed by federal authorities under provisions of the Racketeering Influenced and Corrupt Organizations (RICO) Act. Edwards immediately proclaimed his innocence, sure that he would not be convicted on any charges.

On March 8, 1985, he entered a plea of not guilty in federal court in New Orleans. United States Attorney John Volz, a Republican, conducted the case against the governor, and Edwards often said to reporters that his indictment and trial were politically motivated by Volz and the Republican party. During the course of the trial, Volz attempted to show that Edwards' gambling losses, sustained at a number of Nevada casinos, put the governor in need of money to pay back his growing debts. Meanwhile, after a lengthy trial, Marion Edwards was acquitted of the charges against him. In December, 1985, when the jury failed to reach a unanimous verdict, Judge Marcel Livaudais declared a mistrial in the case against Governor Edwards. The ruling of a mistrial was interpreted by Edwards as confirmation of his innocence, but Volz soon moved for a new trial. The second trial resulted in an acquittal.

Edwards has no doubt earned special treatment in political histories of Louisiana. He was the first governor elected to three terms. He was only the second twentieth-century governor to succeed himself—thanks to a constitutional amendment passed in 1966. He was the first French-speaking, Cajun governor in over a century. Although Edwards has an Anglo-Saxon name, his mother was a Brouillette, and he retains from his childhood in Cajun country a distinct Cajun accent and the zest for life characteristic of Louisiana's French descendants.

Louisiana voters have established clearly over many decades their preference for colorful—even flamboyant—politicians. In large measure, they found in Edwards the quality they admire. Always impeccably dressed and manicured, Edwards has few peers among politicians when it comes to one-liners, and in public he is never without a stage presence. Many call him charismatic. While his detractors might deny his charisma, few would deny that he is a master showman-politician. For example, he once called a press conference to reveal that he had failed to report a campaign contribution from a South Korean lobbyist. When a reporter asked why he did not return the money, Edwards replied without hesitation or a trace of a smile that he did not know whom to return it to since "all Koreans look alike" to him.

Running for an unprecedented fourth term in the open primary of October, 1987, Edwards met an unexpectedly strong set of challengers. The field included Billy Tauzin, a former Edwards floor leader in the state legislature; Jim Brown, the secretary of state; Bob Livingston, the Republican congressman from New Orleans; and Charles ("Buddy") Roemer III, the Democratic congressman from Shreveport. Perhaps all of the state's economic problems and Edwards' own political difficulties of the third term began to catch up with the governor.

In the primary balloting on October 24, Edwards finished second, with 28 percent of the vote, to Roemer, who gathered 33 percent. Roemer had rushed into contention in the final three weeks of the campaign, gaining major newspaper endorsements and showing well in a widely televised multicandidate debate. A result of the first primary would have forced a runoff between Edwards and Roemer, but Edwards

shocked the state and disappointed many of his supporters by announcing his withdrawal from the race on October 25, thus throwing the election to Roemer. The possibility—maybe the likelihood—of failing to
muster the required backing in a hard-fought second primary was evidently not appealing to Edwards. If Roemer had gained most of the
support from the other major candidates, he would have won the
runoff. The various political polls and the division of the votes among
the other candidates on October 24 (Livingston with 18 percent, Tauzin
with about 10 percent, and Brown with about 9 percent) seemed to indicate that reform, or at least the call of newspaper editorials to elect
"anybody but Edwards," would carry the day against the incumbent.

The transition period between administrations (then stretching from
the primary in October, 1987, to March, 1988) was controversial and
filled with contention. Roemer made many proposals to reorganize
state agencies and revise the state budget. Edwards went along with
some proposals but neglected or rejected others. Roemer was inaugurated on March 14, 1988.[2]

෴

Edwards' governorship could boast of numerous accomplishments. He
pushed a plan for a constitutional convention through the legislature in
the first session after his election. That convention (dubbed CC–73)
drafted a new constitution, which was approved by the voters and became effective in January, 1975. The Constitution of 1921, which it replaced, was among the longest in the nation, cluttered with detail and
burdened with the hundreds of amendments approved in the half century of its existence. In accordance with the provisions of the new constitution, Edwards initiated a major reorganization of the executive
branch. Over eighty agencies were abolished, and those remaining were
rearranged on the model of the federal government. In addition,
Edwards was the first governor since Reconstruction to include blacks in
high positions in his administration. In this area, his administration
marked a clear break with the past, when blacks held state jobs only at
the menial level.

Edwards used tax revenues on oil and gas to increase state spending.
He succeeded in getting enacted a legislative proposal that restructured

2. Some representative reports on the 1987 election and its aftermath: Baton Rouge *Morning
Advocate*, October 31, 1987, March 14, 1988; Houston *Chronicle*, October 26, 1987; *Washington
Post National Weekly Edition*, November 9, 1987; *Wall Street Journal*, March 14, 1988.

the severence tax on crude oil to a percentage of the price of each barrel, from a flat fee per barrel. When energy prices soared during the 1970s, the Louisiana treasury was a direct beneficiary of the price-setting power of the Organization of Petroleum Exporting Countries (OPEC). In Edwards' third term, however, this policy came back to haunt him, for oil prices went into a free fall that resulted in massive revenue shortages for the state treasury. Edwards was the moving force behind the Louisiana Superport, an offshore facility designed to handle oil supertankers. During his first two terms, the state's expenditures increased dramatically (163 percent), and still the budget was balanced consistently and with relative ease. But this third term was plagued with budgetary problems from the beginning.

Edwards also worked for a change in election procedures, which he pushed through the legislature during his first term. When he won office in 1972, he had to get through two Democratic primaries and then defeat a Republican candidate in the general election. Edwards quickly set himself to changing that procedure in order to make his re-election easier. He got the legislature to pass a new "open elections" arrangement that put Democrats, Republicans, and independents on the same ballot, with two heats if no candidate received a majority in the first balloting. This procedure was for all elected offices in the state. It worked well for Edwards in 1975, when he won with ease in the first heat. But in 1979, it turned out to help the Republican party, which it was originally designed to thwart. The Republican, Treen, defeated a divided field of five Democrats. The electoral arrangement did serve, however, to stymie the development of Republican representation in the state legislature.

Few observers took a neutral attitude toward Edwards. His critics are as intense in their feelings as his admirers are. The critics find much to criticize. Edwards' terms as governor have found him in several near-entanglements with scandal. His campaign contribution from a Korean lobbyist appeared to some to be of questionable legality. His commissioner of administration, Charles Roemer, was convicted and sentenced to prison in a bribery kickback scheme to place a state insurance contract with a company owned by Carlos Marcello, alleged to be an underworld boss. Edwards was never implicated in that scandal. Camille Gravel, Edwards' close friend and political confidant, once said, "Edwin's greatest strength—and his greatest weakness—is his ability to come within a millimeter of the law without breaking it."[3] By evading conviction in two federal trials, he has proved Gravel's assessment.

Edwards remained one of Louisiana's most popular and colorful figures throughout his years as governor. His first two terms showed excellent political management in the flush times of high oil prices and, consequently, high income from state severance taxes. The state needed a new constitution, and Edwards used his executive authority and power to press for a convention that produced an excellent state charter, certainly an outstanding improvement over the outmoded Constitution of 1921. Furthermore, Edwards accomplished a major reorganization of the executive branch and appointed a significant number of blacks to various offices in state government.

In his third term, however, he faced fiscal and personal crises. Although he claimed that he could manage state resources better than Governor Treen, oil revenues plummeted because of the drastic decline in international oil prices, leaving the state with a staggering revenue shortfall, with inadequate funds to continue some state programs, and with the need to trim the state budget instead of expanding programs and funding departments at higher levels, as had been possible during his first two terms. Moreover, the federal racketeering charges made Edwards a figure of national notoriety. The colorfulness of his character throughout his years in office, the problems of his third term, and his withdrawal from the campaign of 1987 indicate that Edwards will remain controversial in Louisiana history.

JOSEPH B. PARKER

BIBLIOGRAPHY

Bass, Jack, and Walter DeVries. *The Transformation of Southern Politics: Social Change and Political Consequence Since 1945.* New York, 1976.
Bollner, James, ed. *Louisiana Politics: Festival in a Labyrinth,* esp. 15–41, 75–88. Baton Rouge, 1982. Chapters by Mark T. Carleton and Edward Renwick.
Grenier, Charles E., and Perry H. Howard. "The Edwards Victory." *Louisiana Review,* I (1972), 31–42.
Maginnis, John. *The Last Hayride.* Baton Rouge, 1985.
Parker, Joseph B. "New Style Campaign Politics: Madison Avenue Comes to Dixie." In *Contemporary Southern Politics: Continuity and Change,* edited by James F. Lea. Baton Rouge, 1988.
Wall, Bennett H., ed. *Louisiana: A History.* Arlington Heights, Ill., 1984.

---

3. Alan Katz, "The Upcoming Trial of the Century," New Orleans *Times-Picayune,* March 3, 1985, sec. 1, p. 26.

David Treen

Governor, 1980–1984

TREEN, David Connor (b. Baton Rouge, Louisiana, July 16, 1928), congressman and governor. Treen is an anomaly among Louisiana governors.[1] Louisiana's first Republican governor in the twentieth century may turn out to be the state's least colorful governor of the century too. In a state that prefers its governors to entertain as well as govern, Treen is a serious-minded man with a passion for detail and little inclination toward showmanship.

DAVID TREEN. *Photograph courtesy of State Library of Louisiana.*

Treen attended public schools in East Baton Rouge, Jefferson, and Orleans parishes and graduated from Fortier High School, in New Orleans, in 1945. He received both his undergraduate and law degrees from Tulane University and served as a defense and prosecuting counsel in the United States Air Force for two years. He is married to the former Delores Briski, and they have three children.

Treen became involved in politics in the late 1950s. He was initially involved in the States Rights party—running one time under its banner for the United States House of Representatives. He switched to the Republican party, and became chairman of the Jefferson Parish executive committee for several years as well as a member of the state central committee for most of the 1960s and 1970s. He ran unsuccessfully as the Republican candidate for governor in 1972. Later that year he was elected to Congress from the Third District (largely suburban New Or-

1. The author is indebted to several journalists who have written for the New Orleans *Times-Picayune/States Item,* for their factual and interpretive accounts of Treen's performance as governor. The writers include James Gillis, Charles Hargroder, Alan Katz, Iris Kelso, Newton Renfro, and Jack Wardlaw.

leans), to become the first Republican elected to Congress from Louisiana in the twentieth century. He was reelected in 1974, 1976, and 1978.

In 1979, Republican leaders responded to Louisiana's "open election" system—in which all the candidates of all the parties ran on the same ballot, with two heats if no candidate won by a majority in the first canvass—by deciding to field just one Republican in the governor's race, against a number of Democrats. That approach worked well. Five major Democrats were in the race, and Treen, by virtue of being the senior elected Republican in the state, was the Republican candidate. The Democratic candidates generally conceded Treen a place in the second round and fought tenaciously to be there with him. In the first heat, Treen ran first. He faced Louis Lambert, of the Public Service Commission, in the new round, since Lambert had narrowly edged out Lieutenant Governor James Fitzmorris for second place. But the tone of the campaign for the second position was so bitter and intense that the four unsuccessful Democrats gave their endorsement to Treen. All four had substantial campaign debts that Treen helped pay off, and all were appointed to positions in Treen's administration. Some of Treen's critics who thought that he did not know how to play Louisiana's tough game of politics may need to reexamine their opinion. Treen defeated Lambert by fewer than ten thousand votes.

As governor, Treen got a legislative program passed that aimed at improving education. The program included pay incentives for teachers who added to their training, and it imposed higher standards for qualifying to teach in the state. Treen negotiated a settlement with the United States Department of Justice in a long-standing dispute over Louisiana's dual system of predominantly white and predominantly black colleges and universities.

Governor Treen also worked out a plan for flood control and environmental preservation in the Atchafalaya Basin. He obtained the initial legislation for purchasing privately owned land there, but the plan's ultimate success will depend upon action by the national government. Appropriations of more than one billion dollars are necessary to implement the flood-control design. Treen sponsored legislation intended to protect Louisiana's coastal wetlands, but that bill failed.

Treen's governorship had a significant, though perhaps ironic, result for blacks, who may have perceived Treen as a segregationist antipathetic to their interests. He received less than 1 percent of their vote in his unsuccessful race for governor in 1972 and only about 3 percent in 1979. Nevertheless, he appointed more blacks to positions under gubernatorial control than any previous governor has done. Thus he can be credited with a large role in the attempt to change the perception of the Louisiana Republican party from that of a WASPish club to that of a broad-based, competitive party.

❧

Treen had more than a few problems as governor. He came to the office with no experience in state or local government and none as an administrator. His government seemed confused and indecisive as it slowly made its way through the shakedown period of its early weeks. Perhaps Treen's greatest problem was the financial difficulty that the oil glut of the early 1980s created. Because of the dependence of Louisiana's revenue system on severance taxes levied upon oil, the decline in both the production of oil and its prices created a financial nightmare of shrinking revenues during much of Treen's tenure. In addition, there were cutbacks in available federal revenues as a consequence of budget reforms pushed by Treen's fellow Republican, President Ronald Reagan.

Undoubtedly, one of Treen's major problems as governor was his personality and political style. A political observer contends that Louisianians like their politicians like their food: hot and spicy. Treen was neither. And he followed a succession of governors who had provided voters with plenty of entertainment. Instead, Treen exhibited a passion for detail and methodical decision making. Those traits led journalists and politicians to conclude that he was plodding and indecisive. Most of his recent predecessors were gregarious types who enjoyed traveling, speaking, and shaking the hands of voters across the state. Treen seemed uncomfortable in those roles. Instead he preferred to be behind a desk, enmeshed in the details of running the governor's office. As a consequence, he may have turned down more speaking and ribbon-cutting invitations than any other governor in recent times.

In 1983, Treen sought a second term and was opposed by his predecessor, Edwin Edwards. Treen's campaign struggled uphill from the beginning. A Republican in a predominantly Democratic state running against one of the greatest campaigners in Louisiana history, he had the burden of presiding as governor during a severe budget crisis and at a time when unemployment in the state was well above the national average. The problems were a result of the state's heavy depenence upon oil and gas for both employment and tax revenues at a time when an overabundance of oil plagued the industry. Treen began the campaign trailing badly in the polls, and though he fought tenaciously to hold on to the governorship, he was able to gain only 36.8 percent of the vote, and a majority in only two parishes.

Treen's defense of his stewardship as governor was that "leadership is not demonstrated by flamboyance or by glibness. It is demonstrated by accomplishments."[2] Time will tell whether his accomplishments put him among Louisiana's significant chief executives. How the Republican party does in the state in the next few decades will show whether Treen has brought his party to the level of a viable competitor with the Democrats or whether his governorship was only a once-in-a-century aberration akin to an eclipse of the sun or a close encounter of planets.

JOSEPH B. PARKER

BIBLIOGRAPHY

Parker, Joseph B. "New Style Campaign Politics: Madison Avenue Comes to Dixie." In *Contemporary Southern Politics: Continuity and Change,* edited by James F. Lea. Baton Rouge, 1988.

Public Affairs Research Council of Louisiana (PAR). "The Great Louisiana Spendathon." In *PAR Analysis.* Baton Rouge, 1980.

Renwick, Edward. "The Governor." In *Louisiana Politics: Festival in a Labyrinth,* edited by James Bolner, 75–88. Baton Rouge, 1982.

Wall, Bennett H., ed. *Louisiana: A History.* Arlington Heights, Ill., 1984.

---

2. Jack Wardlaw, "Treen's Legacy," New Orleans *Times-Picayune,* October 26, 1983, sec. 1, p. 27.

The Contributors

MATHÉ ALLAIN, a longtime student of French colonial Louisiana, is an instructor in the Department of Languages at the University of Southwestern Louisiana. She has contributed articles to a number of publications, including the *French Review*, the *Modern Language Quarterly*, and *Louisiana History*.

ARTHUR W. BERGERON, JR., holds the Ph.D. in history from Louisiana State University (1980). He has written articles for *Louisiana History*, the *Alabama Historical Quarterly*, and the *Louisiana Review*. He has edited *Reminiscences of Uncle Silas, 18th Louisiana Infantry Regiment* (1982) and has contributed a chapter to *A Guide to the History of Louisiana* (1982), edited by Light T. Cummins and Glen Jeansonne. He is the author of the *Guide to Louisiana Confederate Military Units, 1861–1865* (1989). Bergeron is a historian with the Louisiana Office of State Parks.

F. WAYNE BINNING holds the Ph.D. in history from the University of North Carolina (1969) and has contributed articles to *Louisiana History* and *Southern Studies*.

CARL A. BRASSEAUX, assistant director of the Center for Louisiana Studies, at the University of Southwestern Louisiana, has published articles on Louisiana's colonial period in such journals as *Louisiana History*, the *Southwestern Historical Quarterly*, and the *Alabama Review*. He has edited *A Comparative View of French Louisiana, 1699 and 1762: The Journals of Pierre Le Moyne d'Iberville and Jean-Jacques-Blaise d'Abbadie* (1979) and other works. He is author of *The Founding of New Acadia: The Beginnings of Acadian Life in Louisiana, 1705–1803* (1987). He holds the *doctorat du troisième cycle* from the University of Paris (1982).

MARK T. CARLETON, associate professor of history at Louisiana State University, earned the Ph.D. in history from Stanford University (1970). He is the author of *Politics and Punishment: The History of the Louisiana State Penal System* (1971) and *River Capital: An Illustrated History of Baton Rouge* (1981), as well as articles in *Louisiana History*, *Louisiana*

Studies, and the *Tulane Law Review*. He is also a coauthor of *Louisiana: A History* (1984), edited by Bennett H. Wall, and *Louisiana Politics: Festival in a Labyrinth* (1982), edited by James Bolner. Carleton is coeditor of *Readings in Louisiana Politics* (1975).

MARIUS M. CARRIERE, JR., is associate professor of history at Christian Brothers College. He holds the Ph.D. in history from Louisiana State University (1977). He has contributed articles to *Louisiana History* and is editor of the *Papers* of the West Tennessee Historical Society.

FLOYD M. CLAY is the author of *Coozan Dudley LeBlanc: From Huey Long to Hadocol* (1974) and is associate professor of history at Holy Cross College, in New Orleans. He earned the Ph.D. in history from the University of Mississippi (1972).

BRIAN E. COUTTS is assistant professor of history at Western Kentucky University. He holds the Ph.D. in history from Louisiana State University (1981). He has contributed to historical journals, including *Louisiana History*.

LIGHT TOWNSEND CUMMINS is professor of history at Austin College. He is coeditor of *Guide to the History of Louisiana* (1982) and *Guide to the History of Texas* (1988). He earned the Ph.D. in history from Tulane University (1977). He has contributed articles to *Southern Studies* and the *Louisiana Review*.

JOSEPH G. DAWSON III is associate professor of history at Texas A & M University. He is the author of *Army Generals and Reconstruction: Louisiana, 1862–1877* (1982), which won the General L. Kemper Williams Prize. His articles have appeared in *Civil War History*, *Southern Studies*, *Louisiana History*, the *Red River Valley Historical Review*, and the *Louisiana Review*. He has contributed essays to *The Dictionary of Literary Biography* (1983, 1984). He was a contributor to and an associate editor of *The Dictionary of American Military Biography* (1984), edited by Roger J. Spiller. Dawson earned the Ph.D. in history from Louisiana State University (1978).

CAROLYN E. DeLATTE is associate professor of history at McNeese State University. She received the Ph.D. in history from Louisiana State University (1979). She is the author of *Lucy Audubon* (1982) and a number of articles, including several published in *Louisiana History*.

HENRY C. DETHLOFF is professor of history at Texas A&M University. He earned the Ph.D. in history from the University of Missouri (1964) and is the author of *The Centennial History of Texas A&M University* (1975). He wrote *Americans and Free Enterprise* (1978) and *A History of the American Rice Industry, 1685–1985* (1988), and is coauthor of *History of*

American Business (1983). Dethloff is the editor of *Huey P. Long: Southern Demagogue or American Democrat?* (1967) and has written several articles for various historical journals, including *Agricultural History*, the *Arkansas Historical Quarterly*, *Louisiana Studies*, and *Louisiana History*. He has edited *Southwestern Agriculture, Pre-Columbian to Modern* (1982).

GILBERT C. DIN is professor of history at Fort Lewis College. He holds the Ph.D. in history from the University of Madrid (1960). He edited *Louisiana in 1776: A Memoria of Francisco Bouligny* (1977) and is coauthor of *Imperial Osages* (1983). His articles have appeared in various journals, including the *Florida Historical Quarterly*, the *Southwestern Historical Quarterly*, *Louisiana History*, and the *Arkansas Historical Quarterly*.

BETTY M. FIELD earned a Ph.D. in history from Tulane University (1973). She has taught at the University of New Orleans and Tulane University. Her publications include the chapter "Louisiana and the Great Depression" in *Louisiana Gothic: Recollections of the 1930s* (1984), edited by Glenn Conrad.

PATRICIA KAY GALLOWAY is special projects officer at the Mississippi Department of Archives and History, in Jackson, Mississippi. She holds the Ph.D. in comparative literature from the University of North Carolina (1973). She revised and edited *Mississippi Provincial Archives: French Dominion*, Vol. IV, *1729–1748*, and Vol. V, *1749–1763* (1983), originally edited and translated by Dunbar Rowland and Albert G. Sanders. Galloway also edited *LaSalle and His Legacy* (1982).

JUDITH F. GENTRY earned the Ph.D. in history from Rice University (1969) and is associate professor of history at the University of Southwestern Louisiana. She has contributed articles to the *Journal of Southern History* and *Louisiana History*.

JACK D. L. HOLMES holds the Ph.D. in history from the University of Texas (1959) and served as professor of history at the University of Alabama at Birmingham. He is the author of *Gayoso: the Life of a Spanish Governor in the Mississippi Valley* (1965), winner of the Louisiana Literary Award. He prepared *A Guide to Spanish Louisiana* (1970). His articles have been published in many journals, including *Louisiana History*, the *Tennessee Historical Quarterly*, the *Florida Historical Quarterly*, the *Alabama Historical Quarterly*, *Louisiana Studies*, the *Southwestern Historical Quarterly*, the *Alabama Review*, the *Mississippi Quarterly*, the *Journal of Mississippi History*, and the *Alabama Quarterly*. He has contributed chapters to numerous edited works, among them *The French in the Mississippi Valley* (1969) and *The Spanish in the Mississippi Valley* (1974).

JOY J. JACKSON is professor of history at Southeastern Louisiana University and earned the Ph.D. in history from Tulane University (1961). She is the author of *New Orleans in the Gilded Age* (1969) and has contributed articles to *Louisiana History*.

GLEN JEANSONNE is associate professor of history at the University of Wisconsin at Milwaukee. He holds the Ph.D. in history from Florida State University (1975). He is the author of *Leander Perez: Boss of the Delta* (1977), *Race, Religion, and Politics: The Louisiana Gubernatorial Elections of 1959–1960* (1977), and *Gerald L. K. Smith, Minister of Hate* (1988). He has contributed numerous articles to historical journals, including the *Red River Valley Historical Review, Louisiana History, Louisiana Studies,* and the *Louisiana Review*.

MICHAEL L. KURTZ is professor of history at Southeastern Louisiana University. He holds the Ph.D. in history from Tulane University (1971). He is the author of *Crime of the Century: The Kennedy Assassination from a Historian's Perspective* (1982) and *The Challenging of America, 1920–1945* (1986). His articles have appeared in *Louisiana History,* and he is coauthor of *Louisiana: A History* (1984), edited by Bennett H. Wall, and *The Saga of Uncle Earl and Louisiana Politics* (1990).

DONALD J. LEMIEUX is archivist at the Louisiana State Archives, Baton Rouge, a division of the Office of the Secretary of State. He earned the Ph.D. in history from Louisiana State University (1972) and has contributed to historical journals, including *Southern Studies*.

J. PAUL LESLIE, JR., is professor of history at Nicholls State University. He holds the Ph.D. in history from the University of Missouri (1974) and has contributed articles to *Louisiana History*.

J. PRESTON MOORE was for much of his career professor of history at Louisiana State University; he retired in 1972. He holds a Ph.D. in history from Northwestern University (1942). He is the author of *The Cabildo in Peru* (2 vols.; 1954–66) and *Revolt in Louisiana: The Spanish Occupation* (1976), which won the General L. Kemper Williams Prize. He has contributed a number of articles to historical journals.

C. HOWARD NICHOLS is professor of history at Southeastern Louisiana University. He completed advanced studies in history at Louisiana State University. He is the author of articles in *Louisiana History* and other journals.

JOSEPH B. PARKER is professor of political science at the University of Southern Mississippi and formerly taught at the University of New Orleans. He is the author of *The Morrison Era* (1974). He is coeditor of *Readings in Louisiana Politics* (1975) and contributed to *Louisiana Politics: Festival in a Labyrinth* (1982), edited by James Bolner. Parker earned the Ph.D. in political science from Tulane University (1971).

JERRY PURVIS SANSON earned the Ph.D. in history from Louisiana State University (1984) and is instructor in history at Louisiana State University at Alexandria. He has contributed articles to historical journals, including *Louisiana History.*

MATTHEW J. SCHOTT is associate professor of history at the University of Southwestern Louisiana. He holds the Ph.D. in history from Vanderbilt University (1969). He has written a number of articles, including several for *Louisiana History.*

JOE GRAY TAYLOR (1920–1987) was dean of the College of Liberal Arts and professor of history at McNeese State University. He was the author of *Negro Slavery in Louisiana* (1963), *Louisiana Reconstructed* (1975) (which was the winner of Louisiana Literary Award and the General L. Kemper Williams Prize), *Louisiana: A Bicentennial History* (1976), and *Eating, Drinking, and Visiting in the South* (1982). Taylor edited *The Whip, Hoe, and Sword; or, The Gulf Department in '63* (1979). He wrote numerous articles for historical journals, including the *Georgia Review* and *Louisiana History.* He held the Ph.D. in history from Louisiana State University (1951).

JOSEPH G. TREGLE, JR., taught for many years at the University of New Orleans, where he was professor of history until his retirement in 1979. He earned the Ph.D. in history from the University of Pennsylvania (1954). He is the author of several articles in such journals as the *Journal of Southern History* and *Louisiana History.*

PHILIP D. UZEE was university archivist and Alcée Fortier Professor of History at Nicholls State University until his retirement in 1984. He earned the Ph.D. in history at Louisiana State University (1950). He has contributed articles to *Louisiana History.*

CHARLES VINCENT is professor of history and chairman of the Department of History at Southern University, at Baton Rouge. He earned the Ph.D. in history at Louisiana State University (1973). He is the author of *Black Legislators in Louisiana During Reconstruction* (1976) and *A Centennial History of Southern University* (1981). His articles and essays have appeared in the *Journal of Black Studies,* the *Journal of Negro History,* and *Louisiana History.*

LOUIS VYHNANEK holds the Ph.D. in history from Louisiana State University (1979). He is reference librarian at the library of Washington State University and has contributed articles to *Louisiana History* and the *Red River Historical Review.*

FRANK J. WETTA earned the Ph.D. from Louisiana State University (1977) and is professor of history and dean of social sciences at Galveston College. He has contributed articles to *Louisiana History* and *Southern Studies*.

Index

Bonnie Stewart
Pi Beta Phi

D1542971

Le Nozze di Figaro

MOZART'S *Le Nozze*

di Figaro

A CRITICAL ANALYSIS / BY SIEGMUND LEVARIE

THE UNIVERSITY OF CHICAGO PRESS

The silhouettes on the title-page and jacket
are those of Francesco Benucci and Nancy Storace,
the first Figaro and Susanna

THE UNIVERSITY OF CHICAGO PRESS, CHICAGO 37

Cambridge University Press, London, N.W. 1, England
W. J. Gage & Co., Limited, Toronto 2B, Canada

*Copyright 1952 by The University of Chicago. All rights
reserved. Copyright 1952 under the International Copyright
Union. Published 1952. Composed and printed by The
University of Chicago Press, Chicago, Illinois, U.S.A.*

PREFACE

"Many attempts have been made by writers on art and poetry to define beauty in the abstract, to express it in the most general terms, to find some universal formula for it. The value of these attempts has most often been in the suggestive and penetrating things said by the way. Such discussions help us very little to enjoy what has been well done in art or poetry, to discriminate between what is more and what is less excellent in them, or to use words like beauty, excellence, art, poetry, with a more precise meaning than they would otherwise have. Beauty, like all other qualities presented to human experience, is relative; and the definition of it becomes unmeaning and useless in proportion to its abstractness. To define beauty, not in the most abstract but in the most concrete terms possible, to find not its universal formula, but the formula which expresses most adequately this or that special manifestation of it, is the aim of the true student of aesthetics. . . .

"And the function of the aesthetic critic is to distinguish, to analyse, and separate from its adjuncts, the virtue by which a picture, a landscape, a fair personality in life or in a book, produces this special impression of beauty or pleasure, to indicate what the source of that impression is, and under what conditions it is experienced. His end is reached when he has disengaged that virtue, and noted it, as a chemist notes some natural element, for himself and others; and the rule for those who would reach this end is stated with great exactness in the words of a recent critic of Sainte-Beuve:—*De se borner à connaître de près les belles choses, et à s'en nourrir en exquis amateurs, en humanistes accomplis.*"

WALTER PATER, from the Preface to The Renaissance

These words indicate openly the purpose, and implicitly the method, of the book. A thorough critique of a single work of art intimately increases one's knowledge and therefore one's enjoyment of it. A result of this kind is satisfactory in itself if the work of art merits the circumstantial attention by virtue of being a source of pleasure or profit to men. But the meaning of the investigation may transcend the set boundary by becoming a concrete manifestation of abstract aesthetic principles. The latter need not be specifically stated, although they may be or may become part of a philosophic system. The principles grow out of the developing analysis.

The immediate concern of the present exegesis is, accordingly, the analysis of the composition into its constitutive parts in an attempt to evaluate the effectiveness or appropriateness of musical devices for dramatic and musical purposes. One recognizes the formal mode of criticism.[1] It is closely connected with the scientific mode of criticism, the concern of which with construction and parts supplies an analytic technique and renders available a criterion of unity and structure.

Emphasis on the score will banish from the staked limits any primary consideration of Mozart's life and experience. Only rarely and incidentally will the historical devices of the scholarly mode of criticism be admitted.

The terminology one may expect is, then, not in need of explanation by Mozart's life or by circumstances leading up to the creation of the particular opera. It is taken from "things" in the Aristotelian sense, which would permit the definition of opera as an artificial thing, its action and movement composed of dramatic and musical incidents or "things." It is widened by words yielded by the study of the relationships of the content to the style—a study which determines the musical means that are effective within a given frame. The terminology will thus not be able to avoid loans from universal thoughts and aspirations, not necessarily musical, which are shared by all mankind but given particular expression by the composer.

In the criticism of a musical work of art the problem of terminology alleviates certain difficulties germane to the other arts, but it also creates new ones. The music critic has the advantages of a fairly precise language on his side. Concepts like triad, tonic, dominant, consonance, chromaticism, and many others are exact and clear to an extent unmatched by words from the usual repertory of the literary and art critics, like imagery, feeling, lilt, euphony, mood, representation, material, color, and line. These latter terms are either nonscientific (i.e., not taken from "things") or aesthetically not measurable. The rhythm of a poem, or the color combination of a painting, or the curves of a statue can be subjectively described by metaphor or exactly evaluated in physical rather than aesthetic terms. The knowledge that a verse follows a certain meter, or that a painting favors red shades over blue, or that a line on a figure has a certain length gives a much vaguer in-

1. For this and similar terminology employed, see the useful essay by Richard P. McKeon, "The Philosophic Bases of Art and Criticism," *Modern Philology*, Vol. XVI, Nos. 2 and 3 (November, 1943, and February, 1944).

sight into the work of art than the knowledge that an aria modulates into the subdominant or that a melody suffers a chromatic alteration. In the case of poetry and painting, the aesthetic meaning can be approximated by a description of the grammar. In the case of music, meaning and grammar are identical.

But the same precision of language also acts to the music critic's disadvantage. The very generality of the literary and art critics' terms makes them, without detriment to the professional, intelligible and palatable to the amateur. The music critic, on the other hand, faces the dilemma of amusing the reader by deserting his own technical equipment or of boring the reader by employing the technical jargon. Occasionally, the dilemma is resolved in the hands of a critically endowed poet or a poetically sensitive critic.

The method to be followed is implied by the suggestion that special virtues of the score be disengaged and noted. Unlike the purpose, it cannot and will not be stated openly. What generally recognized method of analyzing a composition exists? How much is accomplished by verbalizing the function of a chord or the name of a form? The method of this book will best be grasped as a by-product of the purpose. Any formula expressing a particular value of the composition becomes acceptable. Any description rendering a mere translation of a musical into a literary event remains excluded as critically meaningless. Nor does the analysis claim the need for enumerating all possible formulas. The resultant eclecticism is unavoidable, perhaps even desirable. To a dialectical mind it is preferable to any self-sufficient system.

The best reader of this book will be the expert. He will take various postulates in his stride and add his own value-judgments to those presented in the text. The amateur, the pure lover of the opera, should find the analysis accessible if he brings a receptive attitude and some rudimentary musical knowledge into the bargain. The book cannot be read like a novel; it becomes intelligible only by constant reference to the score.[2] A vocal score is adequate, although it loses a good deal compared to a full score. Many technical and theoretical terms are explained in the context; others can be looked up in a musical dictionary. The most frequently used concepts of harmony (leaning on Hugo Riemann's sys-

2. The orchestra score published by Peters (Leipzig, 1941)—and reissued by Broude Bros. (New York, 1948)—numbers the measures. Anyone using an edition without printed measure numbers will have to go to the trouble of writing them in. The list of measure numbers in the Appendix (pp. 269 f.) will help avoid errors.

tem of functions) and of form (based on Alfred Lorenz' classification by dynamic proportions) are briefly defined in the Appendix.[3] The technique of analyzing a melody as a drive from a definite beginning to a definite end is developed along with the text.

Recitatives have been omitted from the analysis. They present a problem of their own, which is as much literary as it is musical. The completeness of the investigation which the inclusion of recitatives might have produced is sacrificed for a more condensed representation and sharper isolation of purely musical values.

Early foundations for this book were laid in a graduate seminar under the author's guidance at the University of Chicago. The participation of the students clarified and confirmed many issues. Their response encouraged the elaboration of critical fragments into the present volume.

CHICAGO, 1951

3. See pp. 263 ff..

viii

TABLE OF CONTENTS

SINFONIA

Sinfonia (D MAJOR)

In several respects the purely instrumental pages at the beginning of the score lie outside the opera itself. Most indicative of this fact is Mozart's choice of the title "Sinfonia," rather than "overture" or "introduction," which deliberately severs the opening piece from the rest of the opera. In each of the later operas, *Don Giovanni*, *Così fan tutte*, and *Die Zauberflöte*, he uses the title "Ouvertura" or "Ouverture" and links the composition thus designated closely to the opera itself by a musical idea shared by both: the D-minor section in *Don Giovanni*, the sentence from which the whole opera gains its name in *Così fan tutte*, and the threefold chords in *Die Zauberflöte*. There is no open musical connection between the sinfonia and rest of *Le Nozze di Figaro*, except perhaps for the general mood and tonality.

For this reason, one may do well to skip this chapter and start directly with the analysis of the first act of the opera. The problems of a purely instrumental composition are different from those of a sung operatic number, where the character of the participants and the dramatic situation must be considered. This book is written with the intention of shedding some light on problems of operatic, not of purely instrumental, composing. A chapter on the sinfonia is nonetheless included, partly for reasons of completeness and partly as a suggestion that the methods of analyzing vocal and instrumental compositions need not differ in regard to fundamentals.

As is well known, the sinfonia follows the outline of a sonata form without a development section. Mozart crossed out a few measures originally sketched for a contrasting middle section. Hence all contrast and development in the widest sense are concentrated in the main sections—not merely taken by themselves but primarily heard in their relationship to each other. Exposition and recapitulation here assume the roles of strophe and antistrophe. One may be thought of as a variation of the other. In dynamic terms it is more fruitful to justify the existence of the recapitulation by stating that it fulfils what the exposition leaves undone. The principle of ascribing to musical movement the function of completing a definite musical task will find many illustrations in the course of the opera. There it often serves the purpose of the drama.

3

It can be isolated, however, from any extra-musical factors and still remain valid; for the musical content of any composition can be equated, contrary to all other arts, with its grammar.

The first subject consists of two identical halves (m. 1–17 and 18–34). It therefore belongs to that kind of classical melody structure which has been called the "song type" and which, popular in origin, is basically uncomplicated.[1] The organization of each half in this case belies the simplicity of the over-all structure. The mere fact that the consequent intends to be nothing but a repetition of the antecedent is overshadowed by two added counterpoints in first flute and oboe at the crucial moment of the beginning of the consequent. Mozart employs a similar technique in the first subject of the *Jupiter Symphony:* the counterpoints are sufficiently exposed to distract from the structural repetition.

The antecedent, as well as the consequent, is tripartite and by no means in the nature of a simple song tune. One hears a unison melody of seven measures, which outlines the tonic scale in its neutral form around a central axis; a four-measure arpeggio of the tonic triad in the wood winds and horns; and a seven-measure tutti, which outlines the tonic scale in its descending form across an entire octave. A bow form is the result; new dynamics mark each new section in a steep rise from pianissimo to fortissimo:

Unison scale around central axis; strings————————7 m.

　　Arpeggio; wood winds————————————4 m.

Descending scale; tutti————————————7 m. (incl. elision)

The outer sections are rhythmically surprising by their adherence to seven measures. The elongation of the opening section sets in with measure 4—with the chromatic step toward the sixth degree of the scale, to be exact. Up to that moment, the melody progresses regularly enough. Measures 1 and 3 both are strong measures, corresponding to each other as a real imitation at the fifth would correspond to the model statement. Measure 4, rhythmically weak like measure 2, continues the real imitation at the fifth but is deflected on the fourth eighth-note toward the temporary climax b. An exact imitation would have completed the tonic octave span with the end of the fourth measure. The

1. Wilhelm Fischer, "Zur Entwicklungsgeschichte des Wiener klassischen Stils," *Studien zur Musikwissenschaft*, III (1915), 24–84.

deflection in the fourth measure turns the line back to the starting point with the help of a sequence (m. 5) and then a closing formula (m. 6 and 7). The normal grouping of two phrases into 2 + 2 measures (ab + a′b′) is thus extended into 2 + 5 measures (ab + a′b′b″cadence).

The rhythmic upheaval is considerable. Not only is the balance of 2 against 5 startling, but the two quarter-rests are placed in such a manner as to create misleading caesuras within the course of each phrase while permitting the one phrase to run smoothly into the other. The elongation manifests itself also harmonically, as the following sketch of the main beats of the total section shows:

The dactylic rhythm of the tonic triad (o d d) is answered by the dominant triad in exactly doubled note values (ʜ o o).

The rhythmic irregularities, which begin to be felt after measure 4, help point up the significant melodic irregularity of the chromatic step a-sharp to b and its consequences. Even without the rhythmic pointer, the significance of a-sharp cannot be underrated. It is the event which breaks the norm and thus puts its characteristic stamp on the whole sinfonia. It is the tone which unexpectedly emphasizes b to such an extent that the ascending scale is hindered in its ascent to the octave of the tonic, d. The other chromaticisms which occur are of a secondary nature, both by-products of a real imitation: g-sharp (m. 3) answers the first measure in the symmetry of a binary structure; and d-sharp (m. 5) answers the preceding measure in a sequence. Only a-sharp is an original force—the inventive idea of the whole movement.

The task of the sinfonia lies in the meaningful utilization of the arbitrarily introduced a-sharp and in the eventual completion of the ascending tonic scale past the sixth up to the octave.

The remainder of the antecedent of the first subject does not do much more than absorb the rhythmic shock of the opening section on the secure ground of a tonic organ point. One remains aware of the rhythmic tremor throughout the short middle section (m. 8–11). If one hears measure 8 correctly as a weak measure, then the entrance of oboes and

5

horns (m. 8 and 10) rubs against the metric accents of bassoons, violas, and double basses (m. 9 and 11); and one strong measure follows another when the loud entrance of the closing tutti asserts itself against the masculine ending of the middle section. If one is misguided into accepting the entrance of oboes and horns as an accent, then the conflict with the metric accents of the bass instruments still exists; and one strong measure follows another at the beginning (m. 7 and 8), rather than at the end, of the section.

It is this swinging-out of the rhythmic upheaval which justifies the elongation of the closing section. The procedure here is much simpler than it was in the opening section, for no new task must be set up to complicate matters further within the limited frame of the sinfonia. The middle two measures (14 and 15) are a parenthetical extension, so to speak, of the opening two measures (12 and 13), which they merely twice repeat in diminution. Measure 16 could directly follow measure 13; and a complete descending tonic scale, d^2 to d^1, emerges as the simple melodic content.

The beginning of this descending scale mockingly serves as an impetus for the counterpoint which accompanies the repetition of the whole antecedent (m. 19 ff.).

The content of the bow form sketched earlier may thus be stated more concisely:

> Ascending scale, interrupted by a-sharp————————7 m.
>
>) Arpeggio————————————————4 m.
>
> Descending scale, complete————————————7 m.

With the repetition of this bow form the statement of the first subject is properly completed. The function of the following measures up to the next caesura (35–58) is that of a cadence, as one look at the bass line will reveal. Apart from this fact, they may be said to form an epode to the two preceding strophes of antecedent and consequent; for even the balance in mere measure numbers is convincing if one subtracts the irregular extensions from the strophes $[(3 \times 4) + (3 \times 4) = 24]$. These measures may also be called a coda, for in it one hears a playful summary of past events. The ascending scale occupies the first half of the coda, the main points of the line carefully marked by forte accents. There is a short cut toward the critical sixth degree of the scale (m. 41) and a hurried, though imperfect (c-natural), version of the entire scale in the bass (m. 42). Arpeggios intervene (m. 45–48) before the complete descending tonic scale gets its share (m. 49 and 50). The correspondence with the closing section of each strophe of the first subject (cf. m. 12 ff. and 29 ff.) includes the triple stalling on the first descending tetrachord before the whole scale rushes down to the tonic.

This cadence, or epode, or coda also contains a playful prognostication of the eventual happy solution of the original task. After the short cut to b (m. 41), the ascending scale reaches the tonic one octave above the starting point (m. 45). The erroneous step to c-natural before the corrective leading tone echoes the chromatic nature of the task and points up the achievement of the diatonic completion of the scale (m. 43–45). It is a playful forecast of the happy end, however, and not the real solution; for the complete uninterrupted ascending tonic scale has yet to be heard. In this instance the middle is missing.

The recapitulation presents the first subject in a manner which confirms the submitted interpretation. The antecedent (m. 139–155) is identical with that heard in the exposition. The chromatic problem is exactly restated to leave no doubt in anybody's ears. In the consequent (m. 156 ff.) the melodic movement swerves precisely in the critical fourth measure. The deflecting step a-sharp to b is missing. The unison melody runs out without ever rising beyond the fifth. Briefly touched in the lower octave, a-sharp serves merely as a reminder. It is here not part of the ascending main line. The rhythmic organization is restored to the eight-measure norm. The wind counterpoint again gains its impetus from the preceding descending scale; what was a mocking step in the exposition is here extended to almost an octave (d^2–e^1). One gains the impression that distracting factors heard in the exposition have been eliminated in order to focus all attention on the fragment of the ascending scale and the task of completing it.

The unison scale, having wound its way not higher than a, lands directly in the cadential section remembered from the exposition (m. 164–171).

At this point somebody may be tempted to explain the deviation of the first subject in the recapitulation by a naïvely external reference to the different modulatory plan of any sonata recapitulation as compared with the exposition. He may say that the movement has to change somewhere in order to remain in the tonic rather than progress toward the dominant. Such an explanation is rejected by the score itself; for, regardless

7

of the melodic variant, the following cadence (before the caesura in m. 171) is exactly the same, melodically and harmonically, as it was in the exposition (m. 58). The melodic variant has contributed toward the clarification of the musical content but not toward a change of harmonic direction.

The second subject completely elucidates the plan of the composition. The general conjecture is permissible that in a good sonata form the two subjects are thus dialectically related to one another rather than merely juxtaposed for reasons of external contrast.

In this special case the second subject, as it appears in the recapitulation, gives a quick insight into the musical content. It is the function of a classical sonata recapitulation to present a solution, whereas the exposition, by its nature, remains fragmentary.[2]

Like the first subject, the second subject forms a closed unit with a clear-cut beginning and end (m. 85–107 and 198–220); and, like the first subject, it is binary or an example of the "song-type" melody. The melody one hears (m. 198 ff.) is a concise version of the fragmentary ascending scale of the first subject. From the tonic the line rises as high as the sixth before receding. The chromatic step to the fifth is again utilized; but the significant a-sharp is missing—markedly so, because the omission becomes responsible for the only skip in an otherwise stepwise progression. The short phrase is immediately repeated. To the miniature strophes thus created, the following epode (m. 203–208) gives the supplementary explanation. The note a-sharp is enharmonically reinterpreted as b-flat. Properly resolved, it henceforth ceases to obstruct the completion of the ascending scale.

The consequent of the second subject (m. 209–220) is fundamentally identical with the antecedent. There are slight but revealing variants. A short inserted response at the end of each miniature strophe (m. 210 and 212) furtively indicates how the tonic scale, after reaching b, may be completed by the progression c-sharp to d. The miniature epode emphasizes the importance of b-flat by sustaining it in augmentation in the high strings and imitatively leading the bass line up to it in the low strings. The counterpoint in the solo bassoon is another example of the

2. The synthetic role of the recapitulation has been well established by Arthur Byler in his unpublished dissertation on "First-Movement Form in Mozart's Piano Concertos" (University of Chicago, 1947). Byler proves that the two expositions in the first movements of Mozart's piano concertos are each incomplete, though in different respects, and are reconciled only by the recapitulation.

technique found earlier in the consequent of the first subject (cf. m. 18 ff.).

Before leading into the jubilating coda, Mozart inserts a closing subject (m. 221–236). It is nothing more than a little song, completely free of chromaticisms and entirely regular in structure [(4 + 4) × 2].[3] Harmonically understandable as the *Auskomponierung* of a full cadence, it sounds melodically like a tune anybody might whistle in joy over an accomplished task. Within the simple diatonic framework, the crucial tone b is distinctly marked by ornament (m. 224) and phrasing (m. 226), without ever taking the decisive step upward.

The coda (m. 236 ff.) confirms the solution. It consists primarily of repeated projections of the completed ascending tonic scale. An octave is spanned in the first eight measures, not without jokingly taking the familiar erroneous step to c-natural (cf. m. 42 and 159) before the corrective turn to the leading tone. A second octave is similarly spanned; and one marvels at the placement of the forte indication, together with the entrance of trumpets and timpani, at the precise moment when the crucial sixth of the scale is reached in the middle of the period (m. 250), rather than the octave at the beginning of a new period. The following measures may be reminiscent of the second and third sections of the first subject—the tonic arpeggio (m. 252 ff.) and the subsequent descending scale (m. 260 ff.). But the most significant event is the unison of all strings on the last three steps of the ascending scale—the same steps which heretofore were missing. The written-out grace notes after the trill on the leading tone (m. 263) repeat the wanted progression in diminution. Around the diatonic unison of the strings, brass and timpani outline that part of the scale, the upper tetrachord, which is now finally completed.

It is no accident that the subsequent reiteration of most of the coda (m. 266 ff.) presents these three climactic measures twice more (276 ff. and 280 ff.). What is left afterward merely confirms the basic tonality.

The sections not yet discussed need a short explanation. They are the second and closing subjects in the exposition and the bridge from first to second subject in both exposition and recapitulation.

The structure of the second and closing subjects in the exposition is identical with the corresponding passages in the recapitulation. The tonal orientation—here in the dominant, there in the tonic—is the only dif-

3. Fischer (*op. cit.*) states that the use of a "song-type" melody for the closing subject is characteristic of Mozart's mature style.

ference. The exposition makes a direct, though secondary, contribution to the total plan by fully utilizing the chromatic alterations of the opening measures. The tones g-sharp and d-sharp recur time and again, the former even in its enharmonic reinterpretation, whereas the more crucial a-sharp is spared for the recapitulation, only in passing apprehensively anticipating the eventual establishment of b-flat (m. 102 and 104). Otherwise, no progress is made in the solution of the original task. It is noteworthy that the coda (m. 123 ff.) attempts to climb a scale up one octave, but the scale is not in the tonic and, moreover, is stopped short on the seventh. One is forced to the conclusion that this part of the exposition has gone off the straight path. This expression is meant to connote not merely the obvious trend away from the consonant tonic toward the dissonant dominant but the melodic inadequacy of the second subject against the first in—as we called it earlier—its dialectical opposition. The inadequacy makes necessary the recapitulation, the fresh statement of the whole case. The entire second half of the exposition can best be expounded by its relationship to the more successful corresponding sections in the recapitulation.

The bridge passages (m. 59–85 and 172–198) are each in bar form (8 + 8 + 11). The vigorous accents involving rhythmic and chromatic aberrations sufficiently compensate the epode for being somewhat short. The strophes are each built on a complete descending diatonic scale— the dominant scale in the exposition and the tonic scale in the recapitulation. One remembers that the cadence before the bridge is the same in both exposition and recapitulation. In the latter the need for the descending tonic scale is great, for it is precisely that part of the first subject which was omitted in the variant of the recapitulation (cf. m. 18 ff. and 156 ff., discussed earlier in context). In the exposition, on the other hand, a tonic scale after the caesura at the end of the first subject would sound redundant; and a dominant scale is needed to establish A major not merely as the fifth degree of the prevailing tonality but temporarily as a tonal center of its own.

Against the descending scale of the viola, the first violins play a counterpoint—the third instance in the sinfonia in which a counterpoint is sufficiently attractive and exposed to vie with the main line (cf. m. 18 and 156 ff.; and 102 and 215 ff.). On an ideal level, this peculiar device of covering the serious event by a lighter counterpoint may be brought into analogy with the frivolous *qui pro quo* typical of the plot of the opera. When the counterpoint, halfway through each strophe, becomes

10

lively, various wood winds lend reinforcement to the main line to save it from becoming too obscured. The counterpoint, however, is not without message. In the exposition it elaborates on the chromas of the opening measures, g-sharp and d-sharp (sparing the main chromatic event, a-sharp, for a moment of greater importance). In the recapitulation the counterpoint playfully closes that part of the ascending tonic scale which had been left gaping: the upper tetrachord.

The epode of the bridge (m. 75–85 and 188–198), harmonically not farther in the end than in the beginning, approaches the sought-for final solution more seriously. In both exposition and recapitulation, b-flat is heard, in anticipation of the decisive enharmonic change of the initial chroma above the fifth.

The tone a-sharp, in the fourth measure, has proved to be the generator for the entire musical movement.

FIRST ACT

FIRST ACT

NUMBER 1 / Duettino (G MAJOR)

The dramatic action of the opening duet is minimal. Susanna is trying on a new hat. Figaro is taking measurements of the room which they are to occupy after their wedding. She asks him to admire her hat, and he does. The situation reveals little of the character of the two lovers. Mozart's musical interpretation of this unpretentious situation lends human depth and meaning to the two individualities.

The instrumental introduction (m. 1–18) gives the first indication of the composer's plan. It is clearly divided into two sections, the second of which is slightly longer than the first (m. 1–9 and 9–18). The two sections are contrasted in every possible manner. The melody of the first section impresses the ear with the stolid seven repetitions of the same note, d^1, within the opening eight-note group and the exaggerated jumps away from the repeated notes. The exaggeration of the jump becomes audible at the first occurrence in measure 3, where g^1 is expected instead of a^1 in order to complete the octave of the G-major tonality. The tonic in the bass, deprived of its secure position by the skip of the first-violin melody, is thereby forced to resolve downward. The melody skips of a major sixth (m. 4–5) and a minor seventh (m. 5–6) continue the extravagant motion. The melody of the second section, on the other hand, is all grace by virtue of the many appoggiaturas (m. 10, 11, 12, etc.) and smoothness by virtue of its conjunct motion. The melodic drive of the first section points upward, from a^1 (m. 3) via b^1 (m. 5) and c^2 (m. 6) to d^2 (m. 7), one octave above the springboard of the initial note. The melodic drive of every fragment of the second section points downward. The ascending fourth a^1–d^2 of the first section is here answered by the descending fourth d^1–a (m. 9–10); the descending line returns sequentially in each of the following measures, is emphasized by the explosively interspersed string passages (m. 11 and 13), and is summarized in the flourish of measure 15 and the final cadence (m. 16–18). The over-all construction of the first melody shows a certain impatience. The melodic drives begin without firmly establishing the tonic (the second-violin accompaniment taking care of this problem), the big skips create immediate tension, and the upbeats become shortened and breathless (m. 5, 6, and 7). The over-all construction of the second

15

melody contrasts by deliberate restraint, consisting, before the cadence, of three repeats of the same two-measure phrase. The bass to the first melody maintains a certain contrapuntal independence. It even imitates the main line of the melody a^1–d^2: first one and a half measures behind (m. 4); then closer (m. 5 and 6); and, finally, in apprehension of the approaching cadence, shooting one tone beyond the desired point to e before settling with the whole section on d. The bass to the second melody is the opposite of the liveliness of the first bass: it maintains an obstinate organ point on D, relieved only by the final cadence.

The harmonic structure emphasizes the contrast. The first section creates tension by moving from the tonic to the dominant. The second section resolves the tension by returning from the dominant to the tonic.

The orchestration, finally, corroborates the composer's intention of sharply distinguishing two sections within the orchestral introduction of this opening number. The first section is played by the strings, the winds entering only as occasional reinforcements of the counterpoint in the bass and the dynamic increase of the cadence. The second section is given to the winds, the strings being employed only as occasional reinforcements of the sforzato accents and the dynamic confirmation of the tonic cadence.

The meaning of the contrast between the two sections is clarified by the almost literal repeat of the orchestral introduction in the subsequent measures (18–36). The voices of Figaro and Susanna are added. Figaro sings exclusively during the first section (m. 18–30); Susanna, exclusively during the second (m. 30–36). Hence, we may, for the sake of convenience rather than for any other reason, call the melody of the first section the "Figaro melody" and the melody of the second section the "Susanna melody." These names do not imply the use of any leitmotiv technique. They simply indicate that the listener cannot help associating one kind of melody in this number with Figaro and a contrasting one with Susanna. They further substitute short specific identifications for melodies otherwise referred to in vague general terms. The association of the two themes with Figaro and Susanna, respectively, must not be underestimated. Figaro's dotted rhythm on one note recurs in the duettino between Marcellina and Susanna (No. 5, m. 2 ff.) and reminds the listener that Figaro is the subject of the argument between the two women. Susanna's catching arpeggio (m. 34, 35) is heard at the end of the same duettino (m. 66–67), where, the excited triplet motion suddenly ceasing, Susanna emerges victorious from the altercation; and it

16

is lifted from the cadence where it first occurs into the opening of the aria (No. 27) which signifies her warmest personal feelings.

The repetition of the orchestral introduction by the next eighteen measures at first produces the effect of two strophes. Strophe and antistrophe are of equal length and correspond patently in parts. The voices of Figaro and Susanna present no new musical material. The internal construction of the antistrophe deviates in one significant respect from that of the strophe. Whereas the Figaro and Susanna sections, as we have called them, in their first appearance divided the orchestral introduction into two halves of approximately the same length (the Susanna section being slightly longer), the Figaro section in the antistrophe is deliberately expanded at the expense of the Susanna section so as to occupy about two-thirds of the total length of the antistrophe. The impatient measures 6 and 7, with their shortened upbeats and growing dynamics, are now retarded in the corresponding measures 23–26 by full-length upbeats and with equable dynamics. The expansion of the movement necessitates a longer cadence, which is produced simply by having the end of the progression SR–$\mathbb{D}$–D (m. 8–9 and 27–28) repeated (m. 29–30) in a technique typical of the Vienna classical style. It is noteworthy that the contrapuntal imitation of the bass follows the plan first laid in the strophe of avoiding the root of the dominant—the temporary goal of the movement—up to the cadence. There the bass line unexpectedly jumped from c to e before settling on d. Here the bass line lags behind the melody sufficiently not to reach D before the cadence. Against the retarding tendency of the Figaro section, the Susanna section in the antistrophe sounds accelerated. The triple repeat of her short phrase (m. 9–15) is reduced by one (m. 30–34). Analogously to the Figaro cadence, the Susanna cadence is also modified. It is shortened in agreement with the acceleration of the entire section, Susanna's arpeggio (m. 34–36) being a concise reduction of the original cadential formation (m. 16–18).

The difference between antistrophe and strophe, slight as it is, will not fail to impress the listener in a definite manner. Instead of hearing the expected exact repetition of a strophe, he will experience a psychological retarding in the section sung by Figaro and an accelerating in the section sung by Susanna. The experience will necessarily be associated with the two characters. Figaro emerges as the stodgier partner of the couple; Susanna, as the sprightlier one. This impression is strongly corroborated by the musical material assigned to, and hence associated with, the two characters. We remember that the melody of the Figaro section con-

17

sisted of somewhat stolid repetitions of the same note alternating with inelegant skips, whereas the melody of the Susanna section distinguished itself by graceful appoggiaturas and smooth progressions. Figaro's melody immediately created tensions, which Susanna's melody firmly and spiritedly resolved. Figaro's harmonic drive led straight to the dissonance of the dominant, and only Susanna's modulation back to the tonic eased the complication. Susanna's capriciousness, furthermore, twinkled through the sudden accents of the quick string passages; and her liveliness, through the generally sharp sound of the wood-wind instruments. Thus, the music to an otherwise noncommittal scene makes an early basic distinction between the characters of Figaro and Susanna, which is fully developed in the course of the opera. It is always Figaro who somewhat awkwardly brings about difficult situations which Susanna adroitly resolves.

The continuation of the duettino (after m. 36) first sounds like a third repetition of the same strophe. The original Figaro section of the introduction returns in the original key. Figaro, undisturbed by Susanna's new hat, is measuring the room as before. Susanna, quite disturbed by Figaro's neglect of her fashion display, tries to gain his attention. She succeeds very deftly by first using his language. She sings her admonition, "Guarda un po'," to his melody and rhythm, smoothing the dotted up-beat into two even eighth-notes. Her line, d^1–g (m. 36–37), obligingly completes his fragment, G–D (m. 36). Her response, d^1–a (m. 38–39), to his next exclamation, A–D (m. 38), again suggests complaisance; but she twists the end of the phrase back up to b (m. 40), and from here on she is gradually but decidedly gaining over him. He begins to take the cue from her: B in measure 40 and c in measure 41. Her impatience grows, particularly as at the end of the Figaro section (m. 44) he has not quite given up measuring the room in favor of admiring her. Her melody becomes ever more insistent by the repetition of the same notes. The first violins emphasize the excitement by turning from a metric accompaniment (m. 28–29) into syncopations (m. 45–47); and the second violins, by leading the smooth arpeggios (m. 36 ff.) into a stronger melodic drive (m. 45 ff.). The loudness grows into a real forte (m. 48–49), which coincides with the point of greatest harmonic distance from the tonic [(D)D]. Susanna's outburst—moderate because the situation is trifling, but still an outburst in relation to the prevailing mood—has the desired effect on Figaro. He pays her the solicited compliment not merely by saying, "Si, mio core, or è più bello, sembra fatto in ver per te," but mostly by singing her original tune. Measures 36–55 sound vaguely like a third repeat of the first strophe, at least in regard to the melodic material. The Figaro section is used by Susanna to make him listen to her, and the Susanna section is sung by Figaro in order to pacify her.

From now on (m. 55 ff.), however, the music associated with Figaro disappears completely. Only Susanna's melody remains, sung by both, thereby indicating her victory over him in this little scene. Above an organ point on the dominant, Susanna leads the discussion. To her firm exclamations (*mfp* in m. 55 and 57) he replies acquiescingly (*p* in m. 56 and 58). Susanna resumes a continuous melodic line with the rhythm of her first melody (cf. m. 59–61 with 30–32), and Figaro submits to her completely by following her two measures later in lower parallel tenths. After the fermata and return to the tonic key of G major (m. 67), the lovers show their unity by singing the same tune in parallel motion—Susanna's tune, to be sure, cadential arpeggio and all.

The coda begins in measure 77. It has primarily a confirming cadential function, as the bass line clearly reveals. The few reminiscences of earlier moments—Susanna's peculiar arpeggio (m. 79–81) and the flourish of the final four measures—become intelligible by reference to the over-all form of the duettino. Although strophic construction at first sounded plausible, the disappearance of the Figaro music halfway through the composition leads to another solution, namely, a rondo form in which the Susanna music becomes the ritornello:[1]

---

1. The measure numbers on the right of all tables do not necessarily add up to the total number of measures of each composition, partly because elision measures are counted double and partly because fragments of measures are rounded up.

Introduction, Figaro's music,
tonic, played by orchestra___9 m.

RITORNELLO, 3 repetitions, tonic, played
by orchestra. Characteristic cadential arpeggio missing but later balanced in coda_____9 m.

Figaro's music, tonic, sung
by Figaro. He ignores Su-
sanna_____13 m.

RITORNELLO, including characteristic cadential arpeggio, 2 repetitions, tonic, sung by
Susanna_____6 m.

Figaro's music, modulating
to dominant, sung by Figaro
and Susanna. Exact center
and climax: psychological
change (Figaro finally looks
at Susanna's hat); greatest
harmonic tension; forte___14 m.

RITORNELLO, including characteristic cadential arpeggio, 2 repetitions, dominant, sung
by Figaro_____6 m.

Episode, over organ point
preparing tonic, sung by Susanna and Figaro. He admires
Susanna_____12 m.

RITORNELLO, including characteristic cadential arpeggio, 3 repetitions, tonic, sung by
Susanna and Figaro_____10 m.

Coda, tonic, sung by Susanna
and Figaro. Occurrence of
characteristic cadential arpeggio balances omission of
it in first ritornello_____12 m.

Proportions and relationships between parts make the rondo construction most convincing. The ritornello occurs four times: first presented by the orchestra, then by Susanna, then by Figaro, and, finally, by Susanna and Figaro. The two and three repetitions of the theme, respectively, are grouped symmetrically around the center. Susanna's triad motive follows the ritornello theme in three places: first in the tonic sung by Susanna, then in the dominant sung by Figaro, and again in the tonic sung by both (with a repeat emphasizing the final cadence before the coda). The occurrence of the triad motive in the coda (m. 79–81) balances the omission of it in the orchestral introduction (where it could have been placed at m. 15).

An orthodox rondo might have opened (and closed) with the ritornello. Beginning with an episode, this composition at first creates the impression of a strophic form. There is a good reason for this ambiguity at the beginning. Mozart does not wish to reveal the fact, by placing Susanna's ritornello theme prominently at the head, that she is going to win out in the end. The opening of the duettino shows Figaro and Susanna as apparently equal partners. Only the subsequent musical development will indicate which is the smarter and stronger of the two.

NUMBER 2 / Duettino (B-FLAT MAJOR)

It would mean a risk for any composer other than Mozart to follow the opening duet of an opera immediately by another duet between the same two voices—both duets, moreover, allegro and in duple meter. To Mozart this kind of organization affords the opportunity to develop in greater detail the relationship of the two characters. Contrary to the first duet, the second duet uses throughout the same music for Figaro and Susanna. In such a case an average duet in an eighteenth-century opera would indicate accord between the partners by distributing the melodic material evenly between them or having them sing in parallel thirds. Mozart's construction is subtler. He lets Figaro in simple mind state the fact of the location of the rooms in the tonic. Susanna, with nimbler spirit anticipating possible developments from the proximity of their room to the quarters of the Count and Countess, carries the same musical material through a key in the minor mode. The two sections (m. 1–39 and 40–82) act on each other as strophe and antistrophe, the rest of the duettino forming the epode with comparatively new musical material from the recitative on.

STROPHE, T–D, Figaro		39 m. (1–39)
1st Strophe	20	
2d Strophe	20	
ANTISTROPHE, TR–T, Susanna		43 m. (40–82)
1st Strophe	23	
2d Strophe	20	
EPODE, T, Figaro and Susanna		52 m. (83–134)
Recitative	2	
Strophe (bar form, 4 + 4 + 4)	12	
Antistrophe (4 + 4 + 4)	12	
Epode	27	
Strophe (bar form, 2 + 2 + 4)	8	
Antistrophe (2 + 2 + 4)	8	
Epode	11	
CODA, T		11 m. (134–144)

23

The four measures of the little phrase which supplies the musical material for the strophes gain their tensions from the progression T–D–D–T (m. 2–5, etc.). Their most salient feature, however, is their triple repeat at each occurrence. The formal norm of eight measures is thus stretched to twelve, not by any extension of either antecedent or consequent but by the real buffo technique of exaggerated repetitions of a short phrase. Mozart uses the same device at various other places in this opera. In the sextet, No. 18, for instance, a short two-measure phrase is repeated five times (m. 48 ff.) when Susanna's anger, caused by her misapprehension of a fundamentally comical situation, accumulates until it explodes with her boxing Figaro's ears. Similarly in the second finale, No. 28, the short two-measure sequence which opens the comedy scene between Figaro and Susanna (m. 121–123) is repeated four times after a few moments, and six and a half times later on (m. 233 ff.) in a situation where Susanna again slaps her lover. Many buffo scenes in other operas employ the same technique. An investigation of the psychological reasons for the comical effect of excessive repetitions is difficult. It may suffice to remind one's self of the cumulative effect of a joke or mere phrase broadcast week after week by the same radio comedian or drawn time and again in a continued comic strip.

The first statement of the phrase is given to the orchestra; the second, to Figaro; and the third is divided between instruments and the singer, thus dramatically justifying the third repeat as if it were an afterthought half-expressed by Figaro. The bassoon doubles the melody of the first violins two octaves below (yielding the range to the first entrance of the baritone), perhaps signifying the potential dangers resting below the surface of Figaro's innocent speculation. Susanna's analogous statement (m. 40 ff.) has lost the innocence of an accompaniment in parallel octaves. The counterpoint has come to the surface like her suspicion and is sharply cut through the melody of the first violin by the oboes (a 2!). After the three repetitions the upbeat of the phrase is heard again. Separated from the rest, it is quickly converted into an imitation of a bell.

Music, as we know, is the art which does not imitate phenomena of the material world. It may do so, as is the case in program music, but thereby actually forfeits its true artistic prerogative. When a good composer turns to material imitation, he usually has a specifically strong reason in mind. The thunder in Beethoven's *Pastoral Symphony*, for instance, is—like the whole interpolated movement in which it occurs—

a dramatic preparation for the contrasting lyricism of the finale. Here the direct imitation, rather than a mere mentioning, of the bell is symptomatic of the ebullient spirit with which Figaro meets the situation and against which Susanna's suspicious reaction, ironically tinged by her taking up the bell imitation, provides a particularly dramatic contrast.

Figaro's second strophe (m. 20–39) runs in exact analogy to the first. The two strophes are joined by a half-cadence, which creates a kind of antecedent-consequent relationship between them and pushes the beginning of the second strophe up to the dominant. A few modifications seem to follow the text. The first strophe having described Susanna's duties, the bell tinkled in a high register, and the upbeat of the little phrase took the V–I step upward. The second strophe dealing with Figaro's duties, the bell sounds in a lower register, and the V–I upbeat points downward.

Susanna's antistrophe is so obviously similar to Figaro's strophe that their formal relationship needs little proof. The subdivision into two sections and the triple repetition of the melody phrase can be found in both instances. A few subtle and witty alterations corroborate the impression of Susanna's personality gained in the first duet. The sharp oboe counterpoint and the turn into the minor mode have been mentioned before as indicative of Susanna's awareness of possible unpleasant complications. The varied pitching of her bell imitation (m. 51–54) adds a further innuendo. The significance of the bell to Susanna's mind is emphasized by a formal rearrangement of the content of her two strophes. The bell imitation having thus far been sounded toward the end of each substrophe, it now precedes Susanna's second strophe. This deviation from an exactly parallel construction has various advantages. It differentiates anew Susanna's freer spirit from Figaro's more confined mentality, even more so as Susanna's *din din* now introduces, rather than follows as before, the instrumental tinkling. It moves close together all of Susanna's bell imitations, which, thus accumulated, reverberate all the more. It finally frees the last part of the antistrophe for a gradual cessation of the musical movement in accordance with the text, permitting Figaro to interrupt and stop Susanna at the right musical place in the middle of the phrase, after which another bell imitation would have made little sense. The prominent horn sound characterizing the Count's bell (m. 32–35 and 61–62) creates a peculiarly funny effect, particularly in its second occurrence, testified to by the usual laughter in the audience

25

at this spot. The sudden contrast of pitch, dynamics, and timbre (cf. m. 58–60 and 60–62) is perhaps not the only cause of the joke. The extra-musical association of "horn" in most languages (It. *corno*, Ger. *Horn*, Fr. *corne*) with "cuckold" was close and obvious to everybody in an eighteenth-century audience. Shakespeare had nowise exhausted the pun:

> My lady goes to kill horns; but, if thou marry,
> Hang me by the neck if horns that year miscarry.
>
> *Love's Labour's Lost*, IV, 1, 115

> What woman-post is this? hath she no husband
> That will take pains to blow a horn before her?
>
> *King John*, I, 1, 219

> O! that I knew this husband,
> which, you say, must charge his horns with
> garlands.
>
> *Antony and Cleopatra*, I, 2, 5

The use of horns precisely when reference is made to the Count's adulterous designs on Susanna is probably planned in the same spirit. The horns again become prominent toward the end of the duettino when Figaro chills with fear of becoming a cuckold (m. 134 ff.). The most brutal form of this joke is heard at the end of Figaro's aria (No. 26) on the infidelity of women. With a long catalogue of complaints leading up to the worst possible thing a woman can do to her husband, Figaro cuts himself short with the words, "Il resto nol dico, già ognuno lo sa" ("I won't tell the rest, everybody knows what I mean"). What he means and considers too painful to mention, the solo horns blast out with no ambiguity (m. 102 ff.).

The remainder of the antistrophe (m. 63 ff.) dissolves the musical material as Susanna's words are broken up by Figaro's interruption. Of the three established repetitions of the basic phrase, the second already shows signs of disintegration by wavering dynamics and orchestration (m. 67–70). The third repetition is incomplete, the first half omitted and the second half repeated to balance the missing measures. The cessation of movement, requested by Figaro, begins in the bass, over the organ point of which a full tonic cadence is gradually reduced to a dominant-tonic progression until the final standstill on the fermata.

The two variants of the basic phrase, distinguished by the direction of the upbeat, are employed with planned consistency. Susanna's possible adventures are described with the more buoyant upward leap; Figaro's, with the explosive, but quickly deflated, downward start.

STROPHE

Figaro talks about Susanna, upward
Figaro talks about Figaro, downward

ANTISTROPHE

Susanna talks about Figaro, downward
Susanna talks about Susanna, upward

The epode of the whole number pyramids bar forms, from the smallest unit up to the form of the whole. The dynamic quality of a bar form has repeatedly been pointed out against the static quality of a bow form. Here, too, it serves dramatic intensification as the scene progresses. In the purely quantitative relationship of measure numbers, the epode seems short as compared to the combined strophes. Qualitative factors, however, amply restore a psychological balance. The force of the epode is increased by the impact of the combined voices of the singers against their alternating solos in the strophes; the many sudden accents; upsetting syncopations; three fermatas; and increased harmonic tension, as witnessed by more chromatic alterations. These devices are all also characteristic of Figaro's growing doubts and pangs of jealousy. A similar qualitative balance is achieved within the small bar form opening the epode (m. 85–96), in which the last four measures, though not longer than each single strophe, sound with double intensity by virtue of increased dynamics, motion, orchestration, and melodic range.

The last eleven measures of the duettino form a coda to the whole rather than to the epode alone. Reminiscences of the early strophes are heard most clearly in the string section and to a lesser degree in the wood winds.

The tonality of this composition, with its two flats, contrasts strongly with the G major of the preceding duet. One connecting link is provided by Susanna's excursion into the minor mode, where the relative of the present tonic becomes identical with the parallel of the former (TR of B-flat major equals TP of G major).

NUMBER 3 / Cavatina (F MAJOR)

The *da capo* of the opening twenty measures at the end of the cavatina can hardly escape any hearer. But this fact does not explain the special force of the composition, in particular the relationship of the *da capo* sections to the long middle part between them and the aggressive presto at the end. More revealing is the fact that the cavatina is built in the manner of a theme and three variations. The theme is represented by a minuet (m. 1–20). The first variation maintains the same meter and leads to a closing formula similar to that of the theme (m. 21–42). The second variation, still in 3/4 time, extends up to the first change of tempo (m. 42–63). The third variation fills the entire presto section (m. 64–103). The theme is then repeated in the fashion of a typical variation cycle. A quick coda, with material of the third variation and not at all typical of the form of a variation cycle, follows the last statement of the theme.

The musical sound of the text alone knits theme and variations together. With one exception (*scuola*), each of the nine lines ends on the vowel *o*. Internal rhymes in most of the lines increase the total number of prominent *o* sounds to sixteen.

In order to recognize the variation elements, one must first become well acquainted with the theme itself. The minuet character is undeniable. Even the text conveys the idea of *ballare*; and if the Count really wished to dance, he would certainly do so to the beat of the most popular aristocratic dance of his time, the minuet. The music itself, however, is the strongest proof. Tempo and rhythm are both characteristic of a minuet. There is no upbeat, in accordance with the true nature of the dance and contrary to later practice. (The *Don Giovanni* minuet obeys the same traditional rhythm.) The organization follows the usual dance pattern of pyramiding four-measure phrases into a sixteen-measure entity, in which a regular bar form (4 + 4 + 8) can be discerned. The extension of the theme to twenty measures is one symptom, among others, of a tendency found throughout the cavatina to rebel against traditional patterns by wilfully bursting them. Beneath the apparent calm of the aristocratic dance, Figaro's plebeian wrath is smoldering. The unruly extension occurs at the end of the sixteen-measure period, introduced by a turn toward an imperfect cadence where a perfect cadence may rightly be expected. A second trial remains imperfect, reaching out for the root in a wrong octave range (m. 18). The third attempt finally closes the theme on the right tone, after all other triad tones within the given range have been heard in the course of the extension.

Figaro's rebellious mood breaks through, not only in the over-all rhythm but also in that of each small phrase. On the smooth surface of the courtly dance, strong measures stand at the beginning of each four-measure phrase. Complete caesuras leave no doubt about the boundaries of each phrase. Against this apparently regular meter of the dance, Figaro's rhythm chafes in headstrong consistency. His word accents mark the second and fourth, rather than the first and third, measures of each phrase. The slurred dotted rhythm in his line clarifies any possible misunderstanding. He receives support from the placement of the instrumental pizzicato bass. His explosive accents at the end (m. 16 and 18) are last assertions of his individual expression against the flow of the minuet.

The melodic outline of the theme is extremely simple, partly because it functions as the basis of subsequent variations and partly because it indicates Figaro's popular character. The structure is binary. In the first half the line rises by step from the tonic to the dominant, strophe and antistrophe each accomplishing half the way. With the epode (m. 9 ff.) the line reaches the climax—the free sixth above the dominant—and turns back whence it came. The rhythm of the last phrase of the epode before the extension (m. 13–16) reverts to that of the strophes, thereby creating the impression of a recapitulation bar form. The idea of a scale, ascending and descending, gives life to the variations.

The first variation follows the structure of the theme rather closely. Strophe and antistrophe, in good variation technique, employ a new figuration in the orchestra. Alternating between violins and oboes and horns, the figuration consists of not more than a single note repeated in the winds and trilled in the strings. Nevertheless, it obtains deserved attention by its syncopated entrance and by being first presented in isolation before the voice—a prelude, as it were, anticipating the strophe proper. Strophe (m. 23–26) and antistrophe (m. 27–30), identical in length and sequential organization with strophe and antistrophe of the theme, take up the motive of the descending scale. The lower strings join the solo voice in it. The ascending scale is represented as a counterpoint in the bassoons. The epode (m. 31–42) is marked by a sudden change of dynamics and the abandonment of the figuration by the orchestra. The similarity to the epode of the theme is close. Identical in length, it employs the same extension principle. The expected perfect cadence, this time transposed into the dominant, is twice delayed by imperfect, unruly twists (m. 38 ff.).

Though maintaining the tempo and meter of the minuet, the variation forsakes the character of the aristocratic dance in favor of freer subjective expression by the servant Figaro. The subdued irony of the beginning is yielding to more open aggression. Throughout the variation the regular meter of a sixteen-measure period is again in continual conflict with the rhythmic accents of the voice line.

The first variation having utilized the descending-scale element of the theme, the second variation exploits the ascending-scale element. It supplies the material for a new figuration in the first violins (m. 42, 44, etc.). In augmentation, the ascending scale gives direction to the vocal line (m. 42–51), doubled in the higher octaves by first violins and first oboe and reinforced by the bassoons and middle strings. The violin figuration is a development of that of the first variation, to which it eventually returns (m. 56 ff.). As in the first variation, the figuration is introduced before the solo voice absorbs the hearer's attention. The ascending scale in the solo voice and in the reinforcing instruments is brought out dynamically by carefully planted forte marks. Apart from the rising scale, the voice merely participates in the dominant organ point, on which the first half of the variation is built. The second half shifts the organ point from the dominant proper to that of the relative of the given key, that is, from D to (D)TR. The path from one organ point to the other is that of an upward major sixth. Representing the accomplishment of the vocal line from the first to the last note of this variation (m. 42–63), the major sixth is derived from the melodic compass of the theme—originally in the tonic, F to d, and now in the dominant, C to A. As in so many instances in which a force is driving toward a certain goal, the movement here shoots slightly beyond the goal and then sinks back to it.[1] In this sense the note B-flat (m. 51–52) must be understood. Its quality as an extra is clarified by the surprise break from forte to piano at the moment of its entry and the accompanying fall of

1. Heinrich Schenker describes a similar, and typical, case in his analysis, *Beethovens Neunte Sinfonie* (Vienna, 1912). See First Movement, m. 484–494, in particular the fortissimo in m. 489.

the first violins. Harmonized as a ninth in a diminished seventh chord, it precludes any interpretation as the striven-for point of rest. Withal, it helps build the melodic bridge between the two disjunct elements of the voice line: the scale ascending from C to A and the organ point maintained one octave above C. As soon as the extra B-flat and the underlying diminished seventh chord are resolved, the musical content of the second variation is exhausted. The establishing of the new organ point on the dominant of the tonic relative is all that follows (m. 53 ff.). The first three measures resolve the organ point by contrapuntal movement. The voice drops from the extra B-flat back to A and then temporarily merely changes places, by contrary motion, with the instrumental bass. After measure 55 the new organ point is always really audible. The voice sings it to the exclusion of anything else. The descending scale of the voice (m. 53–55), although of a subordinate function, creates a connection with the descending element of the theme, otherwise neglected in this variation, and with the following measures reminiscent of the first variation, in which the descending scale predominated.

The third variation fills the whole presto section. In actuality, it is no longer than the theme or either of the two preceding variations, for two measures of the faster tempo approximately correspond to one of the allegretto. The variation is most outspoken in breaking down by tempo, meter, rhythm, and figuration the general character of the courtly dance, which Figaro has ironically chosen as a means for expressing his rebellious feelings. Because of the great external difference between this variation and the theme, the melodic outline, in an effort to preserve unity of expression, follows the original model more closely than either of the other variations. One remembers the melody of the theme as rising on the scale from F to c, reaching beyond the dominant to a free and climactic d, and then returning to its point of origin. The vocal melody of the third variation does nothing else. The ascent is accomplished in a regular eight-measure phrase, the three tones between tonic and dominant each occupying two measures (m. 64–71). The descent is more rapid, one measure per tone, but is stalled one tone before the expected destination. The measures gained by the acceleration are employed, in crescendo, to settle the temporary termination on the dominant, thus preserving another eight-measure construction (m. 72–79). The interruption of the descending scale admits the retrieval of the missing climax d, the free sixth above the dominant. One expects the d-sound for another reason: the dominant of it, on which the second variation closed, has so far not been properly resolved. The continuation of the third variation quickly brings the tone above the dominant (m. 81), but in the wrong octave by virtue of an inversion and, moreover, as the basis of a restive harmony [(D^7)SR]. The correct range is regained, after an eight-measure slump caused by the inverted approach to the sixth and an answering sequence (m. 80–87), by a direct restatement of the ascending scale up to the desired climax (m. 88–91). The task accomplished, a quick descent to the tonic, settling on an open unison cadence, closes the movement (m. 92–95). The last eight measures, initially repeating the successful ascent to *d*, serve as a coda to the variation and transition to the *da capo* of the theme (m. 96–103). The bar form of the third variation, as well as of the epode itself, can be easily recognized:

Ascending scale_____STROPHE, 8
Descending scale_____ANTISTROPHE, 8

Retrieving of sixth in wrong range, SR   4 ⎫
Sequence   4 ⎬__EPODE, 16
Retrieving of sixth in right range, cadence 8 ⎭

Part of epode repeated   4 ⎫
Transition   4 ⎭__CODA, 8

Most striking in the form of the third variation is the organization by very regular eight-measure phrases, each of which can be further bisected down to four-measure and two-measure units. This fact and the recurrence of a basic rhythmic figure, ♩ ♪♪♩ | ♩ ♪♩ |, justify the speculation that the third variation follows a dance pattern. The first two variations, although continuing the tempo and meter of the minuet, showed no dance characteristics. The third variation, quite different in tempo and rhythm from the theme, juxtaposes a dance of its own with the initial minuet. An investigation of dance music of the decade during which *Le Nozze di Figaro* was written identifies the rhythm and the construction of the third variation unambiguously as that of a dance popular in England. The name of the dance is not exactly definable, as is the case with so many English dances. (Even the popular hornpipe is transmitted in different meters and rhythms.) The existence of numerous direct sources, however, provides ample proof. In all following examples—which are gleaned at random from a multitude of equally suitable possibilities—the dance pattern of the third variation will be recognized. The quoted dances are all built in eight-measure phrases, which can be as easily bisected as those of the third variation. One may consider measures 88–95 as most completely revealing the pattern of the variation because they include the cadence. Mozart must have felt the typical significance of these measures when he selected them for the final statement of the cavatina after the repetition of the theme. Here is the rhythm of this eight-measure phrase, with which the rhythm of the quoted English dances may be compared:

Here are the rhythms of a few typical English dances:

(*a*)

(*b*)

(*c*)

Example (*a*) is taken from a collection entitled *The Opera Dances as performʼd at the King's Theatre in the Hay Market 1776*, printed by John Welcker in London.[2] The dance bears no title; the dynamic marking is forte. Examples (*b*) and (*c*) can be found in a collection "Humbly Dedicated To the Nobility & Gentry, Subscribers to Willis's Rooms, Festino etc. by Francis Werner. Where he plays the Country Dances and Cotillions on the Harp, and directs the proper Figures." Example (*b*) is from *Book the XVI. For the Year 1783. Twelve new Country Dances, among which are several favorite New Allmands....*[3] Example (*c*) is from *Book the XVIII. For the Year 1785. Twelve new Country Dances....*[4] The melody of the last example is given in full because of its close resemblance to the presto

2. P. 9.
3. P. 20. The transcription doubles the note values.
4. P. 23.

section of Figaro's cavatina. In both instances a run of short notes falls on the accented beats—a figure known as "snap" and one that is characteristically English. The emphasis on England is not accidental. A casual cue is provided by the recitative immediately preceding the cavatina, in which Figaro mentions the prospect of his being sent to London. The idea of an English dance may easily be in his mind as he sings variations on a Continental dance. A more meaningful explanation for the particular choice of an English dance rhythm can be based on an extra-musical association. It involves the political roles played by Spain and England, respectively, at the time Figaro—and Mozart—lived. Spain was an autocratic and reactionary state in which common people like Figaro had very limited human rights compared to men who, like Count Almaviva, danced minuets and ruled with an iron hand. England, in relation to the Continent, was liberal and democratic. Figaro's cavatina, which is meant to express his angry protest against the ruling system represented by the Count, transforms the aristocratic minuet into a popular English dance. Figaro at first sings a minuet in ironic subservience to his master. In the first two variations he frees himself from the symbolic bondage of the dance by dissolving the original pattern. In the third variation he asserts his revolutionary liberalism by blotting out the Continental dance pattern in favor of an English rhythm and tune, just as many of Figaro's contemporaries—Mozart among them—were striving toward the extinction of the Continental aristocracy in favor of a humanistic democracy. The French Revolution exploded three years after the *première* of *Le Nozze di Figaro*.

The importance of the English twist accounts for the surprise coda of the cavatina. The return to the theme after a chain of variations is good musical procedure. The quick outburst after the restatement of the theme of a quotation from the English dance is irregular in technical, and insubordinately rebellious in psychological, terms. It is the same musical fragment which Figaro hums when he enters the Countess' boudoir (in the second act between Nos. 10 and 11) to talk to her, not as a servant to his mistress but as one human being to another.

NUMBER 4 / Aria (D MAJOR)

In many external aspects, this aria follows the pattern of the traditional buffo aria of the day. The form sounds like the conventional *da capo*, the fermatas (m. 29 and 72) clearly separating the three sections of the bow form from one another. There are many sudden accents and quick dynamic changes, as a mere glance at the abundance of dynamic markings in the score will reveal. The extended crescendo carried by alternating chords above a dominant organ point (m. 41–45) remains household equipment in Rossini's comic operas. So does the rapid syllabic recitation of a tongue-twisting multitude of words (m. 58–66). The exaggerated repetition of a short phrase—a device the buffo character of which has been noticed in its earlier appearance in the second duet between Susanna and Figaro—is employed in various spots (m. 23 ff., 56 ff., etc.). The orchestra produces bombastic sounds, in particularly effective contrast to the instrumentation of the preceding number. All these features, however, which certainly help get the aria across to the audience, do not add up to the full characterization of Bartolo as we listen to him. Mozart's technique is more deeply musical.

The exposition gives the first clues which are fully substantiated by the content of the remainder of the movement. We hear two distinct melodic phrases which divide the exposition in half (m. 1–14 and 15–29). The first melody phrase, in the tonic, is four measures long (m. 1–4). It sounds like the antecedent of a period, the consequent to which is loudly displaced by the vacuous arpeggios and runs which finish off this section. The phrase itself is well chosen to give an initial impression of Bartolo. No elegant passing note or ornament, not even an accompanying and harmonizing second voice, embellishes the bare big outline of the triad. The lonely turn in the orchestra (m. 2) seems to reveal Bartolo's trait of maintaining a superficial elegance, which is really not indigenous to him. The boisterous accents—real forte, not just sforzato in piano—surrounded by whispers, fall on normally weak syllables; the natural rhythm of the first exclamation, with accents on the second and fourth measures, is shaken up only by Bartolo's pompousness. The continuation of the four-measure phrase does not complete it, as might normally be expected. The arpeggios and runs rather sound as if Bartolo, too sluggish to finish into a well-formed unit what he has begun to say, gets "stuck" on the *vendetta* triad and keeps repeating it with canonic and other reinforcements of the orchestra. The brass, *a 2* and underscored by the timpani, most convincingly elucidates the motive. The cadence in the orchestra, but not in the voice, fills the hollowness of the triad with a complete scale.[1]

The second melody phrase, establishing the dominant, is three measures long (m. 15–17). The harmonic functions, always in reference to the basic tonality of D major, are: $T(D)(SR\ \underline{D}^9)D$. The introduction of a new melody is justified by a new sentence in the text. A certain connection with the first melody phrase is undeniable, as is often the case, for reasons of unity, in a relatively short composition. The dynamic oscillation is carried over. Together with the repeated tonic note of the preceding cadence, the first measure of this section sounds almost like another *vendetta* triad. But the fifth is perversely raised, altering the whole course of the phrase and giving it the stamp of independence. The melodic line is forced into *B*, which becomes the root of a triad for a fleeting instant. Another forte outburst and another, corrective, alteration are needed to turn the line back to the familiar fifth of the tonic— which a good composition should forget as little as Bartolo, in the same

1. After reading the manuscript, Hugo Kauder, in a letter to the author, made the following comment at this spot:

Introduction

Antecedent   Consequent

"This conception of the structure places Mozart's art of characterization perhaps in a still brigher light. The *intended* adherence to formulas and the shortness of breath throughout the whole piece, in which every attempt at melodic formation collapses; the recapitulation, which merely stretches the initial formula into a series of pompous cadences: these are most ingenious expressions of *unintentional* comicalness.

"(All true comicalness is unintentional; moreover, it has the deeper sense that through it the evil is rendered harmless. Wagner's Beckmesser is not a comic figure but rather a repulsive one, born of malevolence and spite. In the finale of Verdi's *Falstaff*, this kind of comicalness attains consciousness of itself, so to say. It thereby retains the last word and triumphs.)"

breath, wishes to forget the shameful trick played on him by Figaro: "L'obliar l'onte e gl'oltraggi è bassezza." Notwithstanding the organic connection between the melody phrases of the two sections of the exposition, however, the second one, by virtue of content and position, maintains its separate identity. It sounds again like a possible antecedent to a period, but, as before, no consequent follows to round off the period. Instead, a kind of free improvisation is heard, so identified because of the typical bass descent down the scale (from d to A_1), the conformably dependent motion in all other voices, and the final settling on an organ point. The baroque improvisation technique is unmistakable. The first Prelude in Bach's *Well-tempered Keyboard*, to quote only one example, employs exactly the same impromptu devices. It is built on a descending scale in the bass, to which the main line of the melody runs in parallel tenths before the motion swings out over an organ point. Here, the prominent parallel fifths in the violins lend the underlying faux-bourdon a singular ungainliness. The organ point is most clearly heard in the voice, then in the horns and first violins, before finding its proper place in the bass.

The effect is analogous to that of the first section of the exposition. In both instances a short thought is expressed but not properly developed; one half a period is left incomplete. The thought itself is somewhat awkward—what was boisterous emptiness in the first case is distorted bravado in the second; and the logical continuation is replaced by what sounds like rambling in the first case and extemporizing in the second. If the melodic invention alone had not convinced the hearer of Bartolo's vain boisterousness, the progress of the exposition would bear out his unrestrained inelegance.

These clues to the formal structure of the exposition and Bartolo's character are entirely verified by what follows. A comparison between the recapitulation (m. 73 ff.) and the exposition immediately reveals the actual completion of the opening phrase by a regular consequent. In fact, all that happens in the recapitulation before the coda is a reiteration of the completed musical period. The first four measures, which before were so crudely abandoned, are here convincingly rounded off by the answer of the next four measures (m. 77–80). The consequent, by shifting piano and forte measures, also corrects the originally faulty accents; the scanning of "Il birbo Figaro vostro sarà," contrary to that of "Tutta Siviglia conosce Bartolo" and "La vendetta, oh la vendetta," is entirely in order. The consequent further sounds—only faintly and in its outline—like the correction or a smoothened reminiscence of the melody phrase of the second section in the exposition. Starting on the third of the tonic, the line this time fills out the triad by a passing note, reaches *B* in unison with the orchestra instruments without a distortion, and therefore without need for a balancing alteration finds its tonic cadence.

There is great value to the idea of leaving a musical thought unfinished in the exposition and carrying it to a satisfactory end, after various adventures, only in the closing section of a composition. It keeps alive the curiosity and interest of an attentive audience, in the same way in which the early complications of a drama or novel are usually not solved until the last act or chapter. Very soon after the curtain rises on *Hamlet*, for instance, the audience is informed of the hero's intention to revenge his father's death; but the intention remains incomplete, it is not answered by the right deed, before the closing scenes of the play. It seems that this technique was frequently and consciously employed by many composers, particularly of the Vienna classical school, though it has not yet been thoroughly investigated. No documentary evidence or literature is known covering this specific technique. It has been studied in various graduate seminars in the Department of Music at the University of Chicago, primarily under the guidance of Cecil Smith and the writer. A dissertation by Arthur Byler traces it through Mozart's piano concertos.[2] The results have been overwhelmingly persuasive. The works of Mozart and Beethoven are full of rewarding examples. Several will be found in the course of this opera (e.g., No. 10, Cavatina).

The consequent to the interrupted melody phrase of the second section of the exposition is more difficult to find because the antecedent is never repeated; but it can be distinctly heard—twice, in fact, should anybody miss it the first time—immediately after the central climax of the aria (m. 51–53 and, repeated, m. 54–56). The best proof of the unity of the two apparently disjunct phrases, almost forty measures apart, should be aural. Play the two phrases in immediate succession and hear that they belong together. If further proof is needed, notice in both phrases the peculiar and, in this aria, exclusive construction *di tre battute*; the highly characteristic identical rhythms; and the thin unison or parallel motion of the participating instruments. Not only the emphatic reiteration of the consequent but even more so its prominent

2. "First-Movement Form in Mozart's Piano Concertos" (University of Chicago, 1947).

placement marks its importance. The consequent is introduced by the dynamic and harmonic climax of the aria, separated from it by a general pause and followed by the return to the tonic, which was abandoned with the middle section of the bow form.

The rest of the aria now falls into place. At the end of the exposition, in which Bartolo twice started to express a thought without being composed enough to finish either, he seems entirely lost. His extemporizing (m. 17–29) has been exhausted. He appears unable to express a new idea or to finish the old ones. The fermata signifies his moment of hesitation and recollection. Like so many inane persons, he finds fuel for renewed ranting not from the original source of his essential complaint but from the conventional irrelevancy of his closing formula, which, by sheer proximity, is still in his ears. The cadential step g-sharp to a (m. 28–29) is picked up and squeezed dry throughout the next section (m. 30–50) until Bartolo can catch his breath again to find the logical consequent to the second of his abandoned thoughts. It remains first in the exposed register of the first violins, doubled conspicuously (because of its nature as major third of a triad) in the two lower octaves, and in full loudness (m. 30–31 and 34–35). Nor does it disappear in the inserted piano answers, where the lower viola part admits it by deliberately adding a seventh to the secondary dominant chord on B_1 (m. 32–33 and 36–37). Bartolo's blank counterpoint to these measures hardly characterizes the *astuzia, arguzia, giudizio,* and *criterio* of which he is bragging. The joke is on him. The cadential progression g-sharp to a now sinks to the bass, stealthily imitated by the second violins and gingerly creeping into the solo voice (m. 37–40). Sforzato accents have taken the place of the previous forte in acting as signposts for the new line. The alteration of a-sharp pushing up into b and immediately corrected by the step g-sharp leading into a is reminiscent of Bartolo's second melody in the exposition (m. 15–17). Perhaps it actually reminds Bartolo to finish that melody by its proper consequent, as he indeed does right after the current outburst. In any case, it is now his turn to reiterate the step G-sharp to A, supported by almost all participating instruments and sharpened by the diminution of the first violins (m. 41–45). The half-step is summed up by a tutti outburst, the center and climax of the aria, with sforzato accents on top of forte and with two repetitions intensified by double time. The explosive effect is heightened by the omission of the otherwise essential major third, g-sharp, in the immediately preceding chord (m. 45). A

41

quick fall in the dominant concludes this section, which harmonically is no farther than it was at the onset. The varied harmonic tensions of the half-step help Bartolo make the most of an impoverished situation. In relation to the dominant of the basic tonality, A major, which governs this section, the step g-sharp to a is ever newly expounded in the progressions D^7–T; D^{5-6}_{3-4}; D–$\mathbb{D}^7$; $\underset{3}{D^7}$–T^{9-8}_{4-3}; again D^{5-6}_{3-4}; and, finally, $\underset{5}{\mathbb{D}^7}$–T. The augmented sixth chord provides the strongest tension, the altered note not only a direct indication of Bartolo's slightly perverted mind but also a reinterpretation of the earlier alteration a-sharp.

The completion, which now follows, of the theme abandoned thirty-four measures ago has been discussed before as a clue to the structure of the whole. It is typical of Bartolo's sluggish character to resume first, of two interrupted thoughts, the one lying within the easier reach of recency rather than to proceed in the more demanding logical order.

The end of the consequent retrieves the tonic. Probably in order to frame the central outburst symmetrically but also to introduce the special task of the recapitulation more deliberately, Mozart here interpolates a section (m. 56–66). Its undeniable bravura character without significant melodic or harmonic development gives it the imprint of a cadenza for the soloist at the traditional moment before the recapitulation. The cadenza lands on the same conformation with which the exposition closed. There the continuation, expanding into the entire middle section, went astray, as it were. Here the continuation, identical with the recapitulation, finally rounds everything off.

The long-delayed completed version of the first musical thought is emphatically repeated (m. 73–87). The elisions between and after the two statements produce grotesque seven-measure phrases, which sound as if, even in the final phases of an artistically unified composition, Mozart wishes to deny Bartolo a proper classical vesture.

The coda (m. 87 ff.) derives its considerable length from the necessity of balancing the excursive exposition. With the coda, the recapitulation is approximately as long as the opening section of the bow form. The structure of the coda is true to the technique of the Vienna school. The full authentic cadence T–S^6–D–T gains momentum by ever increasing concentration, together with increasing dynamics, into D–T and finally T alone. The cadential fall of the orchestra at Bartolo's last syllable fills in, and reverses, the hollowness of his opening triad by a rushing scale, of which earlier rumblings were heard throughout the forte part of the coda.

NUMBER 5 / Duettino (A MAJOR)

The excitement typical of a squabble runs throughout the entire duet in the triplets of the second violins, chafing against the normal duple rhythm of the other voices. In a few high spots the triplet excitement spreads, as if contagious, to other instruments (cf. m. 16, 29, 34, and others). Most startling, however, is the sudden cessation of the triplet movement and string sound altogether at two places, one exactly in the middle and the other at the end of the duet (m. 36 ff. and 64 ff.). Both places coincide with a full cadence in the tonic. The break in the middle, softly sustained wind chords replacing all instrumental agitation, indicates binary organization of the whole structure. The relationship of the two halves can be established after a separate investigation of each.

The most characteristic melodic invention of the duettino is the motive played by the first violins at their initial entrance. The sharp dots and the pointed slide sequentially mounting in pitch identify it as an emotional quality of the altercation. The motive acts as a nonverbalized current, an instrumental byplay, of the dispute; for the two female voices never take it up. The initial dotted rhythm on the same pitch is identical with the one associated with Figaro in the first duet of the opera. It reveals that he is the real cause of the quarrel, even though the women do not say so.

After the beginning, the motive does not recur until a full cadence in the dominant has marked the end of a section (m. 21). The section emerges musically and dramatically as a closed unit. An introduction of two measures, based on a descending scale in the bass, leads from the hyperexcited last recitative exclamation of Marcellina (d^1-sharp above Susanna's d^1-natural) back into the chosen tonality. The inversion of the bass progression from the dominant to the tonic gives the melodic impetus to the first violins. An inversion of the first-violin phrase, again (one could call it an imitation of the first descending bass, but it is hardly heard as that), supplies Marcellina with material to open the exchange of dubious compliments. At this stage both women preserve external politeness. Susanna's reply is a complaisant, exact imitation of Marcellina's phrase. The surface calm is given the lie not only by the agitation of the melody and accompanying undercurrent but by the haste of the larger rhythm which cuts off the last measure of each intended four-measure phrase by an elision (m. 6 and 9). The same friction beween duple and triple meter which can be found in the melodic content of almost every measure, as described earlier, thus acts as an irritant in larger rhythmic units.

The first verbal exchange between the women forms a musical strophe and antistrophe. With the next rally and the initial modulation to the dominant (d^1-sharp in m. 9) the epode begins. Good cohesion of the melodic substance averts the danger of a break where accumulating continuity is desired. The vocal line in the strophe having resulted from an inversion of the first violin motive from e^1 to a^1, the vocal line in the epode is gained from an inversion of the second, continuing violin motive from e^1 to b^1. Susanna's reply, although not an exact imitation of Marcellina's attack as before, still displays the civility of compliantly taking up Marcellina's line. It continues in the same direction the outline of the dominant triad, the joint in the middle firmly emphasized by six tone repetitions. The binary principle, meaningful in the artistic creation of a dispute, governs the whole epode. The short alternate curtsies are repeated and thereby create two parallel miniature strophes. Against them the miniature epode (m. 13 ff.) is set off in the manner of a refrain. Above an organ point on the dominant (m. 13) the women's voices are heard jointly for the first time in a canonic imitation of the descending dominant scale. A late flute entrance (m. 15) gives the illusion, by its timbre and range, of a third staggered imitation, although in reality it merely doubles the women's voices at the octave. Marcellina maintains her initiative into the canon. The civil repetition of the canon (*non fo inciviltà*) —the binary principle invading the refrain—is the only instance in the duettino where she yields the lead to Susanna.

The whole section, not counting the two introductory measures, is nineteen measures long. It has led from the tonic to the dominant. A second section now follows, analogously constructed, and eighteen measures long (m. 21–38). It leads back from the dominant to the tonic. In the second section the dispute loses much of its former apparent suavity. The external features preserve some of the good manners expressed by the music of the first section; but many musical symptoms appear, bringing into the open the aggression hidden under the false compliments. Susanna's answers cease to be polite imitations of Marcellina's inflection. Instead, they surprise the older woman by their sudden independence and eventually triumph over her. The first exchange of fresh compliments illustrates the new trend. Marcellina's *la sposa novella* is a reiteration of her earlier technique. The line descends within the chord. The dotted motive in the first violins is contained by the same intervals which proved apparently successful before: first a fourth (m. 21) and then a fifth (m. 22). Susanna's reply, the words a two-edged anticipation of her final victorious insult, is anything but complaisant. The direction of her phrase is changed to point up. The sharpness of the instrumental byplay is increased by step, first into an ambivalent sixth and then, simultaneously with Susanna's reply, into a pricking, dissonant seventh. The attack is heightened by a sudden forte, the first in the composition, explosively set off by a full wood-wind chord. The ambivalence of Susanna's remark permits of a temporary soothing of both harmonic and dynamic tensions. The seventh (m. 24) is resolved into a consonant octave (m. 25)—consonant only in the sense of its own framework but not so against the basic tonality—as the loud outburst subsides into the prevalent piano level. If this first verbal give-and-take forms a strophe in the second section of the duettino (analogously to the first section), the following antistrophe (m. 26–29) subtly intensifies Susanna's attack. For when Marcellina falls into the civil routine of imitating Susanna's line at the fifth (m. 26–27), the smart girl turns tables on her by another equivocal compliment (m. 28–29). The melody harks back to the opening of the squabble, desisting from all polite imitation of Marcellina's preceding phrase. The sudden forte and wood-wind chord intensify the blow. The dotted figure of the first violins is again stretched up to a seventh; but this time the dissonance remains melodically unresolved as the quickened temper of the situation, cutting off one measure, prevents the period from being rounded out. In the first section, strophe and antistrophe were each three measures long. Although forming an apparently normal total of eight measures in the second section, they maintain a temperamental irregularity by the subdivision of five against three measures. This barrage of aggressive symptoms must not create the impression that Susanna is obviously rude. On the contrary, the musical deviations from the norm are as subtly submersed in the smooth general flow of the composition as the aggressive feelings are covered by the complimentary curtsies.

The epode of the second section is marked by regaining the tonic (m. 29), just as the epode of the first section was marked by leaving it.

45

The parallelism also influences the form; in both cases a double exchange of compliments is followed by an epode with similar refrain elements. An important variant, however, is produced by Susanna's quick replacement of a compliment by an open insult (*l'età*). The music vouches for the effectiveness of the insult. It is skilfully prepared by the apparent submission of Susanna, who once again courteously imitates the inflection of Marcellina's compliment (m. 30–31). When Marcellina, thus lulled into security, repeats the same notes, Susanna unexpectedly tops them (m. 32–33). In reaction to the affront, Marcellina falls into the formerly self-satisfied refrain, the meaning of which has now changed. There she is left dangling alone; for, instead of Susanna's complaisant canonic imitation, one hears an explosive shaking of the subdominant chord, which can mean nothing else but the victorious laughter of the successful joker. The changed dramatic situation causes the omission of the repetition of the refrain. In its place an original phrase of Susanna's announces her triumph, gloriously emphasized by the sudden cessation of the agitated strings against the background of softly sustained cadential wind chords.

The two sections heard thus far are so parallel in construction, although adverse in direction, that they necessarily act on each other as strophe and antistrophe. Their relationship is summarized in the following diagram:

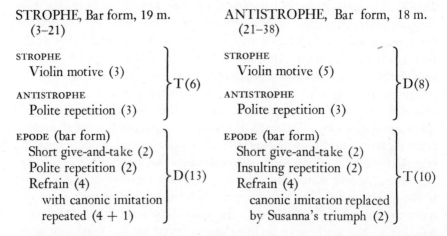

STROPHE, Bar form, 19 m.
(3–21)

ANTISTROPHE, Bar form, 18 m.
(21–38)

STROPHE
  Violin motive (3)

ANTISTROPHE
  Polite repetition (3)
}T(6)

STROPHE
  Violin motive (5)

ANTISTROPHE
  Polite repetition (3)
}D(8)

EPODE (bar form)
  Short give-and-take (2)
  Polite repetition (2)
  Refrain (4)
    with canonic imitation
    repeated (4 + 1)
}D(13)

EPODE (bar form)
  Short give-and-take (2)
  Insulting repetition (2)
  Refrain (4)
    canonic imitation replaced
    by Susanna's triumph (2)
}T(10)

With Susanna's triumph at the end of the antistrophe, the exact middle of the movement has been reached. It is tempting to expect the remainder of the movement to form a crowning epode to the two

46

strophes. The musical substance of the second half, however, foils this expectation. It lacks what is needed in an epode to fulfil its proper function: a synthetic summation of the strophes into a new entity. Rather, it consists of an almost literal repetition of the antistrophe and a prolonged refrain, leading directly into a coda.

The four-measure bridge between the antistrophe and its resumption is dramatically built on a new exclamation by Marcellina, who thereby signifies her unwillingness to accept defeat. Susanna's answer takes up a somewhat condescending line compared to Marcellina's steep curve. The musical function of the bridge is to retrieve the dominant, on which the resumption of the antistrophe, like the original, is to begin. The modulation is accomplished by the easy alteration of the subdominant into the second dominant. The sudden forte on the former, coincident with Susanna's first reaction after her triumph, is reminiscent of her explosive laughter on the same chord at the end of the antistrophe (m. 34).

The repetition of the antistrophe (m. 42 ff.) is almost literal. One may wonder about the uncommon structural procedure of repeating a long section that has returned from the dominant to the tonic and of stringing out, by a similar procedure on a smaller scale, the end refrain of the repetition itself. The psychological situation of the bicker brings the justification. Marcellina, the truly cantankerous party, loses control under the impact of Susanna's successful affront and simply adds repetitive abuse of earlier emotional invention. The only variant lies in an acceleration of the conversational pace. Compliment and repartee follow each other immediately without courteous pauses (cf. m. 43–48 and 22–29). At the same time the edgy violin figure is sharpened by diminution (m. 44 and 47). The resultant contraction of two measures into one in each substrophe is an index of higher tension, which also breaks through in the simultaneous crescendos. In the reiterated controversy, Marcellina displays a certain unimaginative vulgarity by drawing out— a rhythmic change against the original invention—the one real insult she can think of: *Del Conte la bella!* Susanna's ensuing counterattack and laughing withholdal of her part in the canonic imitation are the same as before. Her phrase of triumph (cf. m. 36–37), however, is postponed by a triple repetition of her decisive affront (m. 55), which, evoking a new, furious reaction from Marcellina, thereby becomes responsible for the elongation of the refrain. There is an internal musical reason for the excessive favoring of the refrain. It was cut short at the end of the antistrophe, creating by force of its incompleteness a psychological need for musical compensation. The shortening is now made up for by the prolongation. After Marcellina's solo version of the refrain line, in the manner of the antistrophe, the full refrain is heard twice and is intensified by duet imitation, before the double statement of Susanna's victory. The imitation, although canonic at the head, is no longer at the unison as in the first polite strophe. Susanna asserts herself a major sixth above Marcellina and ends her part of the canon with a flourishing laugh. The descending scale which formed the content of the original refrain is here, in the tonic, divided between the two women. Marcellina sings the first three notes, leaving the longer completion, raised up an octave, to Susanna. The illusion of a third entrance in the imitation, conveyed by the flutes (cf. m. 15) in the original strophe, is here analogously carried out by Marcellina, but ineffectively so below her adversary's main line. Only in the repetition of the refrain does the defeated woman use this spot for a last quick outburst of high temper (m. 62). The first violins, simultaneously raised to double Susanna's pitch at the octave, counteract Marcellina's brief attempt to be on top.

Susanna's phrase of triumph, which after the shortened refrain at the end of the antistrophe first stopped the bickering triplets, also crowns this refrain, doubled like it. The first statement (m. 64–65) experiences the same sudden cessation of all string movement against a sustained wind chord that marked the original. The repetition admits the strings against an unchanged background. They do not resume the excited triplets but rather gloriously add to Susanna's victory by quoting a motive associated with the best in her: the audience heard her characteristic arpeggio of a major triad in her introductory duet with Figaro and will hear it again as the head of the theme of her last, intimate aria. By now, Marcellina has recognized defeat and merely adds a lower counterpoint to Susanna's leading melody. The resumption of the agitated triplets and the pointed first-violin theme in its accelerated form denote Marcellina's furious exit. The widest span worked up to by the first violins is again the sharply dissonant seventh (m. 72). A composer of the romantic school would leave it at that, equating the tense feeling of the situation with the unresolved musical expression. Mozart, however, with a truly classical conception of art, feels the obligation to resolve the dissonance within the musical movement. The first flute, which in the earlier corresponding spots had doubled the dissonance, sounds the resolving octave e^2, covering all the dramatic agitation below.

NUMBER 6 / Aria (E-FLAT MAJOR)

Non so più cosa son, cosa faccio,
  Or di foco, ora sono di ghiaccio,
  Ogni donna cangiar di colore,
  Ogni donna mi fa palpitar.
Solo ai nomi d'amor di diletto,
  Mi si turba, mi s'altera il petto
  E a parlare mi sforza d'amore
  Un desio ch'io non posso spiegar.
    Parlo d'amor vegliando,
    Parlo d'amor sognando,
    All'acqua, all'ombra, ai monti,
    Ai fiori, all'erbe, ai fonti,
    All'eco, all'aria, ai venti,
    Che il suon de' vani accenti
    Portano via con sè.
  E se non ho chi m'oda,
    Parlo d'amor con me.

Cherubino's words, "Non so più cosa son, cosa faccio," could serve as an appropriate motto describing his attitude toward the formation of his aria. There are elements of such open simplicity and well-behaved charm in the music that the hearer becomes inclined to accept the Page as an ingratiating child of good family. But then there are impulsive flights of fancy and unrestrained vagaries of expression which give the hearer flashes of Cherubino's possible development into a Don Giovanni.[1]

What are the immediately ingratiating elements? The melody of the opening stanza (m. 1–15)—the first impression Cherubino makes, so to speak—is among the strongest. The progressions are entirely diatonic, the harmonies uncomplicated. Each little phrase is symmetrically repeated. The over-all line pursues a spirited curve up to a pleasant and polite climax—pleasant because it is part of the tonic triad and polite because it is dedicated to the word *donna*, "woman." The cadence is

1. See Søren Kierkegaard, "The Immediate Stages of the Erotic or the Musical Erotic," in *Either/Or*, I (Princeton, 1944), 60 ff.

authentic and perfect. This type of melody construction is taken from the Vienna *Singspiel* of Mozart's time—the kind of light musical entertainment comparable in popularity to the Broadway musical show of today. Mozart was well aware of the captivating effect of a popular tune in the more earnest surroundings of an opera. Papageno's success depends on it to a great extent. In this light it seems that a real musical and psychological insight, not merely a poetical one, helped Kierkegaard discover a fundamental similarity between the Page and the Bird Catcher—both of them Don Giovannis on a lower level. In this aria the influence of the Vienna *Singspiel* can be stated more directly than just in general terms. The audience at the *première* of *Le Nozze di Figaro* was familiar with Cherubino's first tune, which it had heard the year before in Ignaz Umlauf's popular *Singspiel*, *Der glückliche Jäger*:[2]

The live association with the text of the Umlauf duet, which proclaimed that "Malchen ist eine junge Unschuld vom Lande," certainly assisted in tingeing Cherubino's first appearance with surface innocence. In the instrumentation, moreover, the gentle and elegant clarinets are participating for the first time since the opening curtain.

The simple bow form, appealing to *Singspiel* audiences, seems to have lent another external charm to Cherubino. The repetition of the first stanza after an intermediate contrasting section is exclusively a musical idea, not prescribed by the libretto (m. 37–51). At the end of the repetition, back in the tonic, one believes one has heard a complete little song in bow form.

But not very deep beneath the appearances, and actually more power-

2. Here quoted from Robert Haas, *Wolfgang Amadeus Mozart* (Potsdam, 1933), p. 139.

ful in the musical formation of the aria, lie those free irregularities of expression which disclose Cherubino's rich adolescent fantasy. They become audible in inordinate melodic forms, wilful dynamic fluctuations, uncontrolled dissolution of the formal structure—in short, all those musical devices which violate conventionalized impersonal norms.

The very tune of the captivating opening stanza is far less harmless than it is made to sound. Mozart's Cherubino perhaps has borrowed the costume of Umlauf's Happy Hunter but not his character. In both compositions the first phrase is treated sequentially. In the Umlauf *Singspiel* the sequence is stereotyped and exact. In the Mozart opera the sequence gains spirited personality—not merely because the repetition chooses a higher rather than a lower level but primarily because of the unexpected exaggerated sweep of an octave instead of a sixth (m. 4). The skips are the more striking as they are without any competition, all other tones having progressed by step. The orchestra reacts to the skips with impetuous accents—forte and mezzo forte, plus all winds, against the muted strings, and not just a sforzato in piano. The continuation of the melody in the *Singspiel* model employs another sequence; and the outline of the second group of four measures, moreover, resembles that of the first group. The continuation of Cherubino's melody is more daring. He sings the next text line on a new melodic phrase; and then, with no concern for the developing text and "stuck," as it were, on *ogni donna*, he repeats the same melody phrase. He has now (m. 9) exhausted the four lines of the first poetic strophe but, because of the previous nonprogressing musical repetition, still is faced with the task of completing the melodic stanza. For this purpose he is forced to use the last poetic line over again. The last musical phrase, maintaining the established organization into symmetrical binary groups, leads into a deceptive cadence before its repetition is permitted to end the whole stanza; and for the final repetition the last poetic line is necessarily employed for a third time. In short, there is little planned co-ordination between words and tune. It sounds as if Cherubino allowed his articulate thoughts to run away with him before he found the breath to catch up with them on his emotional level. The irregularity of the text repetitions is accompanied by an upset of rhythm. In the first rendition the four text lines are scanned evenly so as to produce four two-measure units (m. 2–9). Because of the introductory measure in the orchestra, each of these two-measure units begins, apart from the anacrusis, on a weak bar and leads toward a strong bar. The metrical accents in the first eight measures plus the concluding downbeat in the ninth fall, as normally expected, on the odd-numbered measures. The rhythmic accents in the same section offer a certain resistance to subordination under the meter; the even-numbered measures are ready to invite accents, particularly measures 2 and 6 bearing tonic triads. The resistance is not serious, however, and is quickly overcome by the deliberately spaced accents and wind chords in the metrically heavy measures. At the moment, however, when the words have been taken care of and the music alone carries the responsibility as an organizing power (m. 9), the rhythm is openly upset. The former group of two measures is stretched into three measures (cf. m. 8–9 and 10–12). The prolongation begins with the anacrusis, which, hitherto of two hasty eighth-notes, now fills two quarter-notes. The notes of the phrase itself appear almost doubled, the former eighth- and quarter-notes now turned into quarter- and half-notes. Expressive rhythm thus winning out over impersonal meter, the former regular pattern becomes disturbed. At three spots, there is one accented measure following another:

$$m \ldots \acute{7}, \breve{8} \; \acute{9}, \; \acute{10} \; \breve{11} \; \acute{12}, \; \acute{13} \; \breve{14} \; \acute{15}, \; \acute{16} \ldots$$

The *ritmo di tre battute* carries over into the next strophe. Cherubino himself proclaims at that irregular pulsation: "Mi si turba, mi s'altera il petto." As in the opening stanza, the sequence of the second phrase (m. 19–21) is wilfully altered at the end. The expected missing tones f^1 and e^1-flat give the starting fuel to the next phrase. Even after Cherubino finds his breath again (m. 22 ff.), the underlying duple rhythm within each phrase remains disturbed by irregularities between the phrases. The first mentioning of *un desio* (m. 26–27) becomes a sentimental insertion which, like a parenthesis, delays the direct flow from the third to the fourth line of the second poetic strophe. The fourth line does not find its proper end without, by means of a suprise elision (m. 31) which brings about a last reminiscence of the *ritmo di tre battute*, turning back once more to the most sentimental place. Freed of subjective insertion and shortening elision, the second strophe of the poem emerges musically as a bar form:

STROPHE_____3

ANTISTROPHE_____3

EPODE_____8 (+7 Prolongation)

E a parlare, 4
    Insertion, 2
    Un desio—wrong turn into elision, 3   ] Prolongation
    Insertion, 2
Un desio—correct turn into cadence, 4

If closer investigation has unmasked the apparent innocence of Cherubino's opening stanza, similar attention should be given to the rondo-like repetition of the whole stanza at the end of the second text strophe. The repetition is not called for by the poem. Introduced by an apparently flustered boy, it produces the immediate effect of an ingratiating bow form. This effect of orderliness is dissolved by the free subjective flow of the composition after the end of the bow form. It now becomes apparent that the initial charm of a rounded form brings in its wake the surprise of free individualism and the wilful destruction of the literary form on which the aria is based.

The text is clearly in bar form. Two corresponding strophes of four lines each are followed by an epode of contrasting organization and content. A striking feature of the epode is its leading up to a punch line. The very last line twists the romantic cataloguing of the objects to which Cherubino desires to tell of his love into the joke that he will talk to himself about love if nobody else cares to listen. The punch line is carefully prepared by the next to the last line, which is otherwise a superfluous insertion matching, or rhyming with, no other line. The bar form of the poem provides the logical way of leading up to a last line which must not be an expected consequent to, or repetition of, an earlier statement. Cherubino's inordinate though charming presentation of a bow form destroys with youthful *élan* the formal plan and obliges him to lead up to the punch line in a courageously impromptu manner. He does preserve the joke at the end. With all the many text repetitions throughout the aria, the last line is heard only after everything else has been said.

It might be argued that the repetition of the opening stanza still admits of a bar form for the aria as a whole. Such an argument might suggest the following formal solution:

| Stanza, T | } STROPHE |
| Episode, D | (15+22) |

| Stanza, T | } ANTISTROPHE |
| Episode, S | (15+14) |

Che il suon, T	
) Improvisation above organ point, T	} EPODE
Che il suon, T	(7+13+7)

| Preparation and | } CODA |
| Punch line, T | (4+5) |

There are weighty musical reasons against this solution. The episodes in strophe and antistrophe show almost no correspondence. The epode does not provide proper equilibrium to the strophes. The feeling for a completed bow form after the second hearing of the opening stanza, on a perfect authentic tonic cadence, is so strong that it will be difficult to hear a decisive caesura before, rather than after, it. Nor does the harmonic structure favor the submitted solution. The only real movement away from the tonic happens in the first episode. The subdominant elements in the second episode are by no means so independent as the dominant elements in the first episode. They sound rather like a temporarily tonicized fragment within a large full tonic cadence. The first episode begins, progresses, and ends in the dominant. The incidental E-flat major chord in the center (m. 26) can readily be identified as a secondary subdominant of the dominant by virtue of its characteristic added sixth, and not as a functional tonic chord. The second episode, however, may be easily heard as never leaving the tonic:

$$\overset{51 \quad 52 \qquad 53 \ 54 \quad 55 \ 56 \qquad 57 \ 58 \quad 59 \quad 60 \qquad\qquad 65}{|T|(D_5^7|_4^6|_5^7)|S|(D_5^7|_4^6|_5^7)|SR|D^7 \ldots|}$$

The large full tonic cadence emerges in which the subdominant and its relative are each confirmed by three measures of their respective secondary dominants. Classical cadential proportions are preserved:

S (incl. its secondary dominant)_____4 m.
SR (incl. its secondary dominant)_____4 m.
D_____6 m. extended by fermata

54

The aria thus actually never leaving the tonic after the first episode, the sense of completion after the recapitulation of the opening stanza remains fundamentally unchallenged by the consequent harmonic development and increases the reluctance to accept the bar-form solution.

The alternative solution must necessarily focus on the bow form, which is completed when the aria has reached only its mid-point (m. 51). The case for the bow form is literarily weaker, but musically and psychologically stronger, than that for the bar form. The question is not which is right. It is important to remember that a baroque form, more than any other, is by its nature open to varying interpretations which have room next to one another. The formal ambiguity of this aria seems to be the ingenious result of the composer's conscious planning. Mozart wishes to express Cherubino's oscillating character—child and yet man, well bred and yet erratic, well behaved and yet capricious, baroque and yet popular, aristocratic and yet rebellious.

The first arguments in favor of the primacy of the bow form are all those which have just been used against that of the bar form. But proof is yet required for the relationship of the long section that lies outside the bow to the bow itself, the more so as that section is just as long as the bow. It is submitted that Cherubino, after gracefully finishing his early bow form and finding himself with half the poem unfinished on his hands, improvises his way up to the punch line skilfully, charmingly, and—with regard to conventional procedure—disrespectfully. The purely cadential elements of the section following the bow have already been pointed out. The favoring of the subdominant lends the cadence a coda flavor particularly typical of Mozart. The few measures between the first two fermatas take the place of a cadenza, which musically leads directly into the jocose exclamation of the last two measures of the aria. Anybody can easily convince himself of the intimate kinship between the cadenza and the closing measures by playing or singing them as a unit. The closing measures (99–100) answer the preceding measures (68–69) exactly in rhythm, rhyme, harmony, and melody. The exposed third g^1 to e^1-flat in Cherubino's top range, is not answered in the rest of the aria until f^1 to d^1, just before the very last note. The intermediate measures, accordingly, are a long impromptu insertion. The temporary cadence after the second fermata (m. 70–72) forfeits a claim to finality by merely repeating the preceding words, and the sudden drop in dynamics (cf. the forte in m. 99–100) corroborates this impression. The impromptu character of the section up to the next fermata is evinced by the prolonged organ point on which the section is built. Above the organ point, Cherubino knows no better than to sing arpeggios of the tonic triad. The abandoned main line is retrieved by a repetition of the phrase identified above as a cadenza. The subsequent cadence is imperfect this time, opening the way to the as yet unexpected preparation line for the final exclamation. The extra function of the preparation line which makes it stand outside the closed poetic form is consciously expressed by the new adagio tempo, which moves outside the established allegro. The joke of the punch line, *con me*, is heard three times—a poor procedure in a purely verbal narration but a necessary one in any musical situation where the competition given to words by tones sanctions clarifying repetition. Even within the three musical repetitions the surprise element is maintained as much as possible: the first time by odd chromaticism and the second time by subito piano and fermatas. Only the final statement lands the punch forcefully.

The bow-form solution may be represented by the following diagram:

Stanza, 15
) Middle section, 22   } Bow form
Recapitulation, 15   T–D–T

First coda, 14
    Cadenza and cadence, 7 ⎤
) Organ point, 13   ⎥ Insertion   Improvisation
    Cadenza and cadence, 7 ⎦   T
Preparation, adagio, 4
Final coda, 5

The improvisation itself, as shown in the foregoing diagram, forms a regular bow around the center of the section above the organ point. The proportions are exact, for in terms of time rather than of measures the fourteen measures of the first coda are well balanced by the four adagio measures (which last a little longer than twice as many allegro vivace measures) plus the five measures of the final coda.

Whichever of the two solutions seems more cogent, each of them presents a rare mixture of strictness and freedom so characteristic of the Page. In the first solution the over-all bar form is strict, but the relationship of the subordinate parts is free. In the second solution the over-all form of bow plus equally long improvisation seems free, but the relationship of the subordinate parts is exact.

NUMBER 7 / Terzetto (B-FLAT MAJOR)

The supreme joke of this terzetto is the employment of a sonata-form recapitulation for a situation which is no longer identical with that of the exposition. In the beginning the Count's anger is aroused by a malicious remark of Basilio's about Cherubino. Basilio apologizes by calling the basis for his remark a personal suspicion rather than a factual observation. In the development section, Cherubino's unauthorized presence in the room is discovered. This dramatic change justifies a renewed outburst of the Count's anger in the recapitulation. In the due course of the sonata form, Basilio repeats his apologetic remark, which now—Cherubino fully visible to everybody—sounds like the most wicked irony.

The following diagram gives an outline of the sonata form:

EXPOSITION
   1st subject (m. 5)   T   ⎫
   2d subject (m. 43)   D ⎬ 69

DEVELOPMENT (m. 70)   S, D ⎫
FALSE RECAPITULATION AND RECITATIVE (m. 101) T   ⎬ 77

REAL RECAPITULATION   ⎫
   1st subject (m. 147)   T
   2d subject (m. 168)   T ⎬ 75

CODA (m. 201)   T ⎭

The main sections divide the movement into three parts of approximately the same length. The tonal plan and the clear demarcation of the recapitulation by the preceding recitative and fermata, among other characteristics, admit no doubt as to the real employment of a sonata form.

The first four measures serve as an explosive introduction. They establish the tonality by reiterated dominant-tonic cadences, the dissonance far outweighing the consonance. The three singing voices are introduced separately: the two men each with a distinctive and unified melody, but Susanna with a phrase which, above a static bass, sounds like a passing reaction to the situation rather than a significant expression. The melodies of both men are in the tonic, whereas Susanna's line moves in the minor dominant. The statements of all three people are interrupted by pauses, characterizing, in turn, the Count's lordly rhetoric, Basilio's hypocritical servility, and Susanna's agitation. The second subject, given entirely to the two men while Susanna lies in a faint, enters at the precise moment when the minor third makes way for the major third. Susanna regains her voice in the closing cadence, which, as if in a gesture of protest against the lead of the men, substitutes the dominant of the tonic relative for that of the tonic.

The development section, set off from the exposition by a full break, dips to the subdominant with the help of a deceptive cadence. Again, only the two men are heard with musical material taken from the second and first subjects, in this order. Susanna sings by herself only after the dominant organ point of the closing cadence is reached. The false recapitulation and the subsequent recitative technically belong to the development section. They are carefully set off, however, because they provide the real dramatic cause for an otherwise unjustifiable recapitulation of the mood of the exposition. The restatement of the opening phrase in the tonic does not sound false until it dissolves, with the Count's evaporating anger, into ever thinner texture (after m. 109). The insertion of a recitative leaves no doubt about the temporary disruption of the sonata form. The unbroken descending scale of an eleventh, extended by further scale passages in opposite directions, ascribes to the in-tempo section up to the fermata the role of a cadenza in its originally proper place before the recapitulation.

The recapitulation follows the general plan of the exposition without being rigidly exact. Strong tendencies toward tonic cadences seem to rectify the earlier false recapitulation. The Count's opening angry statement recurs, stirred up this time by a real discovery rather than by a slanderous remark. Susanna's fainting escape into the minor mode—there is no escaping this time—is replaced by Basilio's florid jubilation. The substitution reminds one of the original to a certain extent by the excited phrasing of eighth-notes (cf. m. 26 and 162). The second subject is sung by all three voices—for Susanna remains unpleasantly conscious of the situation—before Basilio restates that part of the first subject identified with him. The following repeat of Basilio's jubilation and of the second subject acts as a musical intensification of the prevalent feelings. It can also be understood as a quasi-correction of the irregular order of the recapitulation. Jubilation and second subject followed the Count's part of the first subject without leaving time for Basilio's part; now jubilation and second subject make up for the omission by following in full length Basilio's part of the first subject. The coda helps preserve the equilibrium between recapitulation and exposition.

The melodic material of the terzetto sheds much light on the relations between the three persons. The allotment of the main melodies of both first and second subjects to the Count and Basilio identifies the two men as the active carriers of the situation. The coexistence of two different melodies in the tonic of the first subject is remarkable in its own way, particularly as the second melody (Basilio's) is more catching than the representative opening tune. Actually, there is a close inner connection between the two halves of the tonic subject. The basic melodic element of the Count's sentence is the interval of a third, presented with the intermediate passing tone in conjunct motion and spanning the range of a sixth (the instrumental bass from the tonic up to G, the voice from D up to the tonic). Basilio's statement uses the same melodic element in inversion: the scale is subdivided into units of a third each, the motion is conjunct, and the over-all range spans a sixth (b-flat to g^1). The direction is the main difference. The Count sings with ascending fury; Basilio, with descending malice. The rising and falling melodies are paralleled by rising and falling rhythms. The harmonies bear out the fact that Basilio takes his first cue from the Count. The beginning of the bass progression to his exclamation is identical with that of the cadence just finished, interpolated secondary dominants emphasizing each step:

$$
\text{Count:} \quad \overset{13}{|} \ T \qquad TR \qquad \qquad \overset{14}{|} \ S
$$

$$
\text{Basilio:} \quad \overset{16}{|} \ T \ (D^9) \ \overset{17}{|} \ TR \ \overset{18}{|} \ - \ (D^7) \ \cancel{TR} \ \overset{19}{|} \ S
$$

Basilio appears just about twice as deliberate as the Count: he takes four measures for the same progression that the Count accomplishes in two.

The same power of the interval of a third unites the two men in the second subject, only that here Basilio is in the lead. The melody ascends the scale subdivided into two relays of a third each. The descent from the climax (m. 52) moves in thirds altogether. The outside range is again a sixth (F to d). The two voices, moreover, maintain for the most part the distance of a third from each other. The situation is similar throughout the development section, the melodic material of which is derived exclusively from the first and second subjects just discussed. Basilio retains his superiority by giving the cue to the Count (m. 70 ff.) and finally emerging as the soloist. The interval of the third, and none other, serves the Count in his narrated, and then actual, discovery. By now he has adjusted himself completely to Basilio's descending idiom. If there was anything strong in his original ascending line, it has now lost its dignity under the intriguing influence of the music master. With servile cajoling, Basilio utilized in his first sentence elements of the Count's speech. The flattery, inverted in direction from the start, soon gained independent strength until the nobleman is now using the sycophant's language—almost without knowing it, for the perversion has progressed so skilfully that he may still consider the language his own.

The recapitulation only consolidates Basilio's position as the superior intrigant of the two. His coloratura (encompassing a sixth) is the only new and, at that, most outstanding melodic feature of the recapitulation. His solo is carefully placed to gain full attention. The characteristic interval of a third permeates the structure. Apart from formal repetitions from the exposition, it is responsible for Basilio's first sentence in the recapitulation, the Count's counterpoint to it, and the accompanying figures in the wood winds (m. 155–159); the faux-bourdon in the coda centered around Basilio's line oscillating one third above and below the tonic (m. 201–207); the imperfect final cadence of the voices; and the attempt at perfection of the cadence by the last instrumental chords, in which the top voice of the flute succeeds by force of the very interval of the third, while the imperfect ending on the third gleams through the last chord prominently in all other wind instruments and the first violins.

Against the plotting of the two men, Susanna assumes a relatively passive role. Hers is no solo melody in the opening tonic. She functions primarily in protest against the Count and Basilio on the cadence of each section in which they have had their say. In this manner she finishes the structural unit of the first subject, second subject, and development. Her phrases do not have the individuality of the Count's or, even less, of Basilio's. In the recapitulation she succumbs to the pressure of the situation by joining the ensemble of the men in which she first somehow preserves her independent expression (m. 156 ff.) before she accepts her fate along with Basilio's tune (m. 168 ff.). The music leaves no doubt that she is the loser, temporarily at least, in the encounter. At the end of the terzetto, her voice hits bottom.

The question arises whether her swooning in the exposition is real or sham. The libretto is not very specific, although it conveys the impression that Susanna is feigning. Why else would she suddenly recover as soon as Basilio offers her the compromising chair? Every stage director whose work I have seen has special fun working out her obvious shamming. Does the music clarify the question in any way? By now one has heard Susanna in three duets with two different people and in recitatives with three more people. One knows her well enough to suspect that the turn into the minor dominant and the affected sighs are not her real expression. She is too bright and mature to be earnestly upset in such a girlish manner. Even the more serious complications of the later acts do not draw from her similarly doleful exclamations. The F-minor tonality, the emotional play on the minor sixth, and the girlish sighs are much more characteristic of Susanna's adolescent cousin Barbarina. They can all be heard in Barbarina's cavatina in the fourth act, in which Barbarina sounds inconsolable because of the trifling loss of a pin. From her cousin, Susanna may well have borrowed the mannerisms with which to meet a difficult situation. A teen-ager may honestly swoon in defense against intriguing adults. Susanna uses Barbarina's affected language merely to gain time. The return of phrases from her "fainting" music in the *major* mode at a moment when the men still believe her to be unconscious (m. 57 ff.) sounds more like the true Susanna—as if she were peeping at the scene through half-open lids without completely abandoning the assumed gesture.

NUMBER 8 / Coro (G MAJOR)

The chorus in this opera is treated somewhat incidentally. Unlike the chorus in the later *Zauberflöte*, it does not participate in the two grand finales. Within this number, the four voices are treated as a well-blended unit, moving almost always simultaneously; and the music they sing is simple. Nonetheless, the composer's skill lends dramatic interest even to this noncommittal situation.

The musical form chosen is appropriate to the simple role of the peasants. It is the popular bow form, two corresponding sections symmetrically framing a contrasting centerpiece. The two presentations of the whole movement, Nos. 8 and 8a, themselves form a larger bow around the recitative scene between them. The only difference between the two numbers lies in the orchestra introduction heard before the first chorus and missing in the second. The assumption is therefore permissible that the measures in question are a real introduction and not an integral part of the movement. The psychological explanation is close at hand that the peasants addressing the Count are at their first entrance shy and depend on the orchestra to remind them of what they are to say. At the repetition the peasants, having become accustomed to the situation, start right in with their tune.

Discounting the orchestra introduction, which merely anticipates the opening statement of the chorus, the form emerges as a bow.[1]

OPENING SECTION	m. 1–8
MIDDLE SECTION	m. 9–20 (elision)
RECAPITULATION	m. 20–32

The opening section presents an eight-measure period in the pure, built up symmetrically of four two-measure units.

The middle section, similarly conceived, is extended by a simple device. The second half of its original form (m. 13–16) is moderately led astray by the intrusion of chromaticism and independent figuration of

1. The references to measure numbers apply throughout, for clarity's sake, to the second version of the chorus, No. 8a.

63

the voices. It sounds as if the peasants would suddenly gain some personality—a rebellious sign in the face of the Count. Immediate correction is necessary, even to the minds of the peasants. The same four measures are firmly repeated with familiar innocuousness, purged of individualistic chromaticism and insubordinate figuration (m. 17–20). The correction is so vigorous that it hastily elides the last measure with the opening of the recapitulation.

The recapitulation suffers the processes of both abridgment and expansion, the latter outweighing the former in the over-all structure. The first of the four two-measure units is literally repeated. The second unit seems to be cut in half; but closer scrutiny recognizes in this measure (22) merely a gesture borrowed from the analogous phrase in the opening section. In reality, it means a cessation of the melodic movement, a composed fermata above the tone reached just before (d^1). The fermata resolves, by an elision, into a repetition of the recapitulation measures heard thus far. The external aspect is again reminiscent of the analogous section in the exposition, particularly in regard to the dynamic, and some of the accompanying instrumental, patterns. The musical content, however, differs significantly: there a melodic line was developed, whereas here a melodic line is stopped. The "fermata" measure, as we named it before, is now permitted to swing out—not only into the expected two-measure length (m. 25–26) but, extended beyond it, into the concluding cadence of the piece. Freed of all modifications, the recapitulation can be reduced to an eight-measure period, balancing, although not identical with, the exposition:

The special function of the recapitulation as against that of the exposition can be explained only after an investigation of the melodic content of the whole number. The most striking feature in the over-all structure is the persistently regular alternation of forte and piano. A closer comparison of all phrases according to their dynamic levels shows that—with one exception to be specifically mentioned—all forte phrases follow an upward drive and all piano phrases a downward drive. It becomes manifest that the apparently simple and popular tune is, in fact, composed of two drives pulling in opposite directions. The first two measures, forte, lead the scale from the tonic up to the fifth. Thus tension is created by the need of the fifth eventually to be resolved back to the tonic. The only digression from the scale, the opening mordent on g, fulfilling the task of establishing the tonic, could be explained, and forgotten, as introducing a neighboring note without further contrapuntal obligation. A study of Mozart's style[2] has shown that he prefers in general to treat neighboring notes as real passing dissonances rather than as returning grace notes. The f-sharp in the first measure of the chorus accordingly establishes a moderate trend toward e.

The next two measures, piano, set out to accomplish the task created by the ascending scale by leading from d^1 back to the tonic. The line is marked by the main beats. Grace notes on the weak beats slow up the progress of the descent so that, at the end of the two-measure unit, it has not quite reached the desired goal. The grace notes themselves, bearing out Mozart's handling of them described above, require resolution as passing tones. Like small branches, they lead back into the main current of the ascending drive.

The fifth measure, forte, links with the last point of the first ascent, besides serving as a resolution of the grace note last introduced (c^1). The next measure, simple as it appears, is rich in significance. Loudness and direction identify it with the ascending line of which it becomes the temporary climax. Its position answers the need raised for it by the hitherto unresolved passing note at the beginning of the descent (d^1 in m. 3). Its pitch harks back to the tension created by the very first mordent. Although one octave higher, the substitution is adequate because of the fundamentally weak demands of the mordent. The cascade of the first violins at this moment, furthermore, aurally connects the two ranges. The extension of the ascending drive to the sixth of the scale admits of a new possible development without necessarily changing the nature of the initial task. The sixth degree of the major scale differs from all other steps in its independent quality with respect to consonance or dissonance. In the rest of the scale, consonant and dissonant intervals to the tonic alternate regularly. The tones of the triad are points of relative rest; the passing tones connecting them, of propelling tension. The sixth alone does not qualify as either. Lying outside the tonic triad, it is not a perfect consonance; and, representing the close tonic relative, it is not a disturbing dissonance. The major sixth is free inasmuch as its introduction does not create any special obligation. It

2. In a graduate seminar at the University of Chicago under the direction of the author.

may return to the fifth as a consonant neighboring note; or it may pave the way, in passing, to the leading tone of the scale. Mozart's treatment of neighboring notes, described above, usually also extends to the major sixth. Without special driving power at first hearing, the major sixth prepares the eventual continuation of the scale up to the octave. Similarly here, it satisfies the ear at first by providing a noncommittal climax of the line; but it will at the end become responsible for the completion of the line up to the octave of the beginning point. The busy figuration of the first violins at the same moment e^1 is reached (m. 6, first half) seems to foretell, in diminution, the final outcome. The violin figuration in the phrase is telling in at least one other respect. It appears at its first hearing, in the orchestra introduction to the first chorus (No. 8, m. 5–6), with the dynamic fluctuation, in diminution, characteristic of the composition at large. The ascending halves are marked forte, and the descending halves are marked piano.

The seventh and eighth measures, piano, finish the descending drive, along with the opening section of the bow form. The note e^1, having provided a climax, is treated as a neighboring note. The cadence to g sounds the completion of the descending line, stopped short at its earlier attempt, d^1 reminding the hearer of the beginning of that line. If there is any good reason for continuing the composition from here on after both drives apparently have reached their goals, it is the suddenness of the cadence. The tonic, to be firmly established, should be approached by step, as should the leading tone, from below or above, before it. As if to make this deficiency quite clear, the instruments in the cadence measure outline the possible remedy in unison. The appeal is urgent, for it is played forte in spite of the descending trend of the scale.

The middle section fulfils the function of a second trial. Both ascending and descending movements exercise anew their opposing pulls. They advance in larger arches, twice the length of the former ones. The first four measures of the middle section, forte, are all given to the ascending line; the next four, piano, to the return. The boundaries of the ascending line remain unchanged, and with them the ambivalent position of its highest tone, e^1. The descending line, on the other hand, solves its approach to the tonic by filling the former skip of the descending fifth with melodic passing tones. It does so with such force that its own momentum carries it past the tonic to the leading tone and with such seriousness that imitation and chromaticism suddenly affect the hitherto diatonic movement. The chromatic idea is gained from an orchestra passage

66

in the earliest descending movement (m. 4). It is these irregularities in the line that cause the immediate correction described earlier (m. 17–19). The correction, by its nature, forms the only exception to the plan of projecting each upward line forte and each downward line piano. To be a correction, it has to be loud.

The recapitulation need no longer be concerned with the descending line, which has found its completion in the middle section. To give some balance to the exposition, the piano measures, no longer bound to the descent, are employed to stretch the last tone of the ascent—first by one measure and then by two-times-two measures. Suspense is maintained as to how the fifth, presented as a problem in the first phrase of the composition, will be resolved. The playful runs in the strings point in both directions. The low dynamics seem to presage a downward trend. The ending comes forcefully. The fifth is returned to the tonic by a decisive upward sweep, forte. The high leading tone, surprising at this moment, must be assumed to have been prepared by the early, significant e^1. The ending on the higher octave is daring. The original pitch is immediately restored by the skip of the violins, an imitation by the lower strings confirming the necessity of the restoring octave drop.

The idea of two opposing drives, as most consistently carried out in this piece, is basically a dramatic one. It is a lyric situation that depends on the establishment of a certain mood by one theme. The role of the chorus in the whole opera seems to be not particularly dramatic. There is little doubt, however, that Mozart will permit no particle of an opera to stand outside the dramatic whole. The peasants singing this number are Figaro's friends. They are on his side, supporting his cause against the Count. To Figaro, the cause is both personal and political. To the peasants, who sing as an impersonal chorus, the cause is primarily political. The two drives expressed by their tune may be interpreted as two forces which the peasants experience as they face their aristocratic ruler. Encouraged by the orchestral introduction, they give loud expression to their surging feelings. The presence of the Count cows them into a sudden hushed fall. These opposing forces, one can speculate, fill them throughout their scene with the Count—a typical attitude of a subordinate facing his superior from whom he is about to liberate himself but whom he still fears. The irregularity of coloring the descending, submissive phrase of the middle section with unexpected, most subjective sounds is as revolutionary a symptom as Figaro's protesting parody in his earlier cavatina or as the public reaction to the Necklace Affair which broke in the same season in which Mozart was working on *Le Nozze di Figaro*. Beaumarchais' play had been banned in Habsburg-ruled Vienna, and Mozart's opera on a libretto almost identical with the play was applauded by the emperor. But music can prepare a political revolution as clearly as words: he who has ears to hear, let him hear. The end of the chorus, rising to the tonic one octave above the expected pitch, conveys the courageous spirit of the peasants—and that of the composer who created them in the decade between the American and French revolutions.

NUMBER 9 / Aria (C MAJOR)

This aria became the most popular immediate success of all the numbers in the opera. People sang and whistled it on the street, players and instrumental ensembles arranged it for their own use, and Mozart himself permitted a band to "swing" it as dinner entertainment for Don Giovanni.[1]

The most catching tune in the aria is the opening ritornello, which is heard three times in all. The direct appeal it exercises on anyone's ears has a cause in its clear and strong simplicity. No other harmonies are heard but tonic and dominant. The vocal line follows mostly the arpeggio of the tonic triad, free of complicating passing or ornamental tones and yielding occasionally only to the arpeggio of the dominant triad. There are no difficult dissonant skips. The range of a tenth preserves the singability of the melody for an untrained voice. The accompaniment clarifies and supports the melody rather than complicating it by independent counterpoints. The structure is a symmetrical bar form, the epode of which is emphatically repeated. The parallelism of strophe and antistrophe is sequential. The beginning of the melody is somewhat explosive by virtue of the nature of the fifth entering promptly without being led up to. The epode gains the needed contrast by a change of the hitherto downward direction and the abandonment of accompaniment in favor of an open unison. The middle of the epode brings the climax. The repetition of the entire epode is prepared by as nondeceptive a device as an imperfect dominant cadence.

A casual hearing of the whole aria conveys a similar idea of an immediate simplicity of the large form. The three hearings of the ritornello frame contrasting sections between them into a large bow form. Closer investigation, however, reveals a peculiar lack of balance between the two inclosed contrasting sections and an even more startling musical development after the last ritornello. The irregularities become quite noticeable in the following diagram:

---

1. Finale, Act II, m. 162 ff.

RITORNELLO		T	13
Episode, lyrical (bar form 3 + 3 + 6)		D	12
Cadential scales		D	6
RITORNELLO		T	13
Episode, martial (bar form 2 + 2 + 5, + 6 modulation)		T, DR	15
Drastic transition		T	3
Band music (bar form 2 + 2 + 4)		T	8
Cadential scales		D	9
RITORNELLO		T	13
Band music (2 + 2 + 4, + 4 extension)		T	12
Repeated by full orchestra (same + 3 cadence)		T	15

It is not merely the great discrepancy in length that upsets the balance between the two episodic sections. The second is about twice as long as the first, but the extension seems like part of a wilful plan to destroy what could have been a formal equilibrium. Apart from the unexpected insertion of band music, the second episode is as deliberately stretched as the first one is compressed. Thus the bar form of the first, lyrical episode reduces, through elisions and a co-operating crescendo, the normal sixteen-measure unit by one-fourth of its ideal length; whereas the comparable bar form of the second, martial episode adds six extra measures to its tail. The basically shorter phrases in the second episode, sufficiently balancing the longer phrases of the first one by sheer weight of loudness and orchestration, are by this procedure made to surpass in length the first episode. Similarly, the corresponding cadential scales take at the end of the second episodic section half as much time again as in the first. The composer's intention, not the librettist's, makes it so. Mozart reiterates the phrase, *non più avrai*, before each item of his list—four times instead of only once for all following exclamations, as he did at the end of the first episodic section. The extra insertions are musically distinguished from the main body by regular alternations of forte and piano in the responding orchestra.

The tonal pattern shows a similar disrespect for the preservation of of a formal norm. Whereas the first episodic section stands from beginning to end in the dominant, as may be expected of a contrasting section between two tonic ritornellos, the second episodic section remains in the tonic and modulates only in an afterthought into the dominant relative, which it does not maintain.

As if all these attempts to burst the regular form were not deliberate

70

enough, the forcefully prepared insertion between the episode proper
and the cadential scales of a military march, by band instruments only,
sounds like a most headstrong act. There is something particularly
provoking about the short preparation for the march. After the late
modulation away from the tonic, the fermata on the minor triad of the
dominant relative arouses new expectations. The straight line back to
the tonic, above an agitated steep crescendo of the orchestra, hits the
ears like a slap. The words to these few measures are the strongest
which Figaro, a member of the servant class, uses in his address to
Cherubino, a young nobleman. The transition from *fandango* to *fango*
is compactly presented, whereby the latter Italian word is far sur-
passed in vehement vulgarity by the German equivalent *Dreck* (of special emotional impact on any Viennese audience). The whole moment
is set off the more by the subito piano with which the march begins.

It is the same march for band instruments which, after making an
inroad on the music contained by the ritornellos, now breaks up the
form of the whole aria by establishing itself with individual independence
after the close of the regular bow form. It is impossible to dismiss the
strong twenty-seven measures following the last ritornello as a mere
coda. The music has no coda character in that it does not summarize
in any way the content of the main movement. Moreover, the march
leads too vigorous a life of its own not to be heard as an independently
grown organism. To the surprise return of the band music, before it is
taken up by the full orchestra, Figaro sings nothing but bugle-call
arpeggios of the tonic triad.[2] It is this spot about which Michael Kelly
writes in his report of the first orchestra rehearsal: "When Bennuci
[Figaro] came to the fine passage, 'Cherubino, alla vittoria, alla gloria
militar,' which he gave out with Stentorian lungs, the effect was electricity itself, for the whole of the performers on the stage, and those in
the orchestra, as if actuated by one feeling of delight, vociferated Bravo!
Bravo! Maestro. Viva, viva, grande Mozart. Those in the orchestra I
thought would never have ceased applauding, by beating the bows of
their violins against the music desks."[3] Such enthusiasm cannot have
been based on the melodic invention of the moment, which is negligible

2. Hugo Kauder, in a letter to the author, suggests calling the form of the aria a
strophic song: "Three strophes, each in bar form, but each time taking a different turn.
The military music could be the instrumental postlude of the second and third strophes—
repeated by the orchestra alone at the end and *accompanied* by a parlando of the voice the
first two times."

3. *Reminiscences* (London, 1826), I, 259.

in the solo voice and not new in the orchestra. The cause must be found in the special constellation of musical forces, to which the audience of 1786 proved sensitive.

From the factual recognition of the musical content of the whole aria, the interplay of two forces emerged as the outstanding feature. One force binds the music to the traditional and conventional form of a *da capo* bow. The other force deliberately breaks this bondage, first by expanding a subjective episode within the bow form and then by bursting the conventional bow form altogether. In the context of the opera the final victory of the subjective force over the traditional one was easily understood by the *première* audience as a revolutionary gesture. The spontaneous applause reported by Kelly came at the moment when this victory was established beyond a doubt; for even another ritornello could no longer restore a well-regulated baroque *da capo* aria. The plebeian Figaro tells off the aristocrat Cherubino. The servant expresses in the manner of a free individual what he thinks of a conventionally rigid norm. The audience hears the subjective explosion of an elegant form, and it cheers. Not only an eighteenth-century form of music but the whole eighteenth-century form of living suffers an insult by Figaro's rebellion. The French Revolution is only three years away, translating the spirit of Figaro's aria into political action.

The rebellion of the music is supported by the text. The dialogue all through the opera carefully preserves distinctions of rank. The nobleman Cherubino addresses the servant girl Susanna with the familiarizing *tu*, whereas she respectfully replies *voi* (see, for instance, their first encounter in the fourth scene of the first act). Figaro, similarly, keeps his social distance from the aristocracy before witnesses by asking Cherubino, one minute before this aria: "E *voi* non applaudite?" As soon as he is alone with the youth, however, he not only condescends grammatically (*tu parta, andrai*, etc.) but shows considerable disrespect in his description of the joys of a commissioned officer, the promotion from *fandango* to *fango*.

The rebellious spirit that burst the form of this aria manifests itself strongly also in relation to the form of the entire opera. The first finale of an opera was traditionally given to a tutti ensemble, in which all individual voices were submerged. The audience of 1786 must have been startled to see and hear an individual occupy the prominent place before the first fall of the curtain—a servant at that. The insult is double, against conventionalism and against aristocracy. Among the spiritual forces preparing a revolution, music is not the weakest.

72

SECOND ACT

NUMBER 10 / Cavatina (E-FLAT MAJOR)

The Countess is introduced by a soliloquy—unlike Susanna, Figaro, and the Count, all of whom are first heard in the more social situation of an ensemble. The introduction by solo aria of Bartolo and Cherubino lacks the recluse character of the Countess' cavatina, because the two men address themselves to another person on the stage. The Countess, however, is alone. Her social status, but more so her inward suffering, seems to separate her from her surroundings.

The external appearance of the cavatina discloses a bar form. The strophe ends with the orchestral introduction; the antistrophe, with the fermata. What is important in the evaluation of this, or any other, composition is not so much the general form as the specific solution. The norm must be recognized first, but the modifications of it permit an insight into the expressive qualities intended by the composer.

The first two measures, not recurring anywhere in the movement, are an introduction. There is need for one in order to prevent the possible misinterpretation as introduction of the subsequent orchestra section, which is integral to the whole form. The neutral stateliness of the opening chords reveals its derivation as a curtain raiser. The rhythm of the second measure, which essentially maintains the chordal character of the first (T–D), is later used in analogous situations. Here preceding the strophe, it appears in the cadence preceding the antistrophe (m. 17) and, thus transmuted, in the final cadence (m. 51).

Strophe and antistrophe are of approximately the same length (m. 3–17 and 18–36) and employ the same two musical ideas (cf. m. 3 ff. with 18 ff., and 7 ff. with 26 ff.). The composer's plan of dividing substantial musical material between orchestra and soloist deserves special attention, the more so as he employs it again in the Countess' other aria, No. 19 (where it will be discussed). One gains the impression that the Countess is too full of personal and heavy emotions to be able to find words for all of them. Her aristocratic state also constrains her. Much remains unsaid, and only in the voices of the orchestra are her inner thoughts heard. The absence of the high wood-wind instruments throughout this movement lends these voices a special melancholy tinge.

The leading melody is given to the first violins in the strophe, but it

75

remains an incomplete four-measure phrase (m. 3–6) until it is fully stated and answered by the Countess in the antistrophe (m. 18–25). The best proof of the incompleteness of the statement in the strophe should again be aural. The section following the phrase (m. 7–10) does not fit it as a consequent should fit an antecedent, or as the true answer finally does in the antistrophe (m. 22–25). The melodic disruption in the strophe is emphasized by the simultaneous sudden change of dynamics and orchestration, whereas the melodic cohesiveness in the antistrophe is strengthened by a uniform level of both loudness and instrumental sound.

The complete melody as the Countess sings it (m. 18–25) stands entirely in the tonic, but it ends on a half-cadence. The words express a request; and the normal inflection of any request will leave an opening at the end as if invoking fulfilment. In the entire course of the melody the solo voice soars above the orchestra, doubled only in the last three notes of the cadence. The symmetry of rise and fall in the melody is noteworthy, again in keeping with the text. The words of wishful prayer (*Porgi amor qualche ristoro*) point upward; those referring to her unhappiness (*al mio duolo, a' miei sospir*), downward. Within the symmetric proportion the fall is greater than the rise. The noble calm of the Countess' notes expresses her classical restraint, which is refuted by the emotional quivering of the inner voices. Only the word *duolo*, and later *sospir*, breaks down her controlled demeanor and permits her inner agitation to come to the surface. A similar contradiction between external and internal forces is heard between the meter of the normal eight-measure period and the rhythm of the personal exclamation above it. According to the former, accents would fall on every other, strong, measure (i.e., m. 18, 20, 22, and 24); but the subjective accents of the Countess scan her sentence, both musically and literally, with the exactly opposite current (m. 19, 21, 23, and 25).

The second musical idea of the strophe, following the interruption of the first line, similarly does not seem fully realized until the antistrophe. As in the first melody, only half of a complete eight-measure period is played by the orchestra (m. 7–10); but in this case the reduction is not produced by a simple omission of the consequent to an antecedent. Rather, as the full version in the antistrophe clarifies (m. 26–34), the eight-measure period is broken up into four two-measure units of which every other one is missing in the orchestra strophe. The patchwork character of the incomplete statement is underscored by the persistent fluctuation of dynamics and orchestration. The complete version in the antistrophe observes within its small realm the distribution, noticed in the large form, of the musical material between orchestra and solo voice. While in both media the melodic line is fundamentally the same, descending one, the clarinets—the Countess' unspoken thoughts—are richer in figuration. Moreover, they express first what the Countess' words merely echo, "O mi rendi il mio tesoro, o mi lascia almen morir." The second theme in the antistrophe enters on the dominant, whereas its corresponding parts in the strophe were heard in the tonic. In respect to the tonality of the two themes, strophe and antistrophe of this composition are in the same relationship to each other as the two expositions in the opening sonata-form movement of a classical concerto. Two contrasting themes are stated first in the tonic; in the repetition of the whole section, the second theme appears in the dominant. The analogy is heightened by the orchestra-soloist relationship in the double exposition of a concerto as well as in the two strophes of this cavatina.

The equilibrium between strophe and antistrophe, endangered by the doubling expansion of the latter, is restored by a lengthy coda to the former (m. 11–17). The coda character is best elucidated by the formularized bass progression which leads a full cadence first to a deceptive, and then to a definitive, end. The harmonic functions of this part of the coda (m. 11–15) are: T–S–D–(D)–TR, S–D–T. To this coda the next three measures form a codetta. The need for the codetta is supplied by the yet insufficiently achieved equilibrium. Justification for the codetta is provided by the deceptive cadence and the tense syncopations, which generate a propelling force. The codetta character is evinced by the determined condensation of the preceding cadential bass progression into D–T, D–T, T–T (a typical classical formula, often observed and described) and by the utilization of the whole phrase at the close of the cavatina (m. 49–51).

Compared to the coda of the strophe, that of the antistrophe is very short, there being little need for it. It consists merely of an intensification, accompanied by a crescendo, of the dominant chord by a minor seventh preparing the return to the tonic. The fermata at the end of the antistrophe is the climax of the composition: the Countess' highest note (a^1-flat) and her only forte coincide with the strong emotion of the word *morir*, "to die."

The epode is distinguished from the first half of the bar form by using independent melodic material. The distinction is particularly noticeable at the beginning of the epode, where it helps the listener most. There is considerably more movement in the solo voice so that the first sentence of the text, originally spread over eight measures, is now condensed into two. Together with the melodic intensification, the placidity with which harmonies thus far have changed just about with each measure is disturbed. The chord on the rhyme to *morir* brings the sharpest dissonance of the entire movement, the ninth of the dominant chord to the dominant pointedly projected by the exposed register of the bassoon (m. 38). The dissonant chord is resolved very slowly and deliberately, the drive lasting until the end of the main melodic line of the epode (m. 45). The remaining measures act as a coda to the epode, for much the same reasons that established the similar coda of the strophe. The increased intensity of the epode makes up adequately for its reduced extensity as compared to the sum of strophe and antistrophe.

The over-all line of the vocal melody warrants some attention. It abounds in appoggiaturas and other embellishments which lend a special aristocratic charm to the Countess' expression—quite distant, in the revolutionary atmosphere of the opera, from Figaro's plebeian straightforwardness. The ornaments also cover the fundamental melodic drive, like trimmings of the court obscuring the human being underneath. Freed of all embellishments, the melody reveals as its true content a drive, in the tonality of E-flat major, toward the peak of g^1 and the subsequent resolution down to *e*-flat. The voice, in scientific terminology, tries to reach the goal set by a certain tone. In technical terminology, this goal can be reinterpreted as the Countess' personal desire to achieve something—in this specific case, as we learn from the libretto, the recapture of her husband's affection.

The first measure of the line (m. 18) generates a double drive. The note *b*-flat, by virtue of being the fifth of the tonality, will eventually have to resolve downward to the tonic; but the first interval stepping from it points upward. The downward drive is taken up from the high e^1-flat (m. 19). It is interrupted to make way for the sequential repetition of the first motive which pushes the melody one step higher (m. 20–21). The tone thus reached is f^1, a dissonance against the basic tonality. As such, it will have to be led up to g^1 according to all good principles of counterpoint. This phrase (*ristoro!*) really determines the goal of the whole movement. The tone g^1 (m. 21) does not belong to the main line. It lies outside the sequential repetition of the first motive and is, moreover, too short and unaccented to serve as a real resolution for the pronounced dissonance of f^1. It must be understood as a short indication of what is to come in the future, a fleeting thought of what later becomes an actual achievement. (The embellishment in the analogous spot in the orchestra introduction gracefully points to a similar future development.) The line ascending from e^1-flat (m. 19) to f^1 (m. 21) is stopped short of its desired aim, g^1, and the interrupted descending drive resumes where it has been left. As if to remind the hearer, the step e^1-flat to d^1 (m. 19) is repeated (m. 22), and the whole line sinks down the scale. Like the ascending drive, it is stopped short of the tonic to which it gravitates (m. 25). The two elegant turns within the line up to e^1-flat serve again as reminder of the starting point of the descending line. The device is essential in an art like music which depends on the listener's memory and does not permit him to turn back to the primary statement of a musical problem while following the progress of the composition.

The continuation lifts the melody one octave above its last point (m. 28). The skip of an octave forms an easy bridge. The tone f^1 is meaningful. It was last heard at the moment when the opposing drives divided (m. 21). It formed the last, dissonant barrier to the upward trend. It is also, as the first overtone, representative of the last, dissonant barrier to the downward trend. Temporarily, the latter prevails. The note f^1 turns downward and resolves into a heavily ornamented e^1-flat (m. 28–29). The range, however, is unsatisfactory, the clause on b-flat indicating that the suggested tentative solution presents no progress over the very beginning. A new attempt, after the more encouraging version of elements of the drive by the wood winds, is similarly unsuccessful (m. 32–34). Putting aside the less individualistic downward drive, the voice, with concentrated energy (crescendo, doubled by instruments) and utmost clarity, resumes the entire ascending scale from its original starting point, b-flat. Like so many sudden efforts, this one shoots beyond the desired goal—*morir* is really more than the Countess wants—and comes to a firm halt one half-step above the yearned-for g^1 (m. 36). The exaggerated ornament in the introduction (m. 6), earlier referred to, can now be properly understood. The task of retrieving g^1 is accomplished in a manner analogous to the earlier attempt of the descending line to lead f to e-flat. Then the progression was shifted up an octave into a wrong range (m. 28). Now the step a^1-flat to g^1 is first moved down one octave (m. 37 and 39–40). The a-natural, between the two a-flats, only emphasizes the inherent difficulty of the project (ID^9). The next few measures reconcile the two opposing drives and resolve all created tensions. The descending line, at the farthest point of its development (m. 25), is briefly brought back to memory (m. 40–41) before the strong and elegant ascending scale connects it with the true and desired acme of the whole melody. This g^1 (m. 42) is the real resolution of the early dissonant f^1 (m. 20–21), which created the ascending trend. The descending line is now led all the way down to the tonic (m. 45), but not without pausing for a short, expressive reminiscence of an earlier decisive crisis (appoggiatura in m. 43). The coda fulfils its proper function by summarizing the problems and achievements of the entire movement. The melody, beginning on *b*-flat (m. 46, with upbeat) and pulled up by e^1-flat, soared to a high g^1 and then, regaining the initial tone (m. 48), came to rest on the low tonic, *e*-flat.

This cavatina represents the *lamento* aria, without which no baroque opera could do—from the early Italian *Arianne* by Monteverdi, in which the Cretan princess bewails the faithless departure of her lover, to the late German *Die Zauberflöte*, where Pamina despairs of her fate.

NUMBER 11 / Arietta (B-FLAT MAJOR)

This arietta of Cherubino, being a prepared composition presented to the Countess, is formally more bound than his earlier spontaneous outpouring to Susanna. But the same adolescent speaks both times; and the same abandonment to free fancy, within the decorum of the situation, characterizes both compositions.

Cherubino's attempt to appear like a real nobleman, observing traditionally matured customs, is exhibited in the external forms of both lyrics and tune that he chooses for his *canzone*. The fourteen lines of poetry resemble an Italian sonnet in the manner in which they are organized. Two quatrains are followed by a sestet:

> Voi che sapete   che cosa è amor,
>   Donne vedete   s'io l'ho nel cor.
>   Quello ch'io provo   vi ridirò,
>   È per me nuovo   capir nol so.
> Sento un affetto   pien di desir,
>   Ch'ora è diletto   ch'ora è martir.
>   Gelo, e poi sento   l'alma avvampar,
>   E in un momento   torno a gelar.
> Ricerco un bene   fuori di me,
>   Non so chi'l tiene   non so cos'è.
>   Sospiro e gemo   senza voler,
>   Palpito e tremo   senza saper,
>   Non trovo pace   notte, nè dì,
>   Ma pur mi piace   languir così.

But Cherubino would be untrue to his nature if he had written a really strict sonnet. The rhyme pattern does not at all adhere to that of the regular sonnet. The lines are grouped into naïve couplets, in which the middles of each line are linked to one another by an additional, somewhat childish, rhyme. The conventional design of the poem is even further destroyed by the music to which it is set. The natural bar form of a sonnet, complicated in its strict demands, is made to fit a bow form, the least sophisticated of all. The transformation is accomplished by repeating the first couplet, with sentimental coquetry, at the end. The unfamiliar entity of fourteen lines is thus extended to a convenient sixteen.

A reminiscence of the framing sections in the middle of the song reinforces the symmetrical structure.

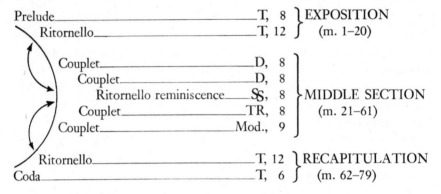

Prelude	T, 8	} EXPOSITION
Ritornello	T, 12	(m. 1–20)
Couplet	D, 8	
Couplet	D, 8	
Ritornello reminiscence	SS, 8	} MIDDLE SECTION
Couplet	TR, 8	(m. 21–61)
Couplet	Mod., 9	
Ritornello	T, 12	} RECAPITULATION
Coda	T, 6	(m. 62–79)

But Cherubino would, this time in musical terms, be untrue to his nature if he were rigidly bound by the outline of a well-organized form. He observes some rules of appearance, as behooves his aristocratic status and in particular his presence in the Countess' boudoir. But underneath the thin surface of proper behavior, he lets his imagination run away with his thoughts.

The first instance of this kind—and one that becomes responsible for the whole chain of subsequent excursions—occurs with the second line he sings. In preparation, the impersonal instruments play a perfectly rounded prelude. In the prelude we hear the melody of the ritornello—for the only time in the whole arietta unadulterated by a subjective whimsey. The melody is a conventional eight-measure period with a half-cadence in the middle and a full cadence at the end. The line rises steadily up to the caesura and, the apex occurring immediately after it, falls from there in due proportion back to the tonic. The distinction between the two parts is emphasized by a change of instrumentation. Now Cherubino repeats the melody. At the caesura he inserts a four-measure phrase, as if he wished to linger on the moment of culmination. The necessary words are found by anticipating the second half of the couplet; there, in their proper place, the same words are heard again. The insertion does not destroy the symmetry of the total line. The first two measures lead up to the same climax, a fifth above the tonic, and the next two measures sequentially prepare the descent. The insertion nonetheless alters the melody by the special charm of irregularity. Besides, the subjective manner of the insertion in the nature of sudden chromaticisms

82

gives the melody a personal and intriguingly lovable character. The irregularities of both form and scale are exclusively Cherubino's doing.

The chromatic passing tones filling in the path to the climax are the more striking as they represent the first accidentals so far, that is, the first tones not belonging to the tonality of the arietta. Their importance is emphasized by doubling in unison in the clarinet and in lower tenths in the bassoon. The use of chromaticism as a symbolic expression of intensified feeling was known to all eighteenth-century composers. The specific association with suffering is most strongly created in a descending line. Here, the ascending chromatic line makes for the touching incongruity of pain with Cherubino's adolescent love. His sentimental, almost romantic, exaggeration is accompanied by a graceful flourish in flute and oboe, which is heard only here and in the analogous place in the recapitulation. Perhaps it is more correct to say that the flourish, occurring in the weak measures after the strong chromatic ones, is not an accompaniment but rather a reaction to the newly intensified progression. The parallel thirds and sixths in the two high-pitched instruments could refer to the Countess and Susanna laughing as they become aware of Cherubino's wilful deviation from the regular tune.

The chromatic idea, once introduced, pervades the rest of the movement. Cherubino's subjective expression remains audible underneath the conventional form of the *canzone*. The sequence within the inserted phrase (m. 15–16) is in two ways the product of the initial chromaticism: first, by virtue of being a sequence of the melody and, second, by imitating the pitch of the originally accompanying bassoon, reinterpreting c-sharp inventively as d-flat. There is no doubt about this process of enharmonic reinterpretation, which can be found as a generating principle throughout the classical style.[1] The clearest proof in this movement is provided by Mozart's orthography in the corresponding place in the recapitulation (m. 65–69). The clarinet, introducing the insertion by anticipating Cherubino's chromaticism and offering the bassoon the possibility of canonic imitation at the octave, spells its first chromatic ascent, to the third of B-flat major, as c^1-sharp; and the same chromatic passage three measures later, to the sixth of F major, as d^1-flat. But in a more important manner, these initial chromaticisms—

1. For examples see Beethoven, Piano Sonata, Op. 10, No. 2: *e*-flat (m. 7) into *d*-sharp (m. 14); *Third Symphony*, First Movement: *C*-sharp (m. 7) into *D*-flat (m. 416); etc.

e, c-sharp, and b—help shape the musical movement of the entire long middle section between the two ritornellos. Without them the unconventional tonal pattern T–D–SS–TR–T would be difficult to understand.

The dominant section before the center (m. 21–36) is established by exactly these accidentals in the very order in which they were initially heard: e is, of course, the decisive step to the dominant of the basic tonality; c-sharp, for the time being, continues its subordinate role as a parallel lower accompaniment to the leading tone to the dominant; and b, by nature a corollary to e, pushes the movement up to the second dominant, which, however, is quickly construed as part of a dominant cadence. Except for the clarifying leading tone to the dominant, the occurring accidentals intensified only the second half of the first of the two couplets forming this section. In the second couplet (m. 29–36), the apparent innocence (no accidentals but e-natural) is preserved up to the last two measures, where the word *martir* provokes a sudden dramatic exaggeration. The bass progression, identical in the two halves of the couplet up to this moment, alters D chromatically into D-flat. What in the first half fulfilled the function of a secondary subdominant to the dominant, in its alteration becomes an augmented five-six chord (i.e., a dominant function) to the second dominant. The change of harmonic function is equivalent to a modulation, which introduces the central section of the arietta (m. 37–44). At least as revealing as the eventual result of the modulation is the meaningful preparation for it. The decisive tone d-flat emerges as a reinterpretation of the original c-sharp. The same d-flat is also responsible for a-flat, first heard in this measure. Keeping the three original chromaticisms in mind, it is possible to infer a-flat as the missing tone in the proportion $e : c\text{-sharp}(d\text{-flat}) = b : x$, or $e : b = c\text{-sharp}(d\text{-flat}) : x$. Needed as a fifth in the chord on D-flat, a-flat is introduced one chord earlier as the minor third of an intended, and earlier (m. 31) actually presented, dominant triad. As part of the modulation, which begins with it, the F-minor triad changes its harmonic function from a secondary subdominant of the second dominant to the tonic relative of the new key of the middle section.

As the tonic of the new section, a-flat becomes established—the farthest dip away from the tonality of the arietta. The underlying text confirms the extreme distance from the calm opening address to the ladies: "Gelo, e poi sento l'alma avvampar, e in un momento torno a gelar." The eight measures of the middle section explore the key of A-flat major. The harmonies are all direct and close functions of the new tonality. The refrain of the ritornello (m. 41–44) lends a familiar stability to the entire section. One nevertheless remembers the power behind the throne: the tone d-flat (the original c-sharp) which first pushed the modulation toward A-flat major. The flute, which helped introduce the first a-flat sound (m. 35), now sustains d^2-flat above the melodic movement as the highest pitch in the couplet. The same power of the tone d-flat has to direct the chromatic way back to the tonic of the *canzone*. The first indication of that way is the natural sign exactly before d^1, in measure 46. The entire return modulation comes most clearly into hearing in the exposed top line of the flute. Various lower voices follow the flute less concisely or cohesively, among them the prominent soprano.

On the highest pitch in the whole composition, the melody, given to the flute, renounces d-flat and re-establishes c-sharp (m. 49). The bassoon, which in the middle section cut through with the progression *e*-flat, *d*-flat, *c*, *B*-flat (m. 41–43), now doubles the corrective flute passage and ends the first couplet of the return modulation with the unaltered version of the same progression: *e*-flat, *d*-natural, *c*, *B*-flat (m. 51–52). The last note becomes the minor third of a retarding tonic-relative triad rather than the final tonic, in order to give the return from the center as much breath as the departure toward it had taken. The task is outlined by the flute, which first lingers on a^1-natural, the complete cancellation of the key of the middle section. The delay assists in turning the cadence to the tonic relative at the moment when the bassoon reaches the tonic, apart from the fact that it averts the danger of consecutive fifths at that point (d/a^1, c/g^1, B-flat/f^1). From g^1, which the flute has now reached (m. 52), to f^1, which is the aimed-for dominant preparation for the recapitulation, is only one step. The flute takes that step on the long route, inverting it by ascending a seventh. This device is part of the plan to extend the couplets on this side of the center in equilibrium with the couplets before the center. The technique of prolongation by inversion of a short interval into a long one was well developed by the time Mozart wrote *Le Nozze di Figaro*. It can be found in Bach (French Suite VI, Allemande, m. 7–8, c^1-sharp to b^1 instead of c^1-sharp to *b*); Haydn (String Quartet, F minor, Op. 20, No. 5, Third Movement, m. 4–8, *a* to f^1 instead of *a* to *f*); and earlier Mozart (Piano Sonata, A major, K. 331, m. 16–18, *b* to a^1 instead of *b* to *a*). Here the detour is not mere prolongation but also serves as a summary of the musical development of the whole *canzone*. It sounds as if Cherubino once more, just before returning to the decorous statement directed to the Countess and Susanna, wished to let his private fancy roam; and his last words before the recapitulation, with their intensified references to himself, are really the most personal of all. Turning on g^1 (m. 52), the inverted line gains b^1-flat, the starting point of the whole composition. It ascends the diatonic scale, just as in the ritornello. The main points—b^1-flat, c^2, and d^2—are held so long that they cannot be missed. Most revealing are the chromatic passing tones between them. They are strongly brought out by deliberate dynamic accents (*mf* in m. 54 and 56) and simultaneous pausing in the movement of the solo voice. The chromatic tones are precisely the ones Cherubino first inserted in the ritornello. The bass takes care of the one of the three original chromatic tones which the flute in its line does not reach (E, in m. 55). The strength of the chromatic idea and the principle of imitation between the outer voices even push the bass up to F-sharp; but the oboe in the next measure, sacrificing doubling the main line of the flute, quickly corrects the extra distracting alteration of the diatonic scale by reinterpreting f-sharp enharmonically as g-flat and leading it back to the essential and desired f^1. The flute reaches e^2-flat. Going above it would surpass the highest pitch reached before (m. 49), thereby introducing a new sound, a new idea, for which there is no proper place in a summary. One step before the goal of f^2, the line of the flute actually reverses its earlier inversion by taking this short step, too, down a seventh instead of up a second. To prevent any possible misinterpretation, the soprano line, which has freely doubled the flute all along in the lower octave, briefly touches f^1 before rejoining the descending flute. Moreover, the bass and the triad above it audibly represent f at the spot where the flute turns back from it. In the final descent to the recapitulation, Cherubino indulges in a last affectional reminiscing of his fanciful chromatics. Instead of coming straight down to earth, he languishes (*languir*, m. 60) on his familiar d^1-flat while the bass supports him on the equally familiar E. When soprano and flute finally reach the tone f, the clarinet and bass gently set right, each for itself, the last chromatic digression.

The recapitulation is almost exact. There are a few changes in the instrumentation, of which the significant clarinet orthography has been discussed. A deceptive cadence (m. 73) admits a coda by extending the ritornello. The formal function of the coda is to balance, in this perfect bow form, the instrumental introduction.

NUMBER 12 / Aria (G MAJOR)

The organization of the *dramma giocoso* into arias, or ensembles, and recitatives is conditioned by the polarity of text and music. Reconciliation of this polarity is one of the main tasks of opera, perhaps the most distinguished task. Different composers have approached it in different ways. Some, like Wagner, tried to merge words and music into a new entity by treating them on the same level. This solution has been criticized by musicians as being too poetic and by poets as being too musical.[1] Other composers, like Peri and Lully, subordinated the music to the text. The tones were at most to increase the emotion of the words, depending entirely on them for movement, rhythm, and formal organization. Such an approach was hailed by rationalists, who in moments of clearer insight away from the opera house conceded to music a role not easily compatible with pure reason. A third group, of which Donizetti and Verdi are good representatives, worked in the opposite direction, employing the libretto as a vehicle for the various emotions which music can directly express. The resulting operas are the musician's delight, although they have often incurred the wrath or ridicule of the intellectual aesthete. The solution of Mozart, and of most of his contemporaries, is a compromise. The unity of an opera is divided into two realms. In one, words rule above music; in the other, music above words. The border line between the two realms is sharply defined. In the recitative sections, words accomplish their mission. Intellectual ideas, which music cannot convey, are projected, and the dramatic action is propelled. In the composed numbers, on the other hand, music exploits the emotional content of the situation to which each preceding recitative has led. Music, by its nature, can be direct in emotional expression where words can at best be symbolic. Figaro's two arias in the first act, for instance, convey no intellectual message, nor do they help develop the plot. The action of the libretto could move right on without them. They clarify the emotional situation; for each expresses the singer's feelings in reaction to the dramatic tension created in the preceding recitative section. In the instance of the Countess' introductory aria, which does not

1. See Thomas Mann, "Leiden und Grösse Richard Wagners," in *Leiden und Grösse der Meister* (Berlin, 1935).

follow a recitative, one learns nothing about her intellectual status as a dramatic agent; but one soon hears that she is unhappy. The cause of her unhappiness cannot be conveyed by the music, that task being proper to the literary realm. The many text repetitions and familiar rhymes will eventually, without self-assertive imposition, give the necessary information to the listener, the visual makeup of the scene contributing extra support.

Susanna's aria in the Countess' boudoir is peculiar, inasmuch as it projects almost nothing of Susanna's concurrent emotions. Even an average audience seems to be aware of this fact; for in spite of the charm and beauty of the melodic invention, this aria is never a "hit." One seldom applauds after it. The historian may add in scholarly fashion that an early Susanna (not Nancy Storace, who sang in the *première*) actually forced Mozart to replace it by another aria, which Otto Jahn describes as "only superficially excited."[2] The critic must look for formal explanations, which proceed from the score. The strongest melodic force in the movement comes from an ingratiating short phrase which recurs five times in refrain-like fashion. It is first heard as a closing turn to Susanna's opening statement (m. 11–14) and subsequently does not quite lose its character as a cadential formula (m. 37 ff. and 47 ff.). Only in its last occurrence does it grow by its own force into a full-fledged period, an imperfect ending shaping it into an antecedent which of necessity begets a corrective repetition with a perfect ending (m. 95 ff.). In each instance the melodic phrase is played by the first violins and first bassoon, the first flute reinforcing the consequent part of the final version. Violins and bassoon are one octave apart in the tonic statements, which lie on the outside, and two octaves apart in the dominant statements, which lie in the middle, of the aria. This mixture of timbre takes a good deal of naïveté away from the phrase, as if the nasal undertones warned against taking the lusher string tones too seriously. A certain ambivalence of mock and grace lies, however, in the melody construction itself.

Its most startling feature is the sudden drop of a ninth and the subsequent regaining of the original range by an octave jump. Such jumps, unless they are symptoms of polyphonic writing within one voice, are usually exaggerations—in a heroic, pathetic, comical, or other manner—of smaller intervals by means of inversion or shift in octave range. The

2. *Life of Mozart* (London, 1882), III, 94.

device has become well established through generations of composers, as the two following illustrations exemplify:

Brahms, *Alto Rhapsody*

Brahms creates the impression of emptiness prescribed by the text by stretching a simple cadential step across one octave. Strauss generates a tremendous emotional sweep by the inversion of a scale progression into an ascending major seventh. The Mozart phrase is of similar technique. The cohesion of the phrase becomes evident if one sings, or plays, the three bottom notes one octave higher in the uniform range of the other notes. What one hears as the essential content is a diatonic scale descending from fifth to prime after a playful detour to the neighboring major sixth. The beginning of the melody is marked by its first note d^1, which must be imagined to be sustained throughout the next two full measures before it moves on. The tones g^1 and b provide the harmonization of the opening tonic by projecting melodically into time what harmonically is an instantaneous experience. The melody has good reason for supplying its own harmonization; for it moves in unison in the crucial beginning where the clarification of a tonal center is the normal task. The merged rendition of melodic and harmonic elements by one continuous voice creates a dualistic effect with a none too obvious outline. It seems to be related to Susanna's mode of expression in certain situations; for one hears it again in the suggestive letter duet (see No. 20) and most strikingly in the *double entendre* of her garden aria (see No. 27). The particular order of breaking the triad in this case, an ascending fourth to the tonic followed by a descending sixth to the third, is even more specifically characteristic by its identity with Susanna's significant arpeggio in the opening duet with Figaro and in her second aria.

The next tone in the phrase, c^1, is the first melody tone after the triad arpeggio. Apart from the high beginning on the unprepared fifth, it is the first symptom of the downward pull, by its delayed continuation a signpost rather than a milestone of the eventual descent by scale to the tonic. Introduced as a passing dissonance against the consonant third of the tonic chord, it points toward d^1 as the required resolution and thereby assists in reintroducing, if not sustaining, the important fifth. A *nota cambiata*, e^1, intervenes. The ambivalent character of the major sixth has been repeatedly experienced in the course of this opera (cf. No. 8 and others). It becomes the main melodic event in this short phrase, attracting attention first in the noticeable shift of octave range and then in a special appoggiatura. It is the direct melodic expression of the same ambivalence which one also hears in the bassoon-violin mixture, the shifting range, and the harmony-melody duality. The indecision of direction brought about by the major sixth is played up to the full. The biggest break in the line, right after e^1, lets the major sixth stick out freely for one full measure; and the trill sixth to fifth is provocatively tried out three times—exaggerated by the drop of an octave, in the new low range, and finally in diminution on the desired level—before a quick descent solves the gently teasing tension. The short flickering at the end of the scale back to the fifth serves as a reminder of the origin of the whole melody.

The rhythmic organization of the phrase corroborates the tendency of combining simplicity with indefiniteness. The length of four measures sounds normal and simple enough. One is inclined to accept the upbeat as a weak anacrusis to a strong bar. The placement of the highest note right after the anacrusis reinforces the strength of the downbeat. Actually, the upbeat stands at the end of the first full measure, and the high note falls on an unaccented measure. Any possible ambiguity is clarified by the continuation of the phrase. The instrumental bass denotes by a carefully placed sforzato the accented nature of the measure, which accordingly is already the third, not the second, measure in the phrase of four. The entrance of the chord-filling middle strings after an empty unisono and the simultaneous significant drop of a ninth increase the strength of the accent by writing it out, as it were, in the composition. Nor can the masculine ending of the whole phrase be doubted after second bassoon, horns, and fresh violin figuration have marked the strong beginning of a new section. The pull of rhythm against meter would not create such an initial feeling of indefiniteness if the possibility of an irregularity had not been shrewdly prepared by the preceding measures.

NUMBER TWELVE / Aria

One may even be justified in thinking that the music before the little phrase has no other function than an introductory one in order to set off the phrase in regard to both its closing cadential nature and its rhythmic ambiguity; for the introductory material, although first in the aria, never returns. The rhythm of the eight-measure period is easily grasped. In both antecedent and consequent, each strong measure is deliberately stressed by long quarter-notes against eighth-notes on all weaker bars. The two-measure extension blurs the rhythm; for not only does it bring two different conflicting accents against the metric one (*mfp* in the winds on the second eighth and *sfp* in the bass on the third), but it also erases its internal rhythmic distinction by being composed of two exact repetitions. The literary excuse for such a procedure is easily found in a baroque exploitation of the exclamation, *restate*. Identified with the meaning of the word, the music does not move on. The musical reason, however, lies in the creation of exactly that indefiniteness of a seemingly simple rhythm which, along with the other devices discussed before, contributes to the duality of the phrase.

One wonders what two trends, so thoroughly and unanimously projected by different musical means, the phrase intends to express. One experiences the polarity and yet cannot associate it with Susanna's person. In most arias the melodies are direct expressions of the singer's emotions. In this aria the lovable short phrase is deliberately maltreated or ignored by the soloist's vocal line. In the first occurrence the most characteristic skip of the descending ninth is replaced by a nondescript harmonic filler. The next time, Susanna neglects the phrase altogether by pausing through three-fourths of it and singing different notes in the cadence. The third time is the same except for a brief participation in the middle measure, the characteristic ninth reduced to a second. Only in the final occurrence does Susanna assume her melodic responsibility by singing the complete phrase; but in the repetition of the phrase she again pauses through the opening as if to maintain her original distance from the melody. The ambivalent content of the invention is thus interpreted by the soloist with equal lack of concentrated seriousness. This is the crux of the matter. The aria deals with the situation more than with the soloist. The listener expects to gain an insight into Susanna's feelings but is kept at a distance. He cannot share Susanna's emotions because she does not really participate in the scene. She comments on it. Such separation of subject from surroundings can be tragic in a heroic setting. In the simple framework of the given melodic invention it is the expression of irony. A human situation taken not quite seriously—there is the dual trend that the music is trying to convey in every possible way by melodic skips, harmonic dissolution in time, rhythm, instrumentation, and vocal interpretation. Even though Mozart could have composed the aria in a different manner, more concerned with Susanna's person than with her ironic detachment from the scene, one must not underrate the force of the libretto. Much dramatic action of an amusingly distracting nature takes place during the aria, contrary to the dramatic inactivity during all other arias. What is more, the distracting action does not come from the soloist but from a silent partner.

Susanna is not serious in her job of singing an aria, just as she is teasing Cherubino while handling him. Her detachment, made obvious by the refrain-like phrase and her relation to it, is even more thorough in relation to another melodic phrase, the second invention of the aria. This phrase enters twice into the movement: first in the dominant (m. 23 ff.) and later in the subdominant realm (SR, T, S: m. 61 ff.). It consists fundamentally of a descending diatonic scale which gains its special gentle charm from many appoggiaturas and the consonant span of an octave, while a certain intensity of purpose is heard in its rhythmic lilt and its basic character as a dominant, not tonic, scale. If the first, refrain-like melody pursued a closing, cadential tendency, this melody clearly opens a new way. Contrary to the first, it sounds like an antecedent without a consequent; for the mere repetition of the phrase, double and later triple, still leaves it open at the end. Four measures long, it too begins on a weak measure. The solo wood winds play it in many possible timbre combinations. Susanna, however, ostentatiously abstains from the melody by pausing two measures and more each time it enters and contrapunting independently against it in its ebbing phase. The musical attention necessarily shifts from the soloist to the wood winds. The personal loss of the former becomes a gain for the dramatic situation. The lyrical phrase undoubtedly reflects Cherubino's innocent flirtation with the Countess. If the audience refrains from applauding Susanna, the cause lies in the singularly impersonal content of the aria.

Nor does Susanna woo the listener by any competing melodic invention of her own. The most superficial examination of her vocal line finds it to be disjunct. Her exclamations are short and seldom flow from one to the next. They consist in most instances of cadential formulas, frequently repetitious (e.g., m. 31 ff., 76 ff.), or of arpeggios extended in time (e.g., m. 17 ff., 53 ff.). The preponderance of the latter is noteworthy, their harmonic essence by nature a negation of melodic development. One may be reconciled in this case by associating the broken major triad with more significant expressions of Susanna's in other instances (cf. Nos. 1, 5, 27).

There are two sections in the aria where Susanna musically holds her own against the byplay of orchestra and stage action. It is typical that these sections lie outside the regular framework of the standard form: they are a free interpolation before the last refrain (m. 80–94) and the coda after it (m. 102–118). The aria itself forms two strophes, which are easily recognized by reference to the placement of the two melodic inventions. The first strophe leads from the refrain in the tonic (m. 10) across a nine-measure bridge to the lyrical theme in the dominant. The subsequent cadence above an organ point initiates the return of the refrain in the dominant; and both cadential figure and refrain are repeated to close the first strophe with full and perfect emphasis (m. 52). The strophe is forty-three measures long and, by force of the refrain, in bow form. The organization of the second strophe is the same, the harmonic drive reversed from dominant to tonic. The two strophes are skilfully spliced by overlapping at the juncture. The repetition of the last refrain in the first strophe (m. 46 ff.) *post festum* proves to be also the opening statement of the second strophe. The same nine-measure bridge follows, this time in the dominant. The lyrical theme after the bridge continues the parallelism to the first strophe. It accomplishes the modulation back to the tonic by reducing the expected second dominant chromatically to the subdominant relative. The ensuing cadential figure above the dominant organ point prepares the final refrain in the tonic; but the refrain is delayed by the interpolation of the special section mentioned above. When it finally assumes its place, it is heard twice, as in the first strophe. The rest is coda. Not counting the interpolation, the second strophe is forty-three measures long, exactly like the first.

Technically, the interpolation can easily be explained as an extension of the dominant organ point, which is actually sustained throughout in the horns. Dramatically, it denotes the completion of Susanna's preoccupation with costuming Cherubino and her first personal reaction to him. The music is, accordingly, for the first time a coherent expression of her direct feelings. They are still full of irony, to be sure; for the now familiar arpeggio of the major triad prevails; and around the

93

hushed tremolo in the middle, alternating tonic and dominant harmonies follow the buffo pattern of accumulating and accelerating reiterations. But at last it is the soloist determining the movement of the aria in a persuasively steady flow. The inflection of the feminine endings in particular makes one suspect that, behind all her teasing, Susanna is not entirely immune to the Page's boyish charm.

Her participation in the last refrain shows warm concern. The coda, with similar intent, yields the melodic lead to her altogether. The whole section is musically well rounded into a perfect bar form $(4 + 4 + 8)$. Although the outline of Susanna's tune is still the tonic arpeggio, the harmony in the strophes is melodically filled with personalizing passing tones; and in the epode its wide, open arch has a tinge of show-off bravura. The instruments are subordinate to the point of a faux-bourdon. Only the exaggerated sforzato leap in the first violins at the beginning of each strophe and the exposed wood-wind comments at the moments when Susanna catches her breath echo the earlier frivolity.

NUMBER 13 / Terzetto (C MAJOR)[1]

Like the other trio, in the first act, this ensemble follows the purely musical rather than literary idea of a sonata form. The basically un-dramatic nature of a complete recapitulation was put to good humorous use in the first terzetto. New implications were cast on the same lines by the change of situation between exposition and recapitulation. No such dramatic change occurs here. Moreover, the most dramatic part of a sonata form, the development section, is entirely missing. Before a criticism is attempted, the facts should be recognized:

EXPOSITION_____61 m. (1–61)
  First subject, T (m. 1)
  Second subject, D (m. 37)

BRIDGE_____11 m. (61–71)

RECAPITULATION_____51 m. (71–121)
  First subject, T (m. 71)
  Second subject, T (m. 101)

CODA_____25 m. (122–146)

The first subject forms a regular eight-measure period. An elision in-troduces the modulation, which, first favoring the subdominant, quickly reinterprets it, in a crescendo, as the affined second dominant. After the dramatic break on the Count's forceful question, *Chi?*, a dominant sub-ject could immediately follow. It is delayed by a touching appeal of the Countess above the old *lamento ostinato* of a descending chromatic tetra-chord. The significance of the interpolation will be strongly experienced at the analogous place in the recapitulation. At the end of the Countess' appeal, the harmony of the second dominant is still waiting, as at the beginning of it, for a resolution into the dominant. The tension is in-creased by a prolonged organ point on the second dominant, a spinning-

1. Because of certain peculiarities of the autograph, there is some doubt as to the exact distribution of the two soprano lines between the Countess and Susanna. This analysis adheres to the most commonly accepted version, printed in the Peters score.

out of the *lamento* bass, and a quadruple pyramiding of a phrase built on the Count's initial rhythm. The Count sets out with the interval of a fourth, which sarcastically harks back to the Countess' fictitious excuse (m. 22–24). The Countess tops him with a sixth, and Susanna tops both of them with an octave. On the peak of the fourth sequential repetition, the two horns and the finally stirring bass increase the movement, while—the voice line on the highest pitch (e^1-flat) and the harmony at the greatest tension ($\mathbf{\mathcal{D}}^9$)—all participating instruments and voices join in forte. The last forte having marked the completed modulation to the dominant and introduced the delaying section before the second subject, this forte announces the end of the delaying section and the logical continuation of the movement into the second subject. The second subject itself, like so many of Mozart's, is a closed eight-measure period. It is constructed in exact bar form $(2 + 2 + 4)$ and leads with an elision on a deceptive cadence into another eight-measure period, which, if such terminology is desired, may be called the closing subject. Two more eliding deceptive cadences (m. 53 and 57) double the length of this section before a bridge on the organ point of the dominant finds a short way to the recapitulation. The recapitulation repeats the exposition almost exactly except for the necessary modification indigenous to a sonata form. The modulation to the dominant via subdominant and second dominant is replaced by a shorter half-cadence in the tonic, the simultaneous emphasis shifted from the Count to the Countess. In the next section, delaying the entrance of the second subject, the Countess' pleading is replaced by the Count's threatening. The subdominant, favored in the modulation section of the exposition and thus far necessarily missing in the recapitulation, is strongly exploited. It is heard in its minor variant, the relative of it, and the Neapolitan sixth chord. The deceptive cadence into A-flat major and the subsequent excursion into other flats are accordingly understood as:

$$
\overset{\text{83 \quad 84 \qquad 85 \qquad\qquad 86} }{}\ \overset{\text{87 88 \qquad 89 \qquad 90 6$\flat$91 \qquad\qquad 92}}{}
$$

$$
|\text{D}|\text{sR}|\,(\text{D}^7)\,|\text{sR}\ \underset{3}{(\mathcal{D}^9)}\,|\text{s}\,|\,(\text{D})\,|\text{s t}\,|\,\text{s}^{[5]}\,|\ \underset{3}{(\mathcal{D}^9)}\,|\text{D}|
$$

From here on, the recapitulation corresponds closely to the exposition. The third of the three deceptive cadences at the end is delayed by a recitative and by the coda, which repeats the entire closing section and, satisfactorily making up for the missing deceptive cadence, completes the terzetto with a perfect dominant cadence.

These are the bare facts. The first question that arises concerns the validity of the use of a sonata form in an operatic ensemble. As in the terzetto of the first act, one must remember that the recapitulation of as long and complex a section as a sonata-form exposition is an artistic procedure deeply musical and dangerously undramatic. It is musical because the principle of repetition is elementary in organizing time-space into an art form. It is dangerous because it contradicts the never repeating continuity of natural life as imitated on a stage. Mozart's awareness of the difficulty is sufficiently documented by the instances of recapitulation in his operas which he ingeniously and deliberately puts to a specific dramatic use—the first terzetto in this opera and Donna Elvira's first aria, for instance. This terzetto seems to afford little dramatic justification. The situation does not change between exposition and recapitulation. The development section in which any dramatic alteration may normally occur, as in the first terzetto, is entirely missing. Two explanations are possible. One focuses on the minute differences between exposition and recapitulation and tries to interpret them as significant modifications, dramatically or psychologically. The other, while recognizing the existence of these differences, minimizes their dramatic impact and tries to justify the sonata form on purely musical, that is, non-dramatic, grounds. Both explanations deserve attention.

The section altered most in the recapitulation is the one which already in the exposition gave this sonata form its individualistic imprint—the long delay of the second subject after the completion of the first. In the exposition a vigorous exclamation of the Count led to the caesura and the subsequent gentle plea of the Countess. In the recapitulation a vigorous denial of the Countess leads to the corresponding caesura and the subsequent subdued threat of the Count. The subdominant region touched by the Count balances and explains *post festum* the path of the modulation in the exposition. Its appearance in the minor mode tinges the threat with real seriousness. The difference between this spot in the exposition and the recapitulation must be interpreted as a psychological, if not dramatic, intensification. The Countess, at first modestly and softly attempting to find her way out of her predicament, is now forced onto losing ground, where she hastily (the modulation section is almost cut in half) and loudly merely shouts a denial. The Count, on the other hand, has grown in his anger from inquiry to threat. The intensification is not brought about by any new discovery between exposition and recapitulation but by the natural progress of any emotional argument in which the participants fail to make concessions. The psychological

97

change in the respective positions of the quarreling couple is carried over into the following pyramiding imitations. In the exposition the Countess found a topping retort to the Count's initial accusation; here the advantage of the repartee is his. The dramatic weight of the whole section is emphasized by its relative length: although functionally only a transition between the first and second subjects, it is longer than either of them. If the recapitulation actually represents a psychological intensification of an externally unchanged dramatic scene, the harmonic plan, substituting the consonant tonic for the dissonant dominant, seems to run counter. But the same harmonic shift is responsible for a general raising of pitch. From the imitative preparation for the second subject until the end of the closing subject, almost every phrase in every voice is higher in the recapitulation than in the corresponding place in the exposition. Susanna's flight up to a high c^2 cannot be missed.

The only other musical event different from the exposition lies in the existence of the coda. In the main, the coda is nothing but a literal repetition of the closing section, the sheer force of the repetition another symptom of intensification. The musical justification for a coda after the recapitulation, which lies partly in corresponding to the bridge after the exposition, is provided by an early interruption of the musical flow. The Count's recitative brutally cuts into the middle of the eight-measure period following Susanna's coloratura. The remaining of the two deceptive cadences gains sharpness by a chromatic passing tone in the bass. The end of the coda not only restores the passage to its original length but also completes the interrupted period by an extra repetition of the cadential phrase, which this time lands on the tonic.

These are the most notable differences between the two halves of this sonata form. One may agree with the idea that the differences tend to increase the emotional intensity of the situation, and yet may wonder whether they are strong enough to offer dramatic compensation for the undramatic fact of a prescribed recapitulation. They actually exist, but they might equally well have been cast in two strophes without the complex demands of a sonata-form exposition. Is it permissible to ignore the dramatic, or undramatic, implications and criticize the terzetto in terms of absolute music?

There are in the ensemble sufficient symptoms that defy any other but a purely musical explanation. The treatment of the rhythmic phrase heard with the Count's first words, for instance, follows musical and not dramatic logic. By its manner of introduction and further use (e.g.,

m. 14–16), it becomes strongly associated with the Count's position in the quarrel and his intimidating command, with either feminine ending (*Susanna, or via sortite*) or masculine ending (*Sortite, così vo'!*). The Countess picks up the rhythm immediately (*Sortire ella non può*). At this point it might be argued that she is hurling the command back at her husband. But the rhythm seems to be entirely her own in the gentle apology presented a few moments later (m. 22 ff.). From here on, this rhythmic phrase expresses her ideas as much as the Count's (e.g., m. 30 ff., 49–51, 69–71, 92 ff., etc.). The lack of rhythmic differentiation between the two adversaries makes for musical unity within the ensemble but is dramatically untenable. One need only bear in mind the sharp rhythmic distinctions between opposite forces in other ensembles in this opera, such as the second-act finale or the sextet, to accept the absence of any such distinction in this trio as deliberately undramatic, in other words, exclusively musical. Somebody might raise an objection to this reasoning by saying that the Count and the Countess are really fighting over the same cause and therefore are similar in their emotional rhythms. Both are giving commands to Susanna: he, to come out; she, to stay in the other room. This objection is quickly overcome by the fact that Susanna herself assimilates the same rhythm, even though she is outside the quarrel to the extent of being almost off the stage (cf. m. 32 ff., 85 ff., etc.). Such unified rhythmic expression is beyond dramatic or psychological justification. In terms of absolute music, however, it is a most valuable device for holding together various musical elements within one movement. It is thus employed in every good sonata form.

Another symptom of the paramountcy of pure music over drama in the terzetto is Susanna's startling coloratura, which is heard three times. Its bravura character is undeniable. Its sensual appeal enchants. Dramatically, it raises doubts even at its first occurrence. Falling on the last syllable of the phrase, *veggiamo come và*, it might with baroque fantasy be interpreted as a symbol of Susanna's uncertain flight of thoughts. The symbol is completely shattered in the recapitulation (*qui certo nascerà*). No fantastic reason supports Susanna's escapade to a high c^2; the stimulus remains purely aural.

The absence of a development section between exposition and recapitulation is another factor establishing the pre-eminence of purely musical elements over dramatic ones.

No further proof is necessary as to Mozart's intention to organize the forces in this ensemble at some expense of dramatic reasoning. Neither need there be any doubt about Mozart's ability to have done otherwise, had he so wished. One must draw the valuable conclusion that in an opera there exists a real need for musical satisfaction which in spots must be completely freed from the distractions of word, stage, and action. Even Wagner and Strauss, who in their philosophies deny the supremacy of music above the other arts contributing to an opera, insert long musical structures in their most playful operas. In these places they are at their best as composers: Wagner writing a quintet *malgré lui* in *Die Meistersinger von Nürnberg;* and Strauss, a crowning finale to *Der Rosenkavalier.* The Mozart trio under discussion is an analogous example. It becomes a dramatic point of rest where—with all the unrest before and after it—only the musical development matters. Why Mozart chose this kind of treatment at this specific moment of the opera eludes the critic. The answer lies in that part of the realm of genius which communicates directly or not at all. It cannot be verbalized, but it can be heard by all of us who respond to this terzetto in a performance of the opera with a pleasure beyond reason.

NUMBER 14 / Duettino (G MAJOR)

The hurried confusion of this scene is projected by many obvious means. The tempo is high. Excited eighth-notes run through every single beat. The furtive exclamations are exchanged pianissimo in a somewhat peeping *tessitura*. The orchestration is reduced to the hustling whisper of the strings. The score, however, permits of a deeper insight into the state of mind of the two scheming youngsters. A comparison of the underlying formal plan with the deviations in the actual execution gives the clue.

The duettino resolves into eight strophes or, more specifically, one strophe and seven variations. The complete, unadulterated version of the strophe occurs only once. The orchestra plays it in the first four measures, as if setting in an impersonal manner a norm against which the incomplete and rather hectic variations may be measured. The little unit is perfect in every way. The melody establishes the tonic in a straightforward, but rhythmically distinctive, triad; swoops up to an explosive climax in the center; returns to the tonic by the short route of a descending scale, the conjunct motion of the descent balancing the skips of the rise; and leads into a strong cadence by varying the steps of the scale into thirds. The fifth spanning the opening triad is answered by the tetrachord of the bass progression, which rounds off the octave of the given tonality. The tetrachord is taken up by the descending melody scale, which gains from it internal organization. The line from b^1 to g runs in three echelons of tetrachords (b^1 to f^1-sharp, g^1 to d^1, and c^1 to g), the cadence slightly rearranging the notes of the last one. The little strophe is cast in bar form. The identity of the first two measures establishes them as strophe and antistrophe. The new melody drive of the last two measures marks the epode, highlighted by the sudden disappearance of the bass and by increased harmonic tension. In relation to the characters involved in this scene, this miniature musical unit may early convey the idea of two fluttering and flustered people (cf. m. 3) who lose their breath in the adventure (cf. the syncopations in m. 4).

The seven variations can be spotted by the characteristic triad which opens each. The following table may serve as a first outline:

I (m. 5–10). Susanna is fearful because of Cherubino's presence and urges him to leave (*Aprite*). T

II (m. 11–14). Cherubino takes a pathetic view of
his fate while Susanna tries to drive him on. T

III (m. 15–25). The attempted escape takes a wrong
turn: they find closed doors. Modulation to D

IV (m. 26–29). Greatest fear (*M'uccide*). D

V (m. 30–42). The attempted escape takes a right
turn: they find an open window. Modulation to S

VI (m. 43–50). Cherubino takes a pathetic view of
his fate while Susanna tries to hold him back. T, t

VII (m. 51–54). Susanna is fearful because of Cherubino's departure and urges him to stay (*Fermate*). T

In relation to one another, the variations clearly form a bow. The equilibrium of the bow emerges even more concisely by reference to the tonal pattern, which groups together two variations on either end:

T_____Susanna   urging_____10 m.

Modulation to D_____Wrong way out_____11 m.

D_____*M'uccide*_____4 m.

Modulation to S_____Right way out_____13 m.

T_____Susanna restraining_____12 m.

The reverse harmonic progression from the dominant to the sub-dominant, rare in a movement in the major mode, makes sense with re-gard to the dramatic situation. Susanna encourages Cherubino while the modulation rises to the dominant; but when she later tries to restrain him, the harmonies drop to the subdominant. Susanna appears alto-gether the more enterprising of the two during the upward modulation. She usually takes the lead in speaking up and making suggestions to which Cherubino responds in utmost dependence. Hers is the first long statement, which fills the first variation. Cherubino is so confused that, instead of acting to his own purpose, he merely repeats Susanna's tune—only the beginning, at that, and Susanna has to prompt him with the continuation (second variation). It is again Susanna who presses for action with a breathless version of her first exclamation; and when Cherubino, still fluttering helplessly, once more merely repeats her tune, she points to a new possible way out, again ahead of Cherubino (third variation). At the moment of greatest tension, Cherubino for the first time takes the lead, roused to action by the thought of the Count's violent temper (fourth variation). From here on, Susanna, frightened by Cherubino's intention to jump out of the window, becomes the retarding force, and the modulation drops to the subdominant. Cherubino is the one to talk first of the window (fifth variation). He finds the solution of the situation, as the harmonic development retrieves the tonic and even has time for a passionate outburst of somewhat puerile chivalry (sixth variation). Only after he has jumped does Susanna end the duettino as she began it (seventh variation).

Considerable modifications, abbreviations, and extensions of the variations against the norm of the original strophe shed light on Susanna's and Cherubino's particular agitation.

The triads characteristic of the first half of the bar form mark each new variation and are therefore of necessity never omitted. In one instance only—the last variation—the triad is not repeated, thus robbing the miniature strophe of its answer. But at that moment Susanna's excitement is high and swallows up any formal considerations. At the beginning of the third variation the first half of the bar form is repeated, the dramatic situation again supplying the musical reason. The G-major triad having got them nowhere at four different places, Susanna now makes a new start. The tone c^1-sharp replaces d^1, and the new harmonic drive leads to the doors. The futility of this attempt is quickly discovered. Through the next three measures the bass moves as little as do the locked doors. The music above the organ point is actually intercalated. The syncopated beats reveal its derivation from the cadential measure, which should not yet follow. It is as if Susanna, imitated by Cherubino, wishes to lead her new idea to a hasty end—the wrong end, as they soon discover. Two more variations, the fifth and sixth, extend strophe and antistrophe of the small bar form. Cherubino, taking the lead after the central variation in the dominant, corrects the inadequate solution suggested by Susanna. He considers the window, through which he finally saves himself, instead of the door, which is locked. In musical terms, he finds the way from a, where Susanna's accidentals had landed him (m. 19), to g^1, the goal of the movement, by a sevenfold sequence up the scale of the opening motive (m. 30–36). The reduction of these seven measures to the original two of the bar form is easily accomplished by understanding the interval of a seventh, which demarcates the distance covered, as the inversion of the interval of a second, which would give a content proper to two measures. What seems like excessive prolongation of the first half of the bar form in this variation following the center is really exactly balanced against the analogous expansion in the variation preceding the center. In both cases two measures are stretched into seven, but by different means: sequence of the head theme in the fifth variation and intercalation of the cadence theme in the third. The sixth variation, finally, expands the strophe and the antistrophe in order to switch into the minor mode, permitting Cherubino to make his romantic declaration.

The epode, too, of the basic musical unit on which the variations are built suffers meaningful modifications. They differ for the fluttering figure of the beginning (m. 3) and the syncopations of the end (m. 4). Indicative of Susanna's and Cherubino's increased state of confusion, the length of the fluttering figure is doubled in the first four variations, in the third variation together with the subsequent cadential syncopations. In the fifth variation, when Cherubino and Susanna are viewing the jump into the garden with highest anxiety, the fluttering measure comes six times and at the highest pitch in the whole movement (c^2) with the exception of Susanna's fright in the very last measure. In the next variation, after Cherubino has made his decision, the fluttering subsides to two-measure length. The typical staccato assumes legato ties when Cherubino, still frightened but amorous, embraces Susanna "for the adored Countess," as he claims. The last variation flutters to pieces when after the statement of the motive a sudden onrush of crescendo and sixteenth-notes—the only time anywhere in the piece—accompanies Susanna's outcry.

Within the course of the variations the fluttering motive itself is heard in two variants. It retains its original descending character (m. 3) only in the two modulating variations, the third and fifth, symmetrically grouped around the center. In all other variations it changes direction so as to point upward, but less uncompromisingly than it had in its descending movement (m. 7, e.g.). At the same time, it is submerged

104

under a new and persistent tremolo. The two variants seem to have some bearing on the situation. The line sinks with the characters' spirits: once when they find the doors locked and again when they realize the danger of jumping out the window. The less decisive ascending version occurs in all other variations where anxiety and confusion rule over planned action. It even briefly invades the descending trend of the fifth variation (m. 39–40), as if adding a slight fluctuation of spirit to the helplessness of the moment.

Whereas the busy first half of the epode has shown a tendency to grow along with the agitation of the scene, the cadential second half seems to vanish as there is less and less time for finished statements. The early first variation doubles the cadence, maintaining a balance to the doubled beginning of the epode; but the second variation, with Cherubino's confusion, hastily omits it altogether. The long extension of the third variation once more justifies the doubling of the cadence, this time together with the fluttering motive as the intact unit of the epode. The excitement mounting, there is no time left from here on for the cadential rounding-off of the form of any variation. Only just before jumping does Cherubino permit himself the luxury of a short *addio* to the breathy pulsation in the orchestra of the last measure of the theme.

The open form and imperfect subdominant cadence of the last variation—both first violin and voice break off on the fifth—leave the listener at the end of this number with a feeling of uncertainty, not a serious one, about Cherubino's landing on the flowerpots.

NUMBER 15 / Finale (E-FLAT MAJOR)

Both Mozart and Da Ponte knew what the audience for which they were writing expected of a finale. In his *Memoirs* the librettist unburdens himself when relating his experiences with Salieri's *Ricco d'un giorno*, about two years before his first collaboration with Mozart: "This *finale*, which must remain intimately connected with the opera as a whole, is nevertheless a sort of little comedy or operette all by itself, and requires a new plot and an unusually high pitch of interest. The *finale*, chiefly, must glow with the genius of the conductor, the power of the voices, the grandest dramatic effects. Recitative is banned from the *finale*: everybody sings; and every form of singing must be available— the *adagio*, the *allegro*, the *andante*, the intimate, the harmonious and then—noise, noise, noise; for the *finale* almost always closes in an up- roar: which, in musical jargon, is called the *chiusa*, or rather the *stretta*, I know not whether because, in it, the whole power of the drama is drawn or 'pinched' together, or because it gives generally not one pinch but a hundred to the poor brain of the poet who must supply the words. The *finale* must, through a dogma of the theatre, produce on the stage every singer of the cast, be there three hundred of them, and whether by ones, by twos, by threes or by sixes, tens or sixties; and they must have solos, duets, terzets, sextets, thirteenets, sixtyets; and if the plot of the drama does not permit, the poet must find a way to make it per- mit, in the face of reason, good sense, Aristotle, and all the powers of heaven or earth; and if then the *finale* happens to go badly, so much the worse for him!"[1]

Much has been said and written about the first *Figaro* finale. The sheer length of it is staggering. One need only set the 939 measures of it in relief against the 521 of the second finale and the 1,699 of the whole third act of Wagner's *Tristan und Isolde*. Nor does the most uncritical listener escape the impact of the steady increase in the num- ber of participants. The beginning of the finale is a duet between the Count and the Countess. By the time the curtain falls, seven singers fill the stage—a large portion of the total cast. The artful arrangement of

1. Here quoted in the English translation of Elisabeth Abbott, from the edition by Arthur Livingston (Philadelphia and London, 1929), p. 133.

keys gives order to the whole structure. Alfred Lorenz has applied to this finale his keen analytic insight.[2] As a proper tribute to him, my words now yield to his:[3]

"First, E-flat major, with its dominant, is established in three sections. Then, at Figaro's unexpected entry, the affair jumps to the fourth dominant; and now the whole finale moves back to the tonic E-flat via G, C, F, and B-flat—each section regularly sinking, in a circle of fourths, to the subdominant. This arrangement alone does not realize the architecture of the composition. One also has to consider the ingenious metric relations of the separate sections. The long stretch, in which the Count looks for the Page and finds Susanna, is organized like a sonata, two very fast *alla breve* movements inclosing an andante in 3/8. The tonality does not complete a circle here. E-flat major ends as if on a half-cadence (B-flat), the feeling for which is created by the prevalence of A-flat major before the reappearance of B-flat major. Now Figaro enters.

"A short scherzo (G major) accompanies his eager entry; an andante (C major), the scene in which all difficulties seem to be solved. The Count is just about to give permission for the wedding, when the troublemakers interfere. There is first the Gardener renewing the Count's suspicion of the Page. The suspicion is weakened by Figaro's lies (in andante, 6/8), just as in the beginning of the finale the suspicion of the Page's actual presence was weakened by Susanna's appearance (also in an andante in triple meter and also in B-flat major). Finally, there is the plotting threesome, which remains victorious in the gigantic E-flat section. This whole episode of the troublemakers thus again forms an entity: fast-slow-fast or 2/2–6/8–2/2, like the formation of the beginning. The spiritual affinity of the opening and closing groups has been noted: both are directed and motivated by the shadow of the absent Page. One distinguishes between the tonal development of the first group from T to D and that of the last group from D to T. If these two groups, which are both in bow form, are interpreted as the main sections of a larger bow, a scherzo and an andante are left as middle movements. Short as these middle movements are, the whole organization is reminiscent of the sonata scheme. In the terms of my theory of form, the entire

2. "Das Finale in Mozarts Meisteropern," *Die Musik*, XIX, No. 9 (June, 1927), 621–632.

3. Translated by S. L.

first *Figaro* finale may be designated as an enlarged bow form, thus represented in a diagram":[4]

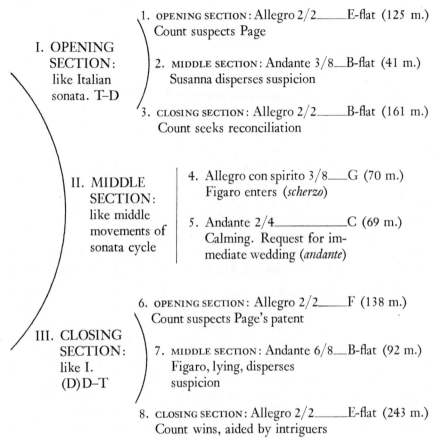

I. OPENING
   SECTION:
   like Italian
   sonata. T–D

1. OPENING SECTION: Allegro 2/2——E-flat (125 m.)
   Count suspects Page

2. MIDDLE SECTION: Andante 3/8—B-flat (41 m.)
   Susanna disperses suspicion

3. CLOSING SECTION: Allegro 2/2——B-flat (161 m.)
   Count seeks reconciliation

II. MIDDLE
    SECTION:
    like middle
    movements of
    sonata cycle

4. Allegro con spirito 3/8—G (70 m.)
   Figaro enters (*scherzo*)

5. Andante 2/4————C (69 m.)
   Calming. Request for immediate wedding (*andante*)

III. CLOSING
     SECTION:
     like I.
     (D)D–T

6. OPENING SECTION: Allegro 2/2——F (138 m.)
   Count suspects Page's patent

7. MIDDLE SECTION: Andante 6/8—B-flat (92 m.)
   Figaro, lying, disperses
   suspicion

8. CLOSING SECTION: Allegro 2/2——E-flat (243 m.)
   Count wins, aided by intriguers

As part of this highly organized framework, the movement of each of the eight separate sections proceeds according to its own inherent musical conditions. The opening duet adheres to sonata form. More important than the mere recognition of this fact is the evaluation of the very special use to which it is put. One distinguishes an exposition (m. 1–54) and a recapitulation (m. 55–121) but no development section between them. The absence of the latter creates the impression of dramatic haste and breathless piling of emotions. In the sinfonia of the opera, the same device was paired with gaiety. Here it is paired with serious tension.

4. Here the quotation ends. The diagram follows Lorenz closely but is expanded to include some additional facts.

Vigorous accents and frequent dynamic shifts pervade the whole duet (cf. m. 1 ff., 8 ff., 96 ff., and others). A tremolo current runs below the surface of many phrases (m. 21–26, 31–39, 44–54, etc.). Forceful strokes of the whole orchestra at one point completely disrupt the melodic flow and threaten to resolve it into a recitative.

The strongest concentration of dramatic excitement conveyed by the music occurs at the beginning of the recapitulation. There is the shock of being deprived of a development section. At the same time, the retrieving of the tonic is not accompanied by a repetition of the opening theme. The recapitulation, at this point at least, is primarily tonal; it is melodic only in so far as a broken tonic triad figures prominently. The new phrase (m. 55 ff.) is not permitted to swing out. Vehement interruptions, leading to a fermata (m. 63), produce the effect of three hectic three-measure phrases. The continuation (m. 64 ff.) sounds the most menacing notes of the entire finale. The Count is apparently contemplating serious vengeance. The turn to F-minor is more than a casual touching of the subdominant relative. The minor mode is confirmed by a cadence of its own (t, sR, s$^6_3$, D^7, t) in which d-flat functions like a somber negation of the basic tonality of the duet. In spite of the dramatic exploitation of this F-minor episode by violent accents, intense tremolos, and final orchestral strokes, its purely musical value is evinced by its role within the sonata form. The dip to the subdominant keeps the recapitulation of the second subject in the tonic—a device well known from many instrumental sonata movements.

The second subject as a whole is musically more significant than the first. One may say that what the first subject sacrifices to drama the second subject salvages for music. The recapitulation is complete (cf. m. 35 ff. and 91 ff.), and the key relationship is the expected one (D versus T). Moreover, the melodic lines form full musical, not dramatic, structures (two strophes, each in bar form); and dramatic repartees yield, as in no other parts of the duet, to ensemble singing.

The discovery of Susanna and the Count's surprise are accompanied by a descending scale organized into three units of a third each (g to e-flat, e-flat to c, and c to A). The figure is reminiscent of the one accompanying the discovery of Cherubino by the Count in the first act (cf. No. 7, m. 129 ff.). The idea of a scale descending into bottomless surprise, which was fully utilized in the first terzetto, recurs here, above the tonic organ point, as a counterpoint to the Count's stammered reaction (m. 145 ff.). With irony, Susanna falls into the inflection of the descending scale when explaining her appearance in lieu of the Page (m. 138 ff.) and suggesting as a parting shot that the Count look for the Page in the cabinet, which she knows to be empty (m. 162 and 166).

Throughout the molto andante, Susanna maintains a clearly superior role, both humanly and musically. The opening section (m. 126–145) is all hers. Even within the regular pattern of the given bar form (4 + 4 + 8, + 4), she preserves a certain independence in the rhythmic irregularities of her first two phrases. Her first word, *Signore*, falls on a weak fourth measure; and the continuation of the phrase, unexpectedly on a strong third measure. The imperfect cadence of the epode (m. 141) causes a repetition of the last four measures, in which Susanna gains a vocal climax on g^1 (m. 143), much needed after five preceding competitive occurrences of f^1. In the middle section (m.145–155) the melodic lines of Count and Countess are insignificantly static compared to Susanna's opening melody and also to her rhythmically sprightly counterpoint. The Countess here sides musically with her husband against Susanna, for her surprise is as great as his. This combination is changed in the allegro part of the trio (m. 167 ff.), where the Count stands musically alone against the united emotions of the two women. In the closing section (m. 155–166) the Count challenges Susanna's superiority for a short moment by attempting to utilize Susanna's opening theme for his own purpose. His effort to balance Susanna's position in the opening section by a kind of recapitulation induced by himself remains abortive. Susanna develops the melody for him (m. 157 ff.). The resulting bar form is half as long as the original one (2 + 2 + 4, + 4). The whole epode corresponds to the cadence only of the original epode (T–S–SR–D–T) and is therefore, by analogy, repeated *in toto*.

Neither tempo nor meter indications can disguise the minuet character of the whole section. The dance rhythm is the ideal one, without upbeat and without any accent on the third beat of the measure. A comparison between the opening measures here and those of the *Don Giovanni* minuet will quickly prove the point. The identification as a dance is significant. One remembers Figaro's choice of a minuet tune as a vehicle for his sharpest irony directed against the Count (No. 3). Susanna is here in a similar situation. Mocking her aristocratic master, she is using a musical language proper to his social class rather than hers. The minuet, not specifically mentioned as such, has become a musical weapon. If taken seriously as a dance at this moment, it indicates Susanna's disrespect toward her master; if taken lightly, her disrespect toward his whole class.

The prominence of the horns in the opening and closing sections of the minuet evokes the same association with marital infidelity and dupery that one experiences throughout the opera. The deliberate absence of the horns in the middle section, where sarcasm is momentarily replaced by stagnant surprise, drives the pun home all the more strongly.

The following allegro movement of the trio is bipartitioned (m. 167–253 and 253–327). The strong cadences of each half coincide with the only ensembles of the three united voices. At the beginning of each half one hears three times a pronounced little figure in a cascade of the violins (m. 175 ff. and 253 ff.). The association with Cherubino's jump from the window is confirmed by the accompanying text, let alone by the utilization of the figure during Antonio's report in a later section of the finale (cf. m. 469 ff. and 548 ff.). The first half moves from B-flat major, the temporary tonic, to A-flat major; and the second half reverses the path.

The dramatic correspondence of the two halves is obvious. In the first half the puzzled Countess asks for, and receives, clarifying information; in the second, the Count. In the first, the repentant Count pleads for pardon, which in the second is granted. The musical development of the two halves preserves the parallelism. The strongest unifying element is a phrase, normally of four-measure length and individualized by rhythm rather than melody (cf. m. 171 ff.), the recurrence of which lends the trio the character of a free rondo.[5] The phrase opening the trio sounds very much like an excited version of the rondo phrase. Identical in length and similar in contour, it precedes the rondo phrase twice in each half like an antecedent (m. 167 ff., 181 ff.; 271 ff., 279 ff.), the immediate relationship in one instance disrupted by an emphatic intercalation (m. 185–195).

The intrinsic identity of two outwardly different phrases becomes the feature of another theme, which opposite the starting quality of the rondo theme assumes a distinct cadential role. It appertains to the women. One version joins their voices in parallel thirds (m. 191 ff., 267 ff.). The other belongs to Susanna alone (m. 207 ff., 222 ff., 293 ff.), although in one instance it attracts her two partners (m. 263 ff.). The fundamental likeness of the two versions of the cadential theme

5. In the style of Karl Philipp Emanuel Bach, according to Robert Haas, *Wolfgang Amadeus Mozart* (Potsdam, 1933), p. 141.

112

pervades dactylic rhythm, binary structure, phrase length, range, and even orchestration without low bass support in the first half.

The double appearance of one idea is not a very common manifestation of the variation technique. This is not a case of a theme and its elaboration or of two themes used vicariously (as, e.g., at the recapitulation in the finale of Brahms's *First Symphony*). The invention here is really Janus-faced—quite deliberately so because it characterizes both the rondo and the cadential phrases. The musical device doubtless reflects the equivocal atmosphere of the scene in which each person indulges in some kind of double talk: the Countess resentful yet tender, the Count confused yet suppliant, and Susanna pleading both sides.

The two structural halves of the trio, even with all correspondence, differ in a few significant regards. The Count's ascendancy over his wife gradually influences the rhythm of her sentences. His expressively reiterated ♩♩♩.♪♩♩𝄾 —grown out of the more excitedly confused rhythm of his opening exclamation, 𝄾♪♩♪♪♩♩♩𝄾 —is first taken up by the Countess with inflamed sarcasm (m. 199 ff. and 231 ff.). Before the end of the first half, her sarcasm already assumes a tinge of pity (m. 234 ff.). In the second half, her yielding to the Count is so complete that his rhythm pulsates even through noncommittal statements (m. 255 ff., 259 ff.), let alone her open surrender (m. 279 ff.). The Count's rhythm, in calm augmentation, reconciles the three voices in the closing ensemble (m. 307 ff.), the counterpart to which in the first half had preserved three individual lines (cf. m. 241 ff.).

Another subtle difference is provided by the new interpretation of a group of explosive chords heard in both halves (m. 212 ff. and 288 ff.). Originally accompanying the Countess' rising passion, they become expressions, together with the inversion of the melodic phrase, of Susanna's irony.

The second half is further emancipated by the new tonal orientation toward E-flat major rather than B-flat major, the structural importance of which for the whole finale was recognized by Lorenz.[6] The crucial role of A-flat major (which changes its function from SS to S) is pointed up by its central position, bridging the two halves of the structure, and the forceful preparation by a fermata. Nor need it be considered an ac-

6. See above, p. 108.

cident that the modulation is placed, with baroque humor, precisely at the words: *Più quella non sono.*

Figaro's entrance brings about a thorough change of mood. His exuberance shifts the meter from duple to triple and the key from a half-cadence in the tonic to the fourth dominant. The triple rhythm, with its rushing accents on the third beat (cf. m. 329, 330, 335 ff., 347 ff.), is taken from popular dance music of the day. The deliberate association is borne out by the consistent use of triple rhythm in instances where folk expression comes to the fore, such as the choruses. Popular expression pervades the structure of Figaro's entire solo passage. Four-measure phrases follow one another in utmost regularity to form a little bow (T–D–T [8 + 8 + (8 + 4)]; the extra four measures lie in the middle of the closing tonic section). The vocal line fills the range of an octave (*D–d*) in an uncomplicated manner. The stepwise ascent from tonic to dominant in the short instrumental introduction is properly answered by Figaro's opening phrase. The melodic material of Figaro's entire song is only a development of this simple first idea: the ascent to the dominant is intensified by a chroma in the middle section and is restored to its diatonic version by the closing section, most succinctly so in the cadence.

The jump to the fourth dominant—which gave Lorenz good reason for placing a decisive caesura at this point of the structure—is startling but logical. The expected dominant of E-flat major, the tonic, is replaced by the dominant of the tonic relative. This substitution is fundamentally a common one.[7] Earlier in the act, in the first three arias, one heard a precedent in the same sequence E♭–B♭–G; and the finale itself, in E-flat major, was preceded by a G-major duet.

The Count's reaction deflates Figaro's exuberance psychologically and musically. The dance pulsation yields to sustained chords. The vigorous accents disappear. The melodic movement becomes stifled. It is actually completed with Figaro's well-rounded song (m. 355). What remains is a slowly descending scale from the height of Figaro's exultation, *d*, to the bottom of his apprehension, G_1. In various configurations the descending scale appears in the orchestra (m. 361 ff. in the strings, 371 ff. in the high winds, 383 ff. in diminution in the bass, etc.). The Count, whose melody is really responsible for pressing the line down, changes his tune at the precise moment when Figaro first

---

7. Cf. the antistrophe of the C-major fugue from the first volume of Bach's *Well-tempered Keyboard*, where E major is substituting for G major, i.e., (D)TR for D.

hits bottom G_1 (m. 375). Against the continued descending trend of the other voices, he sings a rather jaunty ascending counterpoint, doubled by the twang of both bassoons.

At an early moment (m. 358–360) Figaro tries to sweep away the Count's opposition by sheer vigor—almost like a child who, suspecting failure in an attempt to persuade his parents by slow reasoning, will try to score a point by loud and quick liveliness. He succeeds in breaking the regular *ritmo di due battute* by an extra measure; but otherwise he succeeds as little in swaying the Count as do the two women later in the ensemble (m. 383 ff. and 389 ff.), where the direction and dynamics of their expression try to keep up their sinking spirits. The imperfect cadence of the whole section leaves the hearer in apprehension of what is to come. The characteristic step of the imperfect cadence, d^2–b^1, is promptly picked up in sequence, E–C, by the Count's new inquiry, which opens the andante.

The musical essence of the new section is given by a regularly organized sixteen-measure period, which one hears in its entirety after the return of the movement to the prevalent tonic, C major (m. 441–457). The confinement to a fifth of the simple melody of the antecedent is opened in the consequent to a complete octave in Figaro's bass line and widened to higher projections of the fifth in the soprano continuation.

The first half of the quartet presents the sixteen-measure period only incompletely and in fragments. The antecedent (m. 398–406)—complete, though melodically split up among the two male voices and the orchestra—is not followed by the proper consequent but rather by a sequential spinning-out of its closing formula, with an ensuing modulation into the dominant (m. 406–411). The new key is confirmed by a resumption of the antecedent, but the initial eight-measure phrase is broken up into ever shorter and independently developing fragments. Thus one hears only the first half of the antecedent, split up even more than before (m. 411–415) and repeated to round out the eight-measure norm (m. 415–419). The distribution of the melody among the four voices reminds one of archaic hocketing. The consequent is further delayed by the opening measure of the antecedent, developed to self-reliant existence by canonic imitation, repetition, and individual cadence (m. 419–425). When the regular eight-measure consequent finally appears, it is after a spinning-out of the antecedent across twenty interposing measures; and it is in the nonfitting dominant (m. 425–433).

115

The return to the tonic and the concise statement of the intact period is accomplished by two four-measure phrases landing on the familiar organ point supporting a crescendo (m. 433–441). They are balanced at the end of the C-major section by the eight-measure repetition of the consequent (m. 457–465), which thereby also finds compensation for its shorter treatment in the first half.

In the simplicity of the scheme, one can recognize an embryonic sonata form. The antecedent, in the tonic in both halves, corresponds to the first sonata subject; the consequent, first in the dominant and later in the tonic, to the second sonata subject. The technique of spinning out a simple period to sonata-form proportions has been uncovered as basic in the growth of the Vienna classical style.[8] The quartet is a mature atavism. As in the sinfonia of the opera, exposition is followed by recapitulation without separation by a development section. The recapitulation fulfils the fragmentary problems of the exposition.

The intrinsic weight of a sonata form lends support to the suggestion that this section of the finale, short as it is, takes the place of an independent middle movement in the over-all structure.

The opening four-note motive not only reappears rhythmically or melodically in the course of the first subject and the following bridge but shapes directly the second subject and partly the transition to the recapitulation. Even the soprano counterpoint in the second half of the second subject (m. 429 ff., 453 ff.) sounds like an augmentation of the original descending third, the expressive delay on the opening note helping to avoid parallel fifths with the main bass melody. When the sopranos recapture the lead (m. 457 ff.), the basses in turn gain their staccato counterpoint by inverting the motive of the third and stringing it in a chain across the whole octave (C–E, F–A, A–c). This tightly knit melodic organization of the entire number is shared by all four voices, in the same spirit in which they split in hocket fashion the shorter phrases in the exposition. The dramatic situation offers a close analogy: the action has reached a moment which each of the participants expects to employ for his own private benefit.

The two coda measures of the quartet are carried into two introductory measures of the new scene. The latter are individualized by a rhythm which influences the diction of the people present and which recurs, in a similar introductory function, in the subsequent ensemble of

8. See Wilhelm Fischer, "Zur Entwicklungsgeschichte des Wiener klassischen Stils," *Studien zur Musikwissenschaft*, III (1915), 24–84.

the three intrigants (cf. m. 697 ff. and 783 ff.). It doubtless indicates excitement,[9] in this context, of a somewhat aggressive kind. The recurrence lends unity to the whole closing section of the finale, emphasizing the structural correspondence of the parts in F major (6) and E-flat major (8),[10] just as the re-employment of the quick violin figure associated with Cherubino's jump (m. 469 ff., 548 ff.) slings a tie across to an earlier section (cf. m. 175 ff., 253 ff.).

Antonio's characterization is a masterpiece of economy. His initial expression (m. 470–472) is typical of his simplicity: it consists of only one step. The opening pitch on the fourth above the tonic, rather than on a more consonant point of rest, reflects his explosive anger. One notes with amusement that at this moment the Count, who later sets the tone for Antonio, imitates the gardener's inflection, as if anxiously seizing any chance coming his way. Encouraged, Antonio widens his range without abandoning his primitive movement by step (m. 473–475). His next two exclamations (m. 477 ff.) are merely echoes of the end of his last phrase, the sound of his own voice giving him the momentum which his intellect is inadequate to supply.

His report—the reason for his entrance—provides him with the longest solo he ever musters (m. 483–491). His line is void of imagination: it consists of his typical step progression, this time rising from composure to anger, in four identical sequences. The range remains confined to the lower fifth of the scale. The Count tops the sequence in a manner which sets Antonio off on a return movement. One suspects that he would monotonously retrieve the tonic from the fifth, if not arrested on c by the Count's fresh question. When he speaks again after the lengthy interruption (m. 503 ff.), he gains his opening pitch from that of the Count's leading question and then stubbornly resumes his checked descending scale. Irritated by Figaro's laughter, he expands for the first time both his confined range and movement (m. 512 ff.), leaning heavily on the Count in the latter. Antonio seems to find supporting comfort in his dependence on his master; for in the ensuing conversation he merely echoes him (and, in one instance, his mistress) without a new thought of his own (m. 525 ff., 535 ff., 550 ff.). In his last direct altercation with Figaro he reverts to his simple-minded pattern of progression by step and sequence (m. 558 ff., 575 ff.), the sole

9. Cf. Bach's "joy" rhythm. Nor can one easily escape the association with the overture to Rossini's *Guillaume Tell*.

10. See diagram above, p. 109.

interval of a third stamping his impetuous accusation of the Page (m. 565).

In recent years it has become customary to portray Antonio as a drunkard. Neither libretto nor music offers the slightest justification for such a misconception. It is caused, no doubt, by a careless interpretation of Figaro's feeble attempt to discredit the gardener by the well-worn method of calling him a drunkard (m. 497 ff., 517 ff., 528 ff.).

One notices with amusement Antonio's imprint on the music of the other people, all of whom are more sophisticated than he. Even the women cannot quite escape it; the first reaction of the ensemble (m. 475–477) is typical and only one of many instances. The Count's adaptation to Antonio's plain diction is understandable as a conscious and perhaps habitual manner of communicating with subordinates with the specific purpose of making a friendly impression (cf., e.g., m. 472 ff., 491 ff., 501 ff., etc.). Figaro conforms more than anyone else to Antonio's inflection—partly because he is closest in mentality, of all the people present, to the gardener and partly because, as the real antagonist, he is trying to parry the new attack with the gardener's own weapons (cf. m. 517 ff., 538 ff., 584 ff., and others). The arpeggio at Figaro's heroic lie (m. 598–601) is very much in the exaggerated manner of his individual pathos (cf., e.g., No. 28, m. 189–192), but the closing ad libitum performance sounds again like an augmented and chromatic persiflage of Antonio's typical line.

The step progression and triplets of the quintet are carried over into the fresh invention of the following andante. Although the person of the gardener soon drops out, the problem presented by him remains. One recognizes in the main theme (m. 605–609) the trend toward scale fragments, repetition, and sequence, all of which were introduced by Antonio. The steady thumping of the retarded triplets mutates the preceding excitement into cumulative suspense, accentuated by a few brief explosions (m. 629 ff., 651, 667 ff., 681 ff.). The four outbursts have dramatic, as well as structural, significance. They indicate the modulations to D, TR, and back to T. They also coincide with Antonio's dismissal, Figaro's two successful repartees, and the closing ensemble.

The significance of the latter becomes clear after one has traced the main melodic phrase throughout the scene; for only at the end is it permitted to build a complete period. The earlier indecisiveness and lacking termination serve the suspense all the more.

The basic four-measure unit having been formed by a sequence (m.

118

605–609), it is doubled in length by a slightly intensified repetition (m.609–613). These eight measures are not followed up by an answering or developing consequent but by a short cadence which is as ingenuous and unpromising as Figaro's concurrent attitude (m. 613–617). The phrase is reopened with the Count's fresh inquiry but is deflected by the same innocent cadence after only half its former length (m. 617–625). The acceleration continues; for when the phrase makes a third start with Antonio's raillery, it is veered after two measures by the swell of modulation and cadence (m. 625–633). The apparent regularity of the *ritmo di quattro battute* need not mislead anyone into assuming that the melodic idea has at any one point thus far reached its destination.

The modulation to the dominant is confirmed by the ensemble accompanying Antonio's exit (m. 633–641). The period is actually well balanced and self-contained but only half as long as expected; and the melodic line of the little theme is uncouthly twisted upward by Antonio, the alteration up to the sixth (*d*) marked by an explosive forte (m. 635, 637). For Antonio this moment is still that of greatest melodic expression in the whole opera, his earlier remarks in the andante having been confined mostly to recitations on one tone (m. 609 ff., 625 ff.).

The Count, by returning to the direct inquiry of Figaro after the last parenthetical and awkward interruption, sets the phrase right (m. 641–649). It gains, in the new key of the dominant, the full eight-measure length it owned in the tonic. Before it can find the other balancing half of the period, it is checked in a steep crescendo by another modulation, to the tonic relative (m. 649–651). Figaro and the Count are both trying to reach the proper conclusion to the rebounding examination. The movement is renewed in the tonic relative without faring farther than before (m. 651–659) and then sinks in a long sequence by step down to the tonic (m. 659–671). A crescendo heralds the initial pitch of the original phrase (f in m. 665); but the bass, at the same time, contests the tonic by a chroma and thereby delays both Figaro's triumphal elusion and the structural recapitulation.

Back in the tonic, one hears the theme in its familiar eight-measure version (m. 671–679) matched, for the first and only time, by a consequent eight-measure evolution (m. 679–687). The ensemble is united below Susanna's climactic top notes. The accentuated turn of the theme up to the sixth (g^1 in m. 681 and 683) harks back to Antonio's parting remarks, his awkwardness made gracefully subservient to the subdominant element of the cadence. Two deceptive cadences (m. 687 and 691) double the length of the consequent by two repetitions of its second half, in compensation for the many times it was balked.

The dramatic turning point is Figaro's decision to grope for the right answers (*Uh, che testa*). Up to this moment he has been tightly pressed, but from here on he finds the liberating moves. The thorough appropriation of this plot by the music is revealed in the following diagram of the structure:

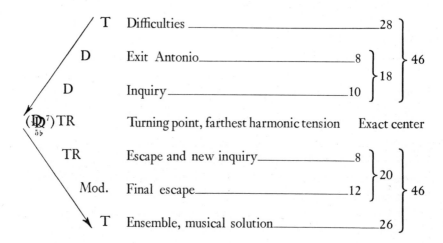

The entrance of the three intrigants coincides with the return of E-flat major, the tonal center of the whole finale. Three successive tempo indications—allegro assai, più allegro, prestissimo—accelerate the scene.

The intrigants first present their claim to the excited rhythm remembered from Antonio's appearance. Their control of the situation permits them to form two parallel four-measure phrases (m. 697–705). When Figaro counters the attack with the same rhythm, the agitation condenses the phrases to three-measure units. The total balance is preserved by an added two-measure cadence (m. 713–721). The Count responds to each party—in a complacent period to his three accomplices and with the agitated figure in clipped three-measure rhythm to Figaro. His continued domineering reactions to the following individual testimonies function as refrains to three similar strophes (m. 729–782). Each strophe consists of a six-measure declaration—Marcellina's in the dominant, Bartolo's in the tonic relative, and Basilio's in the subdomi-

120

nant—provoking an indignant two-measure outburst by the trio of the other party. The Count, in his refrain, balances each strophe by a regular period of his own, extended in the last instance by a six-measure coda and bridge to the faster section. The dactylic Antonio rhythm appears in augmentation in the winds in the quickened second half of each strophe and, intensified by dotting, in the Count's refrain.

It recurs with original force at the beginning of the accelerated section (m. 783 ff.) and generates the formation of two strophes paralleling the beginning of the scene (m. 783 ff. and 803 ff.). The analogy is close (cf. m. 697 ff. and 713 ff.). In both instances the strophe stands in the tonic and the antistrophe in the dominant. The first half of the antistrophe is clipped against that of the strophe, here from six to five measures rather than from four to three. The generally longer phrases are necessary to accommodate the double chorus which has replaced the earlier controversy of individuals, but the faster tempo keeps the phrases to approximately the same time limit. The second halves of both strophe and antistrophe unite the two ensembles in eight-measure periods (m. 795–802, 813–820); but the balance in the antistrophe is again only artificially restored by a two-measure cadence (m. 819–820) after the compressed six-measure body. The parallelism of the beginnings of the allegro assai and the più allegro is made all the more ostensive by the exclusive utilization of the dactylic rhythmic figure.

The scene continues by evolving three distinct structural units of approximately the same length as the preceding strophes. The first unit (m. 821–841) is dominated by the self-satisfied quartet of the temporary victors, against whom the disconcerted trio of Figaro and his two female friends contrapunts in halting confusion. In the second unit (m. 841–857) the trio leads in a chromatically expressive line above the harmonic background of the quartet. The third unit (m. 857–875) combines the two choruses without sacrificing their separate languages. All these sections remain in the tonic. Each section is binary, the second halves of the first two sections an intensification, and the one of the third section an exact repetition, of the correspondent first halves. The nine-measure structure of the third section is produced by the written-out fermata on the climactic a^1-flat. The bass progressively expands the tonic cadence underlying each section—from the unadorned main functions in the first, to the triad and scale outline of the second, to the harmonic bar form of the third ($\overset{858}{T}$ |T |TR |TR $\overset{862}{|}$SR |D |TR |S D|T).

The usual condensation of the cadence toward the end of a movement

121

takes place in two additional sections (m. 875–891, 891–907), which lead to the prestissimo coda. They are, in essence, repetitions of the two preceding sections. The piano ensemble (m. 875 ff.) is built on a simplified version of an earlier bass (cf. m. 841 ff.), Susanna's syncopations now freed into a florid cadenza. The forte section (m. 891 ff.) gains life from the ascending runs heard before (cf. m. 857 ff.), now exclusively above the tonic bass, and from a concise full cadence.

The coda is a bar form of regular proportions (8 + 8 + 17). It reveals the kinship of the scale bass ascending from the third, which characterized two earlier sections, and the runs inspired by *diavol dell'inferno*.

The strophic series formed by the clearly circumscribed and commensurate five sections of the allegro assai and seven sections of the più allegro is grouped in two bar forms by force of the parallel, strong opening strophes. In both cases the tonic is relinquished by the strophes and recaptured by the epode. The epodes, moreover, correspond by obeying ternary internal organization (see diagram on p. 123).

Even with all the excitement, not a single fortissimo effaces the melodic lines. Of the two opposing ensembles, the quartet moves in unified chords with the smug complaisance of the victor, stirred by an occasional outburst of the triumphant Count (cf. m. 858 ff.). The trio projects its disconcertedness by syncopations, chromaticisms, counterpoints, and imitations, which combine to an individual expression of human warmth. The difference in attitude is heard from the very first juxtaposition of the two ensembles (m. 783 ff.), where the calmly regular four-measure phrases of the quartet are inundated by the excitedly clipped triple units of the trio.

Conformably with her role in the opera, Susanna's personality here, too, soars above the rest. Hers are the widest and freest lines, to which even the Countess, her mistress, subordinates herself.

ALLEGRO ASSAI

Intrigants accuse, excited rhythm
Count complacent — $4+4\atop 8$ } 16   T

STROPHE

Figaro counters, excited rhythm
Count agitated — $3+3+2\atop 8$ } 16   D, ĐD

ANTISTROPHE

Marcellina testifies, indignant reaction
Count's refrain — $6+2\atop 8$ } 16   D

EPODE

Bartolo testifies, indignant reaction
Count's refrain — $6+2\atop 8$ } 16   TR

Basilio testifies, indignant reaction
Count's refrain — $6+2\atop 8$ } 16 $\rightarrow$ T   S

PIÙ ALLEGRO

Double chorus, excited rhythm
Diavol dell'inferno runs — $6+6\atop 8$ } 20   T

STROPHE

Double chorus, excited rhythm
Diavol dell'inferno runs — $5+5\atop 8$ } 18   D

ANTISTROPHE

Intrigants smug, confused counterpoint
Ensemble — $6+6\atop 8$ } 20   T

EPODE

Expressive trio
joined by self-satisfied quartet — $8\atop 8$ } 16

Ensemble, *Diavol* runs
repeated — $9\atop 9$ } 18

REPETITION:

Expressive trio leads ensemble
above similar bass as above — $8\atop 8$ } 16

Ensemble, *Diavol* runs
repeated — $8\atop 8$ } 16

CODA

PRESTISSIMO

Earlier bass reveals kinship with *Diavol* runs
Diavol dell'inferno in orchestra — $8+8\atop 17$ } 33

THIRD ACT

THIRD ACT

NUMBER 16 / Duettino (A MINOR–A MAJOR)

Many numbers in this opera bear witness to Mozart's original and independent treatment of the libretto. Rather than being restrained by the given words, he uses the text as a vehicle for carrying his freest and fullest musical imagination. The wit of the duet between the Count and Susanna excels in this respect.

The surface structure of the composition is simple. The change of mode after the fermata and double bar in measure 28 separates an introductory section from the main body of the composition. The latter is clearly ternary. In the framing sections of the bow form the two voices are lyrically joined, whereas in the middle section they are dramatically divorced into questions and answers. The framing sections adhere to regular eight-measure groupings—precisely so in the opening section (m. 29–36) and proportionately extended by a coda in the closing section (m. 54–61, plus 61–68, plus 69–72). The middle section (m. 36–53) adheres to a more breathy six-measure organization, the result of 3×2 (m. 36–41), plus $(3 \times 1) + 3$ (m. 42–47), plus a repetition of the second six measures (m. 48–53).

This last repetition, all by Mozart and not by Da Ponte, exemplifies in a nutshell the musical wit of the duettino. There are two questions that the Count asks: "Verrai?" ("Will you come to the garden?") and "Non mi mancherai?" ("You won't stand me up, will you?"). The first question is to be answered in the affirmative; the second, in the negative. In this form the dialogue actually takes place, each exchange filling one measure (42–44); but the Count in his eagerness reiterates his first question (thereby stretching the two literary questions and answers into the *ritmo di tre battute* described above). Susanna, her last negative answer still in her ears and the Count's conversation not too seriously in her mind, now answers, "No!" instead of the expected "Sì!" The psychology of her wrong answer is perfectly convincing. It is a Freudian slip par excellence, for she really does not wish to keep the rendezvous. Hearing the Count's alarmed reaction (forte, m. 45), she quickly corrects herself (and it is the correction which here extends the phrase to the prevailing three-measure pattern).

Mozart's gain in repeating this little six-measure episode is three-

127

fold. He gives an insight into the character of the Count, who, made insecure by the various deceits wrought on him in the course of the day, insists on hearing Susanna's answers once again. Furthermore, by reversing the order of the questions while repeating the joke of the faulty reply, Mozart adds to the characterization of Susanna; for it must be assumed that her second slip is intentional mockery, in consciously controlled amusement, of the earlier incident. Two similar misstatements in short succession are otherwise psychologically hardly justifiable. The third gain is structural: a musical unit can be literally repeated while propelling the action.

This ingenious treatment of a fundamentally nonhumorous part of the text is the more original inasmuch as questions and answers have already been used up in the composition of the introduction (m. 15–28) and of an earlier section of the A-major bow itself. The libretto is exhausted with the opening section of the bow form. While the words alone are shaped into a ternary form (4 lines, two per person; 4 lines, one each; 4 lines, again two per person), the ternary form of the music does not coincide with that of the words but rather develops independently after an overlap in the middle (at the opening eight-measure period after the double bar).

The different treatments in various places of the duettino of the Count's two questions and Susanna's answers solicit a detailed comparison. But first the opening statements, leading up to the initial exchange, have to be investigated, because they are significantly characteristic of the two persons and the situation.

The libretto gives each person two lines of text, which correspond in meter (7, 6; 7, 6) and rhyme (ab, ab). The music, however, allots ten measures (1–10) to the Count's half and only four (10–14, counting the elision) to Susanna's. The Count's languishing appeal to the girl is thus musically projected by the elongation of his phrase, whereas her prim answer can be contained in a concise four-measure unit. Already the instrumental introduction to his words (m. 1–2) is twice as long as that to hers (m. 10). Harmonically, it is a t–D cadence (with an interpolated altered second dominant, $\text{ĐD}^9_{5\flat}$). The interruption of the ascending tonic scale, in the first violins, at the end of the first measure may have its cause in Mozart's favoring a resolution of the German sixth chord which avoids the usual parallel fifths; but it is precisely this interruption which gives the instrumental introduction, and subse-

128

quently the Count's entire phrase, a characteristic melodic contour. For the elongation of the Count's phrase can best be heard and understood in relation to the two opening instrumental measures, from which it germinates. The Count's vocal line is basically an augmentation of the opening first-violin line: it rises from the tonic and tries to reach the fifth. The noted interruption of the scale at the third is meaningfully utilized.

In technical terms the interruption creates the delay responsible for the elongation. The line breaks on ¢ time and again, always starts anew, and always falls back again. The interruption is first gently introduced by a feminine half-cadence (m. 4); then is confirmed by an accented syncopation (which begets a hemiolic delay of its own by changing the Count's opening three ¢ measures into two 3/2 measures); and is decidedly established by the imperfect cadence at the end of the sentence (m. 6). The remainder of the elongation repeats the delaying interval in a fashion typical of most classical codettas and finally isolates the step from the third to the tonic (m. 9) before the obstructed line settles on the aimed-for fifth one octave below the expected range (m. 10).

In psychological terms the interruption of the scale, the many attempts to reach the high fifth, and the final resignation of the last inverted skip from tonic to dominant are all expressive of the Count's emotions. He languishes for Susanna, tries to gain her by repeated urgent appeals, but does not succeed in finding the right last word for either her or himself.

Compared to his complex approach, her replying melody appears as simple on the surface as the impression she tries to make on him. Within a regular four-measure phrase she outlines a major triad in a thoroughly attractive curve. But the true Susanna peeps through in a number of witty devices. It can be no accident that the highest tone of her curve, which she projects with ease, is the same one, e, which the Count had reached for in vain. She has reinterpreted it in her scintillating and deceitful manner, however, to become the third of a new tonal center rather than to remain the fifth of the old one. She is dodging the Count's request, as it were, by answering in a different, though ostensibly related, key. The modulation itself from t to tR is a masterpiece of dissemblance. The short path employs, in a surreptitious middle voice, a chromatic progression throughout a whole tetrachord, intensified by a crescendo (m. 9–11); and the chromaticism is immediately imitated in augmentation by the bass line, which carries the modulation directly into the cadence (m. 11–14). The apparent primness of Susanna's sentence and melodic line covers up the following evasive harmonic current of a usually short course:

The progression is the more equivocal as the third beat of measure 10 can also be heard as the concord of D̶ and D; and, similarly, the downbeat of measure 12 as the concord of TR and T, produced by two delays in the resolution. The idea of the distinctive augmented three-four-six chord (last beat of m. 12) may be derived from the early augmented five-six chord (m. 1): both instances lead directly to the crucial e.

The rest of the introduction is given to the two questions and answers concerning the rendezvous, one version of which one remembers from the discussion of the central joke of the duet. Here, as there, the insecure urgency of the Count's pursuit is not satisfied with a single exchange of questions and answers. At first (m. 15–22) the dialogue preserves proper order: two-measure phrases follow one another regularly. (The structural period really begins in measure 14. Hence, each vocal phrase must be heard anacrustically, and one strong measure follows another at the joint of this and the next period.) The opening set is in C major; the second, back in the tonic A minor. The Count's melodic line harks back to his initial effort of ascending the scale up to the fifth. The obstructing third c is successfully passed in the first question (m. 15), and the goal e is elegantly attained in the second question (m. 18). The Count's line has finally traversed all steps from the tonic up to the fifth, the scale yielding, with his increasing tension, to the skip of a third and lastly a fourth. The climax is placed in the middle of the second question in order to permit the end on an imperfect cadence to express both the Count's questioning inflection and his need for a reiteration of inquiry and reassurance.

Susanna's answers are singularly alluring. Her graceful portamenti (m. 17 and 21) sound almost as if Rosina were speaking. The intervals of a diminished fifth and a descending minor sixth are enticingly sentimental in the context of her usual tone of voice. Her soaring f^1 (m. 17) is that part of her answer which gives the Count courage and fervor for his climactic *e*. After having thus aroused him, she coquettishly picks up his note of triumph and coyly inverts the whole direction of the conversation downward to the tonic.

The way to a reiteration of questions and answers is now prepared both by the Count's last imperfect cadence and by his inevitable reaction to Susanna's coquettish shyness. The second set (m. 23–28) sounds more urgent in intensity than the first. The eight-measure period is condensed into six measures. The sentences are shorter and breathier, following one another without pause. The Count's melodic line, in terse faux-bourdon with the participating orchestra, is tight in range and anxiously chromatic. By origin it is a quadruple diminution of the top melody of the preceding four measures. The flute unifies model and acceleration by playing both. But the acceleration is further intensified by the chromatic alteration of b to b-flat (creating a Neapolitan by-product), which stands in cross-relation to the emphasized bass of Susanna's short answers.

Susanna's role throughout this second exchange illustrates the progress of their relationship. Her first exclamations (m. 23 and 24) fit right into the Count's line, as if to indicate her thorough yielding to his drive. At the same time she dispels his chromatic anxiousness by forcefully basing her answers on the diatonic b-natural. It is the insistence of this tone which finally convinces the Count of his success. He resolves the two passed cross-relations by finishing his questions on *B*. Susanna reassuringly takes up where he left off, demonstratively supported by a sentimental octave sigh on the same pitch by the first violins. In the last cadential measures (26–28) her surrender sounds complete; for she emphatically gives him with each pulse the fifth of the tonic, which throughout has been meaningful to him. The organ point E_1 in the bass seems to corroborate the achievement.

Compared with the situation in the introduction, the same questions and answers in the center of the A-major section follow an analogous structure. Against the similarity, the actual differences gain in significance. One recognizes the fundamental binary organization in which the second half (m. 42–48) becomes an accelerated intensification of the first (m. 36–42). The repetition of the second half (m. 48–54) is a new feature, the significance of which one remembers as the humorous core of the duet; it merely grows out of, and does not alter, the basic bipartition.

The analogy of the first set of questions and answers here (m. 36–42)

131

with the set in the introduction (m. 14–22) is most clearly heard in the two-measure grouping of the cadential and somewhat obstinate bass and in the anacrustic vocal phrasing. But the orderliness of the dialogue, with pauses between the speakers, yields early (m. 40) to a hasty give-and-take, which, marked by the entrance of the flute in a high register, shortens the period by two measures. The orchestra here really carries the motion in a continuous melody given to first violins and bassoon, in which the singers only occasionally partake. One gains the impression that the emotional undercurrents are stronger than the amorous couple can articulate. As in other places where instruments pronounce what is repressed in words, the subterranean bassoon makes itself noticeable (cf. No. 12, m. 26 ff.; No. 15, m. 145 ff.; and others). In the introduction the orchestra accompanying the analogous dialogue provided at best a suggestive but noncommittal background. The Count himself speaks with much greater self-assurance. Not only is the mode lifted from A minor to A major, but his exclamations sound almost like statements rather than questions. Each phrase begins and ends on the tonic; the contours, jointly, compass the whole ascending tonic scale; and the important *e* tops a secure and elegant tonic triad. Susanna's answers are no longer independent flights of whim. She obediently echoes the Count (m. 39) and modestly keeps to the same line even when the dialogue shifts (m. 41).

The analogy between the second sets of questions and answers (m. 23 ff. and 42 ff.) is close and meaningful. One hears the same acceleration in the repartees, breathiness in the accompanying upper strings, and Susanna's reaffirming employment of the tone *b*. The Count's chromatic anxiousness has given way to a diatonic "dolce" prescribed by the autograph—a rare and therefore doubly significant indication. In this parallel construction a minute change becomes responsible for the unexpected turn in the conversation. In the introduction (m. 24) the Count repeated at the end the second of his two questions warranting two successive negative answers. Here (m. 44) he unexpectedly repeats the first, so that Susanna's slip of the tongue sounds all the more convincing by merely adhering to the old pattern.

What has been discussed so far—the various sets of questions and answers and the opening cadences—comprises about two-thirds of the duettino—all of it, in fact, except for the opening and closing sections of the main bow form. To have thus far neglected the main sections conforms with the structural reversal of the musical content. Whereas in

132

most compositions the outer sections are treated with primary emphasis and the middle section is dealt with as secondary contrast or development or episode, this duettino—in a technique typical of painting rather than music—gains its significant character from the centerpiece. Against the dramatic fixing of the rendezvous by requests and replies, the lyrical melodies at the beginning and end of the A-major section sound almost like contrasting episodes.

At no other time in the opera is the Count so gentle and emotionally untwisted as in the civil eight-measure melody which represents the exposition and the recapitulation of the bow (m. 29 ff. and 54 ff.). The proportions follow a most regular bar form $(2 + 2 + 4)$, which influences in miniature the epode itself $(1 + 1 + 2)$. After the initial joyful excitement over Susanna's surrender, expressed by the new mode, by a small accent (*sfp* in m. 29), and by a fleeting crescendo (m. 30), the melody flows smoothly along, free of chromatic distortions. It is graced by affectionate melismata on many syllables and appoggiaturas in the feminine cadences of the strophes (m. 30 and 32). The line begins with the same interval and aspires to the same contour as in the Count's opening statement in the introduction. But the mood is raised by three sharps, and the full octave, *E* to *e*, is happily spanned in the first onset. Even in the descent to the tonic in the epode, the fifth is abandoned by the Count only after Susanna has repeatedly reassured him of her firm hold on that note. In her first two measures (32 and 33), six out of twelve notes are e^1.

The recapitulation (m. 54 ff.) is almost exact. Two minimal variants indicate the increased firmness of the pair's agreement. One of the Count's gentle appoggiaturas is replaced by a more assertive tone repetition (m. 55); and Susanna's counterpoint, which, anyway, had gained life from the declivous part of the Count's curve, now shows additional dependence by also echoing the opening phrase (m. 54–56). The codetta of the recapitulation (m. 61–65), growing out of a typical extension of the closing cadence, and the coda of the whole duettino (m. 65 ff.) put the final seal on the amorous accord: the voices give up all separate expression and move throughout in parallel tenths. The instrumental coda (m. 69–72) summarizes, as usual, the entire musical content. The top melody, given to the flutes, outlines the curve from the tonic up to the fifth and back. The low octave range is touched, and the assault on the climactic e is twice foiled. The return is accomplished by scale in the flutes and echoed in outline by a skip in the bass. The last two chords remind the listener of the role which the third-to-tonic interval has played in the Count's first statement. Here in major, it sounds like the happy resolution of the early troubles.

The Count's drive toward the compass of a full octave and his repeated repression by a dissonant seventh are characteristic of him throughout the opera. One encounters them again on identical pitches in his aria, which follows (see No. 17, particularly m. 66 ff.), and in other keys in different contexts (e.g., No. 22, m. 21–22). In the duettino under discussion, for instance, the tension of the seventh pervades, aside from the more obvious spots already mentioned, the emotional wave at the Count's reaction to Susanna's faulty answer: it determines the pitch of his explosive exclamation (*d*, m. 45 and 51, against *E* before and below) and is immediately imitated in inversion by the violoncello line (*f*-sharp to *G*-sharp, m. 45–46 and 51–52). Nor does it seem accidental that the Count, having only the promise and not the accomplishment of a conquest, is unable to regain the full octave *E–e* after his early joy in the recapitulation (m. 56). His line in epode and coda is somewhat anxiously confined to the seventh *E–d*, successfully rounded off only by Susanna's voice.

In view of the preponderance of the musical content of the A-minor section and the central part of the A-major section over the exposition and recapitulation of the bow form proper, one may challenge the relegation of the first twenty-eight measures (not too far from half of the total of seventy-two) to the role of mere "introduction." Many elements, however, favor this designation. First, the bow form of what has been called the "main body" of the duettino is one of the clearest in the whole opera, as if to leave no doubt about its structural significance. In this respect the introduction is less purposeful. The weight of the bow form, furthermore, is immeasurably increased by the shift to the major mode. The term "introduction," finally, does not necessarily imply that the section so designated is musically inessential or dramatically inferior.

If the challenger regards these objections as unsatisfactory, he is free to hear the unified duettino as an enlarged bow form:

NUMBER SIXTEEN / Duettino

Opening statements	14
Questions and answers	15
Lyrical duo	8
Questions and answers	18
Recapitulation and coda	19

One knows from experience the ambivalence of certain forms. Two co-existing solutions are compatible with the dramatic content of this duettino, in which Susanna says one thing and means another.

NUMBER 17 / Aria (D MAJOR)

The Count's impulsive character manifests itself in various obvious musical devices. One easily hears, and immediately reacts to, the many oscillations in the aria between loud and soft, high and low, step and skip, and dotted rhythms and meter. His desire to reach happiness by vehement short cuts, his impatience in letting his need for tender feelings swing out fully—these qualities the music expresses by its particular melodic development.

The binary principle which divides the aria into two large sections, a slower and a faster one, governs also the organization within each section. The text of the allegro maestoso is repeated in its entirety (m. 66 ff.), as is that of the allegro assai (m. 117 ff.). Moreover, the text itself consists of two stanzas in each section. In the slower half the stanzas are parallel, each beginning with the word *vedrò* (m. 45 and 56, repeated at 66 and 74). In the faster half the second stanza, beginning with the phrase *già la speranza sola* (m. 107, repeated at 134), is shorter than the first. It sounds like the triumphant result of the intensified drive of its precedent. These stanzas and their repetitions act and interact in the manner of norm and deviation, tendency and interpretation, desire and wilful twist, or emotional expression and impulsive development.

The composition and repetition of the first stanza in the slower section are typical of the chosen process of musical characterization. The movement is set off by the orchestra in a cascade of the tonic scale across two and a half octaves (d^2 to A). Within the scale the step from tonic to leading tone is significantly marked by forte dynamics. The counterpoint in the first oboe imitates it at the fifth. The vocal line continues the descending scale. Beginning on A, where the strings left off, it follows the natural drive to the tonic D, the expected completion of the scale. The Count's temperament bends the line to his own rising emotions just before taking the last step: on E the scale reverts to reach the tonic over the detour of a seventh, the inversion of the expected interval. The technique of inverting a step for specific expressive reasons is the same as that encountered and discussed in Susanna's boudoir aria (see No. 12). The headstrong turn is supported by a tutti crescendo and tremolo of the orchestra. The leading step to the tonic is again forte. The whole period is seven measures long, an irregularity against the normal wave of eight. The remainder of the text stanza re-employs the given musical material. The progress is exactly the same until the step above the expected tonic is reached, E, where the voice inverted the scale. The wilful act is repeated; but in irritable impatience the interval of the seventh is now accomplished in one forceful jump. The accompanying orchestra crescendo is correspondingly steeper. The self-determined achievement, although asserted by four tone repetitions, brings no pleasure: the underlying chord is an intense dissonance ($D^7_{5\flat}$), sharply accented by the whole orchestra; and the voice itself finds no other resolution but by way of a dissonant diminished fifth. The cadential step, G-sharp to A, reminiscent of the early oboe imitation, signifies that the road to the tonic, twice commenced, has been blocked by a modulation to the dominant. To leave no doubt about this fact, the very next vocal phrase, which opens the second text stanza, marks the outline of the tonic triad with a decisive chromatic alteration of the root (m. 57).

The repetition of the first text stanza (m. 66–73) brings two identical four-measure attempts of the Count to retrieve the happy solution which he has forfeited—in musical terms, to continue the scale drive to the tonic from the point where he intentionally lost it. The melody begins on E, the crucial tone of interruption in the first stanza. The weak position in the measure is counteracted by a sforzato in all participating instruments. The melody ascends the scale up to d (the apparent initial skip revealing its portamento nature in the unison passage of strings and flute). The line is identical with that of the inverted seventh in the first stanza. In both instances a crescendo and tremolo in the tutti orchestra support the effort. The sharp climactic step from c-sharp to d is set in familiar relief by a general forte. On the climax, however, the Count finds that his effort has been in vain. The tonic note does not relieve his tension, for the development has shifted its meaning from consonant point of final rest to dissonant seventh denying satisfaction. With a sudden extinction of the dynamic flame, the line drops back to its starting point. A repetition of the attempt is no more successful (m. 70–73). The vocal concern with the set musical problem makes the Count sound at his warmest in these two phrases. Apart from the fact that they obediently fill a conventional eight-bar form, the melodic progression is

138

free of autocratic impulses and honest in its pursuit of the resolution. The disappointment following the effort even evokes a certain human sympathy for the egotistic man. The Count, one must not forget, remains a gentleman throughout.[1] It is this spot which prompted Otto Jahn to concede to the Count "a stream of passion . . . full and unmingled" with "no tinge of Figaro's cunning or Bartolo's meanness."[2]

Against this essential drive contained in the two versions of the first text stanza, the composition and repetition of the second text stanza fulfil a subordinate task. The organ point alone on which each rendition lands, the first on the dominant of the dominant and the repetition on the dominant, denotes the transitory mission of the task. The stanza (m. 55–65) establishes the modulation to the dominant. Whereas the leading tone to the tonic is unexpectedly weakened (c-natural in m. 60 and thereafter), that to the dominant, first heard in the oboe counterpoint one measure before the initial voice entrance, is pointedly played up. From the Count's closing cadence in the first stanza, it finds its way into the ornaments of the violins (m. 55) before assuming a dominating place in the top flute. It is probably also responsible for the appoggiatura in the descending scale of the next section (m. 68) after an appoggiatura in the ascending scale has reinstated the chroma of the legitimate leading tone (m. 67). The repetition of the second text stanza (m. 74–87) is similar to the model in construction, although opposite in direction. One hears the same rhythms in the voice and similar figuration in the instruments. But the characteristic leading tone to the dominant is quickly negated by a double alteration of the second-dominant chord, which thereby receives the function of a diminished seventh chord to the basic tonality (m. 74–75). The flute, which in its exposed register had marked the way to the dominant, now, equally exposed, announces the return to the tonic by the analogous half-step progression (m. 78–79 and 80–81). In the short melodic phrase above the organ point, f-natural recurs. In the first setting it acted as a ninth, or appoggiatura to the octave, in a second-dominant chord. Here it lends the tonic the minor-mode chroma, analogous to the earlier one in the dominant and expressive of the Count's preceding emotional failure. The first symptoms of his undaunted will to proceed and not to accept defeat are the bold upward twists in the feminine endings of two dominant phrases

1. This kind of characterization, which gives an objective view also of the antagonist, becomes perfected in *Don Giovanni*.

2. *Life of Mozart* (London, 1882), III, 90.

(m. 77 and 79) and the simultaneous somewhat martial horn entrance, neither of which was to be found on the way to the dominant section. The voice leaves the low reached at the end of the stanza (m. 83) with forceful leaps, regaining one and a half octaves within two measures. An onrush of polyrhythmic figures in the orchestra generates power for new movement, intermittent cadential chords pointedly isolating the half-tone progression below the tonic. On the last tone of the slower section the voice seems to be no farther than on its first tone in the aria; but the impetuousness with which it first attacked the problem of completing the descending tonic scale and the vehemence with which it recovered from the subsequent passionate failure give sufficient cause to expect a vigorous continuation of the pursuit, in accord with the Count's character. The fermata before the double bar after a tutti chord on the dominant sharpens the expectation.

In the faster section of the aria, which follows, the Count actually succeeds in carrying out his intention; but he does so with much force and little grace. There is hardly a melodic phrase in this part of the aria that any listener might spontaneously hum after the performance, as he is likely to do with melodic material from arias of any other character. The Count triumphs without projecting outward. In this respect the music follows the words; for the jubilation they express is over an imagined success, not a real one. The achievement remains within his own temperament.

The content of the allegro assai section is compressed into less than half its length. In thirty measures everything is said and done. The remainder is an almost literal repetition, extended by a bravura coda. The two text stanzas of the main body contrast in length and meaning. The first, longer, stanza (m. 88–106) conveys the Count's desire for revenge and success; the second, shorter, stanza (m. 107–117), his joyful reaction to the imaginary victory. Both desire and joy are emotions directly expressible by music. They are determined by the interaction and relative weight of tension and resolution, or dissonance and consonance, within the framework set up by natural tonality and artistic task.[3] In this specific case the music of the first stanza, bound by the tonal center of D major and the given problem of an unfinished scale, will drive the movement toward the melodic connection d to D, often attempted and never quite achieved. The music of the second stanza will express joyful

3. See the author's article, "On the Limits of Music," *Chicago Review*, Vol. II, No. 3 (1948).

satisfaction by presenting and firmly maintaining the solution of the problem.

The Count's impetuousness pervades the first stanza. Even the opening two-measure phrase, devoid of charm, is torn by conflicting dynamics. The treatment of the whole phrase is obstinate; for the consequent in no way furthers the movement of the antecedent. It takes a wilful unison break in the line to span the contour of the melodic task for the first time. Impatience hinders a smooth descent aspired to by the coda sweep of the drive. The scale jumps over the leading step and is brutally interrupted at the halfway mark, as if the dominant and its subsemitonus were symbolic representatives of past and future obstacles. At that moment the text, too, is directed against an audacious opponent. The mere sound effect of the interruption is startling: against the unison on g-sharp, brass and timpani alone provide a bass a devilish tritone below. The imitative repetition of the three-measure phrase (m. 95–97) has a corrective function. The obstreperous leading tone to the dominant is overcome by a lowering of the chroma; and the desired leading tone to the tonic, played up so often before, is vehemently reinstated. The remainder of the stanza gives new expression to the basic impulse of the Count: to regain, in musical terms, the tonic scale from its original point of interruption, *E*, up a seventh to *d* for a complete melodic descent to the root, *D*, in the lower octave. In this respect the contents of the following measures (98–106) are very similar to earlier drives in the slower section (cf. m. 46–48, 53–54, 65–67, and 69–71). Although more successful than before, this line—like the nature of the Count's triumph— is self-tortured, as evinced by the chromatic rise, and impetuously unrestrained, as exhibited in the impatient abandonment of the gradual pursuit by a sharply accented and dissonant tritone leap into the seventh of the scale. In the closing cadence in the tonic, the voice really connects octave and prime, not yet melodically, to be sure, but close enough to the desired solution to give a promise of success. The sudden cessation of all wood-wind support and the sweep of the doubling first violins emphasize the achievement.

The second stanza has all the musical characteristics of the jubilant mood expressed by the words. Gay trills in the violins and rising intervals in the wood winds provide the external embellishment. A *basso ostinato*, well known throughout the baroque as a device of final elation,[4] supplies the foundation. The tonic is firmly established by the exclusion

4. Cf. the last scene of Monteverdi's *L'Incoronazione di Poppea*.

of all but primary cadential powers. Against this background the voice sings a regularly rounded and warm eight-measure period. Elements of the set melodic problem are securely manipulated, such as the painful span from E to d (in the over-all range, but particularly from m. 109 to 111) and the marked insistence on the chromatic step below the tonic. Then, all distracting melodic, harmonic, and orchestral forces pausing for one measure, the voice forcefully and elegantly completes the descending tonic scale for which it has so long striven. The accomplishment is acknowledged by a forte outburst of the orchestra, which initiates the final full and perfect cadence.

The only significant change in the repetition of the two stanzas occurs in the opening phrase. After the accomplishment of the first half of the faster section, the dramatic play on the adverse leading tone to the dominant has become superfluous. It is no longer justified by any psychological reasoning. What replaces it is a deliberate nullification of the chromatic step below the dominant by the erection of a full triad, emphasized by accent and anticipation, on the naturalized fourth of the scale. The parallel contrast to the subsequent outburst on the tonic leading tone, voided with the cancellation of the raised fourth, is vicariously provided by the temporary lowering of the seventh. Acting here as seventh in a secondary dominant chord to the subdominant, the naturalized leading tone is reminiscent of the turn toward the minor dominant in the second stanza of the allegro maestoso. The repetition of the opening two-measure phrase, obstinately stagnant in the comparable place in the beginning of the faster section, here gains personal interest by substituting the relative for the subdominant. From the next phrase on, the course is familiar up to the coda. Just as anyone would rejoice in an accomplishment by trying to relive it, so the Count's victorious drive toward the aspired completion of the scale is musically reiterated *in toto*. The reaffirmation helps emphasize the jubilant outcome against the long preceding hardships.

The coda (m. 144–160) begins by repeating in all clarity the solution of the musical task, the full descending tonic scale. The ensuing coloratura is rather brilliant as compared to the Count's style of singing in the rest of the opera but is well enough justified by his momentary elation. Throughout the coda one hears, in the manner of a concluding summary, concise versions of musical elements of the main movement. The dramatic play on the subsemitonus to the tonic recurs in the form of sparkling trills in both voice (m. 147) and highest instruments (m. 155 ff.).

The nullification of the chroma below the dominant is confirmed when the solo voice suddenly doubles the instrumental bass (m. 152 and 154). The crucial octave span of the vocal line is forcefully negotiated three times (m. 149, 151, 153–155), the last time with an exuberant flight to a crowning major third. The instrumental postlude enhances the elating effect of the familiar *basso ostinato* by presenting it, for the first time, in full loudness and with tremolo agitation.

NUMBER 18 / Sestetto (F MAJOR)

In many numbers of this opera a special technique has been uncovered—probably characteristic of Mozart and the classical style in general—of maintaining continuity of movement across long stretches by interrupting a melody at an early hearing and completing it only much later. A similar technique knits various sections of the sextet together. What is interrupted, however, is not so much a melodic phrase—although in one instance, at least, a melody is involved—as a concept of form. Dramatic occurrences during the sextet, of which most other numbers are free, give sufficient reason for the interruptions. There are three moments on which the action throws a spotlight. One is Susanna's entrance (m. 25); the second, her discovery of Figaro's intimacy with Marcellina (m. 40); and the third, her reception of the news that Figaro is Marcellina's son (m. 74). The sections marked off by these spots are in definite musical relationship to one another.

In the beginning, one distinguishes a bar form. The first strophe is given to Marcellina's parental tenderness and Figaro's reaction. The antistrophe is given to Bartolo's parental tenderness and the antagonists' reaction. The epode unites the voices in an ensemble:

Marcellina embraces Figaro. Tender violin
 melody (4)   ⎫
Figaro responds. String tremolo   ⎬ STROPHE, T
 and wind counterpoint (4)   ⎭

Bartolo embraces Figaro. Tender violin
 melody (4)   ⎫
Count and Don Curzio respond. String tremolo   ⎬ ANTISTROPHE, T
 and wind counterpoint (4)   ⎭

Ensemble. Organ point (3 + 3 + 2)   EPODE, T^V

The noteworthy section is the epode. It is obviously too short to balance the strophes, which jointly are twice as long. Nor is its internal structure completely satisfactory; for the promise of its opening phrase is not really fulfilled. Marcellina, doubled by the bassoon in the lower octave,

145

is in the lead; Bartolo, doubled by the oboe two octaves above, replies; and Figaro, his exclamation a miniature epode to the two parental phrases, moves on to a half-cadence. Against this main flow, Don Curzio and the Count are contrapuncting their reaction. Above the dominant organ point the three-measure unit is repeated. Two extra measures, dynamically supported, widen the original half-cadence into a modulation to the dominant. At this moment one may rightly expect a culmination of the ensemble by an epode within its own boundaries. Such early completion, possible in a purely musical situation, entails the risk of slackening the dramatic tension. Mozart promptly utilizes Susanna's entrance for cutting short the ensemble and thereby not only does justice to the action but also leaves himself a musical opening for completing the ensemble at a later time.

The ensemble is actually resumed in measure 33. It is transposed to the dominant, and Bartolo and Marcellina have exchanged their respective phrases and places. Otherwise, the organ point and analogous grouping into two three-measure units are heard again. There is a similar crescendo at the end, accompanying the modulation into the dominant of the prevalent tonality [D(D)]. The second of the two cadential measures suffers an elision caused by a new interruption, namely, Susanna's startled discovery of the embrace between Figaro and Marcellina. From here on, the musical content of the twice interrupted ensemble is abandoned forever. All in all, this resumption of the ensemble sounds like a repetition, rather than a continuation, of the earlier statement. It is a second attempt toward a musical culmination, broken here as there by an abrupt dramatic intervention and serving here as there the purpose of keeping open the musical development.

Both interruptions create musical episodes, which stand in decided contrast to the main stream of the movement. The first episode (m. 25–33) is short and regular. Susanna is the only person singing. In a neat bar form (2 + 2 + 4) she expresses her willingness to pay up Figaro's debt. The two strophes, with new though not unrelated melodic material, run exactly parallel. The epode borrows openly from the earlier configuration preceding, like it, the ensemble (cf. m. 13 ff., particularly the bass). Where Susanna suddenly found the money (*mille doppie* is a large sum), the audience never learns.

The second episode (m. 40–74) is long and can more properly be called the middle section of the whole sextet, for it leads directly into a recapitulation of Marcellina's opening melody and a simultaneous re-

146

capture of the tonic. The prevailing tonality of the middle section itself is the dominant. The pained chromatic alterations in Susanna's initial outburst help establish it by its own dominant. The augmented three-four-six chord (m. 43) leaves no doubt about the dominant character of the following accented G-major triad. The chromatic step down to g is utilized later in the middle section (m. 59 and 63) where—in relation to C major, the dominant of the whole sextet—a subdominant chord replaces the functionally closely related second dominant. The chromatic idea, which is here so properly introduced to accompany Susanna's grief, swings across into the recapitulation and creates progressions like the wind counterpoint in measures 89–91 and, most strikingly, the harmonic and melodic tensions in the ensemble between measures 111 and 124.

Nowhere in the opera does Susanna sound so really hurt as in her reaction to the embrace between Marcellina and Figaro. The ascending melodic scale of the first phrase (m. 40–44) contains, apart from tremolo and vehement accents, two steps across an augmented second. The chord created by the first chromatic alteration (m. 40) is, as Robert Haas has pointed out,[1] borrowed from Gluck. Susanna's voice does not participate in the second of these augmented steps (m. 43), as if she were momentarily too stunned to work herself up to the octave, g^1. The first violins alone complete the line in a crescendo. Her break on e^1-flat produces two additional effects. It emphasizes the very dissonant diminished fourth of which e^1-flat is the upper boundary; and it gives new emphasis to her subsequent recovery, by the leap of a major sixth, up to the corrective e^1-natural.

There are other indications of her recovery from the initial shock. The scales in the first violins become diatonic (m. 44 ff.). The tremolo yields to a more deliberate configuration. C-minor harmonies—(s) 𝕯 rather than d—are abandoned for C-major harmonies (the real D). Notwithstanding all these changes, the general tone of this second phrase (m. 44–48) is still full of pathos, of the kind characteristically voiced by a woman jilted by Don Giovanni. Susanna here anticipates the more tragic feelings of Donna Elvira and Donna Anna (cf. *Don Giovanni*, Nos. 3 and 10).

The short tragedy finds quick musical relief by one of the most obvious buffo devices: the cumulative literal repetition of a short phrase. The simultaneous dramatic relief is provided by slapstick. The repeated

1. *Wolfgang Amadeus Mozart* (Potsdam, 1933), p. 141.

phrase is two measures long. It is placed on an obstinate bass (m. 48–49 ff.), which bisects it harmonically into a T–D progression (or D–𝔇, in relation to the tonality of the whole sextet rather than that of the middle section). The harmonic polarity finds its melodic counterpart in a sequence, which makes the two-measure unit repetitive in itself. This tendency of a *basso ostinato* to be internally repetitively obstinate, besides creating the larger obstinate moves by its whole shape, is typical of the *ostinato* technique in general. It can be found in various civilizations, centuries, and styles.[2] Its effect is to increase the cumulative power of the repeated whole by diminutive repetitions of the smallest melodic, harmonic, and rhythmic particles.

The two-measure unit is repeated five times. The resultant stagnation of progressive musical movement is symbolized by the sustained octave g–g^1 in the oboes. The measures over which the static oboe sound is stretched (m. 50 to first quarter of m. 58) are precisely those which act as a parenthetical prolongation of one short phrase. The movement is resumed with a less obstinate development of the phrase (m. 58 ff.). The *basso ostinato* idea is not entirely dropped. The bass of the ensemble, which for the first time unites all six voices, utilizes the familiar chromatically descending tetrachord—an old *chaconne* stand-by. Another subtle device bridges the dangerous gap between the repetitive buffo section and the ensuing advancing ensemble. A counterpoint in dotted rhythm to the *ostinato* phrase, canonically introduced by the Count and Susanna, becomes the germ cell of a significant motive in the six-voice ensemble. There, in full growth, it expresses the anxiety of Susanna, the Count, and Don Curzio. The first two have good reason to be alarmed by the situation, particularly Susanna, whose voice casts the dotted rhythmic motive into the dissonant melodic mold of two sequential diminished fifths. Don Curzio declares his partiality as a judge by openly sharing the Count's tense concern. Against these three nervous lines, Figaro and his parents move in calm uniformity, pleased by the new development. The music thus groups against each other two sets of three voices each, in keeping with the general attitude of the individuals.

This first organization of six simultaneous voices coincides with the tensest moment of the middle section and the center of the whole sextet. An exact repetition (m. 62–65) heightens the impression. The

2. See the author's dissertation, "Untersuchungen am *Basso Ostinato*" (University of Vienna, 1938).

148

ensemble swings out in a three-measure cadence (m. 66–68), which, in analogy with the main body, is also repeated (m. 69–71). The grouping of the voices into three against three is maintained. The cohesion within each group sounds even tighter than before because of the more striking use of unison (Marcellina and Bartolo), parallel movement (Susanna and Don Curzio), and canon (Figaro following his parents; and Susanna and Don Curzio, the Count). A short instrumental passage (m. 72–73) leads from the dominant key of the middle section back to the tonic.

The application of the term "recapitulation" to the remainder of the sextet is correct only in the widest sense. The intention of presenting a recapitulation is clearly projected by the exposed manner in which the tonic is regained and the actual repetition of Marcellina's opening music by Marcellina herself. The only other direct musical correspondence lies in the treatment of the excited reaction to the discovery of Figaro's parents (cf. m. 80–85 and 89–94 with 13–17). Otherwise, the recapitulation can be recognized in dramatic and conceptional terms. One need not miss an exact musical recapitulation: advancing action in the course of the number runs counter to the true spirit of an emotional recapitulation. The dramatic parallelism between exposition and recapitulation is traced in the comparative table below:

EXPOSITION	RECAPITULATION
FIGARO DISCOVERS THE IDENTITY OF MARCELLINA AND BARTOLO:	SUSANNA DISCOVERS THE IDENTITY OF MARCELLINA AND BARTOLO:
Marcellina explains	Marcellina explains
Figaro reacts	Susanna reacts
Bartolo explains	Bartolo's role explained (by Figaro)
General reaction	General reaction
—	Figaro repeats explanation
Ensemble	Ensemble

The events, touching Figaro in the exposition and Susanna in the recapitulation, correspond exactly, with one minor exception. The exposition lacks the prolonged repetition of an explanatory phrase, which in the recapitulation is given to Figaro (m. 95–102). This deviation is so minimal that an explanation is hardly necessary. If one were attempted, it could proceed from a fundamental difference between exposition and recapitulation, namely, the addition of one extra voice. Figaro, having been the recipient of the initial explanations, now becomes superfluous, so to speak, when Susanna takes his place. His mere presence, however, necessitates his participation, for which the new phrase provides the outlet. The openness of the repeated phrase, moreover, functions as a buffo relief after the tense moments of the middle section. Unison treatment and, in the repetition, the two deceptive twists delaying the final cadence contribute to the frankly comic effect. The usual response of the audience to this phrase is loud laughter, corroborating our speculation.

The other, and perhaps more remarkable, relationship between exposition and recapitulation is based on a conception of form. One remembers that the ensemble forming the epode in the exposition was twice interrupted. The fulfilment of the formal idea was missing. Here, in the recapitulation, a full-grown ensemble crowns the structure. It completes a promise of the exposition. In other similar instances[3] the completion was a melodic one: an interrupted melody was permitted to reach a desired goal. In this sextet the completion is one of formal concept, for the ensemble in the recapitulation is melodically totally unrelated to the one in the exposition. What the two ensembles have in common is their respective placement as an ideal epode after two strophes, which run parallel in exposition and recapitulation. The last ensemble fulfils the formal function—and nothing else—which the first ensemble, for good reason, assumed but left fragmental.

In one spot the completing role of the recapitulation is melodically clarified, as if a sample of the better-known application of the special technique were giving advance notice of the total plan. Marcellina's opening melody, which in the exposition consisted of a repeated two-measure phrase landing on an imperfect cadence, is in the recapitulation rounded out into a complete bar form by an added epode bringing about a perfect cadence (m. 74–80).

In the closing ensemble (m. 102 ff.) the distribution of forces has shifted. Susanna's attitude has changed from anger to contentment. Her personal and musical expressions become identified with those of Figaro and his parents, relegating the two voices of the Count and Don Curzio to a minority opposition. The judge shows his total subservience to his master not merely by singing similar phrases and rhythms as before but by simply doubling him at the higher octave (like an obedient overtone). In the beginning (m. 102–110) he leans on the Count rhythmically, harmonically, and melodically. Afterward (m. 111 to the end) Don

3. Cf. Nos. 4, 10, and others.

Curzio abandons his individuality completely by merging his line with the Count's. Only for two short and intense measures (130–131) do the open octaves yield to parallel tenths. The sharp dotted rhythms characteristic of their anger in the middle section continue to pervade their expressions, while leaving the other four voices, in serene happiness, untouched. Harmonically, as well, the Count and Don Curzio are the sole agents of dissonance. Without them the ensemble would harmonically not go beyond the simplest consonant functions of the given tonality. The chromatic alterations around the dominant (m. 111–112), the germ of which was noticed earlier in the middle section, introduce Neapolitan sounds which eventually become fully realized (m. 116 and 120). This alteration is the more striking as it properly belongs to the minor mode. The manner in which these dissonant distortions (*fiero tormento*) are ignored—one may say, in technical terms, "corrected"— by the happy quartet (*dolce contento*) may be one of the causes of Mozart's calling the sextet his favorite number in the opera.[4] The Count's chromatic B_1-natural (m. 112) is immediately answered by the quartet's tonal b-flat, with complete disregard for the resultant cross-relation. In similar fashion, Don Curzio's and the Count's leap within the Neapolitan harmony from d-flat to g-flat (m. 116 and 120) is topped by Susanna's expressive curve from d^1-flat to g^1-natural. The crucial sound of g-flat itself is an enharmonic reinterpretation of f-sharp sung earlier in the ensemble as a grace note by Susanna (m. 104 and 106) and Marcellina (m. 115). The two women's voices also counteract *post festum* the distortion of g-flat by deliberately employing g-sharp as an ornament in their lines (m. 118, 122, 124, and 127).

At either end of the ensemble, startling coloraturas reach the ear. Susanna's joy, vibrating above all other voices, fills the full range of two octaves in two measures (m. 108–110). The characteristic ornamental turn (on *dolce*, e.g.) becomes inverted in the coloratura of the Count and the judge (m. 125 ff.). A running eighth-note rhythm marks both coloraturas, but the emotional contents of the underlying excitement are as contrary to each other as are the directions of the ornamental lines.

It is this sextet about which Michael Kelly, who sang Don Curzio in the *première* under Mozart's direction, reports the following incident:

"I had a very conspicuous part as the Stuttering Judge. All through the piece I was to stutter; but in the sestetto, Mozart requested I would

4. See Michael Kelly, *Reminiscences* (London, 1826), I, 260.

not, for if I did, I should spoil his music. I told him, that although it might appear very presumptuous in a lad like me to differ with him on this point, I did, and was sure, the way in which I intended to introduce the stuttering, would not interfere with the other parts, but produce an effect; besides, it certainly was not in nature, that I should stutter all through the part, and when I came to the sestetto speak plain; and after that piece of music was over return to stuttering;[5] and, I added, (apologizing at the same time, for my apparent want of deference and respect in placing my opinion in opposition to that of the great Mozart,) that unless I was allowed to perform the part as I wished, I would not perform it at all.

"Mozart at last consented that I should have my own way, but doubted the success of the experiment. Crowded houses proved that nothing ever on the stage produced a more powerful effect; the audience was convulsed with laughter, in which Mozart himself joined. The Emperor repeatedly cried out Bravo! and the piece was loudly applauded and encored. When the opera was over, Mozart came on the stage to me, and shaking me by both hands, said, 'Bravo! young man, I feel obliged to you; and acknowledge you to have been in the right, and myself in the wrong.' There was certainly a risk run, but I felt within myself I could give the effect I wished, and the event proved that I was not mistaken."[6]

The incident reveals, if anything, Kelly's total lack of apprehension of Mozart's aesthetic standards. One senses Mozart's loneliness among his contemporaries, for Kelly was withal one of his most ardent admirers. Not only is Kelly's psychological reasoning incorrect, as he is honest enough to concede in a footnote: "I was not aware at that time of what I have since found to be the fact, that those who labour under the defect of stuttering while speaking, articulate distinctly in singing."[7] More serious is the misplacement of dramatic prominence in the sextet on Don Curzio, which is an inevitable by-product of the exaggerated characterization suggested by Kelly. Most serious, however, is the discrepancy between Mozart's conception of the respective roles of music and drama in an opera and that of even his most sympathetic friends. "In an opera, the poetry must be altogether the obedient daughter of the

5. Where? Don Curzio is not heard in any recitative after the sextet.

6. Kelly, op. cit., pp. 260–261.

7. Ibid., p. 262.

music," Mozart had written a few years before *Figaro*.[8] He understood—as Kelly did not—that music must not imitate natural phenomena, like the other arts, but character itself. Aristotle had made a similar point two thousand years earlier,[9] having learned the distinction between music and imitative arts from Plato.[10] Music forfeits its noblest qualities by trying to become naturalistic. The recitative sections may absorb the extra-musical task of imitating (in the Aristotelian sense) the physical actions of people, such as stuttering. The arias and ensembles serve the deeper, musical function of expressing a person's inner life.

8. Letter of October 13, 1781.

9. *Politics* viii. 1340*a*.

10. *Phaedrus* 248.

NUMBER 19 / Aria (C MAJOR)

> Dove sono i bei momenti
>> Di dolcezza e di piacer,
>> Dove andaro i giuramenti
>> Di quel labbro menzogner!
>
> Perchè mai se in pianti e in pene
>> Per me tutto si cangiò,
>> La memoria di quel bene
>> Dal mio sen non trapassò?
>
> Ah, se almen la mia costanza
>> Nel languire amando ognor,
>> Mi portasse una speranza
>> Di cangiar l'ingrato cor!

The melodic line gains life from a gentle trembling of the tonic note on which the Countess draws her first breath. The beginning on the tonic proper is the firmest and simplest manner of establishing the desired tonality. The trembling of it in this case is written out as a turn filling two measures (26–27). The turn is not merely an ornament characterizing the Countess' special grace; it is here a specific expression of her unstable emotional situation. The words *Dove sono* are not so much a literal question as an indication of the Countess' uncertainty. The melodic grace notes, once introduced, beget melodic obligations. Theoretically, they could be dispensed with as mere ornamental neighboring notes; but Mozart's practice of treating neighboring notes like dissonant passing notes, pointed out before,[1] also prevails here. Accordingly, two drives split from the opening tone c^1: one leads by step upward and the other downward.

The next phrase (m. 28–29) continues the upward trend. Technically, the continuation is gained by a sequence of the first phrase. The content which necessitates the resolution of the first dissonant d^1 into e^1 is anticipated in outline by the first oboe. The voice itself pauses as if with a doleful intake of breath while the instrument provides the link. The silent sigh carries the anacrusis past the bar line, where it conflicts with

1. See pp. 65, 90, and others.

the meter: the accent falls on the syllable *bei*. On the higher pitch e^1 the voice repeats the formal, emotional turn which earlier surrounded the tonic note. Psychologically, the sequential repetition is in line with the Countess' emotional uncertainty, intensifying it by the higher pitch and the additional rhythmic wavering. Technically, the repetition is the product of the baroque and classical styles of composition, in which it serves as the most popular means for immediate continuation. By the end of this phrase, d^1 has been properly resolved into e^1; but b is still waiting for a, and two new dissonances have been created by the nature of the sequence, f^1 and d^1. The first of these points strongly toward g^1, and the first oboe again really offers the resolution. The voice, however, seems to lack the strength or courage to take the last step. It sounds g, but one octave lower than desired. The next two measures signify a valorous attempt of the voice to regain the prescribed range, but it fails again on f^1, one step short of the goal. On the way up to f^1, the dissonant passing tone d^1 of the fourth measure is resolved by c^1 in the fifth measure. The descent from f^1 moves in two parallel lines. The top line follows the scale with three pulse beats on each of the first two tones (f^1 and e^1). The end of the scale restores the normal rhythm of the shortest unit for each dissonance (d^1 and b) and of double its value for a consonance (c^1). The lower line recapitulates, as it were, the earlier secondary drive down from e^1 of measure 29, and in the cadence rejoins the main drive. Of the two opposing drives started in the opening phrase, the ascending one seems to have established its primary importance. Its goal is g^1, which the voice has so far failed to reach. The descending drive, never much emphasized, seems to have served nothing more than an aural preparation for the disappointed drop of the voice to the lower range. Literally, b of measure 27 (re-sounded in m. 31) is not resolved until a in measure 32. There, on the free sixth of the scale, the drive may end. The link with g is closed. Nevertheless, the sound of a retains a certain extra significance in the subsequent development of the aria. The few slight rhythmic irregularities that have lent emotional expression to the calm surface of the smaller phrases radiate into the larger eight-measure period. The metric accents of strong and weak measures conflict ever more with the rhythmic accents of the progressing sentence. Complete coincidence takes place only in the first two-measure phrase, although even there the weak second measure bears a justified accent, underscored by the phrasing of the upper strings. The stress on the strong third measure is replaced, as described earlier, by the delayed anacrusis. In the second half of the period the expressive accents fall on the metrically weak measures (6 and 8), whereas the metrically strong ones (5 and 7) carry an unaccented preposition. The listener hears the Countess' feelings better than he can read about them in words. Below the calm and restrained melodic movement, irregularities and uncertainties are pulsating. The goal of her emotional drive is clear. The line reaches toward the dominant g^1. But as yet the Countess herself is unable to succeed. We hear the complete line in the oboe, a voice outside her physical power of expression—perhaps her inner voice or merely an idea. Her courage is vouched for by two attempts to reach her goal, the first by careful step and the second by quicker leaps. At the end of the period, however, she finds herself back in the situation of the beginning. Only the oboe again holds the ideal before our ears and her thoughts and feelings. The yearned-for g^1 fills the measure between this period and the next. With graceful and extravagant fantasy it even soars to a^1 before resolving into the tonic by the shortest possible route of the descending scale.

The aria continues by repeating the entire opening period. The repetition of the first half is exact, intensified only by the two horns in the wordless ideas linking the shorter phrases. The repetition of the second half is extended in length, although the content remains the same. The ascent from g to f^1, in the first period accomplished in one and a half measures, here lasts twice as long. The earlier daring skips are replaced by a deliberate step progression up the scale. A dotted rhythm gives each step firm determination. The new valorous attempt is no more successful than the earlier one. The Countess' line breaks on the dissonant f^1 short of the aspired goal and drops back to the tonic. Within the descent a last feeble attempt to regain the desired aim touches the hearer's sympathy (f^1, m. 41, on the word *labbro*, her unfaithful husband's lip).

A new section begins. The silenced voice is given fresh hope by the oboe, which does not desist from sounding the ideal g^1. The new melody begins on that tone and reaffirms it by tonicizing it temporarily without any special modulation. The reiterated G in the bass invites the voice to exploit this sound as a triad. The major third of the chord yields to the minor third as the Countess sings, "In pianti e in pene per me tutto si cangiò." It is in the minor mode that the voice for the first time touches g^1, but it is a fleeting and not a final satisfaction. The sound lasts one sixteenth-note on the weakest of all beats in the measure. As if surprised or awed by this sudden achievement, the voice quickly drops an eleventh to its bottom register, accompanied by an equally shocked forte-piano in the orchestra. The excitement of the latter swings out in a tremolo with syncopations of ever shorter breath. The importance of the sound g for the Countess is stressed in her cadential phrase (m. 51). The last note before the half-cadence on d^1, in correspondence to the bass, should normally be c^1; but a most personal drop to g replaces it.

After the full cadence the voice soars for the first time to a satisfactory g^1. No accompanying counterpoint detracts the attention at this moment; the vocal achievement is merely doubled by the violins. The high g^1 coincides with the decisive turn from G minor to G major. Is this the final solution of the given task? In terms of pure counterpoint the note g^1 in this measure (53) is a solution. In terms of artistic composition the solution is too short to make up for the quadruple failure of the opening section. Further confirmation is needed; but the repetition of the phrase—the particular gentleness of which Mozart learned from Johann Christian Bach and, heroically transformed, passed on to Beethoven[2]—shows that the Countess is not yet strong enough for the decisive resolution. Her voice breaks, and it is again the oboe which has to assume the role of a prompter. The Countess does not pick up the line until the range of g^1 has been abandoned (m. 57). The text explains that the one real g^1 sung by her (m. 53) gained its force from *memoria*, the past rather than present reality. The voice finishes the section on g, but it still lies one octave lower than the real goal, which is simultaneously heard in the oboes.

The whole section on the dominant returns to the tonic without particular modulation, just as it left the tonic without one. The fermata gives the hearer time to apprehend the change of function and permits the Countess to gather renewed strength. The return to the tonic brings a full recapitulation. In the second measure the original breathless pause is properly filled by the anacrusis, thereby restoring to the next measure its right accent (cf. m. 64 and 28). It sounds as if the Countess, encouraged by the earlier first symptoms of success, feels slightly less uncertain of herself than before. Otherwise, the recapitulation is exact. The line strives four times toward g^1 and each time fails to attain the goal. On the climax of the last attempt, something happens. Structurally, the

2. Robert Haas (*Wolfgang Amadeus Mozart* [Potsdam, 1933], p. 139) makes a similar observation about m. 91–93.

period is interrupted before the end. Psychologically, the Countess halts on the tone symbolizing the obstacle as if to weigh it, sforzato and fermata, before changing her resigned attitude into one of quickened determination.

The allegro of the aria brings the answer to the problems posed by the andante. The line begins on the same crucial f^1. After one short sentimental reminiscence in the minor mode (*languire*), the voice pushes up the scale toward the dominant. While the bass twice outlines the progression F to G (m. 82 and 84), the voice approaches the prescribed task at first by the old route of stopping at f^1 and reaching g one octave below. But having accumulated enough momentum, it finally accomplishes its mission (*di cangiar l'ingrato cor*, to change her husband's ungrateful heart). The whole task is outlined in this passage (m. 85–88). A melody begins on the tonic, soars to the dominant, and returns. In the eagerness of the ascent the peak is reached by skip and thus somewhat reduced in weight from a primary tone to an appoggiatura. Idea now one with reality, the oboe doubles the voice while both horns reiterate the longed-for pitch. The wind instruments sound the more affirmative as they have not yet been heard in the allegro. In the descent the voice, remembering past unhappiness (*l'ingrato cor*), quickly takes a touching turn back to f^1.

The Countess' accomplishment is acknowledged by a forte of the instrumental tutti—the first in the entire aria. The descending tonic scale is interrupted by dynamics and formation precisely on the dominant. The scale after the interruption exuberantly surpasses the triumphant dominant by the neighboring free sixth, just as the oboe did in its early figuration (m. 33). The continuation of the aria serves to compensate for the frequent earlier failures by reaffirming the achieved g^1. Above the tonic organ point the voice twice reiterates the new success with notable bravura. The first reaffirmation is answered by a renewed instrumental tutti. The second leads back into a repetition of the allegro section heard thus far. Although the task proper has been completed, the repetition of the larger structure is allied to the repetitions of the smaller units as a force emphasizing the final success. The temporary return to the minor mode, harking back to the beginning measures of the allegro, only makes the end sound more triumphant. The repetition of the first half of the allegro becomes modified at the precise spot where the voice first reached g^1. The vigorous decisive approach by scale (m. 85 ff.) is here replaced by an arpeggio cadenza (m. 105 ff.) which is sure of its own power and of the final happy outcome. The exuberance of the cadenza carries the voice beyond the satisfactory tone, g^1, up to a^1, which is forceful enough to determine the root of the harmony in the same measure. The point of greatest vocal height thereby also becomes the point of greatest harmonic distance (third dominant). Only the oboe, persisting in its ideal role, indicates right under the voice where the true melodic climax lies (m. 110). This shooting beyond the goal is psychologically correct for anybody who suddenly succeeds after many long frustrations. It was aurally prepared by the various side lines throughout the aria to and from the tone a.

After a repetition of the climactic phrase, an eight-measure period summarizes the content of the whole conflict (m. 117–124). Beginning on the tonic, the voice rises on the scale but cannot overcome the dissonant fourth. The expected resolution to the dominant first forces the voice to the lower octave. But the repeated attempt is successful. From the triumphant dominant the line drops in the shortest manner, but with decided brilliance, back to the tonic. The remainder is coda—a summary of the summary. In it the exuberant a^1 above the needed g^1 returns, first in the voice and then in the orchestra. The cadence of the four closing measures presents the whole problem in its most concise version: tonic-dominant-tonic-dominant, four times, until there is nothing left but the supreme consonance of the tonic.

It is plain that in the aria a slow *da capo* section is followed by an allegro, as in two concert arias for soprano by Mozart (K. 420 and 505). The allegro acts, across the dividing double bar, as a final cadence to the rounded structure of the andante. Essential is the recognition of the contrapuntal problem presented in the first section and the solution of it in the second. Through it one learns a truth about the Countess' unhappiness and nobility. It is probably no accident that the crucial note g^1 symbolizes the yearned-for happiness not only here but also in the Countess' earlier cavatina. In both compositions the drive of the melodic line is directed toward g^1, there as the major third, here as the perfect fifth, of the tonic. But in the cavatina the Countess' mood does not change. The music gives the hearer a unified impression of her emotional state. In the aria the Countess' mental attitude develops significantly. On the waves of the musical movement it changes from resigned frustration to determined will for success. The change holds true not merely within the frame of this one musical number but for the rest of the opera. Up to the moment of the aria the Countess has been playing a passive role—suffering from her husband's insults and accepting every little intrigue suggested by her servants. But from here on, she leads the game with her own hand. It is she who, in the very next number, dictates the letter bringing about the *qui pro quo* responsible for the happy ending. In the final scene of the opera, she is an active and strong force.

This psychological interpretation of the Countess is all Mozart's. None of it can be found in the libretto. The text of the aria consists of three strophes, in each of which four trochaic lines alternatingly rhyme. A *lamento* atmosphere pervades all three strophes. Baroque librettos abound in similar poetry, which is most easily set in strophic composition. Mozart uses the first strophe for the opening section of the andante, and the second strophe for the following contrasting section. The recapitulation of the first strophe before the change of tempo is Mozart's idea. The third strophe, in which the word "hope" occurs, grows in Mozart's hands to an assurance of a new, happier life.

NUMBER 20 / Duettino (B-FLAT MAJOR)

According to the libretto, the dramatic and poetic materials for this duettino are extremely simple. The Countess dictates a letter to Susanna, who, true to her role as amanuensis, reads the text back to her. The letter is three lines long. A fourth line expresses a personal reflection of the women about the content of the letter and the person to whom it is addressed. The exact manner in which Susanna reads back what she has written—whether sentence by sentence or the completed message—is not prescribed by the libretto. The organization is entirely Mozart's. He chooses to have Susanna repeat short phrases of the dictation as she is catching up with the Countess: some fragmentary, some complete, and one in the form of a question, as if she wanted to make sure that she has heard right. The dictation completed, both women read the letter jointly before sealing it.

Even this organization by the composer seems obvious enough in its demand for a definite musical setting. One may expect two strophes, one for the dictation and the other for the perusal, and perhaps a few echoes or imitations of the main text by Susanna as she is writing. The music accomplishes the miraculous feat of conveying to the naïve listener exactly this impression of two well-balanced strophes with echoed phrases in the first; but the critic soon discovers that the body of the letter, filling twenty-nine measures in the first strophe, takes no more than nine in the second, and that Susanna's echoing repetitions of dictated phrases are neither echoes nor repetitions of the Countess' melody.

It is even more confounding to discover that the body of the letter cannot be reconstructed from the dictation as a continuous melody. Anyone should make the following experiment to become convinced not by the critic's arguments but by the music itself. Sing or play the three sections of the message, which the Countess dictates disjointedly in order to accommodate the writer's slower tempo, in one continuous line. The first phrase coincides with measures 4–6; the second, with measures 11–13; the third, dictated twice because of Susanna's question, with measures 18–21 and again 23–25. The melody, thus unified, does not make sense, whichever version of the third phrase one cares to choose. The separate phrases remain disjointed fragments. The letter does not emerge in the music as an unambiguous and coherent message.

One achieves no better result by comparing the apparently completed version of the letter at the rereading (m. 39–45) with the dictation. The finished message seems to bear little resemblance to the original invention. Only the respective first phrases are identical (cf. m. 4–6 and 39–41). The second musical phrase (m. 41–43) differs thoroughly from the dictated version (m. 11–13); but it was heard before with the text of the third phrase as the Countess' answer to Susanna's inquiry (m. 23–25), and earlier still fragmentally as Susanna's repetition of the first phrase (m. 9–10). The third musical phrase (m. 43–45), finally, is again unlike the original dictation: the first half with the high g^1 is entirely new, and the second half returns to Susanna's closing repetition while she is writing (m. 26–29). The strong discrepancy between dictated version and written result is unrealistic, to say the least.

A similar deviation from obvious echoes characterizes Susanna's repetition of phrases during the dictation. Not one is exact. Most of them are not even similar in casual external features. Only in the most daring flight of the imagination might one carefully wonder whether the Countess' inflection on *zeffiretto* from e^1-flat to d^1 influences Susanna's answer, or whether the Countess' ascent of a fourth on *sotto i pini* with the enveloping appoggiatura prompts Susanna's questioning response.

Another way must be found to retrieve the musical meaning of the scene. The obvious realism of the libretto must be replaced by a subtler one of Mozart's invention. While in the drama the Countess and Susanna remain two distinct characters, for the musical purpose of the duettino they must be understood as merging into one. There is much justification in this scene for identifying the two women with each other. Who is the real author of the letter? The Countess invents it, but Susanna signs it as her own. It transmits Susanna's agreement to a nocturnal tryst with the Count; but the Countess will be the one to keep the rendezvous, in Susanna's clothes. Thus, when Susanna takes the musical lead in rereading the letter—not only by beginning it and carrying two out of the three phrases but also by singing her own musical substance as much as the Countess' model—the reversal of roles as compared with the initial dictation is only a dramatic representation of a psychological situation existing independently of it. Vocally, too, the two women seem to merge. There is no other ensemble in the opera in which the blending of two voices is so deliberately and carefully carried through.

164

The voices twine in and out of each other so that the ear is deceived in attempting to separate the individualities; and when the interlacing yields to simultaneous singing, the voices move in the least individualized manner of parallel thirds and sixths.

A repetition of the first experiment in search of a continuous melody representing the content of the letter brings more satisfactory results if, in consistent execution of the conclusion reached, one obliterates the distinction between dictating and writing persons. The Countess' and Susanna's phrases, taken as a continuum, yield a line which in many respects answers the conditions of a unified melody. The text of the letter does not emerge as a true unit with the melody; for the first two lines are each repeated, and of the third line the first half is heard four times and the second half three times. Musically, however, anyone singing one vocal phrase right after the other, leaping over the few instrumental interludes, will experience no particularly illogical jolts except toward the end. There, between answer and reaffirming repetition, one senses a missing link, as one also earlier may have sensed an occasional weakness in the joints.

A last experiment is necessary, namely, to include the phrases of the oboe, which are mostly doubled at the octave by the bassoon, as essential elements in the structure of the melody; to permit the oboe to merge, as a third partner, with the other two soprano parts. The distribution of a unified melody among vocal and instrumental timbres is no strange procedure. The blend is accomplished partly by the fact that the oboe, like no other instrument, persuasively adapts itself to an expression resembling a human soprano, but more strongly, perhaps, by a long tradition of oboe-soprano duets in the fashion of a trio sonata. In many baroque compositions, as one remembers from Bach cantatas, soprano and oboe weave together the same musical material. So also here. One hears a cohesive melody if one begins with the Countess' first sentence, leads directly into the oboe, then proceeds with Susanna's reply, and thus continues until the end of the letter (m. 29). In the few spots where soprano and oboe are heard simultaneously, the human voice deserves preference, as in Susanna's second reply (m. 15–17). This rule is not to be rigidly executed. One may occasionally follow the oboe rather than the voice (cf. m. 26). The divergence is usually minimal, both voices moving along the same line but not with equally elaborate figuration (e.g., m. 9–10). The musical structure of the first part of the duettino, up to the rereading of the letter, thus rises in convincing bar form:

The equilibrium between sections is excellent. The two strophes correspond closely in internal organization. The epode, extended by Susanna's question, is more complex in its manner of interlacing the voices. The shaping of seven-measure units is somewhat unusual and lends each strophe a certain vagueness of outline. The technical device responsible for both septenary and vague contour is a rich allocation to the melody line of chordal elements. Thus the melody notes not only move according to their own linear drive but at the same time also provide their own harmonization. The line of Susanna's first reply (m. 9–10), if compared with the pure melodic essence sounded simultaneously by the oboe, illustrates the point. The dissolving of the normally instantaneous harmonic experience into one of temporal succession costs time and crisp melodic clarity. All along, one gains the impression that the music, the emotional content, of the letter is far less concise than the text, the verbal message. The reason lies not only in the very indefinite assignment of text lines to musical phrases. In the epode alone, for instance, the exact designation of the place of the rendezvous, *sotto i pini del boschetto*, is transmitted in three quite different musical variants. More impressive is the fact that many characteristic parts of the letter remain unsaid during the dictation. Whether the listener is directly aware of it or not, he becomes witness to the many thoughts and feelings which float through both women as they compose the compromising letter.

Therein lies the true significance of the oboe's participation in the main stream of melody. It conveys a message which the women do not put in the letter. The opening melody of the oboe is the first inspiration which the Countess uses to begin the letter. Then her feelings and Susanna's, expressed by the undulations of oboe and voices, give the real melodic life to the scene. The sentences that find their way into the letter are like incidental drops from the rich flow of the total melody of the women's emotions of the moment. The projection of unspoken feelings by instruments supplementing a voice is one of the most entrancing devices of musical composition. One remembers the role of the oboe in the preceding aria of the Countess. Verdi, similarly, lets the flute express all those high emotions which Gilda, in her aria, like an innocent girl dares not verbalize.

The rereading of the text forms a second strophe (m. 37–62). The compression of the letter text from twenty-nine to nine measures finds considerable compensation in the extension of the reflective coda from nine to eighteen measures. This external restoration of a certain balance is not the only reason for the listener's satisfied impression, mentioned earlier, of hearing two equivalent strophes. The vague contour of the melody is responsible. The recapitulation of the letter is, except for the first line, literally inexact. Nevertheless, one recognizes the letter because the perusal, as initially described, employs elements of the generalized mood of the dictation, if not of the corresponding text sentence. The discrepancy between the two verbalized settings of the letter is only one more proof that the music chooses not to be realistic in regard to words but rather to the total emotional situation. It is realistic in other respects, which easily reconcile an insensitive audience. During the dictation, for instance, the oboe insertions give the slower writer a chance to catch up with the faster-spoken words; and the rereading of the text naturally passes more quickly than the drafting.

In the recapitulation the overlapping sentences reduce the basic *ritmo di tre battute* so that the four three-measure phrases appear as a regular eight-measure period (m. 37–45). The melodic continuity of the line is preserved, even though it is a different melody from the one heard during the dictation. The shorter version sounds like a condensation of all the women's thoughts, feelings, and words. If the process seems fragmentary compared to the complex one experienced during the dictation, one may remember that the words of the letter, too, are merely suggestive and do not form a finished sentence. The difference between recapitulation and exposition is specific: in general terms of outline and interlacing, the mood is kept intact in distilled form. So is the minor detail of formal organization; for the arpeggios establish a harmonic parallelism between the first two sentences (T–D–T) against which the third sentence contrasts by touching the subdominant region (SR–D–T), reaching a new high, and finding support in the wood winds.

The elisions find their way into the coda. An elongation of the coda is nonetheless achieved by a repetition of the miniature strophes in ornamental variation and a consequent climactic doubling of the whole miniature epode. In an appended codetta (m. 56–62) the melodic wave swings above the calmer pulsation of the strings until it, too, comes to rest.

NUMBER 21 / Coro (G MAJOR)

In strong contrast to the highly individualistic expression of the two women's voices in the preceding duet, the chorus—also for two women's voices—employs a number of devices borrowed from the standard equipment of the South German folk song, the Salzburg folk song in particular. Mozart simply is not concerned with realism in the sense in which a nonmusical pedant might expect, or he would have chosen a Spanish tune. He is concerned with the projection of a feeling or mood, a friendly one in this case; and nothing would serve his purpose better than musical phrases unpretentiously absorbed in his childhood.

The most characteristic loan from the Salzburg folk song is the slurred ascending fourth (m. 24, 25, and 28). It is a derivative of the Alpine yodel. Short as the phrase is, it is so typical that Robert Haas has traced it not only in a good many Salzburg compositions of the eighteenth century but all through Wolfgang Amadeus Mozart's work.[1] It can be heard, for instance, in a Salzburg student march of 1777; in various oratorios and masses of Eberlin and Leopold Mozart; and in the earliest sonatas of Wolfgang (K. 8) as well as in his late operas.[2] An immediate repetition of the short turn seems to be typical; and the chorus in *Figaro* does not renounce it, thereby declaring the origin of the phrase all the more clearly.

There are other folk-music sounds in the chorus. The two-part setting for women's voices in parallel thirds and sixths has its model in a song pattern employed by certain street vendors in South German communities. From my own experience I remember the "lavender women" walking through the streets of Vienna and attracting prospective buyers of their plant, as well as simply announcing their presence, by a two-part song, not unlike that of Susanna's friends.

In most of these instances, triple rhythm prevails. Mozart employs it not only here but also in the other chorus in the first act and, for instance, in the countryfolk scene in *Don Giovanni* (No. 5). The over-all simplicity of the whole number is emphasized by the sparing use of any

1. *Wolfgang Amadeus Mozart* (Potsdam, 1933), pp. 7 ff.

2. Haas (*ibid.*) quotes fourteen music illustrations, from which these samples are taken.

counterpoints against the leading melody. Voices other than the main one serve primarily a harmonizing function; and the bass, usually the strongest potential antagonist, rests for the most part on a tonic or dominant organ point.

The musical significance of the movement can be investigated without reference to facts which lie outside the score itself. The eight-measure introduction determines the essence and eventual development of the composition. Complete in the first purely instrumental statement, the eight-measure melody is subsequently heard only in fragments, which are not put together again until the very end. The task of the movement, in terms of scientific criticism, is set by the incomplete repetition of a melody which was first heard in completeness and by the subsequent need for recapturing the melodic entity.

The melody itself, as played by the first violins, is simple enough. It begins on the fifth of the scale, thereby creating sufficient tension for a drive down to the tonic. Simultaneously, like a wave which is part of a larger undulation, a parallel drive moves from the third of the scale down to the tonic. Fifth (d^2) and third (b^1) fill the first measure. Both descend by step to c^2 and a^1, respectively, in the second measure, and once again by step to b^1 and g^1 in the third measure. Dissonant against the tonic, c^2 and a^1 are deliberately placed as passing tones in the weak half of a metrically weak bar. The repeated note d^2 above the descending lines assumes the role of an inverted organ point, so to speak, with the function of a steady reminder of the starting point of the melody. By the end of the phrase (in the middle of m. 3), the two lines have each descended a third, with the result that the secondary line from the third down has reached the destination of the tonic, while the main line from the fifth down has progressed halfway. The phrase is repeated. The masculine ending on the downbeat of measure 5, which replaces the feminine ending of the first phrase, has the effect that the main line is left incomplete, even more poignantly, on the dissonant fourth (c^2) rather than on the more consonant third (b^1) as before. The purpose of this minute change is to project the musical content with the greatest possible clarity and to avoid the chance of a misunderstanding. The imperfect development of the main line begets the need for continuation and eventual completion, as is really accomplished by the remainder of the orchestra introduction. The second four-measure phrase may on the surface appear quite different from the first one, but in essence it supplements it to form a coherent entity. The main line is resumed precisely at the point of the crucial interruption (b^1 in m. 5) and is led down to the tonic in the most direct manner, namely, by scale. The absolute pitch of the goal (g) is one octave below the expected one. The cause for the apparent extension of the line can be found in the initial distribution of voices, in which the first violins soar two octaves above the nearest middle voice. This detached range of the melody generates the drive downward to a more cohesive position of all the voices.

In the middle of measure 7 the melody has completed its proper task. The coda character of the remaining two measures is obvious. The line simply summarizes, in coda fashion, the content of the whole: it retrieves the critical point of the initial interruption, carefully marking both b^1 (m. 7) and c^2 (m. 8), and then returns down the scale to the tonic on low g. Harmonically, the coda is nothing more than a full T–S^6–D^7–T cadence. The running sixteenth-notes, moreover, lend the coda the necessary closing bravura character. What justifies the existence of the coda altogether is a rhythmic disproportion between the four measures of the incomplete statement and only half as many measures for the supplementary answer. The two coda measures re-establish the rhythmic equilibrium.

The orchestration confirms the outlined organization in every detail. There are shifts in the wood winds, which accompany the first-violin line, at each significant point. Flute and bassoon double the melody up to the moment where the break is emphasized (m. 5). Then the sharp oboe takes over to emphasize the resolution in the higher octave range. Flute and bassoon release the oboe only toward the end, as if to indicate their solidarity with a project that they helped launch. The coda is different still. The second oboe enters and assists the first in supplying background harmonies. The horns and low strings, tied to an organ point until now, are set in motion. The second violins support the run of the first; and the flute pauses briefly in order to sparkle all the more on the final run, in which it compasses precisely the full tonic scale.

The complete rendition of the total melodic material in a closed opening period is a baroque, rather than a classical, technique. One finds it quite regularly in a *concerto grosso*, for instance, but hardly ever in a Vienna sonata movement. The baroque composer, starting with something complete, is faced with the task of developing his material by breaking it up, before reuniting all parts in a concluding statement. The classical composer, starting with something fragmentary, is faced with the task of developing his material toward an eventual completion of his idea. The end, in both cases, is the same; but the opening situations differ. In this chorus, with all the popular lightness of the late eighteenth century, Mozart fundamentally employs the old baroque technique.

One becomes aware of it after the chorus has sung the first four-measure phrase. The musical content is identical with that of the opening orchestral four-measure phrase. Freed of some purely instrumental embellishments, the voices make clearly audible the parallel descending lines and the break in the main line. The continuation of the phrase (m. 13 ff.), however, does not answer the demand for the completion of the main line down to g, as it was carried out in the orchestra introduction. Instead, the voices change direction to reach g^1 (m. 16) in the wrong octave range. The approach is systematic: from the point of interruption, the top melody moves, as before, in two lines of parallel thirds:

The idea of inverting a desired step and thereby prolonging the movement has by now been found so frequently, even in this opera alone, that a special explanation at this moment is no longer warranted.[3] It is sufficient to say that the continuation of the sung phrase, as compared to the instrumental model, goes astray. That the high g^1 is not the true goal is emphasized by the harmonization as TR rather than T and its placement on a metrically extremely weak beat. The task of the whole movement is exactly the regaining of the lost path.

The dotted dactylic scale which, prominently doubled by the winds, first resolved the melodic tension in the orchestra introduction (m. 5–7) returns four times in the remainder of the movement (m. 15 f., 26 f., 31 f., and 33 ff.). Each time it acts like a signpost, unambiguously marking the progress of the movement. Each time it is doubled by one or more wood-wind instruments. One remembers that the critical point of interruption was b^1 and that the once-heard completion consisted of a scale descending a tenth to g. In the orchestra introduction this scale was completed in one sweep. In the main body of the composition this scale is completed in instalments. At the first occurrence (m. 15) the

---

3. Cf. pp. 85 f., 104, and others.

dactylic figure resumes the scale on a^1, where it was stopped short, and then strengthens the connection by touching the junction b^1 once more before descending as far as d^1. The potential tonic g^1 is passed by, its character decidedly changed into a restless seventh of a second-dominant chord, in order to insure the continuation to the lower g. The second entrance of the dactylic scale (m. 26) is spliced into the preceding one by its starting point on g^1; but the flute does not enter until the first-violin line has reached e^1, thereby clearly indicating where the actual progress of the movement is resumed. The scale terminates one step above the desired tonic g, making one more scale approach necessary. This final approach coincides with the last phrase of the chorus. While the voices (m. 31–32) really reconcile the divergent drives from b by spanning the full octave g^1–g, the dactylic scale (which is once again presented in the original instrumentation of flute, bassoon, and first violins) is casually dissolved in the end stretch. One more drive toward g becomes necessary. It is allotted *in toto* to the orchestra. The postlude finally gives the complete answer, repressed since the end of the first vocal phrase (m. 13).

The cohesion of the number can be represented in the following diagram:

PHRASE_____(m. 1–5)
ANSWER_____(m. 5–9)

PHRASE_____(m. 9–13)
Episode
Partial answer, 1st instalment
Episode
Partial answer, 2d instalment
Episode
Partial answer, 3d instalment
ANSWER_____(m. 33–37)

The repression of the final answer is accomplished by an interpolation—set off in the diagram above—which, in turn, becomes 'the main section of the choral movement. Being an interpolation, it keeps alive the necessary tension up to the very end of the composition.

The structure of the number can be analogously represented:

```
STROPHE (2+2+4)          ⎫
ANTISTROPHE (2+2+4)      ⎬ 18
Central cadence on dominant (2)  ⎭
EPODE                    ⎫
  Bar form (2+2+6)       ⎬ 18
  Coda (4+4)             ⎭
```

One recognizes a well-balanced bar form. The strophes are each built on a tonic organ point and, at least in their respective first halves, are identical. The discrepancy of the second halves, as well as their correspondence, has been discussed. The epode introduces new figurations. It is in the dominant, quite often also resting on a real or implied organ point. The extension from the norm by two measures in the subepode of the large epode (m. 23–25) is brought about by the exact repetition of the Salzburg "yodel" figure, which has been singled out before. It is noteworthy that Mozart gladly sacrifices an otherwise rigid proportion to the purely musical force of the repetition typical of the popular slur. The large bar form swings out in a recapitulation (after m. 29), established by a return to the tonic as much as by the actual melodic recapitulation. The binary construction of the coda is easily explained by the fact that the first four-measure unit is vocal and the repetition is instrumental.

As may be expected in any good composition, there is no conflict between content and structure. The dactylic scale figure, which gave meaning to the former, always occurs in structurally significant spots: at the ends of strophe, antistrophe, dominant part of the epode, vocal section, and epode itself. The vocal episodes between these main points of the structure literally fall in line. After the detour to high g^1 at the end of the large antistrophe, the soprano melody gradually sinks back to a, which is reached at the end of the miniature antistrophe of the epode (m. 23). The subepode of the epode finally retrieves the long-expected g, simultaneously with the recapitulation of the large form. The coda, as one remembers, summarizes the reconciliation of the "wrong" g^1 with the wanted g.

The whole number is a good example of another specific execution of the general plan, encountered before, by which a given phrase is wilfully interrupted in order to keep alive the musical movement (and the listener's tension) until final completion.

174

NUMBER 22 / Finale (C MAJOR)

The composition of this finale confronted Mozart with a peculiar problem. On the one hand, the number not only ends an act but also contains the scene after which the whole opera was named. On the other hand, the music has to avoid competition with the two great and complex finales of the second and fourth acts, in order not to endanger the over-all binary structure of the work. Mozart solved the problem by choosing popularly appealing and festive music, the mere mass of which absorbs almost completely the emotional development of the individual characters. Thus a logical opening is left for the fourth act, in which the final climax is reached only through the full exploitation of the heroes' subjective emotions left unexpressed at the close of the third act.

Decisive tempo changes provide an easy clue for the formal organization of the finale. The march (m. 1–60) acts as an introduction to the main wedding scene, similar to the opening march in many of Mozart's serenades (cf. K. 63, 239, etc.). The wedding scene itself is in bow form. The framing sections, in C major like the march, are identical in regard to text and musical material. The *da capo* (m. 186–229) is slightly abbreviated as against the exposition (m. 61–131) but compensates for the missing measures by the richer sound of a chorus as compared to two women's voices and by a fuller orchestra. The middle section (m. 132–185) contrasts strongly in mode and rhythm. The minor tonic relative replaces the major tonic; and a dance with three beats to the measure, the surrounding duple pulsation. The short recitative between middle section and *da capo* provides for the return modulation.

The wedding march deserves to be as popular as its countertypes from *Lohengrin* and *A Midsummer-Night's Dream*. It lends itself well to performance by piano, organ, or any instrumental combination. I know of at least one couple who marched to the altar to Mozart's tune and of one young man who intends to inform any girl who may wish to marry him that the playing of Figaro's march at his own wedding is a condition *sine qua non*. With all its propriety, the march has its rhythmic and harmonic surprises. Breaking away from the standard pattern of sixteen-measure periods, it employs a quatorzain as the basic unit. The fourteen measures recur four times, each time divided by a dominant cadence into eight plus six measures. The harmonies before and after the dominant cadence in the middle vary, however, to such an extent that, for example, the tonality of the march is not established until the final cadence of the first quatorzain. The harmonic relationships of the four repetitions reveal an arrangement mirrored at the center, as the following table indicates:

		HARMONY AT		
	BEGINNING	MIDDLE CADENCE	CONTINU- ATION	FINAL CADENCE
March (m. 1–14)	D	D	SR	T
Second time (m. 15–28)	T	D	TR	D
Third time (m. 29–42)	T	D	TR	D
Fourth time (m. 43–56)	D	D	SR	T

In dynamic terms, the march grows steadily from beginning to end in accordance with the dramatic idea of an approaching procession. The first quatorzain is marked pianissimo. The second adds trumpets and timpani and introduces a gradual crescendo toward the next repeat, which is marked forte. The loud dynamics, in full instrumentation, are maintained up to the end. Five coda measures, all on the tonic chord, terminate the procession.

The first two repetitions of the march are skilfully welded by the contrapunting solo voices, which lead across the gap. The melodic significance of the solo lines is minimal, in accordance with the general finale plan described above. The voices merely resolve the given harmonies into arpeggios. The Countess' line at the beginning of the second quatorzain is typical. Only the last short exclamation of the Count projects his sinister craving for vengeance by a scale spanning a dissonant seventh.

The peculiar organization of the march melody into eight plus six measures is justified by the melodic content. The first eight measures encompass the interval of a seventh, d^1 to c^2. (The note c^1 in measure 2 is an auxiliary. It is introduced, no doubt, in order to lessen the tension produced by the dissonant seventh, at the end of the ascending scale, above the starting note. But it is not part of the main line and does not absolve the ascending scale from treating c^2 like a seventh.) The following six measures fulfil the function of completing the octave span by leading the seventh up to d^2. The repetition of the march faces an analogous problem, with the difference that the scale begins one tone higher, on e^1. At the close of the first eight-measure period the scale has again ascended up to a tension-creating seventh, d^2. The next six measures complete the octave by the prominent high e^2 in the first flute, reinforced in pitch by first horn and trumpet. The compass of the scale in each rendition of the march creates a definite tensile relationship between the two large sections. In the basic key of C major the scale running from d^1 to d^2 has a dissonant dominant function as compared to the scale running from e^1 to e^2, which has a consonant tonic function. Because of the mirrored arrangement of the four march sections, the last one is fundamentally the dominant type. Mozart meets the danger of a non-classical ending by the force of the short coda. There is no other explanation for the highest pitch, e^2, in the first flute, in the last chords. The dissonant d^2 is intentionally topped; otherwise, the cadence would be perfect. The impression of an imperfect cadence, slight as it is, furthermore leaves an opening for the main body of the finale.

The opening and closing allegretto sections of the following bow form are worth comparing in regard to the cuts occurring in the latter. The drive toward the final curtain justifies, dramatically and psychologically, the shortening of expression. What the abbreviated version shows, however, is a distinction between measures and phrases which Mozart considered essential and others which, like playful extensions, he could omit in a da capo without impairing the coherence of the expression. These are the measures in the opening section which are cut in the closing section: 61–72, 82–93, 96–97, and 100–109. What remains in the closing section is a recapitulation bar form (4 + 4 + 8). It follows a one-measure introduction which serves to ascribe to the first melody measure the character of an anacrusis. The recapitulation section of the epode (m. 199–202) is repeated. The rest (m. 206 ff.) is coda, itself another bar form (4 + 4 + 8). The orchestra measures after the end of the choral melody are not heard in the exposition, for they are merely a prolonged tonic chord accompanying the lowering of the curtain.

Against this concise form of the closing chorus, the opening duet sounds playfully extended. The bar form of the whole is preserved, but strophes and epode are each blown up to approximately double size. Of the four extra sections in the opening allegretto, the first is an instrumental prelude anticipating the choral melody. The procedure is similar to that of the chorus in the first act (Nos. 8 and 8a), where an instrumental prelude gave a helping cue to the first statement of the chorus but not to the repetition of the whole number. The next extension (m. 82–93) develops in twelve measures the path from tonic to dominant, which the *da capo* covers in one chord. The last four measures of this section are merely a repetition of the preceding phrase. The main body of eight measures acts like an antistrophe to the opening eight measures, which here form the strophe. The parallelism of strophe and antistrophe is very clearly noticeable in the orchestra; but the rhythms of the voices, too, are closely related. The epode begins, as in the *da capo*, with the melodic phrase to which the new sentence, *a un dritto cedendo*, is set. In keeping with the doubled proportions of the strophes, the epode is extended in each of its subdivisions, which (as in the *da capo*) create a bar form of their own. The substrophes are each doubled by jubilant orchestra responses (m. 96–97 and 100–101), which are omitted in the *da capo*. Four measures preceding the recapitulation (i.e., the subepode of the epode) sound, by force of the open octave span in sudden unison, like a composed fermata on the dominant. Their existence is responsible for maintaining an exact two-to-one relationship between the epodes of the two allegretto sections. The recapitulation, finally, gains length by quoting the full strophe instead of only the second half. The coda (m. 117 ff.) is complete.

The formal identity, in different dimensions, of the two allegretto sections is shown in the following table:

OPENING SECTION	DA CAPO
ORCHESTRA PRELUDE (1+12)	ORCHESTRA INTRODUCTION (1)
STROPHE (8)	STROPHE (4)
ANTISTROPHE (8+4 repeated)	ANTISTROPHE (4)
EPODE (24)	EPODE (12)
Strophe (2 sung + 2 orchestra)	Strophe (2 sung)
Antistrophe (2 sung + 2 orchestra)	Antistrophe (2 sung)
Composed fermata (4)	—
Recapitulation (8, complete strophe + 4, second half repeated)	Recapitulation (4, half strophe + 4, repetition)
CODA (4+4+8)	CODA (4+4+8)
	CURTAIN CHORDS (8)

The andante middle section in triple meter (m. 132–175) is melodically far more complex and therefore not only by placement the real centerpiece of the finale. The rhythm is characteristic of a Spanish dance known as the "fandango." The melodic material is a literal loan from Gluck's pantomimic ballet *Don Juan*,[1] which was written a quarter of a century before Mozart's *Le Nozze di Figaro*. Not only are the two main inventions identical (m. 132 ff. and 146 ff.) but also the tonality. Gluck uses the fandango as one of the numbers heard at a party given by Don Juan. It follows the moment when, the guests having fled after the entrance of the statue, Don Juan brazenly extends a supper invitation to his slain antagonist. A detailed comparison of the Gluck and Mozart versions of the fandango lies outside the method pursued by this analysis. In the opera the dance can and must be heard as an autonomous organism, independently of its historical origin. It is noteworthy, however, that Gluck employs a technique of developing the material with the help of alternating interruptions and resumptions of the main line. Mozart's treatment is similar in principle but subjectively different in execution.

As in most dances, the basic construction of Figaro's fandango is an eight-measure period, symmetrically divided into antecedent and consequent. It is heard in this pure form at the very beginning of the section (m. 132–140). The first halves of antecedent and consequent are identical. Each begins explosively on the fifth and moves down the scale to the tonic. The respective second halves vary in the traditional manner which leads the antecedent to a half-cadence (m. 136) and the consequent to a full cadence. The third measures in each phrase are actually less different in content than they sound: the third of the dominant chord moves to the root of the dominant chord, the short way down in the antecedent and the long way up in the consequent (cf. m. 134 and 138). The only real difference occurs in the respective cadential measures (cf. m. 135 and 139). The whole melody adheres closely to the scale. It undulates around the central pivot of the tonic, *a*, the initial *mi supra la* creating a somewhat tense outside range of a ninth. The musical content of this first period of the andante, or the first full statement of the fandango, must be kept in mind and ears in order to understand the subsequent development.

The remainder of the andante consists of three more repetitions of the dance, each extended in a peculiar fashion. For convenience' sake, the four presentations of the fandango will be referred to as A, B, C, and D. They are heard in the following places:

1. *Denkmäler der Tonkunst in Oesterreich*, Vol. XXX/2, No. 19.

The antecedent of fandango B proceeds with utmost regularity, merely transposed from tonic to dominant. The characteristic half-step *mi supra la* appears as an isolated counterpoint (missing in Gluck's ballet) in the high winds. The counterpoint is retained: in fandango C the first bassoon projects it (m. 156 ff.); and in fandango D, again the first flute and oboe (m. 166 ff.). The consequent of fandango B brings the first extension, in a fashion frequently found in compositions of the Vienna classical school. The first two measures of the consequent are a regular transposition of the model, the half-step on top saved by real, rather than tonal, treatment (as was the case in the antecedent). The third measure, in analogous construction to the model of fandango A, should ascend the scale from d^1-sharp to b^1. The content, but not the manner of execution, is preserved. The melody indeed outlines the expected interval, but an arpeggio figure (borrowed from Gluck) replaces the scale. The achievement, moreover, is stretched across three measures against one measure in the original process. The melodically somewhat stagnant character of these three measures is best summarized by the sustained note b^1 in the flute and b in the oboe. The last measure of the dance (cf. m. 139) actually recurs unchanged except for the transposition (m. 151). Maintaining a proper proportion against the tripled third measure, the fourth measure, as well, occupies three times its original length. The two extra measures are interpolated in anticipation of the cadential scale. They effect a lowering by one octave of the range of the melody. Apart from the shifted range, measure 151 could directly follow measure 146, leaving completely intact the continuity of the musical content.

The two bridge measures help regain the original pitch, on which fandango C begins. The extension pattern is now familiar. As in fandango B, the antecedent and the first two measures of the consequent follow the model of fandango A. An upward shift by a third of the scale in the second measure of the consequent (159) accomplishes a simple modulation to the tonic relative, in vicarious function for the tonic. The triple extension of the third measure is again employed, the sig-

180

nificant melodic point this time sustained in the horns. The final measure of fandango C is concise and is not tripled, as in fandango B. In terms of proportion the need for two extra measures is perhaps answered by the bridge passage introducing fandango C. Fandango D, finally, does not break the bounds of the eight-measure dance period but substitutes at the coverage of the ascending sixth, this time in the antecedent, the arpeggio for the scale. The coda drops to a low range in a manner similar to that at the end of fandango B.

While the four repetitions of the dance can rightly be called variations, their internal relationship gives form to the entire andante section. The arrangement is one of mirrored symmetry around a middle axis, which coincides with the two seemingly extraneous bridge measures:

	ANTECEDENT	CONSEQUENT
Fandango A:	4	4
Fandango B:	4	$2+(1\times3)+(1\times3)$
Fandango C:	4	$2+(1\times3)+1$
Fandango D:	4, varied	4

The second half of the large form is poignantly marked from the very beginning by the low vocal counterpoints of the Count and Figaro. The line of the Count shows the characteristic span from E to d, heard earlier in the act in his duettino with Susanna and his aria. Only in the recitative following the dance does the Count muster the friendly grace properly needed for extending a wedding invitation by resolving the dissonant minor seventh into a full octave (cf. m. 176).

As in the finale of the first act, the usual array of all soloists is abandoned in favor of what may be called, in terms of the whole social conflict underlying the plot, the "democratic element" of the cast. There it was the servant Figaro who claimed the curtain scene for himself. Here it is an impersonal and unheroic aggregation of his friends. The disappearance of the soloists behind a group of people is deliberately planned and prepared in both the first and third acts by the same device of placing a chorus number immediately before the finale. In the third act, various qualities of this chorus (No. 21) tie it closely to the finale itself. The strongest tie is the specific sound of two women's voices, moving mostly in parallel thirds and sixths, which surrounds the wedding march. The key of the first, separate chorus is in dominant relation to the following march. The dominant beginning of the march itself acts as a continuation of the tonality of the preceding chorus and is perhaps explained by it. The recitative severing the chorus from the finale proper, moreover, has its counterpart in the recitative section embodied in the finale. Aurally incorporating the chorus (No. 21) in the finale, one gains the impression of a large bow form:

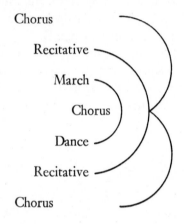

Chorus

    Recitative

        March

           Chorus

        Dance

    Recitative

Chorus

FOURTH ACT

FOURTH ACT

NUMBER 23 / Cavatina (F MINOR)

The girl who sang Barbarina at the first performance under Mozart's baton was twelve years old, and Mozart liked her.[1] These facts explain a few external characteristics of the cavatina: the limited vocal range of one octave, the muted orchestra without any wind instruments, the dependence of the vocal line on instrumental prompting and doubling, and the simple and short construction of the whole. These facts, however, do not explain the real nature of the music. The latter retains its primary significance to the critic. Extra-musical causes serve the composer's inspiration but do not dictate it. Analogously, historical facts assist the critic but do not replace insight.

This cavatina is the only number in the minor mode in the whole opera. (The duet between Susanna and the Count begins in the minor mode but soon shifts to the parallel major.) There are other characters and situations in the drama that might warrant a pathetic turn toward the minor mode more convincingly than a girl in her teens looking for a lost pin. There is an incongruity between the tragic key signature and the innocuous scope of the movement. It is precisely the same incongruity that anyone can notice between the verbal reaction of an emotional, unfledged girl to an event, and the event itself.

The melodic development shows another symptom of the same attitude. It is the divergence of affected exclamations from the simplicity of the main line. The term "affected" should be understood not as a personal banter but in the baroque tradition of signifying a subjectively high emotion. The melody begins on the fifth, a tone of immediate tension as against the self-contained prime. The task of the fifth is to find its resolution down to the tonic. The opening phrase accomplishes half this task before suffering the first interruption. The line in the first violins descends from c^1 in the first two measures via b-flat in the next two to the halfway mark a-flat on the imperfect cadence in measure 5. Even this minute organization is dotted with pathetic little sighs, as which the continual returns to d^1-flat must be heard. The symbolism of the minor sixth pervades the whole baroque; there is hardly a tragic composition which does not use it prominently. As "Dorian repercussion"

1. Anna Gottlieb, who five years later sang the first Pamina.

its expressive quality enriches early Gregorian chant. Here, it is traditionally introduced as a neighboring note to the dominant, bound to it by the semitonus and not free to rise to the octave like the major sixth. But even after the melody begins to descend, the minor sixth retains its emotionally high position. It serves as the ninth in an incomplete dominant ninth chord before it drops back to its point of departure, c^1, at the same time that the main line under it reaches a-flat.

The next phrase (m. 5–9) is not so much an answer to the opening phrase as an interruption of it. The bass stands still on the organ point of the dominant. The strings above, abandoning the established range, undulate in figures reminiscent of an impromptu cadenza. Actually, the chords on the main beats reveal the true nature of the figuration: it is an arpeggio dissolving the dominant triad. Appoggiaturas on each anacrusis echo the half-tone affect sounded in the opening phrase. At the end of the orchestra introduction the hearer is left with the impression that the solution of a task has been attempted (by the descending line from the fifth in the first phrase) but has gone astray by a somewhat undisciplined exploitation of a subjective feeling (the semitonus, hovering above the first line, coloring the dominant arpeggio of the second phrase).

The solo voice repeats the first phrase of the instrumental introduction literally. Again the search for the final resolution is not completed. The interruption occurs at the same place and lands, like the first one, on the dominant triad. The manner in which the interruption proceeds, however, is both more concise and more pathetic. The length is halved to two measures. An impulsive exclamation of the voice soars to the high of the tonic one octave above the desired range. Then it retrieves its original position with the help of a sighing portamento across a diminished fifth. The original minor sixth, d-flat, is at this point moved to the bass—the only, and hence significant, change in the bass progression against that of the instrumental introduction. The resultant augmented five-six chord supports the vocal climax with its own perverse intensity. The half-cadence at the end expresses the character of the grammatical question, "Ah chi sa dove sarà?"

The relationship of Barbarina's statement to the orchestra introduction sounds like that of antistrophe to strophe. The parallelism between the corresponding first halves is exact. The discrepancy in length between the second halves is convincingly compensated by the richer content of the shorter version. It is only logical that the human voice express what happens in a more freely personal manner than the neutral

186

instruments. To strophe and antistrophe, the following return to the tonic (m. 15–23) forms the epode, itself in bar form $(2 + 2 + 4)$. The two miniature strophes augment above the organ point on the dominant the characteristic deviation to the minor sixth. After the half-cadence on the fifth, c^1 (m. 15), the first miniature strophe sustains the minor sixth, d^1-flat, in the first violins and then in the echoing voice; and the miniature antistrophe is dedicated in a sequential pattern to the re-gained c^1. The miniature epode brings crisis and solution (m. 19–23). Barbarina forgoes the resumption of her task of completing the scale down to f. Instead, she indulges in sentimental complaints. The dissonance of an augmented fifth draws her up with a sigh to the range of the earlier interruption, and even her words at this moment bring only an affected reiteration. Her girlish exclamation comes twice before she finds her way back to the pursuit of the main line. While she is thus indulging in her emotional reaction to the loss of the pin, the orchestra takes up the abandoned path. Most noticeable is the arco entrance of the basses, the first in the cavatina after the steady pizzicato. It follows the main line from the dominant downward. The initial accomplishment down to the third serves as a reminder—essential in the time-bound progress of music—of Barbarina's first phrase of similar extent. It also forms a link with Barbarina's last point of departure, the dominant tone clung to by her in the middle of the epode. At the same time, the violas, not muted like the violins, prominently voice the first sigh of the Dorian repercussion; and the first violins, in diminution and quickest motion in the whole number, outline in anticipation the completion of the scale from the third down to the tonic. After her two sentimental exclamations, Barbarina—as if heedful of the corrective efforts of the orchestra—finishes the melody down to the tonic. In doing so, she resumes the whole emotional situation: on the dominant the neighboring sigh is raised and carries its breath into the otherwise directly descending scale. Her brief summarizing of the whole musical content at the end of the epode gives to the large structure the imprint of a recapitulation bar form. The bass, too, initiated into the melodic progress at the arco entrance in the middle of the epode, finds its way down to the tonic. In order to avoid parallel fifths with the soprano (from m. 21 to 22), the leading tone from above is replaced by that from below, the scale thereby being disrupted. The one-measure lead of the bass against the soprano is utilized for a full cadence.

The entire epode of the cavatina is repeated (m. 23–31), be it to compensate for the somewhat scanty extension of the epode as compared to strophe and antistrophe (8 m. versus 15 m.) or to permit Barbarina another plaintive outburst (for the epode is the section most wilfully digressing from the main line). In strophe and antistrophe of the repeated epode, Barbarina still takes her cue from the orchestra; but the straightened line of the suggestive violins shows up all the more her touching appoggiaturas around the dominant.

The coda (m. 31–36) establishes the characterization of Barbarina by tipping the balance in the discrepancy between the completed task of the descending scale and her affected unfocused sighs in favor of the latter. The vocal line abandons the accomplished tonic for pathetic little exclamations around the fifth, on which it had its start. The characteristic minor sixth assumes a strong independence by falling on the accented beats of three successive measures, occupying the center of the surrounding notes, and finally moving into the bass as the foundation of the cadential chord under the dissonant fermata. Barbarina's voice swings out on the sigh of the diminished fifth heard before and ends on the dominant, in both the melodic and the harmonic implications. The half-cadence conveys the impression of the question mark and, in relation to the larger form, the unsuccessful search. The semitone motive fills viola and bass throughout most of the coda.

NUMBER 24 / Aria (G MAJOR)

In external appearance this aria resembles that of the Countess in the preceding act. A slower section is followed by a faster one. The slower section achieves a bow form by means of a real recapitulation (m. 37). The musical content, however, moves on a much simpler level. Not only is Marcellina psychologically less complex than the Countess, but composer and librettist are also decidedly less interested in her characterization than in Rosina's. This is Marcellina's first and only aria. Occurring in the last act, it is meant not so much to give new insight into her personality—apart from the possibility of interpreting the simple facture and expression as means of characterization as valid as the complexity of the Countess' arias—as to provide entertainment on a purely musical level. This point is borne out by Marcellina's minimal emotional involvement in the dramatic situation which evokes this aria and by a number of musical devices which, ingratiating as they may be, are yet conspicuous by their impersonal expression.

One such device is coloratura, which is used excessively in this as compared to any other number in the opera. Not only the mere floridness is surprising but even more so the range. Twice, Marcellina touches high b^1 (m. 82 and 84); seven times, a^1; and repeatedly, almost casually, g^1. Against this achievement one must remember that the highest notes in the Countess' arias are a^1-flat and a^1-natural, respectively, and, in ensembles, a^1-natural. Susanna reaches b^1-flat only once, in the letter duet, and, except for the brilliant runs to high c^2 in the second trio, recognizes a^1 as a top limitation. Another device aimed at aural entertainment rather than musical characterization is the dance rhythm governing both small and large units. The indication, "Tempo di Menuetto," openly professes the derivation of the rhythm of the aria. The same tempo indication is employed in Basilio's aria, which follows Marcellina's, and for the same reason: at this late point of the dramatic development, light amusement becomes preferable to deep revelation. The principle applies to music in general. The last movement of a concerto, symphony, or sonata is usually more playful than the first, just as the closing numbers of a concert will normally be chosen to tax the hearer's attention less than the earlier compositions on the program. In line with this speculation is the fact that Figaro's real minuet in the first act (No. 3)

189

is marked "Allegretto" and not "Menuetto," because at that early dramatic moment the composer's task is the serious one of revealing character rather than the flippant one of providing easy amusement for amusement's sake. In Marcellina's aria the minuet determines the rhythm not only of each measure but also of each phrase and period within the slow section. Apart from the instrumental introduction—the special role of which is the creation of a musical task for the whole, as will be shown—there are caesuras every four measures. Half- and imperfect cadences alternate with full and perfect cadences, shaping the section into regular dance periods. The exposition (m. 13–20) fills the conventional eight-measure pattern with an imperfect tonic cadence in the middle and an imperfect half-cadence at the end. The middle section (m. 21–36) is twice as long as the exposition, not because of expansive new material but rather because of repetitive treatment of motives and phrases. The repetitions are all arranged in such a manner as to preserve the regular dance pattern of four-measure units. Thus the first four-measure phrase is gained through literal repetition of a two-measure motive. The second four-measure phrase, complete in itself, begets by repetition the third, which in turn doubles its length by interpolating a four-measure cadenza before the closing measure. Stripped of extensions, which total eight measures, the middle section is heard as another traditional eight-measure period. It is in bar form $(2 + 2 + 4)$ and thereby contrasts with the freer structure of the exposition, apart from the fundamental contrast provided by the establishment of the dominant tonality. The closing section in the tonic is an exact *da capo* in the manner of the usual dance minuet. The half-cadence at the end, which led into the middle section, here necessitates a coda, which completely submits to the eight-measure dance pattern. Slightly reminiscent of the middle section in rhythm and figuration, it also falls into a regular bar form $(2 + 2 + 4)$ with a little cadenza preceding the final measure.

Against this meticulous regularity of the main body of the section, the instrumental introduction is notably set off by two discrepant elements. One is the chromatic progression, in sequence to the preceding measure, from d^1 via d^1-sharp to e^1 (m. 6–7), which prepares a full tonic cadence. The analogous sung progression (m. 19–20) abandons the chromaticism and forfeits the chance to close the period in the tonic. The other discrepancy is the insertion of four highly figurate measures between the final dominant and tonic chords of the cadence. The result is an exceptional disruption of the conventional eight-measure rhythm.

The influence of the first discrepancy—the chromatic progression—is felt throughout the entire minuet section of the aria. The first phase of the musical problem can be stated in the following terms: a melodious line is presented by the orchestra and noticeably violated by the voice in the subsequent repetition. The violation is startling because it concerns an accepted and familiar norm, according to which a dance tune is struck up by the orchestra in exactly the same way in which the singer eventually projects it. The score does everything possible to call the violation to the hearer's attention. The significance of the chromatic version is set off by an interruption immediately following it. The interruption by the four extra measures mentioned above can do no harm to the structure of the minuet melody, for it occurs before the very last note; but it certainly shocks the hearer into attention at a crucial moment. The playful character of the insertion marks the parenthesis, so to speak, which surrounds it. A figuration in sixteenth-notes replaces the basic movement in eighth-notes. The range suddenly shifts by more than an octave. The bass drops out. A baroque echo is introduced (m. 9 against m. 8), recalling the crucial chromaticism by an imitation at the fifth. The minuet rhythm, most startlingly, is at last totally disrupted by rather complex cross-rhythms projected in a simultaneous dynamic explosion (m. 10–11). Three different rhythms coexist in the forte measures. The basic 3/4 minuet rhythm is implied. Against it, the violins create a hemiolia, the obvious accents falling on the third quarter of measure 10 and the second quarter of measure 11. Below the violins, viola and bass—participating in the 3/2 rhythm in the cadence of measure 11—feign a 6/8 pulse in measures 10 and 12. The listener is not permitted to relax until he hears Marcellina's voice; and then he becomes aware that the chromaticism, which caused all the playful commotion and led to a perfect tonic ending, is partly missing and that the consequent cadence is similarly incomplete. To be more exact: the second half of the chromatic progression (involving d^1-sharp) is missing; and the cadence, by definition, is only a half-cadence.

If the first phase of the musical problem was the violation of an expected norm, the second phase is concerned with the compensation for the missing elements. The composition "owes" the listener the repressed drive promised by d^1-sharp, and a complete tonic cadence. The exploitation of d-sharp gives life to the remainder of the minuet; and the establishment of a full tonic cadence is the central task of the following allegro section.

The middle section of the minuet maintains musical tension by withholding d-sharp consistently while favoring the first chromatic element, c-sharp. The leading tone to the dominant already builds the bridge from exposition to middle section in a bass progression which is the more noticeable as it leads an ascending C-sharp against a simultaneously descending c^1-natural in the voice and first violins (m. 19). Throughout the middle section the chromatic alteration of the fourth recurs in almost every measure. It is reluctantly relinquished shortly before the *da capo*: c^1-sharp moves to c^1-natural (m. 34) but regains the chromaticism once more (m. 35) before yielding to the force of the long-expected crucial d^1-sharp (m. 36). The middle section does not merely totally abstain from sounding d-sharp: it negates it by confirming d-natural as the ruling tonality. Thus the few measures which are free of c-sharp (25, 26, 29, and 30) accomplish nothing more than an arpeggio of the D-major triad, which by its nature is the strongest possible denial of any force generated by d-sharp. The only other chromatic alteration heard in the middle section is a-sharp (m. 34). Its origin is twofold. It was first introduced as an accompaniment to the important c^1-sharp (m. 5) and then repeated as a playful imitation at the fifth of the other meaningful chromaticism, d^1-sharp (m. 8 and 9). In regard to both derivations, the chromatic alteration of a is of a secondary nature as compared to the other two alterations. At the end of the middle section (m. 34), too, it fulfils a mediatory task subservient to both c^1-sharp and d^1-sharp, vicariously reinforcing the former and announcing the return of the latter.

The long-repressed d^1-sharp introduces the *da capo* in an exposed and expressive manner (m. 36). It seems significant that even in this little ornamental turn the rehabilitation of d^1-sharp is tied up with a cancellation of the other chromaticism, c^1-sharp. The final exploitation of this task fills the coda (m. 45–52). The *da capo*, by its nature, brings no new development. The two miniature strophes of the coda take care of nullifying c^1-sharp. The beginnings of both strophe and antistrophe (m. 45 and 47)—where in the analogous spots in the middle section c^1-sharp was firmly proclaimed by the solo voice—place a deliberate c^1-natural on top of a D-major triad. The original chromatic alteration vanishes in a faint trill (m. 44, 46, and 48). The epode of the coda finally gives vent to the promised, but withheld, chromatic alteration of d^1. The solution is delightful in its originality. The note d-sharp is enharmonically reinterpreted as e-flat and supported by its satellite a-sharp in an analogous enharmonic reinterpretation as b-flat. There is no other reason for the peculiar harmonic turn before the allegro. It would be begging the question simply to state that there is a sudden introduction of surprising harmonies, such as the minor subdominant, the diminished seventh chord, and a secondary minor subdominant and altered dominant to the dominant. These chords are chosen not as arbitrary sensual stimuli but as forceful representatives of the musical problem presented in the first measures of the aria by two chromatic alterations. Up to the fermata, e^1-flat ($= d^1$-sharp) is heard as the highest tone in the solo line. It is relayed down to the bass and becomes the foundation of a special chord, stressed by accent and fermata. By name, this chord is easily identified as an augmented sixth chord $[(\mathord{\underset{5\flat}{D}}^7)D]$. Such an identification reveals nothing about its special meaning at this moment. Its content can be explained by reference to the specific chromatic problem of the aria. The augmented sixth chord derives its peculiar tension from the interval of the augmented sixth, which in this case is spanned precisely by e-flat and c-sharp, the two original chromaticisms. Between them, the only note sounded is g, the focal tonality point of the whole aria. Within this dissonant chord, perfect balance is maintained by making E_1-flat the strong foundation, above which the solo voice holds the tonic note before sinking back to c^1-sharp on its way to the ultimate relaxation. By now, c-sharp has accepted a role subordinate to e-flat. Against the powerful bass of the latter, it contents itself first with a passing and ornamental function (last beats of m. 51 and 52) and that of a middle voice (under the fermata, m. 52). The subdued position in the augmented sixth chord is particularly symptomatic in contrast with the typical allocation of the augmented interval to the outer voices.

The allegro section is far less problematic than the minuet section. One remembers how in the Countess' second aria the faster section following the slower one presented a triumphant solution of a melodic problem stated in the beginning. The completion of the interrupted line was tantamount to a character development. Here, in an analogously constructed aria, one experiences far less triumph, because Marcellina's musical problem in the slower section is far less challenging than that of the Countess. Nor does the aria help develop Marcellina's character. For such an attempt, as has been said initially, the time in the opera is too late. The allegro, to be sure, will not ignore the preceding musical content; but it will be more concerned with immediate entertainment than with reflective problems.

The allegro hardly leaves the main harmonic functions of the basic tonality. The middle section rests entirely on a tonic organ point (m. 64–74), which is actually sounding in the first and last four measures and is implied in the central three measures. The framing sections of the allegro are built on simple tonic cadential progressions. The only note in the vocal line not indigenous to G major is the familiar d^1-sharp (m. 82–84). Its double employment at the end of a brilliant and climactic coloratura passage provides the final compensation for its suppression in Marcellina's opening period in the minuet. Orchestral middle voices throughout the allegro contribute to the same goal. The first instrumental chromaticism involves the same d^1-sharp (m. 61); the moment is prominently marked by the resultant augmented triad—a rather uncommon sound in this opera—under a vocal peak. Nor can the next d-sharp escape attention, for it coincides with the dynamically and texturally distinguished entry of the closing section (m. 75 ff.). The immediate corrective naturalization of the dominant by the voice in the very same measure and by the bass in the second half of the phrase does not prevent a renewed assertion of the chromaticism (m. 79), which prepares the final turn of the following coloraturas.

Against this prevalence of d-sharp the fleeting sound of c-sharp (m. 62) is merely a playful recollection of an earlier situation. It is heard in passing while the alto voice and first violins are still holding a c^1-natural; it is immediately canceled by the same bass voice in a determined loud progression; and it recurs no more. The only two other chromaticisms in the allegro section play a secondary role. They neither create new problems nor contribute to the solution of old ones. The note f-natural (m. 64 and 66) is reminiscent of the very first playful cadenza (m. 10) and of the surprise turn at the end of the minuet (m. 50). It probably also imitates at a related interval the preceding naturalization of c. The note g-sharp (m. 89) is in many respects less logical and therefore perhaps intended as a parting jocular surprise. A few loose connections with earlier drives could be traced; suffice it to say that this last chromatic alteration sounds like an attempted negation of the tonic itself at a moment when such a negation is completely fruitless.

The relative simplicity of the allegro section, which, paired with brilliant vocal display, insures its entertainment value, projects directly in the melodies of the opening and closing sections. The opening section (m. 54–63) employs the kind of melody popular in the *Singspiel*. Two four-measure phrases are joined in such a way as to produce a close approximation of the ideal norm called the "song type" by Wilhelm Fischer.[1] The task of the melody is the descent from the fifth to the tonic with a short detour to the neighboring sixth. The antecedent reaches a half-cadence on the supertonic; the consequent, by means of a sequence by step, attains the completion. The two-measure coda reveals its appendix character by word repetition, apart from the chromaticisms discussed earlier and the melodic summarization of the content. The closing section (m. 75 ff.) follows fundamentally the same song-type pattern. Two four-measure phrases correspond in expression and treatment closely enough to the opening section to suggest a bow form for the whole allegro section. The period is extended with the help of an imperfect cadence. The coda to the closing section contains the climactic coloraturas, which lead on a full perfect cadence (m.86) into the coda of the aria itself.

The orchestration, like that of Barbarina's preceding cavatina, creates a specific timbre by being confined to strings alone.

1. "Zur Entwicklungsgeschichte des Wiener klassischen Stils," *Studien zur Musikwissenschaft*, III (1915), 24–84.

NUMBER 25 / Aria (B-FLAT MAJOR)

This aria, like Marcellina's preceding one, has been severely criticized by most people who have given it any thought. Scholars point out that it is a stopgap for one of the few places where Da Ponte left Beaumarchais' secure model. Stage directors and conductors usually omit this number in performances. It contributes nothing to the plot. It tells a story extraneous to the opera. At best it reveals something of Basilio's character; but the characterization is in words more than in music and, moreover, occurs at too late a moment in the opera—it is Basilio's only aria—to warrant new interest in the audience for a mere deuteragonist. By comparison, the only place where one really cares to learn something from the solo aria of a similar intrigant of secondary importance, namely, Bartolo, is at his first appearance, where the aria actually occurs.

Even though all these criticisms are true, a good deal can be said in defense of Basilio's aria. If one does not expect too much of it, it still provides good entertainment. The same reasoning is applicable as to Marcellina's aria. At this late moment of the opera, one should not hope for more than entertainment from as accessory a character as either Marcellina or Basilio. And as pure entertainment this aria offers much— not according to the timeless values of the rest of the opera, to be sure, but certainly according to the gallant rococo taste of the audience for which it was originally written. Opera in the eighteenth century was not solely a plot with music but simultaneously a concert by an ensemble of singers, of whom each wanted his solo. Perhaps this number and the preceding one are the inevitable price one pays for casting secondary parts to good singers.

One hears a variety of three tempos and meters. The longest and richest part, as in Marcellina's aria, is marked "Tempo di Menuetto." The association with the dance, modern to Mozart's contemporaries, alone spells amusement. The subsequent allegro, here as there, is not so much an independent section as an extended closing cadence. The opening andante is an introduction with the primary purpose of setting the stage for the events related during the minuet. The subordinate functions of the outer sections, both in duple meter, help put into sharper focus the central dance.

197

The outstanding entertainment feature in the minuet is the descriptive use of music, imitating events of the physical world. We know, and Mozart knew even better, that imitation of physical objects and events as practiced by the other arts is against the true nature of music.[1] Whenever he stoops to programmatic devices (e.g., the bells in the second duet of this opera; the heartbeat in Belmonte's second aria in *Die Entführung aus dem Serail*; or the triple knock in *Die Zauberflöte*), he incorporates them in the purely musical structure and thereby transforms them into properties of absolute music.

The musical imitations of the storm and the wild beast in Basilio's aria, however, remain on the level of program music. They sound like popular concessions to rococo taste. Mozart's contemporaries knew this kind of musical description from most of the current song literature, which abounded in it. It was usually connected with a narration bound to a dramatic situation. Even though these characteristics reveal the model of the earlier baroque opera, they are typical of the rococo song. Only the later nineteenth-century song convincingly abandons them in favor of consolidated projection of a mood. Accordingly, Basilio's aria is really a song. It tells a story, unlike any other aria in the opera; and it employs devices befitting, in the late eighteenth century, musical entertainers at a social party rather than operatic heroes.

Musical imitation of a storm was an old stand-by in Mozart's days. There is nothing original in Basilio's version (m. 49–56) that cannot be found, for instance, in the opening scene of Gluck's *Iphigénie en Tauride* (1779). The inner strings drive up a dark tremolo before joining the first violins in an imitation of the pelting rain. The bass stirs aggressively and falls heavily across an octave with the hail. The flute whistles. The horns blast (*sf* at *rimbomba il tuono*). The whole orchestra is torn by fluctuating and exploding dynamics. Apart from the program, the musical content is thin. The vocal line is insignificant. It becomes merely a part of the simple harmonic progression T(D)TR.

The description of the wild beast (m. 70–79) is similarly obvious. Chromatic unison slides across a subdominant tetrachord imitate the howling and growling of the voracious animal. Regular alternation of forte and piano throughout the episode (ten changes in all) heightens the effect. When the subdominant moves to the dominant (m. 75), the figuration changes. The obstinate tremolo in the second violins no doubt portrays Basilio's fear. The jumping forte chords in the winds

1. See pp. 24 f., 153.

198

quickly become associated with the threatening animal. The intermediate piano measures echo them, giving Basilio a chance to articulate his story.

The linking of the two episodes by a single sudden chord (m. 69) sounds somewhat casual. Both episodes lead into similar short musical sections marked by persistent afterbeats in the upper strings (m. 57–68 and 80–86). The second of these sections is entirely in unison; the first, partly so. After the storm episode the words corroborate the distinct impression one gains that the shy afterbeats are meant to illustrate Basilio's disappearance behind the sheltering ass's skin, particularly when the softly entering clarinets (m. 64) seem to put a final cover above all other musical movement. After the beast episode the words do not yet narrate the eventual rescue; but analogy with the earlier spot makes one suspect that already at this moment (m. 80 ff.) Basilio is contemplating the particular manner in which he will save himself. The final salvation is thus preserved for the recapitulation of the minuet tune (m. 87 ff.)—a welcome subordination of the literary program to principles of absolute music.

The minuet sections (m. 42–49 and 87–102) help lift the programmatic illustrations from the role of external trimmings to a position within the total musical structure (which, one confesses, is somewhat slight). The episodes become the middle section of the minuet, the chromatic howling of the beast initiating exactly the return to the recapitulation—a point where thematic development and formation properly cease.

The minuet sections are carriers of pure musical ideas in other respects, too. The opening period, simple as it is, yet begets two melodic impulses, which the composition (being by Mozart—program music or not) will have to resolve in its course. One, by far the stronger of the two, springs from the fourth, e-flat (m. 48), which will have to find its way up to the resolving fifth. The import of e-flat as a challenging dissonance, apart from its nature, is pronounced by its position at the acme of the line, isolation by skips (one of them a bad dissonance) on both sides, and harmonization as an extra dissonance in a seventh chord. The second melodic impulse, relatively minute, comes from the leading tone A (m. 44 and again, significantly, 48). Although it can easily be accepted as a neighboring note of B-flat with no further obligation of its own except to return to the tonic, one has learned in the course of the opera (and Mozart's work in general) that the composer favors the treatment of any dissonance as a passing tone. Hence one may expect a resolving G somewhere, to complete—together with the expected ƒ—the full octave scale.

The episodes between exposition and recapitulation are so preoccupied with programmatic descriptions that they thoroughly ignore the melodic problem set out by the opening tune. Such temporary unconcern with the musical task on hand is rare in Mozart, who usually ties every episode—every note, one is tempted to say—to the over-all development of a movement.

The melodic resolutions of the two initial impulses actually make up the musical content of the recapitulation. The recapitulation is twice as long as the exposition. The nonmusical reason may be that the text of the beast episode has not been exhausted after the first eight measures. This reason has a musical origin, anyway, in the deliberate shortening of the preceding syncopated unison section in favor of the emotional impact of the recapitulation. But the real musical reason is the need for resolution of the introduced dissonances, which—as a reminder after the long, diverting middle sections—are first exactly repeated, together with the whole first eight-measure period (m. 87–94). An added chromatic bridge between the two phrases (m. 90) is the only musical indication that the wild beast has not been quite dispensed with.

The new period (m. 94 ff.) ties up all loose ends. The animal finally departs with a last tremolo in the second violins and the familiar anacrustic jumping chords, as the main line of the minuet melody progresses to its destination. The crucial e-flat is first forcefully resumed (the first forte in the recapitulation) and in the next measure, with equal strength, is propelled up to the expected ƒ (m. 96). In the return from the fifth to the tonic, the descending line is interrupted only by the marked low G, the other anticipated resolution. Both resolutions are projected as part of consonant harmonies (T and S, respectively), contrary to the original impulses which were introduced by dissonant seventh chords.

The juncture with the concluding allegro is skilful: the opening phrase (m. 102–106), while already in the new tempo, still belongs by content to the preceding minuet. The first half of the short first-violin phrase (m. 102–103) emphasizes the accomplished resolution of the descending leading tone; the second half joins Basilio in part of his concise and summarizing scale past the fourth up to the fifth and back to the tonic; and the whole unit, although prominently placed in the allegro, never returns.

The rest of the aria is given to a coda. Its nature is simply an extended tonic cadence, most clearly recognizable in the bass line. Its form is a recapitulation bar (8 + 8 + 16), in which the identical strophes sound off a victorious march repeated in the instrumental postlude. The incongruity of a military triumph with Basilio's accomplishment of successfully hiding under an ass's skin is funny. Apart from all these qualities, the purely musical content of the coda provides a melodically meaningful summary. The voice first brags, in unison with the whole orchestra, about the secured f (m. 106–110). The original difficulty was not great, but the shouting is loud. Then the line succinctly relives the initial task and its successful solution by following the scale from the tonic up to the fifth, past the dissonant fourth, and by returning back to the tonic (m. 111–114). The antistrophe (m. 114–122) repeats the strophe exactly, the second half intensified by a few added wood winds.

The line in the epode (m. 122 ff.) is fundamentally the same as in the strophes but is widened by accessory reminiscences. The second melodic accomplishment, g, which has thus far been ignored in the coda, makes itself climactically heard one octave above the expected pitch, soaring as a free sixth above the dominant. The repeated descent from the climax (m. 122–125 and 125–128) harks back to the wild-beast episode by its chromaticism, fluctuating dynamics, and unison treatment. The last vocal phrase (m. 128–132) brings a last musical summary in augmentation: with each downbeat the line slowly ascends the scale until (in m. 131) it joins forces with the magnetic tones f and g, which an implied counterpoint of the upbeats has isolated. Besides constituting the recapitulation of the large allegro bar form, the instrumental postlude, in its only dominant measure (135), employs a melodic contour reminiscent of the beginning of the minuet.

The introductory andante has not yet been discussed. Apart from ushering in the main events of the fable, it owns little to its merit. A few devices tickle the ear with light amusement. Thus the peculiar skips in Basilio's inflection (particularly m. 10 ff.) sound like caricature, and the self-righteous martial cadence at the end of his first sentence (m. 15) anticipates by a short dotted phrase the rhythm of the final march. One's imagination influenced by the prevalence of program music in this aria, one suspects a description of the *piccolo abituro* in the diminution of the accompanying first-violin scale (cf. m. 25–27), and of the *somaro* in the heehaws (*Iah*, to Mozart) of the wind chords, fortepiano across three bar lines, expressively backed by peculiar horn swells (m. 29–32).

The proportions of the aria as a whole emerge well balanced in the following diagram:[2]

INTRODUCTION_____41

MAIN SECTION_____60
    Minuet, 8
      Storm episode, followed by syncopations, 20
        Bridge measure (69), in exact center of aria, 1
      Beast episode, followed by syncopations, 17
    Minuet, 16

CODA_____37
    Bridge, 4
    Recapitulation bar form, 8 + 8 + 16

2. The added numbers of measures of the subordinate sections do not exactly equal the total number of measures of the whole aria because of several elisions, which are counted twice.

NUMBER 26 / Aria (E-FLAT MAJOR)

Apart from a good deal of fun, one notices in this aria at first hearing several very sharp caesuras. They occur in measures 36, 48, 70, 77, and 102. The cadences at these caesuras are all perfect and, except for the next to the last one, also authentic. They alternate regularly between tonic and dominant. Of the six sections set off by the caesuras, the last one (m. 102–111) obviously fulfils a coda function. The third and fifth sections (m. 49–70 and 77–102) are almost entirely identical. The first and fourth sections (m. 24–36 and 71–77) employ the same text but different music. The second section (m. 37–48) stands by itself, recurring in no way. Uncommon in this organization is the ignoring of the music of the opening two sections, usually carrying the most significant invention, in the subsequent movement. The following structure emerges:

Section A_____T_____13 m.
       B_____D_____12 m.
       C_____T_____22 m.
       D (text of A)_____D(T^v)____7 m.
       C_____T_____26 m.
       Coda_____T_____10 m.

Section D can well be eliminated as a formative element. It is extraordinarily short in comparison to the other sections. The musical material is an unimpressive combination of recitative style and cadential formula. Contrary to section B, which really stands in the dominant from beginning to end, the dominant here is heard in relation to the tonic rather than as a temporarily independent harmony. The cadence, accordingly, notwithstanding the uncontradicted a-natural, sounds more like a preparatory half-cadence in the tonic than like a concluding cadence in the dominant. The text, moreover, is not new; it is only a quick condensation of the incomparably richer opening section. Relegating section D, on the basis of these reasons, to a mere bridge passage, one can conceive of the total structure as being in bar form:

STROPHE	T	13 m.
ANTISTROPHE	D	12 m.
EPODE (bar form 4 + 4 + 14)	T	22 m.
BRIDGE	"	
EPODE, repeated	"	
CODA	"	

The logical cohesion of the elemental bar form can readily be explained in spite of a few irregularities. The special purpose of the repetition of the epode will demand an extra reason.

The correspondence between strophe and antistrophe is normally based on identity or at least on similarity of parts. That it can be derived from contrast and lack of similarity has been pointed out by Alfred Lorenz: "Melodic sections of a composition can be vicariously replaced without disregard for correspondence or damage to form. This 'free symmetry' can be developed into a 'symmetry by contrast' when . . . directly contrasting motives are related to each other in such a manner that a convincing rhythm of the whole form can be felt."[1]

Strophe and antistrophe in this aria differ completely in regard to musical content. Yet they are linked by a certain correspondence in the sense defined by Lorenz. They match one another in length and, jointly, the epode. Each is set off by incisive breaks in the flow of the music. Each has a clear-cut beginning and end. The final cadence of each is full and perfect. Each is unified throughout by one ruling tonality. Even in the antithesis of tonic and dominant lies a closeness of relation. The text, finally, reveals indisputably the relationship between strophe and antistrophe. One glance at the libretto shows that the aria consists of two stanzas of four lines each, followed by a lengthy section more freely organized. The meter in the stanzas is iambic, three feet to the line; the rhyme pattern, in a somewhat lax manner, *aabc dffc*. The poetic function of the stanzas is to usher in the unflattering list of female attributes contained in the subsequent long and loose section. The stanzas stand like two heralds at a portal which opens beyond them. They are similar in meaning. The two musical strophes correspond to them.

The fact that the music of neither strophe returns shifts the emphasis onto the epode. Apart from the eventual repetition of the epode, other forces are at play to concentrate on it the listener's best attention. For one, it is a well-organized unit cast in bar form. Strophe and antistrophe

1. *Der Ring des Nibelungen* (Berlin, 1924), p. 123 (translation by S. L.).

are both binary, the former by repetition and the latter by sequence. The figuration of the accompanying orchestra changes with each strophe and the epode. Strings predominate. The mid-point between strophes and epode (m. 57) is marked by the recovery of the tonic. Stronger forces than mere organization, however, make the epode of the larger form the most attractive section of the aria. The music is loaded with tricks of the trade proved as popular charmers. The harmonies do not go beyond the main chords of tonic, subdominant, and dominant until the last cadential phrase, where a few secondary chords sneak in. The voice is free of affected melismata, the rapid syllabic recitation, as in Bartolo's aria, hitting the ears in typical Italian buffo manner. With the increasing rapidity the line rises in pitch and loudness to a bombastic climax, sustained for two and a half measures. The gradual crescendo above an organ point and alternating tonic and dominant harmonies was popularized by the Mannheim school one generation before Mozart and still exercised a strong audience appeal when Rossini used it thirty years after *Figaro*. Not only are rise and fall within the melody straight and counterpoised, but the goal of each line is so obviously in the ear from the beginning that the hearer must feel a complacent satisfaction when he is actually given the expected sound. The principle of repetition runs rampant. Every little phrase is repeated literally or in sequence, or mostly both. The score bears out this point more clearly and directly than words can; but two examples, out of the many possible ones, may be given. The first is taken from the antistrophe within the epode (m. 53–57) where the step descending from the peak is repeated in a sequence down the scale and then four times on the new level before the whole phrase—sequence, repetition, and all—is repeated in a sequence of its own. The second example follows the first in the score: the opening phrase of the epode is repeated four times in just as many measures before the line is permitted to progress. Around all these devices the orchestra sparkles with alluring trimmings. There are trills, tremolos, pizzicati, sforzati, and a deliberate pyramiding of the winds toward the climax. Coincident with the cumulative cataloguing of the treacherously bewitching qualities of women, the epode of the large form—no doubt is left—becomes the *pièce de résistance* of the aria.

Are strophe and antistrophe neglected, and is the second half of the bar form repeated in order to focus the listener's attention on the gaiety of the epode? An affirmative answer is only partly true; it does not fathom the core of the somewhat unusual formal scheme. The casual treatment of strophe and antistrophe shows up the brilliance of the epode, to be sure. But this brilliance is not an end in itself. The repetition does not serve to heighten the emphasis of the epode; rather, the other way around, the first statement of the epode is rigged up to catch the audience' attention in preparation for the repetition. For, with the help of a few small alterations, the repetition becomes the vehicle of a musical joke; and one may rightly suspect that the musical expression of the joke is the primary concern of the composition, responsible for the organization of the whole material with all its irregularities.

The material for the joke is supplied by the next to the last line of the text, which even in the poem is marked by being an extra insertion in an otherwise regular stanza, rhyming with none of the other four lines. Figaro is working his philippic against women up to a culminating invective. These sirens, these frauds and liars, he exclaims, are capable of doing anything to us foolish men. Enough said. "Il resto nol dico." The musical joke lies in exploiting this covert sentence. Music can express the idea of "not saying something" only with the help of an extra-musical trick. The mere negation of expression is paradoxical in an art like music, which lives by always saying something. A composition can convey the idea of "not saying something" only in relation to a prior realization of having said something. It cannot convey the idea directly in absolute terms, as it can, for instance, convey the idea of disappointment or fulfilment. Now one understands the role of the epode and the relationship of the slightly altered repetition to it. The first epode says something in clear and easily remembered terms. The repetition of the epode startles the hearer by a few crude gaps at suggestive points. The second half of each of the two sentences in both substrophes is missing— four gaps, all in all. "Il resto nol dico." The last complete epode actually said what the repetition may now omit. Only in reference to the full epode does the altered version convey the idea that something is not being said. The suggestive interruptions cannot be missed. The solo voice drops from its leading role to that of a supporting bass. The difference in range alone is close to an octave. The accompanying strings yield altogether to a somewhat vulgar band ensemble. One can now comprehend the economic wisdom which excluded wind instruments altogether from the corresponding place in the first epode. The cumulative effect of the four stopgaps of "il resto nol dico" is supported by an assimilation of the retained sentence fragments to each other.

The repetition of the subepode is exact. The most brutal form of the joke is reserved for the coda. What does the whole world know about women that Figaro, as man to men, does not wish to say? The solo horns say it. They illuminated Figaro's fear of being cuckolded the first time he suppressed naming it (m. 68); they identify it here (m. 102 ff.). The association is too obvious to be missed.[2] One quickly laughs about Figaro's wariness of being horned himself.

2. See the pertinent paragraph in the criticism of the duettino, No. 2 (p. 26).

NUMBER 27 / Aria (F MAJOR)

Of all the numbers in the opera, this one is the most elusive. It sounds like a simple *canzonetta*, but it conveys a loving woman's deepest feelings. Susanna sings alone on the stage for the first time in the course of the whole work, but her real figure is sheltered by the Countess' dress she is wearing; and Figaro, moreover, though not visible, is eavesdropping in the wings. The flow of her emotions is directed toward her husband, but in his opinion the philandering Count may well be the desired destination. The critic experiences this elusiveness by a supreme difficulty in verbalizing what reaches him as an entrancingly sensuous event. One marvels at the complete coincidence of musical structure and total impression on people both on and off the stage.

The implied double meaning of the aria comes out in musical symptoms of tempo, instrumentation, form, and melody structure.

In the absence of a specific tempo indication at the beginning of the aria in the autograph, one can only speculate about Mozart's intention; but all considerations seem to favor a much faster tempo than the traditional one commonly heard nowadays. First, one must not underrate the true *canzonetta* character of the piece. It moves in two beats to the measure, not six. The dotted triplet figures are the undeniable inheritance of a quick dance rhythm. The mood of a sprightly serenade is conveyed not only by the call of the words but also by the rhythmic strumming of the strings. Furthermore, one may rightly wonder whether the tempo indication "Allegro vivace assai" at the beginning of the preceding accompanied recitative is not meant to rule the aria as well. It is not likely that Mozart simply forgot to write down the tempo of a number in an otherwise carefully written score, though such an omission is possible (cf. Nos. 5, 10, 11, and 23—four out of twenty-nine). One can speculate more closely by looking at the tempo markings in the other arias which are preceded by an accompanied recitative, namely, Nos. 17, 19, and 26. The Count's and Countess' arias in the third act each strike a new tempo after their respective recitatives. In No. 17, the request for "Allegro maestoso" after "Presto" ["Tempo I"] is as clearly written down as in No. 19 that for "Andante" after "Allegretto" (the tempo indication at m. 10 of the recitative is spurious). In Figaro's aria, however, as in Susanna's, a specific tempo indication is missing. It is not needed, for the probable reason that the "Andante" of the recitative applies also to the main piece. By analogy one is justified in speculating that in Susanna's aria the initial "Allegro vivace assai" is meant to be carried through the entire number. The analogy alone is, of course, no proof, but it supports the directly musical reasons for the relatively fast tempo mentioned earlier. If one accepts the allegro quality of the aria, one must needs be aware of the basic *double-entendre*. The lyrical, almost sentimental, content of the serenade seems to contradict the underlying quick dance pulse. Favoritism for the former is responsible for the one-sided current interpretation in most performances. The peculiar ambiguity of the aria is its main characteristic and charm.

The instrumentation helps project it by the consistent employment of dualisms. Against the strumming strings the wood winds lead throughout a melodically independent life. Within the small wood-wind ensemble itself, oboe and bassoon intimate duplicity by hardly ever leaving a line alone. They play in open octaves, parallel tenths, interwoven arpeggios, or free little canons. The specific timbre of the bassoon manifests the existence of an undercurrent, for it has been repeatedly heard in the course of this opera in a similar suggestive role (cf. No. 16 and others). The double-dealing of the two reed instruments is occasionally covered by an alluring sparkling of the flute, particularly in structurally significant moments such as cadences. The glistening top notes dispel any possible misinterpretation of Susanna's double play as falsehood. The little scale cadenzas in sixteenth-notes always point up in the flute (m. 29, 43, 61, and 73), counteracting the descending trends of the reeds below (m. 29, 61, 73) or before (m. 43, 73).

The form of the aria is equally open to divers interpretations in spite of its apparent external simplicity. The text supplies five rhyming couplets grouped into two strophes of four lines each followed by a single concluding couplet. The first and last couplets are loosely related by containing the direct appeal, *vieni*, whereas the central verses describe the amorous atmosphere of the trysting place. The musical form is clear in so far as it establishes three sections parallel to the text. The end of the first section is marked by a short instrumental postlude and a cadence in the dominant (m. 44); and that of the second section, by a new arco figuration in the first violins and a return to the tonic (elision in m. 56). The outer sections exceed in length, to approximately the same extent, the middle section. The result can be seen in the following table:

FIRST STROPHE (*vieni*)	T	20 m.
SECOND STROPHE	D	12 m.
THIRD STROPHE (*vieni*)	T	19 m.

The bow form follows the recapitulation idea of the text (*vieni*) approximately, but by no means exactly. The greatest divergence lies in the musical emphasis given to the third strophe, which in the poem is the shortest. It is the treatment of this third strophe which creates the ambiguity characteristic of the aria. According to the meaning of the words, tonality, and proportion as expressed in the table above, the third strophe forms the closing section of a ternary bow form. According to the structure of the poem and the weighty musical content, the third strophe can also be heard as the epode of a binary bar form. The poem strengthens this impression by the structural parallelism of the first two strophes, against which the more concise and personal last couplet is decidedly contrasted. The tonal distinctions, too, can be argued either way. The second strophe does not stay away from the tonic longer than the first, except that the directions are inverted (T–D versus D–T). The epode, on the other hand, temporarily dips into the hitherto untouched subdominant region (*e*-flat in m. 62 and 66). Even the proportions can easily be figured in favor of a bar form, for music is subject to other laws than exact mathematics. Strophe and antistrophe become about equal if one considers the orchestra prelude as pertaining to the whole aria rather than merely the first strophe—exactly equal by sung measures (12 each) and approximately equal if one hears the two intermediate instrumental measures (43 and 44) as a postlude to the first strophe rather than a playful central pivot. Against these balanced strophes the third section forms a well-weighted epode. The adequate measure count (17 versus 24, disregarding the purely instrumental measures, or 19 versus 26, including them) is brought up to par by the three fermatas, which in this kind of context signify an indefinite time lapse measurable in psychological rather than mathematical terms.

The over-all rhythm of the phrases broadens the epode in one other persuasive respect. Strophe and antistrophe have pulsated in a *ritmo di tre battute*, which by nature sounds hasty in relation to the norm. With the epode, the wave suddenly swells to a full four-measure rhythm. The expansive effect of the change (m. 56 ff.) is inescapable. It is enlarged

211

by the continued—and always even-numbered—dilation of the quadruple principle in the course of the epode. Two measures (61 and 62) are inserted between the first full phrase and its consequent. The consequent itself (middle of m. 62 to middle of m. 66) participates in the broadening process first by demanding a repetition on the strength of a deceptive cadence. Then the repetition grows by half the original length with the help of two augmentations (m. 68 and 71) and a detour to the subdominant (m. 70). The latter is the outgrowth of the skilful preparation by the earlier flattened seventh (e-flat in m. 62 and 66).

Adding to the weight of the epode are, instrumentally, the change from pizzicato to arco and, vocally, the prominent single climax on a^1 which tops the steep immediate curve of a tenth.

The formal *double-entendre* can be perceived by comparing the following table with the earlier one, a binary solution against the earlier ternary one:

INTRODUCTION, T————————————6

STROPHE, T–D————————————14
    4 three-measure phrases

ANTISTROPHE, D–T————————————12
    4 three-measure phrases

EPODE, T (with new S elements)————————19
    3 four-measure phrases, extended
    Fermatas
    High a^1
    Arco
    Most personal, single text couplet

The ambiguity of form invades the bar form itself, depending on the function one wishes to ascribe to the epode. One can argue that it merely represents a coda, a drawn-out cadence, to the two preceding main strophes. The bass progression and the many fermatas seem to favor this solution. It may, on the other hand, be heard as the crowning synthesis of the loosely joined earlier statements. The intensity of the vocal line leading up to the climax and the new lush string timbre sound as exalted as the most personal appeal of the last sentence of the poem. Independently of these two solutions, recapitulation elements pervade the

212

epode. The return to the tonic on a full cadence in the beginning is as noticeable as the quotation from the instrumental introduction by the postlude. The scales in sixteenth-notes, absent from the second strophe, emphasize the recapitulation quality throughout the epode.

One may wish to utilize the idea of the recapitulation for reconciling the binary and ternary formal concepts of the piece. A recapitulation bar form in many respects approaches a bow form. The specific double meaning of Susanna's aria, however, easily admits of two structural interpretations. One remembers a similar congruity of content and structure from Cherubino's aria in the first act. The same technique is used for different purposes—there to characterize the conflicting impulses of the adolescent, here to indicate the seductive *double-entendre* of the love call.

Susanna's melody structure—as much as tempo, instrumentation, and form—carries out this ambiguity. The most intricate outward symptom is the interweaving of melodic and harmonic elements to the extent that the main line becomes obscured by the sheer sensuality of the movement. It is as if the melody were supplying its own harmonization. Steps expand into arpeggios, and chords are filled in by steps. A similar melodic undulation characterizes the letter duet (No. 20) with the same intriguing effect of elusive charm.

The opening six-measure period of the oboe sets the norm. An arpeggio of the tonic triad across a full octave establishes the tonality. One associates this particular arpeggio with earlier expressions of Susanna's (cf. Nos. 1 and 5). Then the line begins to ascend the scale. Reversing the direction of the arpeggio, it fills the open skips with cogent steps. There is a short halt, coincident with the end of the phrase, on the fifth. It is the same tone which generated the opening impulse of the melody. The detour to g combines various forces. It breaks the rigid path of the scale, lends individuality to the melody, implies a harmonization of the passing tone *b*-flat, acts as a free *nota cambiata* between fourth and fifth, sets off the acme of the fifth, but also marks the fourth as the first real obstacle to the melodic progress. The dissonant character of the fourth is further elucidated by the underlying dominant seventh chord—the first nontonic chord of the aria.

The consequent completes the scale up to the octave and sinks back to the starting point c^1. The full span of the first arpeggio has been answered. A new ascending scale in diminution unexpectedly widens the range of the melody in a most personal manner. The dissonant fourth, marked earlier, soars to the top one octave above its first appearance.

213

The illusion of an even wider range is given by an imitation of the ascending scale in the flute. The third member of the wood-wind ensemble, the bassoon, enhances this illusion by abandoning the parallel octaves to the leading melody for parallel tenths.

Already in this opening statement there is a noteworthy ambiguity of qualities. The interweaving of harmonic and melodic elements, typical of the whole aria, is projected in the very first measures. Ascending and descending trends flow against one another throughout the whole period. The direction changes with every measure in the antecedent and—in good psychological acceleration—with every half-measure in the consequent. The whole oboe melody oscillates between the classical need of being complete in itself and the romantic suggestiveness of being incomplete. Thus the full tonic scale is rounded off by both arpeggio and scale, but the diminutive run above the octave ends on the dissonant fourth. This unresolved climax, on the other hand, is playfully covered by the flute, which vicariously supplies a temporary resolution. The real resolution of the fourth will become the main task of the remainder of the aria.

The idea of the linear double current, too, continues to show its influence in the larger dimension of the whole piece. The oboe cadenza scales in sixteenth-notes change direction with each occurrence: up in measure 29, down in 43, up in 61, down in 68, and up in 72. One suspects the purpose of the penultimate cadenza—singularly marked by the absence of imitation—as an insertion in order to insure all the more the final ascensions. In one instance (at the end of the first strophe, m. 42 ff.) the duality of direction invades the imitation itself.

The melodic drive and content of the vocal line can be understood in relation to the norm established by the opening instrumental period. Any deviation becomes a meaningful expression, necessitates a correction, and sets a task. This specific technique of composition carries Susanna's aria like other numbers in this opera (e.g., Nos. 11, 24) and probably many pieces of absolute music not yet investigated.

Even though the first vocal phrase sounds sufficiently like the oboe model to be recognized as its counterpart, it deviates significantly. The ascent of the second measure is not by step, and the original obstacle of b-flat is not resolved as a passing tone into c^1. It thereby becomes a source of tension. Its position as temporary acme is pointedly corroborated by the short answer of the oboe (which serves as bridge, reminder of the model scale, and echoing summary at the same time) and the re-

mainder of the period. The consequent (m. 34–36) sounds like an extended elaboration of the obstructing *b*-flat and therefore differs completely from the model consequent of the introduction (m. 28–30). The first of the three measures (34) plays on the *b*-flat level, the implied counterpoint on the weak beats polyphonically filling in the third of the scale neglected before (m. 32). The second measure (35), by imitation of the opening interval, sounds like a fresh start after the reiterated halt on the fourth. The incidental resolution by c^1 is spurious, for the vocal line actually recaptures *b*-flat (m. 36), about the temporary supremacy of which the oboe insert, by similar devices as before, can leave no further doubt.

The whole period now becomes an antecedent by force of its new qualities of incompleteness. The answer first imitates the beginning like a second attempt. But on the same *f* where the vocal line first split from the oboe model, the melody again abandons the path, succumbing to the *notturna face* with a mysterious low register. The oboe bridge at the end of the phrase (m. 39) this time has to remind the voice melody of the span of the original task. It succeeds in drawing the line up to the abandoned range of *f* (m. 40). From there the long-expected scale up to the fifth is traversed in one breath (m. 40–42); but it is bent by the naturalization of the fourth away from the life-giving tension and toward the fleeting tonality of the halfway mark c^1 and is obscured by the characteristic harmonization of the line by itself:

At the end of the first vocal strophe, after twelve measures, the melody is as far as it was at the end of the first instrumental phrase, after three measures. The syntactic expansion can be equated with the expressive content. In both places the fifth is the point of temporary rest. Proportionately with the longer wave, the emphasis on the fifth is here strengthened by the chromatization of its own leading tone and, in familiar manner, by the short instrumental postlude, in which the flute gains ascendancy over the oboe.

The second strophe (m. 45–56) twines the double threads characteristic of the aria with masterful subtlety. The self-harmonization of the melody more than ever smothers the linear progress with sensuality. Without clarification by the short wood-wind interludes, one might easily lose the direction. It is outlined by the top notes of the flute: c^2 in the first breathing spell (m. 47); b^1-flat in the second (m. 50–51); and, with the usual acceleration of progress, a^1 to g^1 in the third (m. 53–54). This line counteracts the earlier accomplishment of the scale up to the fifth. Instead of the expected continuation from the fifth up to the octave (cf. m. 28), one hears the scale in inverted direction. It also cancels the chroma of the dominant by restating the original crucial tone b-flat. The descending scale stops short of the completing tonic, thus leaving an opening for the final section of the aria.

The duplicity of this line—right by starting point and scale progress and wrong by direction—is mirrored by a related, though different, kind of duplicity of the voice line. The main points of Susanna's curve are in accord with the clarifying flute. The whole first couplet (m. 45–50) represents the fifth by the closed tonality of the dominant and the rhythmic weight of c^1 on the downbeats of measures 46, 47, and 48 (supported by the lower octave in m. 50). The second couplet (m. 51–56) has b-flat as its first focus (m. 51–52), the functional grace notes serving as ornamental pointers to the seven tone repetitions in the voice around the *ostinato* of the first violins. Then the second couplet continues past a (m. 53) to g (m. 54) and the tonic (m. 56). Simultaneously, however, Susanna's top points take care of the neglected upper part of the scale: f^1 in the first phrase, e^1 in the second, and d^1 in the remaining two. The joint with the dominant c^1 is reserved for the third section of the aria. There is duplicity in the care of the upper part of the scale but in the wrong direction, and in the simultaneous handling of both halves of the scale. Moreover, against the gradual melodic descent, the harmonic leaps create exciting upward billows. The large wave of the four phrases designs a further alternation of rise-fall-rise-fall.

The elision of the second and third strophes (m. 56) is the result of the compellent melodic drive which carries over. The immediate task is to regain the point at which the ascending scale was stopped in the first strophe. The goal, c^1, is identical with the juncture of the two split scale halves of the second strophe. It is reached and established by the first half of the epode (m. 57–62). The voice captures it (*ben mio*) after a seductive reminiscing on the early obstacle b-flat (m. 57) and on the

216

chroma, now appoggiatura, *b*-natural (m. 58). The solo bassoon, for the first time alone, sustains *c* (m. 58–60), while the voice, between grace note and lowest destination, spans the c-octave—no longer dominant dissonance but incorporated in the tonic triad. Then the voice again takes the fifth from the bassoon and spins the first fermata around it (m. 61–62).

There are countercurrents, as one may suspect, but they are subordinate to the main achievement of the final approach. Thus the descending scale elements in the voice line tie up in diminution the similar progress of the second strophe. The notes *a* and *g* (m. 57) must imply polyphony of a secondary order; for the resultant parallel fifths to the bass are only apparent and not real (*C/g* to *F/c¹*, across the bar line between m. 57 and 58). The cadenzas in the three wood winds, now that the immediate task of the epode is mastered, mockingly image the primary assignment of the voice melody: the completion of the ascending tonic scale, impeded from the first phrase. None of the images is perfect: the outer instruments reach the tonic without quite spanning the full octave, and the oboe originates from the dominant.

The second half of the epode (after the fermata in m. 62) brings the final solution. One understands now, from a different angle, why the form of this part of the third strophe consists of the repetition and expansive intensification of one phrase: the content is important and, after the preceding intricacies, should be stated twice rather than risk being missed.

The persuasiveness of the final solution is overwhelmingly direct. The complete tonic scale, *f* to *f¹*, is covered in two concise assaults (m. 62–64). A high third, in a range prepared by the first overflow of the oboe (m. 29), crowns the achievement (*incoronar*). Then an arpeggio of the tonic triad encompasses the tonal field, as it did in the first measure of the aria. It becomes part of the closing cadence, in which the last three notes once more represent the settling scale.

In the repetition of the phrase (m. 66 ff.) the voice is contained by the exact octave. A sustained *f¹* avoids competition with the earlier climax, which is merely intimated by the oboe.

Even with all its directness, the solution is not free of suggestive undercurrents. Against the ascending scale of the voice, the bowed viola (joined in the repeated phrase by the bassoon) plays an expressive descending scale, the tendency of which is presently echoed in the double

lines of oboe and bassoon. The two fermatas in one measure bear an ingratiating innuendo of their own.

The short instrumental postlude combines once more the diverse qualities of the melody. The oboe moves by scale and arpeggio; the first violins descend the scale against the ascending runs of the winds; and the bass, in utmost succinctness, outlines the tonic octave, marking in its course the crucial halfway point.

All these intricacies of tempo, instrumentation, form, and melody are accompanied by the simplest possible harmonies. The bass of the instrumental introduction consists of only two notes carrying the three basic harmonic functions of T, S, and D. The harmonies of the whole aria avoid complications, perhaps in order not to distract the ear from the rich harmonic movement imbedded in the melodic line. The simple harmonic structure succeeds in lending the whole number an air of innocence, with a special delusive charm of its own against the involved entanglement of the rest.

This is the last solo aria before the general finale. Susanna, it seems, has the ultimate word.

NUMBER 28 / Finale (D MAJOR)

Just as in a symphony or concerto the last movement, although often related in form, is usually lighter in spirit, more of a *Musikantenstück*, than the first movement, the last finale of *Le Nozze di Figaro* is constructed in a more simple and carefree manner than its counterpart in the second act. This statement does not imply less ingenuity on the composer's part but rather less complex demands on the listener's ears.

The length of the finale gives primacy in the critic's investigation to the problem of organization. Once the main structure is recognized, subordinate details will fall into place. The spadework done by Alfred Lorenz in exposing the unified form of finales in Mozart's operas has brought to light many beauties of the finale under discussion.[1] Imitation is the most honest form of flattery, it is said. The greatest tribute one can pay to Lorenz at this moment is to follow literally the solution suggested by him. The diagram on the next page copies his original except for the substitution of English words for German and the addition of meter indications.

The perfect bow form is most easily recognized with reference to the key arrangement. The framing sections stay close to the tonic; the middle section dips into distant flats. E-flat major is the Neapolitan key of the tonic and accordingly fulfils a subdominant function ($s_3^{6\flat[5]}$). The tonality flows in the opening section from tonic to subdominant, plays in the middle section on the subdominant element represented by the Neapolitan key and its secondary dominant, and returns in the closing section from the subdominant proper to the tonic. The three formal sections thus are elaborations of a gigantic subdominant cadence. The separate keys are distributed over eight subsections which alternate regularly in tempo: slow-fast-slow-fast and so forth. The tripartition finds rhythmical support; for the outside sections are both in duple meter, whereas the middle section pulsates throughout in triple meter (3/4 and 6/8). The discrepancy in length between the three main sections as expressed by the number of measures is only apparent. Measures do

1. "Das Finale in Mozarts Meisteropern," *Die Musik*, XIX, No. 9 (June, 1927), 630.

219

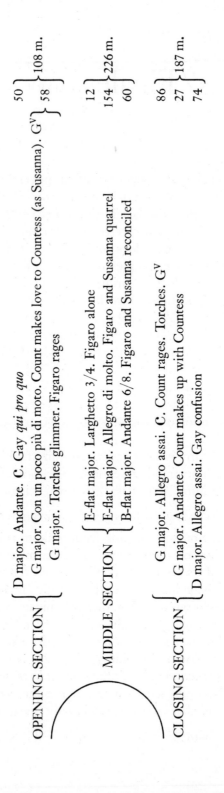

OPENING SECTION { D major. Andante. C. Gay *qui pro quo* — 50
G major. Con un poco più di moto. Count makes love to Countess (as Susanna). G^V — 58 } 108 m.
G major. Torches glimmer. Figaro rages

MIDDLE SECTION { E-flat major. Larghetto 3/4. Figaro alone — 12
E-flat major. Allegro di molto. Figaro and Susanna quarrel — 154 } 226 m.
B-flat major. Andante 6/8. Figaro and Susanna reconciled — 60

CLOSING SECTION { G major. Allegro assai. C. Count rages. Torches. G^V — 86
G major. Andante. Count makes up with Countess — 27 } 187 m.
D major. Allegro assai. Gay confusion — 74

not weigh the same in different tempos. The actual duration of the three main sections is the same—five minutes, almost to the second.

The other big finale, in the second act, was motivated, as one remembers, by the absent Cherubino. The initial power for this finale is generated by the presence of Cherubino. He approaches the Countess (whom he takes for Susanna) to the accompaniment of an elegant three-measure phrase (m. 1–3), which gives the whole opening section in the tonic its characteristic imprint. The three measures may be said to constitute a miniature bar form. The ornamented descending scale of the first measure, with a gracefully recoiling appoggiatura at the end, represents the strophe. It is symmetrically continued by Cherubino's line until the first comma. The strophe remains in the tonic, the antistrophe in the dominant. The epode (m. 3), although no longer than each separate strophe, maintains a good equilibrium against the joint strophes by a greater harmonic density, created by chords changing with each beat, and by collaborating wind reinforcement. The whole phrase is interpreted as the first half of a period. The consequent starts out as a repetition of the antecedent but is deflected at the point of its own miniature epode by a deceptive cadence (m. 6). The deception, supported by a fleeting crescendo of the orchestra, coincides with the Countess' wriggling out of Cherubino's aggressive embrace.

In the remainder of the opening tonic section the phrase recurs twice more (m. 21 ff. and 34 ff.). The first recurrence is in the dominant, the second in the tonic. In both instances a deceptive cadence interrupts the flow at the analogous moments, after the antistrophe of the consequent. In the dominant period the three witnesses outside the love scene take the lead, as Cherubino experiences the interruption, forte-piano, in the middle of his pursuit. In the final tonic instance, Cherubino attacks again; but it is his last chance before the combined efforts of the opposing quartet chase him away for good. The simultaneous dynamic accentuation heard in the analogous earlier spots is here marked by the slap that Figaro receives from the Count. The device of the deceptive cadence so consistently employed serves a double purpose. In each specific instance it breaks into an action and foils its completion. Cherubino's loving pursuit is stopped first by the Countess, then by the appearance of witnesses unseen by Cherubino, and finally by active interference of the witnesses. In a general sense the deceptive cadence expresses the deceitful *qui pro quo* in which everybody is caught.

The three recurrences of the characteristic period support a wide arch

221

containing the structure of the whole period. The symmetry of the arch is increased by the arrangement of subordinate elements. Among them, a contrasting lyrical theme, heard in the dominant in the first third of the bow form and in the tonic in the last third, assimilates the structure to that of a sonata-form rondo.

Characteristic theme, T (m. 1 ff.)
Deceptive cadence, crescendo (m. 6)
Lyrical theme, D (m. 10 ff.)
Rapid soprano sixteenths of Countess on cadence
  (m. 20)

EXPOSITION
20 m.

Characteristic theme, D (m. 21 ff.)
Deceptive cadence, *fp* (m. 26)
Descending bass scale to dominant (m. 26 ff.)

MIDDLE SECTION
13 m.

Characteristic theme, T (m. 34 ff.)
Deceptive cadence, slap (m. 39)
Lyrical theme, T (m. 40 ff.)
Rapid soprano sixteenths of Susanna on cadence
  (m. 47 ff.)

RECAPITULATION
17 m. + fermata

With the elimination of Cherubino, the deceptions and interruptions are by no means ended. The following G-major quartet is full of them. There is the sprightly opening theme in the first violins, a complete and well-rounded melody, which never recurs thereafter. The full four-measure period with which the Count, taking over Cherubino's wooing role, approaches the Countess experiences a response of surface politeness but intrinsic rejection. The answer (m. 55–56) is only half as long as the demand. The rhythm of the Countess' answer displays wilful independence by being set against the norm of the quadruple meter: the true accents fall on the syllables *Giacchè* and *eccomi* in true 3/4 time. The melody, moreover, is created out of an inversion of the Count's initial motive: the tonic triad arpeggio in the first violins from the fifth through the tonic up to the third (m. 51) now expresses the Countess' attitude by being broken in the opposite direction (m. 55). The inverted motive subsequently begins a life of its own in Figaro's ironic complaint (m. 57–58). Although only fragmentary at first—for Figaro is for the moment as frustrated as the Count—it forcefully pervades the whole structure in protest against the apparently illicit love scene.

222

The six repetitions of the note d remind one of Figaro's somewhat heavy-footed behavior at the other end of the opera: the repetitions of the same note in the same key in the first duettino.

Both the Countess' polite reluctance and Figaro's impotent anger are developed throughout the quartet. The Countess' music sounds polite because it always conveys the vague impression of really continuing the Count's courting music, and reluctant because by subtle inversions and amputations it never grows into a fully satisfactory musical response. Such is the case at the Count's next advance (m. 59–60), where the Countess leads his two-measure phrase to the concluding cadence with only four notes filling half a measure. Again her wilfully independent rhythm shifts the straightforwardness of the meter into a unit of five beats extending from the solo of the first oboe (second quarter, m. 60) to the cadence in the middle of the following measure. Her next responses to his ever intenser pleas are so mixed up with Susanna's (m. 69–79) that the aural deception is no smaller than the visual one wrought by the interchanged costumes. The Countess' next individualized response falls into the now familiar pattern: she acknowledges the Count's generous present with a graceful phrase in the same key but of curtailed length (m. 84 ff.). Simultaneously, the self-determined quintuple rhythm runs above the metric pulse of the whole episode; for the accents of the melody as distributed between first violins and first oboe come regularly every five beats beginning with the Countess' answer, until, after five measures in quadruple time or four recurrences of the quintuple unit, meter and rhythm again overlap on the subdominant cadence.[2] When it is at last her turn to make the initial remark in her conversation with her husband, it is only to prepare her escape by a most unlyrical reference to torches intruding on their privacy (m. 89 ff.). The return to the tonic finds her identity again completely merged with Susanna's.

Figaro's anger sounds impotent because it does not actively disturb the tryst until the very end. The "anger" motive (m. 57–58) ironically echoes into the love duet (m. 62) and Susanna's first reaction to the situation (m. 69). By this time the dramatic confusion is so great that the Count's poetic phrase (m. 70) is difficult to hear in its proper relation to the other music floating through the night air of the garden. In

2. The harmonic functions refer to the prevailing tonality of each subsection (the subdominant in this case being C major) and not to the larger tonality of the finale as an entity.

223

scope and rhythm it is reminiscent of the earlier first phrase in the dominant (m. 59–60) without actually developing it. The Count's present phrase is introduced as a consequent to Figaro's anger motive ironically sung by Susanna; truly it does not belong to it, as is demonstrated by the shifting range and timbre of the orchestration and ᵗhe really fitting consequent at the end of the section (m. 100 ff.). There, back in the tonic, Figaro accomplishes what he has been trying in vain to do throughout the quartet (cf. m. 91, 92, and others): complete the anger motive musically by finding for it the proper continuation, and dramatically by successfully breaking up the rendezvous.

As if these were not enough crosscurrents, the Count, who is alone against all others in the conspiracy, tries to stem the general current in his own way. The two repetitions of his intensive cadential figure on the dominant (cf. m. 66–68 and 74 ff.) run counter the closed ensemble in bar form $[2 + 2 + (2 \times 3)]$ beginning with Susanna's entrance (m. 69–79). In the end the current is stronger than he.

The large middle section in E-flat major and its dominant is central also in the sense that it deals exclusively with the two heroes of the opera, Figaro and Susanna. Not only does the drop by four keys in the tonal circle mark its beginning but also the sudden desertion of the stage by all except Figaro. His solitude is romantically exploited by the music. Mellow clarinets and horns carry the melody, the many tone repetitions of which have become characteristically associated with Figaro. String triplets provide the accompaniment. The timbre distribution is similar to that in the trio of the third movement of Beethoven's *Eighth Symphony*, a thoroughly romantic conception like this one. Even the words of the earthy Figaro are mythologically inspired.[3] The larghetto is in obvious bar form $(3 + 3 + 6)$, overlapping lines and elisions at the joints blurring the outlines. Robert Haas gives a clue to the nature of the melodic substance, identifying it as a church litany.[4] He explains that Figaro is so confused by the events of the day that the litany is running through his head. Such an explanation is psychologically perfectly correct for anyone brought up in a church tradition. It is

3. Homer *Odyssey* viii. 266 ff.

4. *Wolfgang Amadeus Mozart* (Potsdam, 1933), p. 140. Without so stating, Haas may be thinking of the Litany SS. Cordis Jesu (*Liber usualis* [1937], p. 1878). To Professor Leopold Nowak, of the University of Vienna, I am indebted for the information that Mozart himself uses a similar melodic formula in the Agnus Dei of his *Litaniae Lauretanae*, K. 195.

a common procedure among peoples of Catholic countries to summon forth and verbalize religious memories when an impasse has been reached with which reason cannot cope for the moment. The situation is described by a common Austrian saying, "Der Katechismus geht mir im Kopf herum" ("The catechism is running through my head"). Mozart was an Austrian Catholic, steeped in the local church tradition in spite of his emancipation in later life; and Figaro, too, born and raised in Spain, was a Catholic, it must be assumed.

In the following duet in E-flat major, one is amused by the many buffo repetitions of a short two-measure phrase, the internal structure of which is repetitive in itself. The opening measures of the duet bring two repetitions and, after a short two-measure interruption, four more. After the modulation to the dominant, the phrase is sounded three times in a row (m. 146–152) and later, back in the tonic, seven times, coincident with Susanna's slapping Figaro. The technique is similar to that employed in the sextet where Susanna slaps Figaro to the music of five cumulative repetitions of another two-measure phrase (cf. No. 18, m. 48 ff.). The buffo effect of the device is tested by experience.

The affectation of Figaro's declaration of love (m. 182 ff.) comes comically across in the music. The inflection of his outpouring is like nothing he has said before. One must not infer that it sounds like a simple man's attempt to employ elegant language; for Figaro's earlier venture into the Count's minuet realm (cf. No. 3) is a convincingly successful satire. Here he is ostentatiously burlesquing. He knows to whom he is talking. The caricature becomes apparent from the exaggerated elongation of all feminine endings (m. 184, 188, 192); the mannered appoggiaturas (m. 184, 188); the sentimental chromaticisms; and, most of all, the absurdly affected jumps down an eleventh, up a ninth, and down a tenth, right in the wake of a half-tone scale. The drop of the eleventh utilizes prime, third, and fifth of the tonic triad in two arpeggios, the regularity of the tone progression submersed under amorous heavings.

A recapitulation of Figaro's love song is quickly interrupted by Susanna's slapping him to the tune of seven repetitions of the opening phrase of the duet (m. 227 ff.). The real recapitulation follows, furiously contrapunted by Susanna (m. 247). Figaro's melody is unchanged, even though he is past making false love. The new dramatic implication of a previously heard musical unit is of the same ironic character as, for instance, the recapitulation in the first trio (No. 7) after Cherubino's discovery.

Buffo phrase, 6 times, T. Figaro recognizes Countess
Cadence, T, with corrective repetition in D
} STROPHE, T
26 m. (121–146)

Buffo phrase, 3 times, D. Figaro recognizes Susanna
Cadence, D, with sequential antecedent
} ANTISTROPHE, D
24 m. (146–169)

Organ point on D
BRIDGE, D
13 m. (169–181)

Figaro's love song (4 + 4 + 7)
Duet leading to sequence and cadence
} EXPOSITION, T (32)

Affected dialogue   MIDDLE SECTION, S and SR (14)

[Figaro's love song interrupted. False recapitulation (20)]
Figaro's love song
Duet leading to sequence and cadence
} RECAPITULATION, T (28)

} EPODE, T
93 m. (182–274)

A recurring cadential figure with sharp cross-accents (m. 135, 142; 165; 209; 266) marks the main points of the structure, preceded by a sequence of antecedent character in all instances except the first, where a repetition of the cadential figure in the dominant completes the period. A recapitulation bar form can be recognized. The epode, in bow form, gains its relative length from the false recapitulation of Figaro's love song and the subsequent interrupting insertion of the opening buffo phrase. The latter provides the recapitulation element in the large bar form (see table on p. 226).

The reconciliation scene in B-flat major is also cast in recapitulation bar form. In the antistrophe (a small bow like the strophe) the middle section is slightly blown up by the Count's search for Susanna. Forte dynamics and orchestration set off the extra measures (297–300). By now it is the Count's turn to be confused; for, trying to find Susanna, he sings the conciliatory melody of Figaro, who has already found her. The epode, in miniature bar form, begins, like that of the preceding duet, with a burlesque declaration of love by Figaro. The melody is new; but the devices, such as exaggerated accents and jumps, are old. The miniature epode brings the recapitulation of the larger bar form. The large epode, in measure numbers no longer than either strophe, more than adequately counterpoises their joint weight by the increased dramatic intensity.

Conciliatory tune (bar form)	T 7	STROPHE
⟩ Susanna's confusion ends	D 4	19 m. (275–293)
Conciliatory tune	T 8	
Conciliatory tune	T 5	ANTISTROPHE
⟩ Figaro's confusion ends	(D)D 8	21 m. (293–313)
Conciliatory tune	D 8	
Strophe: Figaro feigns love, Count rages	D 6	EPODE
Antistrophe: Figaro feigns love, Count rages	TR 7	21 m. (314–334)
Epode: Conciliatory tune	T 8	

The return to G major, the true subdominant of the finale, from the Neapolitan group sounds more abrupt than the earlier modulation in the opposite direction. The suddenness is dramatically warranted by the Count's pouncing on Figaro. The path of the modulation, however, is similar in both directions. G major and E-flat major are connected by the pivot key of G minor, the tonic parallel of the first tonality and the dominant relative of the second. A simple change of chroma initiated the downward move (m. 107), the way having been prepared by the earlier deceptive cadences (m. 6, 26, and 39). The affected turn toward the relative of the prevailing tonality in the last mock love scene points the modulation back up. The stirring G-minor ensemble at the end of the fast section in the regained subdominant, G major, harks back to the accomplished tonal detour of the finale (m. 402–420). Introduced and abandoned, both, by the chromatic alteration of the third, G minor reinterprets the relationship of the two polar keys of the finale, D major and E-flat major, in one progression (m. 415–416).

In the allegro assai section the harmonic excitement is highest, on the dominant of the dominant, at the moment of the expected, but not actual, apprehension of the Countess (m. 367). Her surprise appearance, which brings the final solution of the drama, clears up also the harmonic tensions by cadentially re-establishing G major (m. 398 ff.). Her touching line gains much of its particular *Affekt* by the manner in which it gently continues the preceding violent outburst of the Count. His last exclamations, backed by a unisono orchestra, form a dominant ninth chord without root. A harmonic division of his arpeggio from *e* down to *C* into two chords, first a subdominant relative and then an incomplete dominant seventh, is less likely because of the unified dramatic line and, moreover, provides fundamentally no different explanation; for any dominant ninth chord is but the sum of dominant plus subdominant elements. The ninth of the chord, doubled in the top register of the flute (m. 395), is properly resolved by the same instrument at the Countess' words, while her voice metamorphoses the formerly dissonant tone e into the sentimentally consonant major sixth of the tonic. The effect of the transformed tone e is so magic that the ensemble response of the witnesses dares not touch it and in solemn wonder deflects the melodic line to e-flat. The brightness of e-natural is not heard again until the Countess' final word of forgiveness (m. 425), but then with a similarly enchanting result.

A wilfully bent phrase of the raging Count recurs twice in the allegro assai section, in the tonic (m. 346 ff.) and in the dominant (m. 376 ff.). If we accept it as a cadential refrain to two strophes, it may serve in the organization of a bar form. The strophe is seventeen measures long, ending after the refrain with a full caesura. The antistrophe, after sixteen measures, reaches a "wrong" ending coincident with the discovery

228

of the "wrong" persons. The closing melody of the Count, reminiscent of the refrain but not really identical with it (the characteristic triad undulations are missing), strengthens the illusion of a completed antistrophe. The true ending of the antistrophe with the correct refrain comes ten measures later when the Count pulls out of the pavilion, after three other persons, the one whom he really believes to be his wife. The insertion, although lengthening the antistrophe by more than half, is musically static, as one glance at the basses and first violins will reveal. The epode, beginning after a strong dominant cadence, brings for the first time the sound of women's voices. It is in bow form, the undisguised Countess' appearance in central position. The closing ensemble, again for men's voices only, creates the idea, in terms of timbre, of a recapitulation bar form.

Count rages about Figaro. Men's voices only Refrain, T cadence	]STROPHE } 17 m. (335–351)
Count rages about Countess. Men's voices only [Wrong refrain, wrong discoveries] Refrain, D cadence	} ANTISTROPHE 30 m. (352–381) minus insertion

Perdono ensemble. Women's voices added	18	] EPODE
) Countess appears	4	40 m. (381–420)
Deliro ensemble. Men's voices only	19	

The sentimental major sixth, an unusually warm interval for the Count, finds its way into the andante section. The minor seventh, which he spans by an intensifying sequence, is the same interval which had tortured him in his aria (see No. 17). Here it is gently resolved, as a passing tone from the sixth, into the consonant octave supplied by the Countess. Her reply shows her willingness to conciliate her husband by picking up his sentimental upsweep, harmoniously converted into a perfect fifth but accepted as a model for the subsequent climactic rise to the major sixth. All voices repeat her reply *sotto voce* before crowning with a new epode the Count's request for forgiveness and the Countess' womanly yielding. The accompanying violin figuration gives rich expression to the ensemble by three swelling crescendos, each leading to a subito piano—a play on dynamics not common with Mozart. The crucial tone e is poignantly taken up by the flute, more than two octaves above the subdued unisono of the strings, before a tremolo organ

229

point on the dominant of the over-all tonality announces the near end of the opera.

The closing allegro assai has the main task of retrieving and firmly establishing the basic tonality of the finale and the whole opera. Supplied by the libretto with two parallel four-line strophes, Mozart uses the given poetic form with free exuberance. A baroque exploitation of single words gives him the pretext.[5] The word *tormenti* (m. 451) begets the dissonance of an incomplete second-dominant ninth chord. *Capricci* and *follia* twist the movement momentarily into the minor mode. *Terminar* brings the first full cadence in the tonic. The music does not resist falling into a *lieta marcia* at the mere sound of these words. The distinct character of the march singles it out as the middle section of a loose bow form, even though the corresponding words are taken from the seventh of the eight text lines. A certain free correspondence between the framing sections can be traced. Of approximately the same length—almost exactly so if the repetition within the closing section is not counted doubly—each sets men's and women's voices against each other in the fashion of characteristic double-chorus imitation; and the end of each is marked by triplet flourishes in all strings. The middle section (m. 472–487), apart from being cadentially isolated, mixes men's and women's voices, the tenors going with the latter. It also gives the Count his only, and last, chance to assert his individuality against the united group by a nonconforming vocal line (cf. m. 479 ff.). The last unison measures of the orchestra employ the very same notes that were heard at the first rise of the curtain at the other end of the opera. There the steady repetitions of the tone d and the rising interval d to a, in dissonant relation to the established subdominant key G major, were indicative of Figaro's state of mind on the morning of his wedding day. Here the same repetitions and the supplementary answer a to d, in perfect consonant relation to the basic tonic key D major, indicate that all is well at the end of the day and of the opera.

5. Cf. a similar technique in the last section of the second *Così fan tutte* finale (*turbini*, e.g.).

THE OPERA

AS A WHOLE

1 / Structure

Aesthetic formulas, in Walter Pater's sense, can be isolated from the entity of the opera as much as from its details.

Of primary importance is the organization that holds together the many microcosmic elements. Regardless of the four curtain falls, one recognizes the basic binary structure, in which the first two acts form a unit against the last two. The division into two large sections was traditional in Mozart's day. *Don Giovanni, Così fan tutte,* and *Die Zauberflöte* follow the tradition, the two halves equated with two acts, each of which ends with a big finale. In the first finale the dramatic confusion or tension is usually at its height, and the curtain falls on an unresolved situation.[1] The second finale brings the ultimate solution.

This traditional principle also governs *Le Nozze di Figaro.* The endings of the second and fourth acts are pre-eminently high-lighted by the expected finales. The two curves follow a definite tonal order. The keys at the nodes encompass the opera in a gigantic Neapolitan cadence:

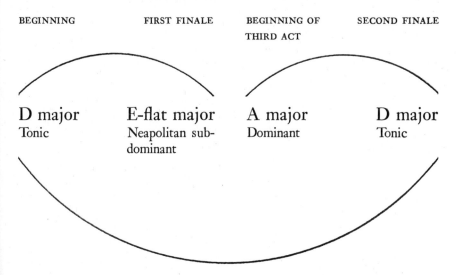

BEGINNING	FIRST FINALE	BEGINNING OF THIRD ACT	SECOND FINALE
D major	E-flat major	A major	D major
Tonic	Neapolitan sub-dominant	Dominant	Tonic

1. The intentional indefiniteness of the first *Don Giovanni* finale, for instance, causes most stage directors unnecessary headaches and traps them into inventing some "clarifying" action.

The crests at the ends of the first and third acts show a planned correspondence to each other. Each scene presents Figaro in a triumphant march—in his fancy as a rebel and in actuality as a bridegroom. Each scene is in C major, the second subdominant, introduced by a chorus in 6/8 meter in G major, its secondary dominant. Each scene has enough dramatic and musical impact to warrant the lowering of the curtain, without seriously competing with the summits of the two big finales.

The tonal organization of each act has been described by Hermann Abert.[2] The first act changes its orientation four times:

1.

G	Susanna, Figaro
B-flat	Susanna, Figaro
F	Figaro

2.

D	Bartolo
A	Susanna, Marcellina

3.

E-flat	Cherubino
B-flat	Susanna, Basilio, Count

4.

G	Chorus
C	Figaro

The tonal caesuras between each two sections coincide with distinct dramatic shifts. Against the predominance of Susanna and Figaro in 1 and 4, the antagonists Bartolo and Marcellina are introduced in 2, and the Cherubino episode fills all of 3. The T–D relationship of the two numbers of 2 is mirrored half a tone higher by the two numbers of 3. Around the strong tritone break in the middle—from the highest to the lowest key employed in the opera—the four sections form a bow in free persuasive correspondence:

2. In his sensitive introduction to the miniature score of the opera (*Kleine Partitur-Ausgabe*, published by Eulenburg [Vienna, 1926]).

1. Susanna, Figaro
   Deteriorating subdominant orientation

   2. Bartolo, Marcellina
      Highest dominant tension
      T–D relationship of two numbers

      Tritone break

   3. Cherubino, Basilio, Count
      Lowest Neapolitan tension
      T–D relationship of two numbers on raised pitch

4. Chorus of friends, Figaro
   Improving subdominant orientation

The tonality of the second act is closed:

1.

| E-flat | Countess |
| B-flat | Cherubino |

2.

G	Susanna
C	Susanna, Countess, Count
G	Susanna, Cherubino

3.

| E-flat | Finale |

Beginning and end are in E-flat major; the central section, which is all Susanna's, is in G major (the secondary subdominant, C major, in the passing middle). The tonal situation approximately reverses that of the first act, in which G major prevailed in the beginning and toward the end and E-flat major was heard in the middle after the startling tonal break. The two keys are related by the context. As functions of the over-all tonic D major, G major is the real, and E-flat major the Neapolitan, subdominant. Parallel with the gradual deterioration of the situation for Susanna and Figaro, the keys sink in the subdominant realm ever farther down until the confusion of the second-act finale strikes the greatest distance below the tonic.

235

The decisive break between the second and third acts employs, in opposite direction, the same tritone as the analogous break in the first act. E-flat and A here represent the crucial members of the large Neapolitan cadence spanning the whole opera. Measured by the keys of all numbers in the work, they are also the points farthest below and above the tonic.

The structure of the third act itself reveals a perfect bow:

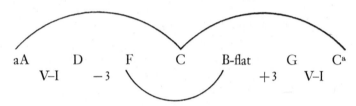

aA   D   F   C   B-flat   G   C^a
  V–I   –3   +3   V–I

The Countess' aria forms the center. One remembers the psychological change occurring in the aria. The coincidence of structural and expressive turning points can be no accident. The central key is repeated identically at the end and is represented by its relative at the beginning. The radiation across the whole act is strengthened by the inclusion of an A-minor section, the fandango, in the finale. The symmetry extends into the tonal progress on either side of the center. The V–I relationship of the first two numbers (A to D) is mirrored by the last two (G to C); and the subsequent drop of three keys (D to F), by the analogous lift (B-flat to G). The two numbers around the center are thus isolated by flats (Nos. 18 and 20). The tonal symmetry parallels, throughout, the organization of the plot:

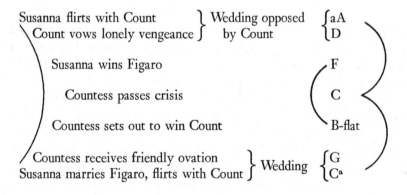

Susanna flirts with Count ⎱ Wedding opposed ⎰aA
  Count vows lonely vengeance ⎰   by Count   ⎱D

    Susanna wins Figaro   F

      Countess passes crisis   C

      Countess sets out to win Count   B-flat

  Countess receives friendly ovation   ⎱ Wedding ⎰G
Susanna marries Figaro, flirts with Count ⎰   ⎱C^a

236

In the Count's aria (No. 17) the tonic of the opera is heard for the first time since the first act (No. 4) and for the last time before the second finale.

The fourth act, according to Abert, falls into three tonal and dramatic sections:

1.

f	Barbarina
G	Marcellina

2.

B-flat	Basilio
E-flat	Figaro
F	Susanna

3.

D	Finale

The first section coincides with the first scene; the second, with the second scene exclusive of the finale; and the finale stands by itself. The middle section coheres by force of the flat signatures, the Neapolitan and tense E-flat again in the middle. The key relationship of the outer sections is given by interpreting F minor as the parallel of the relative of the minor tonic (tRP), and G major as the subdominant (S).

Abert is, no doubt, correct in ascribing to the fourth act a looser structure than to the other acts. The same principle of psychological acceleration or lightening that distinguishes the last movement of a sonata from the first, or the usual second finale from the first—not only in this opera but also, as a good example, in *Così fan tutte*—rightly influences also the structure of the whole closing act. But the tonal organization is firmer than suspected if one juxtaposes the entire development before the finale with that of the finale itself:

NOS. 23–27	FINALE
f	D, G
G, B-flat, E-flat	E-flat, B-flat, G
F	D

237

Two closed arches are the result. The first rises from the minor mode of Barbarina's lament over the lost pin to the major mode of Susanna's serenade—both a source of confusion to the witnessing Figaro. The second rises from the subdominant tinge of the incipient *qui pro quo* to the final establishment of the tonic. The culmination of the first in Susanna's entrancing love call is a worthy counterpart to the culmination of the second in the general happy ending. The contrasting middle sections mirror each other exactly. E-flat major, in both instances, shows Figaro alone on the stage in bottom despair over the unfaithfulness of women, his wife in particular.

Taken one by one in this fashion, the four acts show a strong trend toward the subdominant. The departure from the tonic in the course of the first act, from D major to C major, is answered by the tonal movement of the last act, from F minor back to D major:

D major   D major

                         C major   F minor

     T   SS   s(SS)   T

The two middle acts, as units, sustain the subdominant level by their stabilized tonal orientation toward E-flat major and C major, respectively. The flow of the four acts by themselves can be thus represented:

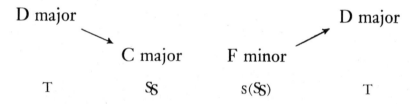

         I   II   III   IV

One is justified in letting one's imagination play with ideas of tonality transcending the boundaries of separate acts. In accordance with the binary organization of the whole opera, one may expect, and will find, a plan of keys binding together the first two acts, and another plan binding together the last two acts. Recognition of the larger wave does not cancel the smaller ones. It joins them and thereby creates a new current.

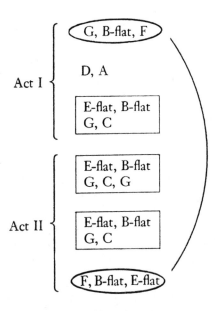

Act I
- G, B-flat, F
- D, A
- E-flat, B-flat G, C

Act II
- E-flat, B-flat G, C, G
- E-flat, B-flat G, C
- F, B-flat, E-flat

The strongest power is generated from the triplicated movement through the same cycle, E-flat, B-flat, G, C. The short extra subdominant duet at the close of the middle cycle (No. 14) does not detract from the significance of the cycle. Each cycle initiates a fresh dramatic situation: E-flat major introduces Cherubino (No. 6), the Countess (No. 10), and the finale (No. 15/1). The second half of each cycle takes a pleasant turn with the G-major tonality of the friendly chorus (No. 8), Susanna's boudoir aria (No. 12), and Figaro's merry entry (No. 15/4). On the way from E-flat major to G major, the three B-flat major sections all deal with Cherubino: he is discovered in the trio of the first (No. 7), sings his arietta to the Countess in the second (No. 11), and is protected by Susanna's surprise appearance in the trio of the third (No. 15/2). There is less dramatic correspondence between the respective last phases. Each C-major section lands on a somewhat indefinite situation (Nos. 9, 13, and 15/5), giving an opening for the resumption of the cycle. The following diagram shows the parallelism of the three cycles:

	1ST CYCLE	2D CYCLE	3D CYCLE
E-flat	Cherubino introduced	Countess introduced	Finale introduced
B-flat	Trio. Cherubino discovered	Cherubino's chanson	Trio. Susanna discovered in Cherubino's place
G	Friendly chorus	Pleasant costuming	Merry entry of Figaro
C	Figaro marching	Excited trio	Request for wedding

Framing the cycles are the three numbers of the first scene between Susanna and Figaro (Nos. 1–3), mirrored at the other end by the three sections governed by the opposing forces of Antonio, Marcellina, Basilio, and Bartolo (No. 15/6–8). Figaro's rebellious F-major song corresponds to Antonio's interference in that key; the B-flat major duet about the location of the nuptial beds, to Marcellina's claim, in the same key, for her place in one of them; and the friendly atmosphere of the G-major opening, to the tense E-flat-major turmoil before the closing curtain. The substitution of E-flat major for G major is nothing more than that of the Neapolitan version of the subdominant for the real subdominant.

The only two numbers not fitting into the perfect over-all symmetry of the first two acts are Bartolo's aria (No. 4) and Marcellina's duet (No. 5). Their sharp keys protrude as noticeably as their acid characters, making the discrepancy from the formal structure appear all the more purposeful.

The joint organization of Acts I and II in no way erases the boundaries set for the various formal sections of the separate acts. The first curtain falls between the first two of the three key cycles, the connecting tonal bridge convincingly built by the interpretation of C major as the parallel of the relative of E-flat major (TRP).[3]

The unified structure of the first half of the opera is answered by an analogous plan for the second half:

3. Perhaps also as (D)SR, in which manner C major is really heard leading from the third to the fourth act.

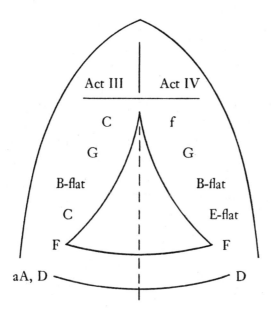

A symmetrical curve encompasses both acts without destroying the formal individuality of the separate acts. The tonic rules the extremes, intensified in the beginning by the preparatory dominant. The tonal correspondence finds its dramatic equivalent in the Count's position— here wooing with supreme seductiveness and emotional vigor (Nos. 16 and 17), there acting out his conquering impulses and conceding ultimate defeat (No. 28). Between the poles of the tonic the ten numbers form a closed F-major entity. It is divided into two equal halves mirrored by the caesura between the two acts. In terms of F major as a temporary tonic, or center of tonal orientation, the harmonic progress is represented by the cohesive symbols:

$$T \quad D \quad S \quad \mathbb{D} \quad D \quad | \quad t \quad \mathbb{D} \quad S \quad \text{\SS} \quad T$$

F major characterizes openly the rich invention and reconciliatory tone of the sextet (No. 18) and Susanna's garden aria (No. 27), and latently the central apex of the wedding (No. 22) leading across the change of scene (D–t) to Barbarina's lament (No. 23). The keys of the remaining mirrored numbers correspond to each other exactly in two instances (B-flat major in Nos. 20 and 25 and G major in Nos. 21 and 24) and vicariously in one (C major in No. 19 against E-flat major in No. 26). The vicariousness is the familiar one of the Neapolitan, for the second, subdominant. The dramatic correspondence of these inner parts of the curve is less strict than the tonal, the loosening of the structure symptomatic of the general lightening toward the end of a work. A tolerant imagination may link the Countess' complaint about her husband's unfaithfulness (No. 19, C major) to Figaro's complaint about Susanna's suspected unfaithfulness (No. 26, E-flat major); the plotting purpose of the letter duet (No. 20, B-flat major) to the plotting character of Basilio's aria (No. 25, B-flat major); and the entertainment proffered by the chorus (No. 21, G major) to the extraneous amusement supplied by Marcellina (No. 24, G major).

The diagram of the tonal curve may accordingly be complemented by the following dramatic juxtaposition:

Act III			Act IV
No. 22. Pin transmitted	C	f	No. 23. Pin lost
No. 21. Chorus entertains	G		No. 24. Marcellina entertains
No. 20. Susanna & Countess plot	B-flat		No. 25. Basilio plots
No. 19. Countess deplores Count's unfaithfulness	C	E-flat	No. 26. Figaro deplores Susanna's unfaithfulness
No. 18. Warm reconciliatory tone of sextet	F		No. 27. Warm reconciliatory tone of garden aria
Nos. 16 & 17. Count prepares tryst, vows conquest	aA, D	D	No. 28. Count comes to tryst, concedes defeat

One more speculation is unavoidable: what is the structural link between the two halves of the opera, below the gigantic arch of the Neapolitan cadence? The sequence of the four keys E-flat, B-flat, G, and C, unfolding three times in succession in the core of the first half, gives the lead. It pervades the second half as well—less rigidly, thereby avoiding monotony, but in a modified manner just as frequently, thereby providing unity.

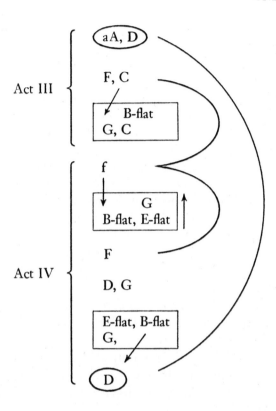

The first cycle is incomplete; but the missing E-flat major of the opening is amply recompensed by the preceding C major in a substitution often heard in the course of the opera.[4] The temporary recognition of this functional vicariousness corroborates the cohesion of each cycle, leading from E-flat major to C major, by an implied unified tonality. Perhaps because of the variant and the intervening big caesura between the two halves of the opera, the dramatic content of this cycle establishes a deliberate connection with the very first cycle: the G-major section breaks away from the preceding B-flat-major situation in a friendly chorus in 6/8 meter (cf. Nos. 21 and 8) and leads into a C-major march of which Figaro is the real hero (cf. Nos. 22 and 9).

The second cycle unrolls in the opposite direction. It, too, is incomplete. The opening part in C major is missing for the good reason, if none other, that by force of the inverted tonal progress the ear is

4. See above, pp. 238 and 240 f.

satiated with the tonal orientation of the preceding numbers (C major and F minor).

The third cycle is again in the expected regular order. The first three segments are intact; but the last one, introduced by the subdominant G major, lands squarely on the final tonic rather than taking the established turn back to the second subdominant.

Besides showing these internal modifications, the three cycles of the second half do not follow each other uninterruptedly, as do those of the first. They are isolated by independent numbers (18, 23, and 27), each built on F (tR of the tonic D major), the outer two in the major mode and the central one in the minor. These are the same numbers that defined the piers and keystone of the inner tonal arch of the joint third and fourth acts.[5]

The structural unity with the first half is emphasized by the symmetrical frame around the three cycles—here imbued with a trend toward the tonic (Nos. 16, 17 against 28/6), there toward the subdominant. It is further perfected by the correspondence of two free parts before the very last cycle (No. 28/1, 2) with the two free parts before the very first cycle (Nos. 4, 5).

The sixfold emphasis on the same tonal cycle raises the question of its psychological significance. It is revealed by the final sequence, which alone leads the subdominant to the tonic rather than twisting it back to the second subdominant. One suspects that the tonic has been the goal all along, carefully prepared in all phases and always foiled in the last moment. The proportion E-flat : B-flat = G : X demonstrates this tendency. The usual break in the middle equates the two sides. The movement of the antecedent defines D major as the only logical solution of X. The progress of the first three members of the proportion is, moreover, in a straight line from the Neapolitan subdominant to its secondary dominant to the real subdominant. A continuation of the line again directly hits the tonic. But the final solution is reserved for the last happy ending. In the course of the opera the line is tonally always turned back into the subdominant region. Dramatically, this turn is always accompanied by an indefinite or incomplete situation.[6] Psychologically, the missing resolution maintains the interest of the listener up

5. See diagram on p. 241, above.

6. One now understands the reason for this indefiniteness, noted earlier (see pp. 239 f.).

to the last curtain, when his expectation is for the first time, and finally, satisfied.

The structural principle of the six cycles strengthens the pillars of the giant cadence. In the following scheme the letters indicate keys; the brackets mark off the free sections; and the circles, crossed through or perfect, symbolize the imperfect or perfect cycles:

D [DA] ɸ ɸ ɸ E-flat|A F ɸ f ɸ F [DG] o D

Substituting functions for keys, one reaches the concise solution:

T　　3 cycles　　S ⟶ |D　3 cycles interspersed with tR　T ⟶

2 / Characterization

The detailed analysis of the various numbers of the opera has revealed most aspects of the acting characters. The purpose of this chapter is not to rehash the old arguments but to investigate devices discernible primarily in a comparison of several numbers.

The significance of the keys to the structure makes one wonder about their power of characterization. A simple equation of a key with a definite character or mood or situation must be rejected for several reasons. It postulates an absolutism typical, for all we know, of the music of some so-called "primitive" civilizations but artificial in our state of culture. Whereas a good deal of non-Western music changes its meaning completely with a change of pitch, we are thoroughly conditioned to recognize the identity of a melody on any absolute pitch.[1]

Furthermore, the equation would reduce the expressive powers of tonal relationships to a narrow symbolism, the rigidity of which would smother any subjective imagination.[2] Western music employs tonalities as functions in relation to a given center rather than as fixed values in an arbitrary personal vacuum.

Finally, nothing in the opera supports the hypothesis of an equation. D major, for instance, is the key of Bartolo's bombastic aria and of the general happy ending; C major, of Figaro's marching song and the Countess' lament; and B-flat major, of Cherubino's amorous arietta and the intrigants' entrance in the first finale.

Keys have a power of characterization if interpreted in a flexible system of relativity. What is meant can best be illustrated by the figure of the Countess. Her first aria is in E-flat major; her second, in C major. In both arias, one remembers from the detailed analysis, the tone g^1 is of paramount importance. It is the goal of the melodic drives, which gain power and content entirely from their orientation toward it. Perhaps

1. This fact is sufficiently proved by the frequency increase of our standard pitch in recent generations, according to which Beethoven, if he were alive today, would hear his *Fifth Symphony* in C-sharp minor. One may further state the curious biological phenomenon that possession of absolute pitch is very common in "primitive" tribes, whereas it is becoming ever rarer in our refined society.

2. The precise case of certain types of antique and oriental music.

Signora Luisa Laschi, the soprano for whom Mozart wrote the part, had a particularly attractive g^1; or perhaps Mozart chose this tone in free imagination. In any case, in both arias it symbolizes the intended achievement, the desired solution. In the specific case of the Countess, as one learns from words and stage action, the object of her desire is to regain her husband's affection; and the tone g^1 becomes musically identified with it. The absolute pitch is flexible in relation to different keys. The shift of the role of g^1 from the third of the first key (E-flat major) to the fifth of the second key (C major) conveys progress in the Countess' endeavor. The word "progress," implying development toward a desired aim, is used deliberately; for the perfect consonance of the fifth is closer to final solution than the imperfect consonance of the major third. The development will be completed with the identification of g^1 with the octave, or tonic, of a given number. This musical solution really characterizes the big reconciliation scene of the last finale (No. 28, m. 335–447).

The Countess' entrance in measure 398 coincides with the return of the section to G major, which was abandoned in the preceding excitement. Her first phrase indicates the straight direction up the scale to g^1 but, for the time being, drops the cadence to the lower g. The answering ensemble (m. 402–420) keeps the G orientation alive by the basic tonality, but the Countess' ultimate reach is safeguarded by the absence of women's voices that might compete with the crucial range and by the subdued chroma of the minor mode. G major is restored by the Count's personal and touching appeal to his wife. The Countess' answer (m. 424 ff.) indicates the solution of her emotional crisis. The six-measure melody begins on the low tonic, the G-major key clearly defined by the opening interval and unadulterated in the continuation. The sixth degree of the scale, quickly approached and gradually relinquished, remains the temporary climax, the compass of this phrase thus being linked to the Countess' earlier exclamation. After a repetition of the phrase with tutti support, the last missing facet of the Countess' character is revealed by the well-prepared reinterpretation of the high g^1. Without struggle or effort—as in the two arias where g^1 was the goal of a major third, and then of a perfect fifth, above the tonic—the voice soars up to the octave. The achievement is prominently marked by the exposed forte dynamics and the unison isolation. The remainder of the section confirms the solution. Before all personal strife is led to rest on the low tonic by the descending scale, the Countess' victoriously consonant g^1 is heard once more in exact reiteration and then in a summarizing climax. The subito change from forte to pianissimo in the latter, occurring exactly after the top octave, sets the accomplishment of g^1 in the strongest possible relief. The words corroborate the direct meaning of the music: "Tutti contenti saremo così." The first oboe, long associated with the Countess, echoes the accomplishment across a sustained three-measure bridge into the closing general jubilation.

The tone g, to synthesize the illustration, does not represent the Countess or express her character. Susanna and Marcellina have G-major arias of totally unrelated meanings. The tone g^1 becomes a dynamic force acting on the Countess in three different contexts. As an imperfect consonance in E-flat major, it presents her with an emotional problem. As the more consonant perfect fifth in C major, it generates in her a desire actively to overcome her difficulties. And as the most consonant octave to the tonic G major, it spells fulfilment of all her wishes.

A similar use of relativity of keys, although of a different kind, assists in the characterization of the Count. His high-strung and contorted sensuality finds expression in the interval of a seventh resulting from an impetuous but imperfect assault on the tonic octave *D–d*. The seventh occurs as *D–c* or *E–d*, often with chromatic alterations of the basic tones; but in all instances one is aware of the frustrated desire of the dissonant seventh to become consonant octave. The conditioning compass of *D–d* coincides with the tonic octave of the whole opera. While all currents lead away from the D major of the overture and are reunited in the D major of the second finale, it is significant that this key is usurped in the course of the opera only by the Count's aria vowing vengeance and Bartolo's parody of the same theme.[3] The Count's strong tie to the tonic is well bound: he is the sole activator of the plot. Without his resistance, the marriage of Susanna and Figaro would be of no dramatic interest; and without his unfaithfulness, the Countess would have no marital problems to solve. The Count's character generates the plot just as the key of D major determines the tonal focus of the opera. With his submission, plot and tonal movement end together.

The specific technique of utilizing the tense seventh which wants to

3. The parallelism between the Count and Bartolo on the two levels of seriousness and parody is consistently developed throughout the plot. Both are eager to marry Marcellina off to Figaro, and both are in a paternal relation to Figaro. It is a realistically grim, but psychologically effective, joke that uncovers the burlesque father as the real one.

become octave is most clearly illustrated, of course, in the Count's solo scene (No. 17). A glance at the score with this design in mind may give a fresh understanding of the details investigated in context: the suggestive d-octaves of the first orchestra measure; the impetuous ascents E–d (m. 46–48 and 53–54); the lyrical transformation of this line (m. 65 ff.); the forceful resolutions, musical and literary (m. 83 ff.); and the occasional setbacks (d–E–d in m. 97–104, 124–131, 142–144; E–d in m. 109–111, 136–138) conquered by the determined vision of success (D–d in m. 92, 104–106, 114–117, 131–133, 141–142, 144–145, 149 ff.). The melodic formula invades even the introductory accompanied recitative (cf. m. 1–2, 7–8, 16–19).

Recognition of the plan lends new meaning to the preceding duet (No. 16). The rare lyricism of the Count (m. 29–32 and 54–57) springs from the rounded octave E–e, an overflowing of the dissonant seventh to an exalted pitch. The true nature of the Count's love and frustration lurks behind this temporary satisfaction: the imperfect octave is immediately shortened to the crucial seventh (E–d in m. 33–34, 44–45, 50–51, 58–59).

For further corroboration of the power of the significant interval, one need only listen to the Count's inflection in many characteristic moments of both finales. In that of the second act, the seventh tightens his first angry address to the Countess (m. 16–17). His plea for forgiveness attempts to straighten the seventh into the octave (*ira.... calmar*, m. 203–206); tinges it with a repentant chroma (*confuso, pentito.... punito*, m. 242 ff.); suggests an exaggerated octave solution (*abbiate pietà*, m. 249); and settles on the status quo (c–D in m. 278, 313–320). The poles of the dissonant seventh circumscribe his mean opposition to Figaro (m. 361–369, 371 ff.), bound to the hope for Marcellina's prompt interference (m. 454–457, 462 ff.). The Count's temporary triumph resolves his strained sevenths into octaves. The consonance expresses his reaction to the welcome news brought by Antonio (m. 531–533) and the other intrigants (m. 863, 864–866, 872, 873–875, 892 ff.). The spuriousness of the triumph is evinced by the D-minor harmonization in the Antonio scene, and the immediate shift to E-flat major in the closing scene, of the D–d octave. Phrases in the Count's line like measures 863–866 remind one that the tension of the tonality of the finale in relation to the tonic of the opera is the result not only of the Neapolitan harmony but also of the elevated pitch.

In the second finale the Count at first thinks himself to be closer to the desired success than ever before. In his inflection the pure *D–d* octave accordingly replaces the earlier tormented sevenths (cf. m. 34, 41, 48 ff.). His melodic outpouring at the height of the love scene is entirely bound by the consonant interval (m. 64–68, 70–79). The subsequent conversation with the woman whom he believes to be Susanna allows him a brief excursion into sentimentality (*c* to *D*-sharp, m. 83) and grandiloquence (*E* to *e*, m. 95), the latter not free of inner friction (*d–E*, m. 94–95; *c–D*, m. 96–97); but the end of the scene finds him again very sure of himself (*d–D*, m. 101, 105). He still does not suspect the trap when he returns (m. 293–295), but the background to his *d–D* octave is no longer the tonic field. His fury explodes on the characteristic seventh (m. 324–326), this time raised in pitch by the excitement. In front of everybody he maintains stubborn control (m. 379–381, 389) before breaking his emotional bounds in a final outburst (*e–C* [!], m. 395–398). The tormented drive of the dissonant seventh toward consonant resolution finds ultimate application in the reconciliation scene. The supplicant inflection, reaching from the bottom *D* up past the sixth to the seventh (m. 420 ff.), sways the Countess to grant pardon by completing the octave in her first interval. The Count takes hold of the perfect consonance, which simultaneously becomes the foundation of the whole ensemble (m. 438), and never lets it go again (m. 464 ff.).

The relative evaluation of a tone in the development of the Countess' character and of an interval in that of the Count's is symptomatic of a system imbuing keys with meanings without absolute rigidity. The interpretation depends on the context and on relationships of various contexts rather than on frozen associations.

The special techniques employed in the characterization of the Count and the Countess meet at a point permitting a clear view of their attitudes toward each other. The Countess' constant g is the harmonic resolution of the Count's grating d–c. The reconciliation of the married couple takes place in G major, the Countess' realm; but the final scene is in D major, in which a straightened-out Count may be expected to prove his dominance over a supporting wife.

The sharp key orientation of the aristocratic couple is shared by its parody counterpart, Marcellina and Bartolo. Their arias are in G major and D major, respectively; and Marcellina's only duet is in A major. Away from the edge of all these forces above or against the wedding of the servant pair, the listener's ear suspects the existence of another tonal center, for two reasons. Of the twenty-nine numbers in the opera, twenty-three plus all subsections of both finales are below the tonic. Susanna and Figaro surely match their opponents by an independent power of their own.

One is carried far by the hypothesis that F major is the second tonal focus. It is the tonic of Figaro's and Susanna's most personal solo arias and of the sextet which centers intimately around their union. F major, one remembers, is a tonal force in the structure of the second half of the opera, forming its own unifying arch below that of D major. It also occupies a governing position in the key distribution of the whole opera:

KEY (AND FREQUENCY)	NUMBER IN OPERA
A (2)	5: Susanna, Marcellina. 16: Susanna, Count.
D (4)	Sinfonia. 4: Bartolo. 17: Count. 28: Finale (opening and conclusion).
G (6)	1: Susanna, Figaro. 8: Chorus. 12: Susanna. 14: Susanna, Cherubino. 21: Chorus. 24: Marcellina. (In Finale I: Figaro enters. In Finale II: Count makes love; rages; asks pardon.)
C (4)	9: Figaro. 13: Trio II. 19: Countess. 22: Wedding. (In Finale I: Request for wedding.)
F (4)	3: Figaro. 18: Sextet. 23: Barbarina (minor). 27: Susanna. (In Finale I: Antonio.)
B-flat (5)	2: Susanna, Figaro. 7: Trio I. 11: Cherubino. 20: Susanna, Countess. 25: Basilio. (In Finale I: Susanna appears; trio; intrigants. In Finale II: Susanna and Figaro united.)
E-flat (4)	6: Cherubino. 10: Countess. 15: Finale (opening and conclusion). 26: Figaro. (In Finale II: Figaro alone.)

Among the five keys below D major, F is central. It reaches easily to the symmetrical flanks of its second dominant (G) and second subdominant (E-flat). The dominant character of C major persuasively imparts the idea of exaltation to Figaro's march, the boudoir trio, and the wedding scene—all situations in which Figaro or Susanna or both have every reason to feel "high." The second dominant, farther still above the tonic but by nature less tense than the dominant and related in function and mood to the subdominant, is well suited to express the friendly atmosphere of the servant pair's opening duet, the two choruses, and Susanna's boudoir aria. It also determines the gay excitement at Cherubino's escape through the window, Figaro's merry entrance in the first finale, and the hiding and finding in the second finale.

The subdominant proper expresses some of the second-dominant trends directly: witness the servant pair's second duet, Cherubino's boudoir chanson, and the letter duet. In the first finale, B-flat major is the key of Susanna's rescuing surprise appearance and, in the second, of Susanna's and Figaro's final reconciliation. But it also represents the dissonant elements below the tonic which are heard in the Basilio trio, the intrigants' ensemble in the first finale, and Basilio's aria. The second subdominant is reserved for the unpropitious situations at the beginning and end of the first finale and Figaro's despair in the last act, both in his aria and in his solo scene in the finale. Cherubino's first aria in the same key builds a tonal bridge from the lowlands of despair or confusion to the noble level of the Countess' lament. The equivocation serves a new warning not to associate definite keys rigidly with definite moods but to recognize them as flexible members of changing relationships. The identification of F major with an auxiliary tonic places the surrounding keys in a certain order but not under an absolute tyranny.

In this sense one need not object to the prevalence of the F mode in two numbers apparently unrelated to Susanna and Figaro, namely, Barbarina's cavatina and Antonio's report in the first finale. One could argue that Barbarina's F-minor key reflects Susanna inasmuch as her little cousin, as has been pointed out in the context, has some of her potentialities and is moreover looking for her pin, and that Antonio is in the family. It might be safer to tie Antonio's F major to the subversive qualities of the following B-flat major. In either case the argument is against an inflexible key symbolism.

The hypothesis of an F-major realm within, or against, the larger D-major one of the whole opera forces one more speculation. What is the relation of F major, the servants' territory, to D major, the opponent aristocrats'?

The antagonism of the two keys is certainly neither so obvious as that of tonic-dominant, typical of Mozart's Italian contemporaries, nor so sophisticated as that of the tritone, typical of many of our contemporaries. One is reminded of the repeated use of the C : E-flat relationship in the course of the opera,[4] to which D : F forms an analogous clause. In the former a functional link could be found by their repeated vicarious orientation toward the tonic of the opera. Here the two keys negate each other. F major counteracts D major by isolating and denying that tone which gives D major its sex. The third is canceled, and the cancellation is inspired with independent life. The only expressed common meeting ground lies far below the tonal and psychological levels of both keys: E-flat major is the Neapolitan subdominant of the one and the second subdominant of the other. The first finale combines both parties at an intersection of currents farthest away from the point of rest.

F proves its ascendancy over D by forcing it into the formation of a B-flat-major triad, the key in which Susanna and Figaro successfully unite after overcoming all obstacles. D, inversely, cannot subjugate F into any compromise key without sacrificing its own basic power as the determining major mode. The re-establishment of D major at the end of the opera occurs, so to speak, outside the F-major arch[5] and only after the servants' marriage has been definitely sealed. The preponderance of the Susanna-Figaro keys in the course of the opera increases their weight as protagonists. The authority of the sharp keys in the beginning and end of the opera sets the frame of the aristocratic rule.

Susanna's and Figaro's characters are brought to the fore by various other musical devices clarified by the course of the whole opera rather than by single numbers. Susanna's scintillating personality emerges in the first act not from any solo aria, as would be conventional, but from four ensembles (three duets and one trio) showing her in relation to four different people. In a recitative she converses with a fifth person, Cherubino. This stereoscopic method of characterization singles her out. She is heard in the remainder of the opera in ensembles of almost every possible combination. Her two arias in the second and fourth acts complete the picture.

She, like Figaro, is introduced in the social situation of a duet. This emphasis on extrovert conversation contrasts strongly to the introspective and aristocratically lonely introduction of the Countess. It is also set off against the excited introduction of the Count by a trio which lacks all intimacy. Neither one of Susanna's masters rises to the rich and manifold expressions of her personality. The Countess maintains

4. See the preceding chapter.
5. See the diagram, p. 241.

enough social decorum not to impress her initial reserve on her conversation with other people, but her most revealing scene (No. 19) is
again a soliloquy. The Count finds in ensembles an outlet for his intense energy. They give him a chance to prove his authority over
other people rather than displaying new facets of his character. His only
aria occurs late in the plot as if he had time for introspection only at a
moment when he cannot act.

Susanna, if anyone, is the leading and most fascinating character of
the plot. It is no accident that the evaluation of the enumerated facts is
corroborated by Susanna's range of over two octaves $(A-c^2)$, surpassing
everybody else's.

Figaro's wit and mental scope are far more limited than Susanna's.
This fact must be stated emphatically in the face of the current tradition which, confusing Mozart's Figaro with Rossini's, expects of the
former the familiar tricks of the latter. At no time does Figaro act with
particular subtlety.[6] He makes the best showing in his somewhat robust
handling of Cherubino in the first act, and he manages to counter
Antonio's report by a somewhat lame lie. Otherwise he finds himself—
usually because of his own simplicity—in one predicament after another, rescued only by Susanna's maneuvering. Mozart's consciousness
of the true relationship of the pair is proved by the very first duet, in
which the music slants a dramatically neutral situation strongly in
Susanna's favor.[7] The second duet finds Figaro slow to understand the
fairly obvious possibilities of the bedroom situation. The trap laid for
the Count snares and vexes Figaro as much as the intended victim.
Even though Figaro first suggests a plot (significantly so in a recitative!), the idea hits him like a boomerang when the women modify the
plot to suit their purposes. In the second-act finale, Figaro sinks in the
subdominant cycle from one plight to the next, until even Susanna's
efforts fail to pull him out. From now on, his role is entirely passive.
Susanna and the Countess carry out their scheme without his help. It is
Susanna who actively tries to overcome the obstacles to their wedding
by paying his debt to Marcellina. Figaro gains her hand only along with
a slap in his face and the ridicule about his parents' discovery. At the
very instant of the wedding ceremony he is duped again, first by not
seeing his wife slip a billet doux to the Count and then, watching the

6. Robert Haas (*Wolfgang Amadeus Mozart* [Potsdam, 1933], p. 139) is one of the
few critics to recognize this fact.

7. See pp. 15 ff.

Count read the note, by glibly suspecting the horns on somebody else's head. The last act finds him thoroughly plagued by jealous misery, slapped by the Count and again by Susanna when he tries to outsmart her.

His simplicity is not without charm, which endears him to a superior girl like Susanna as well as to the audience. His melodies are free of complexities. Their structure is open, their harmonization plain, and their progress immediately appealing. The opening periods of his first two arias are typical expressions of his nature, and rightly the most easily remembered tunes of the opera.

One cannot miss the prevalence of triple meter in many scenes of Susanna, Figaro, and their plebeian friends. A compilation of all spots in the opera governed by triple meter becomes the source for further speculation:

IN 3/8:	No. 15. Susanna enters
	Figaro enters
IN 6/8:	No. 8. Chorus of Figaro's friends
	No. 15. Figaro parries Antonio
	No. 20. Letter duet: Susanna, Countess
	No. 21. Chorus of Susanna's friends
	No. 23. Barbarina
	No. 27. Susanna's garden aria
	No. 28. Susanna and Figaro united
IN 3/4:	No. 3. Figaro's first aria
	No. 13. Trio: Susanna, Countess, Count
	No. 22. Wedding fandango
	No. 24. Marcellina's aria, main section
	No. 25. Basilio's aria, main section
	No. 28. Larghetto: Figaro alone
	Allegro di molto: Susanna and Figaro
TRIPLETS:	No. 4. Bartolo (m. 56–65)
	No. 5. Susanna, Marcellina (throughout)
	No. 15. Antonio (almost entire scene)
	No. 26. Figaro (m. 61–65, 89–93)

One recognizes on the list Susanna's and Figaro's great moments: their intimate solo arias; Susanna's triumph over Marcellina and, later, over the jealous Count; their entrance and successful maneuvers in the

256

first finale; the writing of the billet doux; the wedding dance; and the core of the second finale, dedicated to them alone. These scenes are supplemented by the two choruses of their peasant friends and by the numbers of Antonio and Barbarina, Susanna's family. The only other instances of triple meter are heard in Marcellina's and Basilio's arias, which serve entertainment more than characterization,[8] and in the buffo climaxes of Bartolo's and Figaro's tirades.

Whatever the symbolism of *tempus perfectum* may have meant to a medieval composer, to Mozart and his contemporaries it likely spelled lilt versus stateliness, folk dance and gaiety versus court pace and regulation—in short, that popular freedom of mood and attitude represented by Susanna's and Figaro's class. The aristocrats in the opera stay aloof from the triple measure: Cherubino at all times, and the Count and the Countess touching it only briefly under Susanna's influence (Nos. 13 and 20).

Countess, Count, Susanna, and Figaro are fortified in their leading positions by an accompanied recitative in a solo scene for each of them and for none other. Among the subsidiary characters, Cherubino, the Count's pupil and potential duplicate, stands out by virtue of two arias, one duet, and a prominent place in the last finale. The soprano register allotted to him awakens memories of the baroque *castrato* tradition. His introduction by a solo aria is in accord with his youthful self-consciousness. The clear drawing of his character, as ascertained in the arias, is well displayed in the self-contained tonal circuit of his four numbers, of which the first two stand in the same relationship to each other (E-flat : B-flat) as the next two (G : D). His sensuality belongs to the subdominant realm, whether directed toward Susanna's (and Barbarina's) F or the aristocratic D. His eroticism, like his music, bridges the opposite social classes.

The other six characters find expression in the various numbers in which they appear and in the context of which they have been sufficiently discussed.

---

8. See pp. 189 and 197.

CONCLUSION

Conclusion

What generalizations can be made from the attempt to define the beauty of Mozart's *Le Nozze di Figaro* in concrete terms?

The first generalization concerns the attempt itself. Many virtues of the composition have been disengaged, but many remain untouched. A complete analysis is neither possible nor desirable. Even if all the virtues could be verbalized, their finite sum would ever fall short of the totality of the work. Art has a quality which eludes laboratory approaches. The critic should heed the angels who carry Faust's immortal parts to heaven:

> Uns bleibt ein Erdenrest
> Zu tragen peinlich.

> To us is left an earthly remainder
> Painfully to carry.

The second generalization deals with Mozart's technique of composing. The relationship between conventional and individual devices is unique. Conventions are seldom violated, be they properties of the Italian *opera buffa* or of the absolute musical craft of the time. But all conventional formulas are immeasurably deepened and enriched by Mozart's highly individualized treatment. Each number in the opera bears witness to this accomplishment. One need only recall the unprecedented original utilization of musical repetition (No. 16) and recapitulation (No. 7).

A specific principle that Mozart often seems to follow consists of stating in the opening measures of a number a musical task which the subsequent movement sets out to solve. The task can be created in different ways, but most frequently by one of two devices. In one case the opening statement is incomplete, and the movement gains impetus and direction from the need of completing it. The Countess' second aria gives the clearest illustration; Bartolo's aria falls into the same category. In the other case the opening statement is complete, but the answer to the statement presents a significant deviation from the norm, necessitating a correction. The corrective drive becomes identical with

261

the bulk of the composition. The deviation may be an insertion (as in Cherubino's arietta), a chromatic alteration (as in Marcellina's aria), or simply a new turn (as in Susanna's garden aria). The deviation becomes an easy tool of characterization, and the restoration of the norm determines the musical movement. The existence of a principle underlying the course of a composition helps one understand the speed and infallible surety of Mozart's writing.

The third generalization pertains to the composition of the opera, and perhaps to good composition in general. Everything in the work—not only the tonal forces but also all psychological, descriptive, and other elements—is turned into pure and perfect musical structure. Characters of persons and moods of situations are thoroughly absorbed and reflected by the music alone without extraneous impressionistic or expressionistic aids. The music is never merely an illustration or translation of given characters and situations (in the sense in which Wagner's music is) but always a direct creation. The analysis of every number proves this point, from the very first masterly incorporation of Susanna's and Figaro's distinct personalities in the music of the duet. Mozart himself testifies to this conception of music in a letter to his father (September 26, 1781) describing his composition of Osmin's first aria in *Die Entführung aus dem Serail:* "Osmin's rage is rendered comical by the accompaniment of the Turkish music. In working out the aria I have given full scope now and then to Fischer's beautiful deep notes. The passage 'Upon the Prophet's beard' is indeed in the same tempo, but with quick notes; but as Osmin's rage gradually increases, there comes (just when the aria seems to be at an end) the allegro assai, which is in a totally different measure and in a different key; this is bound to be very effective. For just as a man in such a towering rage oversteps all the bounds of order, moderation, and propriety, and completely forgets himself, so must the music too forget itself. But as passions, whether violent or not, must never be expressed in such a way as to excite disgust, so music, even in the most terrible situations, must never offend the ear, but must please the hearer, or in other words must never cease to be *music*."

APPENDIX

1 / Concepts of Harmony

The text follows Hugo Riemann's interpretation of harmonies as dynamic functions rather than as static phenomena. A few modifications of his ideas and symbols are the result partly of the translation into English (which interchanges the terms "relative" and "parallel") and partly of the author's experiences with the system.

T or t, tonic, the triad on the first degree of the scale. (Capital and small letters bring out the distinction, when necessary, between major and minor modes.)

S or s, subdominant, the triad on the fourth degree of the scale.

D or d, dominant, the triad on the fifth degree of the scale.

TR, SR, DR, the relative triads of the main functions in the major mode, each located a minor third below its major relative. Example: to C major, E minor is DR.

tR, sR, dR, the relative triads of the main functions in the minor mode, each located a minor third above its minor relative. Example: to A minor, F major is sR.

TP, SP, DP, the parallel triads of the main functions. Example: to C major, C minor is TP.

A parenthesis around a symbol marks it as a secondary function. Example: to C major, E major is (D)TR.

(D)D and (S)S may also be written as 𝔻 and 𝕊𝕊.

Any numbers after the symbol indicate chord tones other than those of the triad. Any number below the symbol indicates the bass other than the root. Example: D⁷, the first inversion of the dominant seventh chord.
₃

$\bar{D}$ indicates that the root of D is missing. Hence the symbol for the diminished triad in the major mode is $\bar{D}^7$; for the diminished seventh chord, $\bar{D}^9$.

The diminished triad in the minor mode is $s^{\overset{6}{[5]}}$.

The Neapolitan sixth substitutes for the fifth in the minor subdominant chord, i.e., $s^{\overset{6\flat}{[5]}}$.

A modulation is a change of function. Example: the modulation from C major to G major can be symbolized by $T = S$.

2 / Concepts of Form

The terminology used and tested by Alfred Lorenz in his analysis of Wagner's operas has proved of general value. It is built on proportions of parts to one another and the whole, independent of the absolute length.

A *strophe* is a formal element usually implying repetition ($a\,a\,a \ldots$). If the repetition is not exact, one speaks of variations ($a\,a'\,a'' \ldots$). Example: No. 14.

A *bar form* is the basic binary structure. Two corresponding strophes are balanced by an epode of new material ($a\,a\,b$). The strophes, differentiated as strophe and antistrophe, may be identical, similar, or merely analogous. The epode is normally as long or weighty as the two strophes together ($a + a' = b$). Example: No. 2.

A *recapitulation bar form* repeats elements of the strophes toward the end of the epode ($a + a' = b^a$). The caesura in the middle is preserved. Example: No. 28, Allegro di molto.

An *inverted bar form* is rare, interchanging the two halves of the regular bar form ($b\,a\,a$). The term "epode" is properly replaced by "apode."

A *bow form* is the basic ternary structure. A middle section separates by contrast the framing, corresponding opening and closing sections ($a\,b\,a$). Example: No. 19, Aria (Andante).

An *enlarged bow form* preserves the center axis around which any number of sections arrange themselves either symmetrically ($a\,b\,c \ldots X\ a\,b\,c \ldots$) or mirrored ($a\,b\,c \ldots X \ldots c\,b\,a$). Example: No. 28.

A *rondo* is one version of an enlarged bow form to which a recurring refrain adds one more element of order ($R\,a\,R\,b\,R\,a\,R$). Example: No. 1.

Complex forms may combine several of the basic forms. The various sections of a large bow form, for instance, may each be organized as miniature bar forms, or bow forms, or both.

3 / Measure Numbers

NUMBER IN OPERA	LENGTH IN MEASURES
21	37
22	229

(Allegretto begins at m. 61
Andante   begins at m. 132
Maestoso begins at m. 175
Allegretto begins at m. 186)

23	36
24	93
25	138
26	111

(Aria begins at m. 24)

| 27 | 74 |

(Aria begins at m. 25)

| 28 | 521 |

(Con un poco
   più di moto   begins at m. 51
Larghetto   begins at m. 109
Allegro di molto begins at m. 121
Andante   begins at m. 275
Allegro assai   begins at m. 335
Andante   begins at m. 421
Allegro assai   begins at m. 448)

[PRINTED]
[IN U·S·A·]

This book was designed by Norma Levarie
and set in Monotype Janson
and Foundry Bulmer